A World Bank Group Flagship Report

WORLD DEVELOPMENT REPORT 2020

TRADING FOR DEVELOPMENT

IN THE AGE OF GLOBAL VALUE CHAINS

WORLD BANK GROUP

ISSN, ISBN, e-ISBN, and DOI:

Softcover
ISSN: 0163-5085
ISBN: 978-1-4648-1457-0
e-ISBN: 978-1-4648-1495-2
DOI: 10.1596/978-1-4648-1457-0

Hardcover
ISSN: 0163-5085
ISBN: 978-1-4648-1494-5
DOI: 10.1596/978-1-4648-1494-5

Cover image: The cover image is a screen capture of an interactive visualization depicting the flow of international trade, with each dot representing US$1 billion in value. The interactive map was created by data visualization expert Max Galka, from his *Metrocosm* blog: http://metrocosm.com/map-international-trade/. Used with the permission of Max Galka; further permission required for reuse.

Cover design: Kurt Niedermeier, Niedermeier Design, Seattle, Washington.

Interior design: George Kokkinidis, Design Language, Brooklyn, New York, and Kurt Niedermeier, Niedermeier Design, Seattle, Washington.

Library of Congress Control Number: 2019952802

Contents

Boxes

Figures

Maps

Tables

Foreword

Around the world, the process of delivering goods and services to consumers has become specialized to a degree no one could have ever imagined. Businesses focus on what they do best in their home markets and outsource the rest. Samsung makes its mobile phones with parts from 2,500 suppliers across the globe. One country—Vietnam—produces more than a third of those phones, and it has reaped the benefits. The provinces in which the phones are produced, Thai Nguyen and Bac Ninh, have become two of the richest in Vietnam, and poverty there has fallen dramatically as a result.

The face of global trade has been transformed in the three decades since the World Bank's last major *World Development Report* on the subject. Until 2008, global value chains (GVCs) expanded rapidly. The expansion was revolutionary for many poorer countries, which boosted growth by joining a GVC, thereby eliminating the need to build whole industries from scratch. The experience of the last three decades has proven that it pays to specialize.

Yet GVCs are at a crossroads. Their growth has leveled off since 2008, when GVCs peaked at 52 percent of global trade. The reasons are complex. Slowing global growth and investment are one factor. And value chains have matured, making further specialization more challenging. Meanwhile, the push toward international trade liberalization has stalled. The growth of automation and other labor-saving technologies such as 3D printing may encourage countries to reduce production abroad. Unless trade liberalization is reinforced, value chains are unlikely to expand.

Under the circumstances, do GVCs still offer developing countries a clear path to progress? That's the main question explored in the 2020 *World Development Report*. And the answer is yes: developing countries can achieve better outcomes by pursuing market-oriented reforms specific to their stage of development.

This Report offers a detailed perspective on GVCs. It covers not only the degree to which they contribute to economic growth and poverty reduction, but also the extent to which they lead to inequality and environmental degradation. It discusses how new technologies are reshaping trade, finding that automation will help rather than hurt trade. It also raises concerns about the inadequacies in the global trading system that are fueling disagreements among nations.

In particular, the Report highlights what can be done by countries that have been largely left out of the GVC revolution. Important steps such as speeding up customs procedures and reducing border delays can yield big benefits for countries making the transition from simply exporting commodities to basic manufacturing. Strengthening the rule of law reinforces trade as well. Also helpful are investments that improve connectivity by modernizing communications and roads, railways, and ports. Liberalizing road, sea, and air transport is also important, and it is often less costly.

In the meantime, knowledge and services have become integral to global production, delivering important benefits to developing countries through the supply chain. In Colombia, a program led by a multinational firm induced suppliers to upgrade their coffee farms while planting trees and incorporating more efficient and sustainable practices. About 80,000 farmers and 1,000 villages benefited from the program: the quality of coffee improved, while farmers' profits increased by 15 percent.

Overall, participation in global value chains can deliver a double dividend. First, firms are more likely to specialize in the tasks in which they are most productive. Second, firms are able to gain from connections with foreign firms, which pass on the best managerial and technological practices. As a result, countries enjoy faster income growth and falling poverty.

All countries stand to benefit from the increased trade and commerce spurred by the growth of GVCs.

David Malpass

David R. Malpass
President
The World Bank Group

Preface

The growth of international trade and the expansion of global value chains (GVCs) over the last 30 years have had remarkable effects on development. Incomes have risen, productivity has gone up—particularly in developing countries—and poverty has fallen. The fragmentation of production and knowledge transfer inherent in GVCs are in no small part responsible for these advances. Hyperspecialization by firms at different stages of value chains enhances efficiency and productivity, and durable firm-to-firm relationships foster technology transfer and access to capital and inputs along value chains. GVCs account for around half of world trade today.

At this moment, however, there is reason to worry that this trade-led path to development is under threat. Although trade bounced back after the global financial crisis of 2008, the high growth rates of the 1990s and 2000s have remained elusive. GVC trade—trade in intermediate products—also stalled in 2008, with only modest, intermittent periods of growth since. There are many reasons for this shift, but one is that trade reform has languished and in some cases is even being reversed.

Countries can do much on their own to reinvigorate world trade and GVC expansion. With that in mind, this Report sets out a comprehensive domestic agenda for governments: investments in connectivity, improvements in business climate, and unilateral reductions in trade and investment barriers.

But there is much that countries need to do together to improve the current system. Coordinated trade liberalization is overdue in agriculture and services, the rules applied to foreign investment are uneven, and subsidies and state-owned enterprises are distorting competition.

Unfortunately, international cooperation, too, has begun to falter. Many people are disenchanted with free trade. Some communities have experienced declining wages and unemployment. Businesses are complaining about the limitations of the current multilateral system in dealing with their concerns about lack of access to large markets, the increasing use of "behind-the-border" measures, and "unfair" competition. Governments are inclined to respond by using trade policy as a tool for social protection and to address inadequacies in the current trade rules.

This Report argues that reinvigorating the international trade system will require governments in certain advanced countries to first look inward to address the discontent and inequality associated with openness. More generally, advanced economies need to rethink the priorities of the welfare state to better help workers adjust to structural change.

Developing countries as well need to expand social assistance and improve compliance with labor regulations in order to extend the jobs and earnings gains from participation in GVCs to more people across society. They also need to take steps to ensure that their domestic firms benefit from knowledge transfer from lead global firms. Finally, all countries need to ensure that the growth associated with trade does not lead to environmental degradation.

Meanwhile, governments need to cooperate with one another beyond the traditional trade issues to ensure that trade and GVCs can deliver for development. Cooperation on corporate taxes will enable governments to better tax capital in a global, digitalized economy, so that they have the resources to finance infrastructure projects and social policies. Improved cooperation on competition issues is needed to ensure that firms enjoy a level playing field globally. And finally, new models of cooperation are needed for data flows to strike a balance between the privacy of citizens and the needs of business and innovators.

The expansion of trade and GVCs is at an inflection point. There is still time to reinvigorate growth, trade, and GVCs. Trade is vital for development, but it needs rules to function smoothly. And those rules require cooperation by governments. This Report offers governments a road map for action.

Pinelopi Koujianou Goldberg
Chief Economist
The World Bank Group

Acknowledgments

This year's *World Development Report* (WDR) was prepared by a team led by co-directors Caroline Freund and Aaditya Mattoo (World Bank) and Pol Antràs (Harvard University). Daria Taglioni served as task team leader of the project and as a member of the Report's leadership. Overall guidance was provided by the chief economist of the World Bank, Pinelopi Koujianou Goldberg. The Report is sponsored by the Bank's Development Economics Vice Presidency.

The core team was composed of Erhan Artuc, Paulo Bastos, Davida Connon, François de Soyres, Thomas Farole, Ana Margarida Fernandes, Michael J. Ferrantino, Bernard Hoekman, Claire H. Hollweg, Melise Jaud, Hiau Looi Kee, Bob Rijkers, and Deborah Winkler.

Members of the extended team—Jessie Coleman, Jan De Loecker, Leonardo Iacovone, Kåre Johard, Madina Kukenova, Michele Mancini, Alen Mulabdic, Nadia Rocha, Michele Ruta, Marijn Verhoeven, Michael D. Wong, and Douglas Zhihua Zeng—provided invaluable contributions to the Report. Sources of additional input were Emma Aisbett, Emmanuelle Auriol, Gaëlle Balineau, Christopher Barrett, Benoit Blarel, Alessandro Borin, Fabrizio Cafaggi, Jieun Choi, Ileana Cristina Constantinescu, Wim Douw, Roberto Echandi, Jakob Engel, Dominik Englert, Marianne Fay, Vivien Foster, Sebastián Franco-Bedoya, Emiko Fukase, Gary Gereffi, Tania Priscilla Begazo Gomez, Stephane Hallegatte, Armando Heilbron, Dirk Heine, Etienne Raffi Kechichian, Jana Krajčovičová, Peter Kusek, Somik Lall, Arik Levinson, Yan Liu, Rocco Macchiavello, Maryla Maliszewska, Julien Martin, Denis Medvedev, Josepa Miquel-Florensa, Antonio Nucifora, Carlo Pietrobelli, Obert Pimhidzai, Christine Qiang, Tom Reardon, Kirstin Ingrid Roster, Gianluca Santoni, Abhishek Saurav, Kateryna Schroeder, Victor Steenbergen, Michael A. Toman, and Gonzalo Varela.

Research assistance was provided by Vicky Chemutai, Alexandre Gaillard, Chiara Liardi, Julien Maire, Mitali Nikore, Nicolás Gómez Parra, Xiomara Pulido Ramírez, Juan Miguel Jiménez Riveros, Alejandro Forero Rojas, Maria Filipa Seara e Pereira, Guillaume Sublet, Nicolás Santos Villagrán, and the World Bank's Digital Development program.

The team would like to thank the following colleagues for their guidance during preparation of the Report: Rabah Arezki, Asli Demirgüç-Kunt, Shanta Devarajan, Simeon Djankov, Deon Filmer, Mary Hallward-Driemeier, Daniel Lederman, William Maloney, Martin Rama, Halsey Rogers, Hans Timmer, and Albert Zeufack. The Macroeconomics, Trade, and Investment Global Practice of the Equitable Growth, Finance, and Institutions (EFI) Vice Presidency provided the Report team with support.

The team also benefited at an early stage from consultations on emerging themes with experts from the Bank of Italy, European Commission, French Development Agency, German Agency for International Cooperation (GIZ), German Federal Ministry for Economic Cooperation and Development (BMZ), International Trade Centre, Japan International Cooperation Agency, Organisation for Economic Co-operation and Development, Swedish Chamber of Commerce, Swedish International Development Cooperation Agency, U.K. Department for International Development, United Nations Industrial Development Organization, U.S. Agency for International Development, and World Trade Organization. An event kindly organized by GIZ and BMZ gave the WDR team a unique opportunity to discuss the Report's themes with a diverse range of experts from government, civil society, and the private sector.

Bruce Ross-Larson provided developmental guidance in drafting the Report, which was edited by Sabra Ledent and proofread by Gwenda Larsen. Kurt Niedermeier was the principal graphic designer, with support from Bill Pragluski and Patrick Ibay. Mikael Reventar, Anushka Thewarapperuma, and Roula Yazigi, together with Chisako Fukuda, offered guidance, services, and support on communication and dissemination. Special thanks go to Stephen Pazdan, who coordinated and oversaw production of the Report and to the World Bank's Formal Publishing Program. The team would also like to thank Mary Fisk, who facilitated translation of the overview; Patricia Katayama, who oversaw the overall publication process; and Deb Barker, who managed the printing and electronic conversions of the book and its overview booklets. The team would also like to thank Marcelo Buitron, Michelle Chester, María del Camino Hurtado, Rashi Jain, Gabriela Calderon Motta, Alejandra Ramon, and Consuelo Jurado Tan for fulfilling their coordinating roles.

Background and related research, along with dissemination, have been generously supported by the KDI School Partnership trust fund, the World Bank's Knowledge for Change Program (KCP, a multidonor trust fund), Strategic Research Program, Umbrella Facility for Trade, and Multidonor Trust Fund for Trade and Development.

During preparation of the Report, government officials, researchers, and representatives of civil society organizations (CSOs) attended consultations in Belgium, Chile, China, France, Germany, India, Poland, Sweden, Turkey, the United Kingdom, and the United States. Participants were drawn from many more countries as well. In addition, a diverse group of CSOs participated in two CSO Forum sessions on this Report held during the 2019 World Bank/ International Monetary Fund Spring Meetings and in an e-forum held in March 2019. The team is grateful to these CSOs for their input and to those who took part in these events for their helpful comments and suggestions. Special thanks go to those organizations and individuals who provided written comments and engaged directly with the team, including the Consumer Unity and Trust Society International, International Trade Union Confederation, ISEAL Alliance, Save the Children, and Women in Informal Employment: Globalizing and Organizing (WIEGO). In addition, the team is grateful for those who submitted comments in response to blogs posted on the topic. Steve Commins provided support during consultations with think tanks and CSOs. Further information on these events is available at http://www.worldbank.org /wdr2020.

The team is grateful as well to the many World Bank colleagues who provided written comments during the formal Bank-wide review process. Those comments proved to be invaluable guidance at a crucial stage in the Report's production.

Team members would also like to thank their families for their support during the preparation of this Report.

Finally, the team apologizes to any individuals or organizations that contributed to this Report but were inadvertently omitted from these acknowledgments.

Abbreviations

AfCFTA	African Continental Free Trade Area
AGOA	African Growth and Opportunity Act
ALMP	active labor market policy
APEC	Asia–Pacific Economic Cooperation
ASCM	Agreement on Subsidies and Countervailing Measures
ASEAN	Association of Southeast Asian Nations
AVE	ad valorem equivalent
BCRs	Binding Corporate Rules
BEAT	Base Erosion and Anti-abuse Tax
BEC	Broad Economic Categories
BEPS	base erosion and profit shifting
BIT	bilateral investment treaty
BPO	business processing outsourcing
BRI	Belt and Road Initiative
CBPRs	Cross-Border Privacy Rules
CCAC	Competition and Consumer Affairs Commission (Guyana)
CLOUD Act	Clarifying Lawful Overseas Use of Data Act
CO_2	carbon dioxide
COMESA	Common Market for Eastern and Southern Africa
CORFO	Chilean Innovation Agency
CPEA	Cross-border Privacy Enforcement Arrangement
CPI	consumer price index
CPTPP	Comprehensive and Progressive Agreement for Trans-Pacific Partnership
CVDs	countervailing duties
DBCFT	destination-based cash flow tax
DLTs	distributed ledger technologies
DR–CAFTA	Dominican Republic–Central America Free Trade Agreement
DST	digital services tax
DTA	domestic tariff area
DTRI	Digital Trade Restrictiveness Index
EAC	East African Community
EBA	Everything but Arms
ECOWAS	Economic Community of West African States
ECTEL	Eastern Caribbean Telecommunications Authority
EEA	European Economic Area
EEC	European Economic Community
EIP	eco-industrial park
EKC	environmental Kuznets curve
EPZ	export processing zone
ESG	environmental, social, and governance

EU	European Union
FAO	Food and Agriculture Organization (of the UN)
FDI	foreign direct investment
fintech	financial technology
FTA	free trade agreement
FVA	foreign value added
GATS	General Agreement on Trade in Services
GATT	General Agreement on Tariffs and Trade
GDP	gross domestic product
GDPR	General Data Protection Regulation
GHG	greenhouse gas
GLoBE	global antibase erosion
Gm^3	billion cubic meters
GVC	global value chain
HCI	Human Capital Index
HS	Harmonized System
ICT	information and communication technology
IFC	International Finance Corporation
ILO	International Labour Organization
IMF	International Monetary Fund
IMO	International Maritime Organization
INEGI	National Institute of Statistics and Geography (Mexico)
IP	intellectual property
IPA	investment promotion agency
IPRs	intellectual property rights
ISCO	International Standard Classification of Occupations
ISDS	investor-state dispute settlement
ISIC	International Standard Industrial Classification
ISO	International Organization for Standardization
IT	information technology
ITC	International Trade Centre
ITKIB	Istanbul Textile and Apparel Exporter Associations
LDCs	least developed countries
LPI	logistics performance index
m^3	cubic meters
MENA	Middle East and North Africa
MFA	Multifibre Arrangement
MFN	most favored nation
MIDP	Motor Industry Development Programme
MMT	million metric tons
MNC	multinational corporation
MNE	multinational enterprise
MOU	memorandum of understanding
MRIO	multiregion input–output
NAFTA	North American Free Trade Agreement
NEC	not elsewhere classified
NEET	not in employment, education, or training
NO_x	nitrogen oxides
NTB	nontariff barrier
NTM	nontariff measure
OECD	Organisation for Economic Co-operation and Development

PEA	Privacy Enforcement Authority
PHE	pollution haven effect
PHH	pollution haven hypothesis
PPP	purchasing power parity
PSDC	Penang Skills Development Centre
PTA	preferential trade agreement
PV	photovoltaic
PWT	Penn World Table
QIZ	qualified industrial zone
R&D	research and development
RTA	regional trade agreement
RVC	regional value chain
SACU	Southern African Customs Union
SAR	special administrative region
SCC	Standard Contractual Clause
SDG	Sustainable Development Goal
SDT	special and differential treatment
SEV	Samsung Electronics Vietnam
SEVT	Samsung Electronics Vietnam-Thai Nguyen
SEZ	special economic zone
Sida	Swedish International Development Cooperation Agency
SMEs	small and medium enterprises
SO_2	sulfur dioxide
SOE	state-owned enterprise
SPS	sanitary and phytosanitary
STE	state trading enterprise
STWI	Sweden Textile Water Initiative
System-GMM	System Generalized Method of Moments
TBT	technical barrier to trade
TEN-T	Trans-European Transport Network
TFA	textile, footwear, and apparel
TFA	Trade Facilitation Agreement
TFP	total factor productivity
TiVA	Trade in Value Added
TRIMs	Agreement on Trade-Related Investment Measures
TRIPS	Agreement on Trade-Related Aspects of Intellectual Property Rights
UN	United Nations
UNCTAD	United Nations Conference on Trade and Development
UNIDO	United Nations Industrial Development Organization
USAID	U.S. Agency for International Development
USCBTTA	U.S.–Cambodia Bilateral Textile Trade Agreement
USMCA	United States–Mexico–Canada Agreement
VAT	value added tax
WAEMU	West African Economic and Monetary Union
WDI	World Development Indicators (database)
WEO	World Economic Outlook (database)
WIOD	World Input–Output Database
WITS	World Integrated Trade Solution (database)
WTO	World Trade Organization

All dollar amounts are U.S. dollars unless otherwise indicated.

PART I

Overview

World Development Report 2020: Trading for Development in the Age of Global Value Chains

What is a global value chain (GVC)?

A global value chain breaks up the production process across countries. Firms specialize in a specific task and do not produce the whole product.

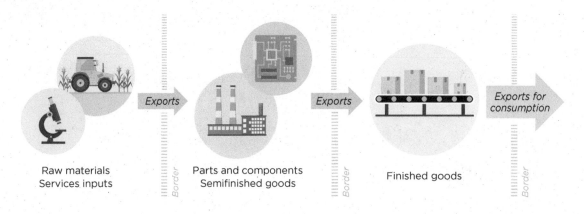

How do GVCs work?

Interactions between firms typically involve durable relationships.

Economic fundamentals drive countries' participation in GVCs. But policies matter—to enhance participation and broaden benefits.

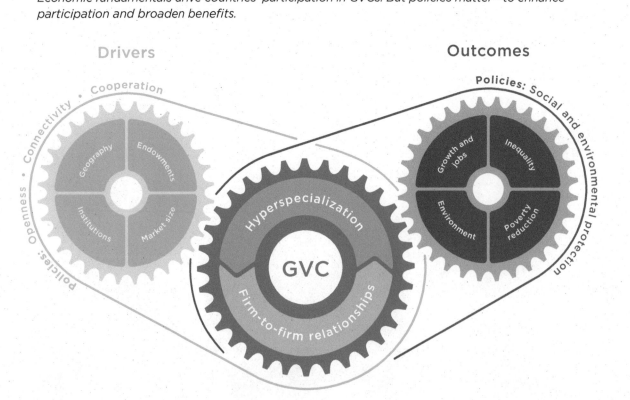

Overview

GVCs can continue to boost growth, create better jobs, and reduce poverty—
provided that developing countries undertake deeper reforms and industrial
countries pursue open, predictable policies.

International trade expanded rapidly after 1990, powered by the rise of global value chains (GVCs). This expansion enabled an unprecedented convergence: poor countries grew faster and began to catch up with richer countries. Poverty fell sharply.

These gains were driven by the fragmentation of production across countries and the growth of connections between firms. Parts and components began crisscrossing the globe as firms looked for efficiencies wherever they could find them. Productivity and incomes rose in countries that became integral to GVCs—Bangladesh, China, and Vietnam, among others. The steepest declines in poverty occurred in precisely those countries.

Today, however, it can no longer be taken for granted that trade will remain a force for prosperity. Since the global financial crisis of 2008, the growth of trade has been sluggish, and the expansion of GVCs has slowed. The last decade has seen nothing like the transformative events of the 1990s—the integration of China and Eastern Europe into the global economy and major trade agreements such as the Uruguay Round and the North American Free Trade Agreement (NAFTA).

At the same time, two potentially serious threats have emerged to the successful model of labor-intensive, trade-led growth. First, the arrival of labor-saving technologies such as automation and 3D printing could draw production closer to the consumer and reduce the demand for labor at home and abroad. Second, trade conflict among large countries could lead to a retrenchment or a segmentation of GVCs.

What does all this mean for developing countries seeking to link to GVCs, acquire new technologies, and grow? Is there still a path to development through GVCs? Those are the central questions explored in this Report. It examines the degree to which GVCs have contributed to growth, jobs, and reduced poverty—but also to inequality and environmental degradation. It spells out how national policies can revive trade growth and ensure that GVCs are a force for development rather than divergence. Finally, it identifies inadequacies in the international trade system that have fomented disagreements among nations and provides a road map to resolving them through greater international cooperation.

This Report concludes that GVCs can continue to boost growth, create better jobs, and reduce poverty, provided that developing countries undertake deeper reforms and industrial countries pursue open, predictable policies. Technological change is likely to be more of a boon than a curse for trade and GVCs. The benefits of GVC participation can be widely shared and sustained if all countries enhance social and environmental protection.

Figure O.1 GVC trade grew rapidly in the 1990s but stagnated after the 2008 global financial crisis

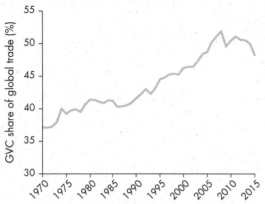

Sources: WDR 2020 team, using data from Eora26 database; Borin and Mancini (2019); and Johnson and Noguera (2017). See appendix A for a description of the databases used in this Report.

Note: See figure 1.2 in chapter 1 for details. Unless otherwise specified, GVC participation measures used in this and subsequent figures throughout the Report follow the methodology from Borin and Mancini (2015, 2019).

The expansion of GVCs could stall unless policy predictability is restored

GVCs have existed for centuries. But they grew swiftly from 1990 to 2007 as technological advances—in transportation, information, and communications—and lower trade barriers induced manufacturers to extend production processes beyond national borders (figure O.1). GVC growth was concentrated in machinery, electronics, and transportation, and in the regions specializing in those sectors: East Asia, North America, and Western Europe. Most countries in these regions participate in complex GVCs, producing advanced manufactures and services, and engage in innovative activities (map O.1). By contrast, many countries in Africa, Latin America, and Central Asia still produce commodities for further processing in other countries.

In recent years, however, trade and GVC growth have slowed (figure O.1). One reason is the decline in overall economic growth, and especially investment. Another reason is the slowing pace and even reversal of trade reforms. Furthermore, the fragmentation of production in the most dynamic regions and sectors has matured. China is producing more at home.[1] In the United States, a booming shale sector reduced oil imports by one-fourth between 2010 and 2015 and slightly reduced the incentives to outsource manufacturing production.[2]

Recent increases in protection could also affect the evolution of GVCs. Protectionism could induce reshoring of existing GVCs or their shifts to new locations. Unless policy predictability is restored, any expansion of GVCs is likely to remain on hold. When future access to markets is uncertain, firms have an incentive to delay investment plans until uncertainty is resolved.

Map O.1 All countries participate in GVCs—but not in the same way

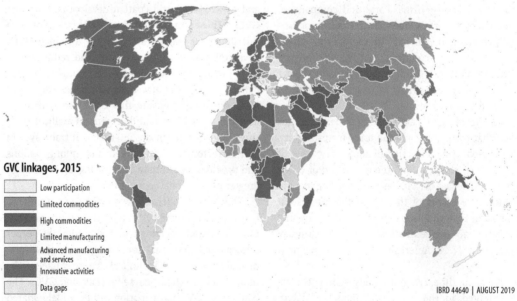

Source: WDR 2020 team, based on the GVC taxonomy for 2015 (see box 1.3 in chapter 1).

Note: The type of a country's GVC linkages is based on (1) the extent of its GVC participation, (2) its sectoral specialization in trade, and (3) its engagement in innovation. Details are provided in figure 1.6 in chapter 1.

GVCs boost incomes, create better jobs, and reduce poverty

Hyperspecialization enhances efficiency, and *durable firm-to-firm relationships* promote the diffusion of technology and access to capital and inputs along chains. For example, in Ethiopia firms participating in GVCs are more than twice as productive as similar firms that participate in standard trade. Firms in other developing countries also show significant gains in productivity from GVC participation. A 1 percent increase in GVC participation is estimated to boost per capita income by more than 1 percent, or much more than the 0.2 percent income gain from standard trade. The biggest growth spurt typically comes when countries transition out of exporting commodities and into exporting basic manufactured products (for example, garments) using imported inputs (for example, textiles) (figure O.2), as has happened in Bangladesh, Cambodia, and Vietnam.

Eventually, however, these high growth rates cannot be sustained without moving to progressively more sophisticated forms of participation. But the transitions from limited manufacturing to more advanced manufacturing and services, and finally to innovative activities (the GVC taxonomy used in this Report is explained further in box 1.3 in chapter 1), become increasingly more demanding in terms of skills, connectivity, and regulatory institutions.

GVCs also deliver better jobs, but the relationship with employment is complex. Firms in GVCs tend to be more productive and capital-intensive than other (especially nontrading) firms, and so their production is less job-intensive. However, the enhanced productivity leads to an expansion in firm output and thus to increases in firm employment.[3] As a result, GVCs are associated with structural transformation in developing countries, drawing people out of less productive activities and into more productive manufacturing and services activities. Firms in GVCs are unusual in another respect: across a wide range of countries, they tend to employ more women than non-GVC firms.[4] They contribute therefore to the broader development benefits of higher female employment.

Because they boost income and employment growth, participation in GVCs is associated with a reduction in poverty.[5] Trade in general reduces poverty primarily through growth. Because gains in economic growth from GVCs tend to be larger than from trade in final products, poverty reduction from GVCs also turns out to be greater than that from standard

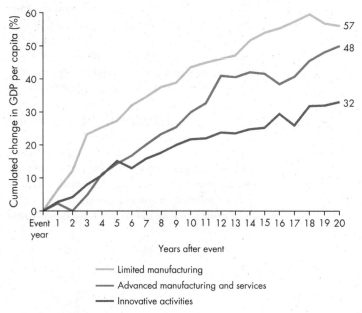

Figure O.2 GDP per capita grows most rapidly when countries break into limited manufacturing GVCs

Sources: WDR 2020 team, using data from the World Bank's WDI database and the GVC taxonomy for 1990–2015 based on Eora26 database.

Note: The event study quantifies the cumulated change in real GDP per capita in the 20 years following a switch from a lower to a higher stage of GVC engagement. See box 3.3 in chapter 3 for the methodology.

trade. In Mexico and Vietnam, for example, the regions that saw more intensive GVC participation also saw a greater reduction in poverty.

The gains from GVCs are not equally shared, and GVCs can hurt the environment

The gains from GVC participation are not distributed equally across and within countries. Large corporations that outsource parts and tasks to developing countries have seen rising markups and profits, suggesting that a growing share of cost reductions from GVC participation are not being passed on to consumers.[6] At the same time, markups for the producers in developing countries are declining. Such a contrast is evident, for example, in the markups of garment firms in the United States and India, respectively.

Within countries, exposure to trade with lower-income countries and technological change contribute to the reallocation of value added from labor to capital. Inequality can also creep upward in the labor market, with a growing premium for skilled work and stagnant wages for unskilled work.[7] Women also face challenges: GVCs may offer more women jobs, but they seem to have even lower glass ceilings. Women are generally found in the lower value-added segments; it is hard to find women owners and managers.[8]

GVCs can also have harmful effects on the environment. The main environmental costs of GVCs are associated with the growing, more distant trade in intermediate goods compared with standard trade. This leads to higher carbon dioxide (CO_2) emissions from transportation (relative to standard trade) and to excess waste (especially in electronics and plastics) from the packaging of goods. The growth generated by GVCs can also strain natural resources, especially if accompanied by production or energy subsidies, which encourage excess production. On a more positive note, the concern that firms may choose to locate the most polluting stages of production in countries where environmental norms are laxer is not borne out by the data.

New technologies on balance promote trade and GVCs

The emergence of new products, new technologies of production such as automation and 3D printing, and new technologies of distribution such as digital platforms is creating both opportunities and risks. But the evidence so far suggests that on balance these technologies are enhancing trade and GVCs.

Innovation is leading to the emergence of new traded goods and services, which contributes to faster trade growth. In 2017, 65 percent of trade was in categories that did not exist in 1992.

Surprisingly, new production technologies are also likely to boost trade. Automation does encourage countries to use less labor-intensive methods and reduces the demand for the labor-intensive products of developing countries. However, the evidence on reshoring is limited,[9] and the evidence on automation[10] and 3D printing[11] suggests that these technologies have contributed to higher productivity and a larger scale of production. As such, they have *increased* the demand for imports of inputs from developing countries (figure O.3).

Similarly, digital platform firms are reducing the cost of trade and making it easier for small firms to break out of their local markets and sell both goods and services to the world. But there are signs that the rising market power of platform firms is affecting the distribution of the gains from trade.[12]

National policies can boost GVC participation

In principle, breaking up complex products such as cars and computers allows countries to specialize in simpler parts and tasks, making it easier for those at an early stage of development to participate in trade. But a country's ability to participate in GVCs is by no means assured.

GVC participation is determined by factor endowments, geography, market size, and institutions. These fundamentals alone need not dictate destiny, however; policies also play an important role. Policies to attract foreign direct investment (FDI) can remedy the scarcity of capital, technology, and management skills.[13] Liberalizing trade at home while negotiating trade liberalization abroad can overcome the constraints of a small domestic market, liberating firms and farms from the limits of domestic demand and local inputs. Improving transportation and communications infrastructure and introducing competition in these services can address the disadvantage of a remote location.[14] And participating in deep integration agreements can spur institutional and policy reform, especially when complemented by technical and financial assistance.[15]

Based on an analysis of the drivers of various types of GVC participation, this Report identifies the policies that promote integration into more advanced GVCs (figure O.4). Importantly, national

Figure O.3 Automation in industrial countries has boosted imports from developing countries

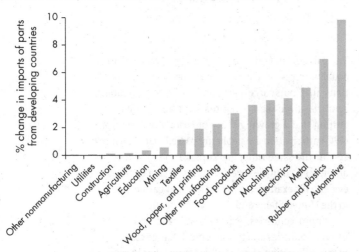

Industries in order of increasing automation

Source: Artuc, Bastos, and Rijkers 2018.

Note: The figure depicts the automation-induced increase in industrial countries' imports of materials from developing countries by broad sector over 1995–2015. The change in imports of parts is measured in log points; a 0.10 increase in log points is roughly equivalent to a 10 percent increase in imports.

Figure O.4 Transitioning to more sophisticated participation in GVCs: Some examples of national policy

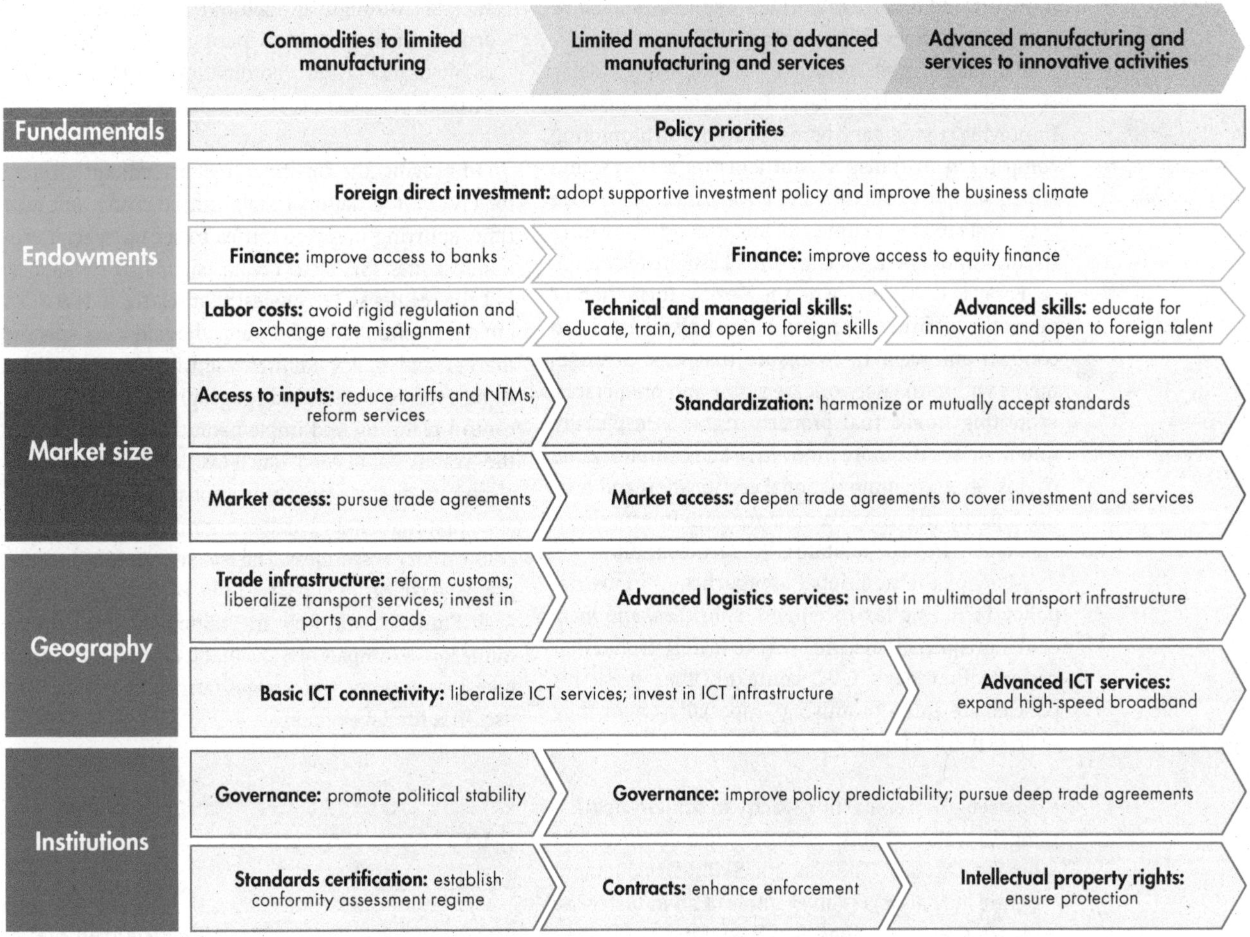

	Commodities to limited manufacturing	Limited manufacturing to advanced manufacturing and services	Advanced manufacturing and services to innovative activities
Fundamentals	Policy priorities		
Endowments	**Foreign direct investment:** adopt supportive investment policy and improve the business climate		
	Finance: improve access to banks	**Finance:** improve access to equity finance	
	Labor costs: avoid rigid regulation and exchange rate misalignment	**Technical and managerial skills:** educate, train, and open to foreign skills	**Advanced skills:** educate for innovation and open to foreign talent
Market size	**Access to inputs:** reduce tariffs and NTMs; reform services	**Standardization:** harmonize or mutually accept standards	
	Market access: pursue trade agreements	**Market access:** deepen trade agreements to cover investment and services	
Geography	**Trade infrastructure:** reform customs; liberalize transport services; invest in ports and roads	**Advanced logistics services:** invest in multimodal transport infrastructure	
	Basic ICT connectivity: liberalize ICT services; invest in ICT infrastructure		**Advanced ICT services:** expand high-speed broadband
Institutions	**Governance:** promote political stability	**Governance:** improve policy predictability; pursue deep trade agreements	
	Standards certification: establish conformity assessment regime	**Contracts:** enhance enforcement	**Intellectual property rights:** ensure protection

Source: WDR 2020 team.

Note: ICT = information and communication technology; NTMs = nontariff measures.

policies can and should be tailored to the specific circumstances of countries and to specific forms of participation in GVCs.

Attracting FDI is important at all stages of participation. It requires openness, investor protection, stability, a favorable business climate, and, in some cases, investment promotion. Some countries, such as those in Southeast Asia that have benefited from foreign investment in goods, still restrict foreign investment in services. Others try to draw in investment through tax exemptions and subsidies, but they risk antagonizing their trading partners, and the net benefits may not be positive. Nevertheless, countries such as Costa Rica, Malaysia, and Morocco have attracted transformative GVC investments by large multinational corporations through the use of successful investment promotion strategies.

Overvalued exchange rates and restrictive labor regulations raise the cost of labor, preventing labor-abundant countries from taking advantage of their endowments. For example, manufacturing labor costs in Bangladesh are in line with its per capita income, but in many African countries, labor costs are more than twice as high.

Connecting to markets through trade liberalization helps countries expand their market size and gain access to the inputs needed for production. For example, large unilateral tariff cuts by Peru in the 2000s are associated with faster productivity growth and expansion and diversification of GVC exports.[16] Trade agreements expand market access, and they have been a critical catalyst for GVC entry in a wide range of countries, including Bangladesh, the Dominican Republic, Honduras, Lesotho, Madagascar, and Mauritius. Because goods and services economies are increasingly linked, reforming services policies—in telecommunications, finance, transport, and a range of business services—should be part of any strategy for promoting GVC activity.

For many goods traded in GVCs, a day's delay is equal to imposing a tariff in excess of 1 percent. Improving customs and border procedures, promoting competition in transport and logistics services, and enhancing port structure and governance can reduce trade costs related to time and uncertainty, mitigating the disadvantages associated with a remote location.

Because GVCs thrive on the flexible formation of networks of firms, attention should also be paid to contract enforcement to ensure that legal arrangements within the network are stable and predictable. Protecting intellectual property rights is especially important for the more innovative and complex value chains. Strengthening national certification and testing capacity to ensure compliance with international standards can also facilitate GVC participation.

Many of the traditional approaches to industrial policy, including tax incentives, subsidies, and local content requirements, are likely to distort production patterns in today's GVC context. Other proactive policies are more promising—especially when they address market failures:

- To strengthen domestic capacity to support upgrading in value chains, countries should invest in human capital.[17] The Penang Skills Development Centre in Malaysia is an example of an industry-led training center that has played an important role in supporting Malaysia's upgrading to electronics and engineering GVCs.
- Targeted policies to unblock constraints to GVC trade can be effective. For example, in Bangladesh the introduction of bonded warehouses, combined with the "back-to-back" letters of credit (ensuring access to working capital), is acknowledged as a catalyst for the country's integration into the apparel GVC.
- Countries can connect domestic small and medium enterprises (SMEs) with lead firms in GVCs—by supporting training and capacity building while providing information to lead firms about supply opportunities. Examples of successful supplier linkage programs include Chile and Guinea in mining, Kenya and Mozambique in agriculture, and the Czech Republic in the electronics and automotive sectors.
- For countries participating in agriculture value chains, policies to help integrate smallholders are particularly important. In Africa, 55 percent of jobs are in agriculture, which is the source of more than 70 percent of the earnings of the poor. Ensuring that smallholders benefit requires additional support, such as through agricultural extension services, access to risk management instruments (such as insurance), and coordination to exploit scale through producer organizations.

Improving the business and investment climate for GVCs on a national scale can be costly and take time, spurring many countries to set up special economic zones (SEZs) to create islands of excellence. But the results so far suggest that relatively few SEZs are successful, and only when they address specific market and policy failures. Getting the conditions right, even in a restricted geographical area, requires careful planning and implementation to ensure that the resources needed—such as labor, land, water, electricity, and telecommunications—are readily available, that regulatory barriers are minimized, and that connectivity is seamless. The few successful zone programs in countries such as China, Panama, the United Arab Emirates, and now in Ethiopia—as well as the numerous examples of SEZs that have failed to attract investors or grow—offer important lessons on how to use SEZs for development.

Other policies can help ensure GVC benefits are shared and sustainable

Beyond policies to facilitate participation in GVCs, complementary policies are needed to share their benefits and attenuate any costs. These include labor market policies to help workers who may be hurt by structural change; mechanisms to ensure compliance with labor regulations; and environmental protection measures.

As GVCs expand, some workers will gain, but others could lose in some locations, sectors, and occupations. Adjustment assistance, which is especially important in middle- and high-income countries, will help workers adapt to the changing patterns of production and distribution that GVCs bring about. Adjustment policies can include facilitating labor mobility and equipping workers to find new jobs.[18] Because unemployment resulting from structural change tends to be persistent, wage insurance can help keep workers employed in lower-paying jobs without experiencing income loss, leading to better long-term outcomes. For example, Denmark's successful "flexicurity" model gives employers the freedom to hire and fire workers with few restrictions, but it supports workers with generous unemployment benefits and active labor market programs.

Labor regulations, when well designed and enforced, help ensure the safety and health of workers. Private firms can contribute, especially when their consumers are sensitive to labor conditions in the firm's global operations. There is also an important role for national policy supported by international cooperation in establishing and monitoring appropriate labor standards. In Vietnam, working conditions improved when firms participated in the International Labour Organization-International Finance Corporation (ILO-IFC) Better Work Programme, alongside complementary government action to publicly disclose the names of firms that fail to meet key labor standards.[19]

Pricing environmental degradation can prevent GVCs from magnifying misallocations of resources.[20] Prices of goods should reflect both their economic and socioenvironmental costs. Appropriate pricing of environmental damage would also encourage innovation in environmentally friendly goods and production processes. Reducing distortions, such as those created by energy and production subsidies, and shifting toward taxing carbon would improve resource allocation and reduce CO_2 emissions.[21] In addition, environmental regulations, especially for specific industries and pollutants, could curb the damage caused by GVC-related production and transport.

International cooperation supports beneficial GVC participation

The international trade system is especially valuable in a GVC world. GVCs span boundaries, and policy action or inaction in one country can affect producers and consumers in other countries. International cooperation can help address the spillover effects of national policies and achieve better development outcomes. Because the costs of protection are magnified when goods and services cross borders multiple times, the gains from coordinated reduction of barriers to trade are even larger for GVCs than for standard trade. In view of the inextricable link between foreign investment and GVCs, creating an open and secure climate for investment is vital for GVC participation, especially by capital-scarce countries.

Developing countries have benefited enormously from the rules-based trade system, particularly its guarantees against trade discrimination, incentives to

reform, market access around the globe, and recourse in case of disputes—even against the trade heavyweights. Today, however, the international trade system is under tremendous pressure. Three decades of trade-led catchup growth in developing countries has contributed to shifts in economic power across countries and increased income inequality within countries. The growing symmetry in the economic size of countries is placing in sharp relief the persistent asymmetry in their levels of protection. Meanwhile, the trade system, which adapted to changes in the past, has faltered in recent years, most notably with the failure of the Doha negotiations. Regional initiatives such as the European Union and NAFTA have also been hurt by disagreements among member countries.

The trade conflict between the United States and China is leading to protection and policy uncertainty, and it is beginning to disrupt GVCs. If the trade conflict worsens and causes a slump in investor confidence, the effects on global growth and poverty could be significant—more than 30 million people could be pushed into poverty (measured as income levels below $5.50 a day), and global income could fall by as much as $1.4 trillion. That said, even in the status quo, adverse effects are likely to have resulted from the trade practices that provoked the conflict.

To sustain beneficial trade openness, it is essential to "walk on two legs." The first priority is to deepen traditional trade cooperation to address remaining barriers to trade in goods and services, as well as other measures that distort trade, such as subsidies and the activities of state-owned enterprises. In parallel, cooperation should be widened beyond trade policy to include taxes, regulation, and infrastructure.

Deepen traditional cooperation

Looking ahead, the first priority should be to deepen traditional trade rules and commitments. International cooperation has so far delivered uneven openness in goods and services. Trade liberalization is overdue in agriculture and services, and some industrial goods remain restricted in certain markets and by nontariff measures. Trade preferences have reduced certain tariffs faced predominantly by the poorest countries—but not the tariffs these countries impose on their imports. Special and differential treatment for developing countries has in some cases accommodated sluggish reform, ultimately inhibiting GVC participation and integration into the global economy.

In addition, the escalation of tariffs in some of the world's largest markets—which serve to protect higher value-added production—is inhibiting processing activities in agroindustry and other labor-intensive areas such as apparel and leather goods in developing countries. Restrictive rules of origin in preferential agreements are curtailing sourcing options. Subsidies and state-owned firms are distorting competition, and the existing rules do not guarantee competitive neutrality. For services, international negotiations have delivered little liberalization beyond that undertaken unilaterally. Important GVC-relevant services, such as air and maritime transportation (which most need coordinated liberalization), have been excluded from negotiations because of the power of vested interests.

Traditional trade negotiations may deliver more meaningful outcomes if the major developing country traders engage as equal partners and even leaders instead of seeking special and differential treatment; if the large industrial countries continue to place their faith in rules-based negotiations instead of resorting to unilateral protection; and if all countries work together to define a negotiating agenda that reflects both development and business priorities.

Widen cooperation on taxes, competition, and data flows

Taxing capital is increasingly difficult in an era of global firms, fragmented production, and growth in intangible assets such as intellectual property. Cooperation should ensure fair access to tax revenues—which rich countries need to help displaced industrial workers and poor countries need to build infrastructure. Ultimately, a joint approach to greater use of destination-based taxation could eliminate firms' incentives to shift profits and countries' incentives to compete over taxes, but the consequences for tax revenue in small developing countries would have to be considered. Meanwhile, other measures to combat tax base erosion and income shifting could alleviate associated challenges for domestic resource mobilization.

Among consumers, concern is growing about data flows and the international expansion of digital firms, both of which play an important role in GVCs. The risks range from privacy abuses in data-based services to anticompetitive practices in platform-based services. Governments are resorting to data localization laws to limit the cross-border mobility of data and to strict rules on the handling of data domestically. Competition laws, too, remain explicitly nationalist in focus, and cooperation in bilateral or regional trading agreements has been limited. The solution may be a new type of bargain: regulatory commitments by exporting firms to protect the interests of consumers abroad in return for market access commitments by importing countries, as is the case in some recent agreements on data flows.

But developing countries must not be left out of such arrangements because that would undermine their productive engagement in GVCs. International support can help them to both make regulatory commitments in areas of export interest (such as in data-based services) and extract commitments from their trading partners when they open their markets (such as for the enforcement of competition policy).

Finally, coordination failures in infrastructure investment affect GVC investment, expansion, and upgrading, especially in the poorest countries. From a global perspective, countries underinvest in trade-related infrastructure because they do not take into account the additional benefits to their trade partners. Countries that share a border can obtain larger gains when they act simultaneously to expedite trade. Guatemala and Honduras, for example, reduced border delays from 10 hours to 15 minutes when they joined a customs union and agreed to accept the same electronic documentation. The World Trade Organization's Trade Facilitation Agreement encourages countries to coordinate improvements in trade facilitation, and provides low-income countries with financial assistance for the necessary investments. A similar approach may help exploit synergies for other investments in transport, energy, and communications infrastructure.

Notes

1. Constantinescu, Mattoo, and Ruta (2018).
2. Constantinescu, Mattoo, and Ruta (2018).
3. In Vietnam, firms that both import and export employ more workers than firms that export only and firms that do not trade, controlling for sector and province fixed effects as well as state and foreign ownership. In Mexico, firms that have relationships with buyers, as well as firms that export and import, also see higher employment than firms that only import or only export. This finding holds even when considering the regional, sector, and foreign ownership characteristics of firms. Across a country, then, firms that both import and export employ more workers than one-way traders or nontraders.
4. Rocha and Winkler (2019).
5. The poverty elasticity of growth depends on various factors, including its incidence (changes in inequality), the initial distribution of land, wealth and income, education levels among the poor, other forms of past public investment, as well as local institutions, including unions (Ferreira, Leite, and Ravallion 2010; Ravallion and Datt 2002). Also see Dollar and Kraay (2002) and Ferreira and Ravallion (2008).
6. Markups can increase because prices are higher, or because costs are lower, or a combination of both when

markets are not perfectly competitive, meaning that firms can affect prices. The effect on firms' markups depends on whether the reduction in costs, or the gains from GVC participation, are passed fully on to the consumer through lower prices.

7. Feenstra and Hanson (1996, 1997); Verhoogen (2008).
8. Rocha and Winkler (2019).
9. Oldenski (2015) provides evidence that reshoring is not widespread in the United States.
10. Artuc, Bastos, and Rijkers (2018).
11. Freund, Mulabdic, and Ruta (2018).
12. See Chen and Wu (2018); Garicano and Kaplan (2001); Höppner and Westerhoff (2018).
13. The positive association between FDI and capital, technology, and management skills is driven by GVC participation in the manufacturing sector only. There is no association between FDI inflows and countries' GVC integration of their agriculture, commodities, or services sectors. This finding could point to a more favorable role for efficiency-seeking or market-seeking FDI that looks for internationally cost-competitive destinations and potential export platforms. See Buelens and Tirpák (2017) for further evidence that bilateral FDI stocks are positively associated with the bilateral backward GVC participation as well as with bilateral gross trade.
14. APEC and World Bank (2018).
15. According to Johnson and Noguera (2017), the European Union and other preferential trade agreements, especially deep ones, play an important role in decreasing the ratio of bilateral value added to gross exports, a sign of growth in global production fragmentation.
16. Pierola, Fernandes, and Farole (2018).
17. Evidence from the Eora database by Lenzen, Kanemoto, Moran, and Geschke (2012), (https://worldmrio.com/) shows a U-shaped relationship between GDP per capita and forward GVC integration across countries.
18. Bown and Freund (2019).
19. Hollweg (2019).
20. Gollier and Tirole (2015); Nordhaus (2015).
21. Cramton et al. (2017); Farid et al. (2016); Weitzman (2017).

References

APEC (Asia–Pacific Economic Cooperation) and World Bank. 2018. "Promoting Open and Competitive Markets in Road Freight and Logistics Services: The World Bank Group's Markets and Competition Policy Assessment Tool Applied in Peru, the Philippines, and Vietnam." Unpublished report, World Bank, Washington, DC.

Artuc, Erhan, Paulo S. R. Bastos, and Bob Rijkers. 2018. "Robots, Tasks, and Trade." Policy Research Paper 8674, World Bank, Washington, DC.

Borin, Alessandro, and Michele Mancini. 2015. "Follow the Value Added: Bilateral Gross Export Accounting." Temi di discussione (Economic Working Paper) 1026, Economic Research and International Relations Area, Bank of Italy.

———. 2019. "Measuring What Matters in Global Value Chains and Value-Added Trade." Policy Research Working Paper 8804, World Bank, Washington, DC.

Bown, Chad P., and Caroline L. Freund. 2019. "Active Labor Market Policies: Lessons from Other Countries for the United States." PIIE Working Paper 19–2 (January), Peterson Institute for International Economics, Washington, DC.

Buelens, Christian, and Marcel Tirpák. 2017. "Reading the Footprints: How Foreign Investors Shape Countries' Participation in Global Value Chains." Comparative Economic Studies 59 (4): 561–84.

Chen, Maggie Xiaoyang, and Min Wu. 2018. "The Value of Reputation in Trade: Evidence from Alibaba." Paper presented at Workshop on Trade and the Chinese Economy, King Center on Global Development, Stanford University, Stanford, CA, April 12–13.

Constantinescu, Ileana Cristina Neagu, Aaditya Mattoo, and Michele Ruta. 2018. "The Global Trade Slowdown: Cyclical or Structural?" World Bank Economic Review. Published electronically May 23. https://doi.org/10.1093/wber/lhx027.

Cramton, Peter, David J. MacKay, Axel Ockenfels, and Steven Stoft, eds. 2017. Global Carbon Pricing: The Path to Climate Cooperation. Cambridge, MA: MIT Press.

Dollar, David, and Aart Kraay. 2002. "Growth Is Good for the Poor." Journal of Economic Growth 7 (3): 195–225.

Farid, Mai, Michael Keen, Michael G. Papaioannou, Ian W. H. Parry, Catherine A. Pattillo, and Anna Ter-Martirosyan. 2016. "After Paris: Fiscal, Macroeconomic, and Financial Implications of Global Climate Change." IMF Staff Discussion Note 16/01 (January), International Monetary Fund, Washington, DC.

Feenstra, Robert C., and Gordon H. Hanson. 1996. "Foreign Investment, Outsourcing, and Relative Wages." In The Political Economy of Trade Policy: Papers in Honor of Jagdish Bhagwati, edited by Robert C. Feenstra, Gene M. Grossman, and Douglas A. Irwin, 89–128. Cambridge, MA: MIT Press.

———. 1997. "Foreign Direct Investment and Relative Wages: Evidence from Mexico's Maquiladoras." Journal of International Economics 42 (3–4): 371–93.

Ferreira, Francisco H. G., Phillippe George Leite, and Martin Ravallion. 2010. "Poverty Reduction without Economic Growth? Explaining Brazil's Poverty Dynamics, 1985–2004." Journal of Development Economics 93 (1): 20–36.

Ferreira, Francisco H. G., and Martin Ravallion. 2008. "Global Poverty and Inequality: A Review of the Evidence." Policy Research Working Paper 4623, World Bank, Washington, DC.

Freund, Caroline L., Alen Mulabdic, and Michele Ruta. 2018. "Is 3D Printing a Threat to Global Trade? The Trade Effects You Didn't Hear About." Unpublished working paper, World Bank, Washington, DC.

Garicano, Luis, and Steven N. Kaplan. 2001. "The Effects of Business-to-Business E-Commerce on Transaction Costs." Journal of Industrial Economics 49 (4): 463–85.

Gollier, Christian, and Jean Tirole. 2015. "Negotiating Effective Institutions against Climate Change." Economics of Energy and Environmental Policy 4 (2): 5–27.

Hollweg, Claire H. 2019. "Firm Compliance and Public Disclosure in Vietnam." Policy Research Working Paper 9026, World Bank, Washington, DC.

Höppner, Thomas, and Phillipp Westerhoff. 2018. "The EU's Competition Investigation into Amazon Marketplace." *Kluwer Competition Law Blog*, November 30, Wolters Kluwer, Alphen aan den Rijn, The Netherlands. http://competitionlawblog.kluwercompetitionlaw.com/2018/11/30/the-eus-competition-investigation-into-amazon-marketplace/.

ILO (International Labour Organization) and IFC (International Finance Corporation). 2016. "Progress and Potential: How Better Work Is Improving Garment Workers' Lives and Boosting Factory Competitiveness." International Labour Office, Geneva. https://betterwork.org/dev/wp-content/uploads/2016/09/BW-Progress-and-Potential_Web-final.pdf.

Johnson, Robert Christopher, and Guillermo Noguera. 2012. "Accounting for Intermediates: Production Sharing and Trade in Value Added." *Journal of International Economics* 86 (2): 224–36.

——. 2017. "A Portrait of Trade in Value-Added over Four Decades." *Review of Economics and Statistics* 99 (5): 896–911.

Lenzen, M., K. Kanemoto, D. Moran, and A. Geschke. 2012. "Mapping the Structure of the World Economy." *Environmental Science & Technology* 46 (15): 8374–81.

Nordhaus, William. 2015. "Climate Clubs: Overcoming Free-Riding in International Climate Policy." *American Economic Review* 105 (4): 1339–70.

Oldenski, Lindsay. 2015. "Reshoring by U.S. Firms: What Do the Data Say?" PIIE Policy Brief 15–14 (September), Peterson Institute for International Economics, Washington, DC.

Pierola, Martha Denisse, Ana Margarida Fernandes, and Thomas Farole. 2018. "The Role of Imports for Exporter Performance in Peru." *World Economy* 41 (2): 550–72.

Ravallion, Martin, and Guarav Datt. 2002. "Why Has Economic Growth Been More Pro-Poor in Some States of India than Others?" *Journal of Development Economics* 68 (2): 381–400.

Rocha, Nadia, and Deborah Winkler. 2019. "Trade and Female Labor Participation: Stylized Facts Using a Global Dataset." Background paper, World Bank-World Trade Organization Trade and Gender Report, World Bank, Washington, DC.

Verhoogen, Eric A. 2008. "Trade, Quality Upgrading, and Wage Inequality in the Mexican Manufacturing Sector." *Quarterly Journal of Economics* 123 (2): 489–530.

Weitzman, Martin L. 2017. "How a Minimum Carbon-Price Commitment Might Help to Internalize the Global Warming Externality." In *Global Carbon Pricing: The Path to Climate Collaboration*, edited by Peter Cramton, David J. C. MacKay, Axel Ockenfels, and Steven Stoft, 125–48. Cambridge, MA: MIT Press.

PART II

Global value chains: What are they?

The new face of trade

Key findings

- **Global value chains (GVCs) expanded in the 1990s and 2000s, but that expansion has slowed since the financial crisis of 2008.** One reason is lower global economic growth and investment. Another is the lack of major liberalization initiatives in recent years.

- **GVCs matter for development.** GVC trade exhibits two features that distinguish it from traditional trade: hyperspecialization and durable firm-to-firm relationships. These features allow firms to raise productivity and income, rendering GVC trade more powerful than traditional trade in supporting growth and poverty reduction.

- **All countries participate in GVCs but in different ways.** Developed and large emerging countries participate in complex GVCs producing advanced and innovative manufactures and services. By contrast, many countries in Africa, Central Asia, and Latin America still produce commodities for further processing in other countries or engage in limited manufacturing.

- **The intensification of GVCs was driven by a handful of regions, sectors, and firms.** GVCs grew in the machinery, electronics, and transportation sectors and in the regions specializing in those sectors: East Asia, North America, and Western Europe. Within countries, a few large trading firms dominate GVC trade, supported by foreign direct investment.

- **More-complex value chains have stronger regional linkages, although GVCs have expanded both globally and regionally.** GVCs in East Asia and Europe are more focused on trade within the region. GVCs in North America depend somewhat more on global partners. Elsewhere, GVC integration has been mostly global and is primarily continuing in that direction.

Production of goods and services was increasingly globalized from 1990 to 2008. The process was more pronounced in some regions and sectors than in others as firms began to organize their production in complex global value chains (GVCs). They designed products in one country, procured parts and components from several countries, and assembled the final products in yet another country. As a result, international trade and investment flows increased considerably, far outpacing the growth of economic output. However, with the 2008 global financial crisis and the great recession that followed, the growth of GVCs and trade slowed, prompting speculation that the phenomenon had run its course.

Some aspects of this wave of globalization are not new. International trade in raw materials and intermediate inputs has been a prominent feature of world trade flows since time immemorial. For example, Assyrian merchants who settled in Kanesh (in modern-day Turkey) in the 19th century BCE imported luxury fabrics and tin from Aššur and traded copper and wool within Anatolia.[1] Past increases in the ratio of trade to the gross domestic product (GDP) have been substantial and sustained. The "First Globalization" during 1870–1914 saw a major increase in international trade flows, largely attributed to the steamship. Similarly, today's wave of globalization has been fueled by falling trade costs due to technological developments such as containerization and policy reforms, particularly the integration of China and Eastern Europe into the world economy and major trade agreements such as the North American Free Trade Agreement (NAFTA) and the Uruguay Round, which established the World Trade Organization (WTO) in 1995.

This wave of globalization has, however, some new features. For example, by integrating in GVCs developing countries can take advantage of richer states' industrial bases rather than having to build up entire industries from scratch. In this way, they accelerate their industrialization and development. Moreover, trade within GVCs intensifies the effects of standard trade integration. Fragmented production makes it possible for firms in developing countries to enter foreign markets at lower costs, benefit from specialization in niche tasks, and gain access to larger markets for their output. Companies can also access cheaper and better inputs, productivity-enhancing technologies, and improved management practices developed elsewhere, and thus grow at a faster rate, contributing to the creation of better, higher-paying jobs. Because

of these features, GVCs are becoming more attractive to policy makers in developing countries.

Given their development potential, the stagnation of trade growth and GVC formation since the financial crisis is a concern. The slowdown is partly cyclical. Trade growth is lower because output growth is lower in the major trading economies, including Europe—which accounts for one-fourth of global output and one-third of world trade—and China. The slowdown is also structural. Trade growth has become less responsive to income growth over the last decade, particularly in China and the United States, both major actors in GVCs. Part of this development reflects changes in the two economies as China moves up the value chain and the U.S. energy sector expands. But it also reflects the absence of major new liberalization initiatives, such as the Uruguay Round, and of major reforms by the large emerging markets—reforms similar to those by China and Eastern Europe in the 1990s.

This chapter analyzes the changing patterns in global trade and investment over the last 30 years and the importance of GVCs in shaping these shifts. Using new data, it characterizes the GVC phenomenon across regions, countries, and sectors. In so doing, it provides a better understanding of what is new in the world of GVCs, setting the stage for the Report's analysis of how GVCs affect economic development, inequality, and poverty alleviation.

This chapter offers three main findings. First, countries participate in GVCs in different ways. Argentina, Ethiopia, and Indonesia are more engaged in simple manufacturing production chains, whereas Algeria, Chile, and Nigeria export commodities or raw materials for further processing. India and the United States produce services that are being increasingly traded and embodied in manufactured goods. And mostly advanced countries and large emerging economies are producing innovative goods and services.

Second, the intensification of GVC trade is concentrated in a handful of regions, sectors, and firms. GVC linkages have expanded fastest in the three trade hubs—East Asia, Europe, and North America—in part because these regions account for a large share of production in the sectors whose production processes have become the most fragmented across countries, particularly electronics, machinery, and transport equipment. In each country, GVCs tend to be concentrated among 15 percent of large firms that both import and export and together account for 80 percent of total trade flows. Related-party trade, such as that through multinational corporations, is especially important.

Third, more-complex value chains tend to have especially strong regional linkages, although the expansion of GVCs has been both global and regional. Europe is the most integrated region, with four times as many regional linkages as global linkages. In East Asia, linkages are more regional than global, and the regional linkages have intensified substantially since 1990. By contrast, GVCs in North America depend somewhat more on global partners than regional partners, and integration has been increasing on both fronts. Elsewhere, GVC integration has been mostly global and has been increasing primarily with global partners. Importantly, in recent decades the differences in GVC participation across regions have been far greater than the changes within regions. The same dynamic applies to sectors.

What is a global value chain?

The bicycle is the world's most popular form of transport. Invented in Germany in the early 19th century, bicycles were mass-produced by the Dutch at the end of that century, sometimes with frames imported from England. Global production later grew from about 10 million units in 1950 to more than 130 million units today.

Bicycles are heavily traded. They are assembled using parts and components from all over the world, especially Asia and Europe (figure 1.1). For example, Bianchi carries out all of its design, proto-typing, and conception work in Italy, and then assembles most of its bicycles in Taiwan, China, using parts and components from China, Italy, Japan, Malaysia, and many other parts of the world. Each parts producer has niche expertise—

Figure 1.1 Where do bicycles come from?

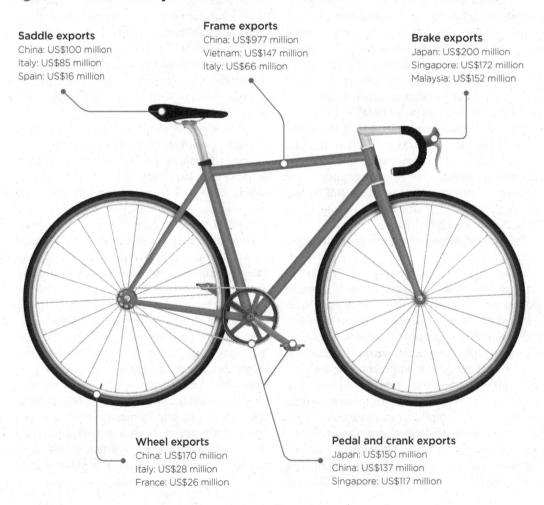

Saddle exports
China: US$100 million
Italy: US$85 million
Spain: US$16 million

Frame exports
China: US$977 million
Vietnam: US$147 million
Italy: US$66 million

Brake exports
Japan: US$200 million
Singapore: US$172 million
Malaysia: US$152 million

Wheel exports
China: US$170 million
Italy: US$28 million
France: US$26 million

Pedal and crank exports
Japan: US$150 million
China: US$137 million
Singapore: US$117 million

Source: WDR 2020 team, using data from UN Comtrade database. See appendix A for a description of the databases used in this Report.

Shimano of Japan, for example, makes brakes for Bianchi, and the handlebars are made in Taiwan, China.

Assembling a bicycle from parts and components made around the world improves efficiency and results in a cheaper and higher-quality bicycle for the consumer. The bicycle frame requires steel, aluminum, or carbon fiber tubing and welding. The wheel must be straightened in both radial and lateral directions to ensure uniform tension.

A quality saddle requires the know-how to produce high-tech gel.

Because of the extensive bicycle value chain, the trade in bicycle parts has outstripped the trade in bicycles by 15–25 percent in recent years. In Finland, 33 percent of value added is from outside the country, including 13 percent from the European Union (EU), 11 percent from Asia, and 5 percent from North America.[2] Boxes 1.1 and 1.2 define GVCs and explain how data are used to estimate GVC participation more broadly.

Box 1.1 Defining global value chains

A global value chain (GVC) is the series of stages in the production of a product or service for sale to consumers. Each stage adds value, and at least two stages are in different countries. For example, a bike assembled in Finland with parts from Italy, Japan, and Malaysia and exported to the Arab Republic of Egypt is a GVC. By this definition, a country, sector, or firm participates in a GVC if it engages in (at least) one stage in a GVC.

Defining spiders and snakes
The definition of a GVC does not specify the form the foreign value added in production will take, although it is often associated with either international trade in raw materials (such as tin or aluminum), in intermediate inputs (such as car parts), or in tasks (such as back-office services). Similarly, the definition does not mention the various configurations that a GVC might take, including simple spiderlike structures, with multiple parts and components converging at an assembly plant, or snakelike structures, with value created sequentially in a series of stages.[a]

Regardless of the shape of GVCs, the possibility of fragmenting production across borders gives rise to a finer international division of labor and greater gains from specialization. GVCs allow resources to flow to their most productive use, not only across countries and sectors, but also within sectors across stages of production. As a result, GVCs magnify the growth, employment, and distributional impacts of standard trade.

In summary, unlike traditional international trade whose transactions involve only two countries (an exporting country and an importing country), GVC trade crosses borders multiple times. This approach to trade not only leads to the rich set of determinants and consequences of GVC participation described in this Report, but also creates challenges for measuring GVC activity in the world.

a. Baldwin and Venables (2013).

Box 1.2 Measuring global value chains

The main challenge in measuring where value is added in a GVC arises from the fact that customs data, the standard source for international trade flows, provide information on *where* the transacted good or service was produced, but not on *how* it was produced—that is, which countries contributed value to it. Similarly, customs data record *where* the transacted good is flowing to, but not *how* it will be used—that is, whether it will be fully consumed (absorbed) in the importing country, or whether it will be reexported after the importing country adds value to it.

A macro view of GVCs
With the goal of tracing value-added trade flows across countries, a body of work has combined information from customs offices with national input–output tables to construct global input–output tables. The most widely used are

(Box continues next page)

Box 1.2 Measuring global value chains *(continued)*

the World Input–Output Database (WIOD), a collaborative project led by researchers at the University of Groningen; the Trade in Value Added (TiVA) database compiled by the Organisation for Economic Co-operation and Development (OECD); and the Eora global supply chain database, constructed by a team of researchers at the University of Sydney.[a] On a very broad level, these collaborative projects can be thought of as "scaled up" versions of product-level studies, such as the bicycle study, which showed that 33 percent of value added came from foreign countries.[b]

Such global input–output tables can be used to devise alternative ways of measuring the extent to which production processes have globalized in recent years and how countries and sectors participate in GVCs. Building on global input–output tables, a natural measure of the importance of GVC trade in total international trade is the share of trade that flows through at least two borders (see Borin and Mancini [2015, 2019] for details on the methodology). Such trade encompasses two broad types of GVC trade:

- *Backward GVC participation,* in which a country's exports embody value added previously imported from abroad. For example, if the bicycles exported by Taiwan, China, use imported intermediates, then its GVC participation is considered backward because the intermediates used in exports are from the previous stage.
- *Forward GVC participation,* in which a country's exports are not fully absorbed in the importing country and instead are embodied in the importing country's exports to third countries. In the bicycle example, if India sends aluminum tubing to Taiwan, China, where it is further used in the production of the bicycle later exported, then India's GVC participation is considered forward because the exporter is at the early stage of production of the bicycle.

Despite their widespread use, global input–output tables have two limitations. First, because they rely on aggregated input–output data, the resulting sectoral disaggregation of GVC flows is coarse. They therefore miss a lot of GVC activity within the broadly defined sectors. For example, one can compute the origin of "fabricated metal products"

in the production of "motor vehicles" in the United States but cannot infer where more specific components such as tires, car engines, or windshield wipers originate. Second, in constructing the tables, researchers are forced to impose strong assumptions to back out some bilateral intermediate input trade flows that cannot be readily read from either customs data or national input–output tables.[c]

A micro view of GVCs

A more granular approach to measuring the fragmentation of production processes across countries, first suggested by Yeats (1998), computes the share of trade flows accounted for by industry categories that can safely be assumed to contain only intermediate inputs (reflected in the words "Parts of" at the outset of the product description). Yeats found that intermediate input categories accounted for about 30 percent of OECD merchandise exports of machinery and transport equipment in 1995, and that this share had steadily increased from 26 percent in 1978. Yeats's classification has continued to be refined in recent years based on the Broad Economic Categories (BEC) product classification of the United Nations Conference on Trade and Development (UNCTAD).[d]

More recently, customs data at the firm level have been used to advance measurement of GVC linkages. An important strength of these data is that transactions between firms and their foreign partner countries can be observed rather than inferred. In addition, firm-level data capture the heterogeneity in GVC linkages across firms that is obscured by aggregated industry-level data and thus allow a finer understanding of firms' input sourcing decisions, how import and export participation are linked, and how multinational firms organize their production networks. However, such data do not trace firm-to-firm transactions across countries. This would require linking customs offices and firm identifiers across the world.[e] Thus in the absence of such data, the best option is to continue improving the measurement of GVC linkages at both the macro and micro levels across a wider range of countries to gain a more complete empirical measurement of GVCs.

a. This chapter and the rest of this Report rely on several global input–output databases for the analysis. The choice of database is dictated by the level of geographical or sectoral coverage needed for the analysis. Eora offers the largest country coverage for the longest continuous time period, but its sectoral coverage is more aggregate and thus less precise than the WIOD and TiVA databases. See Lenzen, Kanemoto, Moran, and Geschke (2012) for a description of EORA; and Borin and Mancini (2019), Johnson (2018), and appendix A for a more detailed description of these and other databases used in this Report.
b. Kalm et al. (2013); OECD (2013).
c. The homogeneity and proportionality assumptions are conveniently imposed to resolve the fact that the available data sets have no

information on which domestic industries buy which imports. However, such assumptions are not necessarily valid. Specifically, under the homogeneity assumption all firms in the same industry are assumed to have the same production function and use the same bundle of inputs. Yet at the country-industry level, input use varies with output because firms exporting to different countries and industries participate in different value chains and face distinct rules of origin (de Gortari 2019).
d. UN Trade Statistics, Intermediate Goods in Trade Statistics, https:// unstats.un.org/unsd/tradekb/Knowledgebase/50090/Intermediate -Goods-in-Trade-Statistics.
e. Johnson (2018).

The evolution of GVC participation

The overall share of GVC trade in total world trade—encompassing both forward and backward linkages—grew significantly in the 1990s and early 2000s, but it appears to have stagnated or even declined in the last 10 years (figure 1.2). Still, about half of world trade appears to be related to GVCs.

What explains the remarkable rise in GVC participation in the 1990s and 2000s? And why has this process stalled since the financial crisis?

The global wave of fragmentation of production in the 1990s and 2000s was driven by a combination of factors. The information and communication technology (ICT) revolution brought forth cheaper and more reliable telecommunications, new information management software, and increasingly powerful personal computers (figure 1.3, panel a). Manufacturing firms then found it easier to outsource and coordinate complex activities at a distance and ensure the quality of their inputs. In addition, firms were able to disperse production across the world because transport costs fell significantly (figure 1.3, panel b). Declining air and sea freight costs boosted the trade in goods, while services benefited from cheaper communication costs.

Successive rounds of trade liberalization have resulted in rapidly falling barriers to trade and investment for both developed and developing countries. Tariffs have declined, especially for manufactured goods, and the gradual, although still insufficient, lowering of nontariff barriers has facilitated the international trade of goods and services (figure 1.4). Finally, the creation of the European single market—together with the integration of China, India, and the Soviet Union into the global economy—created huge new product and labor markets, and so firms could sell the same goods to more people and take advantage of economies of scale leading to the further deepening of GVCs. The new supply of cheap labor encouraged profit-seeking companies to either reallocate their production facilities or find local suppliers in low-wage countries.[3]

Since the global financial crisis in 2008, the dynamics of GVC expansion have changed. Trade has bounced back from its deep crisis level, but it has grown only marginally faster than output. Trade in parts and components also stalled after the financial crisis and even fell between 2011 and 2014, with a modest increase since then.

The factors behind the trade and GVC slowdown are both cyclical and structural in nature. On the one hand, trade growth is lower because global output growth is lower in economies that account for large shares of global trade and global output, such as Europe and China. Trade has also grown at a slower pace because the trade-to-income elasticity—defined as the amount of trade generated as output rises—has decreased. This is especially true in large trading countries, including China and the United States. China is producing more at home, thereby becoming less reliant on imported components for its exports. The share of intermediate imports in exports of Chinese goods dropped from about 50 percent in the 1990s to a little over 30 percent in 2015. In the United States, a booming shale sector reduced oil imports by one-fourth between 2010 and 2015.[4]

As for any major liberalization initiatives that might have set off a new wave of GVC formation, there have been none. The Doha Round stalled, and no large emerging markets are engaging in the types of drastic reforms undertaken decades ago in China and Eastern Europe.

All countries partake in GVCs, but across the world their participation is uneven (map 1.1). Some countries

Figure 1.2 GVC trade grew rapidly in the 1990s but stagnated after the 2008 global financial crisis

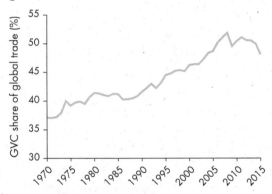

Sources: WDR 2020 team, using data from Eora26 database; Borin and Mancini (2015, 2019); and Johnson and Noguera (2017). See appendix A for a description of the databases used in this Report.

Note: Unless otherwise specified, GVC participation measures used in this and subsequent figures throughout the Report follow the methodology from Borin and Mancini (2015, 2019). The Eora26 database is used because it offers the largest country coverage: 190 countries between 1990 and 2015. GVC participation corresponds to the share of world exports that flow through at least two borders. For 1990–2015, the GVC participation measure is computed as the share of GVC exports in total international exports using the Borin and Mancini methodology. GVC exports include transactions in which a country's exports embody value added that it previously imported from abroad (backward GVC participation), as well as transactions in which a country's exports are not fully absorbed in the importing country and instead are embodied in the importing country's exports to third countries (forward GVC participation). For 1970–90, the GVC participation measure is backcasted using the above data and the time variation of the measure (1-VAX). The VAX by Johnson and Noguera (2017) is an alternative measure of the value-added content of trade. Although the level difference between (1-VAX) and the GVC participation measure is sizable, the correlation of their change over the overlapping years (1990–2009) is 0.97. This method allows reconstructing a long series covering 1970–2015 rather than simply 1990–2015 for which the Eora26 database is available.

Figure 1.3 The ICT revolution spurred the emergence of GVCs

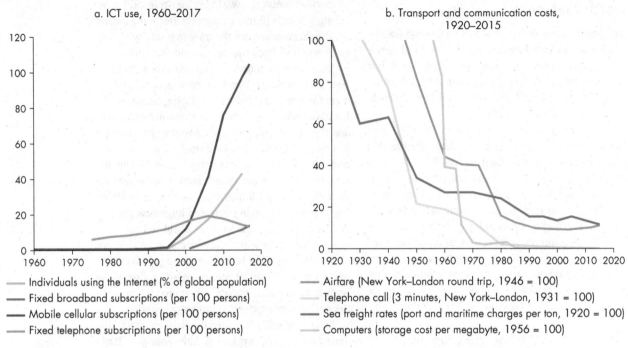

a. ICT use, 1960–2017

b. Transport and communication costs, 1920–2015

—— Individuals using the Internet (% of global population)
—— Fixed broadband subscriptions (per 100 persons)
—— Mobile cellular subscriptions (per 100 persons)
—— Fixed telephone subscriptions (per 100 persons)

—— Airfare (New York–London round trip, 1946 = 100)
—— Telephone call (3 minutes, New York–London, 1931 = 100)
—— Sea freight rates (port and maritime charges per ton, 1920 = 100)
—— Computers (storage cost per megabyte, 1956 = 100)

Sources: WDR 2020 team, using data from ITU's World Telecommunication/ICT Indicators database for panel a and based on Rodrigue, Comtois, and Slack (2017) for panel b.

Note: In panel a, data are available for over 200 countries. Mobile cellular subscriptions per 100 persons may be over 100 as some people may have several mobile phones. In panel b, for each indicator the cost is reported as 100 for the first year with data. ICT = information and communication technology.

Figure 1.4 From 1948 to 2016, tariffs dropped thanks to multilateral and regional trade agreements

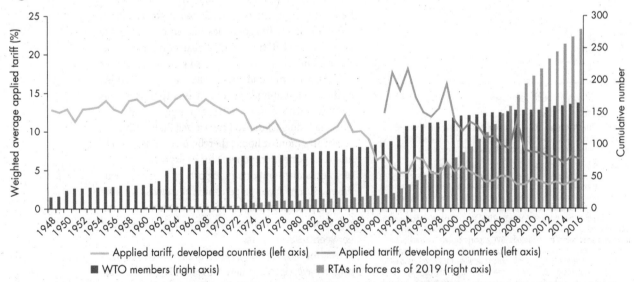

—— Applied tariff, developed countries (left axis)   —— Applied tariff, developing countries (left axis)
■ WTO members (right axis)   ■ RTAs in force as of 2019 (right axis)

Sources: WDR 2020 team, based on Baldwin (2012). Data for regional trade agreements (RTAs) and World Trade Organization (WTO) members are from the WTO's RTAs database. Tariff data prior to 1988 are from Clemens and Williamson (2004), and those for subsequent years are from the World Bank's WDI database using country-level weighted applied tariffs for all products.

Note: The figure plots tariffs computed as simple averages for developed and developing countries. Prior to 1988, the developed country sample covers 35 countries, including 21 industrialized countries (Argentina, Australia, Austria-Hungary, Canada, Chile, Cuba, Denmark, France, Germany, Greece, Italy, New Zealand, Norway, Portugal, Russia, Serbia, Spain, Sweden, the United Kingdom, the United States, and Uruguay) and 14 developing countries at the time: Brazil, Burma (now Myanmar), Ceylon (now Sri Lanka), China, Colombia, Egypt, India, Indonesia, Japan, Mexico, Peru, the Philippines, Siam (now Thailand), and Turkey. After 1988, developed countries are defined as high-income countries and developing countries as not high-income countries based on the World Bank's 2018 country classification.

Map 1.1 All countries participate in GVCs—but not in the same way

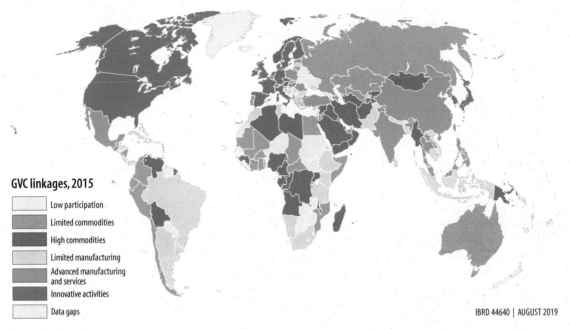

GVC linkages, 2015

- Low participation
- Limited commodities
- High commodities
- Limited manufacturing
- Advanced manufacturing and services
- Innovative activities
- Data gaps

IBRD 44640 | AUGUST 2019

Source: WDR 2020 team, based on the GVC taxonomy for 2015 (see box 1.3).

Note: The type of a country's GVC linkages is based on the country's extent of backward GVC participation, measured as the portion of imports embodied in manufacturing exports as a percentage of a country's total exports, combined with the country's sector specialization of domestic value added in exports and engagement in innovation. Countries in the commodities group have a small share of manufacturing exports and limited backward GVC integration. Their share of commodity exports can be low, medium, or high. Countries specialized in limited manufacturing GVCs engage in some manufacturing exports, often alongside commodities exports, and exhibit medium backward GVC integration. Countries specialized in advanced manufacturing and services GVCs have a high share of manufacturing and business services exports and high backward GVC integration. Countries specialized in innovative GVC activities spend a large share of GDP on research and development, receive a large share of GDP from intellectual property, and exhibit high backward GVC integration.

export raw materials for further processing; others import inputs for assembly and exports; and still others produce complex goods and services. In addition, some are heavily reliant on GVCs for trade, whereas others export largely domestic goods for consumption. To capture these distinct features of participation, countries are classified into four main types—commodities, limited manufacturing, advanced manufacturing and services, and innovative activities—based on the products they export and their participation in GVCs. The rules for classification are described in box 1.3.

This taxonomy reveals clear distinctions among regions. East Asia, Europe, and North America are engaged in advanced manufacturing and services GVCs and innovative GVC activities, whereas Africa, Central Asia, and Latin America are mostly in commodities and limited manufacturing GVCs.

GVC participation intensified between 1990 and 2015, as illustrated by the many countries that transitioned up into more sophisticated forms of GVC participation (figure 1.5). Transitions were especially common in East Asia and Europe, where countries were heavily engaged in the sectors most amenable to GVCs, such as electronics and machinery. Among advanced countries, small open economies tended to

Figure 1.5 Country transitions between different types of GVC participation, 1990–2015

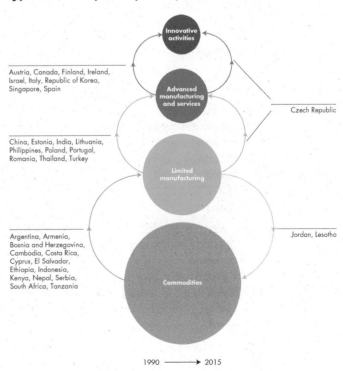

Austria, Canada, Finland, Ireland, Israel, Italy, Republic of Korea, Singapore, Spain

Innovative activities

Advanced manufacturing and services

Czech Republic

China, Estonia, India, Lithuania, Philippines, Poland, Portugal, Romania, Thailand, Turkey

Limited manufacturing

Argentina, Armenia, Bosnia and Herzegovina, Cambodia, Costa Rica, Cyprus, El Salvador, Ethiopia, Indonesia, Kenya, Nepal, Serbia, South Africa, Tanzania

Jordan, Lesotho

Commodities

1990 ⟶ 2015

Box 1.3 Types of GVC participation

Countries participate in GVCs in different ways, but there are regularities in the type of GVC integration and how countries upgrade. In 146 countries over the period 1990–2015, the following four types of GVC participation are particularly notable: (1) commodities; (2) limited manufacturing; (3) advanced manufacturing and services; and (4) innovative activities.

Data and measures

Countries are classified based on (1) the goods and services exported, (2) the extent of GVC participation, and (3) measures of innovation. A country's sectoral specialization of exports is based on the domestic value added in gross exports of primary goods, manufacturing, and business services. A country's extent of GVC participation is measured as backward integration of the manufacturing sector as a share of the country's total exports. Higher backward integration in manufacturing is an important characteristic of countries entering or specialized in noncommodity GVCs. Two measures are used to capture a country's innovative activities: (1) intellectual property (IP) receipts as a percentage of GDP and (2) research and development (R&D) intensity, defined as its expenditure of public and private R&D as a percentage of GDP.

Definitions of GVC taxonomy groups

The rules take into account country size because smaller countries naturally rely on trade to a relatively greater extent.

The following taxonomy groups are defined *sequentially*:

Commodities

Manufacturing share of total domestic value added in exports is less than 60 percent, *and*

- *Small countries:* Backward manufacturing is less than 20 percent.
- *Medium-size countries:* Backward manufacturing is less than 10 percent.
- *Large countries:* Backward manufacturing is less than 7.5 percent.

These criteria ensure that manufacturing is a small share of exports and that backward linkages in manufacturing are limited.

This group is further subdivided as follows:

- ○ *Low participation:* Primary goods' share of total domestic value added in exports is less than 20 percent.
- ○ *Limited commodities:* Primary goods' share of total domestic value added in exports is equal to or greater than 20 percent but less than 40 percent.
- ○ *High commodities:* Primary goods' share of total domestic value added in exports is equal to or greater than 40 percent.

These criteria define countries according to their export dependence on manufacturing.

Innovative activities (based on remaining countries)

- *Small countries:* IP receipts as a percentage of GDP are equal to or greater than 0.15 percent, and R&D intensity is equal to or greater than 1.5 percent.
- *Medium-size and large countries:* IP receipts as a percentage of GDP are equal to or greater than 0.1 percent and R&D intensity is equal to or greater than 1 percent.

These criteria split groups into those that spend a relatively large share of GDP on research and receive a large share of GDP from IP.

Advanced manufacturing and services (based on remaining countries)

Share of manufacturing and business services[a] in total domestic value added in exports is equal to or greater than 80 percent, *and*

- *Small countries:* Backward manufacturing is equal to or greater than 30 percent.
- *Medium-size countries:* Backward manufacturing is equal to or greater than 20 percent.
- *Large countries:* Backward manufacturing is equal to or greater than 15 percent.

Limited manufacturing (rest of sample)

Upgrading trajectories

Based on these definitions, the following countries transitioned from commodities into limited manufacturing GVCs over the period 1990–2015: Argentina, Armenia, Bosnia and Herzegovina, Cambodia, Costa Rica, Cyprus, El Salvador, Ethiopia, Indonesia, Kenya, Nepal, Serbia, South Africa, and Tanzania.

The following countries moved into advanced manufacturing and services from limited manufacturing GVCs: China, the Czech Republic, Estonia, India, Lithuania, the Philippines, Poland, Portugal, Romania, Thailand, and Turkey.

The Czech Republic moved further up into the innovative activities group in 2012 and remained in this group over the

(Box continues next page)

show the highest participation. Emerging economies such as China, Poland, and South Africa experienced rapid growth in GVC participation between 1990 and 2015 and as such moved up GVC groups. South Africa transitioned from commodities to limited manufacturing while China and Poland transitioned from limited manufacturing to advanced manufacturing and services. Other countries remained in the same group over that period. In Brazil, Morocco, and Pakistan, GVC participation grew less rapidly. The high GVC participation for major commodity exporters such as Algeria, Saudi Arabia, and República Bolivariana de Venezuela reflects extensive forward integration because natural resources are the most upstream sectors.

Countries' sectoral specialization shapes the extent of backward and forward participation. Figure 1.6 shows an approximate distribution of backward and forward GVC integration across the four taxonomy groups. Backward integration is lowest for countries specialized in commodities and starts to expand for countries in the limited manufacturing group. Countries specializing in advanced manufacturing and services are highly reliant on imported inputs for exports. Backward participation is slightly lower for the countries in the innovative group because their activities are less dependent on imported inputs.

The abundance of natural resources or agriculture in a country is linked to high forward integration because commodities are used in a variety of downstream production processes that typically cross several borders. Participation in limited manufacturing reduces forward integration because commodities are less important in trade, and the manufacturing output at this stage (such as garments) is less likely to be used as inputs in destination countries. However, moving to advanced manufacturing and services GVCs and especially innovative activities increases forward participation.

Figure 1.6 Average backward and forward GVC participation across taxonomy groups

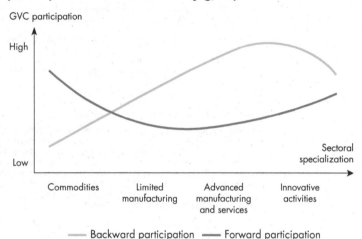

Source: WDR 2020 team.

Note: The approximate distribution is based on backward and forward GVC participation averages by taxonomy group for the period 2010–15. For the definition of taxonomy groups, see box 1.3.

How are GVCs distributed across regions?

GVCs have increased globally and regionally, but the differences across regions remain larger than differences over time. Some regional GVCs are more focused on trade within the region, while others are more dependent on global integration (figure 1.7). Countries' trade with regional (or regional bloc) value chains involves only production partners in the region, whereas extraregional value chain trade involves only partner countries outside the region. Importantly, the differences between regions in the depth of regional integration are stark and vastly dominate changes over time. Europe is the most regionally integrated region, with four times as many regional linkages as global linkages. South Asia and

Figure 1.7 GVC activities increased globally and regionally from 1990 to 2015

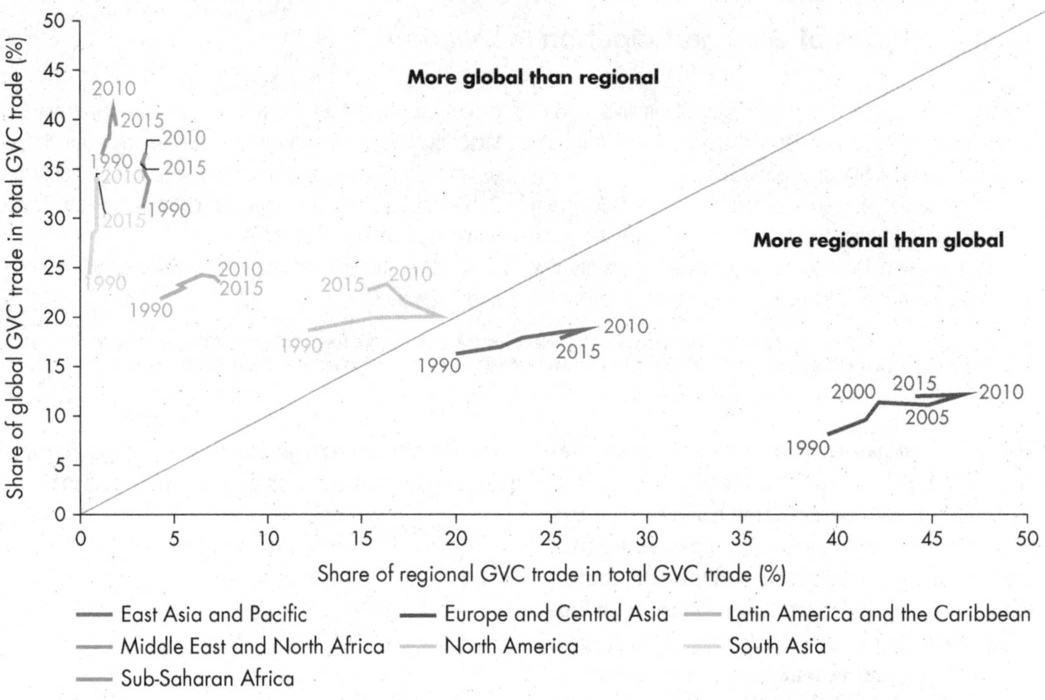

More global than regional

More regional than global

Share of global GVC trade in total GVC trade (%)

Share of regional GVC trade in total GVC trade (%)

— East Asia and Pacific   — Europe and Central Asia   — Latin America and the Caribbean
— Middle East and North Africa   — North America   — South Asia
— Sub-Saharan Africa

Source: WDR 2020 team, using data from Eora26 database.

Note: For each region and intervals of 5–6 years between 1990 and 2015, the figure plots the share of GVC trade involving only production partners in the same region in total GVC trade (regional GVC integration) against the share of GVC trade involving only partner countries outside the region in total GVC trade (global GVC integration). Regional and global GVC participation measures are computed as weighted averages over the countries in each group. The weights are the share of each country in the corresponding region total trade. The economic size of the trading blocs and the number of potential production partners in the region influence these indicators. The 45-degree line marks instances in which the share of regional and global GVC trade in total GVC trade for a given region are equal. In this figure, Mexico is not included in the Latin America and the Caribbean region but in North America, together with Canada and the United States. The economic size of the trading blocs and the number of potential production partners in the region influence these indicators. See the note to figure 1.2 on methodology and data for GVC participation measures.

the Middle East and North Africa are the least regionally integrated regions.

In all regions, the increase in GVC participation between 1990 and 2015 resulted from a combination of regional and global trends:

- In Europe, regional fragmentation of value chains increased through successive rounds of enlargement in which Eastern European countries, including Bulgaria, Hungary, and Poland, progressively joined older members' production networks. But global fragmentation was equally important, driven mostly by the larger European economies such as France, Germany, and the United Kingdom, whose linkages with countries in Asia such as China or India expanded.
- In East Asia, linkages are more regional than global, and GVCs became more internationally fragmented after 1990 because of both regional and global fragmentation in the 1990s and 2000s, although regional integration dominated.

- By contrast, the NAFTA GVCs depend somewhat more on global partners than regional partners, and integration has been increasing on both fronts. GVCs expanded more regionally in the 1990s, reflecting the coming into force of the NAFTA trade agreement in 1994, while the 2000s saw a marked acceleration in global GVC activities in part owing to China joining the world economy.
- In Latin America and the Caribbean, value chains are more globally linked, but they have increased both regionally and globally.
- In the three remaining regions, GVC integration has been mostly global and has been increasing primarily with global partners, with South Asia's GVCs expanding almost entirely outside the region.

A look at backward linkages confirms that production networks in East Asia, Europe, and, to a lesser extent, North America are mostly regional (figure 1.8). In an average European country, 65 percent of the imported intermediates embodied in its exports in

Figure 1.8 Global production networks are organized around three main regions, 2018

Share of foreign value added in exports of each region, by source region

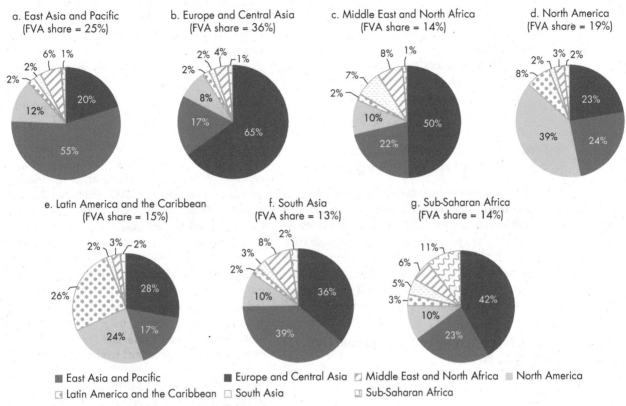

a. East Asia and Pacific
(FVA share = 25%)
20% 6% 1% 2% 2% 12% 55%

b. Europe and Central Asia
(FVA share = 36%)
2% 4% 1% 2% 8% 17% 65%

c. Middle East and North Africa
(FVA share = 14%)
8% 1% 7% 2% 10% 22% 50%

d. North America
(FVA share = 19%)
2% 3% 2% 8% 23% 39% 24%

e. Latin America and the Caribbean
(FVA share = 15%)
2% 3% 2% 26% 28% 24% 17%

f. South Asia
(FVA share = 13%)
2% 8% 3% 2% 10% 36% 39%

g. Sub-Saharan Africa
(FVA share = 14%)
11% 6% 5% 3% 10% 42% 23%

■ East Asia and Pacific ■ Europe and Central Asia ▨ Middle East and North Africa ▨ North America
◩ Latin America and the Caribbean ☐ South Asia ▧ Sub-Saharan Africa

Source: WDR 2020 team, using data from full Eora database (latest year for which data are available is 2018).

Note: The full Eora database is used because it offers the largest country coverage. The geographic breakdown across source countries is available for only one GVC participation index, the foreign value-added (FVA) content of exports. For each region, the figure reports the share of imported intermediates embodied in exports in total exports, computed as the ratio of the FVA content of exports in total gross exports (FVA share is in parenthesis). The figure also reports the contribution of each origin partner region to this FVA share. In this figure, Mexico is not included in the Latin America and the Caribbean region but in North America together with Canada and the United States.

2018 originated from other European countries. This share is about 55 percent for an average East Asian economy, and almost 40 percent for a member country of NAFTA. The other regions are all more integrated globally than regionally. The share of imported intermediates embodied in exports originating from regional partners is 26 percent in Latin America and the Caribbean but as low as 3 percent in South Asia.

In Latin America and the Caribbean, the geographic distribution of the foreign content of exports is almost equivalent across East Asia, Europe, and North America. South Asia is especially integrated in production networks in East Asia and Europe, whereas Sub-Saharan Africa is predominantly integrated in European supply chains followed by those in East Asia. These regional patterns reflect geographical distances and trade costs because intermediate inputs are shipped across borders multiple times. For example, just-in-time manufacturing techniques have pushed firms to locate the production of time-

sensitive components closer to home. Trade costs also determine the optimal location for individual production stages along GVCs.[5]

North and Sub-Saharan Africa have managed to join GVCs in the apparel, food, and automotive industries and in some business services. But Africa remains a small actor in the global economy, accounting for just 3 percent of global trade in intermediate goods. African exports tend to enter at the very beginning of GVCs. A high share serves as inputs for other countries' exports, reflecting the still-predominant role of agriculture and natural resources in African exports. Botswana, the Democratic Republic of Congo, and Nigeria have become integrated in GVCs through exports of oil and other natural resources. But Ethiopia, Kenya, and Tanzania have seen faster GVC integration, sourcing foreign inputs for their export-oriented businesses. Most of their integration has occurred in agribusiness and apparel (especially in Ethiopia and Kenya), in manufacturing (in Tanzania), and to a lesser extent, in transport and tourism. Morocco's efforts to attract major manufacturers in the automotive industries over the past decade are paying off. A new Peugeot facility opened in 2019, following in the footsteps of another French automaker, Renault-Nissan. Overall, GVC participation in some of these Sub-Saharan countries (Ethiopia, Kenya, South Africa, and Tanzania) grew by 10 percentage points or more, approaching what Poland or Vietnam—now success stories—experienced in the late 1990s and 2000s.

Which countries have accounted for most of the GVC expansion?

A few countries in Asia, Europe, and North America have driven GVC expansion over the past 30 years. Between 1990 and 2015, GVC participation worldwide grew by about 7 percentage points, because production processes in some countries and sectors become more fragmented—an intensification effect; or because countries and sectors that were already GVC-intensive boosted their share of world trade—a scale effect.

Figure 1.9 A handful of countries drove global GVC expansion from 1990 to 2015

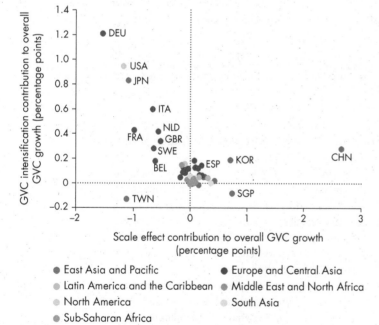

- East Asia and Pacific
- Latin America and the Caribbean
- North America
- Sub-Saharan Africa
- Europe and Central Asia
- Middle East and North Africa
- South Asia

Source: WDR 2020 team, using data from Eora26 database.

Note: The Eora26 database is used because it offers the largest country coverage, covering 190 countries between 1990 and 2015. The GVC participation measure reflects the share of a country's exports that flow through at least two borders. It is computed as the share of GVC exports in total international exports. GVC exports include transactions in which a country's exports embody value added that it previously imported from abroad (backward GVC participation), as well as transactions in which a country's exports are not fully absorbed in the importing country and instead are embodied in the importing country's exports to third countries (forward GVC participation). For country abbreviations, see International Organization for Standardization (ISO), https://www.iso.org/obp/ui/#search.

The top contributors to GVC intensification were Germany, the United States, Japan, Italy, and France, which began using more imported inputs in their exports (figure 1.9). By contrast, China's contribution to the expansion of GVC worldwide was predominantly through an increase in its share of world trade, although its GVC intensification remains significant.

How are GVCs distributed across sectors?

The sectoral composition of GVC flows is also quite diverse. Some countries specialize largely in agricultural GVCs (such as Madagascar) or in the natural resource segments of GVCs (such as Chile and Norway). These types of GVCs are classified as commodity-linked. Developing economies (such as Tanzania) specialize in low-tech simple manufacturing, and more developed economies (such as China, Mexico, and the Slovak Republic) in medium-tech manufacturing. One set of countries (including India and Singapore) largely specializes in the services embodied in GVCs. And a small set of very advanced economies (Germany, Japan, and the United States) provide innovative goods and services.

Most GVCs serve a handful of sectors in manufacturing and services

Some industries have used GVCs heavily for decades. Examples are basic industries that are resource-intensive and make heavy use of imported primary inputs—chemicals, refined petroleum, basic metals, and rubber and plastics. These sectors were already displaying large GVC participation in 1995 because of their high foreign value added in exports (figure 1.10). They have intensified their use of supply chains over time.

By contrast, the fragmentation of value chains in textiles and leather has not changed over the past two decades. Most fragmentation of production in these sectors occurred in the 1970s and 1980s, thus the slower pace. The termination of the Multifibre Arrangement in 2004 further concentrated production chains in fewer countries, with China emerging as the largest producer and capturing many stages of production. For services, construction and transport-related activities are the most fragmented. For transport-related activities, GVC participation increased substantially between 1995 and 2011.

For sectors, most of the GVC intensification over the period was driven by high-tech manufacturing industries, whose use of imported inputs increased. At the other end of the spectrum, very upstream mining and other primary industries accounted for most of the

Figure 1.10 GVC participation by sector, 1995 and 2011

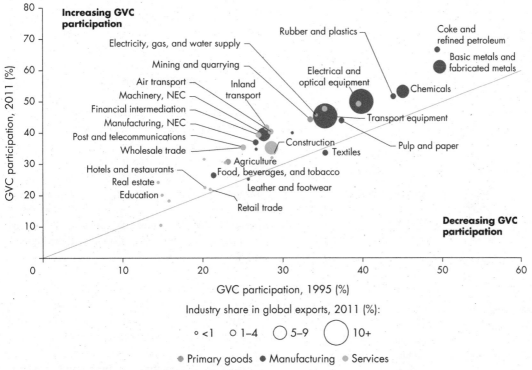

Source: WDR 2020 team, using data from WIOD 2013 release database.

Note: The WIOD 2013 database is used because it offers a finer sectoral classification than Eora26. In addition, the 2013 release (covering 1995–2011) is used instead of the latest 2016 release (covering 2001–14) in order to compare the change in GVC participation in the 2010s with that in the 1990s. The GVC participation measure reflects the share of world exports that flow through at least two borders. For each industry-year, it is computed as the share of GVC exports in total international exports. GVC exports include transactions in which a country's exports embody value added that it previously imported from abroad (backward GVC participation), as well as transactions in which a country's exports are not fully absorbed in the importing country and instead are embodied in the importing country's exports to third countries (forward GVC participation). The 45-degree line marks instances in which GVC participation for a given sector is the same in 1995 and 2011. NEC = not elsewhere classified.

scale effect, consistent with their high share of GVC integration and growing share of world trade following the large price surge over the period (figure 1.11).

GVCs are not just in manufacturing—they have also expanded rapidly in services

Services are an invisible but vital part of GVCs. The fragmentation of goods production has been associated with outsourcing not just manufacturing tasks but also service tasks, with the back office of many U.S. manufacturers now in India. In addition, transportation, telecommunications, and financial services facilitate and coordinate the geographic dispersion of production in all sectors. And service production is itself being fragmented across countries, such as when preliminary architectural designs, tax returns, and magnetic resonance imaging (MRI) readings are performed in one country and finalized and delivered to customers in another. In France, Germany, Italy, the United Kingdom, and the United States, services contribute more than half the total value added embodied

in exports. India, Kenya, and the Philippines also have rapidly expanding ICT and business service sectors. Even in China, traditionally viewed as an exporter of manufactures, more than a third of the value added in its exports comes from services.

For gross exports of services, such as transport, tourism, or business services, the share in trade is fairly flat at about 20 percent. The goods trade is increasingly involving services in production, with the share of services in valued-added trade rising from 31 percent to 43 percent between 1980 and 2009, a result of both forward and backward use of services in production (figure 1.12).

GVCs in agriculture and food industries have also expanded, including those in Africa

Although GVCs in the agriculture and food sectors have expanded over the past two decades, they remain a small share of GVC trade. In 2014 agriculture exports accounted for 2 percent of world exports

Figure 1.11 A handful of sectors drove global GVC expansion from 1995 to 2011

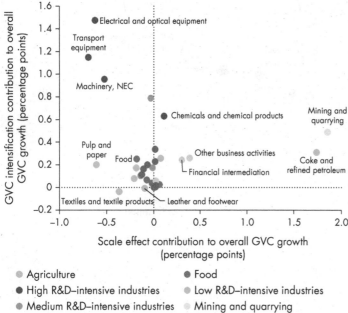

Agriculture
High R&D–intensive industries
Medium R&D–intensive industries
Other services
Trade and transportation

Food
Low R&D–intensive industries
Mining and quarrying
Telecommunications, financial, and business services

Source: WDR 2020 team, using data from WIOD 2013 release database.

Note: The WIOD 2013 database is used because it offers a finer sectoral classification than Eora26. In addition, the 2013 release (covering 1995–2011) is used instead of the latest 2016 release (covering 2001–14) in order to compare the change in GVC participation in the 2010s with that in the 1990s. The GVC participation measure reflects the share of a country's exports that flow through at least two borders. It is computed as the share of GVC exports in total international exports. GVC exports include transactions in which a country's exports embody value added that it previously imported from abroad (backward GVC participation), as well as transactions in which a country's exports are not fully absorbed in the importing country and instead are embodied in the importing country's exports to third countries (forward GVC participation). The 35 WIOD 2013 industries are classified in nine industry groups (see World Bank 2019): (1) agriculture, hunting, forestry, and fishing (ISIC Rev. 3 code 01T05); (2) food (ISIC Rev. 3 code 15T16); (3) mining and quarrying (ISIC Rev. 3 code 10T14); (4) high R&D–intensive industries (ISIC Rev. 3 codes 24, 29T34, 352, 353, 359); (5) medium R&D–intensive industries (ISIC Rev. 3 code 25T28, 351, 37); (6) low R&D–intensive industries (ISIC Rev. 3 codes 17T23, 36); (7) trade and transportation (ISIC Rev. 3 codes 50T52, 55, 60T63); (8) post and telecommunications, financial, and business services (ISIC Rev. 3 codes 64, 65T67, 71T74); and (9) real estate activities, utility, construction, and other services (ISIC Rev. 3 codes 70, 75, 80, 85, 90T93, 95, 40, 41, 45). ISIC = International Standard Industrial Classification; NEC = not elsewhere classified; R&D = research and development.

as contracting and logistics expertise. Taken together, Asia, Latin America, and Sub-Saharan Africa saw their foreign direct investment (FDI) inflows in the agri-food sector grow by a factor of three between 2000 and 2010. But such investments are mainly in large and more developed markets within Latin America (Argentina, Brazil, Chile, and Mexico) and Asia (China, Indonesia, and Vietnam), with little flowing into Sub-Saharan Africa (Ethiopia, Ghana, Tanzania, and Uganda). These investments are mostly aimed at the food industry (processing and retail) instead of agriculture.[7]

In overall participation in agriculture GVCs between 1990 and 2015, Ethiopia, Ghana, Kenya, and Rwanda in Africa and Vietnam in East Asia stand out. They increased their GVC participation by almost 10 percentage points or more. By contrast, the Lao People's Democratic Republic, Lebanon, and the Republic of Yemen—and resource-rich economies such as South Sudan—saw their integration in agriculture GVCs drop by between 5 and 30 percentage points (figure 1.13, panel a). For food GVCs, Sub-Saharan African countries including Ethiopia, The Gambia, and Tanzania also saw significant increase in participation, suggesting that those countries have been successfully developing food processing industries (figure 1.13, panel b). Value chains in the food industry are also important in Eastern European countries such as Bulgaria, Hungary, and Serbia.

Importantly, the participation of most developing countries in agriculture and food GVCs is largely forward because it is limited to supplying a specific product such as coffee by Ethiopia or Uganda, cocoa by Côte d'Ivoire or Ghana, oranges by Brazil, and bananas by Colombia.

Agriculture GVCs are also characterized by the prevalence of informality, which has important consequences for workers' poverty and vulnerability. In developing countries, over 94 percent of employment in agriculture is informal versus 63 percent in manufacturing. In African countries, these shares rise to 98 percent for agriculture and 77 percent for manufacturing.[8] Although firms in GVCs pay higher wages to their formal workers, they also rely heavily on informal workers who do not earn the same premiums. In Peru, 79 percent of all men and 84 percent of all women working on artichoke farms and processing plants have jobs that are not secure. Only about half of the migrant workers in the export pineapple sector in Ghana have permanent contracts.[9] Hiring workers indirectly through subcontractors or agents further contributes to vulnerability within GVCs as firms transfer their social responsibilities to a third party.

in contrast to 60 percent for manufactures and around 20 percent for services. When measured in value-added terms, this share rises to about 5 percent.

This finding reflects the fact that in the agri-food sector, unlike in the manufacturing sector, domestic value chains are dominant and dynamic, with GVCs important but secondary. In Asia and Latin America, supermarkets and small and medium enterprises in the food sector such as chain restaurants, processors, and modern wholesale and logistics companies have spread rapidly.[6]

Another factor in this finding is that GVCs in the agri-food sector typically involve less cross-border movement of goods than capital investments through direct and portfolio means and business practices such

Figure 1.12 Services are playing a growing role in GVCs

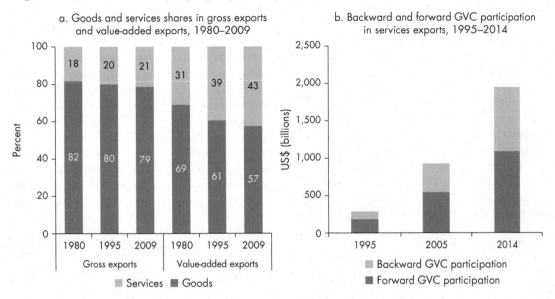

a. Goods and services shares in gross exports and value-added exports, 1980–2009

b. Backward and forward GVC participation in services exports, 1995–2014

Services ■ Goods

■ Backward GVC participation
■ Forward GVC participation

Sources: WDR 2020 team, using data from Johnson and Noguera (2017) for value-added exports measure in panel a and WIOD data from the 2013 release for 1995 and the 2016 release for 2005 and 2014 for panel b.

Note: Panel a reports the share of goods and services in gross exports and value-added exports, and panel b the GVC exports of services broken down into their backward and forward components. The GVC exports reflect exports that flow through at least two borders and indicate the extent to which sectors participate in GVCs. The GVC exports include transactions in which a country's exports embody value added that it previously imported from abroad (backward GVC participation), as well as transactions in which a country's exports are not fully absorbed in the importing country and instead are embodied in the importing country's exports to third countries (forward GVC participation).

Figure 1.13 GVCs expanded in both the agriculture and food industries from 1990 to 2015

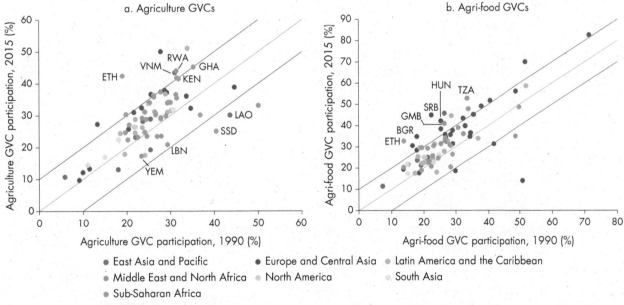

a. Agriculture GVCs

b. Agri-food GVCs

● East Asia and Pacific ● Europe and Central Asia ● Latin America and the Caribbean
● Middle East and North Africa ● North America ● South Asia
● Sub-Saharan Africa

Source: WDR 2020 team, using data from Eora26 database.

Note: The Eora26 database is used because it offers the largest country coverage: 190 countries between 1990 and 2015. Plots report only countries with at least 5 percent of their exports in the agriculture or agri-food sector. Agriculture includes forestry, hunting, and fishing. The GVC participation measure reflects the share of a country's exports that flow through at least two borders. It is computed as the share of GVC exports in total international exports. GVC exports include transactions in which a country's exports embody value added that it previously imported from abroad (backward GVC participation), as well as transactions in which a country's exports are not fully absorbed in the importing country and instead are embodied in the importing country's exports to third countries (forward GVC participation). The blue 45-degree line marks instances in which GVC participation for a given country are the same in 1990 and 2015. The red 45-degree lines mark a 10 percentage point change in the rate of GVC participation between 1990 and 2015. For country abbreviations, see International Organization for Standardization (ISO), https://www.iso.org/obp/ui/#search.

A few large trading firms account for most GVC trade

In practice, it is firms, not countries or industries, that participate in international trade (box 1.4). In line with this simple observation, economic research on international trade underwent a dramatic transformation in the last 20 years, placing firm-level international strategies at center stage. Fueling this shift was the growing availability of longitudinal plant and firm data sets that permitted researchers to unveil new facts challenging the validity of existing models. An important stylized fact from this literature is that in all countries, rich and poor, trade is highly concentrated in a small share of large firms that both import and export. Similarly, firms that both import and export dominate GVC participation (figure 1.14).

Because firms are the main actors in GVCs, another way to illustrate an individual country's GVC participation is to look at its share of firms engaged in two-way trade—that is, firms that both import and export (figure 1.14). For example, 41 percent of trading firms in China, 32 percent in South Africa, and 22 percent in Mexico both import and export—and all three have large GVC participation. The concentration of trade in a few importing–exporting firms is extreme. Two-way traders account for about 15 percent of all trading firms on average in the sample of countries, and yet they capture almost 80 percent of total trade. These

Box 1.4 A firm-level approach to GVCs

While most conceptual frameworks and empirical measures related to GVCs are at the country or country-industry level, in practice, it is not *countries* or *industries* that trade, but rather firms. In line with this observation, research in international trade has undergone a dramatic transformation in the past 20 years, placing firm-level international strategies at the center stage. This intellectual revolution was fueled by the increased availability of longitudinal plant and firm-level data sets that allowed researchers to unveil new facts that challenged the validity of existing models. At the theoretical level, a seminal paper was that of Melitz (2003), which focuses on the exporting decisions of heterogeneous firms within an industry. In Melitz's framework, firms are assumed to produce differentiated products using technologies featuring increasing returns to scale. Product differentiation confers market power on firms, whereas scale economies are associated with firms facing fixed costs of production and distribution. The decision of a firm to export to a given foreign market is shaped by a comparison of the potential operating profit obtained in that foreign market with the fixed costs associated with distributing products in that market.

This firm-level approach to international trade initially involved only the exchange of final goods, but an active literature has adopted similar ideas to understand the rise of GVCs. Because of the fixed costs of engaging in global sourcing (that is, of importing parts and components), one would expect that the use of imported inputs in production would require importers to attain a minimum efficient scale of production, thereby excluding smaller and less productive firms in an industry from GVC participation.[a]

Using a firm-level approach, one can also distinguish GVCs organized by a lead firm, which incurs the bulk of the fixed costs associated with setting up the network of producers for a given production process, from those that are more decentralized, with individual producers incurring the costs to set up links upstream and downstream.[b]

Firm-level data sets containing information on the import and export transactions of firms can be used to construct measures of GVC participation similar to those based on the country-industry information in global input–output tables. Specifically, transaction-level customs data sets of the type available from the World Bank's Exporter Dynamics Database can identify the set of firms in a country that participate in trade, further distinguishing firms that export, firms that import, and firms that both export and import. When a given firm in a given country both imports *and* exports, it is natural to conclude that this firm participates in GVCs.

To map this definition more precisely to the definition of backward GVC participation developed in country-industry studies, one would ideally also resort to product-level information to verify that the goods imported by an exporting firm are indeed intermediate inputs (rather than final goods), so that one can more comfortably conclude that this firm is indeed using foreign value added in its production destined for exports. Without linking customs data across countries, it is much harder to come up with analogous firm-level measures of forward GVC participation. Even when a firm is identified as an exporter of intermediate inputs (instead of final goods), it is almost impossible to establish whether those inputs are fully absorbed in the importing

(Box continues next page)

"superstar" firms, many of them multinational,[10] drive country trade performance.[11]

Sticky buyer–seller relations

Modeling global production sharing as simply an increase in the extent to which foreign inputs (or foreign value added) are used in production misses distinctive characteristics of the recent rise of GVCs. That rise entails much more than the intensification of the trade in raw materials and homogeneous intermediate inputs that has been undertaken since the Bronze Age. It is also much more than import and export firms transacting with each other in world markets. The expansion of GVCs entails a finer international division of labor, but it also involves several additional features, four of them especially important: (1) matching buyers and sellers, (2) making relationship-specific investments, (3) exchanging intangibles, and (4) living with limited contractual security.

Matching buyers and sellers in GVCs is not frictionless. The fixed costs of exporting and importing reflect in part the costs of finding suitable suppliers of parts and components or suitable buyers of a seller's products. For this reason, these fixed costs are better understood as sunk costs, which naturally create "stickiness" among participants in a GVC.

A source of lock-in for GVC relationships is that participants often make *relationship-specific investments* (such as purchasing specialized equipment or customizing products), and so they would obtain a much lower return if GVC linkages were broken. The need to customize inputs, coupled with quality sensitivity, makes matching buyers and sellers particularly important. If a firm suddenly faces an increase in the demand for its goods, it cannot easily scale up by buying more foreign inputs from some centralized market. Typically, only a handful of suppliers worldwide can provide the additional customized inputs to scale up.

Meanwhile, GVCs are more likely to lead to technology transfer and standards upgrading. Firms in GVCs do not engage only in trade in tangible goods with other members of their value chains. They often benefit from large *flows of intangibles*, such as technology, intellectual property, and credit. Lead or parent firms may also provide good managerial practices, saving resources and lifting productivity, or labor and environmental standards. The exchange of these intangibles is much more complex than that of simple goods or services.

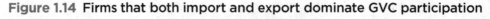

Figure 1.14 Firms that both import and export dominate GVC participation

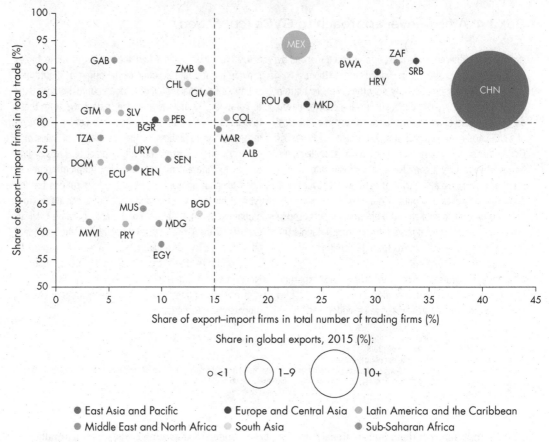

Source: WDR 2020 team, using firm-matched export–import customs data collected for 32 countries by the Trade and International Integration Unit of the World Bank Development Research Group, as part of efforts to build the Exporter Dynamics Database described in Fernandes, Freund, and Pierola (2016).

Note: The figure plots the share of two-way trading firms (firms that both import and export in a given year) in the total number of trading firms (firms that import, export, or do both) against their share in a country's total trade value (imports plus exports). For each country, the average of each measure is computed over 2005–15 for the largest available sample of countries. The dashed lines mark the average across countries for each measure on the x-axis and y-axis. For country abbreviations, see International Organization for Standardization (ISO), https://www.iso.org/obp/ui/#search.

The lock-in effects and flows of intangibles within GVCs are particularly relevant because of the *limited contractual security* that governs transactions within these chains. GVCs often engage in transactions that require a strong legal environment to bind producers together and avoid technological leakage. And yet GVCs often lack this strong legal environment because cross-border exchanges of goods cannot generally be governed by the same contractual safeguards that typically govern similar exchanges within borders. As a result, GVC participants must have repeated interactions to ensure implicit contract enforcement. As with matching frictions and relationship-specificity, this force contributes to the "stickiness" of GVC relationships.

In summary, these features of GVCs lead to a novel, relational conceptualization of GVCs that shifts the focus away from the mere allocation of

value added across countries through anonymous spot exchanges of goods and services. Instead, the identity of the agents participating in a GVC is crucial, and within GVCs, relationships are more likely to exhibit persistence.

Transactions within firm boundaries

An extreme version of relational contracting arises when parties in a GVC bypass the market mechanism altogether and undertake transactions within the boundaries of firms by having the buyer vertically integrate with the seller or vice versa. Indeed, many value chains are managed and controlled by multinational enterprises that organize their production across different locations. In some cases, goods are closer to new customers and the costs of trade fall (market-seeking investment). In others, it is a matter of taking advantage of lower costs of factors of production (efficiency-seeking investment). Both types of investment have contributed to the international dispersion of production, but the second has been especially important for GVC growth, which is evident from the growth of FDI flows and GVCs, especially since the 1990s (figure 1.15).

FDI flows into countries in the South and North (inward FDI) are positively correlated, suggesting that the expansion of foreign investments in one market did not come at the expense of the other. For foreign investment flows out of developed and developing countries (outward FDI), those from emerging economies have grown quickly, if from a very low base.[12] Since the early 2000s, companies in the South have sought opportunities to sell products locally, such as when the Kenyan supermarket chain Tuskys opened stores in Uganda. In other instances, firms have focused on taking advantage of cheaper labor, such as when Chinese firms invested in Madagascar's agriculture and textile sectors. From 2000 to 2015, the outward direct investment of firms in Brazil, China, India, the Russian Federation, and South Africa surged—from $7 billion to $200 billion, or almost one-third of global FDI.[13]

Intrafirm trade flows in world trade flows also exemplify the relational aspects of the growth of GVCs. For example, U.S. Census data from 2016 show that more than 40 percent of U.S. goods trade involves related-party transactions. At the global level, intrafirm trade has been estimated to be about one-third of world trade flows. In addition to having their own affiliates abroad, multinational companies rely on independent suppliers, including small firms in domestic and foreign markets.

The hierarchy and direction of knowledge flows between the multinational (or lead) firm and its suppliers vary across types of GVCs, depending on the complexity of products, the ability to codify transactions, and the capabilities of supply firms.[14] In producer-driven chains, the lead firm controls the design and most of the assembly of products by affiliates and captive suppliers, who are prevented from sharing technology with competitors. Such chains are typical in industries relying heavily on technology and R&D, such as electronics, automotive, aerospace, and pharmaceuticals, where production requires the assembly of thousands of customized parts into one

Figure 1.15 Foreign direct investment accompanied the fragmentation of production from 1970 to 2018

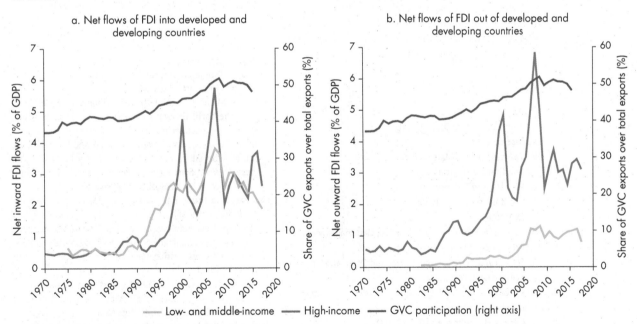

a. Net flows of FDI into developed and developing countries

b. Net flows of FDI out of developed and developing countries

— Low- and middle-income — High-income — GVC participation (right axis)

Source: WDR 2020 team, using data from the World Bank's WDI database.

Note: Panel a reports the net inflows of investment to the reporting economy from foreign investors divided by GDP, and panel b reports the net outflows of investment from the reporting economy to the rest of the world divided by GDP. To avoid composition effects, the definitions of income groups are time-invariant and based on the World Bank's 2018 country classification. The GVC participation measure reflects the share of countries' exports that flows through at least two borders. It is computed as the share of GVC exports in total international exports. GVC exports include transactions in which a country's exports embody value added that it previously imported from abroad (backward GVC participation), as well as transactions in which a country's exports are not fully absorbed in the importing country and instead are embodied in the importing country's exports to third countries (forward GVC participation). FDI = foreign direct investment.

high-end product. Large manufacturers such as Apple, General Motors, Samsung, Sony, and Toyota are typical of producer-driven global supply chains.

By contrast, when production is less complex and can be modularized or knowledge can be codified, captive relationships are less likely. In GVCs driven by the purchasing firms—so-called buyer-driven GVCs—the lead company has few factories of its own and sources its products almost entirely from a large network of independent suppliers, leaving it to concentrate instead on marketing and sales. This type of GVC is mostly found in the textile and apparel industries, where products such as clothes, housewares, or toys require relatively little capital and skills. Large retailers such as JCPenney and Walmart and big brands such as Nike are examples.

From this relational concept of GVCs emerges a richer analysis of them, one that puts on center stage the major actors (such as multinational firms and lead firms in GVCs) that shape GVC activity and FDI flows. Such an analysis underscores the role of institutional factors in shaping the location of global production. By explicitly modeling the mechanisms for dividing the gains from specialization across firms, this relational approach also delivers novel lessons about the implications of GVC participation for inequality and for development, as the following chapters review. It also provides a rich set of predictions about how an increase in automation or digital technologies may affect the landscape of the international economy and the different agents in society.

Notes

1. Barjamovic et al. (2019).
2. Kalm et al. (2013); OECD (2013).
3. Freeman (2007).
4. Constantinescu, Mattoo, and Ruta (2018).
5. Antràs and de Gortari (2017).
6. Reardon and Timmer (2012).
7. Reardon and Barrett (2019).
8. ILO (2018).
9. Barrientos at al. (2009); Chan (2013); Gammage (2009).
10. Freund and Pierola (2015).
11. Freund and Pierola (2015); Mayer and Ottaviano (2008).
12. See also UNCTAD (2019).
13. Cusolito, Safadi, and Taglioni (2016); Gómez-Mera et al. (2015).
14. Gereffi, Humphrey, and Sturgeon (2005).

References

Antràs, Pol, and Alonso de Gortari. 2017. "On the Geography of Global Value Chains." NBER Working Paper 23456 (May), National Bureau of Economic Research, Cambridge, MA.

Antràs, Pol, Teresa C. Fort, and Felix Tintelnot. 2017. "The Margin of Global Sourcing: Theory and Evidence from U.S. Firms." *American Economic Review* 107 (9): 2514–64.

Antràs, Pol, and Elhanan Helpman. 2004. "Global Sourcing." *Journal of Political Economy* 112 (3): 552–80.

Baldwin, Richard E. 2012. "Global Supply Chains: Why They Emerged, Why They Matter, and Where They Are Going." CEPR Discussion Paper 9103 (August), Centre for Economic Policy Research, London.

Baldwin, Richard E., and Anthony J. Venables. 2013. "Spiders and Snakes: Offshoring and Agglomeration in the Global Economy." *Journal of International Economics* 90 (2): 245–54.

Barjamovic, Gojko, Thomas Chaney, Kerem Coşar, and Ali Hortaçsu. 2019. "Trade, Merchants, and the Lost Cities of the Bronze Age." *Quarterly Journal of Economics* 134 (3): 1455–1503.

Barrientos, Stephanie Ware, John Kwasi Anarfi, Nicolina Lamhauge, Adriana Castaldo, and Nana Akua Anyidoho. 2009. "Social Protection for Migrant Labour in the Ghanaian Pineapple Sector." DRC Working Paper T-30 (September), Development Research Centre on Migration, Globalisation, and Poverty, University of Sussex, Brighton, U.K.

Bernard, Andrew B., Andreas Moxnes, and Karen Helene Ulltveit-Moe. 2018. "Two-Sided Heterogeneity and Trade." *Review of Economics and Statistics* 100 (3): 424–39.

Borin, Alessandro, and Michele Mancini. 2015. "Follow the Value Added: Bilateral Gross Export Accounting." Temi di discussione (Economic Working Paper) 1026, Economic Research and International Relations Area, Bank of Italy.

————. 2019. "Measuring What Matters in Global Value Chains and Value-Added Trade." Policy Research Working Paper 8804, World Bank, Washington, DC.

Chan, Man-Kwun. 2013. "Informal Workers in Global Horticulture and Commodities Value Chains: A Review of Literature." WIEGO (Global Trade) Working Paper 28 (June), Women in Informal Employment Globalizing and Organizing, Cambridge, MA.

Clemens, Michael A., and Jeffrey G. Williamson. 2004. "Why Did the Tariff-Growth Correlation Change after 1950?" *Journal of Economic Growth* 9 (1): 5–46.

Constantinescu, Cristina, Aaditya Mattoo, and Michele Ruta. 2018. "The Global Trade Slowdown: Cyclical or Structural?" *World Bank Economic Review.* Published electronically May 23. https://doi.org/10.1093/wber/lhx027.

Cusolito, Ana Paula, Raed Safadi, and Daria Taglioni. 2016. *Inclusive Global Value Chains: Policy Options for Small and Medium Enterprises and Low-Income Countries.* Directions in Development: Trade Series. Washington, DC: World Bank and Organisation for Economic Co-operation and Development.

de Gortari, Alonso. 2019. "Disentangling Global Value Chains." NBER Working Paper 25868 (May), National Bureau of Economic Research, Cambridge, MA.

Fernandes, Ana Margarida, Caroline L. Freund, and Martha Denisse Pierola. 2016. "Exporter Behavior, Country Size and Stage of Development: Evidence from the Exporter Dynamics Database." *Journal of Development Economics* 119 (March): 121–37.

Freeman, Richard B. 2007. "The Great Doubling: The Challenge of the New Global Labor Market." In *Ending Poverty* in America: How to Restore the American Dream, edited by John Edwards, Marion Crain, and Arne L. Kalleberg, 55–65. Chapel Hill, NC: Center on Poverty, Work, and Opportunity, University of North Carolina at Chapel Hill; New York: New Press.

Freund, Caroline L., and Martha Denisse Pierola. 2015. "Export Superstars." *Review of Economics and Statistics* 97 (5): 1023–32.

Gammage, Sarah C. 2009. "Gender and Pro-Poor Value Chain Analysis: Insights from the GATE Project Methodology and Case Studies." With inputs from Cristina Manfre and Kristy Cook. May, U.S. Agency for International Development, Washington, DC.

Gereffi, Gary, John Humphrey, and Timothy J. Sturgeon. 2005. "The Governance of Global Value Chains." *Review of International Political Economy* 12 (1): 78–104.

Gómez-Mera, Laura, Thomas Kenyon, Yotam Margalit, Josó Guilherme Reis, and Gonzalo J. Varela. 2015. *New Voices in Investment: A Survey of Investors from Emerging Countries.* World Bank Study Series. Washington, DC: World Bank.

Gopinath, Gita, and Brent Neiman. 2014. "Trade Adjustment and Productivity in Large Crises." *American Economic Review* 104 (3): 793–831.

Halpern, Laszlo, Miklos Koren, and Adam Szeidl. 2015. "Imported Inputs and Productivity." *American Economic Review* 105 (12): 3660–3703.

ILO (International Labour Organization). 2018. *Women and Men in the Informal Economy: A Statistical Picture*, 3d ed. Geneva: ILO.

Johnson, Robert Christopher. 2018. "Measuring Global Value Chains." *Annual Review of Economics* 10 (1): 207–36.

Johnson, Robert Christopher, and Guillermo Noguera. 2017. "A Portrait of Trade in Value Added over Four Decades." *Review of Economics and Statistics* 99 (5): 896–911.

Kalm, Matias, Mika Pajarinen, Petri Rouvinen, and Timo Seppälä. 2013. "The Rise of Baltic Sea Value Chains—A Bicycle Producer's World Tour." In *State of the Region Reports: The Top of Europe—Plowing Ahead in the Shadows of a Fractured Global Economy*, 10th ed., edited by Christian Ketels, 126–35. København, Denmark: Baltic Development Forum.

Kee, Hiau Looi, and Heiwai Tang. 2016. "Domestic Value Added in Exports: Theory and Firm Evidence from China." *American Economic Review* 106 (6): 1402–36.

Lenzen, M., K. Kanemoto, D. Moran, and A. Geschke. 2012. "Mapping the Structure of the World Economy." *Environmental Science & Technology* 46 (15): 8374–81.

Mayer, Thierry, and Gianmarco I. P. Ottaviano. 2008. "The Happy Few: The Internationalisation of European Firms." *Intereconomics* 43 (3): 135–48.

Melitz, Marc J. 2003. "The Impact of Trade on Intra-Industry Reallocations and Aggregate Industry Productivity." *Econometrica* 71 (6): 1695–1725.

OECD (Organisation for Economic Co-operation and Development). 2013. *Interconnected Economies: Benefiting from Global Value Chains.* Paris: OECD.

Reardon, Thomas, and Christopher B. Barrett. 2019. "The Evolution of Agri-Food Value Chains in Developing Countries." Background paper, World Bank, Washington, DC.

Reardon, Thomas, and Charles Peter Timmer. 2012. "The Economics of the Food System Revolution." *Annual Review of Resource Economics* 4 (August): 225–64.

Rodrigue, Jean-Paul, Claude Comtois, and Brian Slack. 2017. *The Geography of Transport Systems*, 4th ed. New York: Routledge.

UNCTAD (United Nations Conference on Trade and Development). 2019. *World Investment Report 2019: Special Economic Zones.* New York and Geneva: United Nations.

World Bank. 2019. *Global Value Chain Development Report 2019: Technological Innovation, Supply Chain Trade, and Workers in a Globalized World.* Washington, DC: World Bank.

Yeats, Alexander J. 1998. "Just How Big Is Global Production Sharing?" Policy Research Working Paper 1871, Washington, DC, World Bank.

2

Drivers of participation

Key findings

- **Global value chain (GVC) participation is determined by fundamentals such as factor endowments, market size, geography, and institutional quality, but these fundamentals need not dictate destiny.** Choosing the right policies can shape each one of these fundamentals and thus GVC participation.

- **Factor endowments matter.** Low-skilled labor and foreign capital are central to backward participation in GVCs at early stages. An abundance of natural resources drives forward GVC integration. Foreign capital, whether efficiency-seeking or resource-seeking, can enhance host country integration in GVCs.

- **Market size matters.** Small countries are more dependent on imported inputs and foreign markets. Trade liberalization can expand effective market size and promote participation in GVCs.

- **Geography matters.** Overcoming remoteness by improving connectivity can promote GVC participation. Trade in parts and components within international production networks is highly sensitive to logistics performance and uncertainty in bilateral international transport times.

- **Institutional quality matters.** Entering deep preferential trade agreements (PTAs) can enhance institutional quality and increase GVC participation. Deep PTAs cover legal and regulatory frameworks, harmonize customs procedures, and set rules on intellectual property rights.

Vietnam's electronics sector expanded dramatically in less than a decade. Today, Vietnam is the second-largest smartphone exporter, producing 40 percent of Samsung's global mobile phone products and employing 35 percent of its global staff.

Vietnam's success can be attributed to a combination of factors. Trade liberalization—driven by World Trade Organization (WTO) accession and an agreement with the United States—a favorable investment climate, and a large pool of low-cost labor determined Vietnam's attractiveness as a global value chain (GVC) location. The result was large foreign direct investment (FDI) inflows, including from Samsung. Vietnam's geographical proximity to regional suppliers of electronics parts and components such as China, Japan, the Republic of Korea, and Thailand helped foreign investors gain access to high-quality inputs from abroad. And improved connectivity enabled Vietnam to import and export in a timely manner.

The story of Vietnam demonstrates that GVC participation is determined first and foremost by fundamentals such as factor endowments, market size, geography, and institutions (box 2.1). But these fundamentals need not dictate destiny. Choosing the right policies can shape each one of these fundamentals and thus GVC participation. Attracting FDI can remedy a scarcity of capital, technology, and management skills. Liberalizing trade at home and negotiating trade liberalization abroad can overcome the constraints of a small domestic market, freeing firms and farms from dependence on limited local inputs and narrow domestic demand. Improving transport and communication infrastructure and introducing competition in these services can address the disadvantage of a remote location. Participating in deep trade integration agreements that encompass policy areas beyond traditional trade policy, such as investment, competition, and intellectual property rights protection, can improve domestic institutions by helping countries commit to domestic reform and receive technical and financial assistance.

Factor endowments matter. Low-skilled labor and foreign capital are central to backward participation in GVCs. The abundant supply of low-cost labor in lower-income countries is often an entry point for participation in the labor-intensive manufacturing segments of GVCs. But upgrading skills becomes necessary for integration in more complex GVCs. An abundance of natural resources drives forward GVC integration. Foreign capital, whether efficiency-seeking or resource-seeking, can enhance host country integration in GVCs. Indeed, it is strongly and positively correlated with backward GVC participation. It also promotes domestic upstream sectors, as happened in the case of apparel in Bangladesh, electronics in Vietnam, and automotives in Morocco.

Market size matters. Trade liberalization can expand market size and promote participation in GVCs. Lower tariffs on manufacturing goods foster backward GVC participation in manufacturing. Manufacturing tariffs fall sharply in the years before a country's transition from commodity to limited manufacturing GVCs. Sectors facing lower tariffs in destination markets exhibit stronger backward and forward GVC participation. Market access for low-income countries provided by the Everything but Arms initiative of the European Union (EU) or the African Growth and Opportunity Act (AGOA), a U.S. trade pact, can stimulate their exports and GVC integration. In the long run, however, the effects depend on rules of origin and their impacts on developing a local supplier base.

Geography matters. Overcoming remoteness by improving connectivity can promote GVC participation. Longer geographical distances to the major GVC hubs—China, Germany, and the United States—have a strong negative impact on both backward and forward GVC participation in manufacturing. By contrast, longer distances increase a country's likelihood of specializing in commodity GVCs. High transport costs impede entering, establishing, and upgrading in GVCs. Inefficient transport and logistics services and weak competition in these services amplify those costs in many manufacturing GVCs. Trade in parts and components within international production networks is highly sensitive to logistics performance and uncertainty in bilateral international transport times. Connectivity also includes effective communication among the participants in GVCs, which can be improved by access to the Internet. Higher Internet usage is linked to stronger backward GVC integration.

Institutional quality matters. Entering deep preferential trade agreements (PTAs) can enhance institutional quality and increase GVC participation. Deep PTAs cover legal and regulatory frameworks, harmonize customs procedures, and set the rules on intellectual property rights. Weak contract enforcement deters traditional trade flows, and GVCs are particularly sensitive to the quality of contractual institutions. Sectors relying more on contract enforcement see faster growth in GVC participation in countries with better institutional quality. Greater political stability reduces the likelihood of specializing in commodity GVCs.

Box 2.1 Vietnam's integration in the electronics GVC

Today, Vietnam is the second-largest smartphone exporter, producing 40 percent of Samsung's global mobile phone products and employing 35 percent of its global staff. Vietnam's backward participation in electronics GVCs increased from 47 percent in 2000 to 67 percent in 2010, and then declined slightly after 2012 (figure B2.1.1, panel a). Import tariffs in the sector dropped from about 8 percent in 2000 to less than 3 percent by 2015 (figure B2.1.1, panel b).

Vietnam has been a member of the Association of Southeast Asian Nations (ASEAN) since 1995, and after entering the World Trade Organization in 2007 the country's number of preferential trade partners increased from 10 to 16 by 2014. Most free trade agreements were between ASEAN and third countries (Australia, China, India, Japan, the Republic of Korea, and New Zealand), but some were bilateral with Chile, Japan, and the European Union. The coverage in Vietnam's trade agreements expanded substantially from 13 core provisions in 2007 to 86 in 2014.

Vietnam owes its success in the electronics sector to the following factors.

Stable investment climate. Vietnam's foreign direct investment (FDI) stock picked up from around $400 per person in the early 2000s to $500 in 2008 and $880 in 2015 (figure B2.1.1, panel c). FDI inflows to the electronics sector included mostly large investments from Korea's Samsung Group, which launched Samsung Electronics Vietnam in

2008. Samsung's presence in Vietnam now includes the world's largest smartphone production facility, a smartphone and tablet display assembly facility, an electromechanical assembly operation for camera modules, and the Samsung Vietnam Mobile Research and Development Center. Samsung has about 160,000 workers in Vietnam, and lead firms LG, Canon, and Panasonic, contract manufacturers Foxconn and Jabil Circuit, and platform leaders Intel and Microsoft also operate there. FDI benefited from generous incentives, including tax concessions provided by the Vietnamese government.

Abundant low-skilled, low-cost labor. Vietnam's large pool of low-skilled, low-cost labor was an important determinant of its attractiveness as a GVC location. Over half of the workforce in Vietnam's population of more than 95 million was estimated to be low-skilled in 2006. But the quality of education in Vietnam is a significant barrier, and extensive training is still necessary. Samsung's software engineers are trained at the Samsung Vietnam Mobile Research and Development Center, with 90 percent of them attaining Samsung's global standards. The improved technological skills of the Vietnamese workforce may have actually contributed to the country's declining share of low-skilled workers—down to less than 40 percent by 2015.

Proximity. Most of the electronic inputs imported by Vietnam are from China; Hong Kong SAR, China; Japan;

Figure B2.1.1 Vietnam's backward GVC integration increased from 2000 to 2015 as tariffs declined and foreign direct investment (FDI) expanded

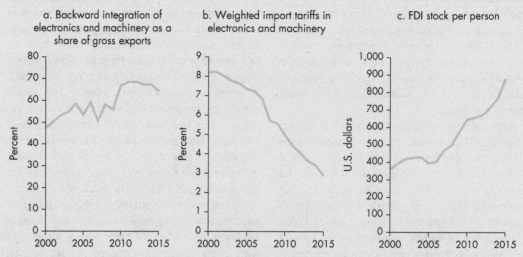

Sources: WDR 2020 team, using data from Eora and World Bank's WDI and WITS databases. See appendix A for a description of the databases used in this Report.

(Box continues next page)

Korea; Singapore; Taiwan, China; and Thailand. Although the import content of electronics exports reached two-thirds of gross exports in recent years (figure B2.1.1, panel a), the reliance on imported inputs declined slightly as the role of local suppliers increased. Samsung's local suppliers include not only foreign-owned suppliers that co-located with Samsung in Vietnam, but also 29 domestic suppliers (such as in display making and plastic molding) in 2016, up from just four in 2014, all trained by Samsung to meet quality standards.

Connectivity. Vietnam reduced the average time to import by two days—to roughly three weeks over 2006–15—and yet this is still one week longer than in the Philippines or Thailand, which have been involved in manufacturing GVCs for much longer. Meanwhile, Vietnam's Internet usage shot up from 17 percent of the population in 2006 to 43 percent in 2015—higher than the 27 percent in the Philippines and 25 percent in Thailand—reflecting an effort to dominate the information and communication technology GVC, not only in hardware but also in business services.

Sources: Nikkei Asian Review (2018); Sturgeon and Zylberberg (2016); *Viet Nam News* (2015).

Factor endowments matter

GVCs entail a finer international division of labor than standard trade, with countries specializing in segments of GVCs rather than in industries (chapter 1). Traditional trade theory postulates that factor endowments are an important determinant of specialization in GVCs, and they also shape the positioning of countries in GVCs. For example, an abundance of natural resources in a country is naturally linked to high forward GVC integration because agricultural products and commodities are used in a variety of downstream production processes that typically cross several borders. Vietnam's electronics GVC illustrates how abundance in low-skilled labor is often an entry point to backward participation.[1]

A large pool of low-skilled workers matters for joining manufacturing GVCs, but higher skills matter for upgrading

When Samsung decided to invest in Vietnam, it was attracted to the young, cheap, and abundant workforce.[2] On average, Vietnamese workers could be hired at half the cost of their Chinese counterparts and were seven years younger. This cheap labor lowers costs in Samsung's factories, giving the smartphone maker an edge over Apple in the less expensive handsets. Likewise, Bangladesh's success in apparel exports after conclusion of the Multifibre Arrangement's quota regime in 2004 is linked to its large pool of low-skilled, low-cost workers. At less than $200 a month, the average wage of an apparel sector worker in Bangladesh is lower than that in China ($270), India ($255), and Vietnam ($248).[3]

The abundance of low-skilled labor in countries is positively linked to the extent of their backward integration in GVCs, based on evidence from a large sample of countries in the Eora database (box 2.2).[4] This pattern is driven by backward GVC participation in the manufacturing and services sectors. Countries with larger endowments of low-skilled labor in the 2000s were also more likely to be among the group of countries specializing in either limited manufacturing or advanced manufacturing and services in 2011. Among countries engaged in limited manufacturing, Vietnam had by far the highest average percentage of low-skilled workers in its labor force (over 42 percent) during 2006–15, followed by Ethiopia (37 percent) and El Salvador (31 percent). Using labor costs as an alternative measure of low-skilled labor endowments for the same large sample of countries in the Eora database confirms the positive link with backward integration. According to evidence for 87 countries, lower wages facilitate participation in the final assembly stages of GVCs, mostly in the apparel sector.[5]

But labor costs could rise with a country's continued involvement in and upgrading of GVCs, as has happened in China. Improved technological skills contributed to a declining share of low-skilled workers in Vietnam (see box 2.1). Upgrading workforce skills becomes necessary to export more advanced manufacturing goods and services (box 2.2).[6] A firm-level analysis of Bangladesh confirms that the higher skill intensity of a workforce and higher wages (relative to other firms in the country) are positively associated with the likelihood of being a GVC firm.[7]

Box 2.2 Modeling results on the drivers of GVC participation

From imports of pistons used as intermediates in car manufacturing in Morocco (foreign content of exports/backward participation) to Chilean exports of copper used in refrigerators produced by firms in China and Mexico (domestic value added in exports used by partner countries for export production/forward participation), GVC participation is multifaceted and diverse across countries.

This assessment of the drivers of GVC participation across countries relies on GVC participation measures from Borin and Mancini (2019) using the Eora database, which covers 190 countries and draws on a combination of international input–output tables, domestic production, and trade data (see appendix A for a description of the databases used in this Report). The econometric model assesses the marginal impacts on

GVC participation of seven broad types of determinants emphasized in the trade literature: (1) factor endowments, (2) geography, (3) market size, (4) trade policy and foreign direct investment (FDI), (5) quality of institutions, (6) connectivity, and (7) financial and business environment factors.

This assessment estimates the impact of country averages of the determinants in the previous decade (e.g., the 1990s) on country average GVC participation in the following decade (e.g., the 2000s). It considers the following dependent variables: (1) the share of backward or forward GVC participation in gross exports, which captures the intensity of GVC trade relative to that of traditional exports; (2) backward or forward GVC participation levels (logs); and (3) gross exports (logs). Comparing the factors that affect

Figure B2.2.1 What explains backward and forward GVC participation?

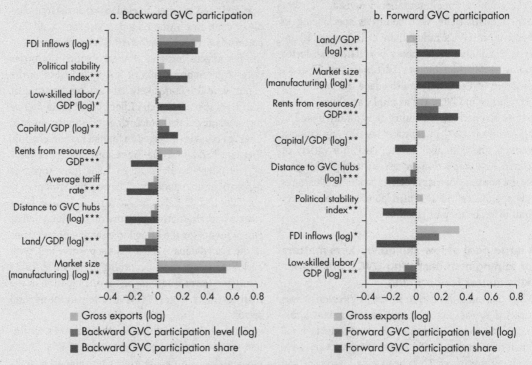

Sources: WDR 2020 team, using data from CEPII, Eora, ILO, PWT 9.0, UNCTAD, WDI, WGI, and World Bank. See Appendix A for a description of the databases used in this Report. For more detail, see Fernandes, Kee, and Winkler (2019).

Note: The graphs show standardized coefficients for each variable on the y-axis. The coefficients are based on a between-effects regression. The dependent variables are average exports and backward or forward GVC participation levels and shares. The determinants are measured as averages in the previous decade and include manufacturing import tariffs, FDI inward inflows, distance to major GVC hubs (China, Germany, and the United States), manufacturing value added, political stability index, ratio of low-skilled labor to GDP, ratio of resource rents to GDP, ratio of land to GDP, ratio of capital stock to GDP, nominal exchange rate appreciation, and decade fixed effects. Significance is based on the GVC participation share regressions. Only determinants with statistically significant coefficients are shown. Standardized coefficients refer to how many standard deviations the dependent variable will change per standard deviation increase in the explanatory variable. FDI = foreign direct investment.

Significance level: * = 10 percent, ** = 5 percent, *** = 1 percent.

(Box continues next page)

Box 2.2 Modeling results on the drivers of GVC participation (continued)

GVC participation shares with their influence on GVC participation levels and on export levels indicates which determinants matter beyond traditional exports. This assessment also decomposes backward and forward country-level GVC participation measures into the four broad sectors of agriculture, mining, manufacturing, and services to shed light on which sectors are driving the overall cross-country results. The estimated impacts of the drivers in the baseline model are shown in figure B2.2.1 (these drivers explain more than half the variation in GVC participation shares):

- Low-skilled labor fosters backward GVC participation, while endowments of natural resources and land foster forward GVC participation.
- Controlling for factor endowments, liberal trade policy, higher FDI presence, and better institutional quality are important in determining backward GVC participation, while they do not matter (tariffs) or they matter in the opposite direction (FDI, political stability) for forward GVC participation.
- Domestic market size provides a larger pool of local input suppliers, which lowers backward GVC participation but increases forward GVC participation.

Decomposing the country-level backward GVC participation measures by broad sector suggests that the findings in figure B2.2.1 are driven largely by backward GVC participation of the manufacturing sector. The role of other drivers of GVC participation shares is also tested. Membership in preferential trade agreements and the depth of those agreements increase backward GVC participation. The time required to clear imports weakly reduces backward

GVC participation, whereas a better score in the logistics performance index (LPI) is linked to stronger backward GVC participation. Female labor market participation increases backward GVC participation. And the share of population speaking English as a second language weakly increases both forward and backward GVC participation.

To better understand what determines how countries participate in GVCs, measures of backward and forward GVC participation at the country-sector level are used in another econometric model that combines country endowments (capital, skilled labor, and natural resources), institutional quality, and input, output, and market access tariffs.[a] The model allows sectors to differ (largely for technological reasons) in their intensity of using endowments and contracts, and it allows results to be given a causal interpretation (figure B2.2.2):

- Sectors using high-skilled labor or capital more intensively exhibit stronger GVC participation and gross exports in countries relatively more endowed with skilled labor or capital.
- Countries with better institutional quality exhibit stronger GVC participation and exports in their more contractually intensive sectors.
- Input tariffs and market access tariffs reduce GVC participation and gross exports.

In a separate additional test, sectors using the Internet more intensively exhibit stronger GVC participation and gross exports in countries with a higher number of Internet users, controlling for all other determinants.

(Box continues next page)

Different types of engagement in GVCs require different types of workers. The average annual labor costs for countries with limited manufacturing GVCs (such as Costa Rica, Morocco, South Africa, and Sri Lanka) were about $11,000 per worker over 2006–15. Labor costs reached $16,500 for countries specializing in advanced manufacturing and services GVCs (such as Mexico, Poland, Thailand, and Turkey). In countries focusing on innovative GVC activities—such as Germany, Japan, the United Kingdom, and the United States—the employee cost was about $55,000 a year on average, reflecting their higher skill intensity and productivity (figure 2.1).

Cross-country evidence supports the positive correlation between skills and integration in innovative GVCs. Countries that entered the group of advanced manufacturing and services GVCs at some point over

1990–2015 (such as China, the Czech Republic, Poland, and Turkey) saw their labor costs increase sharply. Even countries with limited manufacturing GVCs (such as Cambodia, Indonesia, Nicaragua, and South Africa) show strong increases in their labor costs in the five years before transitioning (figure 2.2, panel a). Sectors using skilled labor more intensively see faster growth in GVC participation (and in gross exports) in countries relatively more endowed with skilled labor (see box 2.2). The estimated impacts are large: if Ghana increased its skilled labor share (7.5 percent) to the cross-country median (20 percent), its backward GVC participation and its gross exports would grow by an estimated 42 percent, and its forward GVC participation would grow by 39 percent. Further evidence for Sub-Saharan Africa shows that skilled labor and higher values of the World Bank's Human Capital

Box 2.2 Modeling results on the drivers of GVC participation *(continued)*

Figure B2.2.2 What explains a country-sector's GVC participation levels and gross exports?

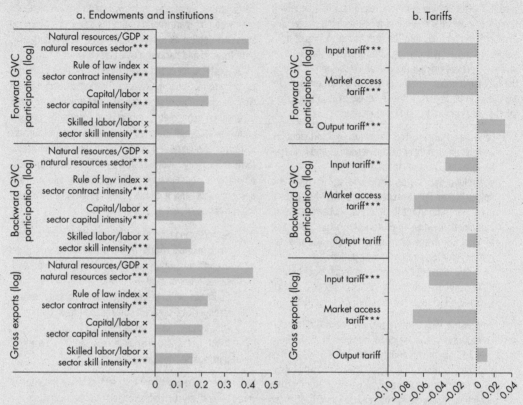

a. Endowments and institutions

b. Tariffs

Sources: WDR 2020 team, using data from Eora, ILO, NBER-CES Manufacturing Industry Database, PWT 9.0, TRAINS, UNIDO, WGI, WITS, Braun (2003), Felbermayr, Teti, and Yalcin (2019), and Nunn (2007). See Appendix A for a description of the databases used in this Report. For more detail, see Fernandes, Kee, and Winkler (2019).

Note: The graphs show standardized coefficients for each variable on the y-axis from three separate regressions using forward GVC participation, backward GVC participation, and gross exports as dependent variables. The regressions use a three-year lag of each of the determinants shown in panels a and b and control for country-year fixed effects and sector fixed effects. Standardized coefficients refer to how many standard deviations the dependent variable will change per standard deviation increase in the explanatory variable.

Significance level: * = 10 percent, ** = 5 percent, *** = 1 percent.

---

a. This analysis focuses only on differences across countries in the seven subsectors within the overall manufacturing sector in the Eora database.

Index[8] are positively associated with GVC participation in the region.[9]

Female labor market participation is linked to higher backward GVC participation (see box 2.2). Evidence from manufacturing firms across 64 developing countries confirms that the female share of total employment is higher for firms participating in GVCs (defined as those that both import intermediate inputs and export).[10] Verified in all sectors, this pattern is especially strong in the apparel and electronics sectors. A causal link is not warranted, however, because female labor market participation and GVC

integration can mutually reinforce one another. But the link between firm GVC participation and female corporate leadership is negative. Majority female-owned and female-managed firms are less likely to participate in GVCs. Chapter 3 discusses further the relationship between GVC participation and female employment, ownership, and management.

Automation, robotics, and 3D printing could pose a challenge to the GVC participation of countries whose comparative advantage lies predominantly in abundant low-cost workers. These enterprises require higher skills, and they enable customized production close to the end markets, such as the 3D printing of shoes. Producers in lower-income countries typically rely more on low-skilled manual labor than do producers in higher-income countries. But this could become more difficult in the context of new technologies in GVCs because new technologies are associated with higher-quality standards and high-skilled labor, raising the hurdle for lower-income countries wishing to participate in GVCs.[11] (Chapter 6 discusses the potential impacts of new technologies on countries' prospects for GVC participation.)

Natural resources are a driving force for forward GVC participation

Higher relative endowments of land or natural resources are both strongly positively correlated with forward GVC participation (see box 2.2). In other words, countries with abundant extractive resources, such as copper, iron ore, and other minerals, exhibit higher shares of domestic value added embodied in their partner countries' exports downstream. Sub-Saharan countries rich in non-oil natural resources exhibit greater forward linkages to manufacturing GVCs than other countries exhibit.[12] Almost a fifth of GDP originates from natural resources in countries specializing in commodities, compared with 3 percent or less for countries operating in limited manufacturing GVCs (see figure 2.1).

FDI acts as a catalyst for GVC integration, providing foreign capital and technical know-how

Higher capital endowments stimulate GVC integration and upgrading, but for those countries with scarce

Figure 2.1 Countries specializing in limited manufacturing rely on low labor costs, and countries specializing in commodities derive almost a fifth of GDP from natural resources

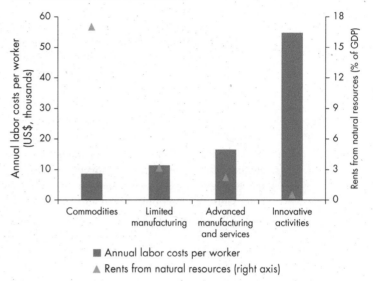

■ Annual labor costs per worker
▲ Rents from natural resources (right axis)

Sources: WDR 2020 team, based on Penn World Table; World Bank's WDI database; GVC taxonomy for the year 2011.

Note: The left axis shows average annual labor costs and the right axis the average rents from natural resources as a share of GDP by GVC taxonomy group, with averages over 2006–15. Labor costs were obtained by multiplying a country's (deflated) GDP by its labor share and dividing by the number of employees. The average of labor costs for countries specializing in commodities includes several high-income countries (such as Australia, Norway, and Saudi Arabia). See box 1.3 in chapter 1 for a description of the GVC taxonomy used in this Report.

capital FDI offers a solution. Cross-country cross-sector evidence from the Eora database shows that a relative scarcity of capital deters stronger GVC participation in capital-intensive sectors (see box 2.2). Countries moving from commodities to limited

Figure 2.2 Increases in labor costs and capital stock accompany upgrading in GVCs

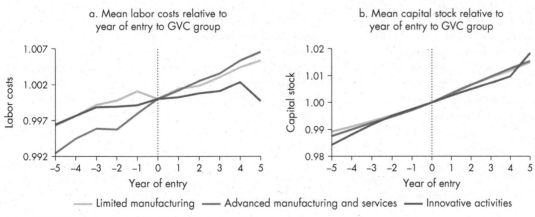

Sources: WDR 2020 team, based on Eora; World Bank's WDI database; GVC taxonomy.

Note: The year of entry is normalized to 0 for all countries in a particular GVC group, and the sample used to compute the means shown is based on countries with at least five years of observations before and after entry to the GVC group. Labor costs and capital stock are measured relative to the year of entry. Additional analysis confirms that labor costs and capital stock increase significantly in the five years before and after a switch.

manufacturing GVCs exhibit a strong increase in capital stock in the five years before the transition (figure 2.2, panel b). Because countries can attract FDI to overcome relative capital scarcity and thus integrate into GVCs, GVC activity and FDI inflows go hand in hand. When tight control over foreign production processes is necessary (perhaps because of weak contractual enforcement or weak protection of intellectual property), lead firms might prefer vertical integration of suppliers over an arm's-length relationship, resulting in intrafirm trade and FDI flows (see chapter 1).

It is hard to imagine a GVC in which a multinational firm is not involved at some stage of the production chain. Vietnam's success in smartphones stemmed from investments by Samsung in Vietnam to set up Samsung Electronics Vietnam (SEV) in 2008 and Samsung Electronics Vietnam-Thai Nguyen (SEVT) in 2013 (see box 2.1). Likewise, the Moroccan automotive industry has relied on investments by the French Renault-Nissan Alliance and PSA Group car companies. Singapore's Olam, one of the world's largest suppliers of cocoa beans, contributed to Ghana's cocoa exports reaching over 23,000 customers worldwide.[13] And then there were the earlier success stories such as Intel in Costa Rica (until 2014) and Volkswagen in South Africa.[14] In addition, investors from Taiwan, China, in the 1990s and South African investors in the 2000s were instrumental in developing and expanding the apparel value chain in Lesotho, whereas Mauritian investors played a similar role for apparel in Madagascar.[15] In all these cases, foreign-owned firms were instrumental in jumpstarting the domestic economy and integrating production into GVCs. And yet the reliance on FDI inflows also poses risks: Costa Rica lost many manufacturing jobs to Vietnam in 2014 after Intel abruptly relocated its operations.

Although many of these success stories (particularly in East Asia) are linked to FDI in manufacturing GVCs, much of the growth in FDI over the past two decades has come through natural resource–based sectors. Such investment differs considerably from traditional manufacturing FDI. Investors tend to be resource-seeking rather than efficiency-seeking or market-seeking. Investment is also likely to be dispersed across a wider set of countries and to emerge from a widening set of investors (including large investors from the global South).[16]

FDI inflows play a strong role in the extent of backward GVC participation shares and levels (see box 2.2), driven by GVC integration of the manufacturing sector.[17] The lack of foreign-owned firms in manufacturing is an important reason for low backward GVC participation in Sub-Saharan Africa.[18] Meanwhile, FDI is linked to lower forward GVC participation shares driven by GVC integration of agriculture and services. Countries attracting FDI in manufacturing may reduce their exports of raw agricultural goods and intermediate services (such as transportation) embodied in exports of resource-intensive goods, thereby lowering their forward GVC participation.[19]

Foreign-owned firms may also promote domestic upstream sectors. They increase the demand for local intermediate inputs and cultivate local suppliers that may subsequently supply other downstream domestic firms and even export. FDI can ease the entry of domestic firms into GVCs by, for example, conferring technical know-how and transmitting managerial practices. According to the Moroccan minister of industry, trade, and new technologies, Moulay Hafid El Alami, when Renault-Nissan set up plants in the north of Morocco's small city of Melloussa, it aimed to build an "industry ecosystem." Later, in fact, it attracted many other companies specializing in auto parts production and seeking to supply Renault-Nissan. Meanwhile, the government of Morocco is looking at ways to deepen the country's backward linkages. FDI in the apparel sector in Bangladesh led to new local input suppliers producing zippers, buttons, and fabrics, which also benefited domestic apparel firms and ensured the country's competitiveness in global apparel exports (box 2.3).[20] Such linkages of sectors and firms through FDI can further deepen countries' participation in GVCs.[21] Indeed, China has defied the global decline in the share of domestic value added in exports because its large domestic manufacturing capacity is supplying the downstream GVC parties through favorable FDI and trade policies (box 2.4).[22]

The link between FDI and GVC participation makes it difficult to disentangle their determinants. In their responses to the World Bank's Global Investment Competitiveness survey, executives at multinational corporations involved in efficiency-seeking FDI viewed country endowments as crucial for their investment decisions. Endowments included the available talent and skill of labor, the low cost of labor and inputs (including ease of access to imported inputs), and the capacity and skills of local suppliers.[23] Favorable exchange rates, good physical infrastructure, and low tax rates are also important, as are PTAs, bilateral investment treaties, and investment incentives. (Some of these policy-amenable factors are discussed throughout the chapter as important drivers of GVC participation. Other factors are covered in chapter 7.)

FDI is critical, particularly for countries upgrading their type of participation in GVCs. From 1990 to 2015,

Box 2.3 Sharing suppliers: How foreign firms benefit domestic firms

In the development of Bangladesh's apparel sector, foreign firms created incentives for local suppliers to improve their quality and productivity. Domestic firms that shared local suppliers with foreign firms gained access to newer and better local inputs. The spillover effects of shared suppliers helped explain a quarter of the expanded product scope and a third of the productivity gains of Bangladesh's domestic firms in the apparel sector from 1999 to 2003. In Bangladesh, foreign apparel firms also fostered the local market supplying intermediate inputs (figure B2.3.1).

But the reverse is true when foreign firms leave. In Malaysia, a local supplier sold a special plastic resin to Panasonic for its fax machines and to local manufacturers of box cutters. When Panasonic closed the plant, manufacturers of box cutters suffered as well.

Source: Kee 2015.

Figure B2.3.1 In Bangladesh, local suppliers grew as FDI grew from 1985 to 2003

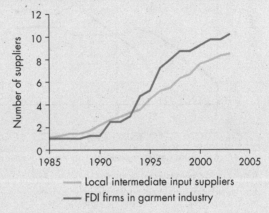

Source: Kee 2015.
Note: FDI = foreign direct investment.

Box 2.4 How liberalizing trade and FDI helped China move up in GVCs

Global production fragmentation has allowed firms to rely less on domestic inputs for production, as is evident in the growing backward GVC participation and the declining ratios of value added to gross exports across the world. China is an intriguing exception. How did it defy the global decline in domestic content in exports, despite its deep engagement in GVCs?

Firm-level customs transaction data and manufacturing firm survey data are used to measure China's domestic content in exports (its ratio of domestic value added in exports to gross exports). From 2000 to 2007, the share of domestic content in Chinese exports rose from 65 percent to 70 percent (figure B2.4.1). This upward trend was driven mainly by China's processing exporters, who substituted domestic for imported intermediate inputs in both volume and variety. After 2000, China's structural transformation was fueled by trade and foreign direct investment liberalization that encouraged intermediate input producers in China to expand their product varieties. Exporters in China began to buy more domestic intermediate inputs and to rely less on imported inputs. Other factors—such as rising wages, firm entry and exit, and the changing composition of

Chinese exports toward industries with high domestic value added or in nonprocessing sectors—cannot explain the upward trend.

Figure B2.4.1 Domestic value added in exports from China increased from 2000 to 2007

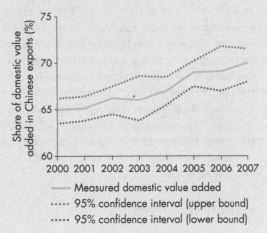

Source: Kee and Tang 2016.

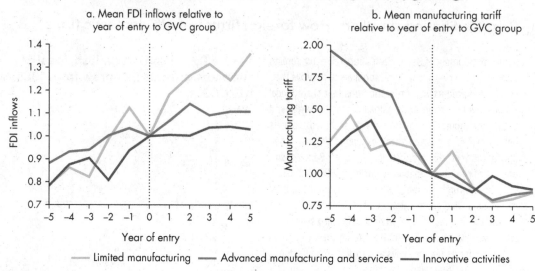

Figure 2.3 FDI increases and tariff declines accompany GVC upgrading

a. Mean FDI inflows relative to
year of entry to GVC group

b. Mean manufacturing tariff
relative to year of entry to GVC group

——— Limited manufacturing ——— Advanced manufacturing and services ——— Innovative activities

Source: WDR 2020 team, based on World Bank's WDI database and GVC taxonomy.

Note: The year of entry is normalized at 0 for all countries in a particular GVC group, and the sample to compute the means is based on countries with at least five years of observations before and after entry to the GVC group. FDI inflows and manufacturing tariffs are measured relative to the year of entry. Additional analysis confirms that FDI inflows increase significantly in the five years before and after a switch, whereas manufacturing tariffs decline significantly over that same period. FDI = foreign direct investment.

net FDI inflows picked up substantially for all countries in the years before transitioning into a new GVC group (figure 2.3, panel a). The growth of FDI inflows continues after countries transition into limited manufacturing GVCs (such as in Argentina, Cambodia, Indonesia, and South Africa) and to a lesser degree for countries transitioning into advanced manufacturing and services GVCs (such as in China, the Czech Republic, Romania, and Turkey) or into innovative GVC activities (such as in Austria, Italy, Korea, and Singapore).

To attract FDI, lower-income countries that face substantial infrastructure and regulatory gaps can establish special economic zones (SEZs) or export processing zones with less burdensome rules for business and better access to inputs than in the rest of the country. This approach was central to Bangladesh, Cambodia, Lesotho, and recently Ethiopia successfully entering the apparel GVC. Such sites account for a large share of exports and employment in GVCs, but linkages to the local economy tend to be small.[24] However, many other countries have struggled to establish successful zones. Chapter 7 dives deeper into SEZs and their role for GVCs.

Market size matters

Backward GVC participation in manufacturing as a percentage of total exports is lower in large economies, including China, Japan, and the United States.

To minimize cross-hauling of semiprocessed goods in GVCs, countries often specialize in contiguous stages of production. Because larger countries have a larger industrial capacity, they tend to attract a larger set of contiguous stages and reduce the use of imported inputs relative to domestically sourced inputs in their exports (lower backward GVC integration).

By their sheer size, large countries are likely to be geographically close to the consumers of final goods, so their more "central" location should make them more prone to specialize in downstream stages of production embodying more foreign value added.[25] Moreover, a large domestic supplier base reduces search frictions and facilitates the replacement of domestic suppliers if there are production disruptions.

Market size and the role of domestic suppliers

A story from Poland highlights the relationship between market size and GVCs and how industry linkages through the role of domestic suppliers can affect outcomes. In 1992 General Motors, one of the world's largest automakers, set up General Motors Poland to import Opel cars for the large Polish domestic market. Two years later, GM Poland commenced production activities, and today Poland has become one of the world's major auto exporting countries. Through intensive cooperation with Polish auto part suppliers, GM Poland has contributed to the significant growth in their number and also plays a role in expanding their sales to other GM units around the world.

The effect of market size on GVC participation is crucially mediated by links to domestic industries. Markets with larger manufacturing sectors are characterized by larger forward GVC participation and smaller backward GVC participation, highlighting the importance of domestic suppliers for GVC participation (see box 2.2). A larger manufacturing sector in the 2000s also increased the likelihood of countries participating in advanced manufacturing and services GVCs or in innovative GVC activities in 2011.

Enhancing market size by liberalizing trade policies

The constraints of a small market and limited local inputs can be overcome by liberalizing trade at home and negotiating liberalization abroad in order to liberate firms and farms from dependence on local inputs and narrow domestic demand. Regulatory barriers on both imports and exports, such as tariffs or quotas, increase trade costs, with consequences for countries' GVC participation and positioning. Trade barriers increase the cost of imported intermediate inputs and thus can reduce backward GVC participation. They also translate into higher costs for a country's exports, lowering forward GVC participation. Because tariffs imposed by partner countries increase the costs of exports, reducing tariff barriers can amplify the benefits for internationally fragmented production.

Costly imported intermediates are a barrier to GVC integration

Successive rounds of trade negotiations and unilateral trade liberalization efforts have been a driving force for GVC integration over the last three decades. China's accession to the WTO in 2001 and the accompanying requirement to reduce more than 7,000 tariffs ushered in a new era of globalization that stimulated GVC participation not only for its home firms but also for those in partner countries in East Asia and beyond. Meanwhile, accession to the world's largest customs union—the EU—was critical in bringing the Czech Republic, Hungary, Poland, and the Slovak Republic, and later Bulgaria and Romania, into GVCs.[26]

Lower tariffs on manufacturing goods encourage countries' backward GVC participation (see box 2.2). A 1 percentage point decrease in a country's average manufacturing tariff is associated with an increase of 0.4 percentage points in that country's backward GVC participation share in gross exports. In Sub-Saharan Africa, the negative impact of tariffs on GVC

participation is especially acute.[27] Higher import tariffs on manufacturing in the 2000s reduced the propensity of being in the group of countries specializing in advanced manufacturing and services GVCs in 2011. Tariffs on intermediate inputs have a strong negative impact on both GVC participation and gross exports (see box 2.2).

Tariffs on imported intermediates shape countries' export bundles, often preventing them from upgrading to more sophisticated or more profitable products. For example, Nepal exports tea almost entirely in bulk to India at about one-tenth of the price for tea sold packaged to Germany or the United Kingdom. To scale up the exports of branded, packaged tea, Nepalese entrepreneurs need intermediate inputs such as filter bags. But those are subject to a tariff of 30 percent, plus a 5 percent excise duty, increasing the world price of filter bags for Nepalese exporters by 36.5 percent and hampering their competitiveness.[28]

Exporters can often circumvent high tariffs on imported intermediates by using duty suspension mechanisms, but these often do not function efficiently. Two examples from South Asia illustrate this point. Pakistan's tariffs on intermediates average 8 percent—four times the average in East Asia—and its regulatory and additional duties (para-tariffs) are high. Thus, Pakistani exporters of textiles and apparel—the country's major export sector—rely mostly on domestic cotton rather than on imported artificial fibers such as polyester (the leading input to the fast-growing global imports of apparel).[29] In principle, Pakistani exporters have access to duty suspension schemes for their imported intermediates, such as the Duty and Tax Remission on Exports. In practice, approvals for remission takes on average 60 days—twice the time specified by law—and clearing customs after approval takes an extra 5–10 days. For that reason, a mere 3 percent of textile and apparel exporters use the scheme. In Bangladesh, by contrast, obtaining approval for duty suspension on intermediates takes on average 24 hours, and about 90 percent of textile and apparel firms use the scheme.[30]

Despite the gradual decline in tariffs over the last decades, especially for manufactured goods, there are still important differences in the restrictiveness of trade policies across countries. Countries specializing in commodities imposed manufacturing tariffs averaging 7.5 percent from 2006 to 2015, and those with limited manufacturing GVCs imposed tariffs averaging 6.5 percent. Tariffs drop sharply to less than 3 percent for countries with advanced manufacturing and services GVCs and to less than 2 percent for those with innovative GVC activities (figure 2.4).

Figure 2.4 Manufacturing tariffs are high and preferential trading partners few in countries connected to commodity GVCs

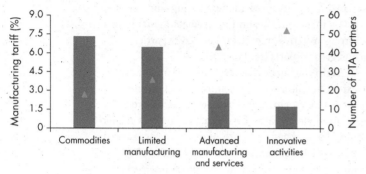

■ Manufacturing tariff ▲ Number of PTA partners (right axis)

Sources: WDR 2020 team, based on World Bank's WDI and Deep Trade Agreements databases and GVC taxonomy for the year 2011.

Note: The left axis shows average manufacturing import tariffs and the right axis the average number of preferential trading partners by GVC taxonomy group, with averages over 2006–15. PTA = preferential trade agreement.

Table 2.1 South Asian countries impose higher barriers to trade on each other (overall trade restrictiveness index, 2011)

Importing country	Origin of imports	
	South Asia	Rest of world
Afghanistan	3.84	4.65
India	4.59	0.50
Nepal	10.59	6.87
Pakistan	3.00	0.51
Sri Lanka	1.01	0.33

Source: Updated estimates by UNCTAD and World Bank (2018), based on their methodology.

Note: The overall trade restrictiveness indexes are computed using applied tariffs that take into account bilateral preferences.

For countries upgrading their participation in GVCs, manufacturing tariffs fall substantially in the years prior to such transitions (see figure 2.3, panel b). For countries establishing limited manufacturing GVCs at some point during 1990–2015—such as Argentina, Cambodia, Indonesia, and South Africa—the average manufacturing tariff rates were on average 25 percent higher five years before the transition compared with the year of the transition. Countries joining the group of advanced manufacturing and services GVCs—such as China, the Czech Republic, Romania, and Turkey—saw their tariffs drop by half from five years before the transition to the time of upgrading and saw a continued decline in the five years after upgrading.

Low tariffs are necessary but insufficient for high backward GVC participation because nontariff measures and other barriers at the border also matter. In South Asia, nontariff barriers—including para-tariffs and other regulatory constraints—increase firms' production costs and alter their input mix, thereby affecting their long-term export competitiveness. This outcome hurts the already low trade and GVC participation in South Asia.[31] The overall trade restrictiveness index for South Asia countries—capturing the trade policy distortions that each country imposes on its import bundle—shows greater protection for imports from South Asia than from the rest of the world (table 2.1).[32]

Brazil's large automotive sector, which employed more than 500,000 workers in 2016, developed under the shelter of high tariffs and high nontariff measures. But these policies have also been behind the sector's poor integration into GVCs, reflected in the lack of export orientation of its major auto producers and its domestic suppliers.[33] High local content requirements in the country's industrial policy toward the auto sector—the Inovar-Auto policy (2011–17)—prevented the sector from participating in GVCs.

Market access can jumpstart GVC participation

Market access, captured by the tariffs in destination markets, also plays a role in GVC participation. Sectors facing on average lower tariffs in destination markets exhibit stronger backward and forward GVC participation (see box 2.2). A 1 percentage point decline in the average tariff facing a sector in destination markets is associated with an increase in the country-sector's backward (forward) GVC participation by 6 percent (7 percent).

Preferential access is one aspect of special and differential treatment and its objective has been to encourage export-led growth in developing countries. But whether preferential access can help developing countries' exports has sparked disagreement, with skeptics arguing that trade preferences dilute the case for policy reform at home and lure beneficiaries into sectors in which they lack a comparative advantage.[34] Preferential access to foreign markets such as that provided by the Everything but Arms initiative of the European Union and the AGOA of the United States can help developing countries' exports in the short run.[35] In the long run, however, the effects are more nuanced, depending on the prevalent rules of origin and their impacts on the development of domestic suppliers (box 2.5). There is great heterogeneity across African countries in the response to AGOA market access preferences. Evidence suggests that for export

Box 2.5 Trade preferences as catalytic aid?

Immediately after the European Union granted duty-free and quota-free access to Bangladesh under the Everything but Arms (EBA) initiative in 2001, knitwear exports from Bangladesh to the European Union more than doubled, from $1.3 billion in 2000 to $3 billion in 2004. During the same period, knitwear exports from Bangladesh to the United States also increased by $30 million. Much to the surprise of many, such generous trade preferences resulted not in trade diversion from the rest of the world to the preference-granting markets, but in trade creation to the rest of the world. What could explain this finding?

Trade preferences can result in a long-term win-win scenario for all parties concerned.[a] The European Union gained from giving trade preferences to Bangladesh under the EBA because its lost tariff revenues were outweighed by gains from the lower prices resulting from higher entry into exporting in Bangladesh. Preferences raised the profits of potential exporters in Bangladesh, inducing greater firm entry exports to the European Union. But as firms overcame the fixed costs of production and exporting, some began to export to other markets, and exports from Bangladesh to all markets rose. Moreover, Bangladesh solidified its position as a major apparel exporter to the European Union, even after the conclusion of the Multi-fibre Arrangement (MFA) quota regime in 2004. The strict origin requirements of the European Union's EBA and its potential encouragement of greater local value added through nurturing stronger domestic suppliers may have helped explain these durable benefits.

The long-term impacts of the African Growth and Opportunity Act (AGOA) on the apparel export performance of African countries were more nuanced. At first, aggregate African apparel exports to the United States boomed after AGOA was enacted, and they then declined after MFA quotas ended in 2004 and preference erosion ensued (with competition from Asian giants). They have stagnated in recent years. The aggregate picture, however, is based on four different country-level stories (figure B2.5.1). Countries mostly in Central and West Africa, such as Cameroon, never took meaningful advantage of AGOA (panel a). Countries mostly in Southern Africa, such as Eswatini (formerly Swaziland), experienced a boom right after AGOA was enacted, followed by a bust (panel b). Countries such as Lesotho experienced growth and then stagnation (panel c). And countries in East Africa, such as Ethiopia, saw fairly sustained success, albeit starting late in some cases (panel d).[b]

As for other countries in these regions, in Madagascar the contraction in apparel exports to the United States after the MFA phase-out was driven by a tremendous exit of firms. In Mauritius, firms did not exit but contracted their exports sharply until a relaxation of the AGOA rules of origin in 2009 prompted a revival. The sustained dynamism of Kenya and the late growth in Ethiopia were driven largely by new firms entering the market after 2010 rather than by incumbent firms that benefited from large preference margins during the early AGOA period. Thus trade preferences do not seem to have nurtured longer-term comparative advantage in African countries.

(Box continues next page)

success, preferential access per se is not sufficient but needs to be complemented by specific domestic policies: lower tariffs, a reduced regulatory burden, and enhanced connectivity.[36] In some cases, as in Ethiopia, trade preferences are fundamental to offsetting a country's cost disadvantages stemming from lower labor productivity and higher logistics costs (relative to countries such as Vietnam) and so help attract FDI.[37]

Geography matters

Proximity to the hubs in the global trade network—China, Germany, Japan, and the United States—matters for GVC participation. Many value chains are not global but regional. Vietnam's proximity to its regional suppliers of electronic inputs—such as China, Japan, Korea, and Singapore—clearly helped

its GVC participation in the electronics sector (see box 2.1). Has remoteness prevented countries in Latin America and Sub-Saharan Africa from participating in GVCs? The total distance from Argentina or Chile to the GVC hubs is almost 40,000 kilometers and that from Malawi or Mozambique is more than 30,000 kilometers. These distances contrast with those for countries specialized in advanced manufacturing and services GVCs and innovative GVC activities, which average 18,000 kilometers.

The automotive sector relies heavily on fairly short regional value chains for at least three reasons. Automotive components such as car seats or engines can be heavy, bulky, and easily damaged, thereby increasing transportation costs. Just-in-time production and high product variety often require that subcomponents be produced near final assembly. And

Box 2.5 Trade preferences as catalytic aid? *(continued)*

Figure B2.5.1 Four stories of AGOA apparel exports from Africa

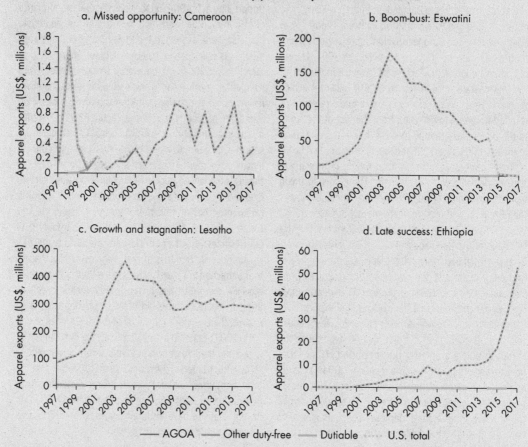

Source: WDR 2020 team, using data from the World Bank's Developing Countries' Trade and Market Access in the European Union and the United States database (U.S. section).

Note: Exports are classified by tariff regime eligibility by product-country-year and do not account for preference use. AGOA = African Growth and Opportunity Act.

a. Cherkashin et al. (2015).
b. Fernandes et al. (2019).

final assembly often happens in large end markets with local content requirements in return for market access, such as in Brazil, China, India, and South Africa.[38] Morocco took advantage of its geographical proximity to the EU market to become Africa's largest producer of passenger vehicles in 2017, surpassing South Africa.[39]

Inefficient infrastructure and delays in clearing customs are important sources of high trade costs. The performance of a GVC is often severely impaired by its weakest link, such as customs delays. Supply chain disruptions are especially costly when firms cannot easily resort to alternative suppliers. Trade delays associated with inefficient connectivity can be a large deterrent for relational GVCs requiring coordination and "just-in-time" delivery. Weak contract enforcement and the need for stronger cooperation and repeated interactions among the several agents participating in the chain may be severely curtailed by a remote location or inadequate air connectivity.

Trade costs can also shape a country's positioning in GVCs. In sequential (or snakelike) GVCs, trade costs compound along the value chain and occur at a higher incidence in the downstream stages than in the upstream stages. This situation may give remote countries an incentive to specialize in upstream stages and more central countries an incentive to specialize in downstream stages.[40] Inefficient transport and logistics services and weak competition in these services amplify the trade costs in many manufacturing GVCs with multiple border crossings and can offset other competitive advantages such as low labor costs.[41]

Strong evidence of the negative role played by longer geographical distances for GVC participation, both backward and forward, can be found using the Eora database. This evidence is driven mainly by manufacturing sector GVCs (see box 2.2).[42] The longer geographical distances to the GVC hubs in China, Germany, and the United States increase a country's likelihood of specializing in commodities, whereas countries closer to the GVC hubs are more likely to participate in limited manufacturing GVCs. Geographical proximity also matters more for trade in GVCs than for trade in final goods.[43]

Enhanced connectivity can overcome geographical barriers and promote GVC participation

The disadvantage of a remote location can be addressed by improving transport and communication infrastructure as well as the regulatory framework—especially competition—governing these services. The most remote countries, such as landlocked ones, have policies for important "linking" services such as transport and telecommunications that are perversely restrictive.[44] Better connectivity would influence the predictability, reliability, and timeliness of GVCs.[45]

Transport costs remain, according to developing country suppliers, the main obstacle to entering, establishing, or upgrading in GVCs.[46] The geographic centrality of a country can attract downstream production stages in GVCs. But geographic centrality is more related to centrality in the transport network than to distance. Perhaps more important for GVC participation is economic distance. Countries in Central Asia, while central in the distance to neighbors, are isolated because of their poor-quality transport networks, their lack of affordable transport services for containers, and the missing links along main infrastructure corridors.[47] These issues impair their participation in the downstream stages of GVCs. Similarly, slow and unpredictable land transport keeps most Sub-Saharan African countries out of the electronics value chain.[48] Estimates suggest that improving trade facilitation halfway to global best practices would stimulate trade in the Sub-Saharan Africa region to a far greater extent than eliminating all import tariffs.[49] And although air transport could help bridge slow land transport or long geographical distances, its high cost limits low-income country exports to goods with very high unit values (such as gold and silver), time-sensitive goods (fast fashion clothing), and perishable goods (cut flowers).[50] A day of delay in transit due to a different transport mode choice has a tariff equivalent of 0.6–2.1 percent, and the most sensitive trade flows are those involving parts and components.[51] Meanwhile, the private provision of cold storage logistics infrastructure has enabled the development of the Ethiopian floriculture value chain, whereas lack of such infrastructure is limiting the upgrading potential in Bangladesh's aquaculture value chain.[52]

High logistics costs inhibit landlocked countries from participating in GVCs for electronics and fruits and vegetables.[53] The average number of days from a warehouse in the origin economy to a warehouse in the destination country in 2006–15 varied greatly for different types of GVC participation (figure 2.5). Imports by countries specializing in innovative GVC activities need less than nine days on average to reach a warehouse, but one additional week is required for countries specializing in advanced manufacturing and services GVCs, such as the Philippines, Portugal, and Thailand. By contrast, the average time to import exceeds one month in countries specializing in commodities (not shown in figure 2.5): 42 days to import in Ghana and 92 days to import in Iraq. Infrastructure gaps are partly responsible for longer delays in Africa, while the lack of electronic systems and to a lesser extent customs administration and inspections account for more than half of the total delays, according to the Doing Business database (figure 2.6). A large portion of long transport times in Sub-Saharan Africa is attributed to cargo dwell times at ports.[54] Despite an already favorable location, Vietnam reduced its average time to import during the period the electronics GVC sector expanded, but its connectivity remains worse than that of its regional competitors such as Thailand (see box 2.1).

An inability to meet requirements for timely production and delivery hurts GVC participation. Trade in parts and components in international production networks is more sensitive to logistics performance than trade in final goods and is more likely to suffer

Figure 2.5 Connectivity is associated with specialization in more advanced GVCs

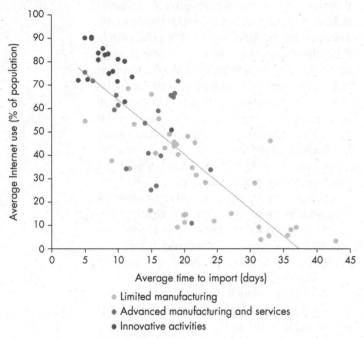

Sources: WDR team, based on World Bank's WDI and Doing Business databases and GVC taxonomy for the year 2011.

Note: The bivariate regression line between average time to import and average Internet use is shown in blue. Figure excludes countries specializing in commodities. Averages are over 2006–15.

Figure 2.6 Improving customs and introducing electronic systems are as important as infrastructure for African trade

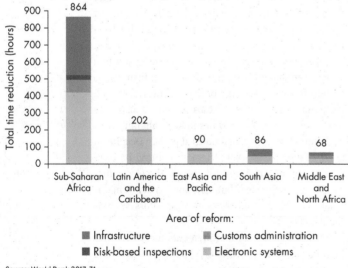

Source: World Bank 2017, 31.

Note: The time reduction captures reforms that were implemented and had a positive impact on the time for trading across borders indicator from 2016 to 2017. The reforms recorded during this period are aggregated in four wide-ranging categories: electronic systems, customs administration, risk-based inspections, and infrastructure. Regions with no reforms on time are excluded from the figure.

in the face of higher uncertainty in bilateral international transport times.[55] Evidence from the Eora database indicates that better scores in the logistics performance index are linked to stronger backward GVC participation (see box 2.2). Unpredictability in border clearance times for imports lowers survival rates for manufacturing exporters in 48 developing countries.[56] Moreover, the quality of the national road infrastructure matters for timely delivery to global markets. For Indonesian manufacturing firms, a higher road density in a firm's province and in neighboring provinces increases the probability of exporting.[57]

Connectivity is not confined to the physical supply chain of goods; it also includes effective communication between the participants in GVCs. Two ways that improve effective communication are use of the Internet and of the English language.

Stronger Internet usage could be linked to stronger GVC integration for at least two reasons. First, a large percentage of inputs embodied in exports—about 30 percent—are services such as logistics, information and communication technology (ICT), and other business services that rely on the Internet. Second, firms in GVCs need to communicate with both their suppliers and their customers through Internet-based technologies.

Countries in which a higher average share of the population is using the Internet exhibit stronger backward GVC integration (see box 2.2). In China, expanding Internet access from coastal provinces to hinterland provinces increased the density of manufacturing exporters in hinterland provinces, controlling for differences across provinces in changing skills, capital, and transport infrastructure (map 2.1).[58]

But many countries still have very low Internet coverage, particularly those specializing in commodities. Over 2006–15, only 21 percent of the population of these countries used the Internet, and coverage was even lower than 5 percent in Burkina Faso, Burundi, and Mali. This coverage contrasts sharply with that in countries participating in advanced manufacturing and services GVCs, where half the population on average are online. And this share exceeds three-quarters in countries focusing on innovative GVC activities, with coverage of over 85 percent in Denmark, Finland, and Sweden (see figure 2.5).

English skills have helped India and the Philippines become attractive offshore destinations for business services, including not only call centers but also increasingly complex services such as information technology and finance serving the United Kingdom and the United States. Morocco and Tunisia have become destinations for French firms.

Map 2.1 Growth in Internet density and exporter firm density across provinces in China, 1999 and 2007

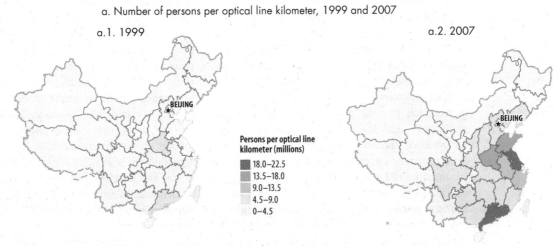

a. Number of persons per optical line kilometer, 1999 and 2007

a.1. 1999

a.2. 2007

Persons per optical line
kilometer (millions)
- 18.0–22.5
- 13.5–18.0
- 9.0–13.5
- 4.5–9.0
- 0–4.5

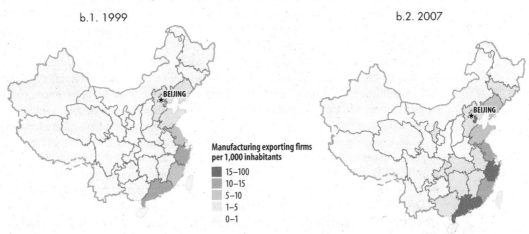

b. Number of manufacturing exporting firms per 1,000 inhabitants, 1999 and 2007

b.1. 1999

b.2. 2007

Manufacturing exporting firms
per 1,000 inhabitants
- 15–100
- 10–15
- 5–10
- 1–5
- 0–1

Source: Fernandes et al. 2017.

IBRD 44646 | AUGUST 2019

A higher portion of people speaking English in a country is positively correlated with forward GVC participation (see box 2.2), and proximity has been shown to be more relevant for GVC trade than for trade in final goods.[59] Language frictions inhibit knowledge spillovers in GVCs, such as in Myanmar, where high communication barriers between domestic managers and Chinese, Japanese, and Korean managers limit the productivity spillovers from FDI.[60]

Institutional quality matters

Among the top 25 most politically unstable countries over 2006–15, only the Philippines and Thailand participated in advanced manufacturing and services GVCs, and only Israel in innovative GVC activities. How important is the quality of institutions, all else being equal, for countries' participation in GVCs?

Weak contract enforcement is a significant deterrent of traditional trade flows, and GVCs are particularly sensitive to the quality of contractual institutions. Because the performance of a GVC depends on the strength of its weakest link, production delays driven by weak contract enforcement could be particularly harmful to GVCs. The presence of relationship-specific investments (such as for the customization of products) and the exchange of large flows of intangibles (such as technology, intellectual property, and credit) reinforce the potential role of institutional quality as a significant determinant of relational GVC participation.[61] GVC linkages relying heavily on institutional quality also tend to be particularly "sticky," which calls for reputational mechanisms of cooperation that partly substitute for the absence of formal contracting. Under some circumstances, vertical integration through FDI may serve as a direct (albeit imperfect) substitute for strong contract enforcement in the host countries.

Evidence based on the Eora database reveals that political stability greatly matters for backward GVC integration (see box 2.2). Sectors that rely more on contract enforcement see greater increases in GVC participation (and in gross exports) in countries with better institutional quality, after controlling for resource endowments, geography, tariffs, and macroeconomic cycles (see box 2.2). If Mozambique increased its rule of law index to the cross-country median, its backward GVC participation level would rise by 29 percent, while its forward GVC participation level and its exports would grow by 32 percent.[62] By contrast, countries characterized by lower political stability exhibit higher forward GVC participation (see box 2.2). On average across countries, this is driven by participation of the mining sector in GVCs. Indeed, higher average political stability in the 2000s reduced the likelihood of countries specializing in commodities in 2011. Poor institutional quality linked to land and property rights in Côte d'Ivoire and Ghana has hampered growth in their agriprocessing GVCs (pineapples and cocoa).[63]

PTAs, especially those with deep provisions, can improve domestic institutions because they help import both reform and technical and financial assistance and so result in stronger GVC participation.

Over the last decades, most tariff liberalization has arisen from the negotiation of bilateral and regional PTAs by developing and developed countries. Tariff reductions (and certainty about those reductions) are an important benefit of PTAs, but more countries are signing bilateral and regional PTAs that go beyond simple market access. The depth of trade agreements is associated with the international fragmentation of production because behind-the-border policies need to be disciplined in trade agreements for GVCs to operate efficiently.

Participation in more advanced GVCs goes hand in hand with countries' engagement with more PTA partners (see figure 2.4). The Eora database reveals a supportive role for regional trade blocs and deep trade agreements in promoting countries' backward integration in GVCs. Specific trade agreements, such as those represented by the European Union and the Association of Southeast Asian Nations (ASEAN),[64] are linked to substantially higher backward GVC integration for their members, and a positive if weak effect is also found for the North American Free Trade Agreement (see box 2.2).[65] The depth of trade agreements is particularly relevant now that countries are signing more deep trade agreements exhibiting higher backward GVC participation (chapter 8 discusses deep trade agreements in more detail). The African Continental Free Trade Area, which came into force in 2019, is expected to unleash opportunities for strong GVC participation in Africa. The channels for PTAs to nurture GVC participation include lower tariffs, larger FDI inflows, shorter distances to GVC hubs, and stronger regulatory frameworks that increase political stability.

But not all PTAs have been conducive to GVC participation. Mercosur has, if anything, impeded its members' backward GVC participation (see box 2.2).[66] Argentina exhibits low backward integration into GVCs because of its restrictive trade policies, but high forward GVC integration because of its rich natural resources. If Mercosur were to add deep provisions, such as commitments to investment and reforms to remove entry barriers and tackle anticompetitive business practices, Argentina's GVC integration would gain substantially.[67] Argentina now has only three PTA partners encompassing 57 enforceable deep provisions, compared with 18 PTA partners for Colombia and 19 for Peru (covering 250 and 263 deep provisions, respectively). With a Mercosur agreement as deep as the agreement among the EU, Colombia, and Peru in terms of the number of enforceable provisions, Argentina could increase its exports of parts and components to Mercosur members by 1–9 percent. Large potential gains for GVC participation from deepening existing PTAs (and from engaging in new deep PTAs) are also possible for the other Mercosur giant, Brazil.[68] But the impacts of PTAs on GVC participation can be subtle because the rules of origin under PTAs can influence how GVCs form and expand (box 2.6).

Transitioning up the GVC typology

Over 1990–2015, many countries upgraded their GVC categories. The Czech Republic moved from limited manufacturing GVCs in the 1990s to advanced manufacturing and services GVCs in the 2000s and to innovative GVC activities after 2010.

Several determinants identified here as conducive to stronger GVC integration help to explain the Czech Republic's transitions. After the downfall of the Soviet Union in 1991, the geographical proximity of the Czech Republic (Czechoslovakia until 1993) to neighboring Austria and Germany and its supply of skilled labor at lower labor costs made the country an attractive location for FDI. In the 1990s, its shares of high-skilled workers (35 percent) and medium-skilled workers (57 percent) were almost identical to Germany's, while the average labor costs of a Czech worker were around $13,800, or less than a third of Germany's $49,000. The country's appealing labor picture led to strong FDI inflows, particularly in automotive and business services, and it was bolstered by the newfound political stability.

Although average manufacturing import tariffs were already low in the Czech Republic in the early 1990s at around 5 percent, they had fallen to less than 2 percent by 2000. The Czech Republic's accession to the European Union in 2004 opened the doors for PTAs—the European Union being one of the deepest PTAs—and the number of PTA partners jumped from 0 to 45. The 2000s also launched a new era in which the country emphasized skill building and innovation. Internet use rose from 35 percent of the Czech population in 2005 to 75 percent in 2015. The share of high-skilled workers further climbed, reaching 40 percent by 2007, while R&D expenditure as a percentage of GDP grew from 1.1 percent in 2000 to 1.9 percent in 2015, ranking the Czech Republic among the countries with the highest innovation potential in the world.[69]

Box 2.6 PTAs and GVCs: The role of rules of origin

Rules of origin, a central element of preferential trade agreements (PTAs), state that the eligibility of a final good for preferential tariff treatment requires the production or sourcing of some of its inputs within the PTA area. PTAs can affect firm-level decisions on intermediate input sourcing, and thus their GVC linkages, through two channels: preferential tariffs and rules of origin.

For preferential tariffs, inputs imported from PTA members face lower (often zero) tariffs than inputs sourced from nonmembers. Rules of origin distinguish goods originating from PTA members from goods originating from nonmembers with the objective of ensuring that goods imported by one PTA member from another benefiting from lower PTA tariffs truly originate from the PTA area and are not simply assembled from components originating in nonmembers.

Rules of origin can constrain PTA members by not allowing them to select the globally most efficient suppliers of intermediate inputs. In recent surveys, manufacturing firms in developing countries repeatedly pointed to rules of origin as a crucial nontariff barrier.[a] Rules of origin are difficult to measure because of their legal complexity, but such measurements did improve for the world's largest PTA, the North American Free Trade Agreement (NAFTA).

A novel mapping of all input–output linkages embedded in NAFTA's rules of origin is constructed for each final good, identifying all intermediate inputs required for its production subject to rules of origin, and for each intermediate good, identifying all final goods that impose rule of origin restrictions on its sourcing.[b] Regressions performed on the impact of these sourcing restrictions show that NAFTA's rules of origin significantly reduced the growth rate of Mexican imports of intermediate goods from nonmembers relative to the growth rate of imports of intermediate goods from members. On average, NAFTA's rules of origin have reduced the growth rate of imports of affected goods from nonmembers relative to NAFTA members by 30 percentage points. These findings reveal an effective strengthening of the regional GVC, Factory North America.[c] But they also point to the trade diversion of PTAs through the deterrence of imports of intermediate goods from nonmembers.

Exemplifying the dramatic changes in sourcing decisions—and thus changes in patterns of GVC participation stemming from changes in rules of origin under a PTA—is the Mauritius apparel sector since 2000. Mauritius had been eligible for U.S. nonreciprocal trade preferences under the African Growth and Opportunity Act (AGOA) since 2001, but it experienced a swing between stringent rules of origin (2001–09) and liberal rules of origin (2009–15) in its exports of apparel to the U.S. market (figure B2.6.1). A shift across sources of fabric imports followed closely the swing in rules of origin, with fabric originating in African countries or the United States until 2009 and then almost entirely from outside Africa and the United States (mostly from Asian countries) from 2010 on.[d]

(Box continues next page)

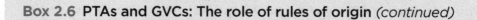

Box 2.6 PTAs and GVCs: The role of rules of origin *(continued)*

Figure B2.6.1 Mauritius's exports of apparel to the United States, by origin of fabric, 2001–15

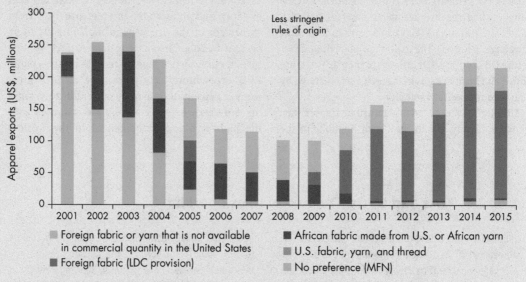

Legend:
- Foreign fabric or yarn that is not available in commercial quantity in the United States
- Foreign fabric (LDC provision)
- African fabric made from U.S. or African yarn
- U.S. fabric, yarn, and thread
- No preference (MFN)

Source: Office of Textiles and Apparel (OTEXA), International Trade Administration, U.S. Department of Commerce

Note: LDC = least developed country; MFN = most-favored-nation.

a. ITC (2015).
b. Conconi et al. (2018).
c. The term was coined by Baldwin (2013).
d. Fernandes et al. (2019).

The productivity of the workforce and the availability of high-quality suppliers are major reasons for the country's continuing attractiveness to German and other multinationals.

The relative importance of different determinants for GVC participation depends on the type of GVC engagement and on the characteristics of countries. Bottlenecks specific to different regions and groups of countries hamper their backward GVC participation (box 2.7). To transition across types, all determinants and policy areas must be improved, including tariffs, FDI, political stability, customs, and logistics. For countries in different regions, the relative importance of these determinants differ. For example, in Sub-Saharan Africa low FDI inflows are the most important factor deterring backward GVC participation, while for countries in the Middle East and North Africa (MENA) and in fragile and conflict situations, low political stability is the severest obstacle. Countries in South Asia, Latin America and the Caribbean, MENA, and the Pacific Islands stand to benefit the most from tariff liberalization.

Box 2.7 Most important determinants of GVC participation, by taxonomy group and region

The determinants of backward GVC participation differ across countries, depending on their type of GVC participation (table B2.7.1):

- An average country in the *commodities* group is characterized by low political stability (–0.6), low foreign direct investment (FDI) inflows, high manufacturing import tariffs (6.6 percent), low customs efficiency (35 days to import), and low scores in the logistics performance index (LPI, 2.6).
- Countries in the *limited manufacturing* group see on average improved political stability, 60 percent higher FDI inflows, 1 percentage point lower average tariffs (5.6 percent), improved customs efficiency (20 days to import), as well as improved LPI scores (2.8), relative to the commodities group.
- Countries in the *advanced manufacturing and services* group exhibit on average further improved political stability, substantially (150 percent) higher FDI inflows, substantially lower average tariffs by 3 percentage points (2.6 percent), better customs efficiency (13 days to import), as well as a higher LPI (3.3), compared with the limited manufacturing group.
- Countries part of the *innovative activities* group show on average improved political stability, 90 percent higher FDI inflows, lower tariffs by 0.9 percentage points (1.7 percent), higher customs efficiency (8.9 days to import), and a better LPI (3.8), relative to the advanced manufacturing and services group.

Overall, it is clear that to transition across different types of GVC participation, several policy areas require substantial improvements. The color-coded averages shown in table B2.7.1 suggest that the time to import improves substantially from the commodities to the limited manufacturing group, while tariff rates fall drastically from the limited manufacturing to the advanced manufacturing and services group. The relative importance of lower tariffs coincides with backward integration being much higher for countries specializing in advanced manufacturing and services than for countries in limited manufacturing (39.8 percent versus 24.1 percent). The innovative activities group sees improvements on all fronts, most notably in political stability and in logistics performance.

Based on the evidence from the cross-country regressions (see box 2.2), the most important bottlenecks hampering backward GVC participation shares of each World Bank region or group of countries can be summarized as follows, along with the hypothetical impacts of their improvements (table B2.7.2):

- *Backward GVC integration in South Asia, Sub-Saharan Africa, fragile and conflict situations, and the Caribbean and Pacific Islands would benefit the most from attracting FDI.* South Asia and Sub-Saharan Africa rank lowest among all regions in terms of FDI inflows. If South Asia and Sub-Saharan Africa were to improve their average FDI levels to those of the best-performer Europe and Central Asia (ECA) region, backward GVC participation for each would increase by an estimated 16 percent.[a] If fragile and conflict situations improved

Table B2.7.1 Backward GVC participation and determinants, by taxonomy group

Taxonomy group	Average backward GVC participation share (%)	Average political stability index	Average FDI inflow (log)	Average tariff rate (%)	Average days to import	Logistics performance index
Commodities	13.9	–0.6	6.7	6.6	35.4	2.6
Limited manufacturing	24.1	–0.3	7.3	5.6	19.9	2.8
Advanced manufacturing and services	39.8	0.1	8.8	2.6	13.0	3.3
Innovative activities	37.3	0.8	9.7	1.7	8.9	3.8

Source: WDR 2020 team.

Note: Averages shown cover the period 2010–15, using the GVC taxonomy for the year 2015. See box 1.3 in chapter 1 for a description of the GVC taxonomy used in this Report. Dark blue relates to the best performance across taxonomy groups, dark red to the worst performance, and lighter shades to intermediate performance. FDI = foreign direct investment.

(Box continues next page)

Box 2.7 Most important determinants of GVC participation, by taxonomy group and region (continued)

Table B2.7.2 Backward GVC participation and determinants, by region and group of countries

	Average backward GVC participation share (%)	Average political stability index	Average FDI inflows (log)	Average tariff rate (%)
East Asia and Pacific	20.0	−0.2	7.3	5.6
Europe and Central Asia	28.9	−0.2	7.4	3.0
Latin America and the Caribbean	18.1	−0.2	7.2	6.3
Middle East and North Africa	14.7	−1.3	7.3	8.8
South Asia	16.1	−1.1	6.1	11.0
Sub-Saharan Africa	17.3	−0.5	6.0	8.6
Fragile and conflict situations	11.6	−1.3	5.4	9.0
Caribbean Islands	17.5	0.1	5.7	9.5
Pacific Islands	15.3	0.1	4.2	8.4

Source: WDR 2020 team.

Note: Averages shown cover the period 2010–15. In each region or group of countries, averages are computed based only on World Bank client countries. These groups include only countries that are eligible for lending and are part of the Eora database. Dark blue relates to the best performance across regions or country groups, dark red to the worst performance, and lighter shades or white to intermediate performance. FDI = foreign direct investment.

FDI levels to those of the ECA, backward GVC participation could increase by 34 percent on average. For the Caribbean Islands, GVC participation is estimated to grow by 19 percent under that scenario, while for the Pacific Islands the increase would be a dramatic 40 percent.

- *Backward GVC participation in South Asia, the Middle East and North Africa (MENA), and the Pacific Islands would increase the most from import tariff liberalization.* South Asia imposes the highest average manufacturing import tariff rates across all regions (11 percent). If it reduced its tariff rates to those of the best-performer ECA (3 percent), backward GVC participation could increase by 20 percent. Under the same scenario, MENA and the Pacific Islands are estimated to experience growth in backward GVC participation rates of 14–16 percent.

- *Backward GVC integration in MENA, South Asia, and fragile and conflict situations would increase the most from improved institutional quality.* MENA and South Asia rank lowest among all regions in terms of political stability. If MENA and South Asia improved their political stability to that of the best-performer East Asia and Pacific region, backward GVC participation in MENA would increase by an estimated 28 percent and by 20–36 percent in South Asia and in fragile and conflict situations.

- *For Latin America and the Caribbean (LAC), lower tariffs could have a high payoff for GVC integration.* If LAC reduced its tariff rates from their average of 6.3 percent to the average rate of the best-performer ECA, 3 percent, backward GVC participation would increase by an estimated 7 percent.

a. For any given determinant, the magnitudes reported are obtained as a ratio of (1) the product between the difference in the determinant in the best-performer region and the determinant in the considered region/group and the estimated coefficient on the determinant in cross-country regressions and (2) the average backward GVC participation share in the considered region/group. Estimated coefficients are shown in Fernandes, Kee, and Winkler (2019).

Notes

1. In this chapter, the definition of *low-skilled worker* or *low-skilled labor* is based on International Standard Classification of Occupations (ISCO) categories, and it covers "elementary occupations," labeled skill level 1 by the International Labour Organization (ILO). See https://www.ilo.org/public/english/bureau/stat/isco/isco08/index.htm.

2. *Economist* (2018).

3. Stitchdiary (2018).

4. See appendix A for a description of the databases used in this Report. These results appear to contrast with those of the McKinsey Global Institute (MGI 2019), which argues that labor-cost arbitrage is a small share of the GVC activity that declined between 2007 and 2017. The difference in interpretations stems from differences in definitions and methodology. MGI defines *labor-cost arbitrage* as exports from countries whose GDP per capita is one-fifth or less than that of the importing country, and so convergence between developing and advanced countries will reduce labor-cost arbitrage. Importantly, it finds that the overall share of labor-cost arbitrage in goods value chains remained roughly constant at 18–19 percent from 2007 to 2017. Only for labor-intensive goods, such as textiles and apparel, does it note a significant decline in labor-cost arbitrage, albeit from high levels. Consistent with the analysis presented in this Report, it also observes a sharp increase in labor-cost arbitrage from 1995 to 2007 and finds labor-cost arbitrage is high and rising even in the most recent decade in some sectors, such as autos, and in some countries, such the United States.

5. See Pathikonda and Farole (2017), who extend the traditional theory of factor content of trade to construct measures capturing the capabilities most relevant in the trade of GVC products, as defined by Athukorala (2010) and Sturgeon and Memedovic (2011).

6. Evidence from the Eora database shows a U-shaped relationship between GDP per capita and forward GVC integration across countries.

7. Engman, Farole, and Winkler (2018).

8. The Human Capital Index (HCI) database provides data at the country level for each of the components of the HCI as well as for the overall index, disaggregated by gender. The index measures the amount of human capital that a child born today can expect to attain by age 18, given the risks of poor health and poor education that prevail in the country where she lives.

9. See Yameogo and Jammeh (2019), based on Eora cross-country data for 23 African countries and their comparison to global evidence for 115 countries.

10. See Rocha and Winkler (2019) for a study using data from the World Bank's Enterprise Surveys.

11. Rodrik (2018).

12. See the evidence in Abreha et al. (2019) based on the Eora database contrasting GVCs of Africa's manufacturers to GVCs of other developing regions (including in South Asia and East Asia).

13. Olam (2016).

14. See Freund and Moran (2017) on how governments were successful in using FDI to increase Costa Rica's and Morocco's GVC participation.

15. See Godfrey (2015); Morris and Staritz (2014).

16. Farole and Winkler (2014).

17. This positive association is driven by GVC participation in the manufacturing sector only, while there is no association between FDI inflows and countries' GVC integration of their agriculture, commodities, or services sectors. This could point to a more favorable role of efficiency-seeking or market-seeking FDI that looks for internationally cost-competitive destinations and potential export platforms. See Buelens and Tirpák (2017) for further evidence that bilateral FDI stocks are positively associated with the bilateral backward GVC participation as well as with bilateral gross trade.

18. Liu and Steenbergen (2019) use the World Bank's Enterprise Survey data for 139 countries for 2006–18 to show that a lower foreign ownership presence is linked to lower backward GVC participation, measured by exporting and importing at the firm level. Based on the same source of data, Gould (2018) shows evidence of a strong link between foreign participation and integration into global production chains via exporting and importing for firms in the East and Central Asia region.

19. However, FDI inflows are important for forward GVC participation levels according to the Eora cross-country evidence (see box 2.2). The negative impact of FDI on forward GVC participation shares may also reflect the fact that some of the countries abundant in natural resources that exhibit very high values of those shares have low institutional quality (as shown later in this chapter) and attract relatively less FDI.

20. Kee (2015).

21. Alfaro-Ureña, Manelici, and Vasquez (2019) also highlight similar positive improvements for local suppliers that joined multinational supply chains in Costa Rica.

22. Kee and Tang (2016).

23. World Bank (2018).

24. Taglioni and Winkler (2016).

25. Antràs and de Gortari (2017).

26. World Bank (2018).

27. See Abudu and Nguimkeu (2019) focusing on Eora data for African countries and exploiting variation in countries' tariff policies over time.

28. Narain and Varela (2017).

29. Rocha and Varela (2018).

30. The importance of lower tariffs on intermediate inputs to foster the use of imported inputs and improve export performance at the firm level is true both in countries poorly integrated into GVCs such as Nepal and Pakistan, as well as Peru (see Pierola, Fernandes, and Farole 2018) and in countries highly integrated into GVCs such as China (Bas and Strauss-Kahn 2015).

31. Kathuria (2018).

32. The overall trade restrictiveness index measures the uniform tariff equivalent of a country's tariff and nontariff barriers that would generate the same level of import value for the country in a given year. See UNCTAD and World Bank (2018) for details on the methodology.

33. Sturgeon, Chagas, and Barnes (2017).
34. Hoekman and Özden (2005); Ornelas (2016).
35. An example of the loss of that market access illustrates its importance. The suspension of AGOA market access benefits by Madagascar because of its domestic political unrest in 2009 led to an outflow of Asian FDI and a reduction in exports of apparel to the United States by $156 million, or 75 percent, within a year.
36. See Fernandes, Forero, et al. (2019).
37. Interviews with enterprises in Ethiopia and testimonies of foreign investors discussed in Fernandes, Forero, et al. (2019) indicate that lead apparel companies in GVCs would not have set up their production plants in Ethiopia had AGOA trade preferences not been in place.
38. Sturgeon and Thun (2018).
39. *Morocco World News* (2018).
40. Antràs and de Gortari (2017).
41. APEC and World Bank (2018).
42. A study by Kowalski et al. (2015) finds an important role for geographical distance from GVC hubs, based on Trade in Value Added (TiVA) data on GVC participation from the Organisation for Economic Co-operation and Development.
43. Johnson and Noguera (2017) find distance to be a friction for bilateral value added in exports (as well as for bilateral gross exports), whereas Buelens and Tirpák (2017) find that distance plays a bigger role in GVC trade relative to trade in final goods.
44. Arvis, Raballand, and Marteau (2010) emphasize the crucial role of an uncompetitive market structure in the transport sector in explaining the high logistics costs in landlocked countries. Using the World Bank's Services Trade Restrictiveness Index, Borchert et al. (2017) show that landlocked countries have more restrictive policies in the transport and communication sectors than coastal countries.
45. WEF (2013).
46. OECD and WTO (2013).
47. The evidence is provided by Briceño-Garmendia, Lebrand, and Abate (2018) using a novel measure of country connectivity that captures the cost, time, and reliability of the transport network that enables users to reach relevant economic destinations, including global GVC hubs.
48. Christ and Ferrantino (2011).
49. WEF (2013).
50. Arvis et al. 2011.
51. The estimates obtained by Hummels and Schaur (2013) are based on transport mode choices by U.S. importers. Similar magnitudes for the cost of a one-day delay in inland transit were found in the World Bank's Doing Business database by Djankov, Freund, and Pham (2010).
52. See Ponte et al. (2014).
53. Arvis, Raballand, and Marteau (2010).
54. Raballand et al. (2012).
55. A gravity model of trade is used to relate bilateral trade in parts and components or in final goods to the logistics performance index by Saslavsky and Shepherd (2014) and to transit times measured by Ansón et al. (2017) using the database of parcel deliveries compiled by the Universal Postal Union.

56. Vijil, Wagner, and Woldemichael (2019).
57. Rodríguez-Pose et al. (2013).
58. See Fernandes et al. (2017), who also provide econometric results for a causal impact of Internet access on firm export participation in China. .
59. Buelens and Tirpák (2017).
60. Khandelwal et al. (2018).
61. Levchenko (2007); Nunn (2007).
62. These computations assume an average (mean) sectoral contractual intensity.
63. See Amanor (2012).
64. ASEAN is a regional intergovernmental organization comprising 10 countries in Southeast Asia.
65. Johnson and Noguera (2017) also find that the EU and other preferential trade agreements, especially deep agreements, play an important role in decreasing the ratio of bilateral value added to gross exports, a sign of growth in global production fragmentation.
66. Mercosur is an economic and political bloc comprising Argentina, Brazil, Paraguay, Uruguay, and República Bolivariana de Venezuela.
67. This is one of the trade liberalization scenarios for Argentina, whose impacts are obtained from a dynamic computable general equilibrium model, as discussed by Martínez Licetti et al. (2018).
68. This finding is shown by Hollweg and Rocha (2018), based on the impact of deep PTAs in a gravity model of trade on bilateral trade in parts and components.
69. OECD (n.d.).

References

Abreha, Kaleb Girma, Emmanuel K. K. Lartey, Taye Alemu Mengistae, Solomon Owusu, and Albert G. Zeufack. 2019. "Africa in Manufacturing Global Value Chains: Cross-Country Patterns in the Dynamics of Linkages." Background paper, Office of the Chief Economist, Africa Region, World Bank, Washington, DC.

Abudu, Derrick, and Pierre Nguimkeu. 2019. "Public Policy and Country Integration to Manufacturing Global Value Chains: The Roles of Trade and Competition Policies, Labor Market Regulation, and Tax Incentives." Background paper, Office of the Chief Economist, Africa Region, World Bank, Washington, DC.

Alfaro-Ureña, Alonso, Isabela Manelici, and José P. Vasquez. 2019. "The Effects of Joining Multinational Supply Chains: New Evidence from Firm-to-Firm Linkages." Unpublished working paper, University of California, Berkeley, Berkeley, CA.

Amanor, Kojo Sebastian. 2012. "Global Resource Grabs, Agribusiness Concentration, and the Smallholder: Two West African Case Studies." *Journal of Peasant Studies* 39 (3–4): 731–49.

Ansón, José, Jean-François Arvis, Mauro Boffa, Matthias Helble, and Ben Shepherd. 2017. "Time, Uncertainty, and Trade Flows." ADBI Working Paper 673 (February), Asian Development Bank Institute, Tokyo.

Antràs, Pol, and Alonso de Gortari. 2017. "On the Geography of Global Value Chains." NBER Working Paper 23456 (May), National Bureau of Economic Research, Cambridge, MA.

APEC (Asia–Pacific Economic Cooperation) and World Bank. 2018. "Promoting Open and Competitive Markets in Road Freight and Logistics Services: The World Bank Group's Markets and Competition Policy Assessment Tool Applied in Peru, The Philippines, and Vietnam." Unpublished report, World Bank, Washington, DC.

Arvis, Jean-François, Robin Carruthers, Graham Smith, and Christopher Willoughby. 2011. *Connecting Landlocked Developing Countries to Markets: Trade Corridors in the 21st Century*. Directions in Development: Trade Series. Washington, DC: World Bank.

Arvis, Jean-François, Gaël Raballand, and Jean-François Marteau. 2010. *The Cost of Being Landlocked: Logistics Costs and Supply Chain Reliability*. Directions in Development: Trade Series. Washington, DC: World Bank.

Athukorala, Prema-chandra. 2010. "Production Networks and Trade Patterns in East Asia: Regionalization or Globalization?" Working Paper Series on Regional Economic Integration 56 (August), Asian Development Bank, Manila.

Baldwin, Richard E. 2013. "Global Supply Chains: Why They Emerged, Why They Matter, and Where They Are Going." In *Global Value Chains in a Changing World*, edited by Deborah Kay Elms and Patrick Low, 13–60. Geneva: World Trade Organization.

Bas, Maria, and Vanessa Strauss-Kahn. 2015. "Input-Trade Liberalization, Export Prices, and Quality Upgrading." *Journal of International Economics* 95 (2): 250–62.

Borchert, Ingo, Batshur Gootiiz, Arti Grover Goswami, and Aaditya Mattoo. 2017. "Services Trade Protection and Economic Isolation." *World Economy* 40 (3): 632–52.

Borin, Alessandro, and Michele Mancini. 2019. "Measuring What Matters in Global Value Chains and Value-Added Trade." Policy Research Working Paper 8804, World Bank, Washington, DC.

Braun, Matias. 2003. "Financial Contractibility and Asset Hardness." Mimeo, University of California, Los Angeles.

Briceño-Garmendia, Cecilia, Mathilde Lebrand, and Megersa Abate. 2018. "Transport Connectivity: Cost, Time, and Networks in Europe and Central Asia." Unpublished working paper, World Bank, Washington, DC.

Buelens, Christian, and Marcel Tirpák. 2017. "Reading the Footprints: How Foreign Investors Shape Countries' Participation in Global Value Chains." *Comparative Economic Studies* 59 (4): 561–84.

Cherkashin, Ivan, Svetlana Demidova, Hiau Looi Kee, and Kala Krishna. 2015. "Firm Heterogeneity and Costly Trade: A New Estimation Strategy and Policy Experiments." *Journal of International Economics* 96 (1): 18–36.

Christ, Nannette, and Michael Joseph Ferrantino. 2011. "Land Transport for Export: The Effects of Cost, Time, and Uncertainty in Sub-Saharan Africa." *World Development* 39 (10): 1749–59.

Conconi, Paola, Manuel García-Santana, Laura Puccio, and Roberto Venturini. 2018. "From Final Goods to Inputs: The Protectionist Effect of Rules of Origin." *American Economic Review* 108 (8): 2335–65.

Djankov, Simeon, Caroline L. Freund, and Cong S. Pham. 2010. "Trading on Time." *Review of Economics and Statistics* 92 (1): 166–73.

Economist. 2018. "Why Samsung of South Korea Is the Biggest Firm in Vietnam." April 12. https://www.economist.com /asia/2018/04/12/why-samsung-of-south-korea-is-the -biggest-firm-in-vietnam.

Engman, Michael, Thomas Farole, and Deborah Winkler. 2018. "Firm Performance and Job Characteristics of Global Value Chain Participants in Bangladesh: Evidence from New Survey Data." Unpublished working paper, World Bank, Washington, DC.

Farole, Thomas, and Deborah Winkler, eds. 2014. *Making Foreign Direct Investment Work for Sub-Saharan Africa: Local Spillovers and Competitiveness in Global Value Chains*. Directions in Development: Trade Series. Washington, DC: World Bank.

Felbermayr, Gabriel, Feodora Teti, and Erdal Yalcin. 2019 (forthcoming). "Rules of Origin and the Profitability of Trade Deflection." *Journal of International Economics*.

Fernandes, Ana Margarida, Alejandro Forero, Hibret Maemir, and Aaditya Mattoo. 2019. "Are Trade Preferences a Panacea? The African Growth and Opportunity Act and African Exports." Policy Research Working Paper 8753, World Bank, Washington, DC.

Fernandes, Ana Margarida, Hiau Looi Kee, and Deborah Winkler. 2019. "Factors Affecting Global Value Chain Participation across Countries." Policy Research Working Paper, World Bank, Washington, DC.

Fernandes, Ana Margarida, Aaditya Mattoo, Huy Nguyen, and Marc Schiffbauer. 2017. "The Internet and Chinese Exports in the Pre-Ali Baba Era." Policy Research Working Paper 8262, World Bank, Washington, DC.

Freund, Caroline L., and Theodore H. Moran. 2017. "Multinational Investors as Export Superstars: How Emerging-Market Governments Can Reshape Comparative Advantage." Working Paper 17-1 (January), Peterson Institute for International Economics, Washington, DC.

Godfrey, Shane. 2015. "Global, Regional and Domestic Apparel Value Chains in Southern Africa: Social Upgrading for Some and Downgrading for Others." *Cambridge Journal of Regions, Economy and Society* 8 (3): 491–504.

Gould, David Michael. 2018. *Critical Connections: Promoting Economic Growth and Resilience in Europe and Central Asia*. Europe and Central Asia Studies Series. Washington, DC: World Bank.

Hoekman, Bernard, and Çağlar Özden. 2005. "Trade Preferences and Differential Treatment of Developing Countries: A Selective Survey." Policy Research Working Paper 3566, World Bank, Washington, DC.

Hollweg, Claire H., and Nadia Rocha. 2018. "GVC Participation and Deep Integration in Brazil." Policy Research Working Paper 8646, World Bank, Washington, DC.

Hummels, David L., and Georg Schaur. 2013. "Time as a Trade Barrier." *American Economic Review* 103 (7): 2935–59.

ITC (International Trade Centre). 2015. "The Invisible Barriers to Trade: How Businesses Experience Non-Tariff Measures." Technical Paper MAR-15-326.E, ITC, Geneva.

Johnson, Robert Christopher, and Guillermo Noguera. 2017. "A Portrait of Trade in Value-Added over Four Decades." *Review of Economics and Statistics* 99 (5): 896–911.

Kathuria, Sanjay, ed. 2018. *A Glass Half Full: The Promise of Regional Trade in South Asia.* South Asia Development Forum. Washington, DC: World Bank.

Kee, Hiau Looi. 2015. "Local Intermediate Inputs and the Shared Supplier Spillovers of Foreign Direct Investment." *Journal of Development Economics* 112 (January): 56–71.

Kee, Hiau Looi, and Heiwei Tang. 2016. "Domestic Value Added in Exports: Theory and Firm Evidence from China." *American Economic Review* 106 (6): 1402–36.

Khandelwal, Amit Kumar, Louise Guillouet, Rocco Macchiavello, and Matthieu Teachout. 2018. "Communication Frictions and Knowledge Transfers: Evidence from FDI." Paper presented at "Macroeconomics, Trade, and Finance Seminar," World Bank, Washington, DC, October 18.

Kowalski, Przemyslaw, Javier Lopez Gonzalez, Alexandros Ragoussis, and Cristian Ugarte. 2015. "Participation of Developing Countries in Global Value Chains: Implications for Trade and Trade-Related Policies." OECD Trade Policy Paper 179, Organisation for Economic Co-operation and Development, Paris.

Levchenko, Andrei A. 2007. "Institutional Quality and International Trade." *Review of Economic Studies* 74 (3): 791–819.

Liu, Yan, and Viktor Steenbergen. 2019. "The Role of FDI in Global Value Chains (GVCs): Implications for Sub-Saharan Africa." Unpublished working paper, World Bank, Washington, DC.

Martínez Licetti, Martha, Mariana Iootty, Tanya Goodwin, and José Signoret. 2018. *Strengthening Argentina's Integration into the Global Economy: Policy Proposals for Trade, Investment, and Competition.* International Development in Focus Series. Washington, DC: World Bank.

MGI (McKinsey Global Institute). 2019. *Globalization in Transition: The Future of Trade and Value Chains.* New York: McKinsey.

Morocco World News. 2018. "WSJ: Morocco Is Leading Africa's Automotive Industry." October 1. https://www.moroccoworldnews.com/2018/10/254381/morocco-africa-automotive-industry/.

Morris, Mike, and Cornelia Staritz. 2014. "Industrialization Trajectories in Madagascar's Export Apparel Industry: Ownership, Embeddedness, Markets, and Upgrading." *World Development* 56 (April): 243–57.

Narain, Ashish, and Gonzalo J. Varela. 2017. "Trade Policy Reforms for the Twenty First Century: The Case of Nepal." World Bank, Washington, DC.

Nikkei Asian Review. 2018. "Samsung Suppliers in Vietnam Branch Out to New Frontiers." July 3. https://asia.nikkei.com/Business/Business-trends/Samsung-suppliers-in-Vietnam-branch-out-to-new-frontiers.

Nunn, Nathan. 2007. "Relationship-Specificity, Incomplete Contracts, and the Pattern of Trade." *Quarterly Journal of Economics* 122 (2): 569–600.

OECD (Organisation for Economic Co-operation and Development). No date. "Business Brief: The Czech Republic's Fourth Industrial Revolution." http://www.oecd.org/innovation/czech-republic-fourth-industrial-revolution.htm.

OECD (Organisation for Economic Co-operation and Development) and WTO (World Trade Organization). 2013. *Aid for Trade at a Glance 2013: Connecting to Value Chains.* Geneva: WTO; Paris: OECD.

Olam. 2016. *Olam: Maximising Value and Purpose: Annual Report 2015.* Singapore: Olam. http://olamgroup.com/investor-relations/annual-report-2016/.

Ornelas, Emanuel. 2016. "Special and Differential Treatment for Developing Countries." In *Handbook of Commercial Policy,* vol. 1A, edited by Kyle Bagwell and Robert W. Staiger, 369–432. *Handbooks in Economics.* Amsterdam: Elsevier.

Pathikonda, Vilas, and Thomas Farole. 2017. "The Capabilities Driving Participation in Global Value Chains." *Journal of International Commerce, Economics and Policy* 8 (1): 1–26.

Pierola, Martha Denisse, Ana Margarida Fernandes, and Thomas Farole. 2018. "The Role of Imports for Exporter Performance in Peru." *World Economy* 41 (2): 550–72.

Ponte, Stefano, Ingrid Kelling, Karen Sau Jespersen, and Froukje Kruijssen. 2014. "The Blue Revolution in Asia: Upgrading and Governance in Aquaculture Value Chains." *World Development* 64 (December): 52–64.

Raballand, Gaël, Salim Refas, Monica Beuran, and Gözde Isik. 2012. *Why Does Cargo Spend Weeks in Sub-Saharan African Ports? Lessons from Six Countries.* Directions in Development: Trade Series. Washington, DC: World Bank.

Rocha, Nadia, and Gonzalo J. Varela. 2018. "Unlocking Private Sector Growth through Increased Trade and Investment Competitiveness in Pakistan." Unpublished working paper, World Bank, Washington, DC.

Rocha, Nadia, and Deborah Winkler. 2019. "Trade and Female Labor Participation: Stylized Facts Using a Global Dataset." Background paper, World Bank-World Trade Organization Trade and Gender Report, World Bank, Washington, DC.

Rodríguez-Pose, Andrés, Vassilis Tselios, Deborah Winkler, and Thomas Farole. 2013. "Geography and the Determinants of Firm Exports in Indonesia." *World Development* 44 (April): 225–40.

Rodrik, Dani. 2018. "New Technologies, Global Value Chains, and Developing Economies." NBER Working Paper 25164, National Bureau of Economic Research, Cambridge, MA.

Saslavsky, Daniel, and Ben Shepherd. 2014. "Facilitating International Production Networks: The Role of Trade Logistics." *Journal of International Trade and Economic Development* 23 (7): 979–99.

Stitchdiary. 2018. "What Makes Bangladesh—A Hub of Garment Manufacturing?" July 18. https://medium.com/@stitchdiary/what-makes-bangladesh-a-hub-of-garment-manufacturing-ce83aa37edfc.

Sturgeon, Timothy J., Leonardo Lima Chagas, and Justin Barnes. 2017. *Inovar Auto: Evaluating Brazil's Automotive Industrial Policy to Meet the Challenges of Global Value Chains.* Washington, DC: World Bank.

Sturgeon, Timothy J., and Olga Memedovic. 2011. "Mapping Global Value Chains: Intermediate Goods Trade and Structural Change in the World Economy." Development Policy and Strategic Research Branch Working Paper 05/2010, United Nations Industrial Development Organization, Vienna.

Sturgeon, Timothy J., and Eric Thun. 2018. "China: New Drivers of Growth: Case Studies of China's Automotive and ICT Hardware Sectors." Background paper, World Bank, Washington, DC.

Sturgeon, Timothy J., and Ezequiel Zylberberg. 2016. "The Global Information and Communications Technology Industry: Where Vietnam Fits in Global Value Chains." Policy Research Working Paper 7916, World Bank, Washington, DC.

Taglioni, Daria, and Deborah Winkler. 2016. *Making Global Value Chains Work for Development*. Trade and Development Series. Washington, DC: World Bank.

UNCTAD (United Nations Conference on Trade and Development) and World Bank. 2018. "The Unseen Impact of Non-tariff Measures: Insights from a New Database." Report UNCTAD/DITC/TAB/2018/2, UNCTAD, Geneva.

Viet Nam News. 2015. "Samsung R&D Centre Hitting Stride." December 3. https://vietnamnews.vn/economy/279340 /samsung-r-d-centre-hitting-stride.html.

Vijil, Mariana, Laurent Wagner, and Martha Tesfaye Woldemichael. 2019. "Import Uncertainty and Export Dynamics." Policy Research Working Paper 8793, World Bank, Washington, DC.

WEF (World Economic Forum). 2013. "Enabling Trade: Valuing Growth Opportunities." WEF, Geneva.

World Bank. 2017. *Doing Business 2019: Reforming to Create Jobs*. Washington, DC: World Bank.

———. 2018. *Global Investment Competitiveness Report 2017/2018: Foreign Investor Perspectives and Policy Implications*. Washington, DC: World Bank.

Yameogo, Nadege Desiree, and Kebba Jammeh. 2019. "Determinants of Participation in Manufacturing GVCs in Africa: The Role of Skills, Human Capital Endowment, and Migration." Policy Research Working Paper 8938, World Bank, Washington, DC.

PART III

What are the effects of GVCs?

3

Consequences for development

Key findings

- **Hyperspecialization and durable firm-to-firm relationships promote efficient production and the diffusion of technology, as well as access to capital and inputs along value chains.** The result is increased productivity and income growth—more so than what countries achieve through domestic production but also than what they achieve through trade in finished goods.

- **How countries participate in global value chains (GVCs) matters for the impact on development.** Countries experience the biggest growth spurt during the transition out of commodities into basic manufacturing activities.

- **GVCs deliver more productive jobs, primarily through scale effects that result from increased productivity and expanded output.** Because they boost income and productive employment, participation in GVCs is associated with reduced poverty.

- **The gains from GVC participation are not distributed equally across and within countries.** Inequalities arise in the distribution of firm markups across countries; in the distribution of capital and labor, between skilled and unskilled workers as well as between male and female workers; and geographically within countries.

- **The expansion of GVCs has magnified the challenges facing the international tax system.** The tax revenue losses from profit shifting and tax competition are substantial, particularly for lower-income countries.

angladesh is a powerful example of how participation in global value chains (GVCs) has supported economic growth and structural change.
In 1988 Bangladesh's exports of apparel and footwear
were negligible, accounting for less than 1 percent of
the global total. Since then, the business of exporting
apparel made from imported textiles has grown on
average by nearly 18 percent a year. Bangladesh now
exports 7 percent of the world's apparel and footwear—
third only to China (which increasingly sources from
Bangladesh) and Vietnam.[1] The sector accounts for 89
percent of the country's exports and 14 percent of GDP,
and it employs 3.6 million workers, 55 percent of them
women.[2] Diversification is also under way. The plastics sector has benefited from complementarities with
the ready-made garment sector because garments
are enclosed in plastic packaging. Leather goods and
footwear are growing rapidly (second-largest export
category). Meanwhile, agriculture's share of GDP fell
from 70 percent in 1988 to 38 percent in 2018, and the
share of people in extreme poverty from 44 percent to
15 percent in 2016.[3]

Navigating globalization has been challenging.
Low wages drive Bangladesh's export success, and in
the past 30 years there has been little upgrading to
better-paid tasks. Demands for higher wages in the
factories recently spilled into social unrest in the streets
in the form of strikes and protests.[4] Tragic incidents,
such as the April 2013 collapse of the Rana Plaza building in Dhaka and the garment factory it housed, where
1,134 lives were lost, highlighted the poor safety conditions in some parts of the value chain, particularly in
the more peripheral but numerous contractor factories.
Moreover, unplanned growth of the sector has strained
scarce land resources as well as water resources—the
sector consumes nearly twice as much water as the
entire population of the capital, Dhaka, and ground-
water levels are dropping at more than 2 meters a year.

The relational nature of GVCs may help gradually
to mitigate these problems. Large, formal exporters in
GVCs tend to pay well and offer safe conditions, unlike
the less visible subcontractors further up the value
chain. But because those suppliers are associated with
global brands, poor working conditions, safety and
environmental concerns, and worker dissatisfaction
have captured the attention of global consumers and
civil society, who are urging improvement. With the
support of donors and in coordination with local public
institutions, some international buyers have ramped
up monitoring of indirect suppliers and undertaken a
series of initiatives to improve the governance of the
value chain, together with social and environmental
practices. Among others, they have begun to enforce

better fire, building, and worker safety, and they have
taken steps to reduce water waste and environmental
damage.[5] In response to demands from international
buyers, and learning from international best practices,
Bangladeshi producers are increasingly recognizing
that they must not only improve their practices, but
also ensure that improvements can be independently
verified by third parties.

Is Bangladesh an isolated experience? This chapter
examines whether GVC participation promotes development beyond what countries can achieve through
standard trade, or whether it makes the development
path harder. It considers cross-country evidence, but
also dives deeper into firm-level evidence from a few
countries—especially Ethiopia, Mexico, and Vietnam—to demonstrate the complexities of GVC participation. The evidence indicates that the challenges,
opportunities, successes, and failures of Bangladesh
reflect how other countries are forging their development path in a GVC world. However, their outcomes
are also shaped by national choices about policies,
institutions, and other factors.

GVCs support productivity gains and income
growth because of their two defining characteristics:
long-term firm-to-firm relationships and hyperspecialization in specific tasks. In cross-country studies,
a 10 percent increase in the level of GVC participation
is estimated to increase average productivity by close
to 1.6 percent and per capita GDP by 11–14 percent—
or much more than the 2 percent income gain from
increasing trade in products fully produced in one
country by a comparable amount.

In GVCs, domestic firms become interdependent
with foreign firms that share know-how and technology with their buyers and suppliers. Because of hyperspecialization, exporting no longer requires mastering
the entire production process of a good; countries can
specialize in only a few tasks in the production process. For these two important reasons, firms in developing countries that participate in GVCs tend to be
more productive, and all forms of GVC participation
are associated with higher income growth than standard trade. The biggest growth spurt, however, comes
when countries such as Bangladesh, Cambodia, and
Vietnam break out of commodities or agriculture into
basic manufacturing. Empirical evidence suggests
that within three years of joining a manufacturing
GVC, a country is more than 20 percent richer on a per
capita basis.

Alongside the productivity and income gains, GVCs
deliver more and better jobs. Production is more capital-intensive, perhaps because machines allow production on a large scale and can deliver the precision

required for compatible parts. Because of the greater reliance on machinery, GVC exports require fewer units of human work per unit of production compared with non-GVC exports. But the overall effects on employment in the relevant firms and sectors have been positive because of the large boost to exports. The new activities that GVCs bring to countries pull workers out of less productive tasks and into more productive manufacturing jobs. Between 2000 and 2014, for example, the labor force of Ethiopian firms that became importers and exporters—a measure of GVC participation—grew by 39 percent relative to when they were nontraders, despite the fact that they also utilized 145 percent more capital per worker than nontrading firms.

GVC firms also tend to employ more women than other firms, improving their livelihoods and those of their families. In Bangladesh, for example, young women in villages exposed to the GVC-dominated garment sector delay marriage and childbirth, and young girls gain an additional 1.5 years of schooling.

By boosting income and employment growth, GVC participation also reduces poverty. Because economic growth and employment gains from GVCs are larger than from conventional trade, poverty reduction from GVCs can also be expected to be larger than that produced by such trade.

GVCs, however, create some challenges. First, the gains from GVC participation may be distributed unequally within and across countries. Large corporations that outsource parts and tasks to developing countries have seen an increase in markups, suggesting that cost reductions are not being passed on to consumers.[6] At the same time, markups for the producers of these inputs in developing countries are declining. So, too, is the share of income accruing to labor in both developed and developing countries. Technological change and higher markups reallocate value added from labor to capital within countries. Inequality can also arise within the labor market, with growing premiums for skills. Women are generally employed in lower-value-added segments, and women owners and managers are largely missing in GVCs. Inequality has a geographic dimension too, with GVCs concentrated in urban agglomerations and in border regions for countries neighboring GVC partners.

Second, in some countries and sectors, firms could be stuck in dead-end tasks with few opportunities to innovate, upgrade, and diversify. The skill mix of the domestic workforce, the organization and governance of some value chains, and the nature of certain technologies may not favor the process of learning and innovation typical of relational GVCs.

Finally, GVCs do not cause tax avoidance and tax competition, but their evolution has magnified the challenges facing the international tax system. The growth of intangibles in global business and the digital delivery of services are further exacerbating a preexisting problem. Moreover, in GVCs that involve affiliates of the same firm, fragmentation of production also leads to greater intrafirm trade and more opportunities for tax avoidance by manipulating where profits are recognized for tax purposes. The tax revenue losses from profit shifting are substantial, and they are particularly large for developing countries. In 2013 non-OECD (Organisation for Economic Co-operation and Development) countries missed out on $200 billion in tax revenue as a result of this practice.

Policy intervention is important to address the challenges, attenuate the costs, and share the benefits of GVC participation. Although GVCs have been able to drive pro-poor growth over the past 30 years, with the steepest declines in poverty occurring in precisely those countries that became integral to GVCs, only additional efforts can pull the remaining 2 billion people out of poverty without exceeding environmental limits. The policy chapters of this Report discuss these considerations in detail.

Economic growth

Trade openness and GVC integration are contributing to better economic performance (figure 3.1).[7] The rise of GVCs has generated even greater income gains than a commensurate expansion of traditional trade.[8] These gains stem from the productivity effects of GVCs. Figure 3.2 depicts the positive association between growth in manufacturing productivity and growth in GVC participation. Backward participation in GVCs is particularly important—a 10 percent increase in the level of GVC participation increases in turn average productivity by close to 1.6 percent.[9]

Because GVCs are a firm-level phenomenon, the greater productivity gains are attributable to firms becoming more productive. In the cashew value chain in Mozambique, for example, processors for international brands introduced new semiautomatic equipment that increased capacity, reduced costs, and boosted productivity.[10] Firm-level empirical evidence supports the association of GVC participation with higher productivity observed in cross-country data and anecdotally. Firm-level data can identify the set of firms in a country that participate in trade, further distinguishing between firms that export, firms that import, and firms that both export and import. When a given firm in a country both imports *and* exports,

Figure 3.1 GVC participation is associated with growth in exports and incomes

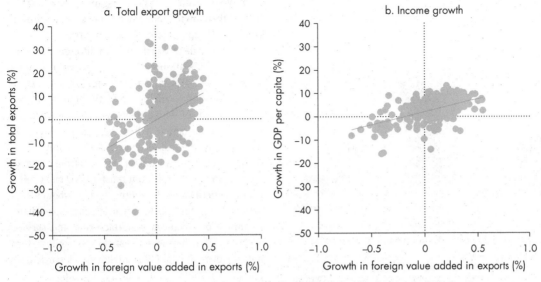

a. Total export growth

b. Income growth

Source: WDR 2020 team, using data from World Bank's WDI database. See appendix A for a description of the databases used in this Report.

Note: Each dot is a country-year observation. In both panels, the x-axis is the average annual growth in foreign value added in exports between 1990 and 2015. In panel a, the y-axis is the average annual growth in total exports between 1990 and 2015. Total export growth includes exports of goods and services. In panel b, the y-axis is the average annual growth in per capita GDP in purchasing power parity terms between 1990 and 2015. *R*-squared is 0.73 for total export growth and 0.25 for GDP per capita growth.

the likely conclusion is that this firm participates in GVCs. In Ethiopia and across a large sample of countries, GVC firms in manufacturing show higher productivity (labor productivity, controlling for capital intensity) than one-way traders or nontraders (figure 3.3). Firms that both import and export are 76 percent more productive than nontrading firms, compared with a 42 percent difference for export-only firms and a 20 percent difference for import-only firms.[11] In Vietnam, this relationship holds across firms in all sectors: manufacturing, services, and agriculture alike.

Intuitively, there are two complementary explanations for higher growth and productivity. First, GVCs allow countries to benefit from the efficiency gained from a much finer international division of labor. GVCs exploit the fact that countries have different comparative advantages not only in different sectors, but also in different stages of production within sectors. By breaking up complex products, GVCs allow countries to specialize in specific parts or tasks of production, escaping domestic supply and demand constraints. China's "Button Town," where hundreds of factories produce more than 60 percent of all buttons on Earth, is an extreme example.[12]

Second, growth and productivity gains stem from better access to a greater variety of higher-quality or less costly intermediate inputs.[13] In traditional trade, where products cross borders only as finished products, greater openness to imports entails greater

Figure 3.2 GVC participation is associated with growth in productivity

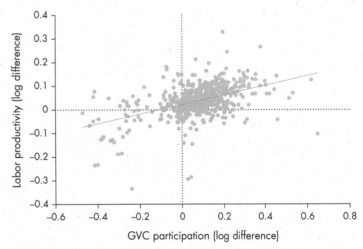

Source: Constantinescu, Mattoo, and Ruta 2019.

Note: Each dot represents a country-year combination for 1995–2009. GVC participation is measured as the sum of the foreign value added embodied in a country's gross exports (backward linkages) and the country's domestic value added embodied in other countries' gross exports (forward linkages). Labor productivity is computed as the real value added divided by the number of persons employed in manufacturing (excluding petrochemicals). *R*-squared is 0.22.

competition for domestic producers. In GVC trade, openness also increases imports of intermediate inputs, and domestic firms using those inputs observe positive effects on their productivity. Because of these mechanisms, export growth can be expected to raise domestic income and employment even when exports

Figure 3.3 Firms that both export and import are more productive

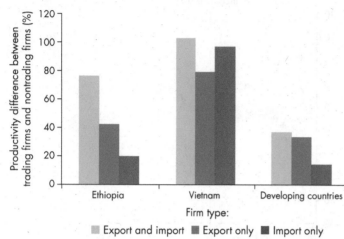

Firm type:
■ Export and import ■ Export only ■ Import only

Sources: Ethiopia: Choi, Fukase, and Zeufack (2019), based on 2000–2014 manufacturing census (firms with 10 or more employees). Vietnam: WDR 2020 team, based on 2014 Enterprise Surveys (firms with more than five employees). Developing countries: WDR 2020 team, based on World Bank's Enterprise Surveys (sample of 81 developing countries).

Note: The figure reports the percentage difference in productivity between nontrading firms and (1) firms that both export and import or (2) firms that only export or (3) firms that only import. The results are obtained by regressing firm labor productivity (log sales per worker) on dummy variables marking the type of firm (export and import, export only, or import only), controlling for log capital per worker and fixed effects. The Ethiopia estimation controls for sector, year, and region fixed effects, as well as for whether the firm is state owned. The Vietnam estimation controls for sector and region fixed effects as well as for whether the firm is state- or foreign-owned. The developing countries estimation controls for country-sector, subnational region, and year fixed effects. All coefficient estimates are statistically significant. The percent differences reported in the graph are obtained as 100 multiplied by the exponential of the coefficient estimates minus 1.

have lower domestic content (discussed shortly).[14] Reinforcing this productivity enhancement is the fact that exporting to the global market allows for greater economies of scale.[15]

These observations are consistent with empirical findings. Increasing direct and indirect exports and imports of goods, services, parts, and components produced through GVCs has been associated with much larger per capita income growth than other forms of trade openness (box 3.1).

Relational GVCs are a vehicle for technology transfer

It is well accepted that real income grows when episodes of trade liberalization boost the diffusion of new technology.[16] Those positive effects are even greater in relational GVC trade. As observed in chapter 1, in contrast to "standard" trade carried out in anonymous markets, GVCs typically involve longer-term firm-to-firm relationships. This relational nature of GVCs makes them a particularly powerful vehicle for technology transfer along the value chain. Firms have a shared interest in specializing in specific tasks, exchanging technology, and learning from each other.

Interdependent firms may share know-how and technology with suppliers because such sharing boosts their own productivity and sales, leading to faster catch-up growth across countries. Unlike in traditional trade in which firms in different countries compete, GVCs are networks of firms with common goals. Those goals include minimizing the costs of production or maximizing the profits of the entire production chain of which they are part.[17] Downstream firms typically benefit when their suppliers become more productive and vice versa. A direct implication of this simple observation is that firms from countries specializing in innovation-intensive GVC tasks might find it beneficial to share process and product innovations with their GVC coparticipants specializing in simple or advanced manufacturing and services GVC tasks. Furthermore, the stickiness—or long-term nature—of relational GVCs makes firms particularly prone to benefit from learning-by-importing and learning-by-exporting through repeated interactions with highly productive firms at the global frontier of knowledge.

In Kenya, South Africa, and Uganda, for example, improved processes in horticulture were induced by demand for higher quality and sourcing requirements by global and regional supermarket chains, allowing in turn diversification and higher yields of fresh fruit and vegetable exports.[18] In Kenya, incomes increased after contract farmers adopted the quality standards demanded by their international buyers, and these firms supported better traceability of the product along the entire supplier network.[19]

Trade between firms engaging in GVCs has characteristics very similar to those of intrafirm trade because external international sourcing requires the same high levels of coordination, intense bilateral information flows, and harmonization and integration of many business services as intrafirm internationally fragmented production.[20] In the coffee value chain in Costa Rica, trade transactions conducted within integrated firms (intrafirm) and those conducted within long-term relationships with other firms (interfirm) are similar to one another but starkly different from trade transactions conducted between anonymous firms.[21]

Additional empirical evidence supports the hypothesis that firms in GVCs work toward common goals. A 2018 survey of 1,476 apparel, textile, and information and communication technology (ICT) firms in Ethiopia and Vietnam found that the probability of a buyer providing its suppliers with some form of assistance is greater in strongly relational GVCs—that

Box 3.1 Dynamic estimations of the relationship between GVC participation and per capita income growth

Growth regressions have been estimated for a panel of 100 countries across income groups for the period 1990–2015. A standard Solow growth model was augmented with measures of GVC participation. Specifically, the log GDP per capita was regressed on its lagged value, a vector of the standard determinants of growth, and measures of backward and forward GVC participation. To reflect the dynamic nature of growth, the equation was estimated in a dynamic panel setting, through a System Generalized Method of Moments (System-GMM).

A 1 percent increase in GVC participation is associated with a more than 1 percent increase in per capita income in the long run. The point estimates of the relationship are reported in figure B3.1.1.

The estimation is robust to various statistical tests, including reverse causality, diagnostic tests for weak instruments, and those for the strength of the chosen instruments.

The difference in coefficients for backward and forward GVC integration suggests that the development impact for a commodity producer integrated in GVCs only through forward linkages is much lower than that for a country producing intermediate inputs, which benefits from both forward and backward linkages.

Figure B3.1.1 GVC trade is associated with larger per capita income than non-GVC trade

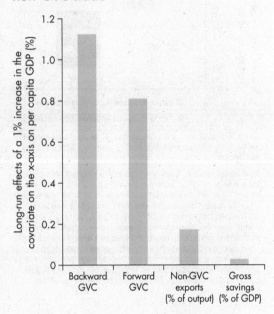

Sources: WDR 2020 team, using data from World Bank's WDI database.

---

is, firms selling exclusively to a single buyer are 38 percent more likely to receive assistance than firms with a diversified client base. Firms without strong relationships are 29 percent less likely to receive assistance from a client (figure 3.4). The survey also asked about know-how assistance specifically: firms selling exclusively to a single buyer are 34 percent more likely to receive know-how than firms with a diversified client base, while firms without strong relationships are 31 percent less likely. Lead firms may be more willing to share knowledge and know-how that benefit the supplier firm if they believe those benefits will not be passed on to other buyers. The survey also shows that suppliers' main support from their foreign partner is in capacity building, which may help firms overcome skill constraints.

Through firm-to-firm relationships, GVC firms can also play an important role in on-the-job learning, and employer-sponsored training within GVCs can be an effective mechanism for skill development, economic

growth, and wage increases: a 1 percent increase in training is associated with 0.6 percent increase in value added per hour and a 0.3 percent increase in the hourly wage.[22] A case study of the impact of a Japanese multinational company on skilled labor in Malaysia shows that the integration of the subsidiary's production network into its GVC spurred greater needs for skill development, particularly in management and engineering services.[23] The development implications of GVC firm efforts in the on-the-job training in supplier companies are of primary importance: employer-sponsored training is the most important source of further education in OECD countries, and it is more effective than both government-financed active labor programs and training self-financed by employees.[24]

Buyer support can take other, sometimes surprising, forms. For example, Samsung, which in 2018 employed 160,000 people in Vietnam to produce its Galaxy smartphones, is trying to build a stronger local supplier base—not only through its own initiative, but

Figure 3.4 GVC firms with relationships receive more assistance

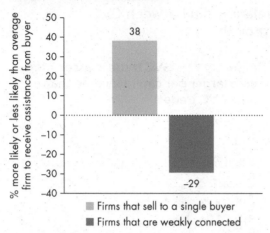

Source: WDR 2020 team, using data from a 2018 survey of 1,476 apparel, textile, and information and communication technology firms in Ethiopia and Vietnam.

Note: Survey question: "Is any type of assistance—financial, technology, know-how, or material assistance—provided by the largest client?" The survey further asks the respondent to characterize the largest client. *Single buyer* is a variable that takes the value of 1 for firms whose total sales (100 percent) are to a single client. Finally, the survey asks respondents to identify their "GVC connectedness." A *weakly connected firm* is a firm with no direct linkages to GVCs. The variable takes on a value of 1 when a firm is not connected to the industry leader as either buyer or supplier, and it does not participate in exporting activity or in trade with foreign entities directly or indirectly through intermediaries. The regressions control for country, sector, and size fixed effects. All coefficient estimates are statistically significant.

also by pushing its suppliers from other countries to help in the effort and instructing them to train local firms in customizing production to Samsung's needs. Sometimes, lead firm involvement benefits the wider educational system of the host country. For example, Synopsys, one of the world's leading companies in chip design and testing, established a presence in Armenia. Today, Synopsys is one of the largest information technology (IT) employers in the country, with 800 employees—mostly engineers—in Yerevan. With the goal of preparing qualified microelectronics specialists, it initiated bachelor's, master's, and PhD programs at both its own educational centers and five Armenian universities.

In the agri-food sector, long-term relational contracts can also be beneficial by helping improve connectivity, provide better access to technology and capital inputs that increase quality and yield for local producers, achieve higher and more stable prices for farmers, lead to new managerial practices, and achieve a better reputation. Recent research has investigated the effects of becoming a supplier to multinational corporations (MNCs) using administrative data tracking all firm-to-firm transactions in Costa Rica.[25] Estimates from event studies reveal that after starting to

supply MNCs, domestic firms experience strong and persistent improvements in performance, including gains in total factor productivity (TFP) of 6–9 percent four years later. Moreover, the sales of domestic firms to buyers other than the first MNC buyer grow by 20 percent through both a larger number of buyers and larger sales per buyer.

The relational nature of GVCs does not automatically result in technology transfer, however. Lead firms can use relational dependence to prevent technologies from spilling over from their supplier network to potential competitors. As a result, new capabilities may be especially difficult to gain when lead firms in GVCs tightly control their technology.

In the car industry, where production is complex, lead firms maintain control over the supply chain, and the technology is not easily diffused. Brands systematically coordinate production from start to finish, and incentives for suppliers to innovate, upgrade, and diversify into new market opportunities are relatively weak.

Recent research from the mining industry has similarly shown that the hierarchical form of governance typically prevailing in the mining sector has often served as an obstacle to learning and innovation.[26] Though the industry is evolving, rarely do mining companies forge long-term formal links with local suppliers or collaborate with them on innovation projects. When new technological challenges arise that offer new technological opportunities for the mining industry in developing countries, they rely on solutions from their headquarters abroad or international suppliers to the disadvantage of their new local suppliers (box 3.2).

The extent to which a GVC relationship supports the growth potential of GVC participants from developing countries is therefore likely to be determined by a multitude of factors. The sensitivity and value of the intellectual property embedded in a lead firm's relationship with its suppliers, technical dependence, codification of transactions, the complexity of both the product and the value chain, and the technical and managerial competence of suppliers all converge to determine suppliers' upgrading opportunities.[27]

How countries participate in GVCs matters

Because of the forces just described, how countries participate in GVCs matters. Backward participation and forward participation drive the positive association between GVC participation and growth in per capita GDP. Inputs that are high in services content—a proxy for knowledge-intensive products—and exports that are high in domestic manufacturing content have the strongest associations with per capita GDP growth. Meanwhile, trade in unprocessed agricultural goods and commodities has no systematic and statistically significant relationship with growth in per capita GDP.

Countries such as Bangladesh, Cambodia, and Vietnam leveraged GVCs to move out of commodities into basic manufacturing activities and experienced large growth spurts during this transition. Firms in GVCs contribute to their country's economic transformation

---

Box 3.2 Mining GVCs: New opportunities and old obstacles for local suppliers from developing countries

Mining activities are no longer always organized as huge, vertically integrated (multinational) corporations. The shift toward focusing on core activities while outsourcing and subcontracting many others is surfacing in this sector and allowing for the emergence of relational GVCs. Lead companies in mining GVCs must contain costs, and so their activities have become more knowledge-intensive. They are increasingly searching for *local* innovative solutions from *local* firms to problems such as falling ore grades, falling productivity, rising production costs, exposure to local labor and environmental disputes, and the challenges of extreme geographical conditions such as in Bolivia, Chile, and Peru, where mines are operated at high altitudes, in narrow veins, and in very dry climates.

Mining companies are relying on local suppliers not only for simple intermediate products, but also increasingly for knowledge-intensive ones. According to recent research, scientific advances and new forms of innovation have opened new technological opportunities for the mining industry in developing countries.[a] These include revolutionary advances in information and communication technologies, computer vision systems, satellites and other remote sensing applications, advances in molecular and synthetic biology for bioleaching (extracting heavy metals from minerals with living organisms), and bioremediation of pollutants for copper and gold. It is precisely these and similar advances that open opportunities for new suppliers to access and add value to mining value chains.[b]

That said, the organization and governance of the value chain do not appear to favor learning and innovation by mining suppliers, as sometimes happens in other sectors.

The hierarchical form of governance typically prevailing in the mining sector has often proved to be a true obstacle.[c] Information is highly asymmetric; power between the lead mining companies or buyers and their (local) suppliers is unbalanced; and many other market imperfections and failures affect transactions along the value chain. As a result, the demand for locally and sometimes even internationally provided suppliers is not easily fulfilled.

Can public policies help? The World Class Supplier Program in Chile attempts to do so by matching demand and supply with an open innovation approach, but it has had mixed results thus far.[d] Public intervention can help address other obstacles, particularly when these require a long-term commitment or do not happen because of coordination failures. An example of a long-term commitment is developing the skills required by the mining industry, while an example of the coordination required is bringing together the many different stakeholders. In the mining industry, the latter is an important obstacle because many actors beyond the mining industry must concur to create the enabling environment needed for firms to thrive. These actors range from local communities in the mining regions to water and energy interests, education and training institutions, and regulatory institutions—notably, those dealing with the environment.[e] Most important, time is of the essence for this sector. Technology is hardly modifiable once in use, and the opportunities for local firms to meet mining firms' demands and become suppliers can be generated only in the early stages of extraction process design and implementation. Once exploitation is under way, opportunities for developing country producers may shrink.

Source: Prepared by Carlo Pietrobelli, Roma Tre University and UNU-MERIT, drawing on Pietrobelli and Olivari (2018).

a. Pietrobelli, Marin, and Olivari (2018).
b. For example, in Chile the company Micomo has developed highly innovative monitoring technologies that assist the extraction process through fiber optics. Power Train has entered the market with new remote-control systems for trucks operating at high temperatures and with wireless monitoring systems that predict where crucial equipment will wear and have to be replaced, thereby preventing stoppages. In Brazil, Geoambiente has developed sophisticated geological maps, sensors, and radar images that help in the exploration phases, predicting the contents of minerals or areas prone to erosion in order to monitor environmental impacts. This company is now Google's largest partner in Brazil. The use of new materials is also revolutionizing the industry. For example, Verti in Brazil has developed dust suppressors that run on excess glycerin from biodiesel plants. Meanwhile, Innovaxxion in Chile has applied new approaches to mechanical, robotic, and electrical engineering to substantially reduce the waste generated in copper mining.
c. Pietrobelli, Marin, and Olivari (2018).
d. Navarro (2018).
e. Katz and Pietrobelli (2018).

by becoming suppliers of materials and components to a global buyer. Previously only marginally and intermittently involved in exporting or importing, these firms now source foreign goods and services to process and reexport as part of a global buyer's value chain. During this initial phase of manufacturing engagement, domestic per capita income grows steeply, reflecting firms' learning of new processes and capabilities, access to large-scale international demand, and inflow of know-how and technology from GVC partners.[28]

Productive firms drive the transition from limited to advanced GVC participation in manufacturing and services by growing in sophistication and size. They adopt a more complex production structure and improve managerial practices. They hire more workers in nonproduction functions, including in supply chain management, product development, ICT, and professional services. They become more capital- and data-intensive, and also tend to expand middle-management functions to handle the bigger scale of operations and the growing complexity. In this enhanced phase, relation-specific feedback loops with GVC partners become more relevant. Success requires not only continued access to markets, capital, and opportunities, but also learning more cutting-edge technologies and skills.[29]

Consistent with these observations, regression results reveal that from 1990 to 2015 cumulative per capita GDP growth was largest for countries as they moved away from being commodity or agriculture suppliers and relatively closed to foreign inputs and began to build international linkages in simple manufacturing GVC tasks—that is, "limited" manufacturing GVCs (figure 3.5 and box 3.3). In the first year after entering limited manufacturing GVCs, countries' GDP per capita is 6 percent higher than in the year of entry. In the first year after entering advanced manufacturing and services GVCs their GDP per capita is 2 percent higher. And in the first year after entering innovative tasks of GVCs, they are 3 percent higher. However, there are diminishing—and even negative—returns in staying indefinitely in this phase of development. Higher rates of growth can be sustained by transitioning into advanced manufacturing and services, and then into innovative activities. The Czech Republic, which upgraded from limited to advanced manufacturing and services in 2000 and then to innovation in 2012 (see chapter 2) is now the most productive economy in Eastern Europe and the OECD country with the lowest share of population having a disposable income below the poverty line (measured as 60 percent of median household income). The economy is thriving. Growth is balanced. Internal demand and household consumption are strong, supported by both per capita income growth and private investment. Finally, the unemployment rate has steadily declined since the country's accession into the European Union (EU) in 2004, and it is now below 3 percent, one of the lowest rates in the OECD.

What does this all mean for countries' industrialization options? It is well understood that GVCs can facilitate industrialization by reducing the range of "capabilities" required to produce and export industrial goods. For example, in the auto industry countries can participate through GVCs even when they do not have any domestic car makers or any domestic provider of car engines.

But more sophisticated tasks in value chains require skills and capabilities that many developing countries lack. As a general rule, learning to handle simple products and production processes is likely to be easier than acquiring the capabilities to transition from simple production tasks to specializing in intangible capital and breaking into new industries. The wrong skill mix could end up providing few opportunities to innovate, upgrade, and diversify after new GVC ties with international partners are created. Suppliers may find it difficult to upgrade beyond a certain task complexity because doing so may require an ability to handle growing firm size and more sophisticated management, sourcing, and learning strategies.[30]

Figure 3.5 GDP per capita grows most rapidly when countries break into limited manufacturing GVCs

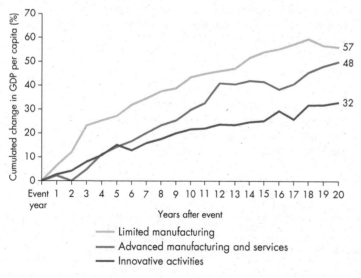

Sources: WDR 2020 team, using data from the World Bank's WDI database and the GVC taxonomy for 1990–2015 based on Eora26 database.

Note: The event study quantifies the cumulated change in real GDP per capita in the 20 years following a switch from a lower to a higher stage of GVC engagement. See box 3.3 for the methodology.

Box 3.3 Assessing outcomes of GVC participation using event studies

Event studies are used in this chapter and in chapter 5 to quantify the changes in outcomes in the 20 years following a switch from a lower to a higher stage of GVC engagement. Based on data for 146 countries over the period 1990–2015, four types of GVC engagement were identified: (1) commodities, (2) limited manufacturing, (3) advanced manufacturing and services, and (4) innovative activities (see box 1.3 in chapter 1 for a detailed description).

The event study involves computing average within-country deviations in a given outcome in each year following the year of a transition for all countries that stay at least four years in a particular GVC engagement stage, had one transition toward a more advanced GVC engagement stage, and had no transitions back to a lower stage.

The econometric specification is expressed as

$$ln(\text{outcome variable}_{it}) = \alpha_0 + \sum_{n=1}^{20}(\delta_{t+n}^{switch}) + \delta_t + \delta_i + e_{it}$$

where the outcome variables are real income per capita (in logarithms); employment, aggregated and by skill level (in logarithms); inequality as measured by the Gini coefficient; $5.50 per day poverty share; and CO_2 emissions (kilograms of CO_2 per $1 of GDP at 2011 values, purchasing power parity–adjusted).

The explanatory variable, δ_{t+n}^{switch}, is a vector of dummy variables taking a value of 1 in the nth year after a transition to a more advanced GVC engagement stage and 0 otherwise; δ_t and δ_i are time and country fixed effects to control for conditions in different calendar years and in different countries, respectively; and e_{it} is the error term. The analysis quantifies the effect of transitions into limited manufacturing GVC participation ("limited"), into advanced manufacturing and services GVC participation ("advanced"), and into innovation GVC participation ("innovation"). The estimated coefficients on each dummy variable are multiplied by 100 to give the percent change in the outcome variable relative to the outcome level at the time of the transition. Figures 3.5, 3.9, and 3.13 and figure 5.2 in chapter 5 plot those coefficients.

As discussed earlier, in some cases the organization and governance of the value chain, the nature of technology, and large bargaining power imbalances may trap suppliers from developing countries in dead-end tasks instead of favoring the processes of learning and innovation typical of relational GVCs.

The rise of GVCs may thus lead countries engaged in highly hierarchical or captive GVCs, or those that lag behind in skills and human capital, connectivity, and institutional quality (chapter 2), to become locked in in relatively low value-added segments of production with little scope for upgrading. Bangladesh's and Cambodia's experiences in the apparel sector are examples of the difficulties developing country firms face in upgrading from basic assembly functions to more sophisticated segments of the value chain, which require a very different skill set (box 3.4). They may, then, find it simpler to "industrialize" in the age of GVCs, but the returns to doing so by replicating the strategies of earlier developers may not be as high as they were in the past. Moreover, the gradual increase in automation may compound these effects (chapter 6).

China's experience suggests, however, that industrialization may still be possible, but it requires new approaches to development. Chinese firms that upgraded in the smartphone market used two strategies: strong connectivity to international technology ecosystems, and investments in design and marketing capabilities. These strategies allowed firms to develop innovative and cost-efficient products compatible with global markets by using cutting-edge technologies and capabilities in marketing and design to respond rapidly to changes in market demand and consumer taste. A few successful companies started developing their own research and development (R&D) capabilities and high-technology expertise, but they did so as part of the global ecosystem of technology, not through just indigenous innovation.

Because of deepening global integration, Whittaker et al. (2010) suggest that the viable growth path for developing countries is now "compressed development"—that is, leveraging globally engaged production systems rather than nationally integrated production systems. GVCs introduce international interdependencies that are unlike those faced by earlier developers (chapter 4). Accordingly, the efficacy of industrialization and development strategies depends on how well policy makers understand these new conditions and learn, seize opportunities, adapt, and develop innovative solutions in concert with a wide range of actors, domestic and foreign. These issues are discussed further in the chapters on policies.

Box 3.4 Skills and upgrading in Cambodia's apparel value chain

The foreign direct investment that Cambodia's apparel sector has attracted over the past two decades has been important for jobs and growth. Foreign investors set up manufacturing locations in Cambodia 20 years ago to take advantage of lower production costs stemming from a mix of lower minimum wages and trade preferences. These multinational manufacturing firms have head offices in Hong Kong SAR, China; Taiwan, China; or the Republic of Korea. They also have manufacturing facilities in other Asian countries. Despite the presence of these firms, Cambodia has not moved up the apparel GVC and is still performing many of the same assembly activities largely carried out by the same original foreign investors. More than 95 percent of its apparel exporters are branch plants of foreign-owned firms.

All the activities associated with functional upgrading take place at the headquarters location, leaving little or no room for branch manufacturing sites to take on more activities. These activities include textile sourcing and sales/buyer acquisition and technical product development.

This experience is not unique to Cambodia. It is, in fact, difficult for countries to upgrade in this industry because of relationships between global lead firms, multinational apparel manufacturers, and their foreign branch plant locations.

Opportunities for functional upgrading of these multinational corporations (MNCs) is also limited because the apparel industry is buyer-driven. The company or brand responsible for setting the final price and selling the product is not the same company that owns manufacturing facilities. Apparel manufacturers (whether at the headquarters or branch locations) do not control retail, marketing, branding, or creative new product development, which are the most lucrative and knowledge-intensive activities in the sector. Thus branch plants of foreign operations therefore have little opportunity for functional upgrading.

And yet there are still opportunities for upgrading in three areas. The first is in the preproduction and production stages currently performed in Cambodia by foreigners. The second is in the sourcing of inputs and arranging the logistics of shipments, currently carried out abroad at the headquarters of foreign MNCs with manufacturing locations in Cambodia, but that could be transferred to Cambodia. The third is in creative design and branding; which could be done by private domestic firms that are locally headquartered.

Source: Based on Frederick (2018).

Finally, integration in agricultural GVCs can also support economic transformation in the sector wherever lead firms are able to encourage the upgrading of farmers through long-term relationships. Formal or informal contractual arrangements that regulate the provision of production inputs, such as fertilizer, technology, extension services, and market information, have positively affected the upgrading of farmers in Ghana, Kenya, and Zambia who are growing maize, cassava, or sorghum. Having a contract with a buyer is significantly and positively associated with upgrading to higher-value intermediate processes and moving to higher-value-added products. Farmers under contract seem to have better access to inputs and technologies through the out-grower company or other external sources. In a random sample of 1,200 farmers in Ghana, Kenya, and Zambia, over 50 percent of surveyed contract farmers attributed their use of fertilizer to their contractual arrangement. Extension services, seeds and pesticides, and tractors were other cited forms of support. Moreover, the majority of the farmers under contract said the scheme had a positive to very positive impact on their production and income. For example, many farmers reported that their income and output increased by half or more as a result of contractual arrangements.[31]

Employment

Apart from higher overall productivity, firms in developing countries that participate in GVCs tend to be more capital-intensive. Machines can be equipped to deliver the precision needed for the compatibility of parts. They can also deliver the higher-quality output demanded by foreign consumers and help firms achieve higher productivity and greater scale. It may therefore make sense for firms to adopt more capital-intensive methods, even those in poor countries with relatively large labor forces. The costs of accessing capital may also be lower for GVC firms because of the relational dimension of participation—they have easier access to finance, foreign machinery, and training for their operations. In Vietnam, firms that both import and export use more capital inputs per worker than firms that export only or firms that sell exclusively to the domestic market.[32] Firms in Ethiopia that export and import are also more capital-intensive than one-way traders or nontraders. This observation holds across a sample of developing countries.[33]

Can GVCs deliver higher productivity and greater capital intensity, as well as more and better-paying jobs? Or is economic growth through GVCs at the expense of job growth? GVCs are becoming more important for exports (chapter 1), but at the same time exports are becoming less job-intensive.[34] In some countries, exports are contributing a smaller share of total jobs,[35] leading some observers to conclude that the employment consequences of GVCs have been dis-appointing.[36] According to these observers, rather than contributing to more and better-paying jobs in developing countries, capital-intensive production by GVC firms may lead to stagnant or lower overall employment, and the path to development by moving workers from agriculture to manufacturing may be suppressed.

Because GVCs boost exports, their overall effects on employment in developing countries have been positive. Even though production is becoming more capital-intensive and less job-intensive, the positive productivity effects at the firm level are (unexpectedly) good for scale and employment. Through scale effects, higher productivity is expanding aggregate output and employment. GVC firms tend to employ more workers than other firms.[37] When the higher productivity of these firms leads to sufficient scale—through more competition and market restructuring, demonstration effects, demand effects, technology spillovers, and investment in infrastructure—the overall effect on jobs is positive. In Ethiopia, firms that both export and import are more capital-intensive *and* increased their labor force faster than other firms between 2000 and 2014 (figure 3.6). These firms utilized 145 percent more capital per worker than nontrading firms between 2000 and 2014, compared with a 102 percent difference for export-only firms and a 19 percent difference for import-only firms.[38] Ethiopian firms that became two-way traders saw their labor force grow by 39 percent (relative to when they were nontraders), while the growth for firms becoming exporters was 29 percent and for firms becoming importers was 6 percent. Employment in manufacturing expanded from 2000 to 2014, and GVC firms accounted for an increasing share of manufacturing employment.[39] In Mozambique, despite adopting more mechanical technologies in the cashew value chain, as discussed earlier, employment also increased alongside output in the sector.[40]

Vietnam is another powerful example. Between 2004 and 2014, total jobs in firms that both import and export expanded faster than in firms that import only or export only.[41] As a result, GVC firms increased their

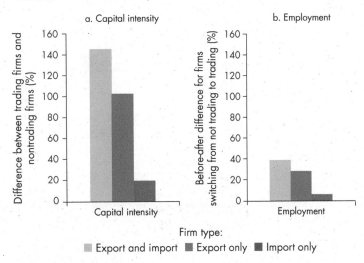

Figure 3.6 In Ethiopia, GVC firms are relatively more capital-intensive but their employment is increasing fastest

Sources: Choi, Fukase, and Zeufact (2019), using data from Ethiopia 2000–2014 manufacturing census (firms with 10 or more employees).

Note: For the period 2000–2014 panel a reports the percentage difference in capital intensity between nontrading firms and trading firms. The results are obtained by regressing firm capital intensity (log capital per worker) on dummy variables if a firm exports and imports (GVC firm), exports only, or imports only, controlling for whether the firm is state-owned, as well as sector, year, and region fixed effects. Panel b reports the percentage difference in employment before and after the switch for firms that switched from nontrading to trading status. The results are obtained by regressing firm employment (log number of workers) on dummy variables if a firm exports and imports (GVC firm), exports only, or imports only, controlling for whether the firm is state owned, as well as year and firm fixed effects. All coefficient estimates are statistically significant. For the capital intensity and employment regressions, the coefficients for export-only and GVC firms are not statistically different. The percent differences reported in the graphs are obtained as 100 multiplied by the exponential of the coefficient estimates minus 1.

share in total employment, albeit slightly.[42] In fact, the provinces that became more GVC-intensive also experienced faster growth in the employment share of the population (map 3.1). No province experienced net job losses. Net job creation nationally exceeded 12 million, and the share of employment in the population (ages 15 and over) increased from 70 percent to 76 percent.[43] It is likely these experiences would extend to other low-income countries that have been able to integrate into basic manufacturing, such as textiles or agribusiness.

In Mexico, employment expansion is more strongly linked to GVCs than one-way trade (figure 3.7). Between 1993 and 2013, municipalities in Mexico with a larger share of employees in manufacturing firms that both export and import experienced stronger growth in their total employment and increased their share in the country's total employment.

The new activities that GVCs bring to countries can also induce shifts in type of employment. In Vietnam, the number of self-employed, wage, and salaried workers, as well as employers, all increased between 2004 and 2014. But wage and salaried jobs nearly doubled, outpacing other employment types, and the

Map 3.1 In Vietnam, employment expansion was linked to GVC firms

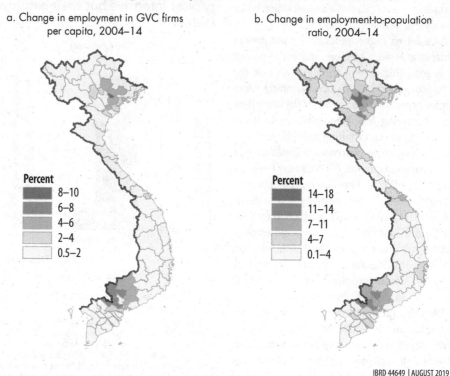

a. Change in employment in GVC firms per capita, 2004–14

b. Change in employment-to-population ratio, 2004–14

Percent
- 8–10
- 6–8
- 4–6
- 2–4
- 0.5–2

Percent
- 14–18
- 11–14
- 7–11
- 4–7
- 0.1–4

IBRD 44649 | AUGUST 2019

Sources: WDR 2020 team, using data from GSO (2012) and General Statistics Office of Vietnam's Enterprise Surveys.

Note: GVC firms are firms that both export and import. Employment is measured as the total number of employees reported by registered firms, summed across firms with more than five employees within each province. The employment-to-population ratio is measured as employment relative to population in the province.

Figure 3.7 In Mexico, employment expansion is more strongly linked to GVC expansion than non-GVC trade

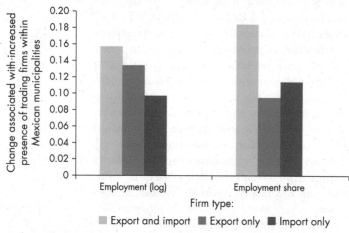

Firm type: ▢ Export and import ▣ Export only ■ Import only

Sources: WDR 2020 team, based on INEGI (2014) and CONEVAL and World Bank (2013).

Note: Standardized coefficient estimates are reported for the period 1993–2013 from a regression of log of municipality employment or municipality employment share in total employment on the number of employees per capita in manufacturing firms that export and import, export only, and import only, controlling for total population of the municipality, distance of the municipality to the U.S. border, and state and year fixed effects. All coefficient estimates are statistically significant. Standardized coefficients refer to how many standard deviations the dependent variable will change per standard deviation increase in the explanatory variable.

share of total employment increased 11 percentage points, from 25 to 36 percent. Formal employment (jobs covered by social security) in the manufacturing sector also grew as GVC firms assumed greater importance in formal manufacturing employment in Vietnam.[44] However, as discussed shortly, informal or noncontract work can also be important in agriculture and manufacturing value chains.

The overall result is that GVCs are associated with structural transformation, with exports pulling people out of less productive activities and into more productive manufacturing jobs. In Vietnam, manufacturing absorbed nearly 2.5 million workers between 2005 and 2014, increasing its share of the country's total employment from 12 to 14 percent.[45] This is not unique to Vietnam. The 2016 World Bank report *Stitches to Riches?* reveals that, based on data on the apparel sector in South Asia between 2000 and 2010, when a country experienced a 1 percent increase in apparel output (a proxy for apparel exports), there was a 0.3–0.4 percent increase in employment. This rise in employment increased overall welfare as workers moved out of agriculture or the informal sector toward better-paying, higher-value-added jobs.[46] Similarly, Lesotho's integration in the global apparel sector accounted for 10 percent of the country's workforce and half of manufacturing employment in 2009, helping to transform an agrarian economy.[47] In Haiti, the apparel sector employed 37,000 workers in 2014.[48]

GVCs support employment of not just men, but also women. Female employment grew faster than male employment in Vietnamese provinces where GVC participation expanded the most.[49] Notably in the apparel and electronics sectors, where assembly of many small parts must be done manually, firms report preferences for female employees because of the high levels of dexterity required. In Ethiopia, women constitute 75 percent of the workforce in the apparel sector,[50] 65 percent in Haiti,[51] and 77 percent in Sri Lanka.[52]

Across the world, firms that both export and import tend to employ more women than firms that do not participate in GVCs (figure 3.8). Foreign-owned firms as well as firms that export *or* import also have higher female labor shares on average than firms that do not, but the relationship is stronger for GVC participants. These jobs have positive effects on other aspects of women's livelihoods. In Bangladesh, for example, young women in villages exposed to the garment sector delay marriage and childbirth, and young girls gain an additional 1.5 years of schooling (box 3.5).[53] The gender dimension of GVCs though is not without challenges.

Not only do GVC firms employ more people, but they also pay better. In Ethiopia, manufacturing firms that both import and export paid significantly higher

Figure 3.8 Worldwide, GVC firms hire more women than non-GVC firms

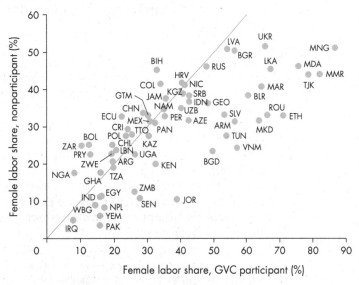

Source: Rocha and Winkler (2019), using data from World Bank's Enterprise Surveys.

Note: Each dot represents a country-year observation. The x-axis plots the employment-weighted share of female workers of total workers in firms that both export and import (GVC participant). The y-axis plots the employment-weighted share of female workers of total workers in firms that do not export and import (nonparticipant). For country abbreviations, see International Organization for Standardization (ISO), https://www.iso.org/obp/ui/#search.

wages in 2000–2014 than did those that exported only or imported only, controlling for sector, location, and year effects. In Mexico, wages are also significantly higher in firms that both import and export than in firms that do not. Firms that have relationships with buyers or suppliers also pay higher wages than

---

Box 3.5 GVC participation can lead to indirect welfare improvements for women

How does getting a job change one's life beyond the income itself? Bangladesh is an interesting case study because the country's ready-made garment industry employs 3.6 million people, 53 percent of whom are women.[a] Meanwhile, the country has seen remarkable progress in health and education. How might these factors be related? One study used an innovative approach, looking at 1,395 households in 60 villages to identify how the arrival of ready-made garment jobs may have affected various welfare-related indicators.[b] Exposure to the sector was associated with a drop in both marriages and childbirths for girls ages 12 to 18—an important finding because of the long-term

negative effects of early marriage and childbirth. Girls in villages close to garment factories had on average significantly higher educational attainment—they appeared more likely to stay in school than those with no factory nearby. This effect was particularly strong for younger girls ages 5–9. The most plausible explanation appears to be that the chances of getting a job increase the returns to staying in school and improving literacy and numeracy. In addition, parents, through higher income from these jobs, can better afford to send their children to school.

The study compared these demand-led welfare effects with a more supply-side intervention in the form of a

(Box continues next page)

Box 3.5 GVC participation can lead to indirect welfare improvements for women (continued)

large-scale conditional cash transfer program to encourage girls' school enrollment. The demand-led welfare effects were much larger than the effects of conditional cash transfers. In other words, expanding light manufacturing provides not only benefits in the form of jobs but also, more indirectly, benefits for education, health, and workers' children. That said, there was a small negative effect on school enrollment of girls ages 17–18. For them, the opportunity cost of getting a garment factory job may outweigh the returns to staying in school. As discussed in box 3.6, the relationship between human capital formation and participation in GVCs is heterogeneous across countries' contexts.

Together, these results suggest that the type of job matters, and that as countries move into more value-added and skill-intensive activities, the returns to education for girls will improve, and dropout rates are likely to fall. Evidence from India seems to confirm this point. An investigation of the more skill-intensive business processing outsourcing (BPO) industry in the country showed that women in villages linked to the industry had higher aspirations and invested more in computer or English courses than did

those in other villages. There were also indirect positive effects from BPO employment on girls' school enrollment, nutrition, health, delayed marriage, and childbirth.[c]

Evidence of improved welfare for women working in GVCs can be found elsewhere as well. One study looked at the subjective well-being of women employed in Senegal's export-oriented horticulture industry.[d] Employment improved subjective well-being for the poorest women, generally through improved living standards, but not as much for women whose incomes were well above the poverty threshold. For low-income women employed in Ethiopia's cut flower industry, savings in relation to their incomes are higher than for those employed in other sectors, and the subjective valuation of their jobs is also higher.[e]

Finally, by analyzing workers' experiences in the Kenyan cut flower industry through interviews, the authors of one article found a clear link between employment and women's empowerment—such as in greater independence, new opportunities, and decision making within the household.[f] The strength of the effect, however, depends on the quality of the job.

a. Moazzem and Radia (2018).
b. Heath and Mobarak (2015).
c. Jensen (2012).
d. Van den Broeck and Maertens (2017).
e. Suzuki, Mano, and Abebe (2018).
f. Said-Allsopp and Tallontire (2015).

firms without relationships in Mexico.[54] In China, GVC engagement improved firms' wages (more so in capital-intensive and foreign-invested firms) both by improving productivity within firms and by reallocating labor to more productive firms.[55] Again, across a sample of developing countries, firms that both export and import pay higher wages than import-only and export-only firms and nontraders.[56]

How countries participate in GVCs also matters for wage growth. From 1990 to 2015, wage growth was the largest for countries that broke out of commodities or agriculture into basic manufacturing ("limited manufacturing" in figure 3.9).

Poverty and shared prosperity

By supporting employment and income growth, GVCs also support poverty reduction and shared prosperity. The classical trade literature suggests that trade creates growth, better jobs, and higher incomes,

which reduces poverty. However, GVCs may have additional channels through which trade affects poverty. Labor-saving productivity growth through the hyperspecialization of GVCs may directly displace jobs. However, adoption of techniques and technologies that save on labor can spur job creation through three indirect channels that are more challenging to conceptualize and measure. First, productivity gains in supplier industries can yield steep increases in the demand for labor because of input–output linkages. Second, productivity growth can boost final demand. And, third, such growth may lead to compositional shifts in the structure of the economy and could support jobs by spurring the growth of sectors with high labor shares.

In a cross section of countries, growth in GVC participation is indeed associated with a decline in the number of people living on less than $5.50 a day (in 2011 international prices)—see figure 3.10. Openness affects poverty primarily through growth, the main driver of the remarkable reduction in global poverty since 1990.[57] Where economic growth from GVCs is larger than from conventional trade, poverty reduction from GVCs will also likely be larger.

In Mexico, municipalities with a larger share of employees in internationalized firms experienced a greater reduction in poverty between 1993 and 2013 for the poorest as well as vulnerable households. A greater presence of import and export firms is positively associated with the poorest households' ability to obtain a basic food basket. Municipalities with greater GVC participation also experienced a lower incidence of capabilities poverty and asset poverty—that is, their access to enough financial resources to provide for other needs, including health, education, and transport, improved.[58] They also experienced a decline in the marginalization index, which captures deprivation and inaccessibility to basic goods and services for welfare. The relationship among poverty, marginalization, and international integration is generally stronger for firms that both export and import than for those that export only or import only (figure 3.11). All this said, even though GVCs can create opportunities for poor households, they have also been found to create risks for the accumulation of human capital throughout the life cycle, such as in Mexico (box 3.6).

In Vietnam, provinces with more internationalized firms also experienced greater reductions in poverty between 2004 and 2014 (figure 3.12). This decline likely worked through the employment and ultimately the income channels, as just discussed. Provinces with more internationalized firms similarly experienced higher growth in the incomes of the bottom 40 percent of the population between 2004 and 2014. The impacts were not restricted to those provinces with more GVC participation, and poverty also fell in neighboring provinces in Vietnam.[59]

The positive effects of GVC participation on income growth are likely to extend to everyone in society—if the welfare state works. GVC integration in certain regions of a country can give people the incentive to migrate within their country, which can be a powerful mechanism for reducing poverty. Higher incomes will also generate more demand for a greater number and diversity of goods and services, imported and domestic. This demand will lead to diversification of the economy, which will increase opportunities for a broader and more diverse set of agents. GVCs are also likely to make a larger variety of goods more affordable, such as cell phones, thereby allowing the poor to participate more widely in society.

Figure 3.9 The boost to wages is largest in countries after they first enter limited manufacturing GVCs

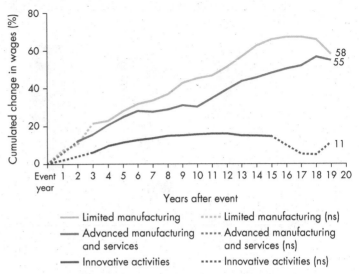

Sources: WDR 2020 team, using data from the World Bank's WDI database and the GVC taxonomy for 1990–2015 based on Eora26 database.

Note: The event study quantifies the cumulated change in wages in the 20 years following a switch from a lower to a higher stage of GVC engagement. Dotted lines indicate statistically nonsignificant (ns) coefficients. See box 3.3 for the methodology.

Figure 3.10 GVC participation is associated with poverty reduction

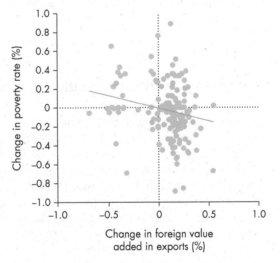

Sources: WDR 2020 team, using data from Eora and World Bank's WDI database.

Note: Each dot is a country-year observation. The x-axis is the average annual growth in foreign value added in exports between 1990 and 2015. The y-axis is the average annual growth in the poverty rate between 1990 and 2015. The poverty rate is measured as a percentage of the population living on less than $5.50 a day (in 2011 international prices).

Agriculture value chains can be a particularly powerful factor in poverty reduction by integrating rural households and smallholder farmers into supply chains. In Madagascar and Senegal, more high-value

Figure 3.11 In municipalities in Mexico, the expanded presence of GVC firms is more strongly associated with poverty reduction than the presence of firms that export only or import only

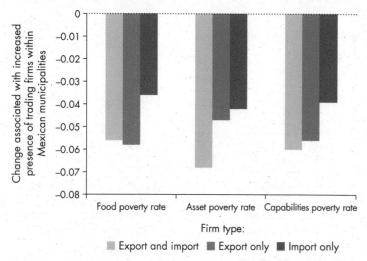

Firm type:
■ Export and import ■ Export only ■ Import only

Sources: WDR 2020 team, using data from INEGI (2014) and CONEVAL and World Bank (2013).

Note: Standardized coefficient estimates are reported for the period 1993–2013 from a regression of food poverty, asset poverty, and capabilities poverty rates at the municipal level on the number of employees per capita in manufacturing firms that export and import, export only, and import only, controlling for total population of the municipality, distance of the municipality to the U.S. border, and state and year fixed effects. Ratios are defined as the number of food, asset, or capabilities poor over total population in the municipality. All coefficient estimates are statistically significant. Standardized coefficients refer to how many standard deviations the dependent variable will change per standard deviation increase in the explanatory variable. For definitions of food poverty, asset poverty, and capabilities poverty, see note 55 at the end of this chapter.

exports and the modernization of export supply chains of green beans and tomatoes had important positive welfare effects. Most notable were higher incomes for these farmers, particularly those in the lower quartile of the income distribution. The result was a reduction in the absolute poverty levels.[60]

There is no apparent relationship between GVC participation and growth in income inequality in Vietnam or Mexico, as measured by the Gini coefficient using household data at the provincial or municipal level.[61] Despite this finding, there can be important distributional implications of GVC participation across and within countries.

The lack of a systematic relationship between GVC participation and growth in income inequality for developing countries is at first sight confirmed by the cross-country event study described in this chapter (see box 3.3). Greater income inequality within countries, as measured by the Gini coefficient, is observed only in the group of countries that switch to the innovation stage of GVC engagement, and it becomes statistically significant only after about a decade (figure 3.13).

Distribution of gains

Paralleling the gains that GVCs have delivered for countries, a large majority of people in both high- and lower-income countries view two elements of GVCs

---

Box 3.6 Does GVC participation lead to human capital accumulation?

By boosting productivity and enabling structural transformation, participation in GVCs has been associated with rising incomes and less poverty. But the extent to which countries reap long-term development gains from GVC participation hinges critically on its consequences for the human capital of workers and their children.

Many developing countries are giving priority to raising human capital formation while deepening GVC participation and pursuing export-led industrialization. The experience of East Asia—such as Korea in the 1980s and 1990s and more recently China and Vietnam—suggests that these two goals are compatible and may reinforce one other. GVC participation fosters industrialization and urbanization, boosting parental income and productivity. It also raises tax collection and creates room for larger private and public investments in education. Human capital formation further supports GVC participation and industrial development.

But the rates of human capital formation differ significantly among countries that increased their participation in GVCs. Although Mexico experienced an increase in openness after the launch of the North American Free Trade Agreement (NAFTA), income growth and human capital formation remained disappointing, despite rising public spending on education.

What explains these different experiences? Recent empirical evidence suggests that the skill intensity of newly created manufacturing jobs may play a critical role. Subnational evidence from Mexico reveals that the school dropout rate rose with the local expansion of export manufacturing industries: for every 25 jobs created, one student dropped out of school at grade 9 instead of continuing through grade 12.[a] These effects are driven by the export-manufacturing jobs that require fewer skills and therefore raised the opportunity cost of schooling for

(Box continues next page)

students at the margin. Subnational evidence from China reveals that high-skill export shocks raise both high school and college enrollments, whereas low-skill export shocks depress both.[b] The amplified differences in skill abundance across regions reinforce the initial patterns of industry specialization. Broader cross-country evidence for 102 countries over 45 years points in the same direction: growth in less skill-intensive exports depresses average educational attainment, whereas growth in skill-intensive exports raises schooling.[c] At the same time, in China rising imports of capital goods raised the demand for skills and led to greater educational attainment.[d]

These findings point to a mutually reinforcing relationship between the skill intensity of tasks and skill acquisition. On balance, participation in GVCs may still support human capital formation via income growth and the weaker financial constraints facing parents and governments. But these positive effects may be offset by reduced skill formation in areas in which participation in GVCs leads to an expansion of low-skill-intensive sectors and tedious tasks.

a. Atkin (2106).
b. Li (2018).
c. Blanchard and Olney (2017).
d. Li (2019).

positively: free trade and international business ties. However, the number of skeptics in all countries grew between 2002 and 2014 (figure 3.14). Although the discontent is greater in high-income countries, the number of those perceiving themselves to be losers from global integration is also nonnegligible in developing countries.

GVCs may have fueled some of this public discontent. Rather than being distributed equally across and within countries, the gains have been concentrated, accruing to specific firms, workers, and locations. People can feel left out, even if they are not worse off.

Markups and firms

The public sentiment on trade and international business ties captures the fact that since the 1980s there has been a widespread rise in firms' profits. In 134 countries, the average global markup increased by 46 percent between 1980 and 2016, with the largest increases accruing to the largest firms in Europe and North America and across a broad range of economic sectors.[62]

The growth of GVC activity appears to be a contributor to the rise in markups for several reasons. First, GVCs lower the costs of inputs for companies, through importing, and increase their productivity, through the scale of expansion afforded by exporting. Second, in the presence of economies of scale GVCs disproportionately favor large firms that can afford the fixed costs of exporting and importing.

Figure 3.12 In Vietnam, poverty reduction was greater in locations with a higher presence of GVC firms

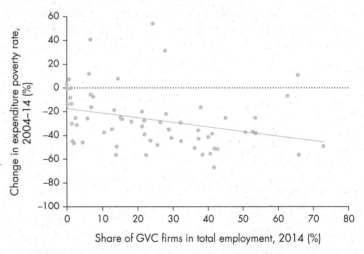

Sources: WDR 2020 team, using data from GSO (2012) and General Statistics Office of Vietnam's Enterprise Surveys.

Note: GVC firms are firms that both export and import. Employment is measured as the total number of employees reported by registered firms, summed across firms with more than five employees within each province. The expenditure poverty rate is measured as the poverty headcount. The presence of firms that export only had no additional relationship with poverty reduction.

Firms that import and export are not constrained by domestic inputs and domestic demand, which helps them grow and realize economies of scale. This factor is especially important in the mass production manufacturing that dominates the limited manufacturing GVC group. The size distribution of firms is likely to

Figure 3.13 Rising income inequality is a greater problem for countries breaking into the innovation stages of GVC engagement

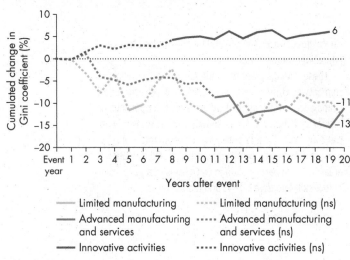

Sources: WDR 2020 team, using data from the World Bank's WDI database and the GVC taxonomy for 1990–2015 based on Eora26 database.

Note: The event study quantifies the cumulated change in the Gini coefficient in the 20 years following a switch from a lower to a higher stage of GVC engagement. Dotted lines indicate statistically nonsignificant (ns) coefficients. See box 3.3 for the methodology.

Figure 3.14 A majority worldwide views trade and international business ties positively, but skepticism grew from 2002 to 2014

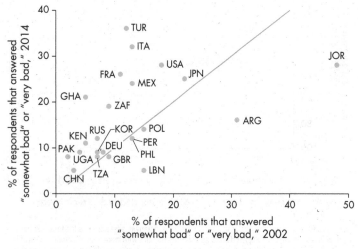

Source: Pew Research Center 2014.

Note: Each dot is a country-year observation. The figure shows the share of respondents that answered in 2002 and in 2014 "somewhat bad" or "very bad" to the question "What do you think about the growing trade and business ties between [survey country] and other countries—do you think it is a very good thing, somewhat good, somewhat bad, or a very bad thing for our country?" For country abbreviations, see International Organization for Standardization (ISO), https://www.iso.org/obp/ui/#search.

be significantly more skewed in a world of GVCs than in a world without them, which is consistent with evidence that firms participating in GVCs tend to be larger than other firms.

Third, markups increase only if these cost reductions are not fully passed on to consumers through lower prices.[63] Participating in GVCs justifies some markup increase to cover the greater fixed costs of more complex sourcing or exporting. But the markup growth in GVC-intensive sectors is also likely to have increased the profit rate of these companies. It is well established empirically that large firms pass through a smaller share of a price shock to consumers. Consistent with this, these large firms are also likely to only partly pass on lower costs due to offshoring to consumers. The California company Everlane, which is committed to transparent pricing, reports the cost breakdown of all its products as well as the average price of its items in the market. According to the company's website, a pair of jeans that customarily sells for $170 is produced for $34, which includes cost, insurance, and freight.

Indeed, U.S. industries are increasingly concentrated, with a small number of productive firms accounting for large shares of the market and large profits.[64] This rise of "superstar" firms in the United States and other advanced economies may be associated in part with the rise of GVCs and in part with technological change and innovations. In other words, GVCs have boosted superstar firms that earn superstar profits and may dominate the market. In Ethiopia, for example, measures of markups are also highly correlated with industry concentration in manufacturing.[65]

There is evidence that firms in developed countries that outsource parts and tasks to suppliers in developing countries have seen higher profits. In the textile sector, for example, markups of Japanese firms have increased since 1990 in line with backward GVC participation (figure 3.15, panel a). This positive association holds for other developed countries and other sectors that have also transferred large parts of their production to developing countries.[66]

Within developing countries, there is also evidence of incomplete pass-throughs of cost reductions to consumers through lower prices, resulting in higher profits. After India's trade liberalization in the 1990s, when input tariffs on intermediate inputs fell, both costs and prices dropped, but markups went up by about 13 percent when the economy opened to trade.[67] Consumers still benefited through lower prices (as well as higher quality and greater variety), but they were worse off than if firms had fully passed on those cost reductions.

GVC activity—and the relational nature of GVCs in particular—similarly appear to be a likely contributor to the international dispersion of the markups that

Figure 3.15 Increasing GVC participation is associated with rising markups in developed countries but falling markups in developing countries

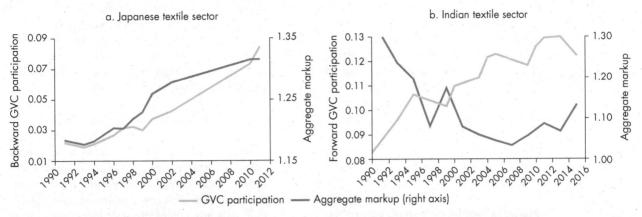

a. Japanese textile sector

b. Indian textile sector

— GVC participation — Aggregate markup (right axis)

Sources: WDR 2020 team, using data from Eora and Worldscope.

Note: Graphs plot data between 1991 and 2011 for panel a and between 1990 and 2015 for panel b. The left y-axis in panel a measures the share of foreign value added in gross exports of the Japanese textile sector (backward GVC participation). The left y-axis in panel b measures the share of domestic value added in India embodied in importing countries' exports to third countries (forward GVC participation). The right y-axis in both panels measures the share-weighted average markup of listed companies in the textile sector. Markups are calculated following De Loecker and Eeckhout (2018). Similar results hold across countries and sectors.

GVCs generate.[68] The implications of GVCs for the emergence of superstar firms huge in scale, high in market power, and large in profit rates are exacerbated by the disproportionate bargaining power that these large lead firms may have over their suppliers.

Although buyer firms in developed countries are seeing higher profits, supplier firms in developing countries are getting squeezed. Across 10 developing countries, the relationship between markups and forward participation is negative for developing countries in the textile and apparel sector (see figure 3.15, panel b, for India).[69] Some developing countries, including China, enjoy a positive correlation. This finding is consistent with a growing number of firms from emerging economies graduating from supplier to lead firms in GVCs.

Other country-level evidence suggests markups have increased mostly in advanced economies but not in emerging markets.[70] In Ethiopia, firms that buy inputs abroad to sell in the external market have lower markups than other types of firms (one-way traders or nontraders).[71] And the more intensely a firm is integrated into a GVC (measured as the share of the export value added and imported inputs in total sales), the lower is its markup. As Ethiopian firms become integrated into GVCs, they also experience reductions in their markups, which are strongest for two-way traders (figure 3.16). In Poland, increased GVC participation—including the use of imported components in production as well as the rising presence of domestic firms in foreign markets—is associated with the observed decline in markups between 2002 and 2016.[72]

Figure 3.16 In Ethiopia, firms entering GVCs experience greater declines in markups, 2000–2014

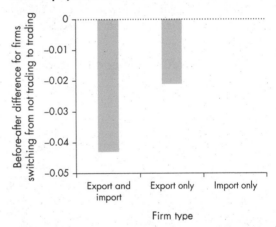

Sources: Choi, Fukase, and Zeufack (2019), using data from Ethiopia: 2000–2014 manufacturing census (firms with 10 or more employees).

Note: Standardized coefficient estimates are reported for the period 2000–2014 from a regression of the log of markup at the firm level on dummy variables for firm type (export only, import only, export and import), controlling for state ownership, labor (log), capital (log), firm fixed effects, and year fixed effects. No data shown for "Import only" because only statistically significant coefficient estimates are reported. Standardized coefficients refer to how many standard deviations the dependent variable will change per standard deviation increase in the explanatory variable.

In South Africa, markups charged by manufacturing exporters are on average significantly lower than those charged by nonexporters. Firms with a relatively small proportion of exports (up to 10 percent) charge markups that are about 1.2 percent lower than nonexporters, while firms with a medium (11–25 percent) and large (more than 25 percent) share of exports charge markups that are 1.8 percent and 2.3 percent lower than those of nonexporters, respectively.[73] The risk that firms from developing countries experience limited profits after becoming suppliers for global firms mirrors the rise in profits in developed countries.

In short, GVCs primarily reward large international firms by reducing their production costs. However, these gains are only partly passed on to consumers or shared with suppliers. Because suppliers are predominantly in developing countries, the gains may be distributed unequally, even across countries in the value chain.

Markups and labor's share of profits

The rise in the market power of firms is contributing to the changing distribution of capital and labor in countries. The share of income accruing to workers—or how much of a country's GDP accrues to labor through wages as opposed to physical capital and profits—is the other side of the markup phenomenon: profits are rising, but labor's share of income is falling (figure 3.17, panel a).

There are, of course, many possible explanations for the observed global decline in the so-called labor

share,[74] but the rise in GVC activity appears to be a contributor. By increasing the profit rate of companies, GVCs also generate a force that results in a lower share of an economy's income being paid to labor. In the United States, superstar firms that are more productive and earn higher profits also have lower labor shares, and their increasing concentration has contributed to the declining labor share within industries.[75] It may be that producers are not passing on their cost savings to both workers and consumers.

Similarly, the movement of relatively labor-intensive tasks from developed to developing countries could explain why the composition of production becomes more capital-intensive with GVC participation in developed countries. In developing countries, this could also reduce the labor share insofar as it accompanies production that has become relatively more capital-intensive than before.[76]

In 63 developed and developing economies, GVC integration as well as other domestic within-industry forces, such as technology or markups, contributed significantly to the reallocation of value added from labor to capital within countries between 1995 and 2011. The labor share declined by 2.2 percentage points, with GVCs contributing 0.6 percentage point (figure 3.17, panel b). Similarly, global integration, particularly

Figure 3.17 **GVCs have contributed to the declining labor share within countries**

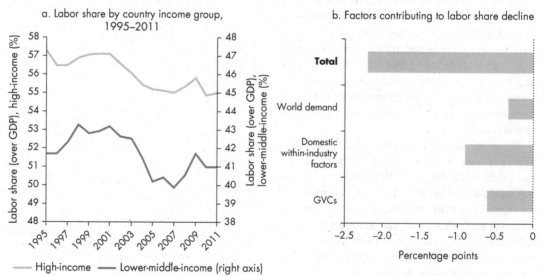

a. Labor share by country income group, 1995–2011

b. Factors contributing to labor share decline

— High-income   — Lower-middle-income (right axis)

Source: WDR 2020 team, using data from OECD's TiVA database.

Note: In panel a, the green line plots the labor share in 29 advanced economies, and the blue line plots the labor share in 34 developing economies. In panel b, the decomposition explores the contribution of world demand, domestic within-industry factors, and GVCs to the total percentage point decline in the average labor share of 63 developed and developing economies between 1995 and 2011. V is the diagonal matrix of the share of value added in gross output; B is the Leontief inverse; and Y is the diagonal matrix of final goods and services produced in a country and sold worldwide. The results are obtained from three counterfactual exercises to decompose the relative contribution of each component by asking what the contribution to the observed overall changes in labor share would be if only domestic within-industry factors (V), GVCs (B), or world demand (Y) are allowed to change over time. The decomposition follows the methodology of Reshef and Santoni (2019).

the expansion of GVCs, has been identified as the primary trigger of the rise of overall capital intensity in production in emerging markets and developing economies.[77] Alongside globalization, explanations have also focused on economies of scale, innovation, and new technologies.[78]

Skills and wage inequality

Inequality can also arise within the labor market, with a growing wage premium for the skilled. The Stolper-Samuelson theorem, one of the key tenets of traditional international trade, indicates that rising trade integration is likely to increase wage inequality (skilled versus unskilled workers) in relatively advanced countries with abundant skilled labor. But rising integration would be expected to reduce wage inequality in lower-income countries in which skilled labor is scarce. In a world of fragmentation, however, the theorem's validity is undermined. And, indeed, it is widely accepted both theoretically and empirically that greater fragmentation of production increases wage inequality in countries at all income levels for at least three reasons.[79] First, when production is moved across countries, the workers in those economies find themselves employed in new production processes and tasks. In higher-income countries, these processes and tasks may be considered low-skilled and labor-intensive, but in lower-income countries they are considered skilled labor-intensive when compared with the outside opportunities of workers.[80] Thus offshoring increases the demand for skilled workers in low- and middle-income economies and puts upward pressure on wage inequality.

A second reason for increased wage inequality in low- and middle-income economies is that GVCs are often more skill-sensitive than traditional trade flows, in part because they often produce goods destined for quality-sensitive consumers in rich countries,[81] and in part because of the high complementarities among the various stages of production carried out in different countries.[82]

The disproportionate importance of the matching between buyers and sellers in GVCs may also drive up wage inequality. Because the identity of these producers matters, especially when sensitivity to quality is high, relational GVCs may set off "a war for talent," with the price of particularly attractive producers or the wage of particularly skilled individuals bid up disproportionately relative to that in a world without relational GVCs.

A third reason for the increase in wage inequality in countries in which skilled labor is scarce is that

firms in GVCs tend to adopt more capital-intensive techniques than comparable domestic firms.[83] Physical capital deepening and upgrading contribute to the increase in the relative demand for skilled workers because of the capital–skill complementarity—physical capital (and especially capital equipment) is less substitutable with skilled labor than with unskilled labor.[84] Consistent with this finding, in countries participating in GVCs and in the more capital-intensive parts of the value chain firms demand more-skilled workers.[85] The result is that as workers tend to move toward less routine and more interactive tasks, GVCs produce more jobs for skilled workers.[86]

Firm-level analysis confirms a positive and significant relationship between GVCs and skilled employment—that is, between the number of skilled workers and firms with international links that export or are foreign-owned.[87] In 27 transition economies, importing inputs increases the demand for skilled labor.[88] In fact, global sourcing explains more than a quarter of the unconditional difference between importers and nonimporters in the employment share of high-skilled workers. In Madagascar, upgrading by diaspora- and Mauritian-owned firms in the apparel sector corresponded with in-firm training and skills upgrading.[89] In Africa more broadly, with Chinese import penetration firms increase their share of skilled workers by almost 4 percent, which is associated with a shift in production from low-skill to high-skill-intensive products.[90]

Geographical disparities

Inequality arising from GVCs also has a geographical dimension. GVC integration is strongly associated with greater concentration in cities,[91] as well as border regions for countries neighboring GVC partners. This finding is consistent with evidence from Mexico and Vietnam showing that economic integration across national borders is associated with greater spatial concentration within national borders (map 3.2).

Because some regions grow faster than others, regional inequalities in developing countries can increase when labor is not perfectly mobile. In Vietnam, the only areas with double-digit job growth were concentrated around Hanoi and Ho Chi Minh City. By contrast, in developed countries some regions are being hollowed out by GVCs. In the United States, the outsourcing of manufacturing tasks and the exposure of industries to foreign competition have led to the emergence of a "rust belt."[92] Such a phenomenon can result in localized and persistent income losses for years for people in negatively affected regions or

Map 3.2 In Mexico and Vietnam, GVCs are spatially concentrated

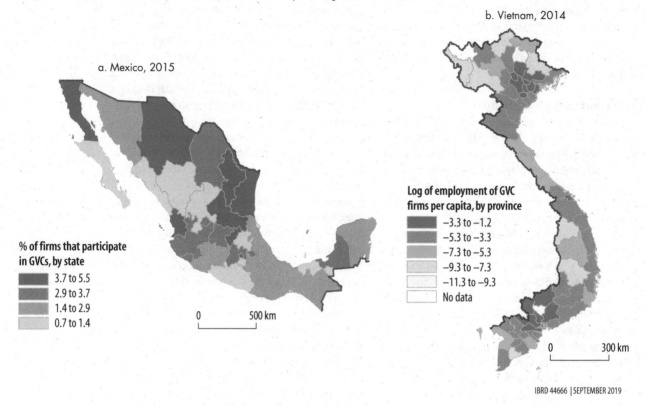

a. Mexico, 2015

b. Vietnam, 2014

% of firms that participate in GVCs, by state
- 3.7 to 5.5
- 2.9 to 3.7
- 1.4 to 2.9
- 0.7 to 1.4

0   500 km

Log of employment of GVC firms per capita, by province
- −3.3 to −1.2
- −5.3 to −3.3
- −7.3 to −5.3
- −9.3 to −7.3
- −11.3 to −9.3
- No data

0   300 km

IBRD 44666 | SEPTEMBER 2019

Sources: Mexico: WDR 2020 team, using data from ENAPROCE 2015. Vietnam: WDR 2020 team, using data from GSO (2012) and General Statistics Office of Vietnam's Enterprise Surveys.

Note: In Mexico, state-level GVC participation is measured as the percent of firms that participate in GVCs. In Vietnam, province-level GVC participation is measured as log of employment of GVC firms per capita.

sectors when people cannot move easily.[93] Both experiences highlight the need for internal mobility of labor to distribute the gains from trade. Place-based policies that could reduce the negative consequences of the economic forces that disproportionately benefit some areas are discussed in the final chapters of this Report.

Unequal work conditions

Small-scale farmers and home-based workers form the base of some value chains, often on unequal terms. A review of 49 studies related to the commodities and horticulture value chains concluded that "informality is the norm rather than the exception: informal workers make up the majority of the workforce, even in formal enterprises."[94] In a random sample of 1,200 farmers in Ghana, Kenya, and Zambia growing maize, cassava, or sorghum, between 82 percent of farmers in Zambia and 97 percent in Kenya had no contract. For those with a contract, informal contracts dominated the landscape. In Kenya, 86 percent of contracts were informal.[95]

Subcontracted home-based workers (so-called homeworkers) make up significant shares of employment in other supply chains. Among other things, they weave textiles, package products, process rice, and make food products. An estimated 5 million homeworkers are part of India's garment and textile supply chains alone. Most homeworkers are informally employed without employer contributions to their social protection, and the vast majority are women. Their average earnings are not only lower than those of factory workers but also erratic, and subcontracted homeworkers also pay for many of the nonwage costs of production, such as workplace, equipment, utilities, and transport. Integrating homeworkers into supply chains on fairer terms will require better regulation from above and better integration from below (box 3.7).

GVC participation can increase casual employment. A case study in Ghana and Côte d'Ivoire on participation in the pineapple and cocoa value chains found that, although participation benefits successful farmers through improved growing processes, higher yields, and higher incomes, it is also associated

Box 3.7 Home-based work in GVCs

By organizing in collectives, homeworkers can link to global supply chains in efficient ways and on fair terms. To do this, collective enterprises of homeworkers—cooperatives or other collective forms—would have to seek the following types of support:

- Management and business training, including how to forecast market demand and how to manage businesses
- Professional managers and knowledge of how to recruit and retain managers
- Professional advice and assistance on how to link to global supply chains, how to upgrade products and production systems, and how to reduce dependence on intermediaries

- Capital—physical and social networks
- More appropriate and enabling laws and regulations regarding cooperatives and commercial transactions because the existing laws in most countries are not appropriate for cooperatives and the commercial transactions of those at the base of the economic pyramid.

Additional spillovers from forming collective enterprises include greater bargaining power in market transactions and an enhanced ability to challenge the social norms that constrain women's time, mobility, and access to resources (such as the social norms governing inheritance and property rights) and the economic policies that ignore or undervalue their economic activities and contributions.

---

with an increase in casual labor hiring, as well as displacement of farmers from land because of their low bargaining positions and lack of knowledge on their rights to land ownership.[96] Earlier research has documented the growing use of casual and seasonal contract labor both on farms and in packhouses in South Africa (fruit exports) and Kenya (fresh vegetable exports).[97]

GVCs may also be associated with poor worker conditions. Work practices often fall short of international standards in supplier countries, ranging from violations of core labor standards to unsafe working conditions, low wages, excessive working hours, and precarious contracts.[98] This problem is particularly associated with labor-intensive GVCs, where outsourcing to developing country locations is often motivated by low-wage labor.[99] This situation has led many observers to question the social value of the GVC business model, pointing to incidents at contract manufacturers such as the 2013 collapse of the Rana Plaza garment factory in Bangladesh. In the copper-cobalt belt of the Democratic Republic of Congo, for example, children often work in the mining sector.[100] And yet putting a halt to sourcing from these artisanal mines as a way to counter child labor could have unintended negative effects for household income, where poverty and then social norms are the main reasons for children working in mining.

There are signs that GVCs can transmit sensitivities about working conditions in host countries and induce remedial actions. In Indonesia, for example, anti-sweatshop campaigns in the 1990s brought attention to poor working conditions in the textile, footwear, and apparel (TFA) sector.[101] As a result of activist pressure, multinational enterprises (MNEs) signed codes of conduct pledging to raise wages and improve working conditions in factories producing their products. The result was large real wage increases in the targeted enterprises, by as much as 30 percent in large foreign-owned and exporting TFA plants relative to other TFA plants. In fact, wages were no worse in MNEs than in domestic plants to begin with. Within the TFA sector, real annual wages in domestic plants were lower than those in foreign-owned or exporting plants.

Relationships within value chains can also catalyze improved working conditions. CocoaAction, promoted by nine main global producers of chocolate and cocoa, was set up to regenerate the cocoa plantations in West Africa. It also sought to help smallholder cocoa farmers who often subsist on incomes below the poverty line and who face deficits in literacy, low school attendance rates, child labor, and gender inequality. In launching CocoaAction, the leading chocolate and cocoa companies recognized that their individual commitments could not solve the complex and systemic challenges and that more sustainable production of cocoa would also be good for their profits. Similar efforts were made in Ethiopia, Mexico, and Vietnam.

However, this may not be enough. While private firms can play an important role, there is also a clear role for policy action supported by international cooperation to determine the appropriate standards and ensure their enforcement. These policies are addressed in the final chapters of this Report.

The gender gap

Although firms in GVCs tend to employ more women than other firms, women are generally in lower-value-added segments of the value chain, mostly in labor-intensive production jobs and in occupations that require lower skills and pay less.[102] The positive relationship between GVC participation and the female labor share is much higher for production workers than for administrators or sales workers in manufacturing firms (figure 3.18, panel a). Many countries have few women-owned or women-run GVC firms. Firms that import and export are significantly less likely to be majority female–owned than other firms and are significantly less likely to have a top female manager. Thus GVCs do not appear to be breaking the glass ceiling (figure 3.18, panel b).

The asymmetry between production, on the one hand, and management and ownership, on the other, is particularly visible in agriculture, but it is on view in other sectors as well (table 3.1). In southern Africa's fish-aquaculture sector, women contribute mostly to primary production and make up 90 percent of the

processing workforce, but they are poorly represented in enterprise management. The trends are similar in aquaculture in Nigeria and Vietnam,[103] cocoa and coffee in Papua New Guinea,[104] and horticulture in Azerbaijan[105] and Afghanistan.[106] In the cashew value chain in Mozambique, lack of gender equality limits the access of women farmers to agricultural inputs, credit services, and markets. Despite the fact that more than half of the industry's workforce are women, almost no women hold leadership positions within factories.[107] In call centers in the Arab Republic of Egypt, women make up the majority of call agents, whereas men dominate jobs in higher-value segments and management.[108] In Kenya, women are overrepresented in the accommodation and excursion segments of tourism, but they tend to work as low- to mid-skilled employees, unless engaged as entrepreneurs.[109]

Why are so few GVC firms owned or run by women? Women's placement in value chains stems in part from the same reasons that hold back women in the non-GVC economy. These include disadvantages in endowments, such as assets, education, skills, experience, networks, and social capital, as well as gender-biased regulations or discriminatory social norms. According to the World Bank's Women, Business, and the Law database, 20 countries have yet to grant men and married women equal ownership

Figure 3.18 Women are more likely to be production workers and less likely to own or manage GVC firms

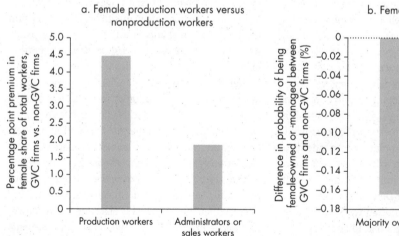

a. Female production workers versus nonproduction workers

b. Female owners and managers

Source: Rocha and Winkler (2019), using data from the World Bank's Enterprise Surveys.

Note: Exporters are firms with an export share (direct or indirect) of at least 10 percent of total sales. Importers are firms with an imported input share of at least 10 percent of total inputs. GVC participants are firms classified as both exporter and importer. Panel a plots the coefficient of estimations of the female labor share (production workers and nonproduction workers) on a dummy variable if the firm is a GVC participant, controlling for capital intensity, sales, and total factor productivity (TFP), as well as country-sector, subnational region, and year fixed effects. Panel b plots the coefficient of estimations of whether a firm is majority female-owned or has a female top manager on a dummy variable if the firm is a GVC participant, controlling for country-sector, subnational region, and year fixed effects. All coefficient estimates are statistically significant.

Table 3.1 Sample of results from case studies on gender in specific GVCs

Author and year of publication	Sector and country(ies)	Results
Veliu et al. (2009)	Aquaculture, Nigeria and northeast Vietnam	Women represent a significant share of employment, especially in processing and packaging, but they are poorly represented in enterprise management.
World Bank and IFC (2014)	Cocoa, coffee, and fresh produce value chains, Papua New Guinea	Women provide substantial labor in both coffee and cocoa cultivation and predominate in the fresh produce sectors, especially in tasks relevant for the quality of exports such as postharvesting.
IFC (2018)	Horticulture, Azerbaijan	A higher share of women are employed in horticulture than in other sectors. For products that depend on manual harvesting, women constitute more than 50 percent of harvesters.
World Bank (2011)	Horticulture, Afghanistan	Women provide the majority of labor in the lower levels of the value chains for horticulture—harvesting and postharvesting—although this is often unpaid household work.
Ahmed (2013)	Call centers, Arab Republic of Egypt	Women make up the majority of call agents, whereas men dominate jobs in higher-value segments and management.
Christian (2013)	Tourism, Kenya	Women are overrepresented in the accommodation and excursion segments of the tourism sector, although they tend to work as low- to mid-skilled employees, unless they are engaged as entrepreneurs.
Barrientos (2014)	Apparel, globally	In 2014 on average 60–80 percent of production workers in the top 27 apparel-exporting countries were women.

rights to property, and 41 countries do not grant sons and daughters equal rights to inherit assets from their parents. Even when the legal system does not discriminate against female ownership of assets, social norms inhibiting land ownership by women are a recurring theme across low- and middle-income countries. In Afghanistan's rural areas, social and cultural norms severely limit women's access to services, including credit, training, extension, inputs, and trading and marketing networks.[110] In Honduras, efforts by female entrepreneurs to enter value chains and upgrade into higher-value activities appear to be complicated by limited access to important inputs such as land, finance, and market information.[111] In call centers in Egypt, limited access to education, training, promotion, and networks made it difficult for women to take advantage of the rising demand for higher technical skills generated by product upgrading.[112] These gender-intensified constraints can restrict a country's ability to remain competitive and upgrade to higher-value segments of the chain—a topic discussed in a forthcoming report by the World Bank and World Trade Organization on trade and gender, "How Can 21st Century Trade Help to Close the Gender Gap?"

Removing legal restrictions that make it harder for women to start businesses and access productive

Figure 3.19 Gender equality in business regulations ensures that women are more fairly rewarded

Source: World Bank 2019b.

Note: Each dot represents a country observation. The x-axis plots the country score for gender equality in business regulation. The y-axis plots the expected percentage increase in wages for each additional year of experience for women. The World Bank's Women, Business, and the Law database (2019) documents the gender legal disparities for 189 economies.

resources can be an effective first step. The larger the number of legal restrictions women face, the lower is the payoff from work experience (figure 3.19). Simply mandating a nondiscrimination clause in hiring increases women's employment in formal firms by 8.6 percent.[113]

Taxation

Raising tax revenue is a challenge in today's globalized and digitalized economy. GVCs have magnified the challenges facing the international tax system. The current system of international taxation relies principally on identifying the physical place where value is created by firms. The mobility of certain factors of production, combined with the fragmentation of production processes across countries, make firms even more sensitive to the differences in taxation from country to country. In GVCs that involve affiliates of the same firm, fragmentation of production also leads to greater intrafirm trade and more opportunities for tax avoidance by manipulating where value is recognized for tax purposes. Exacerbating the problems are the growth of intangibles in global business and the digital delivery of services.[114]

Countries are under pressure to engage in tax competition by lowering the burden of corporate income tax to retain domestic and attract foreign investment. Meanwhile, lower communication and transport costs are facilitating the relocation of firms and the fragmentation of production across countries. Indeed, firms can locate production chains and procurement across the globe, choosing countries that make the most sense from a business perspective. That includes taking advantage of differences between national tax systems to shift production to lower-tax jurisdictions. Countries compete by

lowering corporate income tax rates and granting tax incentives such as tax holidays and preferential tax zones. Such measures can help countries achieve development objectives by promoting job growth and technology transfer. But they can also be inefficient if such benefits do not outweigh the cost of lower tax revenues.[115] In a race to the bottom, corporate income tax rates have declined by almost half since 1990 (figure 3.20).[116]

Revenues from corporate income taxes are further eroded by international tax avoidance, which takes advantage of loopholes and weaknesses in the international tax architecture. In GVCs that involve affiliates of the same common corporate structure, firms can locate activities that generate high profits with relatively little input, or "substance," in jurisdictions where those profits are taxed at low rates. Such practices are legal, but they run counter to the principle of taxing activities where value is created. Firms can also manipulate transfer prices between their affiliates to shift profits to lower-tax jurisdictions.

In principle, transactions between affiliates of a multinational corporation are "priced" according to the arm's-length principle, which means that they are in line with comparable transactions between unrelated enterprises under comparable circumstances. These rules for affiliated-party transactions are intended to ensure that profits of MNCs are registered in countries where value is created. In practice, however, the arm's-length principle is hard to apply, leaving scope for manipulating transfer prices to shift profits (but not substantial activities) to low-taxed entities without violating transfer pricing rules.[117]

Figure 3.20 Corporate income tax rates have declined by almost 50 percent since 1990

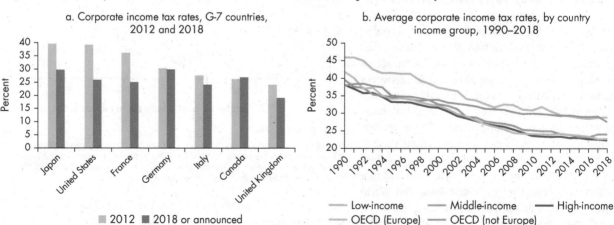

a. Corporate income tax rates, G-7 countries, 2012 and 2018

b. Average corporate income tax rates, by country income group, 1990–2018

■ 2012 ■ 2018 or announced

— Low-income   — Middle-income   — High-income
— OECD (Europe)   — OECD (not Europe)

Source: IMF 2019.

Note: Data include average subnational rates. OECD = Organisation for Economic Co-operation and Development.

Figure 3.21 As a share of GDP, non-OECD countries lose the most from profit shifting

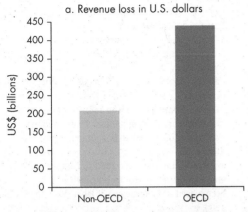

a. Revenue loss in U.S. dollars

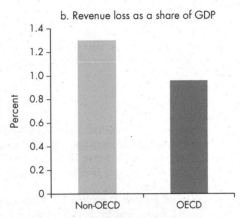

b. Revenue loss as a share of GDP

Source: Crivelli, de Mooij, and Keen 2016.

Note: OECD = Organisation for Economic Co-operation and Development.

Other avenues for international tax avoidance include debt transactions between affiliated parties in low-tax jurisdictions (lender) and high-tax jurisdictions (borrower), locating intangible assets in low-tax jurisdictions, and treaty shopping.[118]

Tax revenue losses from profit shifting are substantial: an estimated 30 percent of global cross-border corporate investment stocks are routed through offshore hubs, and the associated tax losses for developing countries are estimated at about $100 billion.[119] In 2013 non-OECD countries missed out on $200 billion in tax revenue as a result of profit shifting, a relatively larger loss than in OECD countries (figure 3.21).[120]

The growth of intangibles in GVCs and the digital delivery of services pose special challenges. Intangible assets such as data, patents, and trademarks are inherently more mobile than the traditional physical factors of production. Such assets are hard to value, and their share in overall capital goods is rising in the digital economy. In the United States, the share of intangible assets in the nonresidential capital stock doubled between 1966 and 2016.[121] Firms can choose to move only certain parts of the production process abroad, thereby minimizing any associated risk and maximizing the potential gains.[122] Thus small changes in tax policy can prompt large locational shifts by GVC firms, increasing pressure on countries to compete for economic activity through their national tax systems.

Notes

1. Harmonized System (HS) categories 61, 62, and 64, using mirror data for 2017. The HS trade statistics coding system is an internationally standardized system of names and numbers to classify traded products.

2. Moazzem and Radia (2018); Solotaroff et al. (2019).
3. World Bank, Women, Business, and the Law (database). See appendix A for a description of the databases used in this Report.
4. *Guardian* (2019).
5. International buyers have joined together to work in a coordinated way through the Fire and Building Safety Accord (mostly European companies and unions) and through the Alliance for Bangladesh Worker Safety (a group of mostly North American buyers). These groups have committed to inspecting their supplier factories and developing plans for training and remediation. In March 2013, the government, business organizations, and trade unions signed the National Action Plan on Fire Safety, which calls for action to improve legislation, expand labor inspection capacity, and implement systematic inspections of all factories. The Accord, the Alliance, and the National Action Plan have agreed to use a common standard for certification to ensure that building structural integrity and fire safety are adequate. The World Bank Group has also been working with the private sector on improving water usage through the Partnership for Clean Textiles and labor standards through ILO-IFC Better Work (ILO and IFC 2016). In April 2018, after the five-year anniversary of the Rana Plaza disaster, a crowdsourcing effort to map all garment factories in Bangladesh and make the mapping publicly available was initiated by the private sector, with collaboration among Sourcemap, the C&A Foundation, and BRAC University.
6. Markup is a measure of market power. It is the ratio of the price to the marginal cost of production after all tangible and intangible factors of production have been remunerated.
7. (See also UNCTAD 2013.)
8. Quantitative methods that trace the internationally fragmented nature of GVCs through global input–output links typically predict larger gains from trading across borders than models without those international links (Antràs and de Gortari 2017; Caliendo and Parro 2013).

9. Based on regression results from Constantinescu, Mattoo, and Ruta (2019).

10. Costa (2019).

11. Output per worker controlling for capital as well as foreign ownership status, sector, and regional differences. The percent differences are obtained by multiplying 100 by the exponential of the coefficient in figure 3.3 minus 1.

12. Doane (2015).

13. Amiti and Konings (2007); De Loecker et al. (2016); Goldberg et al. (2010).

14. For example, Antràs, Fort, and Tintelnot (2017) show that U.S. firms that began importing from China after that country's accession to the World Trade Organization also increased their sourcing from domestic suppliers in the United States.

15. Amiti and Konings (2007); Constantinescu, Mattoo, and Ruta (2017); Goldberg et al. (2010); Halpern, Koren, and Szeidl (2015); Taglioni and Winkler (2016).

16. Sampson (2015).

17. The benefits for producers in developing countries that relational GVCs produce are sizable. In Colombia, a program led by a multinational firm induced suppliers to upgrade their coffee farms while planting trees and incorporating more efficient and sustainable practices. About 80,000 farmers and 1,000 villages benefited from the program: the quality of coffee improved, while farmers' profits increased by 15 percent (Macchiavello and Miquel-Florensa 2019).

18. Barrientos et al. (2016).

19. Krishnan (2017).

20. Gereffi, Humphrey, and Sturgeon (2005).

21. Macchiavello and Miquel-Florensa 2017).

22. Dearden, Reed, and Van Reenen (2006).

23. Iberahim (2013).

24. Hansson (2008).

25. Alfaro-Ureña, Manelici, and Vasquez (2019).

26. Pietrobelli, Marin, and Olivari (2018).

27. Gereffi, Humphrey, and Sturgeon (2005).

28. De Loecker (2007, 2013); Iacovone and Crespi (2010).

29. Kugler and Verhoogen (2012).

30. More abundant use of capital and skills is important for upgrading (Bustos 2011). Handling greater product complexity requires reinforcing intermediate management layers relative to plant workers (Caliendo et al. 2015). Sourcing strategies are also essential for upgrading. As part of this process, the organization of procurement practices and sourcing becomes an integral part of a firm's strategy and an increasingly important part of its competitive advantage (Antràs, Fort, and Tintelnot 2017). It not only matters which international linkages a firm creates, but also which domestic supplier linkages it creates (Eslava, Fieler, and Xu 2015). Connections with demanding and refined customers supports learning (Fieler, Eslava, and Xu 2014). But these customers have high standards of quality and delivery that may be more difficult to learn than simpler tasks, even with deep relationships within the GVC. A firm's ability to quickly absorb increasing amounts of more complex technology, know-how, and an ability to produce at high quality

determine outcomes (Costinot, Oldenski, and Rauch 2011).

31. Dihel et al. (2018).

32. General Statistics Office (GSO), Vietnam, Enterprise Surveys, 2014 (database).

33. World Bank, Enterprise Surveys (database). The surveys are administered to a developing country sample of 81 countries.

34. Calì et al. (2016). In a sample of 39 countries, the number of jobs supported by $1 million in gross exports declined from 38 in 2001 to 16 in 2011. The number of manufacturing jobs supported by $1 million in gross exports declined from 20 in 2001 to 12 in 2011. Similarly, the number of jobs per unit of domestic value added in exports declined between 2000 and 2014 in seven developing countries, where technical change in GVCs has been biased against the use of labor (Pahl and Timmer 2019).

35. Calì et al. (2016). In a sample of 39 countries with data for 2001 and 2011, 26 countries experienced a decline in export jobs' share of total jobs. On average, 28 percent of jobs were supported by exports in 2011, compared with 31 percent in 2001.

36. Rodrik (2018).

37. In Vietnam, firms that import and export employ more workers than firms that export only and firms that do not trade, controlling for sector and province fixed effects as well as state- and foreign-ownership. In Mexico, firms that have relationships with buyers, as well as firms that export and import, also see higher employment than firms that only import or only export. This holds even when considering regional, sector, and foreign ownership characteristics of firms. Across developing countries, firms that import and export employ more workers than one-way traders or nontraders.

38. The percent differences are obtained as 100 multiplied by the exponential of the coefficient in figure 3.6 minus 1.

39. Manufacturing firms with 10 or more workers. The share of GVC firms in total employment increased from 19 percent to 23 percent between 2000 and 2014.

40. Costa (2019).

41. In the nonagricultural enterprise sector. Employment in GVC firms increased by 130 percent between 2004 and 2014, compared with 115 percent for import-only and 47 percent for export-only firms (with six or more employees). Total employment in nontrading firms increased slightly faster, by 136 percent, although this difference is likely not statistically significant.

42. From 30 percent to 31 percent.

43. World Bank, World Development Indicators (database).

44. Total manufacturing employment increased from 2.7 million to 5.7 million between 2004 and 2014. Formal manufacturing jobs (covered by social security) in formal enterprises increased from 2.4 million to 4.5 million. GVC firms accounted for 14 percent of formal jobs in 2004 and 17 percent in 2014.

45. According to the General Statistics Office (GSO) of Vietnam, the number of employees age 15 and older in

manufacturing was 5,031,200 in 2005 (first year of available data) and 7,414,700 in 2014 (see annual employed population and annual employed population 15 years of age and above, with breakdown by kind of economic activity, items, and year).

46. Lopez-Acevedo and Robertson (2016).

47. Kumar (2017).

48. Faucheux et al. (2014).

49. Within provinces, a 1 percentage point increase in the share of firms that participate in GVCs is associated with a 3.2 percent increase in female employment and a 2.1 percent increase in male employment.

50. Staritz, Plank, and Morris (2016).

51. Faucheux et al. (2014).

52. World Bank (2018).

53. Heath and Mobarak (2015). There is a 28 percent decrease in the likelihood of getting married and a 29 percent decrease in the likelihood of childbirth.

54. There is no additional wage premium for relational firms over export-only or import-only firms.

55. Using firm-level and customs transaction–level data covering the period 2000–2006 with the methods of propensity score matching, difference in differences, and generalized propensity score. See Lu et al. (2019).

56. Shepherd and Stone (2012) also find that firms with the strongest international linkages—export, import, and foreign-owned—pay higher wages.

57. The poverty elasticity of growth depends on various factors, including its incidence (changes in inequality); the initial distribution of land; wealth and income; education levels among the poor; other forms of past public investment; and local institutions, including unions (Ferreira, Leite, and Ravallion 2010; Ravallion and Datt 2002). Also see Dollar and Kraay (2002) and Ferreira and Ravallion (2008).

58. *Food poverty* is defined as the inability, even if all available income is used in the home, to buy only the goods of a basic food basket. *Capabilities poverty* is defined as the insufficiency of disposable income to acquire the value of the food basket and carry out the expenses necessary in health and education, even dedicating the total income of the home to nothing more than these purposes. *Asset poverty* is defined as the insufficiency of income available to acquire the food basket, as well as to make the necessary expenses in health, clothing, housing, transportation, and education, even if the entire household income is used exclusively for the acquisition of these goods and services.

59. This is consistent with the observation that migrant workers are more likely to work in the formal sector in Vietnam (McCaig and Pavcnik 2015).

60. Maertens, Minten, and Swinnen (2012).

61. Foreign direct investment (FDI) inflows—an important determinant of GVC participation—has similarly been associated with poverty reduction, but also income inequality in Ethiopia, Vietnam, and Turkey (World Bank 2019a). In Ethiopia, the overall effects of FDI are largely positive, with large effects on poverty reduction and limited effects on income inequality. In Vietnam, FDI has significantly benefited shared prosperity, but some increases in income inequality emerged as well. In Turkey, the average worker has experienced some benefits, although many of the benefits have accrued to high-skilled workers, thereby revealing the greatest increase in income inequality.

62. De Loecker and Eeckhout (2018).

63. Markups can increase because prices are higher or because costs are lower, or it may be a combination of both when markets are not perfectly competitive, meaning that firms can affect prices. The effect of GVC participation on firms' markups depends on whether the reductions in costs, or the gains from GVC participation, are fully passed on to the consumer through lower prices.

64. Autor et al. (2017).

65. Including the Herfindahl index and the number of firms within an industry.

66. Based on regression analysis that considers country- and industry-specific characteristics. It is possible that these producers focus on tasks that have the highest value added because of demand (such as for a particular design, concept, or service—that is, where market power is the result of innovation or merit), and they outsource those tasks that have lower value added (such as producing homogeneous parts). Ideally, one would disentangle the channels and the different effects, but this is not possible with the data.

67. De Loecker et al. (2016).

68. De Loecker and Warzynski (2009).

69. Excluding China and controlling for country fixed effects. The negative correlation also holds without controlling for country fixed effects for samples that exclude and include China.

70. Diez, Fan, and Villegas-Sánchez (2019).

71. Choi, Fukase, and Zeufack (2019). Controlling for state ownership, firm size, and capital intensity.

72. Gradzewicz and Mućk (2019).

73. Dauda, Nyman, and Cassim (forthcoming).

74. Karabarbounis and Neiman (2013).

75. Barkai (2016) finds that in the United States profits have risen as a share of GDP and that the pure capital share of income (defined as the value of the capital stock times the required rate of return on capital over GDP) has fallen alongside the labor share.

76. Autor et al. (2017) also point to outsourcing as a possible explanation for the declining labor share in the United States.

77. Reshef and Santoni (2019) investigate the same phenomenon in a sample of 26 EU countries over the period 1995–2014. They suggest that the labor-reducing effect of capital intensity may be a short-run phenomenon. The authors document a recovery from 2007 onward, explained by within-industry changes, notably for skilled labor associated with the complementarities between capital intensity and skilled labor. Domestic within-industry factors also explain a recovery in the labor share from 2007 on in the larger sample of 63 developing and developed economies.

78. Oxera Consulting (2019).

79. Goldberg and Pavcnik (2007).

80. Feenstra and Hanson (1996, 1997).

81. Verhoogen (2008).
82. Antràs, Garicano, and Rossi-Hansberg (2006); Kremer and Maskin (2006).
83. Bernard, Moxnes, and Ulltveit-Moe (2018).
84. Griliches (1969); Krusell et al. (2000).
85. Becker, Eckholm, and Muendler (2013); Bloom and Van Reenen (2011); Dearden, Reed, and Van Reenen (2006); Hansson (2008).
86. Hijzen et al. (2013); Javorcik (2014); Markusen and Trofimenko (2009); te Velde and Morrissey (2003). Other studies link GVC participation to increased wage disparity between skilled and unskilled labor in developed countries, although little literature exists for developing countries. Using matched employer-employee data for Denmark for 1995–2006, Hummels et al. (2014) characterize the link between offshoring and wages across skill levels and find that offshoring increases (lowers) the high-skilled (low-skilled) wage. Similarly, using matched employer-employee data for Italy, Borghi and Crinò (2013) confirm that offshoring contributes to widening the wage gap between skilled and less skilled employees.
87. Shepherd and Stone (2012).
88. Crinò (2012).
89. Morris and Staritz (2014).
90. Darko, Occhiali, and Vanino (2018).
91. World Bank staff estimates. Analysis of OECD's TiVA database for 61 countries shows that a one-unit standard deviation increase in domestic value added in exports of intermediate products is associated with a 0.1 decline in the dispersion of the urban size distribution within countries.
92. Autor, Dorn, and Hanson (2016).
93. de Vries (2017); Farole, Hollweg, and Winkler (2018).
94. Chan (2013).
95. Dihel et al. (2018).
96. Amanor (2012).
97. Dolan and Sutherland (2003); Kritzinger et al. (2004).
98. ILO (2016).
99. ILO and IFC (2016).
100. Faber, Krause, and Sánchez de la Sierra (2017).
101. Harrison and Scorse (2010).
102. Staritz and Reis (2013).
103. Veliu et al. (2009).
104. World Bank and IFC (2014).
105. Muñoz-Boudet (2018).
106. World Bank (2011).
107. Costa (2019).
108. Staritz and Reis (2013).
109. Christian (2013).
110. World Bank (2011).
111. Staritz and Reis (2013).
112. Ahmed (2013).
113. World Bank, Women, Business, and the Law (database).
114. This section focuses on direct taxation. However, GVCs also pose challenges for indirect taxes, such as the value added tax (VAT), although these are more tractable (see Clavey et al., forthcoming).
115. See IMF, OECD, United Nations, and World Bank (2015).
116. As corporate profits have gone up, the average revenue from corporate income tax has remained stable over the same period. But as other sources of income (such as wage income) as a share of GDP have gone down, these factors have indirectly reduced the scope for governments to secure adequate tax revenue.
117. Cooper et al. (2016).
118. For a more complete listing, see Beer, de Mooij, and Liu (2018).
119. UNCTAD (2015).
120. Crivelli, de Mooij, and Keen (2016).
121. Auerbach (2017).
122. de Mooij and Ederveen (2008).

References

Ahmed, Ghada. 2013. "Global Value Chains, Economic Upgrading, and Gender in the Call Center Industry." In *Global Value Chains, Economic Upgrading, and Gender: Case Studies of the Horticulture, Tourism, and Call Center Industries*, edited by Cornelia Staritz and José Guilherme Reis, 73–105. Report 83233 (January). Washington, DC: World Bank.

Alfaro-Ureña, Alonso, Isabela Manelici, and José P. Vasquez. 2019. "The Effects of Joining Multinational Supply Chains: New Evidence from Firm-to-Firm Linkages." Paper presented at the National Bureau of Economic Research conference, "Firms, Networks, and Trade," Cambridge, MA, March 15.

Amanor, Kojo Sebastian. 2012. "Global Resource Grabs, Agribusiness Concentration, and the Smallholder: Two West African Case Studies." *Journal of Peasant Studies* 39 (3–4): 731–49.

Amiti, Mary, and Jozef Konings. 2007. "Trade Liberalization, Intermediate Inputs, and Productivity: Evidence from Indonesia." *American Economic Review* 97 (5): 1611–38.

Antràs, Pol, and Alonso de Gortari. 2017. "On the Geography of Global Value Chains." NBER Working Paper 23456 (May), National Bureau of Economic Research, Cambridge, MA.

Antràs, Pol, Teresa C. Fort, and Felix Tintelnot. 2017. "The Margins of Global Sourcing: Theory and Evidence from U.S. Firms." *American Economic Review* 107 (9): 2514–64.

Antràs, Pol, Luis Garicano, and Esteban Rossi-Hansberg. 2006. "Offshoring in a Knowledge Economy." *Quarterly Journal of Economics* 121 (1): 31–77.

Atkin, David. 2016. "Endogenous Skill Acquisition and Export Manufacturing in Mexico." *American Economic Review* 106 (8): 2046–85.

Auerbach, Alan J. 2017. "Demystifying the Destination-Based Cash Flow Tax." NBER Working Paper 23881 (September), National Bureau of Economic Research, Cambridge, MA.

Autor, David H., David Dorn, and Gordon H. Hanson. 2016. "The China Shock: Learning from Labor-Market Adjustment to Large Changes in Trade." NBER Working Paper 21906 (January), National Bureau of Economic Research, Cambridge, MA.

Autor, David H., David Dorn, Lawrence F. Katz, Christina Patterson, and John Van Reenen. 2017. "Concentrating on the Fall of the Labor Share." *American Economic Review: Papers and Proceedings* 107 (5): 180–85.

Barkai, Simcha. 2016. "Declining Labor and Capital Shares." Working Paper 2, Stigler Center for the Study of the Economy and the State, Booth School of Business, University of Chicago.

Barrientos, Stephanie. 2014. "Gender and Global Value Chains: Challenges of Economic and Social Upgrading in Agri-Food." EUI Working Paper RSCAS 2014/96, Robert Schuman Centre for Advanced Studies, European University Institute, San Domenico di Fiesole, Italy.

Barrientos, Stephanie, Peter Knorringa, Barbara Evers, Margareet Visser, and Maggie Opondo. 2016. "Shifting Regional Dynamics of Global Value Chains: Implications for Economic and Social Upgrading in African Horticulture." *Environment and Planning A: Economy and Space* 48 (7): 1266–83.

Becker, Sascha O., Karolina Eckholm, and Marc-Andreas Muendler. 2013. "Offshoring and the Onshore Composition of Tasks and Skills." *Journal of International Economics* 90 (1): 91–106.

Beer, Sebastian, Ruud Aloysius de Mooij, and Li Liu. 2018. "International Corporate Tax Avoidance: A Review of the Channels, Magnitudes, and Blind Spots." IMF Working Paper WP/18/168 (July 23), International Monetary Fund, Washington, DC.

Bernard, Andrew B., Andreas Moxnes, and Karen Helene Ulltveit-Moe. 2018. "Two-Sided Heterogeneity and Trade." *Review of Economics and Statistics* 100 (3): 424–39.

Blanchard, Emily, and William W. Olney. 2017. "Globalization and Human Capital Investment: Export Composition Drives Educational Attainment." *Journal of International Economics* 106: 165–83.

Bloom, Nicholas, and John Van Reenen. 2011. "Human Resource Management and Productivity." In *Handbook of Labor Economics*, vol. 4B, edited by David Card and Orley Ashenfelter, 1697–1767. San Diego: Elsevier.

Borghi, Elisa, and Rosario Crinò. 2013. "Service Offshoring and Wages: Worker-Level Evidence from Italy." LIUC Papers in Economics 264 (April), Serie Economia e Impresa 70, Carlo Cattaneo University, Castellanza, Italy.

Borin, Alessandro, and Michele Mancini. 2015. "Follow the Value Added: Bilateral Gross Export Accounting." Temi di discussione (Economic Working Paper) 1026, Economic Research and International Relations Area, Bank of Italy.

———. 2019. "Measuring What Matters in Global Value Chains and Value-Added Trade." Policy Research Working Paper 8804, World Bank, Washington, DC.

Bustos, Paula. 2011. "Trade Liberalization, Exports, and Technology Upgrading: Evidence on the Impact of MERCOSUR on Argentinian Firms." *American Economic Review* 101 (1): 304–40.

Calì, Massimiliano, Joseph Francois, Claire H. Hollweg, Miriam Manchin, Doris Anita Oberdabernig, Hugo Alexander Rojas-Romagosa, Stela Rubinova 2016. "The Labor Content of Exports Database." Policy Research Working Paper 7615, World Bank, Washington, DC.

Caliendo, Lorenzo, Giordano Mion, Luca David Opromolla, and Esteban Rossi-Hansberg. 2015. "Productivity and Organisation in Portuguese Firms." CEPR Discussion Paper 10993, Centre for Economic Policy Research, London.

Caliendo, Lorenzo, and Fernando Parro. 2013. "Estimates of the Trade and Welfare Effects of NAFTA." *Review of Economic Studies* 82 (1): 1–44.

Chan, Man-Kwun. 2013. "Informal Workers in Global Horticulture and Commodities Value Chains: A Review of Literature." WIEGO (Global Trade) Working Paper 28 (June), Women in Informal Employment Globalizing and Organizing, Cambridge, MA.

Choi, Jieun, Emiko Fukase, and Albert Zeufack. 2019. "Global Value Chain (GVC) Participation, Competition, and Markup: Firm-Level Evidence from Ethiopia." Background paper, World Bank, Washington, DC.

Christian, Michelle. 2013. "Global Value Chains, Economic Upgrading, and Gender in the Tourism Industry." In *Global Value Chains, Economic Upgrading, and Gender: Case Studies of the Horticulture, Tourism, and Call Center Industries*, edited by Cornelia Staritz and José Guilherme Reis, 43–71. Report 83233 (January). Washington, DC: World Bank.

Clavey, Colin, Jonathan Leigh Pemberton, Jan Loeprick, and Marijn Verhoeven. Forthcoming. "International Tax Reform, Digitization, and Developing Economies." World Bank, Washington, DC.

CONEVAL (Mexico, Consejo Nacional de Evaluación de la Política de Desarrollo Social [National Council for the Evaluation of Social Development Policy]) and World Bank. 2013. "Desigualdad, pobreza, y politica social en Mexico: Una perspectiva del largo plazo." CONEVAL and World Bank, Mexico City.

Constantinescu, Cristina, Aaditya Mattoo, and Michele Ruta. 2017. "Does Vertical Specialization Increase Productivity?" Policy Research Working Paper 7978, World Bank, Washington, DC.

———. 2019. "Does Vertical Specialization Increase Productivity?" *World Economy*. Published electronically April 10. https://doi.org/10.1111/twec.12801.

Cooper, Joel, Randall Fox, Jan Loeprick, and Komal Mohindra. 2016. *Transfer Pricing and Developing Economies: A Handbook for Policy Makers and Practitioners*. Directions in Development: Public Sector Governance Series. Washington, DC: World Bank.

Costa, Carlos. 2019. "The Cashew Value Chain in Mozambique." With contributions by Christopher Delgado. Jobs Working Paper 32, World Bank, Washington, DC.

Costinot, Arnaud, Lindsay Oldenski, and James Rauch. 2011. "Adaptation and the Boundary of Multinational Firms." *Review of Economics and Statistics* 93 (1): 298–308.

Crinò, Rosario. 2012. "Service Offshoring and the Skill Composition of Labor Demand." *Oxford Bulletin of Economics and Statistics* 74 (1): 20–57.

Crivelli, Ernesto, Ruud Aloysius de Mooij, and Michael Keen. 2016. "Base Erosion, Profit Shifting, and Developing Countries." *FinanzArchiv: Public Finance Analysis* 72 (3): 268–301.

Darko, Christian K., Giovanni Occhiali, and Enrico Vanino. 2018. "The Chinese Are Here: Firm Level Analysis of Import Competition and Performance in Sub-Saharan

Africa." FEEM Working Paper 014.2018 (April), Note di Lavoro Series, Fondazione Eni Enrico Mattei, Milan.

Dauda, Seidu, Sara Nyman, and Aalia Cassim. Forthcoming. "Product Market Competition, Productivity, and Jobs: The Case of South Africa." Policy Research Working Paper, World Bank, Washington, DC.

Dearden, Lorraine, Howard Reed, and John Van Reenen. 2006. "The Impact of Training on Productivity and Wages: Evidence from British Panel Data." *Oxford Bulletin of Economics and Statistics* 68 (4): 397–421.

De Loecker, Jan K. 2007. "Do Exports Generate Higher Productivity? Evidence from Slovenia." *Journal of International Economics* 73 (1): 69–98.

———. 2013. "Detecting Learning by Exporting." *American Economic Journal: Microeconomics* 5 (3): 1–21.

De Loecker, Jan K., and Jan Eeckhout. 2018. "Global Market Power." NBER Working Paper 24768 (June), National Bureau of Economic Research, Cambridge, MA.

De Loecker, Jan K., Pinelopi Koujianou Goldberg, Amit Kumar Khandelwal, and Nina Pavcnik. 2016. "Prices, Markups, and Trade Reform." *Econometrica* 84 (2): 445–510.

De Loecker, Jan K., and Frederic Warzynski. 2009. "Markups and Firm-Level Export Status." NBER Working Paper 15198 (July), National Bureau of Economic Research, Cambridge, MA.

de Mooij, Ruud Aloysius, and Sjef Ederveen. 2008. "Corporate Tax Elasticities: A Reader's Guide to Empirical Findings." *Oxford Review of Economic Policy* 24 (4): 680–97.

de Vries, Gaaitzen J. 2017. "Drivers of Job Polarization: A Global Supply Chain Perspective." With Laurie Reijnders, WTO Trade Dialogues Lecture Series, presented at Groningen Growth and Development Centre, Faculty of Economics and Business, University of Groningen, Groningen, the Netherlands, March 2.

Diez, Federico J., Jiayue Fan, and Carolina Villegas-Sánchez. 2019. "Global Declining Competition." IMF Working Paper WP/19/82, International Monetary Fund, Washington, DC.

Dihel, Nora, Arti Grover Goswami, Claire H. Hollweg, and Anja Slaney. 2018. "How Does Participation in Value Chains Matter to African Farmers?" Policy Research Working Paper 8506, World Bank, Washington, DC.

Doane, Seth. 2015. "A Look at China's 'Button Town.'" *CBS Evening News*, October 8. https://www.cbsnews.com/news /welcome-to-button-town-china/.

Dolan, Catherine, and Kirsty Sutherland. 2003. "Gender and Employment in the Kenya Horticulture Value Chain." Globalisation and Poverty Discussion Paper No. 8, Globalisation and Poverty Research Programme, Institute of Development Studies, Brighton, U.K.

Dollar, David, and Aart Kraay. 2002. "Growth Is Good for the Poor." *Journal of Economic Growth* 7 (3): 195–225.

Eslava, Marcela, Ana Cecília Fieler, and Daniel Yi Xu. 2015. "(Indirect) Input Linkages." *American Economic Review: Papers and Proceedings* 105 (5): 662–66.

Faber, Benjamin, Benjamin Krause, and Raúl Sánchez de la Sierra. 2017. "Artisanal Mining, Livelihoods, and Child Labor in the Cobalt Supply Chain of the Democratic Republic of Congo." Policy Report (May 6), Center

for Effective Global Action, University of California, Berkeley.

Farole, Thomas, Claire H. Hollweg, and Deborah E. Winkler. 2018. "Trade in Global Value Chains: An Assessment of Labor Market Implications." Jobs Working Paper 18 (July 16), World Bank, Washington, DC.

Faucheux, Benoit, J. R. del Rosario, Gomera Economistas Asociados, and Ayitika. 2014. "Analyse des Chaînes Logistiques en Haïti, Fiche Filière: Textile." World Bank, Washington, DC; Catram Consultants, Paris. https://www .catram-consultants.com/portfolio-item/logistiques -haiti/#tab-id-2.

Feenstra, Robert C., and Gordon H. Hanson. 1996. "Foreign Investment, Outsourcing, and Relative Wages." In *The Political Economy of Trade Policy: Papers in Honor of Jagdish Bhagwati*, edited by Robert C. Feenstra, Gene M. Grossman, and Douglas A. Irwin, 89–128. Cambridge, MA: MIT Press.

———. 1997. "Foreign Direct Investment and Relative Wages: Evidence from Mexico's Maquiladoras." *Journal of International Economics* 42 (3–4): 371–93.

Ferreira, Francisco H. G., Phillippe George Leite, and Martin Ravallion. 2010. "Poverty Reduction without Economic Growth? Explaining Brazil's Poverty Dynamics, 1985–2004." *Journal of Development Economics* 93 (1): 20–36.

Ferreira, Francisco H. G., and Martin Ravallion. 2008. "Global Poverty and Inequality: A Review of the Evidence." Policy Research Working Paper 4623, World Bank, Washington, DC.

Fieler, Ana Cecília, Marcela Eslava, and Daniel Yi Xu. 2014. "Trade, Skills, and Quality Upgrading: A Theory with Evidence from Colombia." NBER Working Paper 19992, National Bureau of Economic Research, Cambridge, MA.

Frederick, Stacey. 2018. "Apparel Skills Mapping and Functional Upgrading in Cambodia: Jobs Diagnostic." World Bank, Washington, DC.

Gereffi, Gary, John Humphrey, and Timothy Sturgeon. 2005. "The Governance of Global Value Chains." *Review of International Political Economy* 12 (1): 78–104.

Global Reporting Initiative and United Nations Global Compact. 2017. "Business Reporting on the SDGs: An Analysis of the Goals and Targets." https://www.globalreporting .org/resourcelibrary/GRI_UNGC_Business-Reporting-on -SDGs_Analysis-of-Goals-and-Targets.pdf.

Goldberg, Pinelopi Koujianou, Amit Kumar Khandelwal, Nina Pavcnik, and Petia Topalova. 2010. "Imported Intermediate Inputs and Domestic Product Growth: Evidence from India." *Quarterly Journal of Economics* 125 (4): 1727–67.

Goldberg, Pinelopi Koujianou, and Nina Pavcnik. 2007. "Distributional Effects of Globalization in Developing Countries." *Journal of Economic Literature* 45 (1): 39–82.

Gradzewicz, Michał, and Jakub Mućk. 2019. "Globalization and the Fall in Markups." Warsaw School of Economics, Warsaw. https://www.nbp.pl/badania/seminaria/20ii2019 .pdf.

Griliches, Zvi. 1969. "Capital-Skill Complementarity." *Review of Economics and Statistics* 51 (4): 465–68.

GSO (General Statistics Office, Vietnam). 2012. *Result of the Viet Nam Household Living Standards Survey 2012*. Hanoi: GSO.

Guardian. 2019. "Bangladesh Strikes: Thousands of Garment Workers Clash with Police over Poor Pay." January 13. https://www.theguardian.com/world/2019/jan/14/bangladesh-strikes-thousands-of-garment-workers-clash-with-police-over-poor-pay.

Halpern, Laszlo, Miklos Koren, and Adam Szeidl. 2015. "Imported Inputs and Productivity." *American Economic Review* 105 (12): 3660–3703.

Hansson, Bo. 2008. "Job-Related Training and Benefits for Individuals: A Review of Evidence and Explanations." OECD Education Working Paper 19, Organisation for Economic Co-operation and Development, Paris.

Harrison, Ann, and Jason Scorse. 2010. "Multinationals and Anti-sweatshop Activism." *American Economic Review* 100 (1): 247–73.

Heath, Rachel, and A. Mushfiq Mobarak. 2015. "Manufacturing Growth and the Lives of Bangladeshi Women." *Journal of Development Economics* 115 (July): 1–15.

Hijzen, Alexander, Pedro S. Martins, Thorsten Schank, and Richard Upward. 2013. "Foreign-Owned Firms around the World: A Comparative Analysis of Wages and Employment at the Micro-Level." *European Economic Review* 60 (May): 170–88.

Hummels, David L., Rasmus Jørgensen, Jakob Munch, and Chong Xiang. 2014. "The Wage Effects of Offshoring: Evidence from Danish Matched Worker-Firm Data." *American Economic Review* 104 (6): 1597–1629.

Iacovone, Leonardo, and Gustavo Crespi. 2010. "Catching Up with the Technological Frontier: Micro-Level Evidence on Growth and Convergence." *Industrial and Corporate Change* 19 (6): 2073–96.

Iberahim, Hadijah. 2013. "Vertical Integration into Global Value Chains and Its Effects on Skill Development." In *IEEE Business Engineering and Industrial Applications Colloquium*, 28–33. Piscataway, NJ: Institute of Electrical and Electronics Engineers.

IFC (International Finance Corporation). 2018. "Horticulture: Value Chain Analysis, Azerbaijan." South Caucasus Gender Assessment Technical Assistance (P160432) Report (April), IFC, Washington, DC.

ILO (International Labour Organization). 2016. *Sectoral Studies on Decent Work in Global Supply Chains: Comparative Analysis of Opportunities and Challenges for Social and Economic Upgrading*. Geneva: International Labour Office. https://www.ilo.org/public/libdoc/ilo/2016/490742.pdf.

ILO (International Labour Organization) and IFC (International Finance Corporation). 2016. "Progress and Potential: How Better Work Is Improving Garment Workers' Lives and Boosting Factory Competitiveness." International Labour Office, Geneva. https://betterwork.org/dev/wp-content/uploads/2016/09/BW-Progress-and-Potential_Web-final.pdf.

IMF (International Monetary Fund). 2019. "Corporate Taxation in the Global Economy." Policy Paper 19/007 (March 10), IMF, Washington, DC.

IMF (International Monetary Fund), OECD (Organisation for Economic Co-operation and Development), United Nations, and World Bank. 2015. *Options for Low-Income Countries' Effective and Efficient Use of Tax Incentives for Investment: A Report to the G-20 Development Working Group by the IMF, OECD, UN, and World Bank*. Washington, DC: World Bank.

INEGI (Mexico, Instituto Nacional de Estadistica y Geografia [National Institute of Statistics and Geography]). 2014. "Economic Censuses." INEGI, Aguascalientes, Mexico. https://en.www.inegi.org.mx/programas/ce/2014/.

Javorcik, Beata Smarzynska. 2014. "Does FDI Bring Good Jobs to Host Countries?" Policy Research Working Paper 6936, World Bank, Washington, DC.

Jensen, Robert. 2012. "Do Labor Market Opportunities Affect Young Women's Work and Family Decisions? Experimental Evidence from India." *Quarterly Journal of Economics* 127 (2): 753–92.

Karabarbounis, Loukas, and Brent Neiman. 2013. "The Global Decline of the Labor Share." NBER Working Paper 19136 (June), National Bureau of Economic Research, Cambridge, MA.

Katz, Jorge, and Carlo Pietrobelli. 2018. "Natural Resource-Based Growth, Global Value Chains, and Domestic Capabilities in the Mining Industry." *Resources Policy* 58 (October): 11–20.

Kremer, Michael R., and Eric Maskin. 2006. "Globalization and Inequality." Weatherhead Center for International Affairs, Harvard University, Cambridge, MA.

Krishnan, Aarti. 2017. "The Origin and Expansion of Regional Value Chains: The Case of Kenyan Horticulture." *Global Networks* 18 (2): 238–63.

Kritzinger, Andrienetta, Stephanie Barrientos, and Hester Rossouw. 2004. "Global Production and Flexible Employment in South African Horticulture: Experiences of Contract Workers in Fruit Exports." *Sociologia Ruralis* 44 (1): 17–39.

Krusell, Per, Lee E. Ohanian, José-Victor Ríos-Rull, and Giovanni L. Violante. 2000. "Capital-Skill Complementarity and Inequality: A Macroeconomic Analysis." *Econometrica* 68 (5): 1029–53.

Kugler, Maurice, and Eric A. Verhoogen. 2012. "Prices, Plant Size, and Product Quality." *Review of Economic Studies* 79 (1): 307–39.

Kumar, Ruchira. 2017. "Global Value Chains: A Way to Create More, Better, and Inclusive Jobs." *Jobs and Development* (blog), July 12. https://blogs.worldbank.org/jobs/global-value-chains-way-create-more-better-and-inclusive-jobs.

Li, Bingjing. 2018. "Export Expansion, Skill Acquisition and Industry Specialization: Evidence from China." *Journal of International Economics* 114 (September): 346–61.

———. 2019. "Skill-Biased Imports, Human Capital Accumulation, and the Allocation of Talent." https://pdfs.semanticscholar.org/1497/7c5d507017f14afaeec804011564af95514b.pdf.

Lopez-Acevedo, Gladys, and Raymond Robertson, eds. 2016. *Stitches to Riches? Apparel Employment, Trade, and Economic Development in South Asia*. Directions in Development: Poverty Series. Washington, DC: World Bank.

Lu, Yue, Yunlong Lu, Rui Xie, and Xiao Yu. 2019. "Does Global Value Chain Engagement Improve Firms' Wages: The Empirical Evidence from China." *World Economy*. Published electronically April 16. https://doi.org/10.1111/twec.12805.

Macchiavello, Rocco, and Josepa Miquel-Florensa. 2017. "Vertical Integration and Relational Contracts: Evidence from the Costa Rica Coffee Chain." CEPR Discussion Paper No. DP11874, Centre for Economic Policy Research, London. SSRN: https://ssrn.com/abstract=2924734.

———. 2019. "Buyer-Driven Upgrading in GVCs: The Sustainable Quality Program in Colombia," CEPR Discussion Papers 13935, Centre for Economic Policy Research, London.

Maertens, Miet, Bart Minten, and Johan F. M. Swinnen. 2012. "Modern Food Supply Chains and Development: Evidence from Horticulture Export Sectors in Sub-Saharan Africa." *Development Policy Review* 30 (4): 437–97.

Markusen, James, and Natalia Trofimenko. 2009. "Teaching Locals New Tricks: Foreign Experts as a Channel of Knowledge Transfers." *Journal of Development Economics* 88 (1): 121–31.

McCaig, Brian, and Nina Pavcnik. 2015. "Informal Employment and a Growing Globalizing Low-Income Country." NBER Working Paper 20891 (January), National Bureau of Economic Research, Cambridge, MA.

Moazzem, Khondaker Golam, and Marzuka Ahmad Radia. 2018. "'Data Universe' of Bangladesh's RMG Enterprises: Key Features and Limitations." Centre for Policy Dialogue, Dhaka.

Morris, Mike, and Cornelia Staritz. 2014. "Industrialization Trajectories in Madagascar's Export Apparel Industry: Ownership, Embeddedness, Markets, and Upgrading." *World Development* 56 (April): 243–57.

Muñoz-Boudet, Ana María. 2018. "Value Chain Selection: Azerbaijan." South Caucasus Gender Assessment Technical Assistance (P160432) Report (May), International Finance Corporation, Washington, DC.

Navarro, Lucas. 2018. "The World Class Supplier Program for Mining in Chile: Assessment and Perspectives." *Resources Policy* 58 (October): 49–61.

Oxera Consulting. 2019. "Increased Market Power: A Global Problem That Needs Solving?" *Oxera Agenda* (January), Oxera Consulting, Oxford, U.K. https://www.oxera.com/wp-content/uploads/2019/01/Increased-market-power.pdf.

Pahl, Stefan, and Marcel Peter Timmer. 2019. "Jobs in Global Value Chains: A New Measurement Framework and Analysis for Fourteen Countries in Africa and Asia." Background paper, World Bank, Washington, DC.

Pew Research Center. 2014. "Faith and Skepticism about Trade, Foreign Investment." Pew Report (September 16), Pew Research Center, Washington, DC. https://www.pewresearch.org/global/2014/09/16/faith-and-skepticism-about-trade-foreign-investment/.

Pietrobelli, Carlo, Anabel Marin, and Jocelyn Olivari. 2018. "Innovation in Mining Value Chains: New Evidence from Latin America." *Resources Policy* 58 (October): 1–10.

Pietrobelli, Carlo, and Jocelyn Olivari, eds. 2018. "Special Issue on Mining Value Chains, Innovation, and Learning." *Resources Policy* 58 (October).

Ravallion, Martin, and Guarav Datt. 2002. "Why Has Economic Growth Been More Pro-Poor in Some States of India than Others?" *Journal of Development Economics* 68 (2): 381–400.

Reshef, Ariell, and Gianluca Santoni. 2019. "Are Your Labor Shares Set in Beijing? The View through the Lens of Global Value Chains." Working paper (May), Paris School of Economics, Paris.

Rocha, Nadia, and Deborah E. Winkler. 2019. "Trade and Female Labor Participation: Stylized Facts Using a Global Dataset." Background paper, *How Can 21st Century Trade Help to Close the Gender Gap?*, World Bank and World Trade Organization.

Rodrik, Dani. 2018. "New Technologies, Global Value Chains, and Developing Economies." NBER Working Paper 25164, National Bureau of Economic Research, Cambridge, MA.

Said-Allsopp, Muhaimina, and Anne Tallontire. 2015. "Pathways to Empowerment? Dynamics of Women's Participation in Global Value Chains." *Journal of Cleaner Production* 107 (November): 114–21.

Sampson, Thomas. 2015. "Dynamic Selection: An Idea Flows Theory of Entry, Trade, and Growth." *Quarterly Journal of Economics* 131 (1): 315–80.

Shepherd, Ben, and Susan Stone. 2012. "Global Production Networks and Employment: A Developing Country Perspective." OECD Trade Policy Paper 154 (May 14), Organisation for Economic Co-operation and Development, Paris.

Solotaroff, Jennifer L., Aphichke Kotikula, Tara Lonnberg, Snigdha Ali, Rohini P. Pande, and Ferdous Jahan. 2019. *Voices to Choices: Bangladesh's Journey in Women's Economic Empowerment.* Washington, DC: World Bank.

Staritz, Cornelia, Leonhard Plank, and Mike Morris. 2016. "Global Value Chains, Industrial Policy, and Sustainable Development: Ethiopia's Apparel Export Sector." ICTSD Country Case Study (November), International Centre for Trade and Sustainable Development, Geneva.

Staritz, Cornelia, and José Guilherme Reis, eds. 2013. *Global Value Chains, Economic Upgrading, and Gender: Case Studies of the Horticulture, Tourism, and Call Center Industries.* Report 83233 (January). Washington, DC: World Bank.

Suzuki, Aya, Yukichi Mano, and Girum Abebe. 2018. "Earnings, Savings, and Job Satisfaction in a Labor-Intensive Export Sector: Evidence from the Cut Flower Industry in Ethiopia." *World Development* 110 (October): 176–91.

Taglioni, Daria, and Deborah E. Winkler. 2016. *Making Global Value Chains Work for Development.* Trade and Development Series. Washington, DC: World Bank.

te Velde, Dirk Willem, and Oliver Morrissey. 2003. "Do Workers in Africa Get a Wage Premium if Employed in Firms Owned by Foreigners?" *Journal of African Economies* 12 (1): 41–73.

UNCTAD (United Nations Conference on Trade and Development). 2013. *World Investment Report 2013: Global Value Chains: Investment and Trade for Development.* Geneva: United Nations.

———. 2015. *World Investment Report 2015: Reforming International Investment Governance.* Geneva: United Nations.

Van den Broeck, Goedele, and Miet Maertens. 2017. "Does Off-Farm Wage Employment Make Women in Rural Senegal Happy?" *Feminist Economics* 23 (4): 250–75.

Veliu, Atdhe, Nebiyeluel Gessese, Catherine Ragasa, and Christine Okali. 2009. "Gender Analysis of Aquaculture Value Chains in Northeast Vietnam and Nigeria."

Agriculture and Rural Development Discussion Paper 44, World Bank, Washington, DC.

Verhoogen, Eric A. 2008. "Trade, Quality Upgrading, and Wage Inequality in the Mexican Manufacturing Sector." *Quarterly Journal of Economics* 123 (2): 489–530.

Whittaker, D. Hugh, Tianbiao Zhu, Timothy Sturgeon, Mon Han Tsai, and Toshie Okita. 2010. "Compressed Development." *Studies in Comparative International Development* 45 (4): 439–67.

World Bank. 2011. "Understanding Gender in Agricultural Value Chains: The Cases of Grapes/Raisins, Almonds, and Saffron in Afghanistan." Report 62323-AF (May), Agriculture and Rural Development Unit, Sustainable Development Department, South Asia Region, World Bank, Washington, DC.

———. 2018. "Apparel GVC Analysis: Sri Lanka." World Bank, Washington, DC. https://www.theciip.org/sites/ciip/files /Apparel%20GVC%20analysis.pdf.

———. 2019a. "Global Investment Competitiveness Report 2019/2020." World Bank, Washington, DC.

———. 2019b. *World Development Report 2019: The Changing Nature of Work*. Washington, DC: World Bank.

World Bank and IFC (International Finance Corporation). 2014. "The Fruit of Her Labor: Promoting Gender-Equitable Agribusiness in Papua New Guinea." Report ACS10004 (June 30), World Bank and IFC, Washington, DC.

World Bank and World Trade Organization. Forthcoming. "How Can 21st Century Trade Help to Close the Gender Gap?" Washington, DC, and Geneva.

Macroeconomic implications

Key findings

- **Global value chains (GVCs) are associated with greater synchronization of economic activity across countries.** When production in one country relies on inputs from another country, then economic activity in the two countries is linked.

- **GVCs create strong links in price formation, implying that inflation in one country is more likely to spill over to its direct and indirect trading partners.** In this sense, GVC participation is associated with the rising synchrony in inflation across countries.

- **In GVC countries, episodes of export growth are linked to episodes of import growth.** This finding implies that the consequences of currency movements for export volumes are likely to be dampened.

- **GVCs amplify the costs of protectionism for trade and growth.** The back-and-forth movement in tasks and parts across borders means that trade barriers are incurred multiple times. Protectionism is therefore costlier for growth and welfare.

- **Trade agreements have the potential to reshape the geography of production.** The prevalence of rules of origin as well as the productivity gains associated with a reduction in the price of imported inputs imply that trade agreements have systemic consequences for the allocation of production across countries in GVCs.

Global value chains (GVCs) strengthen the economic connections between countries. Instead of individually selling final goods and competing for the same customers, countries are increasingly related through rigid production linkages that bind them to a common fate. This international interdependence means that policies and economic conditions in one country affect its trading partners and propagate to the rest of the world. As a result, the benefits of international coordination (and the costs of not coordinating) have increased. Four are investigated in this chapter.

First, production linkages are associated with greater synchrony of economic activity across countries. When production in one country relies on inputs from its trading partners, the economic conditions in other countries affect its domestic activity and its ability to thrive. Although international trade in finished products cannot be associated with any change in the synchronization of GDP across countries, trade in intermediate inputs can be.

Second, input–output linkages create strong links in price formation, implying that inflation in one country is more likely to spill over to its direct and indirect trading partners. In this sense, GVC participation is associated with the rising synchrony of both real economic activity and inflation across countries. At the same time, the actions of national central banks, through production linkages between domestic and foreign firms, can have important consequences in other countries as well.

Third, because of the interconnections in production, episodes of export growth are linked with similar growth in imports. Thus the consequences of currency movements for export volumes are likely to be reduced and become harder to predict. Export volumes do not react to the exchange rate with the direct partner; they react to the exchange rate in the country of final consumption. When a government changes the value of its currency, it affects the trade flows of other countries throughout the production chain.

Fourth, the rise of GVCs influences the impact of regional trade agreements and how policy makers should think about the possible diversion of trade flows. When firm-to-firm relationships are rigid, the benefits of accessing new markets can be shared throughout the production chains with countries not part of the trade agreement. Conversely, the disruption created by trade wars and dismantled agreements may be transmitted to other trading partners and may not be easily avoided by reorganizing buyer–seller relationships.

Posing new challenges for governments and policy makers, these realities require closer cooperation between countries. National policies are now transmitted to other countries, and the GVC feedback loop can reduce their effectiveness. Because of the high interdependence of production structures, decisions by governments and central banks are more likely to have a systemic impact, and their effectiveness depends on policies in various parts of the world. Moreover, regional agreements can have global ripples, and economic issues are more global, calling for coordinated solutions. In view of their rigid ties, GVCs would benefit from multilateral institutions helping to coordinate policy worldwide, including through the formulation of product standards, investment and intellectual property protections, or the timing of fiscal adjustments.

Synchronizing economic activity

When the production of a good in Vietnam requires inputs from Indonesia and is then used for production in China, it is only natural that supply and demand shocks in one country will be felt by its suppliers and customers. One example of such an arrangement is Nike, one of the world's most valuable sport brands. It has segmented its footwear production across these three South Asian countries.

Over the past 30 years, the co-movement of economic activity has surged globally. In the 1980s, economic cycles in different countries were largely independent of one another, especially in middle- and low-income countries, with correlations of less than 0.1. But economic activity has since become much more correlated—the most for high-income countries followed by middle-income and low-income countries (figure 4.1).

The recent worldwide increase in economic synchrony stems in part from the rise of GVCs. Production is increasingly organized according to a "world factory" view, which drastically changes how shocks are transmitted across borders. To understand the importance of those changes, one could start by taking a look at the world before the recent increase in international production linkages.[1]

If two countries were open to trade and produce a similar final good—say, clothes—their firms competed in the same markets for the same customers. As a result, a country's increase in productivity could enhance consumer welfare everywhere, but it could also mean tougher competition for its competitors. In this sense, good news in one country could be bad

Figure 4.1 In all income groups, countries' economic activity has become more synchronized since the mid-1990s

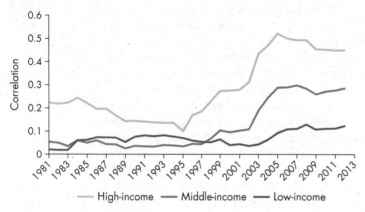

Source: WDR 2020 team, using data from the World Bank's WDI database. See appendix A for a description of the databases used in this Report.

Note: Each year represents the midpoint of a 10-year moving window. Each line represents the average of all country-pair GDP correlations, taken over all country-pairs containing at least one country in the income group considered (high, middle, and low).

Figure 4.2 Greater synchrony of economic activity is associated with GVCs

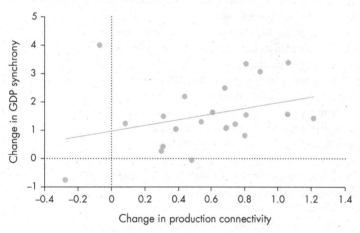

Sources: WDR 2020 team, using data from the World Bank's WDI and WITS databases.

Note: Each dot represents a pair of regions—for example, East Asia and Pacific and Sub-Saharan Africa are one region-pair, and Latin America and the Caribbean and South Asia are another. The x-axis measures the change in production connectivity defined as the total trade in intermediates as a share of GDP of both regions, taken between the 2002–11 and 1982–1991 time windows. The y-axis measures the proportional change in the GDP correlation over time. Region-pair values are computed by taking the simple average of all country-pairs between two regions.

news for its trading partners. For example, higher efficiency in the garment industry in Bangladesh could be linked to a contraction in production in India.

In a world dominated by GVCs, however, countries increasingly trade intermediate inputs and are tied by rigid production linkages. From the iPhone to Nutella,

the design, production, and after-sales services of many goods are spread over many countries. This new reality changes the extent to which economic fluctuations are transmitted across countries. If a country's productivity rises, the consequences are good for trading partners buying its goods as inputs as well as for the country's own suppliers: they can share the competitive gains throughout all production stages, and they are less likely to cannibalize each other's market shares.[2]

The positive historical association between total trade and business cycle co-movement was driven by trade in intermediate inputs (figure 4.2). Although GVCs are not the only factor explaining the surge in GDP correlation across countries, evidence about their role is growing. From both a microdata and firm perspective[3] and a more macroaggregate perspective,[4] studies have shown that the recent increase in input–output linkages enhanced the co-movements in economic activity.

The economic fates of countries participating in GVCs are tied to one another. Even if at the microeconomic level individual firms in different countries continue to compete, the aggregate health of an economy now depends on the health of other economies supplying inputs or buying outputs. Based on a panel of 150 countries for the last 50 years, one study finds that moving from the 25th to the 75th percentile of trade in intermediate inputs is associated with an increase in the GDP correlation of 28 percentage points.[5]

Synchrony of economic activity across countries is a key indicator for many macroeconomic policies. For example, the extent to which the West African Economic and Monetary Union (WAEMU) can be considered an optimal currency area largely depends on the synchrony of business cycles among all member countries. And beyond currency considerations, the synchrony of economic activity among countries signals interdependence, so both good news and bad news are transmitted from one country to the next.

Large firms dominate the global economy. For 32 developing countries, the five largest exporters in a country account on average for a third of its exports and nearly half of its export growth.[6] Although the importance of large firms in driving economic growth is not new, their impact reached a more global scale with the expansion of GVCs. With production more fragmented across countries, any local decision that improves a global firm's ability to thrive will have a positive impact on many countries.

Propagating shocks

The strength of propagating shocks across firms and countries is a function of the "specificity" of the input–output relationship, which is not always well represented by simply looking at cost shares across countries. When an input is needed for production, losing access to it can be disastrous, even though the input may not represent a large share of total production costs (box 4.1). The interdependence of firms and countries thus increases to the extent that GVCs involve custom products that cannot be easily replaced.

GVCs are also linked to greater synchrony of financial cycles and stock market returns. Looking at the consequences of natural disasters, firms experience a larger drop in stock market returns when disasters hit their specific suppliers than their non-specific ones.[7] A specific supplier is a supplier that produces an input tailored just for its customers. When such a relationship exists, both buyer and supplier may face less flexibility in changing their business partners when needed, as it takes time to find another firm willing and able to produce or buy specific inputs.

Box 4.1 The Japanese earthquake and the costs of supply chain disruptions

Businesses tend to focus on the possibility that inputs will increase in price or be delivered late. But disruptions by extreme events are a rising threat. In 2018 extreme weather caused $81 billion in global losses; in 2017, $300 billion.[a] Natural disasters can have unanticipated cascading impacts along GVCs, shocking distribution and supply networks worldwide.

In March 2011, the Tōhoku earthquake, measuring 9.0 on the Richter scale, hit Japan's northeast coast. Several tsunamis followed, devastating coastal areas, flooding and disabling local nuclear power stations, and creating a national nuclear crisis. The triple disaster was catastrophic for GVCs, particularly the automotive, computer, and consumer electronics producers that rely heavily on Japanese suppliers of specialized parts and components. As Japanese production of automotive equipment drew to a halt, senior executives at Toyota, Honda, Opel, Nissan, and General Motors froze production lines in several factories worldwide, leading to losses of $70 million a day.[b]

Famously, automakers temporarily stopped orders for cars in colors that required a specialty pigment called Xirallic, which gives cars a glittery shine. Xirallic is produced only in Japan, and its production was badly affected during the nuclear crisis.

In electronics, the problems were similar. The many specialized connectors, speakers, microphones, batteries, and sensors produced in Japan had few or no substitutes. At the time, it was estimated that about a third of Apple's flash drives came from Toshiba, Japan, and the rest from the Republic of Korea.[c]

Quantifying the global impact of such a disaster is not easy. For the transport equipment industry, the disruption cost an estimated $139 billion (in value added), with Japan suffering about 40 percent of the impact and the rest falling mainly on the United States (25 percent), China (8 percent), the European Union (8 percent), and Canada (7 percent).[d]

The substitutability of inputs is a critical determinant of supply chain shocks. In one study of U.S. affiliates of Japanese firms, the degree of the shock depended not on the level of Japanese ownership, but on the U.S. affiliate's ability to replace in the short run imported intermediates from Japan with alternative inputs.[e] In the month following the crisis, U.S. manufacturing output fell about 1 percent and remained significantly below previous levels for the next six months.

These findings are particularly relevant to buyers and suppliers holding low inventories and relying heavily on just-in-time production to keep inventory costs low. Risk management strategies to diversify suppliers and reduce firm sensitivity to inventory shortages and delays in logistics will become more important as environment-related disasters increase.

a. Swiss Re (2019).
b. *Automotive News* (2011).
c. Lohr (2011).
d. Arto, Andreoni, and Rueda Cantuche (2015).
e. Boehm, Flaaen, and Pandalai-Nayar (2019).

Synchronizing inflation

International input–output linkages also create strong links in price formation, implying that inflation in one country is more likely to spill over to its direct and indirect trading partners (figure 4.3). Such linkages account for an estimated half of the global component of producer price index inflation.[8] Although imported inflation has been a factor in the consumer price index, its extension to producer prices has policy implications for central banks.

When designing their monetary policy and targeting a given inflation rate, authorities need to account for the economic conditions and strategies of their direct and indirect trading partners. In this sense, GVC participation is associated with the rising synchrony of not only real economic activity but also inflation across countries.

Backward GVC participation is associated with an increase in the globalization of inflation. For each country, the change in the correlation between domestic and world inflation over the past decade is associated with an increase in the amount of imported inputs used in production.

The fragmentation of production across countries also plays a role in the synchrony of inflation expectations, which feeds back into current inflation (figure 4.4). For example, although economists have long recognized domestic and global output gaps (measures of

the "slack" in an economy) in estimating the inflation pressure in the economy, GVCs have been shown to significantly increase the global factors at the expense of purely domestic ones.

Furthermore, an increase in imports and exports of intermediate inputs is associated with a decline in the relative weight of the domestic output gap in favor of global economic conditions in the formation of inflation (figure 4.5). Because imported intermediates can be used to produce goods that are either reexported further or consumed in the domestic economy, such a result points to a synchronization of inflation across all sectors. This finding is in line with Ha, Kose, and Ohnsorge (2019), who show that inflation synchronization has been significant across all inflation measures since 2001, whereas it was previously prominent only for inflation measures that included mostly tradable goods.

Finally, GVCs are not only associated with the co-movement of inflation patterns but also may be linked to the global reduction in inflation. The emergence of independent central banks and better monitoring in many countries has played an important role, but a recent study by the Organisation for Economic Co-operation and Development (OECD) also suggests that GVCs have contributed to lower inflation via downward pressures on labor through heightened competition across countries to attract tasks, in particular when low-wage countries are integrated in supply chains.[9]

Figure 4.3 **The synchrony of inflation increased between 1988 and 2010**

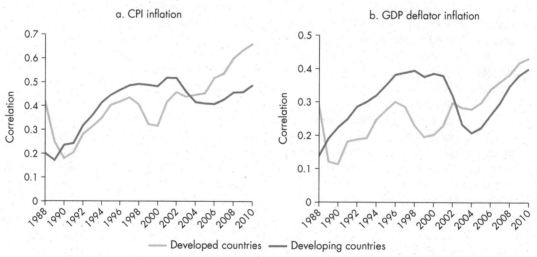

Source: WDR 2020 team, using data from the World Bank's WDI database.

Note: For each country, the correlation between domestic and world inflation was determined using two measures of price levels: the consumer price index (CPI) in panel a and the GDP deflator in panel b. An average was then taken across two income groups in order to plot the evolution of this average correlation. Each year represents the midpoint of a 15-year rolling window.

Reducing the effect of devaluations

Economics textbooks presume a relationship between movements in a country's exchange rate and its export volumes. When the currency depreciates, export volumes are expected to increase by some amount, and that amount is called the exchange rate elasticity of exports. Yet some recent significant exchange rate movements, such as those in the United Kingdom in 2007–09 and in Japan in 2012–14, were not associated with large movements in trade volumes.[10] This perceived unresponsiveness of exports to exchange rate fluctuations has raised the question of whether the exchange rate elasticity of export volumes has changed or even dropped to zero.

For all country income groups, changes in a country's exports and imports have become more correlated over time (figure 4.6). Upper-middle-income countries especially, many of whom are engaged in GVCs in Europe, have seen a sharp rise.

Over the last decades, short-term growth in exports has been accompanied by import growth. Contrary to what the standard quantitative trade models of importing predict, a country's aggregate imported input share increases after large depreciations.[11] This can be explained by the fact that exporting firms are often also importers, and export opportunities are accompanied by a need to import.

The latest research suggests that all production linkages can have an impact on export elasticities and that GVCs can have complex effects on devaluation. By loosening the effectiveness of devaluations, the expansion of GVCs complicates the task of policy makers and creates the need for international coordination (box 4.2).

Greater participation in GVCs is expected to generate larger *bilateral* balances, but it is not necessarily associated with a larger *overall* trade balance. Indeed, current accounts at the country level are mostly determined by savings, investments, and cross-border finance and are little affected by changes in trade policy or by the links between imports and exports.

Policy makers in countries participating in GVCs should track not only the currency composition of inputs for production, but also the currency in the country of final absorption (figure 4.7).[12] In doing so, they should keep in mind the following points:

- An increase in an export's share of foreign value added from a country with a different currency

Figure 4.4 GVCs are associated with greater inflation synchrony in some countries

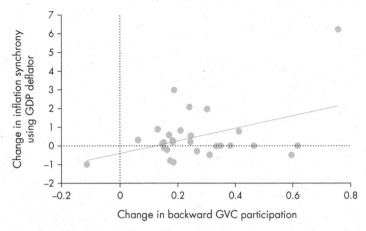

Sources: WDR 2020 team, using data from the World Bank's WDI database.

Note: Each dot represents a pair of regions—for example, East Asia and Pacific and Sub-Saharan Africa are one region-pair and Latin America and the Caribbean and South Asia are another. The x-axis measures the change, taken between the 2000–2009 and 1990–1999 time windows, in production connectivity defined as the total trade in intermediates as a share of GDP of both regions. The y-axis measures the proportional change in inflation correlation for the same time windows, where inflation is measured by the changes in the GDP deflator.

Figure 4.5 Trade in intermediate inputs increased the weight of global factors in inflation formation from 1983 to 2006

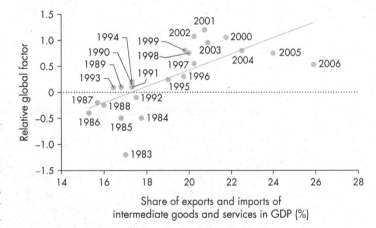

Source: Auer, Borio, and Filardo 2017.

Note: The relative global factor is the difference between domestic and global output gaps in the formation of inflation. The upward-sloping line shows the positive relationship between the global weight in domestic inflation (y-axis) and participation in GVCs (x-axis).

reduces the change in export price in response to exchange rate movements, thereby lessening the associated change in export volumes.

- A greater share of exports that return as imports to a country sharing the same currency weakens the

Figure 4.6 Export boosts tend to coincide with import boosts—more now than 30 years ago

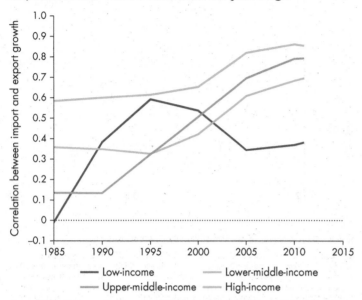

Sources: WDR 2020 team, using data on annual trade flows from the World Bank's WITS database and income group classification from the World Bank (2017 version).

Note: The year-on-year growth rate of total imports and exports was computed for each year. Then the correlation between these growth rates was computed for a rolling window of 10 years. Each year represents the midpoint of the 10-year rolling window.

exchange rate responsiveness of exports. Simply put, if the final demand driving exports is located at home or in a country with the same currency, a devaluation can do little to boost those trade flows.

• An increase in the share of exports used in the destination country to produce further reexports that are ultimately consumed in a third country increases the responsiveness of trade flows to the direct trading partner's nominal effective exchange rate, creating significant interdependence across countries. This mechanism underlines the international interconnections that characterize today's production processes.

With the international fragmentation of production across countries, export performance in one country can be driven by the demand addressed by firms located in other countries. In this sense, the consequences of devaluing a country's currency value propagate upstream in the supply chain and trigger export growth from its suppliers.

Interestingly, greater participation in international production decreases the exchange rate elasticity of exports, and a currency devaluation could also *reduce* a sector's exports to a specific destination. This happens whenever a sector has both a high share of foreign value added in exports and a high share of exports reimported and consumed in a country with the same currency.

Current GVC participation around the world already accounts for a significant decline in the efficiency of devaluation in boosting exports (figure 4.8). Sectors in the top decile of the backward GVC participation have an export elasticity that is only two-thirds

Box 4.2 Blunting the effects of devaluation on Turkey's exports

Changes in imports and exports are driven by many elements, and the value of currency is only one of them. Other important determinants are economic and financial conditions and the uncertainty in both direct and indirect trading partners, as well as possible changes in tariffs and nontariff barriers and the design of industrial policy in both domestic and foreign economies.

Without accounting for all these other factors, it is difficult to draw strong conclusions about the way GVCs are changing the link between devaluations and export volumes. With those caveats in mind, the recent devaluations in Turkey illustrate the mechanisms described in this chapter.

Turkey has moved rapidly from a current account that was relatively in balance up to 2000 to sustaining relatively

large current account deficits over the past 15 years. In 2015 the country was well integrated in GVCs, with its share of foreign value added in exports reaching 30 percent, almost 10 percentage points above the world average. Between 2015 and 2018, the real effective exchange rate depreciated by 25 percent, and such a large movement translated into only a modest 5 percent in export growth (much slower than the world's export growth of 8 percent during the same period) and 11 percent in import growth.

This relatively small adjustment is especially striking because recent World Bank studies have shown that historically Turkey's current account balance has been less persistent than is typically found in the cross-country literature, suggesting that it adjusts more rapidly to shocks.[a]

a. Knight, Nedeljkovic, and Portugal-Perez 2019.

Figure 4.7 With GVCs, devaluations can have complex consequences

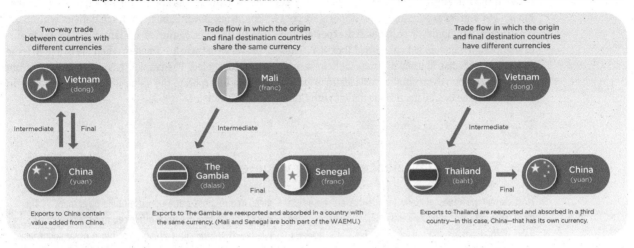

Exports less sensitive to currency devaluations | Exports sensitive to the exchange rate of trade partner

Source: WDR 2020 team.

Note: This figure summarizes the different channels through which GVCs can influence the elasticity of exports to devaluations. WAEMU = West African Economic and Monetary Union.

Figure 4.8 GVCs dampen the reaction of export volumes to currency movements

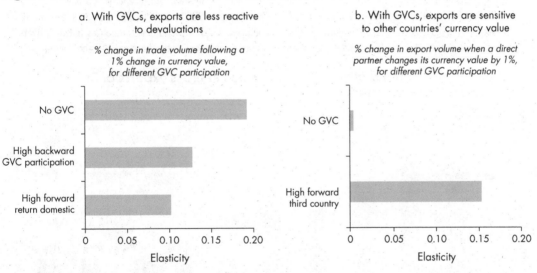

a. With GVCs, exports are less reactive to devaluations

% change in trade volume following a 1% change in currency value, for different GVC participation

b. With GVCs, exports are sensitive to other countries' currency value

% change in export volume when a direct partner changes its currency value by 1%, for different GVC participation

Source: WDR 2020 team.

Note: In panel a, the bars plot the value of the exchange rate elasticity for the 10 percent highest GVC participation indexes. "High backward GVC participation" refers to the foreign value added embedded in exports. "High forward return domestic" refers to the domestic value added embedded in exports and reexported back in the domestic economy. In panel b, the bars plot the value of the elasticity of export volume to the change in the nominal effective exchange rate of a direct partner. The values displayed in this figure use the estimation coefficients from de Soyres et al. (2018) on the elasticity of exports to exchange rate, as well as the interaction of this elasticity with a variable marking the intensity of GVC participation.

of the elasticity corresponding to sectors with no participation in GVCs. Moreover, the rise of production interconnections is associated with a significant sensitivity of export volume to foreign devaluations.

The relationship between exchange rate movements and export growth is also affected by the choice of invoicing currency as well as possible changes in markups. For example, because many international transactions are invoiced in U.S. dollars, some countries are more sensitive to the U.S. dollar exchange rate than the bilateral exchange rate.[13] Moreover, foreign investment enterprises in China are absorbing currency movements to partially stabilize their prices in local currency terms. By contrast, the prices charged by private, locally owned Chinese firms exhibit much more sensitivity to currency movements.[14]

Most current measures of trade imbalances are based on gross trade data, reflecting the difference between the value of total exports and total imports. But for GVCs, gross exports and gross imports are poor measures of the domestic value added exported and of the foreign value added consumed (box 4.3). Thus GVCs bias the distribution of trade deficits across trading partners, which might mislead trade policy. For example, the U.S. bilateral trade deficit with China is smaller when measured in trade in value added than when measured in gross trade. The reason? China buys many of the inputs for its exports from other countries. But U.S. bilateral trade deficits with many of those other countries are larger (or U.S. trade surpluses with them are smaller) when measured in trade in value added. The reason? Many U.S. imports from China incorporate the value of inputs originating in these countries.

Box 4.3 Trade imbalances in using value-added data

Most current measures of trade imbalances are based on gross trade data and simply reflect the difference between the value of total exports and total imports. For GVCs, however, gross exports and gross imports are not accurate measures of the domestic value added exported and of the foreign value added consumed. Thus over the past few years several researchers have highlighted the importance of building a more accurate picture of bilateral trade flows and the need to account for the evolution of bilateral value-added balances.[a]

For example, the U.S. bilateral trade deficit with China is smaller when measured in trade in value added than when measured in gross trade because China buys many of the inputs for its exports from other countries. However, U.S. bilateral trade deficits with some of those other countries are larger when measured in value-added terms because many U.S. imports from China contain inputs originating in these countries.

Based on the Trade in Value Added (TiVA) database from the Organisation for Economic Co-operation and Development (OECD) for 2015, figure B4.3.1 shows the 10 country-pairs with the largest differences between bilateral trade balances using gross exports and value-added

Figure B4.3.1 Computing bilateral trade balance in gross exports or in value-added exports matters

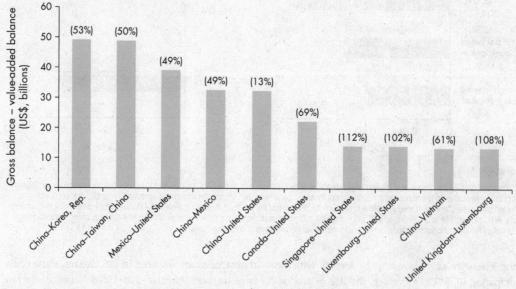

Source: WDR 2020 team, using data from OECD's TiVA database.

Note: The figure shows the 10 pairs of countries with the largest differences between their gross trade balance and their value-added trade balance. At the top of each bar, the difference in the gross and value-added balance is also expressed as a *share* of the gross trade balance. The indicator used to compute the gross trade balance is "EXGR: gross exports" in the TiVA database. The value-added trade balance is given by "BALVAFD: Value added embodied in final demand, balance" in the TiVA database. It is computed as the difference between domestic value added in foreign final demand, FFD_DVA, and foreign value added in domestic final demand, DFD_FVA.

(Box continues next page)

Box 4.3 **Trade imbalances in using value-added data** *(continued)*

exports, respectively. The difference, also expressed as a share of gross balance, shows how important it is to account for the value-added balance.

One method often used to compute value-added trade flow is based on manipulation of input–output tables to calculate the share of value added coming from any country embedded in any gross flow. Such a method, however, relies on strong proportionality assumptions. For example, when looking at the automotive industry in Mexico, this method assumes that the share of inputs from the United States is the same regardless of the destination of the trade flows—in other words, it assumes the same production process for all destinations for a given industry in a given country.

New findings from de Gortari (2019) reveal that this assumption does not hold in the data. Using data from the automotive industry, de Gortari finds a strong link between the destination of exports and the origin of the imported inputs: about 74 percent of all the foreign parts used by vehicle assemblers in Mexico that export to the

United States are imported from the United States itself. By contrast, only 18 percent of the imported parts used by Mexican firms exporting to Germany come from the United States. This finding implies that just looking at sectors to understand trade flows is not enough: one needs to deepen the analysis at both the sector and destination levels.

Finally, even though greater participation in GVCs is expected to generate larger bilateral balances, such an outcome is not necessarily associated with a larger overall trade balance. According to the International Monetary Fund's 2019 *World Economic Outlook*, there is a strong positive relationship between a country's participation in GVCs and the size of its absolute bilateral balances, whereas the relationship is much weaker when it comes to the size of the overall trade balance. Moreover, it has been shown that targeting bilateral trade deficits does not, in general, reduce a country's overall current account deficit. Indeed, macroeconomic policies as well as financial conditions tend to be the key forces explaining countries' overall trade balances.[b]

a. Johnson and Noguera (2012a, 2012b, 2017); Koopman, Wang, and Wei (2014).
b. IMF (2019). See also Ahn et al. (2019) for more on this subject.

Moreover, as noted by Amiti, Freund, and Bodine-Smith (2017), production linkages across countries lead to bilateral imbalances across countries, in the same way that large companies routinely run deficits with their suppliers: the company purchases inputs but sells little to these smaller firms. For example, Germany, despite running a large aggregate trade surplus, runs bilateral trade deficits with the Czech Republic, Hungary, and the Slovak Republic, the main low-cost suppliers in the European production chain.[15] Indeed, a bilateral deficit has little meaning for the aggregate trade balance. The same is true for the U.S.–Mexico relationship, where new measures from de Gortari (2019) highlight the high integration in the automotive industry (box 4.3).

Mitigating trade diversion and increasing trade

Production fragmentation knits together the economic interests of firms (and workers) up and down the supply chain. Before the proliferation of GVCs, trade liberalization often benefited local consumers at the expense of local producers. But with these new linkages, the producer gains from trade that used to

accrue only to foreign exporters are shared—and often divided differently—on both sides of the border.[16]

GVCs also change another standard paradigm of trade policy: the diversion of trade from a more efficient producer outside of a trade agreement to a less efficient producer inside of it. Traditionally, signing a trade agreement has been associated with an increase in trade flows within the agreement zone as well as a decrease in trade flows between the agreement zone and the rest of the world.[17] However, because of production linkages within GVCs, this standard view has been challenged.

A look at all regional trade agreements over the past 60 years reveals that agreements are associated with strong, positive trade creation: on signing the agreement, exports between member countries grow significantly, with estimates ranging from less than 10 percent to more than 80 percent, depending on the agreement and the countries. But there is also trade diversion: exports from nonmember to member countries can decrease, while exports from member to nonmember countries tend to increase slightly.

The reduction in imports within the agreement zone is, among other things, related to rules of origin on final goods. Those rules are defined to prevent nonmember countries from transshipping products through low-tariff agreement members to avoid high tariffs. In effect, the rules act as an input tariff in the sense that they distort sourcing decisions and divert trade in intermediate goods to higher-cost agreement members. Those mechanisms are quantitatively quite relevant: on average, Mexican imports of intermediate inputs from third countries relative to its partners in the North American Free Trade Agreement (NAFTA) would have been 45 percent higher without rules of origin.[18]

GVCs thus fundamentally change how local trade agreements affect global trade flows. With production fragmented across countries, rigid linkages have the potential to mitigate the diversion usually associated with regional trade agreements. For example, if a member country relies significantly on intermediate inputs from other member countries, signing a trade agreement actually strongly increases its exports to nonmember countries. The explanation comes from the supply side: firms gaining preferred access to their supplier within the free trade zone have a lower marginal cost and can expand their market share in other countries. In other words, countries forming a trade agreement import less from and export more to the rest of the world. Such an effect can lead to efficiency gains not only within the regional free trade zone but also in other parts of the world.[19]

Despite the rules of origin, when the share of intermediate goods increases between a nonmember country and a member country, the trade diversion of exports from the nonmember country to the member country is largely mitigated. Indeed, firms in member countries gaining access to larger markets within a free trade zone can transmit this positive shock to their own suppliers outside the agreement zone.

Moreover, an increase in the share of intermediate inputs between two countries is associated with higher trade creation upon signing a trade agreement and lower trade diversion when one of the two countries enters a separate trade agreement with other partners. This finding has consequences for trade negotiations. If signing a trade agreement creates positive spillovers to nonmember countries, the whole design of trade negotiations could be adapted to allow for more cross-country coordination, including countries that are not directly part of the trade agreement.

The return of protectionism

Protectionism saw a resurgence over the last two years, fueled by tensions between the United States and China. In 2018 the two countries imposed tariffs on each other, covering more than half of their bilateral trade (approximately 70 percent of U.S. exports to China and almost half of U.S. imports from China). The United States also imposed tariffs on other countries covering solar panels, washing machines, steel, and aluminum, sparking retaliation from the affected trading partners. At the same time, negotiations continued over the terms and timing of the United Kingdom's departure from the European Union (EU).

In the age of GVCs, this new wave of protectionism is likely to have significant costs:

- The hyperspecialization in tasks and parts across borders means that trade costs are incurred multiple times.
- Protective measures against any country have knock-on effects on all its trading partners in the value chain.
- GVCs also amplify the costs of trade policy uncertainty because firms are more reluctant to make further investments in new or existing relationships with foreign suppliers.
- Significant tariffs on inputs can force firms to incur large costs to reshape their existing supply chains, thereby causing potentially long-lasting disruptions in global investment and production.

According to a recent estimate, the tariffs already implemented would lead to a decline in U.S. imports of intermediate goods from China over the longer term by over 40 percent, much more than the declines in consumption and investment goods.[20] Furthermore, if the trade conflict worsens and leads to a slump in investor confidence, effects on global growth and poverty could be significant—up to 30.7 million people could be pushed into poverty measured as an income level of less than $5.50 a day, and global income could fall as much as $1.4 trillion in a worst-case scenario.[21] Low- and middle-income countries other than China would bear roughly half of the global income loss.[22]

GVCs amplify the costs of protection for trade and growth

A large body of empirical research has shown that an increase in trade costs significantly reduces trade flows. GVCs are affected to an even greater extent. The hyperspecialization in tasks and parts across borders means that trade barriers are incurred multiple times. Recent evidence reveals that protection and disintegration reduce both backward and forward linkages.[23] As shown in chapter 3, GVC trade has a bigger effect on growth and employment than standard trade. Protectionism is therefore costlier for growth and welfare.

Protection not only affects whether and how much countries participate in GVCs; it also affects *how* they participate. In sequential (or snakelike) GVCs, trade costs compound along the value chain and have a bigger effect on the downstream stages than on the upstream stages. This effect leads remote countries to specialize in upstream stages and more central countries to specialize in the more downstream stages.[24] An implication is that the effect of trade costs would be more significant for backward GVC participation than for forward participation and therefore would have stronger negative impacts on growth. Consistent with this view, recent studies estimate that the negative impacts of Brexit on trade and employment will be considerably larger than commonly expected because of backward linkages.[25]

GVCs fuel the transmission of protection

In a world of GVCs, bilateral trade barriers may spill over to products and countries not directly targeted by those barriers. As noted, protective measures against any country have knock-on effects on all its trading partners in the value chain.[26] For example, China's exports to the United States have significant value added from developed countries such as Japan, the Republic of Korea, or the United States and from developing countries including Indonesia or Malaysia (figure 4.9). U.S. tariffs on Chinese final goods therefore affect the intermediate producers in those economies. Similarly, Chinese tariffs on U.S. goods affect producers in Canada and Mexico. The supply chain *diffusion channels* determine how the local effects of a shock propagate upstream and downstream to trade partners in the same supply chain.

Protection may cause lasting disruptions in supply chains

Bilateral measures of protection create incentives for firms to reorganize their supply chain. The effects of protection on GVC participation may differ when GVCs are relational in nature. Because of protectionism, some of the links in the chain may be unable to provide parts, components, or services in time or under prespecified terms. These supply chain disruptions are particularly costly when firms cannot easily resort to alternative suppliers.

The lock-in effects associated with costly search and relationship-specific investments also have implications for the role of market size in attracting GVC activity. With relational GVCs, a large market may reduce search frictions.[27] Trade barriers imposed on large markets such as China or the European Union may therefore be particularly disruptive for firms in the country that imposes protection. For example, U.S. tariffs on the car industry would penalize U.S. companies reliant on Chinese parts, which are often difficult to source at home. Brexit will likely hit the U.K. producers relatively harder than those in the EU-27 because the United Kingdom is losing a larger market for suppliers.[28]

Evidence reveals that in the months after tariffs were imposed by the United States in 2018, they were paid in full by U.S. importers, generating aggregate welfare losses.[29] The resulting price hikes also affected supply chains. Imports of products subject to tariffs declined sharply, in part because importers turned to domestic products, but in part because companies shifted their sourcing to more expensive nontargeted sources such as Mexico and Vietnam.[30]

The effects of protection on consumer prices and welfare are likely to be even stronger if tariffs are applied globally, leaving firms unable to shift to other suppliers. Recent evidence reveals that when global tariffs on washing machines were applied in early 2018, their prices climbed about 12 percent for U.S. consumers—foreign manufacturers could no longer shift production to other countries.[31] Because protection and disintegration create incentives for firms to restructure their supply networks, the consequences of even a temporary increase in protection could persist.

If U.S.–China trade tensions are not resolved, they could disrupt GVCs. In particular, tariffs imposed by the United States on intermediate goods are likely to lead to a reallocation of sourcing of inputs across value chains between the United States and China, possibly causing adjustment costs in the sectors and locations affected by trade diversion.

Recent evidence also reveals how the impact of U.S.–China tariffs changes with time, the magnitude of protection, and the nature of products. Econometric analysis of the value and quantities of imports in the United States in 2018 and the first quarter of 2019 finds that the tariffs have led to significant declines in the affected imports by the United States from China.[32] This decline is relative not only to imports of affected products prior to tariff implementation, but also to imports of unaffected products, whether from China or third countries. The analysis also shows that higher tariff rates lead to larger declines and that declines become bigger over time as the policy change is perceived to be ongoing and agents adjust to the new situation (figure 4.10).

The U.S.–China tariffs have also affected products traded via GVCs. For intermediates likely to be associated with GVCs, such as parts and components and

Figure 4.9 The multilateral dimension of the U.S.–China trade war

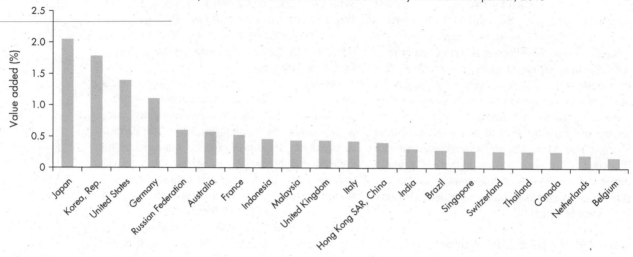

a. Chinese exports to United States: Share of value added by Chinese trade partner, 2015

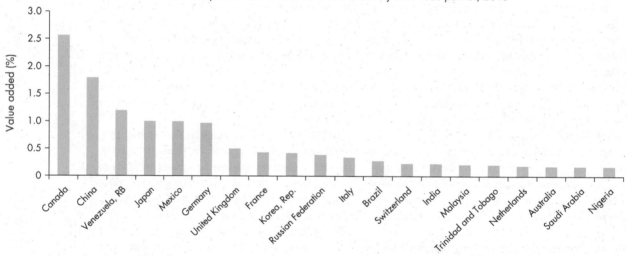

b. U.S. exports to China: Share of value added by U.S. trade partner, 2015

Source: WDR 2020 team, using data from Eora database.

Note: All countries including self are considered as sources of value added in U.S. and Chinese bilateral exports. That is, we include U.S. and Chinese domestic value added into the respective total value added in exports. The figures, however, plot only the share of the top 20 foreign partner countries in the total value added embedded in the U.S. and Chinese bilateral exports. Exports of goods and services are considered.

processed industrial supplies, the decline in import values and quantities are smaller than those for other products. This finding is consistent with the existence of long-term relationships in GVCs. Moreover, the finding that declines are larger and statistically significant for products targeted by higher tariff rates holds for GVC products as well. Although more data are needed, this result points to the first signs of GVC disruptions associated with the trade tensions.

Analysis using a computable general equilibrium model suggests that the longer-term effects may be even larger. It is estimated that U.S. imports of intermediate goods from China are likely to decline in the longer term by over 41 percent, or much more so than the declines in consumption goods by 9 percent and investment goods by 26 percent.[33]

Policy uncertainty is costlier under GVCs

GVCs also amplify the costs of sudden increases in trade policy uncertainty because firms may wait to invest in relationships with foreign suppliers until the uncertainty is resolved.[34] Firms experiencing more

Figure 4.10 Impact of U.S. tariffs on imports from China (average decline)

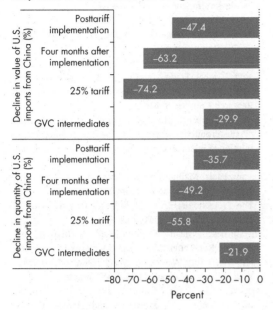

Source: WDR 2020 team, using data from U.S. Census (as of April 2019).

Note: Intermediates are defined as categories 42 and 53 in the Broad Economic Categories (BEC).

permanent uncertainty in specific countries are likely to shift sourcing to more expensive nontargeted markets and diversify their set of suppliers. Generalized and long-lasting trade policy uncertainty is likely to have even stronger negative impacts on GVC trade and investment. The increase in policy uncertainty in 2018 likely contributed to the recent trade slowdown. The negative association between economic policy uncertainty and trade growth emerges from a broader sample spanning 18 countries over 30 years.[35]

Notes

1. Burstein, Kurz, and Tesar (2008).
2. Johnson (2014).
3. Boehm, Flaaen, and Pandalai-Nayar (2019); di Giovanni, Levchenko, and Méjean (2018); Liao and Santacreu (2015).
4. de Soyres and Gaillard (2019a, 2019b).
5. de Soyres and Gaillard (2019a).
6. Freund and Pierola (2015).
7. Barrot and Sauvagnat (2016).
8. Auer, Borio, and Filardo (2017); Auer, Levchenko, and Sauré (2019).
9. See Andrews, Gal, and Witheridge (2018) and de Soyres and Franco (2019).
10. IMF (2015).
11. Blaum (2018).
12. See Amiti, Itskhoki, and Konings (2014) for a discussion of upstream GVC participation as well as its link with

markup fluctuations. See Ahmed, Appendino, and Ruta (2017) and de Soyres et al. (2018) for the role of downstream GVC participation. See Mattoo, Mishra, and Subramanian (2017) for related evidence on the role of third-country effects.
13. Boz, Gopinath, and Plagborg-Møller (2017).
14. Corsetti et al. (2018).
15. See Amiti, Freund, and Bodine-Smith (2017) for more details.
16. Blanchard (2010, 2017).
17. Mattoo, Mulabdic, and Ruta (2017).
18. Conconi et al. (2018).
19. de Soyres, Maire, and Sublet (2019).
20. Corong et al. (2019).
21. Constantinescu et al. (2019).
22. Constantinescu et al. (2019).
23. Laget et al. (2018).
24. Antràs and de Gortari (2017).
25. See Vandenbussche, Connell, and Simons (2017).
26. Bellora and Fontagné (2019).
27. Grossman and Helpman (2005).
28. Sampson 2017; Vandenbussche, Connell, and Simons (2017).
29. Amiti, Redding, and Weinsein (2019); Fajgelbaum et al. (2019).
30. Amiti, Redding, and Weinstein (2019).
31. Flaaen, Hortaçsu, and Tintelnot (2019).
32. Constantinescu et al. (2019).
33. Corong et al. (2019).
34. Graziano, Handley, and Limão (2018) find that Brexit uncertainty induced a net exit of traded products and a reduction in U.K.–EU bilateral trade flows, especially in industries with high sunk costs. Crowley, Exton and Han (2018) estimate that in 2016 over 5,200 U.K. firms declined to export new products to the European Union, and almost 4,000 U.K. firms halted product exports to the European Union. Entry (exit) in 2016 would have been 5.1 percent higher (4.3 percent lower) if firms exporting from the United Kingdom to the European Union had not faced greater trade policy uncertainty after June 2016.
35. Constantinescu, Mattoo, and Ruta (2017).

References

Ahmed, Swarnali, Maximiliano Appendino, and Michele Ruta. 2017. "Global Value Chains and the Exchange Rate Elasticity of Exports." *B.E. Journal of Macroeconomics* 17 (1): 1–24.

Ahn, JaeBin, Emine Boz, Maurice Obstfeld, and Petia Topalova. 2019. "Bilateral Trade Balances and Global Value Chains." Paper presented at 2019 International Economics and Finance Society–East Asian Economic Review Joint Seminar, "Structural Changes in the Global Economy: Global Value Chains and Financial Risks," Seoul National University Asia Center, June 5.

Amiti, Mary, Caroline L. Freund, and Tyler Bodine-Smith. 2017. "Why Renegotiating NAFTA Could Disrupt Supply Chains." *Liberty Street Economics* (blog), April 18, Federal Reserve Bank of New York. https://libertystreet

economics.newyorkfed.org/2017/04/why-renegotiating
-nafta-could-disrupt-supply-chains.html.

Amiti, Mary, Oleg Itskhoki, and Jozef Konings. 2014. "Importers, Exporters, and Exchange Rate Disconnect." *American
Economic Review* 104 (7): 1942–78.

Amiti, Mary, Stephen J. Redding, and David Weinstein. 2019.
"The Impact of the 2018 Trade War on U.S. Prices and
Welfare." NBER Working Paper 25672 (March), National
Bureau of Economic Research, Cambridge, MA.

Andrews, Dan, Peter Gal, and William Witheridge. 2018. "A
Genie in a Bottle? Globalisation, Competition, and Inflation." OECD Economics Department Working Paper 1462,
Document ECO/WKP(2018)10 (March 20), Organisation
for Economic Co-operation and Development, Paris.

Antràs, Pol, and Alonso de Gortari. 2017. "On the Geography
of Global Value Chains." NBER Working Paper 23456
(May), National Bureau of Economic Research, Cambridge, MA.

Arto, Iñaki, Valeria Andreoni, and José Manuel Rueda Cantuche. 2015. "Global Impacts of the Automotive Supply
Chain Disruption Following the Japanese Earthquake of
2011." *Economic Systems Research* 27 (3): 306–23.

Auer, Raphael, Claudio Borio, and Andrew Filardo. 2017.
"The Globalisation of Inflation: The Growing Impor-
tance of Global Value Chains." BIS Working Paper 602
(January 9), Bank for International Settlements, Basel,
Switzerland.

Auer, Raphael, Andrei A. Levchenko, and Philip Sauré. 2019.
"International Inflation Spillovers through Input Linkages." *Review of Economics and Statistics* 101 (3): 507–21.

Automotive News. 2011. "Opel, Renault Production Hit by
Shortage of Japanese Parts." March 18. https://www
.autonews.com/article/20110318/COPY01/303189860/opel
-renault-production-hit-by-shortage-of-japanese-parts.

Barrot, Jean-Noël, and Julien Sauvagnat. 2016. "Input Specificity and the Propagation of Idiosyncratic Shocks in
Production Networks." *Quarterly Journal of Economics* 131
(3): 1543–92.

Bellora, Cecilia, and Lionel Fontagné. 2019. "Shooting Oneself
in the Foot? Trade War and Global Value Chains." Paper
presented at Global Trade Analysis Project's 22nd Annual
Conference on Global Economic Analysis, "Challenges
to Global, Social, and Economic Growth," University of
Warsaw, Poland, June 19–21.

Blanchard, Emily J. 2010. "Reevaluating the Role of Trade
Agreements: Does Investment Globalization Make the
WTO Obsolete?" *Journal of International Economics* 82 (1):
63–72.

———. 2017. "Renegotiating NAFTA: The Role of Global
Supply Chains." In *Economics and Policy in the Age of Trump*,
edited by Chad P. Brown, 175–84. London: Centre for
Economic Policy Research.

Blaum, Joaquin. 2018. "Global Firms in Large Devaluations."
2018 Meeting Paper 593, Society for Economic Dynamics,
Department of Economics, Stonybrook University, Stonybrook, NY.

Boehm, Christoph Emanuel, Aaron B. Flaaen, and Nitya
Pandalai-Nayar. 2019. "Input Linkages and the Trans-
mission of Shocks: Firm-Level Evidence from the 2011

Tōhoku Earthquake." *Review of Economics and Statistics* 101
(1): 60–75.

Borin, Alessandro, and Michele Mancini. 2019. "Measuring
What Matters in Global Value Chains and Value-Added
Trade." Policy Research Working Paper 8804, World
Bank, Washington, DC.

Boz, Emine, Gita Gopinath, and Mikkel Plagborg-Møller.
2017. "Global Trade and the Dollar." NBER Working
Paper 23988 (November), National Bureau of Economic
Research, Cambridge, MA.

Burstein, Ariel, Christopher Kurz, and Linda Tesar. 2008.
"Trade, Production Sharing, and the International Trans-
mission of Business Cycles." *Journal of Monetary Economics*
55 (4): 775–95.

Conconi, Paola, Manuel García-Santana, Laura Puccio, and
Roberto Venturini. 2018. "From Final Goods to Inputs:
The Protectionist Effect of Rules of Origin." *American
Economic Review* 108 (8): 2335–65.

Constantinescu, Ileana Cristina, Aaditya Mattoo, and
Michele Ruta. 2017. "Trade Developments in 2016: Pol-
icy Uncertainty Weighs on World Trade." Global Trade
Watch (February 21), World Bank, Washington, DC.

Constantinescu, Ileana Cristina, Aaditya Mattoo, Michele
Ruta, Maryla Maliszewska, and Israel Osorio-
Rodarte. 2019. "Global Trade Watch 2018: Trade Amid
Tensions." Global Trade Watch (May 29), World Bank,
Washington, DC.

Corong, Erwin, Maryla Maliszewska, Maria Pereira, and
Dominique van der Mensbrugghe. 2019. "Global and
Regional Impacts of Trade Tensions on Global Value
Chains." World Bank, Washington, DC.

Corsetti, Giancarlo, Meredith Allison Crowley, Lu Han, and
Huasheng Song. 2018. "Markets and Markups: A New
Empirical Framework and Evidence on Exporters from
China." CFM Discussion Paper 1803, Centre for Macro-
economics, London School of Economics and Political
Science, London.

Crowley, Meredith Allison, Oliver Exton, and Lu Han. 2018.
"Renegotiation of Trade Agreements and Firm Export-
ing Decisions: Evidence from the Impact of Brexit on
UK Exports." Cambridge-INET Working Paper 2018/10
(December), Institute for New Economic Thinking, Uni-
versity of Cambridge, Cambridge, U.K.

de Gortari, Alonso. 2019. "Disentangling Global Value
Chains." NBER Working Paper 25868 (May), National
Bureau of Economic Research, Cambridge, MA.

de Soyres, François, and Sebastian Franco. 2019. "Inflation
Synchronization through GVCs." Unpublished working
paper, World Bank, Washington, DC.

de Soyres, François, Erik Frohm, Vanessa Gunnella, and
Elena Pavlova. 2018. "Bought, Sold, and Bought Again:
The Impact of Complex Value Chains on Export Elastic-
ities." Policy Research Working Paper 8535, World Bank,
Washington, DC.

de Soyres, François, and Alexandre Gaillard. 2019a. "Trade,
Global Value Chains, and GDP Comovement: An Empir-
ical Investigation." Unpublished working paper, World
Bank, Washington, DC.

———. 2019b. "Value Added and Productivity Linkages across Countries." Unpublished working paper, World Bank, Washington, DC.

de Soyres, François, Julien Maire, and Guillaume Sublet. 2019. "An Empirical Investigation of Trade Diversion and Global Value Chains." Unpublished working paper, World Bank, Washington, DC.

di Giovanni, Julian, Andrei A. Levchenko, and Isabelle Jeanne Méjean. 2018. "The Micro Origins of International Business-Cycle Comovement." *American Economic Review* 108 (1): 82–108.

Fajgelbaum, Pablo D., Pinelopi K. Goldberg, Patrick J. Kennedy, and Amit Kumar Khandelwal. 2019. "The Return to Protectionism." NBER Working Paper 25638, National Bureau of Economic Research, Cambridge, MA.

Flaaen, Aaron B., Ali Hortaçsu, and Felix Tintelnot. 2019. "The Production, Relocation, and Price Effects of U.S. Trade Policy: The Case of Washing Machines." BFI Working Paper 2019-61 (April), Becker Friedman Institute for Research in Economics, University of Chicago.

Freund, Caroline L., and Martha Denisse Pierola. 2015. "Export Superstars." *Review of Economics and Statistics* 97 (5): 1023–32.

Graziano, Alejandro, Kyle Handley, and Nuno Limão. 2018. "Brexit Uncertainty and Trade Disintegration." NBER Working Paper 25334 (December), National Bureau of Economic Research, Cambridge, MA.

Grossman, Gene M., and Elhanan Helpman. 2005. "Outsourcing in a Global Economy." *Review of Economic Studies* 72 (1): 135–59.

Ha, Jongrim, Ayhan Kose, and Franziska Lieselotte Ohnsorge. 2019. "Global Inflation Synchronization." Policy Research Working Paper 8768, World Bank, Washington, DC.

IMF (International Monetary Fund). 2015. *World Economic Outlook, October 2015: Adjusting to Lower Commodity Prices.* World Economic and Financial Surveys Series. Washington, DC: IMF.

———. 2019. *World Economic Outlook, April 2019: Growth Slowdown, Precarious Recovery.* Washington, DC: IMF.

Johnson, Robert Christopher. 2014. "Trade in Intermediate Inputs and Business Cycle Comovement." *American Economic Journal: Macroeconomics* 6 (4): 39–83.

Johnson, Robert Christopher, and Guillermo Noguera. 2012a. "Accounting for Intermediates: Production Sharing and Trade in Value Added." *Journal of International Economics* 86 (2): 224–36.

———. 2012b. "Fragmentation and Trade in Value Added over Four Decades." NBER Working Paper 18186 (June), National Bureau of Economic Research, Cambridge, MA.

———. 2017. "A Portrait of Trade in Value-Added over Four Decades." *Review of Economics and Statistics* 99 (5): 896–911.

Knight, David Stephen, Milan Nedeljkovic, and Alberto Portugal-Perez. 2019. "Turkey: An Empirical Assessment of the Determinants of the Current Account Balance." Policy Research Working Paper 8982, World Bank, Washington, DC.

Koopman, Robert B., Zhi Wang, and Shang-Jin Wei. 2014. "Tracing Value-Added and Double Counting in Gross Exports." *American Economic Review* 104 (2): 459–94.

Laget, Edith, Alberto Osnago, Nadia Rocha, and Michele Ruta. 2018. "Deep Agreements and Global Value Chains." Policy Research Working Paper 8491, World Bank, Washington, DC.

Liao, Wei, and Ana Maria Santacreu. 2015. "The Trade Comovement Puzzle and the Margins of International Trade." *Journal of International Economics* 96 (2): 266–88.

Lohr, Steve. 2011. "Stress Test for the Global Supply Chain." *New York Times,* March 19. https://www.nytimes.com/2011/03/20/business/20supply.html.

Mattoo, Aaditya, Prachi Mishra, and Arvind Subramanian. 2017. "Beggar-Thy-Neighbor Effects of Exchange Rates: A Study of the Renminbi." *American Economic Journal: Economic Policy* 9 (4): 344–66.

Mattoo, Aaditya, Alen Mulabdic, and Michele Ruta. 2017. "Trade Creation and Trade Diversion in Deep Agreements." Policy Research Working Paper 8206, World Bank, Washington, DC.

Sampson, Thomas. 2017. "Brexit: The Economics of International Disintegration." *Journal of Economic Perspectives* 31 (4): 163–84.

Swiss Re. 2019. "Swiss Re Estimates Its Fourth Quarter 2018 Claims Burden from Large Natural Catastrophes at USD 1.0 Billion; Large Man-Made Losses Caused Additional USD 0.3 Billion of Claims." News release, January 15, Swiss Re Insurance Co., Zurich. https://www.swissre.com/media/news-releases/nr-20190115-q4-2018-claims.html.

Vandenbussche, Hylke, William Connell, and Wouter Simons. 2017. "Global Value Chains, Trade Shocks, and Jobs: An Application to Brexit." Discussion Paper DPS17/13 (September), Center for Economic Studies, Department of Economics, University of Leuven, Belgium.

World Bank. 2017. "New Country Classifications by Income Level: 2017-2018." *Data Blog,* July 1, World Bank, Washington, DC. https://blogs.worldbank.org/opendata/new-country-classifications-income-level-2017-2018.

Impact on the environment

Key findings

- **Global value chains (GVCs) are a mixed blessing for the environment.** Scale effects—which refer to the rapid growth of GVC economic activity—are bad for the environment, whereas composition effects—which refer to how tasks are distributed across the globe—have ambiguous effects. Technique effects—which refer to the environmental cost per unit of production—are positive for the environment.

- **GVCs are associated with more shipping and more waste in the aggregate than standard trade.** Both have environmental costs.

- **One important concern has been that industries might migrate to jurisdictions where environmental regulations are lax, but that concern is not borne out by the data.** Rather, by locating production where it is most efficient, GVCs can lower the net resource intensity of global agricultural production.

- **The relational aspect of GVCs can attenuate environmental concerns.** Knowledge flows between firms can enable the spread of more environmentally friendly production techniques throughout a GVC. The large scale of lead firms in GVCs can accelerate environmental innovation and push for higher standards.

- **GVCs also facilitate the production of new environmentally friendly goods.** Products such as solar panels, electric cars, and wind turbines are produced at lower costs in GVCs and help reduce the environmental costs of consumption.

The $4,995 Pedego Conveyor electric bike is produced in Vietnam with parts from all over the world (figure 5.1).[1] Gears, pedals, brakes, and other components are shipped from China, Europe, Indonesia, Japan, and other economies to Vietnam for assembly, and then the bike itself is shipped to the United States for final sale. Roughly 60 percent of the bike's value is from outside Vietnam.

Because parts are crisscrossing the globe, producing the Conveyor through a global value chain (GVC) has greater environmental costs than standard trade. Even more worrisome, some of the most environmentally damaging parts, such as the batteries and tires, may end up being produced in countries with the weakest regulations, leading to more environmental degradation.

But GVCs are also engines of innovation that help drive the creation and diffusion of less-damaging products and processes. GVCs make new environmentally friendly products like this electric bike possible. Big international brands can use GVCs to encourage the global adoption of clean and efficient technologies and processes aimed at enhancing both profitability and sustainability.

Environmental consequences arise from features of GVCs, including the hyperspecialization of tasks, geographic dispersion of production, economies of scale, and the market power of lead firms. The total environmental impact of GVCs is considered here along three dimensions:

- *Scale effect*. If GVCs spur the growth of economic activity, and if composition, consumer preferences, and production techniques remain the same in the sense that pollution per unit of output is constant, then growth leads to environmental deterioration. GVCs also have some consequences that extend beyond those of standard trade. In particular, GVCs are associated with more waste and more shipping in the aggregate, both of which have environmental costs.
- *Composition effect*. GVCs, by promoting trading in tasks, prompt certain types of economic activity to relocate internationally, thereby transforming patterns of production and trade. Shifts in production toward countries with abundant natural resources allow the preservation of scarce resources, helping to sustain global resources such as land and water. However, the redistribution of "dirty" and "clean" tasks among countries may create environmental benefits for some countries and environmental costs for others.

- *Technique effect*. GVCs can also promote improvements in production techniques. The knowledge flows among networks of firms can enable the development or quicker application of more environmentally friendly techniques. With their large scale, the lead firms in GVCs are able to sustain high rates of innovation. Market concentration can lower the difficulty in managing common pool resources such as fisheries and forests. The relational aspect of GVCs is also important in this context because lead firms are increasingly transferring environmentally friendly technologies to their suppliers and pushing for higher standards.

Policies can influence the net impact of GVCs. Subsidies on fuel, for example, can exacerbate the overproduction of fuel-intensive exports. But subsidies for environmental goods can promote their production and further innovation. GVCs in new environmental goods, from solar panels to LED light bulbs, many subsidized over the years, expanded rapidly, thereby facilitating the diffusion of low-carbon technology. Variations in regulation can also lead to net global increases in environmental damage if polluting tasks migrate to countries with lax regulations—part of the composition effect called the pollution haven hypothesis (PHH). However, a large body of literature does not find evidence in support of this hypothesis. Comparative advantage for many of the most polluting industries rests primarily on factors such as capital and resource abundance, and so these industries tend not to migrate to the least regulated countries. However, low- and middle-income countries are often reluctant to raise environmental standards because in a world of liberalized trade and investment they fear losing the interest of foreign investors.[2] Policies for preserving the environment in a world of GVCs are discussed in chapter 8.

Scale effects of trade and growth

As GVCs grow and economic activity expands, emissions increase—a simple scale effect. The effect would be greater if production increased more in higher-polluting industries—a composition effect. Absent technological innovation, the scale effect of GVC trade tends to be negative for the environment because, although production-related pollution and carbon dioxide (CO_2) emissions fall with a country's income, consumption-related environmental emissions and degradation tend to increase.

Figure 5.1 The complexity of producing the Pedego Conveyor electric commuter bike in Vietnam with parts from all over the world

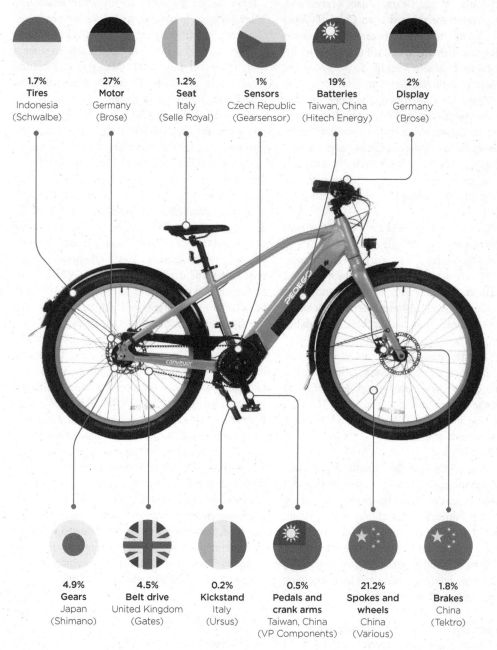

1.7%
Tires
Indonesia
(Schwalbe)

27%
Motor
Germany
(Brose)

1.2%
Seat
Italy
(Selle Royal)

1%
Sensors
Czech Republic
(Gearsensor)

19%
Batteries
Taiwan, China
(Hitech Energy)

2%
Display
Germany
(Brose)

4.9%
Gears
Japan
(Shimano)

4.5%
Belt drive
United Kingdom
(Gates)

0.2%
Kickstand
Italy
(Ursus)

0.5%
**Pedals and
crank arms**
Taiwan, China
(VP Components)

21.2%
**Spokes and
wheels**
China
(Various)

1.8%
Brakes
China
(Tektro)

Source: Frothingham 2018.

Note: Diagram shows the percent of total value added from each component.

Countries that recently transitioned into limited manufacturing-linked GVCs tend to experience faster growth of production-related CO_2 emissions relative to the previous period, although some countries have also seen their emissions growth decline—which is why the effect of transitioning is not statistically significant (figure 5.2). Indeed, in some countries manufacturing has expanded without rising emissions. Meanwhile, countries that recently transitioned into advanced manufacturing and services GVCs, as well as into innovation hubs, typically experience a decline in average production-related CO_2 emissions.

In these countries, which tend to be at a higher stage of development, consumers may demand more regulations, and the technology of production becomes more environmentally friendly.

These contrasting results are consistent with the literature. On the one hand, the environmental Kuznets curve (EKC),[3] an inverted-U, reveals that economic growth increases the presence of local pollution and production-related CO_2 emissions when country incomes are low. Beyond a certain turning point, it is instead associated with improvements in environmental indicators, and rising country incomes appear to lead to an increase in demand for environmental quality.[4] On the other hand, there is a clearly positive correlation between higher GVC activity and a number of indicators of global environmental damage. Because of the urgency of the global environmental challenge, relying on countries growing first and cleaning up later may be misguided, and such an approach may fail to deliver the reductions in emissions needed to avoid a climactic catastrophe.

One way in which GVCs can encourage manufacturing while also protecting the environment is by inducing GVC firms to opt for industrial parks that have higher standards and encourage environmentally friendly production techniques. More than 300 industrial parks now consider themselves to be eco-industrial parks (EIPs)—a number that is expected to rise. In many countries, governments have become more conscious of green approaches to manufacturing, and lead firms, concerned about reputation, are eager to improve the sustainability of production (see box 8.5 in chapter 8).

Transportation

One concern about GVCs is their more intensive use of transportation than other types of trade. Parts and components are shipped to a country only to be shipped out after assembly. This back-and-forth transport of goods across long distances generates CO_2 emissions through the combustion of fossil-based fuels, thereby directly contributing to climate change. CO_2 emissions from international freight transportation account for about 7 percent of total CO_2 emissions globally.[5] By 2050, CO_2 emissions related to international freight are estimated to quadruple, which threatens the temperature goals of the Paris Agreement.[6] In the past, industries more heavily into offshoring produced the greatest increases in carbon emissions related to international trade.

GVCs are most closely linked to maritime transport. More than 80 percent of world trade by volume

Figure 5.2 Production-related CO_2 emissions drop in countries that recently transitioned into advanced GVCs and innovation hubs

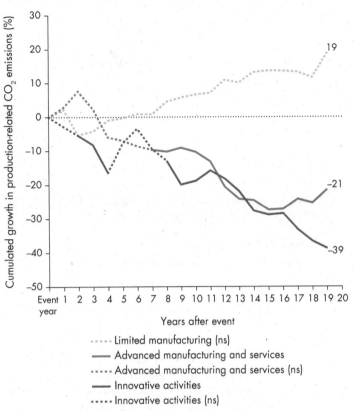

Sources: WDR 2020 team, using data from the World Bank's WDI database and the GVC taxonomy for 1990–2015 based on Eora26 database. See appendix A for a description of the databases used in this Report.

Note: The event study quantifies cumulated CO_2 emissions in the 20 years following a switch from a lower to a higher stage of GVC engagement. Carbon emissions are normally expressed in kilograms per 2011 dollars, adjusted for purchasing power parity (PPP). Dotted lines indicate statistically nonsignificant (ns) coefficients. See box 3.3 for a discussion of the methodology.

and more than 70 percent by value is transported by sea.[7] The capacity of the merchant shipping industry has surged since 1990, and so have emissions from shipping. In 2016, CO_2 emissions from international shipping were about 2.0 percent of global CO_2 emissions (figure 5.3, panel a). This is not a small number: if a country had the same percentage of emissions, it would be the seventh-largest emitter, ranking between Germany and the Republic of Korea.

Under business-as-usual conditions, these emissions are projected to increase by 50–250 percent by 2050[8]—that is, if the maritime sector continues to expand at an annual rate of more than 3 percent, as it has over the past 40 years.[9] Although emissions from other sectors have begun to decline or are expected to peak soon, none of the business-as-usual scenarios for shipping foresee a decline in emissions before 2050.

Figure 5.3 International shipping emissions are increasing

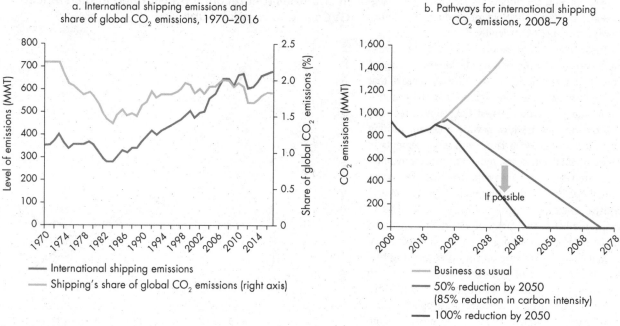

a. International shipping emissions and share of global CO$_2$ emissions, 1970–2016

b. Pathways for international shipping CO$_2$ emissions, 2008–78

- International shipping emissions
- Shipping's share of global CO$_2$ emissions (right axis)

- Business as usual
- 50% reduction by 2050 (85% reduction in carbon intensity)
- 100% reduction by 2050

Sources: Panel a: Muntean et al. 2018; panel b: UCL Energy Institute, London (https://www.ucl.ac.uk/bartlett/energy/research/themes/transport/shipping).

Note: MMT = million metric tons.

As a result, the United Nations Conference on Trade and Development predicts that the maritime sector's share of global CO$_2$ emissions could account for 10–17 percent by 2050.[10] Technological advances and ambitious climate policy will have to counter this trend. As transport technology has improved, growth in emissions since 1990 is already less (1.85 times) than the near tripling of capacity over the same period (figure 5.3, panel a).

Aware of these rapidly rising emissions challenging the world's remaining carbon budget, the International Maritime Organization (IMO) has committed to at least halving CO$_2$ emissions by 2050, aiming to eliminate CO$_2$ emissions from shipping as quickly as possible (figure 5.3, panel b).[11] Although technical and operational efficiency measures could reduce emissions by 30–55 percent by 2050, according to the Intergovernmental Panel on Climate Change,[12] technological innovations will be required to achieve full decarbonization of the sector as envisaged by the IMO.

This energy transition in shipping toward zero-emissions fuels could be facilitated by effective policy support in the form of carbon taxes, emissions trading, low-carbon fuel standards, and a gradual ban of fossil fuels, among other measures. From an environmental perspective, maritime activities are currently undercharged. For example, unlike in domestic

transportation, fuels in international transportation are not subject to excise taxes. Charging for maritime fuels based on their true social cost could support fully exploiting the potential of existing energy efficiency and developing alternative fuels. The challenge is that ships are highly mobile: they travel mostly in international waters and can easily be registered anywhere. Thus pricing emissions appropriately would work best with a global solution such as taxing maritime fuels at a single international carbon rate.[13] And yet because a global solution is not in place yet, and notwithstanding potential market distortions, some governments are exploring unilateral measures. The European Parliament, for example, is considering regional carbon pricing on maritime fuels in the absence of a global agreement.[14] Other options include taxing ships based on the type of vessel or taxing based on bills of lading that show the distance the imported cargo traveled. These and other policy considerations are discussed in chapter 8.

Maritime shipping also poses major pollution challenges in other areas. However, some international solutions have begun to emerge and lead to improvements:

- *Air pollution.* Shipping accounts for roughly 15 percent of global emissions of sulfur dioxide (SO$_2$) and nitrogen oxides (NO_x). Ship engines burn the dirtiest fuel possible (heavy fuel oil, a residual product of the refinery processes of gas, diesel, kerosene, among other fuels). A recent study by the International Council on Clean Transportation attributed 60,000 premature deaths a year to shipping emissions.[15] The IMO therefore recently decided to reduce the mandatory sulfur limit from 3.5 percent to 0.5 percent as of 2020 for maritime fuels.

- *Maritime litter.* Although most plastic waste that ends up in the ocean comes from land-based sources and is transported through rivers into the sea, about 20 percent originates directly from ships and other sea-based sources, including aquaculture, fishing, and dumping of waste and other matter from deep-sea platforms. Next to environmental misconduct, a big problem is that port reception facilities—waste disposal facilities provided for ships by authorities—are often nonexistent, or they are inadequately equipped, complicated to use, or too expensive. Shipbreaking (that is, scrapping vessels) is also a problem.[16]

- *Invasive species.* To float in a balanced way, ships often have to take on board ballast water. This water is then discharged at another location when the weight and volume requirements change. Invasive species are transported around the globe in this water and released at locations where they may not have any natural predators and can pose a threat to sensitive ecosystems.

- *Water pollution.* Other pollution-related problems are linked to oil spills, sewage disposal (from ship operations), and bilge water (a cocktail of oil and chemicals leaking from the engines and machinery and water that accumulates in the lowest part of vessels and must be pumped out from time to time).

Road and rail transport are two additional sources of the impacts of GVCs on the environment because of their predominance in domestic value chains. The efficiency and performance of the trucking industry can have a significant impact on the carbon footprint of GVCs. The adoption of more fuel-efficient vehicles reduces associated emissions, and the reduction of empty backhauls improves overall efficiency, results in less waste, and contributes to lower prices. For example, when the Lao People's Democratic Republic abolished restrictions on backhauling by foreign trucking companies, road transport prices declined by 20 percent. Substitution between road and rail modalities and the associated development of more seamless containerized logistics are another important area that will determine the overall impact of GVCs on

the environment. Rail is the lowest emitter of CO_2 (3 percent of the total), whereas road freight is over 50 percent of the total.

GVCs and waste

GVCs can influence the amount and type of waste generated during the production and transport of goods from source to consumer. They have contributed to a large share of the waste in the electronics and other GVC-intensive sectors, but they are also well positioned to be part of the solution.

E-waste is the fastest-growing waste stream in the world, accounting for more than 70 percent of the toxic waste in U.S. landfills (figure 5.4).[17] GVCs have enabled rapid declines in the cost of electrical and electronic devices,[18] benefiting large numbers of people who otherwise could not afford even low-cost items. GVCs also drive the rate of technological innovation that leads to high replacement rates worldwide.

But GVCs have the potential to close the loop and turn e-waste into valuable resources. The United Nations University conservatively estimated the value of recoverable materials in last year's e-waste to be $55 billion, or more than the 2016 gross domestic product of most countries.[19] Some countries such as Japan have e-waste management laws that make manufacturers and retailers responsible for taking back used home appliances, recycling them, and publishing the costs of recycling.

E-waste flows should be viewed as sources of inputs for next-generation products.[20] The World Economic Forum's call for a circular electronics value chain represents a model of sustainability that is difficult to envisage without GVCs.[21] Inputs from retired electronics should be removed and recycled by the very companies that produce them.

The global trade in plastic waste grew in lockstep with the expansion of GVCs through the 1990s and 2000s. In 1990 worldwide imports of plastic waste were worth less than $1 billion, and by 2010 they had peaked at around $10 billion. In the last decade, they have begun to level off and even decline.[22] Meanwhile, plastic and microplastic waste have proven to be a major challenge for solid waste management and have become a global crisis for the environment, especially the oceans. In 2018 the Center for Biological Diversity estimated that swirling convergences of plastic make up about 40 percent of the world's ocean surfaces and that at current rates they could outweigh all the fish in the sea by 2050.[23]

Gross trade data from UN Comtrade are not well suited to portraying what is happening to plastic

Figure 5.4 The world produced 50 million metric tons of e-waste in 2018

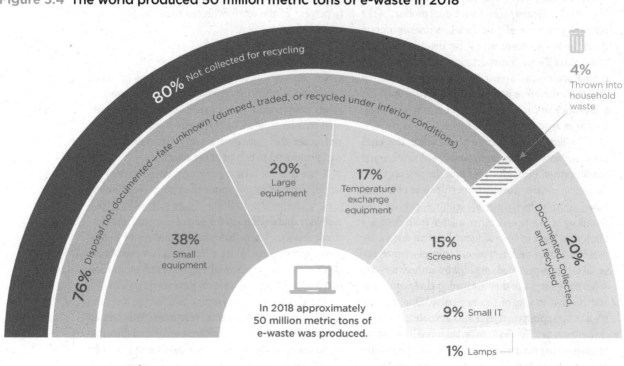

In addition, an estimated 100 million old devices or more are stored in homes.

Source: Adapted from Ryder and Zhao (2019).

Note: IT = information technology.

waste worldwide. Input–output data are in principle better able to track plastic waste, but in both statistical sources the information is too aggregated to track international flows. The two most common polymers, PET and PP, lack specific codes in UN Comtrade because trade codes for these waste materials are not yet harmonized across countries, and the available multiregion input–output data do not include a category for waste. Thus calculating plastic waste urgently requires better statistical measurement.

Today's recycling technologies cannot handle the rapidly growing quantities of global waste. For many years, China was accepting a large share of the world's plastic waste, but eventually the environmental costs of recycling "dirty" plastics became formidable, and China raised the import standards in 2017, all but cutting off acceptance of plastic waste (box 5.1). With most plastic waste now ending up in landfills or incinerators, reducing waste and developing better technology for packaging goods and recycling are environmental priorities in many countries. These countries are promoting a shift away from plastics in bags and water bottles, encouraging reuse, and using more economical and environmentally friendly packaging of parts, components, and goods traveling the world.

Changes in the composition of production

Falling trade costs, tighter environmental regulations, and pollution havens

Because trade costs are falling while environmental regulations are tightening in many countries, polluting manufacturers may respond to new environmental regulations by relocating to countries with less strict standards. Moreover, because GVCs foster hyperspecialization, with tasks moved to the most productive location, lead firms from countries with tight environmental regulations may locate "dirty" production in countries where environmental norms are lax—that is, in so-called pollution havens. Relocating conventional local pollutants thus improves the air and water quality in places with strict regulations at the expense of environmental quality in pollution havens.

In theory, concerns about pollution havens are well founded.[24] Pollution is a production input, just like labor and capital. One could think of pollution as the disposal services of the environment, where the unregulated price is zero. Countries export the goods in which they have a comparative production

Box 5.1 The ban on plastics by China disrupted the waste GVC

One way GVCs extended a product's life was through recycling of paper and plastic waste. In recent decades, goods shipped from China to the United States were consumed, and paper and plastic containers, along with domestic plastic and paper waste, were sent back to China for recycling.

At the end of 2017, China stopped accepting large amounts of imported waste for recycling because a large share was "dirty" and causing environmental damage. The prices of plastic scrap and low-grade paper then collapsed, disrupting the global recycling industry. In the first half of 2017, China and Hong Kong SAR, China, absorbed 60 percent of the plastic waste exported by G-7 countries. A year later, they imported less than 10 percent.[a]

In their place, Malaysia, Thailand, and Vietnam, among other East Asia and Pacific countries, experienced significant increases in contaminated and plastic waste imports. However, many containers were misrepresented as plastic scrap, and when their contents could not be recycled it was burned or dumped. As a result, Indonesia, Malaysia, the Philippines, Thailand, and Vietnam have announced they would ban and send contaminated waste back to the countries of origin, with the threat of abandoning the waste in countries' territorial waters if the waste is not accepted.

Reducing the paper and plastics in packaging and using cleaner technology for recycling has become a priority for environmentally concerned countries. In May 2019, 187 countries—not including the United States—agreed to amend the Basel Convention on the Control of Transboundary Movements of Hazardous Wastes and Their Disposal[b] to better regulate the global trade of plastic waste and make it more transparent. Among the commitments, private companies will have to secure the consent of receiving countries before they can trade contaminated and most mixes of plastic waste.

a. Hook and Reed 2018.
b. The Basel Convention on the Control of Transboundary Movements of Hazardous Wastes and Their Disposal was adopted on March 22, 1989, by the Conference of Plenipotentiaries in Basel, Switzerland, in response to a public outcry following the discovery in the 1980s in Africa and other parts of the developing world of deposits of toxic wastes imported from abroad.

---

advantage—that is, their costs of producing those goods are lower relative to their costs of producing other goods. Countries with lax pollution regulations have a comparative advantage in goods whose production is pollution-intensive, and they will export those goods—becoming pollution havens.

Evidence of the pollution haven effect (PHE) has, however, been very limited so far. Polluting industries—paper, metals, cement, and refineries—tend to be costly to relocate, and production is tied to local factor or product markets. Paper plants locate near the trees, and cement plants near their customers. It is therefore not obvious that countries with lax regulations will have a comparative—or even an absolute—advantage in polluting goods. Environmental regulations are a small part of costs. Consistent with this, empirical evidence shows that strict environmental regulation of polluting industries has not led to large relocations to countries with less-strict standards.[25] In some cases, polluting industries and strict regulations are in fact positively correlated.[26] Of all the recent papers finding a PHE, few attempt to untangle the causal negative effect of pollution regulations on polluting industries. Those that do untangle that effect find a statistically significant but quantitatively modest effect for the most polluting industries. One study showed that a 10 percent increase in pollution abatement costs in the United States leads to a 0.6 percent increase in net imports from Mexico and a 5 percent increase in net imports from Canada.[27]

The association of falling trade costs and tighter environmental regulations could drive polluters to flee to developing countries. But this has not happened. Take, for example, what happened to the types of goods produced in the United States compared with U.S. imports as trade costs declined and U.S. environmental standards became stricter (see chapter 1).[28] Emissions from U.S. domestic manufacturing fell by 60 percent from 1990 to 2008, stemming from changes in environmental policy.[29] Meanwhile, the structure of imports shifted toward cleaner goods. Contrary to the conventional wisdom about industrialized countries "offshoring" production of polluting goods, imports to the United States have been shifting away from pollution-intensive goods even faster than U.S. domestic production (figure 5.5). As trade costs fall, the U.S. increasingly imports goods in which it has a comparative disadvantage, which happen to be those that are relatively less pollution-intensive. Trends in Europe are similar, with imports becoming progressively less pollution-intensive, especially from low-income countries.

Figure 5.5 U.S. output has increasingly shifted away from polluting goods, but imports have done so even faster

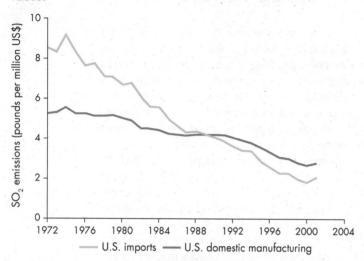

— U.S. imports — U.S. domestic manufacturing

Source: WDR 2020 team, using data from Levinson (2010).

Note: The figure shows the pounds of sulfur dioxide (SO₂) air pollution per million U.S. dollars of value produced by the U.S. manufacturing sector between 1972 and 2001 and those of imported value. Those totals are calculated using the World Bank's Industrial Pollution Projection System, which is simply a list of emission intensities for each of more than 400 manufacturing industries in 1987 (Hettige et al. 1995). Averaging across industries, weighted by their values shipped in each year, gives the average pollution intensity of the entire U.S. manufacturing sector each year. The blue line in the figure plots that average, holding pollution intensities fixed as of 1987. The green line in the figure reports the same calculation for imports. These averages drop over time because of changes in the composition of the manufacturing sector. U.S. output has increasingly shifted away from goods that generate the most pollution per dollar of output toward cleaner goods. Graphs for nitrogen oxides, volatile organic compounds, and carbon monoxide look similar, with the pollution intensity of U.S. domestic manufacturing falling less quickly than that for imports.

Although the PHE has been overplayed to date, it may become more relevant as some countries adopt more ambitious climate policies to reduce emissions rapidly.

Environmental effects of agriculture and commodity GVCs

Much of the literature on trade and the environment and the nascent literature on GVCs and the environment focus on carbon emissions and, to some extent, other forms of pollution. However, land use changes such as deforestation and overfishing are equally important from a purely environmental and human health perspective. These are conceptually distinct issues, with very different impacts from trade and GVCs.

In agriculture, GVCs can help save scarce resources by ensuring that raw materials are sourced closest to natural resources. But they can also lead to overuse because of specialization and a growing global demand. The pernicious effects are magnified when resource use is subsidized.

GVCs allow countries to preserve scarce resources by importing raw agricultural products from countries with more abundant resources. A good example is the water embodied in cereals and oils. Arid countries that do not have a comparative advantage in water-intensive culture no longer need to grow these products domestically. They can import them for consumption or further processing with considerable savings in water usage (box 5.2). Trade in "virtual water," the water embodied in agricultural production, is estimated to have saved 4 percent of the global water footprint.

National policies can make the environment worse by subsidizing activities that lead to environmental problems. Subsidizing fisheries can lead to overfishing, which has been recognized as a major global issue since at least the 1990s.[30] When agriculture is subsidized, deforestation, soil erosion, and chemical runoff into bodies of water are greater than they would be otherwise, and natural biodiversity will decline.[31]

Even in the absence of subsidies, GVCs and trade create some concerns about hyperspecialization and degradation of land for agricultural use, a major driver of forest loss. Four products—soy, cattle, palm oil, and wood products—alone are responsible for 40 percent of global deforestation, at an average rate of 3.8 million hectares a year.[32] But many more commodities—such as cocoa, coffee, spices, vanilla, bananas, cut flowers, orange juice, and natural rubber—are experiencing a growing global demand that threatens the environment in the hotspots where these goods grow. Some fear that this demand may translate into the depredation of resources from developing countries—especially because incomplete markets mean that the biodiversity contained in forests is not valued sufficiently. Through more efficient production and lower prices, trade and GVCs increase the global quantity demanded of certain agricultural resources and commodities. The result can be deforestation, biodiversity loss, and other environmental problems in countries where resources are concentrated.

However, GVCs also present an opportunity to use value chain connections with concerned consumers to address these issues through voluntary standards and regulated changes. Meanwhile, large-scale operations and upstream connections allow lead firms to efficiently provide information and services that give small-scale producers an opportunity to demonstrably meet standards that they otherwise could not. The appropriate regulations and policies will, however, have to be put in place for achieving large scale impact.

The challenges and the possible solutions in a GVC world are well illustrated by the cocoa and chocolate industry. Cocoa—the primary ingredient in the world's chocolate—has been identified as a major driver of deforestation in West Africa. For many years, the soaring global demand and expanding cocoa production

Box 5.2 Virtual water

Are countries that have scarcer water reserves importing water-intensive goods?

The global water footprint in 1996–2005 was estimated at 9,087 billion cubic meters per year: 74 percent green (the rainwater stored in the soil used to produce agricultural goods), 11 percent blue (the freshwater used to produce goods and services), and 15 percent gray (polluted water from production). Agricultural production contributes 92 percent to this total footprint, and about one-fifth of the global water footprint is attributed to production for export.

Because water-efficient countries can export water-intensive goods, especially agricultural products, to less efficient countries, trade has helped reduce the amount of water used in aggregate production. The global water savings related to trade in agricultural products in 1996–2005 was an estimated 369 billion cubic meters per year (58.7 percent green, 26.6 percent blue, and 14.7 percent gray), which is equivalent to 4 percent of the global water footprint related to agricultural production (map B5.2.1).

Map B5.2.1 Global water savings associated with international trade in agricultural products, 1996–2005

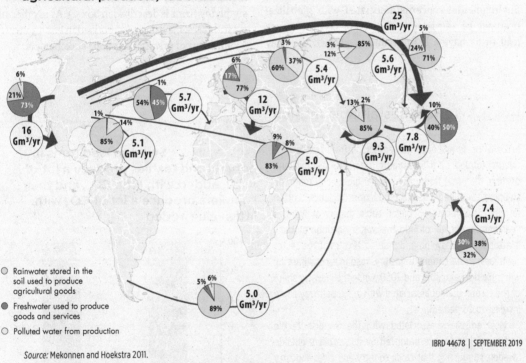

○ Rainwater stored in the
    soil used to produce
    agricultural goods

● Freshwater used to produce
    goods and services

○ Polluted water from production

IBRD 44678 | SEPTEMBER 2019

Source: Mekonnen and Hoekstra 2011.

Note: Virtual water balance per country and direction of gross virtual water flows related to trade in agricultural and industrial products over the period 1996–2005. The thicker the arrow, the bigger the virtual water flow. Only the biggest water savings are shown—more than 5 billion cubic meters per year (Gm³/yr).

have degraded forests. Suitable land is shrinking because of climate change, and trees are aging and need to be replanted, particularly in Côte d'Ivoire and Ghana. However, the 5–6 million smallholder farms that produce almost the entire global supply of cocoa lack good agricultural practices to address these challenges. They also face difficulties in obtaining farming supplies and financing any improvements they may want to make. Ongoing deforestation to increase cocoa production is not sustainable.

Certification schemes are one possible means of addressing the environmental and socioeconomic issues in the industry. This opportunity for moving to more sustainable methods of cocoa production is supported by the downstream industry. Processing is dominated by a few large traders, grinders, and chocolate producers.[33] Six companies alone process and trade 89 percent of the annual global cocoa production, and five chocolate producers buy 39 percent of it. Because a few large companies dominate and compete at the downstream stages of production, they are well placed to cooperate in fighting environmental degradation, a huge threat to their productivity, particularly as climate change is making cocoa harvest yields extremely unpredictable. And yet despite the strong incentives to work together to improve the social and environmental footprint of the upstream operations, the private sector commitments are not translating into improved sustainability of the supply chain in the absence of regulatory change. To improve sustainability of the cocoa value chains, domestic regulators and international development partners need to work together with the private sector.

Relational GVCs and production techniques

Environmental concerns associated with globalization may be alleviated in the age of GVCs. Because lead firms have a brand name to protect, they pay attention to how their supply chains function in terms of social and environmental standards. Typically, the lead firms in GVCs are well known, and so their behavior can be easily monitored. Some firms actively promote standards along the value chain, including by assessing the monetary value of better social and environmental standards in their balance sheets. Consumers are demanding more sustainable products, and so producing such products can have positive economic returns from either cost savings, risk mitigation, or product recognition.[34]

Recent studies provide empirical evidence that stricter regulation can enhance business performance.[35] At the country-industry level, higher compliance with social and environmental standards is correlated with economic upgrading.[36] An example of how higher standards help save the water and energy of supplying firms is described in box 5.3. As in other successful cases, the example described in box 5.3 involves a joint effort of private and public stakeholders.

Box 5.3 Toward sustainable fashion

In 2018 the greenhouse gas emissions from textile production totaled 1.2 billion metric tons of CO_2 equivalent, or more than that from international flights and maritime shipping combined.[a] Textile production (including cotton farming) uses about 93 billion cubic meters of water a year, and 20 percent of industrial water pollution globally is attributable to dyeing and treating textiles. If the sector continues on its current trajectory, resource consumption will triple between 2015 and 2050, while the industry share of the carbon budget associated with a 2°C pathway could increase to 26 percent.

Most emissions associated with the Swedish textile and apparel sector are produced by its suppliers outside Sweden, suggesting that cross-country and cross-industry collaboration is needed to reduce emissions (figure B5.3.1). A partnership between Swedish textile producers and the Swedish International Development Cooperation Agency (Sida) reveals how higher standards can help save the water and energy of supplying firms, with environmental and economic gains.

The Sweden Textile Water Initiative (STWI), launched in 2014 and supported by Sida, was a public-private development partnership with 24 textile and leather companies. Its goal was to help establish a network of private companies committed to improving the efficiency of water use by the

Figure B5.3.1 Swedish lead firms in apparel and textiles produce a lot of value added with little CO_2, and their suppliers produce a lot of CO_2 with little value added

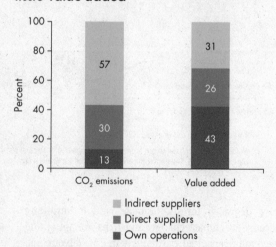

Sources: WDR 2020 team, using data from OECD's TiVA database; WIOD; Exiobase.

Note: Estimates were obtained through a multiregional input-output model extended with satellite accounts for carbon emissions. The direct and indirect suppliers of the Swedish textile and apparel sector include upstream industries from both Sweden and foreign countries.

(Box continues next page)

Box 5.3 Toward sustainable fashion (continued)

suppliers and subsuppliers associated with their brands in Bangladesh, China, Ethiopia, India, and Turkey. Sida provided the financing; clothing brands contributed by engaging their factories; and the Stockholm International Water Institute oversaw implementation. This collaboration generated significant cost savings and time savings in terms of rolling out the initiative.[b] Although Sida exited in 2018, the network continues to expand globally and to pursue its mandate of supporting sustainability champions with business intelligence, networking, and advice on resource efficiency.

In the first three years, STWI supported 276 factories in the five initial countries, training more than 1,300 managers and 37,000 staff. The savings amounted to almost 11 million cubic meters of water and almost 80 million kilowatt-hours of electricity (table B5.3.1). Despite some variation in savings among countries and across factories, the factory investments were generally sustainable because of the cost savings in water and chemicals over time, and companies' awareness and capacity increased. These numbers confirm that development interventions can play a catalytic role in improving the sustainability of GVCs by raising awareness and providing technical assistance. But cost sharing with companies is important to ensure ownership and engagement.

The initiative had a limited impact on national water governance practices in each country. The STWI's upcoming Mill Improvement Alliance hopes to extend the program to a larger number of factories to achieve broader sector- and economywide impacts. But governments also will have to join the effort, particularly in updating their water governance frameworks. Private actors in initiatives such as the STWI can submit recommendations for regulatory change—and possibly counter pushback that might otherwise come from affected companies.

Table B5.3.1 Total reported savings generated by the Sweden Textile Water Initiative in its five partner countries, 2015–17

Savings	Bangladesh	China	Ethiopia	India	Turkey	Total
Water (m³)	2,680,005	6,316,597	99,323	339,659	1,085,973	10,521,557
Electricity (kWh)	18,364,890	45,526,706	21,780	6,074,612	9,599,713	79,587,701
Thermal use (metric tons)	1,708,103	4,695,729	115,881	0	0	6,519,714
Chemical use (kg)	1,187,505	18,611,056	5,185	281,635	2,497,178	22,582,559
Waste water (m³)	16,319	2,435,680	0	0	229,860	2,681,859
Natural gas (m³)	20,798,126	1,407,313	0	24,514	5,130,815	27,360,768
Fossil fuel (metric tons)	702,334	0	444	1,904	625	705,309
Coal (kg)	0	1,002	0	6,319,396	3,823,737	10,144,135
GHG emissions (metric tons)	45,365	353,277	0	41,274	24,850	464,766

Source: Swedish International Development Cooperation Agency (Sida).

Note: GHG = greenhouse gas; kg = kilograms; kWh = kilowatt-hours; m³ = cubic meters.

a. Ellen MacArthur Foundation (2017).
b. Andersson et al. (2018).

The relational nature of GVCs can also promote the transfer of clean technology and know-how. Firms that have a brand to defend naturally tend to align practices within the corporation. The clothing firm Puma, in collaboration with the International Finance Corporation, the bank BNP Paribas, and the fintech firm GT Nexus launched a program in 2016 that offers better receivable financing terms to suppliers who score high on Puma's sustainability index. Levi's has a comparable arrangement with its suppliers through the International Finance Corporation's Global Trade Supplier Finance Program. Investment firms are also pushing for more sustainable practices among the major brands. They are paying more attention to environmental, social, and governance (ESG) performance and pushing the major brands to adopt higher standards.

Box 5.4 Demanding environmental standards in GVC upstream firms

Saitex International (Vietnam) and Zakład Pierzarski Konrad Ożgo (Poland) are GVC suppliers whose comparative advantage includes their ability to meet demanding voluntary environmental standards.

Saitex produces denim jeans in a LEED (Leadership in Energy and Environmental Design)-certified facility for the California company Everlane, whose "radical transparency" is the core of its marketing strategy. According to Everlane's website,[a] Saitex recycles 98 percent of its water, relies on alternative energy sources, and repurposes by-products to create premium jeans minimizing the waste. Standard denim manufacturers use "belly" washing machines, which consume as much as 1,500 liters of water to produce one pair of jeans. Saitex instead consumes only 0.4 liter of water per pair of jeans thanks to state-of-the-art recycling.

On-site rainwater collection pools allow Saitex to minimize the impact of the consumption it does have, and its sophisticated five-step filtration process separates water from toxic contaminants and then sends the clean water back into the system. Saitex is also committed to using renewable energy resources such as solar power and

cutting energy usage by 5.3 million kilowatt-hours a year—and CO_2 emissions by nearly 80 percent. It also plants trees to offset its emissions. Furthermore, it minimizes the waste from production. All denim creates a toxic by-product called sludge, but at Saitex the sludge is extracted and shipped to a nearby brick factory. Mixed with concrete, the toxic material can no longer leech into the environment. The resulting bricks are used to build affordable homes.

Zakład Pierzarski Konrad Ożgo, which preprocesses white goose down for the outdoor clothing firm Patagonia, has a fully traceable supply chain to comply with its brand philosophy. Internal audits and third-party verification ensure that the birds are neither live plucked nor force-fed and that they are raised in humane conditions. The adoption of this costly technology allows this supplier to have a long-lasting relationship with the buyer, Patagonia, which in this way can trace its supply back to the more than 100 individual smallholder farms—including parent farms, hatcheries, and raising farms—whose output passes through the preprocessor.

a. https://www.everlane.com/factories/denim-saitex.

The long-term nature of firm-to-firm relationships and contracts in relational GVCs can be a force for convincing companies in their supply chain to adopt new costly technology (box 5.4). This point is important because many of the environmental impacts are borne upstream, by the suppliers, even if most of the value is created downstream, as in the Swedish example in box 5.3.

The positive role of relational GVCs does have its limits, however. First, the technology transfer tends to benefit direct suppliers the most, and to a much lesser extent second- and lower-tier suppliers, which in some cases are invisible to the GVC lead firm. Second, the positive local effects of relational GVCs may not translate into an overall gain for the environment globally. When a lead firm relocates production to a developing country, and it produces there with carbon intensity that is lower than the prevailing carbon intensity of the host country, that is not in itself a reduction in pollution and emissions. The carbon intensity can still increase overall relative to a counterfactual where the firm did not relocate.

Green goods

One of the biggest contributions of GVCs to the environment may be the many new and innovative environmental products they make possible. Trade and GVCs have a positive impact on the environment by promoting innovation and by making these clean technologies and environmental goods more affordable. This section describes some of the most important green goods value chains.[37]

Solar energy

The solar value chain relies on innovation and complex production systems. Countries may be part of the value chain through producing silicon, manufacturing solar cells, or assembling modules, inverters, mounting systems, combiner boxes, and other components.[38] Older companies appear to be more vertically integrated, whereas newer entrants tend to source from multiple locations for assembly on-site.

Solar photovoltaic (PV) products are generally tradable. Map 5.1 illustrates the supply chain of a PV company. Solar cell production is concentrated

Map 5.1 Supply chain of a solar photovoltaic company

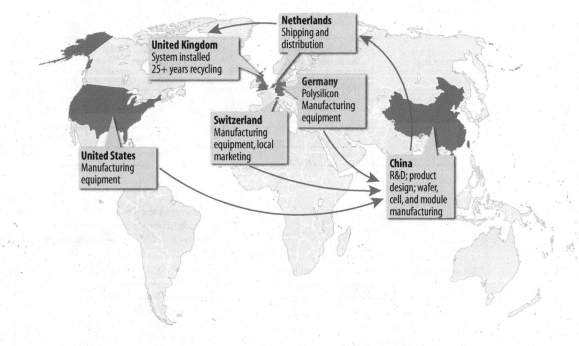

Netherlands
Shipping and distribution

United Kingdom
System installed
25+ years recycling

Germany
Polysilicon
Manufacturing
equipment

Switzerland
Manufacturing
equipment, local
marketing

United States
Manufacturing
equipment

China
R&D; product
design; wafer,
cell, and module
manufacturing

IBRD 44662 | SEPTEMBER 2019

Source: European Commission 2016.

Note: Solar cell production is primarily concentrated in China and elsewhere in Asia and is dependent on the production of components from several countries. Europe and the United States lead upstream service provision, including shipping, distribution, installation, and recycling. R&D = research and development.

primarily in China and elsewhere in Asia and is dependent on the production of components from several countries. Europe and the United States lead upstream service provision, including shipping, distribution, installation, and recycling.

Large parts of the supply chain have generally been located in countries or regions with strong demand, such as the European Union. Low labor costs, natural resources, and government policies have driven some production to China. Meanwhile, policies to encourage deployment have expanded in other countries.[39]

Value created along the solar value chain starts with polysilicon and ends with the PV module (table 5.1). Downstream activities generally account for a large share of value added, especially for services such as installation, system design, and research and development.

Other examples of green goods

The wind energy supply chain, though not as globalized as solar, has grown increasingly complex and fragmented. A single wind turbine has more than 8,000 parts. And major components include rotor blades, towers, and nacelles. In the U.S. supply chain,

only about 50 percent of the value of components is from domestic sources. Several European countries, such as Denmark and Germany, used to be the main manufacturing hubs, but the sector is growing increasingly diverse geographically, with more than 50 percent of suppliers from China, India, and other Asian countries, as well as Brazil.[40]

In the electric vehicle industry, global sales of new vehicles passed a million units for the first time in 2017. On current trajectories, this figure could quadruple by 2020, to about 5 percent of the total global light vehicle market.[41]

China is the largest global market for electric vehicles, and it is dominated by independent domestic firms. China's electric vehicle industry showcases how trade liberalization and greater access to foreign suppliers, combined with government intervention and strong competition in the traditional automotive market, allow independent domestic companies to enter the niche market of electric vehicles and become both innovative and cost-competitive. In the years after China joined the World Trade Organization, the import volumes of parts for electric motors and generators picked up, as exports of electronic motors also increased.

Table 5.1 Estimation of value added at stages of the supply chain of a solar photovoltaic (PV) module

US$ per kilowatt

Stage of production	Sales receipts (turnover or gross output)	Cost of intermediate products and services	Value added
Polysilicon	150	50	100
Silicon wafer	330	150	180
Solar cell	460	330	130
Final product (PV module)	660	460	200
Total	1,600	990	610

Source: Jha 2016.

Notes

1. Roosevelt (2018).
2. This phenomenon, known as the pollution haven effect (PHE), is different from the pollution haven hypothesis (PHH). The empirical literature provides much more support for the PHE than for the PHH (Copeland and Taylor 2004; He 2006; Kellenberg 2009; Levinson and Taylor 2008). The PHE and the associated problem of "carbon leakage" hold even when the PHH does not. Although environmental policy is not a predominant determinant of comparative advantage, it does matter at the margin, particularly for countries whose competitiveness is based on producing at low cost.
3. The environmental Kuznets curve (EKC) describes a relationship between per capita income in a location and environmental outcomes. See Grossman and Krueger (1991, 1995).
4. Copeland and Taylor (2004); Stern (2017).
5. ITF (2015).
6. ITF (2015).
7. UNCTAD (2017, 2018).
8. IMO (2015).
9. UNCTAD (2017).
10. ETC (2018); European Parliament (2015).
11. The initial strategy, launched in April 2018, envisages reducing total greenhouse gas (GHG) emissions from international shipping, which should reduce the total annual GHG emissions by at least 50 percent by 2050 compared with 2008, while pursuing efforts toward phasing them out entirely by that date (IMO 2018b).
12. Sims et al. (2014).
13. Keen, Parry, and Strand (2012).
14. Dominioni, Heine, and Martínez Romera (2018).
15. Anenberg et al. (2019).
16. For more information, see IMO (2018a).
17. Holgate (2018).
18. UNU (2018).
19. UNU (2018).
20. Lepawsky (2015).
21. Ryder and Zhao (2019).
22. Brooks, Wang, and Jambeck (2018).
23. Center for Biological Diversity (n.d.).
24. See Copeland and Taylor (2004) for a formulation of the pollution haven hypothesis.
25. Cherniwchan, Copeland, and Taylor (2017); Dechezleprêtre and Sato (2017); Ederington, Levinson, and Minier (2005).
26. Demsetz (1967).
27. Levinson and Taylor (2008).
28. Shapiro and Walker (2018).
29. Shapiro and Walker (2018).
30. Jackson et al. (2001).
31. van der Werf and Petit (2002).
32. Kroeger et al. (2017).
33. Kroeger et al. (2017).
34. Impact Valuation Roundtable (2017).
35. Lanoie et al. (2011).
36. Kummritz, Taglioni, and Winkler (2017).
37. Not all green goods have a positive environmental footprint. In some cases, such as in the mining of rare minerals, this is not the case.
38. Jha (2016).
39. Jha (2016).
40. Jha (2016).
41. Hertzke et al. (2018).

References

Andersson, Jens, Reza Iftekhar Patwary, Weronika Rehnby, and Emilie Pellby. 2018. "Evaluation of STWI Projects 2014–2018: Final Report." November 19, NIRAS Sweden, Stockholm.

Anenberg, Susan, Joshua Miller, Daven Henze, and Ray Minjaresicct. 2019. "A Global Snapshot of the Air Pollution–Related Health Impacts of Transportation Sector Emissions in 2010 and 2015." International Council on Clean Transportation, Washington, DC.

Brooks, Amy L., Shunli Wang, and Jenna R. Jambeck. 2018. "The Chinese Import Ban and Its Impact on Global Plastic Waste Trade." *Science Advances* 4 (6). doi: 10.1126/sciadv.aat0131.

Center for Biological Diversity. No date. "Ocean Plastics Pollution: A Global Tragedy for Our Oceans and Sea Life." Center for Biological Diversity, Tucson, AZ. https://www.biologicaldiversity.org/campaigns/ocean_plastics/.

Cherniwchan, Jevan, Brian R. Copeland, and M. Scott Taylor. 2017. "Trade and the Environment: New Methods,

Measurements, and Results." *Annual Review of Economics* 9 (August): 59–85.

Copeland, Brian R., and M. Scott Taylor. 2004. "Trade, Growth, and the Environment." *Journal of Economic Literature* 42 (1): 7–71.

Dechezleprêtre, Antoine, and Misato Sato. 2017. "The Impacts of Environmental Regulations on Competitiveness." *Review of Environmental Economics and Policy* 11 (2): 183–206.

Demsetz, Harold. 1967. "Toward a Theory of Property Rights." *American Economic Review* 57 (2): 347–59.

Dominioni, Goran, Dirk Heine, and Beatriz Martínez Romera. 2018. "Regional Carbon Pricing for International Maritime Transport: Challenges and Opportunities for Global Geographical Coverage." Policy Research Working Paper 8319, World Bank, Washington, DC.

Ederington, Josh, Arik Levinson, and Jenny Minier. 2005. "Footloose and Pollution-Free." *Review of Economics and Statistics* 87 (1): 92–99.

Ellen MacArthur Foundation. 2017. *A New Textiles Economy: Redesigning Fashion's Future.* Cowes, Isle of Wight, U.K.: Ellen MacArthur Foundation. https://www.ellenmacarthur foundation.org/publications/a-new-textiles-economy -redesigning-fashions-future.

ETC (Energy Transitions Commission). 2018. *Mission Possible: Reaching Net-Zero Carbon Emissions from Harder-to-Abate Sectors by Mid-Century.* London: ETC. http://www .energy-transitions.org/sites/default/files/ETC_Mission Possible_FullReport.pdf.

European Commission. 2016. *Trade Sustainability Impact Assessment on the Environmental Goods Agreement.* Final report. Brussels: Directorate-General for Trade, European Commission.

European Parliament. 2015. "Emissions Reduction Targets for International Aviation and Shipping." Report IP/A/ENVI/2015-11 (November), Policy Department A: Economic and Scientific Policy, Directorate General for Internal Policies, European Parliament, Brussels.

Frothingham, Steve. 2018. "Pedego Shifts Some E-Bike Production to Vietnam in Response to Tariffs. *Bike Retailer and Industry News,* September 12. https://www.bicycle retailer.com/international/2018/09/12/pedego-shifts-some -e-bike-production-vietnam-response-tariffs#.XVrgOp NKiCd.

Grossman, Gene M., and Alan B. Krueger. 1991. "Environmental Impacts of a North American Free Trade Agreement." NBER Working Paper 3914 (November), National Bureau of Economic Research, Cambridge, MA.

———. 1995. "Economic Growth and the Environment." *Quarterly Journal of Economics* 110 (2): 353–77.

He, Jie. 2006. "Pollution Haven Hypothesis and Environmental Impacts of Foreign Direct Investment: The Case of Industrial Emission of Sulfur Dioxide (SO_2) in Chinese Provinces." *Ecological Economics* 60 (1): 228–45.

Heine, Dirk, and Susanne Gäde. 2018. "Unilaterally Removing Implicit Subsidies for Maritime Fuels." *International Economics and Economic Policy* 15 (2): 523–45.

Hertzke, Patrick, Nicolai Müller, Stephanie Schenk, and Ting Wu. 2018. "The Global Electric-Vehicle Market Is Amped Up and on the Rise. *Our Insights* (blog), May. McKinsey and Company, New York. https://www.mckinsey.com /industries/automotive-and-assembly/our-insights/the -global-electric-vehicle-market-is-amped-up-and-on-the -rise?.

Hettige, Hemamala S., Paul Jonathan Martin, Manjula Singh, and David R. Wheeler. 1995. "The Industrial Pollution Projection System." Policy Research Working Paper 1431, World Bank, Washington, DC.

Holgate, Peter. 2018. "How Do We Tackle the Fastest Growing Waste Stream on the Planet?" *Global Agenda: Circular Economy,* February 9, World Economic Forum, Geneva. https://www.weforum.org/agenda/2018/02/how -do-we-tackle-the-fastest-growing-waste-stream-on-the -planet/.

Hook, Leslie, and John Reed. 2018. "Why the World's Recycling System Stopped Working." *Financial Times,* October 25. https://www.ft.com/content/360e2524-d71a -11e8-a854-33d6f82e62f8.

IMO (International Maritime Organization). 2015. *Third IMO Greenhouse Gas Study, 2014.* London: IMO.

———. 2018a. "Marine Litter." In Focus, IMO, London. http:// www.imo.org/en/MediaCentre/HotTopics/marinelitter /Pages/default.aspx.

———. 2018b. "UN Body Adopts Climate Change Strategy for Shipping." Press Briefing 06, April 13, IMO, London. http://www.imo.org/en/MediaCentre/PressBriefings /Pages/06GHGinitialstrategy.aspx.

Impact Valuation Roundtable. 2017. "White Paper: Operationalizing Impact Valuation: Experiences and Recommendations by Participants of the Impact Valuation Roundtable." Geneva, World Business Council for Sustainable Development.

ITF (International Transport Forum). 2015. "The Carbon Footprint of Global Trade: Tackling Emissions from International Freight Transport." Policy Brief, November 30, ITF, Paris. https://www.itf-oecd.org/carbon-footprint -global-trade.

Jackson, Jeremy B. C., Michael X. Kirby, Wolfgang H. Berger, Karen A. Bjorndal, Louis W. Botsford, Bruce J. Bourque, Roger H. Bradbury, et al. 2001. "Historical Overfishing and the Recent Collapse of Coastal Ecosystems." *Science* 293 (5530): 629–37.

Jha, Veena. 2016. "Building Supply Chain Efficiency in Solar and Wind Energy: Trade and Other Policy Considerations." Issue Paper (May), International Centre for Trade and Sustainable Development, Geneva.

Keen, Michael, Ian W. H. Parry, and Jon Strand. 2012. "Market-Based Instruments for International Aviation and Shipping as a Source of Climate Finance." Policy Research Working Paper 5950, World Bank, Washington, DC.

Kellenberg, Derek K. 2009. "An Empirical Investigation of the Pollution Haven Effect with Strategic Environment and Trade Policy." *Journal of International Economics* 78 (2): 242–55.

Kroeger, Alan, Haseebullah Bakhtary, Franziska Haupt, and Charlotte Streck. 2017. "Eliminating Deforestation from the Cocoa Supply Chain." March, World Bank, Washington, DC.

Kummritz, Victor, Daria Taglioni, and Deborah Elisabeth Winkler. 2017. "Economic Upgrading through Global

Value Chain Participation: Which Policies Increase the Value Added Gains?" Policy Research Working Paper 8007, World Bank, Washington, DC.

Lanoie, Paul, Jérémy Laurent-Lucchetti, Nick Johnstone, and Stefan Ambec. 2011. "Environment Policy, Innovation, and Performance: New Insights on the Porter Hypothesis." *Journal of Economics and Management Strategy* 20 (3): 803–42.

Lepawsky, Josh. 2015. "The Changing Geography of Global Trade in Electronic Discards: Time to Rethink the e-Waste Problem." *Geographical Journal* 181 (2): 147–59.

Levinson, Arik. 2010. "Offshoring Pollution: Is the United States Increasingly Importing Polluting Goods?" *Review of Environmental Economics and Policy* 4 (1): 63–83.

Levinson, Arik, and M. Scott Taylor. 2008. "Unmasking the Pollution Haven Effect." *International Economic Review* 49 (1): 223–54.

Mekonnen, Mesfin M., and Arjen Y. Hoekstra. 2011. "National Water Footprint Accounts: The Green, Blue, and Grey Water Footprint of Production and Consumption." Value of Water Research Report 50 (May), IHE Delft Institute for Water Education, Delft, the Netherlands.

Muntean, Marilena, Diego Guizzardi, Edwin Schaaf, Monica Crippa, Efisio Solazzo, Jos G. J. Olivier, and Elisabetta Vignati. 2018. *Fossil CO_2 Emissions of All World Countries, 2018 Report.* JRC Science for Policy Report EUR 29433 EN. Luxembourg: Joint Research Center, European Union.

Roosevelt, Margot. 2018. "Can Southern California's Electric Bike Industry Survive Trump's Tariffs?" *Orange County Register*, September 10. https://www.ocregister.com/2018 /09/10/can-southern-californias-electric-bike-companies -survive-trumps-tariffs/.

Ryder, Guy, and Houlin Zhao. 2019. "The World's e-Waste Is a Huge Problem: It's Also a Golden Opportunity." *Global*

Agenda: Digital Economy and Society, January 24, World Economic Forum, Geneva. https://www.weforum.org /agenda/2019/01/how-a-circular-approach-can-turn-e -waste-into-a-golden-opportunity/.

Shapiro, Joseph S., and Reed Walker. 2018. "Why Is Pollution from U.S. Manufacturing Declining? The Roles of Environmental Regulation, Productivity, and Trade." *American Economic Review* 108 (12): 3814–54.

Sims, Ralph, Roberto Schaeffer, Felix Creutzig, Xochitl Cruz-Núñez, Marcio D'Agosto, Delia Dimitriu, Maria Josefina Figueroa Meza, et al. 2014. "Transport." In *Climate Change 2014: Mitigation of Climate Change; Contribution of Working Group III to the Fifth Assessment Report of the Intergovernmental Panel on Climate Change*, edited by Ottmar Edenhofer, Ramón Pichs-Madruga, Youba Sokona, Jan C. Minx, Ellie Farahani, Susanne Kadner, Kristin Seyboth, et al., 599–670. New York: Cambridge University Press.

Stern, David I. 2017. "The Environmental Kuznets Curve after 25 Years." *Journal of Bioeconomics* 19 (1): 7–28.

UNCTAD (United Nations Conference on Trade and Development). 2017. *Review of Maritime Transport 2017.* Report UNCTAD/RMT/2017 (October 25). Geneva: UNCTAD.

————. 2018. *Review of Maritime Transport 2018.* Report UNCTAD/RMT/2018 (October 3). Geneva: UNCTAD.

UNU (United Nations University). 2018. "E-Waste Rises 8% by Weight in 2 Years as Incomes Rise, Prices Fall." Press release, December 14, UNU, Tokyo. https://unu .edu/media-relations/releases/ewaste-rises-8-percent-by -weight-in-2-years.html.

van der Werf, Hayo M. G., and Jean Petit. 2002. "Evaluation of the Environmental Impact of Agriculture at the Farm Level: A Comparison and Analysis of 12 Indicator-Based Methods." *Agriculture, Ecosystems, and Environment* 93 (1–3): 131–45.

Technological change

Key findings

- **Trade costs are likely to continue to fall.** New digital technologies enhance opportunities for global value chain (GVC) participation. Developing countries, which exhibit the highest costs and biggest impediments to trade, stand to gain the most.

- **Platform firms and e-commerce generate uneven benefits across firms and households.** Platform firms facilitate participation but also foster concentration, which affects the distribution of gains from participation in GVCs.

- **Anxiety that automation will hinder export-led industrialization may not be warranted.** Evidence of reshoring is limited. New production technologies have promoted North–South trade, although the effects are heterogeneous across countries and sectors.

- **Increased automation in manufacturing is likely to have distributional impacts.** Adoption of robots is driving down the labor share of income and increasing the demand for skilled workers, thereby exacerbating inequality in the labor market and increasing the need for adjustment policies to support disrupted workers.

- **Restricting trade to promote manufacturing is counterproductive.** It lowers efficiency, raises prices of both inputs and outputs, and undermines incentives to innovate.

Supply chains are rapidly changing under the pressure of digital innovation. Robotics, 3D printing, big data, blockchain technologies, cloud computing, the Internet of Things, and the rise of platform firms are transforming production and distribution processes in many industries. Digital technologies raise productivity but are also disruptive, especially when they lead to a reduction in demand for workers. Meanwhile, a substantial share of exports from low-wage developing countries is in sectors being rapidly automated by their trade partners. These developments have sparked fears that industrialization led by labor-intensive exports may no longer be a viable model for developing economies seeking to develop by joining and then moving up the value chain—and that labor costs are becoming a less important determinant of competitiveness. Moreover, changing skills demands associated with technological progress could place developing countries at a disadvantage.

This chapter reviews the evidence on how emerging digital technologies, including advanced robotics and 3D printing, are affecting global value chains (GVCs), trade flows, and the prospects for export-led industrialization. In doing so, it reviews the channels through which technological progress could have impacts on GVCs—reducing trade costs, inducing quality upgrading and product churning, and changing productivity and relative costs across countries and sectors, thereby changing comparative advantage. It then explores how changes in trade policy might alter these effects[1] and offers a tentative assessment of the potential for continued expansion of global supply chains and export-led development. New technologies will likely change GVCs and the trade and jobs they create. But forecasting exactly how is fraught with uncertainty, not least because technological progress is difficult to predict.

Trade costs are likely to continue to fall because of new digital technologies, offering greater opportunities for GVC participation. Developing countries may stand to gain the most from emerging digital technologies because they face the highest trade costs and biggest distortions. Extending access to high-speed Internet and expanding e-commerce will facilitate greater GVC participation. But the gains from e-commerce are unevenly distributed across households, and not all firms benefit equally from Internet access. Artificial intelligence applications, such as machine translation, can further reduce trade and logistics costs, and might also help reduce red tape. Platform firms make it easier to participate in global markets. But the reputation mechanisms they rely on to verify seller and buyer quality may foster concentration, which makes it harder for entrants to compete. Platform firms also pose new challenges for regulators seeking to ensure fair competition and prevent abuse of market power. Meanwhile, because of technological progress more goods and services, as well as new ones, are likely to become tradable over time.

Anxiety that automation will hinder export-led industrialization may not be warranted. Evidence of companies moving operations back to their home country (reshoring) is very limited, and new production technologies such as industrial robots and 3D printing have promoted North–South trade, although the effects are heterogeneous across countries and sectors. Those that mainly compete with robot-adopting countries in output markets are at risk of being outcompeted by foreign robots and may suffer substantial reductions in employment. Adoption of robots is driving down the share of income accruing to labor and increasing the demand for skilled workers that perform tasks that complement those performed by robots, thereby exacerbating inequality.

Robot adoption improves productivity, which leads to an expansion in output and increased demand for material inputs. It also leads to the creation of new tasks. In spite of these benefits, robot adoption will likely entail substantial labor market pain.

Increasing tariffs to shield domestic industries from intensified competition associated with the adoption of new production technologies in other countries is likely counterproductive because it lowers efficiency, raises the prices of both inputs and outputs, and undermines incentives to innovate.

Declining trade costs

The Internet facilitates GVC participation

The information and communication technology (ICT) revolution that emerged in the mid-1990s has been an important enabler of the expansion of GVCs. The share of the global population using the Internet grew from less than 1 percent in 1993 to 46 percent in 2016. By 2014, almost all firms (with at least five employees) in high-income Organisation for Economic Co-operation and Development (OECD) countries used a broadband Internet connection. Among firms in lower-income countries, broadband usage remains lower, but it is rising rapidly.[2] At the same time, the cost at which information can be transmitted via an optical network has fallen dramatically. In fact, today the time it takes to download a high-definition movie through a modem connected to fiber optics is almost imperceptible. This ICT revolution has not only reduced trade costs by lowering the cost of processing and transmitting information over long distances, but it also has enabled firms to improve productivity and has led to a new range of information technology (IT)–related services. These advances have contributed to a rise in global trade and production sharing because firms are increasingly spreading their production process across borders and sourcing more intermediate inputs and services from abroad.[3]

High-speed Internet enables firms in developing countries to link to GVCs. The introduction of fast Internet in Africa and China has spurred employment and export growth, as recent studies of the economic effects of the rollout have shown.[4] In Africa, the gradual arrival of submarine Internet cables led to faster job growth (including for low-skilled workers) in locations that benefited from better access to fast Internet relative to those that did not, with little or no job displacement across space. Increased firm entry, productivity, and exporting are among the drivers of the higher net job creation in these locations. Similarly, in China provinces experiencing an increase in the number of Internet users per capita also witnessed faster export growth, with more firms competing in international markets and a higher share of provincial output sold abroad.[5] These examples attest to the potential of ICTs to help countries become part of international supply chains. They also show that the uneven provision of ICT infrastructure can aggravate spatial inequalities if already productive regions are the prime beneficiaries of infrastructure upgrading.

Digital technologies are lowering logistics and coordination costs

Digital technologies can improve customs performance by automating document processing and making it possible to create a single window for streamlining the administrative procedures for international trade transactions. In Costa Rica, a one-stop online customs system increased both exports and imports.[6] Similarly, in Colombia computerizing import procedures increased imports, reduced corruption cases, bolstered tariff revenues, and accelerated the growth of firms most exposed to the new procedures.[7]

Digital technologies also facilitate trade in existing services and may promote new services (such as videoconferencing and telecommuting) supporting GVCs. The services trade is becoming more important, and the World Trade Organization projects it will rise from approximately 21 percent of world trade today to 25 percent by 2030.[8]

Meanwhile, cloud computing offers a pay-as-you-go subscription model for storage and software, facilitating file sharing between cross-country teams and lowering the fixed costs of investments in IT infrastructure.

Some robotics and artificial intelligence applications might further reduce logistics costs, the time to transport, and the uncertainty of delivery times (box 6.1). At ports, autonomous vehicles might unload, stack, and reload containers faster and with fewer errors. Blockchain shipping solutions may lower transit times and speed up payments. The Internet of Things has the potential to increase the efficiency of delivery services by tracking shipments in real time, while improved and expanded navigation systems may help route trucks based on current road and traffic conditions. Although the empirical evidence on these impacts is limited, it is estimated that new logistics technologies could reduce shipping and customs processing times by 16 to 28 percent.[9]

Investments in digital technologies may be especially beneficial for developing countries

Ongoing technological progress, more widespread adoption of existing digital technologies, and investments in transport infrastructure are likely to reduce trade costs, promote trade, and lead to a continued expansion of GVCs. These developments may especially benefit developing countries, which currently face higher trade and transport costs and have comparatively limited ICT infrastructure. For example, 4G network coverage remains low in large parts of Africa compared with that in richer countries (map 6.1). Tariffs and nontariff measures continue to pose a significant restriction to trade by low-income countries, despite preferential access programs.[10] In addition, developing countries face large intranational trade costs, which determine the extent to which producers and consumers in remote locations are affected by changes in trade policy and international prices. For example, the effect of distance on trade costs within Ethiopia or Nigeria is four to five times larger than in the United States. Intermediaries capture most of the surplus from falling world prices, especially in more distant locations. Therefore, consumers in remote locations see only a small part of the gains from falling international trade barriers.[11] Despite recent advances in the provision of ICT infrastructure, the scope for further expanding access to high-speed Internet in developing countries remains huge.

In part because of high trade costs, firms in low-income countries tend to operate on a small scale and

Box 6.1 Digital innovation and agricultural trade

Distributed ledger technologies (DLTs) are decentralized systems for recording transactions of assets in which the transactions and their details are recorded in multiple places at the same time. DLTs could increase efficiency and transparency in agricultural supply chains by improving product traceability and integrity, contract certainty, verification of geographic origin, and compliance with sanitary and phytosanitary requirements. They could also improve the implementation and monitoring of provisions of World Trade Organization agreements relevant to the agricultural trade. DLTs can ensure that gains from trade accrue more directly to producers and consumers.[a] Meanwhile, the food losses in food systems could be reduced by up to 30 million tons a year if blockchains monitored information in half the world's supply chains.[b]

Blockchain technology is still in its infancy, but pilots testing its use are rapidly spreading. One of the most successful initiatives is the Food Trust consortium run by IBM. It uses blockchain technologies to improve the traceability of food, and it has brought together large retail and food industry companies from across the world, including Dole, Driscoll's, Golden State Foods, Kroger, and McCormick. As part of this consortium, Carrefour, a supermarket chain in France, uses blockchain technology to provide consumers with detailed information on purchased chicken, such as veterinary treatments, freshness, and other metrics.[c] Similarly, Barilla, an Italian pasta and pesto sauce manufacturer, uses blockchain technology to improve transparency and traceability in its pesto production cycle along the entire supply chain—from farm to fork.

Meanwhile, many start-ups are aiming to shorten agriculture value chains and reduce the role of intermediaries. INS, an e-commerce platform, uses DLTs to directly connect producers and consumers through data integration. And AgriDigital, an Australian company, uses blockchain-enabled contracts to facilitate interactions among the various players in the grain supply chain.

To ensure their scalability and accessibility, DLT solutions require the appropriate ecosystems. Although some elements of such ecosystems are technology-specific, they also largely rely on enabling policy, regulatory, and institutional conditions, as well as basic requirements for infrastructure, literacy (including digital), and network coverage.[d] As one example, according to a recent PricewaterhouseCoopers survey,[e] regulatory uncertainty around blockchain-based solutions was identified as a major scale-up challenge across various sectors. Other major challenges are interoperability and the potential failure of different blocks within the chain to work together.

a. Jouanjean (2019).
b. WEF (2018).
c. OECD (2019).
d. Tripoli and Schmidhuber (2018).
e. PwC (2018).

are less likely to export or import. A typical modal manufacturing firm in the United States has 45 workers, and larger firms tend to be more productive and pay higher wages and are more likely to export and import.[12] By contrast, a modal firm in most developing countries has one worker, the owner. Among firms that do hire additional workers, most hire fewer than 10. In India, Indonesia, and Nigeria, firms with fewer than 10 workers account for more than 99 percent of the total.

Developing countries tend to have a smaller number of exporters and a lower concentration of export revenue in their top exporters, suggesting that these firms face greater distortions.[13] Investments in reducing barriers to competition and minimizing frictions may thus be especially beneficial for developing countries.

Digital marketplaces are on the rise, fostering GVC participation—and concentration

Greater access to (and more extensive use of) broadband Internet and digital-enabled devices would also connect more consumers and firms in low-income countries to online markets and business-to-business platforms.

Digital marketplaces and online retailers are on the rise. Platforms such as Alibaba, Amazon, eBay, Taobao, and Mercado Libre are becoming an increasingly important interface between global manufacturers and consumers. At the same time, manufacturers and traditional retailers are seeking to achieve a stronger online presence, alongside their standard distribution channels. Consumers worldwide purchased approximately $2.86 trillion in goods and services online in

Map 6.1 4G network coverage, 2018

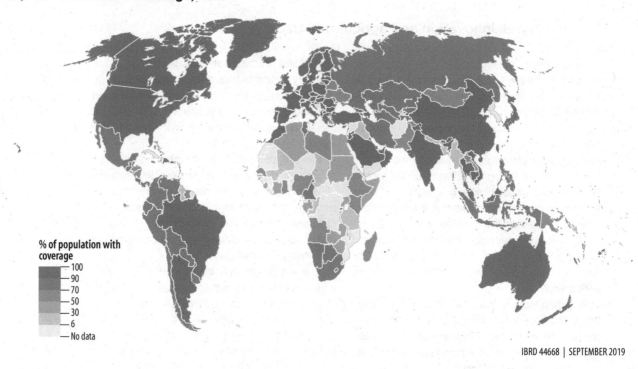

% of population with coverage
- 100
- 90
- 70
- 50
- 30
- 6
- No data

IBRD 44668 | SEPTEMBER 2019

Source: GSMA Intelligence (https://www.gsmaintelligence.com).

2018, up from $2.43 trillion in 2017. The share of online sales in total retail sales increased from 11.3 percent in 2016 to 13.3 percent in 2017.[14]

E-commerce is growing especially rapidly in China. The United States and China—the world's two largest economies—accounted for more than half of global e-commerce sales in 2017. China is the largest e-commerce market, with sales of $877 billion in 2017, up 28 percent from 2016.[15] In China, the share of online sales in total retail sales reached 15 percent in 2017, up from 12.6 percent in 2016. In the United States, consumers spent $449.88 billion on retail sites in 2017, up 15.6 percent from 2016; online penetration reached about 13 percent of total retail sales.[16] E-commerce sales are likely to continue to rise in developing countries as Internet access and usage expand. Improvements in enabling infrastructure, such as e-payment systems, logistics, third-party authenticators, and dispute resolution support services can further augment e-commerce.

Platform firms have emerged as the largest companies in the world, but geographically they are not distributed evenly. Seven of the 10 largest global companies by market capitalization in the first quarter of 2019 were platform firms, up from only three in 2015 and two in 2011 (table 6.1). These platform firms

are predominantly from North America and East Asia; Africa and Latin America are greatly underrepresented. The role of first-mover advantages in the establishment of platform firms may make it difficult for Africa, Latin America, and even Europe to bridge the gap.

A limited number of e-commerce platforms dominate most markets (figure 6.1). Amazon ranks first by traffic share in North America, Western Europe, and parts of the Middle East and India; Alibaba is the most visited site in China and some parts of the Middle East; and Mercado Libre tops Latin America (map 6.2). The activities of platform firms are thus highly concentrated among a few large megafirms.

Platforms enable GVC participation (box 6.2), but they may lead to concentration because their business model relies on building and exploiting network effects. They reduce transaction costs and help verify the quality and reputation of suppliers and match them to potential foreign buyers.[17] One study finds that the extent to which distance reduces trade is 65 percent smaller for eBay than for total trade flows (for the same set of goods and countries).[18] Although platform firms offer opportunities for new actors to connect and integrate into GVCs, the mechanisms that they typically use to overcome information

Table 6.1 Ten largest global companies, by market capitalization, 2011, 2015, and 2019

Year	Ranking	Company	Country	Market value (US$, billions)
2019	1	Apple	United States	961.3
	2	Microsoft	United States	946.5
	3	Amazon	United States	916.1
	4	Alphabet	United States	863.2
	5	Berkshire Hathaway	United States	516.4
	6	Facebook	United States	512.0
	7	Alibaba	China	480.8
	8	Tencent Holdings	China	472.1
	9	JPMorgan Chase	United States	368.5
	10	Johnson & Johnson	United States	366.2
2015	1	Apple	United States	724.8
	2	ExxonMobil	United States	356.5
	3	Berkshire Hathaway	United States	356.5
	4	Google	United States	345.8
	5	Microsoft	United States	333.5
	6	PetroChina	China	329.7
	7	Wells Fargo	United States	279.9
	8	Johnson & Johnson	United States	279.7
	9	Industrial and Commercial Bank of China	China	275.4
	10	Novartis	Switzerland	267.9
2011	1	ExxonMobil	United States	417.2
	2	PetroChina	China	326.2
	3	Apple	United States	321.1
	4	Industrial and Commercial Bank of China	China	251.1
	5	Petrobras	Brazil	247.4
	6	BHP Billiton	Australia/United Kingdom	247.1
	7	China Construction Bank	China	232.6
	8	Royal Dutch Shell	United Kingdom	228.1
	9	Chevron	United States	215.8
	10	Microsoft	United States	213.3

Sources: Financial Times Top 500 Companies (https://www.ft.com/ft500); *Forbes* Global 2000: The 2019 World's Largest Public Companies (https://www.forbes.com/global2000/).

Note: The table lists the top 10 global companies by market capitalization for 2011, 2015, and 2019. Over time, platform firms (shown in bold) have become progressively more important.

frictions, such as consumer ratings that help firms establish a credible reputation, tend to favor concentration. Although platforms enable small and medium enterprises to penetrate export markets, they also make their reputations more widely visible, favoring the emergence of superstar exporters.[19] They make it easier, then, to connect, but harder to compete.

Artificial intelligence applications are facilitating e-commerce

GVCs and e-commerce may be further supported by recent advances in machine learning. The current generation of artificial intelligence represents a revolution in prediction capabilities, with potentially broad implications for transaction costs both within and across countries. Enabling this transformation are the greater availability of data, significantly improved algorithms, and substantially more powerful computer hardware.[20] Large firms, multinational enterprises, and big online retailers such as Alibaba and Amazon are increasingly relying on big data and machine learning to understand and forecast consumer behavior and manage their supply chain more efficiently.[21]

Machine learning also reduces the linguistic barriers to trade and GVC participation. One application

Figure 6.1 Large platform companies are concentrated in North America and Asia

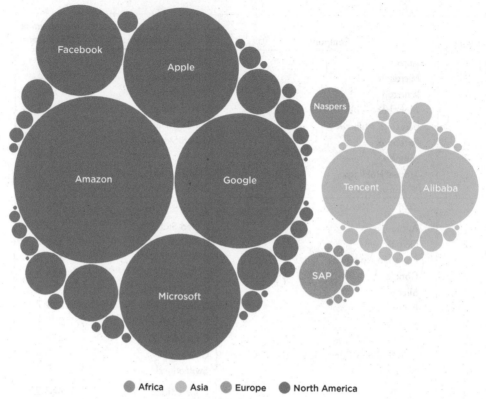

● Africa   ● Asia   ● Europe   ● North America

Source: Peter C. Evans, Global Platform Database, Platform Strategy Institute, 2019.

Note: The figure shows the concentration of the world's 75 largest platform firms by region, with bigger circles representing firms with more market capitalization.

Map 6.2 Top e-commerce platforms, by traffic share, 2019

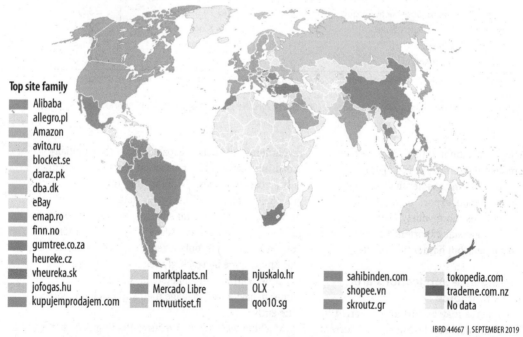

Top site family

- Alibaba
- allegro.pl
- Amazon
- avito.ru
- blocket.se
- daraz.pk
- dba.dk
- eBay
- emap.ro
- finn.no
- gumtree.co.za
- heureke.cz
- vheureka.sk
- jofogas.hu
- kupujemprodajem.com
- marktplaats.nl
- Mercado Libre
- mtvuutiset.fi
- njuskalo.hr
- OLX
- qoo10.sg
- sahibinden.com
- shopee.vn
- skroutz.gr
- tokopedia.com
- trademe.com.nz
- No data

IBRD 44667 | SEPTEMBER 2019

Source: Alexa, SimilarWeb (https://www.similarweb.com/website/alexa.com#overview).

Box 6.2 GVC linkages and cross-border connections between people move together

To operate effectively, GVCs rely on efficient processing of information. This is the point at which platform firms enter the picture because they enable other firms to connect and communicate as well as encourage the formation of new linkages. Professional networks enable the operation of GVCs. To explore the linkages between networks and trade, the World Bank has partnered with LinkedIn, a professional platform with more than 630 million members in over 200 countries and territories. Members of LinkedIn, who provide information on their educational and career backgrounds, are part of a network and thereby "linked" to other professionals in other firms, sectors, and countries. Analysis of the LinkedIn data (figure B6.2.1) reveals that exports (panel a) and both backward and forward GVC participation (panels b and c, respectively) are strongly correlated with the number of foreign connections indicated by members of LinkedIn. Although causality is more difficult to establish, these patterns suggest that professional networks are complementary to the expansion of GVCs.

Figure B6.2.1 Relationship of exports and GVC participation to online foreign connections

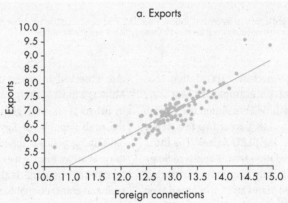

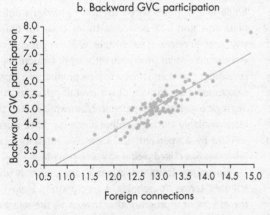

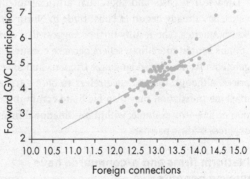

Sources: World Bank Group–LinkedIn Digital Data for Development, Jobs, Skills, and Migration; OECD's TiVA database. See appendix A for a description of the databases used in this Report.

Note: The graphs show the correlation between the three GVC measures and the foreign connections of members of LinkedIn. The y-axis is based on data from the TiVA data set of the Organisation for Economic Co-operation and Development (OECD) at the sector level (36 sectors) for 64 countries. The variables are the natural log of total exports in millions of U.S. dollars (panel a) and backward and forward participation in GVCs (panels b and c, respectively), also measured in logs of millions of U.S. dollars. The x-axis data are from the Economic Graph at LinkedIn (https://economicgraph.linkedin .com/), showing the natural log of the total number of foreign connections in a given sector in the same 64 countries for 2015–18. Each point in the scatterplot represents the mean of the y-axis variable in each of the 100 chosen bins of the x-axis data. The diagonal line represents the prediction of the dependent variable, calculated using a linear regression with additional country and sector fixed effects. Therefore, its slope represents the elasticity between the y-axis and x-axis measures.

Figure 6.2 From 2013 to 2015, U.S. exports to Latin America through eBay increased after the introduction of machine translation

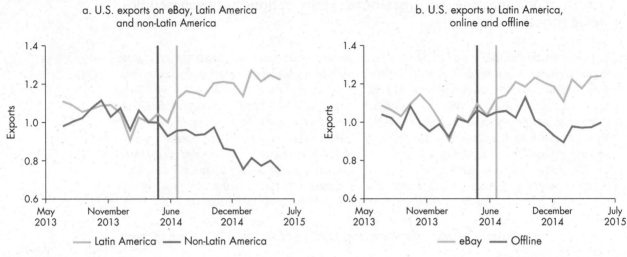

a. U.S. exports on eBay, Latin America and non-Latin America

b. U.S. exports to Latin America, online and offline

— Latin America — Non-Latin America

— eBay — Offline

Source: Brynjolfsson, Hui, and Liu 2018.

Note: Exports in panel a are measured in quantity and normalized to the level in April 2013. Exports in panel b are measured in U.S. dollars and normalized to the level in April 2013. The red vertical line marks the introduction of query translation, and the aqua vertical line marks the introduction of item title translation.

of machine learning—machine translation—has improved in recent years. For example, the best score at the Workshop on Machine Translation for English to German rose from 15.7 to 28.3, according to a widely used comparison metric, the BLEU score.[22] The introduction of machine translation from English to Spanish by eBay has significantly boosted international trade between the United States and Latin America on this platform, increasing exports by 17.5 percent (figure 6.2). These effects reflect a reduction in translation-related search costs and show that artificial intelligence has already begun to boost trade in North and South America. The results further suggest that consumers benefit more than sellers because consumers gain both from reduced language frictions and lower prices. Although the evidence refers to online trade, machine translation may also facilitate communication offline—for example, within multinational firms or across trading partners.

Platform firms and e-commerce have uneven benefits

Besides fueling GVCs and cross-border trade, deeper integration of e-commerce may also help it reach more firms and households in rural markets in developing countries. In China, the largest e-commerce market, the number of people buying and selling products online grew from essentially zero in 2000 to more than 400 million in 2015. A clear upward trend was

also observed in many other developing countries. Although most of this growth has so far been observed in urban areas, emerging economies such as China, the Arab Republic of Egypt, India, and Vietnam are developing policies aimed at expanding e-commerce to rural areas. But such expansion requires more than Internet access alone. It also means overcoming logistical and transactional barriers, such as the dearth of modern commercial parcel deliveries and rural households' lack of familiarity with how to navigate online platforms and lack of access to (or trust in) online payment services. The sizable welfare gains from e-commerce stem predominantly from reductions in consumer prices and access to new products. In Japan, e-commerce has driven down overall prices, raising aggregate welfare by 1 percent. Meanwhile, new varieties available through online shopping have raised welfare by 0.7 percent, and increased intercity price arbitrage has raised welfare by 0.06 percent.[23]

The gains from e-commerce are unevenly distributed across households. A recent study looked at the effects of a program that invests in the logistics needed to ship products to and sell products from tens of thousands of Chinese villages that were largely unconnected to e-commerce.[24] Between the end of 2014 and middle of 2016, nearly 16,500 villages in 333 counties and 27 provinces in China were connected to e-commerce through the program. The sizable gains from e-commerce trading in both number of

Figure 6.3 **Effects of an e-commerce program on the number of buyers and online transactions in Chinese villages**

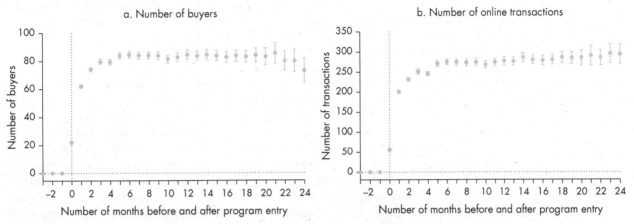

a. Number of buyers

b. Number of online transactions

Source: Couture et al. 2018.

Note: The figure shows point estimates from a regression of depicted outcomes on months since program entry with village and month fixed effects. Outcomes are the number of buyers (panel a) and the number of online transactions (panel b). The data are from a major e-commerce firm's internal database and contain the universe of village purchase transactions from November 2015 to April 2017 in five provinces: Anhui, Guangxi, Guizhou, Henan, and Yunnan (roughly 11,900 villages in total). The last point estimate of each plot pools months 24–28. The graphs show 95 percent confidence intervals based on standard errors that are clustered at the village level. Overall, the figure indicates that the introduction of e-commerce was associated with an increase in both the number of buyers and the number of online transactions.

buyers and number of online transactions (figure 6.3) have, however, tended to accrue to a minority of rural households who are younger, richer, and better positioned to take advantage of the opportunities e-commerce offers. Importantly, the gains have been significantly stronger among villages not previously serviced by commercial parcel delivery, suggesting that the impacts of the program stem mainly from overcoming a logistical barrier rather than from additional investments aimed at adapting e-commerce to transactional barriers specific to rural households.

E-commerce benefits consumers by reducing the cost of living, especially in remote rural areas. On the income side, e-commerce has displacement effects. In the United States, the growth of e-commerce from 3.8 percent of retail sales in 2010 to 8.3 percent in 2017 was associated with a reduction in employment in brick-and-mortar retail stores. In counties with retail fulfilment centers, the labor income of retail workers fell by 2.4 percent after the establishment of such a center, with both younger and older workers experiencing sharper decreases in labor income.[25] Consumption gains thus come at the expense of labor market adjustments.

Platforms create new regulatory challenges

As platform firms grow, gain access to more private data, and wield market power, so do concerns about anticompetitive behavior. At least for now, however,

the scope for raising consumer prices appears to be fairly limited. Online platforms still account for a fairly small share of the overall retail market. Recent evidence points to strong substitution between online and offline sales for personal computers, news, and advertising.[26] Meanwhile, services such as Google Shopping facilitate price comparisons across online merchants and marketplaces, many of which are still in their infancy.

The interdependencies between platforms' third-party sales for retailers and their own online retail operations can result in potential conflicts of interest and may enable anticompetitive conduct.[27] Hybrid platforms such as Amazon, JD.com, and Flipkart sell their own inventory and also act as an online marketplace for other retailers to sell their products, taking a commission for each order. Operating as both an upstream intermediation market for other firms and a downstream retail market for its final customers may give rise to conflicts of interest. Online shoppers may not be able to tell the difference between a platform's own retail services and its marketplace activities for other merchants. Moreover, hybrid platforms may use the data they collect while operating as a marketplace to identify successful products in the marketplace so that they can then market their own branded version in the same platform.

Another, more traditional, form of potential abuse is predatory pricing, whereby platforms use their privileged access to third-party data to temporarily charge prices below cost on their own products to gain a permanent competitive edge over other merchants. The concern is not that platforms offer their own products at a lower price than that offered by the original seller, thereby benefiting consumers. It is that hybrid platforms may be able to offer such prices only because of their use of third-party data. They could then adopt temporary pricing strategies to gain more permanent advantages over their competitors and subsequently raise prices. At the same time, it is important to recognize that pricing structures are complex. Subsidies across users can help a platform increase its volume of transactions and benefits. In other words, a platform can charge prices below marginal cost to some participants, which does not necessarily mean that it is engaged in predatory pricing. Alternatively, charging prices above marginal cost to other participants does not necessarily mean market power is at work.

Concerns about anticompetitive behavior are not unique to platform firms. Markups have been rising in many sectors of the economy, and especially so in digital-intensive sectors.[28] The average U.S. markups have risen from 18 percent above marginal cost in the 1980s to the present 67 percent. Similar trends in markups have been documented in other countries. According to OECD, markups have grown more in digital-intensive sectors than in others, with the growth driven by firms at the top end of the distribution. These superstar firms are thus accounting for a higher share of profits, which increasingly are unevenly divided.

New products

Since the 1990s, many new types of products have entered global trade, primarily intermediate goods, further demonstrating the increasing fragmentation of production and the emergence of entirely new products (figure 6.4). Indeed, the trade in new products has grown dramatically. In 2017, 65 percent of trade was in categories that either did not exist in 1992 or were modified to better reflect changes in trade. Trade in intermediate goods (parts and components and semifinished goods) expanded, and entirely new products entered global trade. For example, trade in IT products tripled over the past two decades, as trade in digitizable goods such as CDs, books, and newspapers steadily declined from 2.7 percent of the total goods trade in 2000 to 0.8 percent in 2018.[29] Technological developments are likely to continue to produce product churning.

Because of technological progress, more goods and services are likely to become tradable over time. For

Figure 6.4 Globally, the number and trade share of new products increased from 1996 to 2017

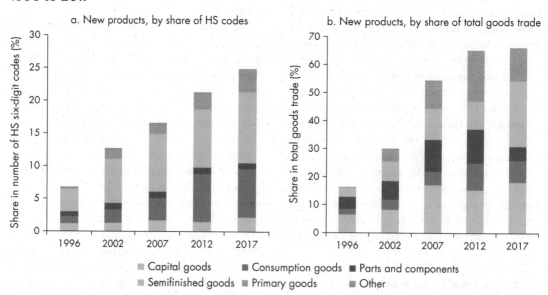

a. New products, by share of HS codes

b. New products, by share of total goods trade

Capital goods Consumption goods Parts and components
Semifinished goods Primary goods Other

Source: UN Comtrade (International Trade Statistics, Import/Export Data).

Note: Products are classified by a Harmonized System (HS) six-digit code. New products are classified relative to the set of products in the first HS classification in 1988/1992. New codes are either genuinely new products, or old product codes that split into two new codes, or two old codes that merged into one new code. Products are further classified as final (consumption and capital), intermediate (parts and components and semifinished), or primary and other goods using the Broad Economic Categories revision 4 classification from the United Nations Conference on Trade and Development. The figure shows that over time trade in new products has grown dramatically.

example, platforms such as Upwork and Mechanical Turk make it easier for businesses to outsource tasks to workers who can perform them virtually. And new goods and services are likely to be developed, including ones not even imaginable today, thereby boosting the incentives to trade.

Automation anxiety

Robotization is on the rise, raising concerns about the future of GVCs

The spread of new production technologies, such as advanced robotics and 3D printing, has raised concerns about the future of trade and of GVCs. Robotics technology, having advanced greatly in the last two decades, is predicted to develop further in the coming years. The average price of an industrial robot has fallen by half in real terms and even more relative to labor costs. Global sales of industrial robots reached a record 387,000 units in 2017, up 31 percent from 2016. Figure 6.5 shows that robotization is higher in countries with higher income per capita, where wages are higher, and in sectors in which robotization is feasible. Robots are used predominantly in high-wage countries in Asia, North America, and Western Europe (panel a). In recent years, China saw the largest growth in demand for industrial robots and was projected to have the largest operational stock of robots by the end of 2018, but still relatively low robot density.[30] Robotization is most pronounced in the automotive, rubber and plastics, metals, and electronics sectors, reflecting differences in the feasibility of automation (panel b). It is still limited in traditionally labor-intensive sectors such as textiles, suggesting that export-led industrialization in these sectors is still a viable development path. Robot adoption is projected to increase greatly over the coming decade, reflecting further reductions in quality-adjusted robot prices.[31]

Modern industrial robots can be programmed to perform a variety of repetitive tasks with consistent precision, and they are increasingly used in a wide range of industries and applications. If tasks previously performed by low-skilled workers in the South (low-wage developing countries) are performed by relatively inexpensive robots in the North (industrial countries), there may be a reversal in North–South trade flows and a greater reliance on domestic production. Moreover, the skill and capital content of inputs that countries in the North demand from the South may increase now that the North can use robots and other technologies more intensively, as discussed in more depth shortly.[32] The criteria for becoming an attractive production location may

Figure 6.5 Robot adoption is greater in high-income countries and in sectors in which tasks are easily automated

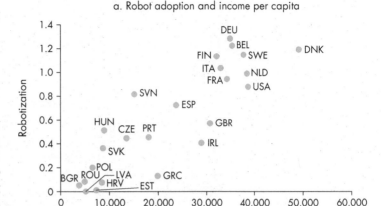

a. Robot adoption and income per capita

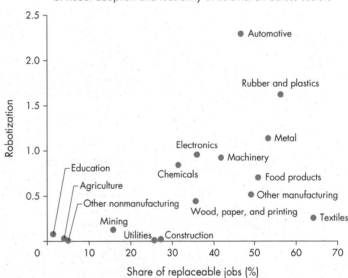

b. Robot adoption and feasibility of automation across sectors

Source: Artuc, Bastos, and Rijkers 2018.

Note: Robotization is the logarithm of 1 plus the ratio of the average stock of robots to the number of working hours (in millions) between 1993 and 2015 (or the subsample of years over this period for which robot data from the International Federation of Robotics [IFR] are available). The stock of robots is estimated using the perpetual inventory method based on the observed stock of robots in the IFR data and using a depreciation rate of 10 percent. The share of jobs that is potentially replaceable by robots is based on the task makeup of the job. See Artuc, Bastos, and Rijkers (2018) for a detailed explanation of how replaceability is measured. For country abbreviations, see International Organization for Standardization (ISO), https://www.iso.org/obp/ui/#search.

change as well, with low labor costs becoming a less important determinant of competitiveness (at least in sectors in which automation is feasible), and complementary factors, such as the availability of skills and sound infrastructure, becoming more important.[33] Although the risk of displacement of jobs or exports currently seems low, middle-income countries such

Map 6.3 A substantial share of exports from developing countries is in goods that can be produced by robots

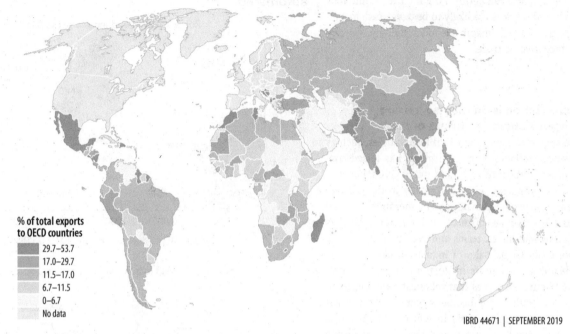

% of total exports
to OECD countries

- 29.7–53.7
- 17.0–29.7
- 11.5–17.0
- 6.7–11.5
- 0–6.7
- No data

IBRD 44671 | SEPTEMBER 2019

Source: WDR 2020 team, based on Artuc, Bastos, and Rijkers (2018).

Note: The map shows exports (by quintile) as a percentage of total exports to high-income OECD (Organisation for Economic Co-operation and Development) countries, weighted by the share of jobs in sectors that produce the exported goods that are potentially replaceable by robots based on their task makeup. See Artuc, Bastos, and Rijkers (2018) for a detailed explanation of how replaceability is measured.

as Mexico, Tunisia, and Pakistan would seem most exposed to the threat of robotization-induced reshoring because their exports are heavily concentrated in goods that robots can help produce (map 6.3). Commodity exporters, however, seem somewhat shielded from the threat of robotization-induced reshoring.

The advent of 3D printing led to predictions that many goods would be printed locally, shortening GVCs and limiting trade. The concern is that if 3D printing becomes cheap, then firms capable of creating a solid 3D object from a digital file will prefer to 3D print products at home rather than import them. 3D printers may therefore perform the tasks previously performed by workers engaged in production and assembly activities located abroad.

These concerns are in part predicated on a few high-profile examples. For example, the sporting goods manufacturer Adidas recently established two "speedfactories" in Germany and the United States that use robots and 3D printing to more quickly produce customizable running shoes for high-income domestic consumers. Adidas hopes the two factories can produce 1 million pairs of shoes a year by 2020, which is still a tiny share of the 403 million pairs it

produced in 2017. Adidas's competitor Nike has several automated platforms under development.

Robotization and 3D printing have promoted North–South trade with heterogeneous impacts across countries

Despite the concerns about the effects of automatization, the evidence that reshoring will result is very limited.[34] Moreover, these technologies may enhance GVCs and boost trade. The spread of automation in richer countries can improve productivity and income, thereby raising the demand for inputs and final goods from countries with large pools of low-wage labor as a comparative advantage. Furthermore, developed countries with similar factor endowments and technologies trade a great deal among themselves. Even if the labor advantage of low-income countries is (partially) canceled out by robotization, there will still be opportunities for trade in differentiated goods and for specialization in some stages of production.

Thus far, the rising adoption of industrial robots and 3D printing seems to have promoted North–South trade. Greater robot intensity in production has led to more imports sourced from lower-income countries in the same broad industry—and to an even stronger increase in gross exports (which embody imported inputs) to those countries. The surge in imports from the South has been concentrated in intermediate goods such as parts and components. The positive impact of automation on imports, particularly on imports of intermediates, attests to the importance of examining the effects of robotization on trade through a GVC framework. More-traditional trade models would predict the increase in exports by the North but fail to foresee the surge in imports from the South in the same industry.[35] Rather than reducing North–South trade, robotization seems to have been boosting it, although it is uncertain whether this trend is likely to continue.

These average effects mask heterogeneity across countries and sectors (figure 6.6). The biggest automation-induced increase in trade has been in the quick-to-automate automotive sector. Countries already supplying inputs to automating producers in the North are well positioned to benefit from the higher demand for their exports. But countries directly competing with them in output markets could lose export revenue and manufacturing employment if their workers are outcompeted by foreign robots. The negative effects of reduced manufacturing employment could outweigh the welfare gains associated with the lower import prices resulting from automation in the North, at least in the short run. But these countries might benefit from automation-induced increases in global productivity and income, which could translate into more exports and activity in sectors where they retain a comparative advantage.

A related dynamic of innovation-induced trade can be observed in goods that can be produced using 3D printers, such as hearing aids (box 6.3). In 2007 hearing aids shifted almost entirely to 3D printing, and trade increased when compared with similar goods (figure 6.7). Estimates that take into account industry growth and the standard determinants of trade reveal that trade in hearing aids was boosted by 60 percent following the introduction of 3D printing. Other industries producing goods that were partially 3D printed have demonstrated that the technology has similar positive effects on trade. The results are at odds with the view that 3D printing will shorten supply chains and reduce trade, at least for this set of products. The findings do suggest that gains may disproportionately accrue to middle- and high-income countries, and thus they serve as a reminder that the gains from the introduction of new production technologies are likely to be unevenly distributed across countries.

Figure 6.6 Automation in industrial countries has boosted imports from developing countries

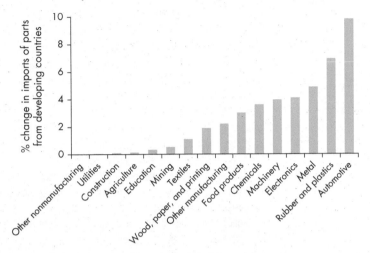

Industries in order of increasing automation

Source: Artuc, Bastos, and Rijkers 2018.

Note: The figure depicts the automation-induced increase in imports of parts by developed countries (North) from developing countries (South) by broad sector from 1995 to 2015. The change in imports of parts is measured in log points; a 0.10 increase in log points is roughly equivalent to a 10 percent increase in imports.

Automation is compressing labor's income share but not necessarily reducing employment

As automation improves productivity, it also compresses labor's share of income in advanced economies. Higher robot density at the industry level is associated with a lower labor share of income, defined as total labor compensation over sales (figure 6.8). This pattern has implications for inequality because it suggests that the primary beneficiaries of automation are the owners of capital. Moreover, technological progress and the accompanying cost reductions in the relative price of capital goods may be contributing to the global decline in labor's share of income observed across countries over the past few decades.[36] Although the jury is out on the drivers of this decline, the fall in the labor share across sectors is highest in sectors undergoing concentration and the emergence of superstar firms. These firms make high profits and typically have a lower share of labor in sales and value added, in part because they are harnessing technological innovations.[37]

Robot adoption among OECD countries has reduced the employment share of low-skilled workers in robot-intensive industries. Across local labor markets in Mexico and the United States, workers with a high exposure to domestic robotization have witnessed a reduction in employment and wages relative to those with more limited exposure.[38]

Box 6.3 Fully automating the production of hearing aids

A common refrain is that automating production, such as with 3D printing, will allow companies to produce goods closer to markets. Companies will drastically shorten their value chains, which will reduce international trade. Lower-income countries will be most affected because their exports are often intermediate products based on abundant, low-cost labor. One attempt to quantify and predict the trade impacts of 3D printing stated it could eliminate as much as 40 percent of trade by 2040.[a] By contrast, new research on the production of, and trade in, hearing aids suggests quite the opposite.

Similar to a standard ink printer, 3D printing uses very little labor and can generate customized products from the same machine. In 2007, following a series of inventions in 3D scanning, software development, and biocompatible materials, the production of hearing aids shifted almost entirely to 3D printing. In the decade that followed, trade increased overall by 60 percent, and because of lower production

costs, prices fell by about 25 percent.[b] Meanwhile, the product underwent improvements: 3D printing allowed for high levels of customization and cosmetic improvements in hearing aids, which reduced discomfort and the stigma for users. Demand increased and trade expanded.

There is no evidence that 3D printing shifted the product closer to consumers or displaced trade—the comparative advantages of different countries in the hearing aid value chain remained the same. Nor does this trend seem to be exclusive to hearing aids. A preliminary analysis of 35 other products[c] that are partially 3D printed found similar positive effects on trade, although to a smaller degree. Perhaps 3D printing had not yet been fully adopted for those products across the entire industry. Unlike the results of the hearing aids analysis, the results of this analysis point to a reshuffling of comparative advantage from labor-abundant countries to countries that adopted 3D printing technologies for each product.

a. Leering (2017).
b. Freund, Mulabdic, and Ruta (2018).
c. Freund, Mulabdic, and Ruta (2018).

Figure 6.7 Trade in hearing aids increased with the adoption of 3D printing in 2007

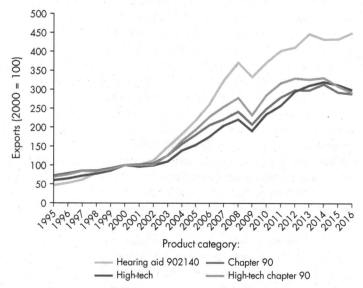

Product category:

— Hearing aid 902140 — Chapter 90
— High-tech — High-tech chapter 90

Source: Freund, Mulabdic, and Ruta 2018.

Note: The Harmonized System (HS) code for hearing aids is 902140. Three additional categories are included for comparison. Chapter 90 covers optical, photographic, cinematographic, measuring, checking, precision, medical or surgical instruments and apparatus, and parts and accessories thereof. High-tech are other goods similar to hearing aids found both in and outside chapter 90. High-tech chapter 90 includes high-tech products selected from chapter 90.

Figure 6.8 Higher robot density is associated with lower shares of income for labor

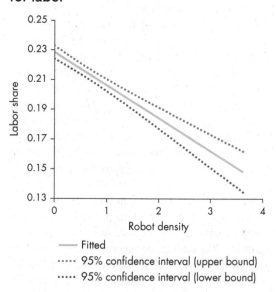

— Fitted
···· 95% confidence interval (upper bound)
···· 95% confidence interval (lower bound)

Source: Artuc, Bastos, and Rijkers 2018.

Note: The figure shows the association between labor's share of income, defined as total labor compensation over sales, and robot density, defined as the number of robots per million work-hours, for industries in the EU-KLEMS data set for the period 1993–2015.

Although automation is no doubt causing pain in the labor market, it would be incorrect to assume that because robots replace workers they always reduce aggregate employment. Robots are a labor-saving form of technological progress and may directly displace jobs, but their adoption can in fact spur job creation through three indirect channels that are challenging to measure. First, the productivity gains in supplier industries can yield steep increases in the demand for labor because of input–output linkages, as shown earlier. Second, productivity growth can boost final demand. And, third, adoption of robots may lead to compositional shifts in the structure of the economy and could create jobs by spurring the growth of sectors with high labor shares. Across member countries of the OECD, industry-level productivity growth has been associated with job losses in the industries in which it originates, but these losses have been more than compensated by indirect gains in customers and supplier industries and growth in final demand. Since the early 1970s, aggregate employment in OECD countries has grown, even though relative employment in industries experiencing the fastest growth in productivity has fallen. Although it is not clear whether automation ultimately helps or hurts net job creation, it certainly causes significant, and costly, labor market adjustments.

Automation is changing the demand for skills and comparative advantages

The intuition behind these findings is that automating tasks that can be performed by robots almost surely raises the economic value of the complementary tasks and thus the demand for laborers to perform them.[39] Automation may also lead to the creation of new tasks and products in which human labor has a comparative advantage both at home and abroad. These forces give rise to a *reinstatement effect*, raising the demand for labor by expanding the set of tasks allocated to workers.[40] For example, in industrial sectors where robotization is more prevalent in the United States, low-skilled occupations such as assemblers and production workers experienced sizable job losses over the past decades, while occupations such as sales representatives, engineers, and programmers experienced strong increases in net employment (figure 6.9). Meanwhile, rising incomes due to automation may lead not only to new tasks, but also to new products

Figure 6.9 Change in U.S. employment in robot-intensive industries, by occupation, 1990–2010

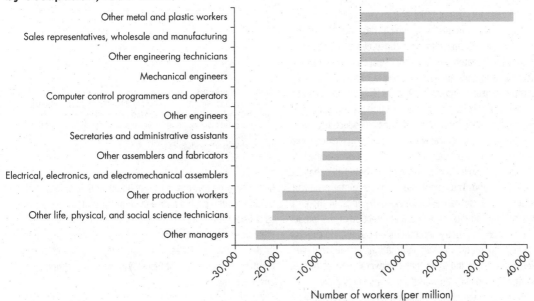

Number of workers (per million)

Source: WDR 2020 team, based on tabulations of IPUMS-USA data using the 2010 Harmonized Occupation Classification Scheme.

Note: Data refer to the automotive, machinery, electronics, rubber and plastics, and metal industries. The figure depicts changes in employment for the five occupations with higher and lower net employment creations. The total number of workers in these sectors is normalized to 1 million per year. Occupations labeled as "Other" refer to those not listed separately. Other metal and plastic workers include electrical discharge machine setup operators, metal rivet machine operators, and tin recovery workers. Other engineering technicians include agricultural, biomedical, metallurgical, and optical engineering technicians. Other engineers include optical, ordinance, photonics, and salvage engineers. Other assemblers and fabricators include air bag builders, crate builders, and doll makers. Other production workers include chemical processing machine setters, operators, and tenders; crushing, grinding, polishing, mixing, and lending workers; and cutting workers. Other life, physical, and social science technicians include meteorological aides and polygraph examiners. Other managers include clerks of court, social science managers, and utilities managers.

and services. Greater product customization may require tasks that robots cannot perform.[41] A glance back at the U.S. economy reveals that between 1990 and 2010 the occupational category "retail salesperson" experienced greater net employment gains in the U.S. economy, along with other service occupations such as food preparation (which includes restaurant chefs and sandwich makers). These findings align with those of the *World Development Report 2019: The Changing Nature of Work*, which documents how new technologies are changing the demand for skills and the nature of work.[42]

Future automation in developed and emerging economies will likely affect worker groups differently, and it may exacerbate inequality. Low-skilled workers performing repetitive tasks are more likely to be displaced by robots. In developing countries, however, middle-skill jobs may also be at risk (box 6.4). Women

Box 6.4 Mexico and technological change

Global value chains link the fates of workers living in different countries because technological progress in one country can affect employment in others.

Over the last two decades, car manufacturers in Detroit have gradually incorporated the use of robots to automate the production of engines, thereby displacing workers. Because some of the engine components are produced elsewhere within GVCs, workers living thousands of miles from Detroit in cities such as Chihuahua, Mexico, where U.S. companies assemble car parts, are exposed to the threat of robotization. In other words, automation in the United States could produce unemployment in Mexico by bringing jobs back to . . . U.S. robots.

But the story is not quite so simple: robots have also increased U.S. productivity, which has led to greater demand for intermediate and consumer products from Mexico and created new jobs for Mexicans (although not necessarily in Chihuahua). For example, roughly 70 percent of the electrical wiring components of U.S. cars are currently produced in Mexico, and their production process cannot be automated. After automation induces a productivity spike, the demand for electrical wiring produced in Mexico could be expected to increase. This productivity boost in the U.S. car industry also increases aggregate income and enhances overall demand. Thus the demand for consumer products, in addition to car parts, from Mexico expands. In the end, it is difficult to predict the size and direction of the impact of high-income country automation on developing country workers operating through international trade channels. Recent evidence indicates that the overall impact of U.S. automation on Mexican workers has been negligible.

Does this mean that Mexican workers have been immune to the negative distributional effects of robotization? No. The use of industrial robots is not limited to high-income countries. In the last 15 years, manufacturers in Mexico have also adopted new automation technologies, but less intensively than manufacturers in the United States. Production technologies in Mexico and the United States are

Figure B6.4.1 Automation reduces the wage employment of high school graduates

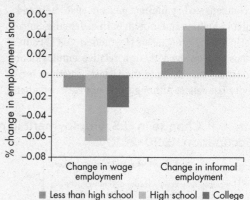

Source: WDR 2020 team, based on Artuc, Christiaensen, and Winkler (2019).

Note: Figure shows the estimated percentage change in wage employment and informal employment of different skill groups between 2011 and 2016 that can be attributed to local automation in Mexico. The impact is statistically significant for high school graduates, who constitute a larger share of employment in robotized industries, such as automotive, compared with other industries.

linked by large corporations, foreign direct investment, and GVCs. The relationship between domestic and foreign firms as subsidiaries or as arm's-length suppliers of parts accelerates transfers of technology and eases access to capital in developing countries. And even when different parts are produced by different firms, using similar technologies ensures compatibility.

As producers in Mexico have begun to use industrial robots in the footsteps of their counterparts in the United States, Mexican workers, like U.S. workers, are beginning to be displaced (figure B6.4.1). However, contrary to speculation, the impact has not been through reshoring, but through the diffusion of technological shocks with the global integration of production processes.

also tend to perform more routine tasks than men across all sectors and occupations—tasks most prone to automation. Female workers thus face a higher risk of automation than male workers, with significant heterogeneity across sectors and countries. Less well-educated older female workers are disproportionately exposed to automation, even though the gender pay gap weakens incentives to automate tasks performed by women, who tend to be paid less than men.[43] The potentially dis-equalizing effects of automation are likely to be compounded by the increase in the relative returns to capital that automation is likely to entail, at least in the short run.

This evidence is well aligned with results from model-based counterfactual simulations of the impact of further reductions in robot prices.[44] As robot prices decline, increased automation displaces workers in the North in a wider range of tasks, which initially depresses wages. Welfare nevertheless increases because the income losses associated with lower labor income are more than offset by the higher income from the rental rate of robots and lower consumer prices. The adverse impacts of automation on labor markets may eventually be overturned by further reductions in robot prices. As robot adoption proceeds in the North, production continues to expand and may raise the labor demand for the tasks in which robotization is technologically unfeasible. This situation potentially leads to an increase in the demand for labor and in real wages. Workers in the South may benefit from robotization.

That robot adoption can at times go hand in hand with job creation is illustrated by the U.S. automotive industry, which in recent decades has adopted more robots than any other sector in the United States, both in absolute terms and per worker. From 2010 until 2016, the operational stock of U.S. robots in the automotive sector rose by 52,000 units. At the same time, the number of jobs increased by 260,600, according to the Bureau of Labor Statistics, partly recovering from the steady decline in the previous decade.

Openness and innovation

How are these patterns affected by trade policy? Inflating trade costs by, for example, imposing tariffs will not only diminish trade, but also influence patterns of technology adoption. Model simulations suggest that developing countries may themselves be *more* likely to adopt labor-saving technologies when trade costs are high. They would then be somewhat shielded from foreign competition in sectors where these technologies are used more intensively as it

would be much more expensive to import goods produced in developed countries using these technologies. But this does not mean that protectionism stimulates innovation. Instead, it likely prevents efficiency-enhancing specialization across countries. By contrast, by opening up opportunities in new markets and fostering competition in domestic markets, trade liberalization tends to incentivize competition and scale and, by implication, innovation. About 7 percent of the increase in knowledge creation during the 1990s was attributable to trade reforms lowering barriers to foreign markets.[45]

Recent firm-level studies point out that international sourcing strategies could serve as a conduit to innovation. For example, evidence from Denmark suggests that offshoring allows firms to devote a larger share of their labor force to innovation-related activities, thereby facilitating technological upgrading. These findings align with evidence from Norway showing research and development (R&D) and international sourcing to be complementary.[46] Cheaper access to imported intermediate inputs raises the returns to R&D. These estimates are also in line with broader cross-country evidence pointing to greater functional specialization in trade: high-income countries tend to specialize in R&D, lower-income countries tend to specialize in fabrication, and specialization in management and marketing is unrelated to income.[47]

Inflating the costs of international sourcing by raising trade protection could thus undermine gains from specialization and stunt productivity growth. Put differently, openness stimulates innovation. The positive impacts of trade openness on technological progress are an often overlooked source of gains from trade.

Export-led industrialization

Although predicting the future is a treacherous exercise, new technologies will likely reduce trade costs and make it easier to participate in global markets. Such outcomes may offer developing countries new opportunities to link into GVCs. However, the attendant intensification of competition may make it more challenging for countries to succeed. Platform firms, for example, are making it easier to connect, but their reputation mechanisms for verifying supplier quality tend to foster concentration and make it harder for entrants to grow. They are creating new challenges for regulators both because they wield market power and because their interactions with agents in different parts of the value chain may create potential conflicts of interest and enhance the scope for anticompetitive conduct.

Automation anxiety is not warranted for all developing countries. Although some countries are likely to lose manufacturing employment because of greater competition in output markets, countries that are part of GVCs and supplying inputs to other countries that are automating may see an increase in the demand for their goods, and consumers everywhere will enjoy lower prices. The primary challenge arising from new production technologies is to ensure that the benefits are shared and that losers are compensated both across and within countries. Among the countries adopting these technologies, labor market disruptions are likely to be significant, skill premiums are likely to rise, and labor's share of income may decline further. These outcomes point to the importance of sound social safety nets and redistributive and tax policies to ensure that gains are widely shared without distorting incentives to innovate. These policies will be discussed in chapter 8.

Notes

1. Artuc, Bastos, and Rijkers (2018); Bown et al. (2017); de la Torre et al. (2015); Dutz (2018); Lopez-Acevedo, Medvedev, and Palmade (2017).
2. In lower-middle-income countries, the share of firms (with at least five employees) using broadband Internet rose from 39 percent in 2006–09 to 68 percent in 2010–14. According to the *World Development Report 2016: Digital Dividends*, the share in low-income countries in 2010–14 was about 38 percent (World Bank 2016).
3. Antràs, Garicano, and Rossi-Hansberg (2008); Costinot, Vogel, and Wang (2013); Fort (2017); Freund and Weinhold (2002, 2004); Grossman and Rossi-Hansberg (2008).
4. See, for example, Hjort and Poulsen (2019).
5. Fernandes et al. (2019).
6. Carballo et al. (2016).
7. Laajaj, Eslava, and Kinda (2019).
8. The McKinsey Global Institute argues that traditional trade statistics do not duly account for the rising importance of trade in services, notably by underestimating (1) the services embodied in goods; (2) the intangibles sent by firms to foreign affiliates; and (3) the proliferation of free digital services made available to global users (MGI 2019).
9. MGI (2019).
10. Hoekman and Nicita (2008).
11. See Atkin and Donaldson (2015).
12. Hsieh and Klenow (2014); Hsieh and Olken (2014); McKenzie (2017).
13. Fernandes, Freund, and Pierola (2016).
14. Young (2019).
15. Young (2019).
16. Young (2019).

17. See Chen and Wu (2018) and Garicano and Kaplan (2001).
18. Lendle et al. (2016).
19. Chen and Wu (2018).
20. Agrawal, Lacetera, and Lyons (2016); Brynjolfsson and McAfee (2017); Mullainathan and Spiess (2017).
21. Columbus (2018).
22. Brynjolfsson, Hui, and Liu (2018), citing http://matrix .statmt.org/matrix.
23. Jo, Matsumura, and Weinstein (2019).
24. Couture et al. (2018).
25. Chava et al. (2018).
26. Duch-Brown, Martens, and Mueller-Langer (2017); Gertner and Stillman (2001); Goldfarb and Tucker (2011); Goolsbee (2001); Prince (2007); Seamans and Zhu (2014).
27. Höppner and Westerhoff (2018).
28. Calligaris, Criscuolo, and Marcolin (2018).
29. WTO (2018).
30. IFR (2018).
31. A study by the Boston Consulting Group predicts that growth in installed robotic systems will rise from the current 3 percent annually to around 10 percent annually in the next decade (BCG 2016).
32. See Rodrik (2018) for a detailed discussion of this "technological-compatibility" channel.
33. Hallward-Driemeier and Nayyar (2018).
34. Oldenski (2015) provides evidence that reshoring is not widespread in the United States.
35. Artuc, Bastos, and Rijkers (2018).
36. Karabarbounis and Neiman (2014).
37. Autor et al. (2017).
38. Acemoglu and Restrepo (2018); Artuc, Christiaensen, and Winkler (2019); Graetz and Michaels (2018).
39. World Bank (2019).
40. Acemoglu and Restrepo (2019).
41. For example, in 2016 the car manufacturer Mercedes-Benz decided to replace some of its assembly-line robots with more capable humans at its Sindelfingen plant in Germany. The wide variety of options for the cars demands adaptability and flexibility, two attributes for which humans currently outperform robots. Skilled humans can change a production line in a weekend, whereas weeks are required to reprogram and realign robots.
42. World Bank (2019).
43. Brussevich et al. (2018).
44. Artuc, Bastos, and Rijkers (2018).
45. Coelli, Moxnes, and Ulltveit-Moe (2016).
46. Bøler, Moxnes, and Ulltveit-Moe (2015).
47. Timmer, Miroudot, and de Vries (2019).

References

Acemoglu, Daron, and Pascual Restrepo. 2018. "Low-Skill and High-Skill Automation." *Journal of Human Capital* 12 (2): 204–32.

———. 2019 "Automation and New Tasks: How Technology Displaces and Reinstates Labor." *Journal of Economic Perspectives* 33 (2): 3–30.

Agrawal, Ajay, Nicola Lacetera, and Elizabeth Lyons. 2016. "Does Standardized Information in Online Markets

Disproportionately Benefit Job Applicants from Less Developed Countries?" *Journal of International Economics* 103 (November): 1–12.

Antràs, Pol, Luis Garicano, and Esteban Rossi-Hansberg. 2008. "Organizing Offshoring: Middle Managers and Communication Costs." In *The Organization of Firms in a Global Economy*, edited by Elhanan Helpman, Dalia Marin, and Thierry Verdier, 311–40. Cambridge, MA: Harvard University Press.

Artuc, Erhan, Paulo S. R. Bastos, and Bob Rijkers. 2018. "Robots, Tasks, and Trade." Policy Research Working Paper 8674, World Bank, Washington, DC.

Artuc, Erhan, Luc Christiaensen, and Hernán Winkler. 2019. "Does Automation in Rich Countries Hurt Developing Ones? Evidence from the U.S. and Mexico." Policy Research Working Paper 8741, World Bank, Washington, DC.

Atkin, David, and Dave Donaldson. 2015. "Who's Getting Globalized? The Size and Implications of Intra-national Trade Costs." NBER Working Paper 21439 (July), National Bureau of Economic Research, Cambridge, MA.

Autor, David H., David Dorn, Lawrence F. Katz, Christina Patterson, and John Van Reenen. 2017. "The Fall of the Labor Share and the Rise of Superstar Firms." NBER Working Paper 23396, National Bureau of Economic Research, Cambridge, MA.

BCG (Boston Consulting Group). 2016. "Inside OPS: Are Your Operations Ready for a Digital Revolution?" July, BCG, Boston.

Bøler, Esther Ann, Andreas Moxnes, and Karen Helene Ulltveit-Moe. 2015. "R&D, International Sourcing, and the Joint Impact on Firm Performance." *American Economic Review* 105 (12): 3704–39.

Bown, Chad P., Daniel Lederman, Samuel Pienknagura, and Raymond Robertson. 2017. *Better Neighbors: Toward a Renewal of Economic Integration in Latin America.* Latin American and Caribbean Studies Series. Washington, DC: World Bank.

Brussevich, Mariya, Era Dabla-Norris, Christine Kamunge, Pooja Karnane, Salma Khalid, and Kalpana Kochhar. 2018. "Gender, Technology, and the Future of Work." IMF Staff Discussion Note SDN/18/07 (October), International Monetary Fund, Washington, DC.

Brynjolfsson, Erik, Xiang Hui, and Meng Liu. 2018. "Does Machine Translation Affect International Trade? Evidence from a Large Digital Platform." NBER Working Paper 24917 (August), National Bureau of Economic Research, Cambridge, MA.

Brynjolfsson, Erik, and Andrew McAfee. 2017. "The Business of Artificial Intelligence: What It Can—and Cannot—Do for Your Organization." *Harvard Business Review* (July 18).

Calligaris, Sara, Chiara Criscuolo, and Luca Marcolin. 2018. "Mark-Ups in the Digital Era." OECD Science, Technology, and Industry Working Paper 2018/10, Organisation for Economic Co-operation and Development, Paris.

Carballo, Jerónimo, Alejandro Graziano, Georg Schaur, and Christian Volpe Martincus. 2016. "The Border Labyrinth: Information Technologies and Trade in the Presence of Multiple Agencies." Working Paper IDB-WP-706 (June), Inter-American Development Bank, Washington, DC.

Chava, Sudheer, Alexander Oettl, Manpreet Singh, and Linghang Zeng. 2018. "The Dark Side of Technological Progress? Impact of E-Commerce on Employees at Brick-and-Mortar Retailers." Paper presented at Northern Finance Association's 30th Annual Conference, Charlevoix, Quebec, September 21–23.

Chen, Maggie Xiaoyang, and Min Wu. 2018. "The Value of Reputation in Trade: Evidence from Alibaba." Paper presented at Workshop on Trade and the Chinese Economy, King Center on Global Development, Stanford University, Stanford, CA, April 12–13.

Coelli, Federica, Andreas Moxnes, and Karen Helene Ulltveit-Moe. 2016. "Better, Faster, Stronger: Global Innovation and Trade Liberalization." NBER Working Paper 22647 (September), National Bureau of Economic Research, Cambridge, MA.

Columbus, Louis. 2018. "10 Ways Machine Learning Is Revolutionizing Supply Chain Management." *Forbes*, June 11. https://www.forbes.com/sites/louiscolumbus/2018/06/11 /10-ways-machine-learning-is-revolutionizing-supply -chain-management/#360c6d223e37.

Costinot, Arnaud, Jonathan Vogel, and Su Wang. 2013. "An Elementary Theory of Global Supply Chains." *Review of Economic Studies* 80 (1): 109–44.

Couture, Victor, Benjamin Faber, Yizhen Gu, and Lizhi Liu. 2018. "E-Commerce Integration and Economic Development: Evidence from China." NBER Working Paper 24384 (August), National Bureau of Economic Research, Cambridge, MA.

de la Torre, Augusto, Tatiana Didier, Alain Ize, Daniel Lederman, and Sergio L. Schmukler. 2015. *Latin America and the Rising South: Changing World, Changing Priorities.* Latin American and Caribbean Studies Series. Washington, DC: World Bank.

Duch-Brown, Nestor, Bertin Martens, and Frank Mueller-Langer. 2017. "The Economics of Ownership, Access, and Trade in Digital Data." JRC Digital Economy Working Paper 2017-01, Joint Research Center, European Commission, Seville, Spain.

Dutz, Mark A. 2018. *Jobs and Growth: Brazil's Productivity Agenda.* International Development in Focus Series. Washington, DC: World Bank.

Fernandes, Ana Margarida, Caroline L. Freund, and Martha Denisse Pierola. 2016. "Exporter Behavior, Country Size and Stage of Development: Evidence from the Exporter Dynamics Database." *Journal of Development Economics* 119 (March): 121–37.

Fernandes, Ana Margarida, Aaditya Mattoo, Huy Le Nguyen, and Marc Tobias Schiffbauer. 2019. "The Internet and Chinese Exports in the Pre-Ali Baba Era." *Journal of Development Economics* 138 (May): 57–76.

Fort, Teresa C. 2017. "Technology and Production Fragmentation: Domestic versus Foreign Sourcing." *Review of Economic Studies* 84 (2): 650–87.

Freund, Caroline L., Alen Mulabdic, and Michele Ruta. 2018. "Is 3D Printing a Threat to Global Trade? The Trade Effects You Didn't Hear About." Working paper, World Bank, Washington, DC.

Freund, Caroline L., and Diana Weinhold. 2002. "The Internet and International Trade in Services." *American Economic Review* 92 (2): 236–40.

————. 2004. "The Effect of the Internet on International Trade." *Journal of International Economics* 62 (1): 171–89.

Garicano, Luis, and Steven N. Kaplan. 2001. "The Effects of Business-to-Business E-Commerce on Transaction Costs." *Journal of Industrial Economics* 49 (4): 463–85.

Gertner, Robert H., and Robert S. Stillman. 2001. "Vertical Integration and Internet Strategies in the Apparel Industry." *Journal of Industrial Economics* 49 (4): 417–40.

Goldfarb, Avi, and Catherine E. Tucker. 2011. "Privacy Regulation and Online Advertising." *Management Science* 57 (1): 57–71.

Goolsbee, Austan. 2001. "Competition in the Computer Industry: Online versus Retail." *Journal of Industrial Economics* 49 (4): 487–99.

Graetz, Georg, and Guy Michaels. 2018. "Robots at Work." *Review of Economics and Statistics* 100 (5): 753–68.

Grossman, Gene M., and Esteban Rossi-Hansberg. 2008. "Trading Tasks: A Simple Theory of Offshoring." *American Economic Review* 98 (5): 1978–97.

Hallward-Driemeier, Mary, and Gaurav Nayyar. 2018. *Trouble in the Making? The Future of Manufacturing-Led Development.* Washington, DC: World Bank.

Hjort, Jonas, and Jonas Poulsen. 2019. "The Arrival of Fast Internet and Employment in Africa." *American Economic Review* 109 (3): 1032–79.

Hoekman, Bernard, and Alessandro Nicita. 2008. "Trade Policy, Trade Costs, and Developing Country Trade." Policy Research Working Paper 4797, World Bank, Washington, DC.

Höppner, Thomas, and Phillipp Westerhoff. 2018. "The EU's Competition Investigation into Amazon Marketplace." *Kluwer Competition Law Blog*, November 30, Wolters Kluwer, Alphen aan den Rijn, the Netherlands. http://competitionlawblog.kluwercompetitionlaw.com/2018/11/30/the-eus-competition-investigation-into-amazon-marketplace/.

Hsieh, Chang-Tai, and Peter J. Klenow. 2014. "The Life Cycle of Plants in India and Mexico." *Quarterly Journal of Economics* 129 (3): 1035–84.

Hsieh, Chang-Tai, and Benjamin A. Olken. 2014. "The Missing 'Missing Middle.'" *Journal of Economic Perspectives* 28 (3): 89–108.

IFR (International Federation of Robotics). 2018. *World Robotics 2018.* Frankfurt: IFR.

Jo, Yoon Joo, Misaki Matsumura, and David Eli Weinstein. 2019. "The Impact of E-Commerce on Urban Prices and Welfare." Paper presented at International Trade Seminar, Department of Economics, Stanford University, Stanford, CA, April 3.

Jouanjean, Marie-Agnès. 2019. "Digital Opportunities for Trade in the Agriculture and Food Sectors." OECD Food, Agriculture, and Fisheries Paper 122, Organisation for Economic Co-operation and Development, Paris.

Karabarbounis, Loukas, and Brent Neiman. 2014. "The Global Decline of the Labor Share." *Quarterly Journal of Economics* 129 (1): 61–103.

Laajaj, Rachid, Marcela Eslava, and Tidiane Kinda. 2019. "The Costs of Bureaucracy and Corruption at Customs: Evidence from the Computerization of Imports in Colombia." Documento CEDE 8 (February), Center for Economic Development Studies, Department of Economics, Universidad de Los Andes, Bogotá, Colombia.

Leering, Raoul. 2017. "3D Printing: A Threat to Global Trade." September 28, Economic and Financial Analysis Division, ING Bank NV, Amsterdam.

Lendle, Andreas, Marcelo Olarrega, Simon Schropp, and Pierre-Louis Vézina. 2016. "There Goes Gravity: eBay and the Death of Distance." *Economic Journal* 126 (591): 406–41.

Lopez-Acevedo, Gladys, Denis Medvedev, and Vincent Palmade, eds. 2017. *South Asia's Turn: Policies to Boost Competitiveness and Create the Next Export Powerhouse.* South Asia Development Matters Series. Washington, DC: World Bank.

McKenzie, David. 2017. "Identifying and Spurring High-Growth Entrepreneurship: Experimental Evidence from a Business Plan Competition." *American Economic Review* 107 (8): 2278–2307.

MGI (McKinsey Global Institute). 2019. *Globalization in Transition: The Future of Trade and Value Chains.* New York: McKinsey.

Mullainathan, Sendhil, and Jann Spiess. 2017. "Machine Learning: An Applied Econometric Approach." *Journal of Economic Perspectives* 31 (2): 87–106.

OECD (Organisation for Economic Co-operation and Development). 2019. "Digital Opportunities for Trade in Agriculture and Food Sectors." Report TAD/TC/CA/WP(2018)4/FINAL (January 16), Joint Working Party on Agriculture and Trade, OECD, Paris.

Oldenski, Lindsay. 2015. "Reshoring by U.S. Firms: What Do the Data Say?" PIIE Policy Brief 15–14 (September), Peterson Institute for International Economics, Washington, DC.

Prince, Jeffrey T. 2007. "The Beginning of Online/Retail Competition and Its Origins: An Application to Personal Computers." *International Journal of Industrial Organization* 25 (1): 139–56.

PwC (PricewaterhouseCoopers). 2018. "Blockchain Is Here: What's Your Next Move?" August, PwC, London. https://fcibglobal.com/pdf/handouts/03_Blockchain-DS.pdf.

Rodrik, Dani. 2018. "New Technologies, Global Value Chains, and Developing Economies." NBER Working Paper 25164, National Bureau of Economic Research, Cambridge, MA.

Seamans, Robert, and Feng Zhu. 2014. "Responses to Entry in Multi-sided Markets: The Impact of Craigslist on Local Newspapers." *Management Science* 60 (2): 476–93.

Timmer, Marcel Peter, Sébastien Miroudot, and Gaaitzen J. de Vries. 2019. "Functional Specialization in Trade." *Journal of Economic Geography* 19 (1): 1–30.

Tripoli, Mischa, and Josef Schmidhuber. 2018. "Emerging Opportunities for the Application of Blockchain in the Agri-food Industry." Issue Paper (August), Food and Agriculture Organization of the United Nations, Rome; International Center for Trade and Sustainable Development, Geneva.

WEF (World Economic Forum). 2018. "Innovation with a Purpose: The Role of Technology Innovation in Accelerating Food Systems Transformation." Prepared in collaboration with McKinsey and Company, January 23, WEF, Geneva.

http://www3.weforum.org/docs/WEF_Innovation_with _a_Purpose_VF-reduced.pdf.

World Bank. 2016. *World Development Report 2016: Digital Dividends*. Washington, DC: World Bank.

———. 2019. *World Development Report 2019: The Changing Nature of Work*. Washington, DC: World Bank.

WTO (World Trade Organization). 2018. *World Trade Report 2018: The Future of World Trade; How Digital Technologies Are Transforming Global Commerce*. Geneva: WTO.

Young, Jessica. 2019. "Global E-Commerce Sales Grow 18% in 2018." *Internet Retailer*, August 7. https://www.digital commerce360.com/article/global-ecommerce-sales/.

PART IV

What domestic policies facilitate fruitful participation?

Policies to enhance participation

Key findings

- **Factor endowments matter: Eliminating restrictions in factor markets enables countries to exploit their comparative advantage.** Avoiding overvalued exchange rates and restrictive regulations ensures labor is competitively priced. A favorable business climate and effective investment promotion facilitate foreign direct investment.

- **Market size matters: Liberalizing trade expands access to markets and inputs.** By reducing tariffs and eliminating nontariff measures, a country expands its sources of supply. Liberalization in destination markets through trade agreements expands market access.

- **Geography matters: Remoteness can be overcome by improving connectivity and lowering trade costs.** Costs related to delay and uncertainty can be reduced by customs reform, introducing competition in transport services, and improving port structure and governance.

- **Institutional quality matters: It can be improved by strengthening contract enforcement, protecting intellectual property rights, and improving standards regimes.** Deep trade agreements can help lock in institutional reforms.

- **Proactive policies can enhance and upgrade global value chain (GVC) participation.** Coordinating, informing, and training domestic small and medium enterprises helps link them to GVC lead firms. Investment in education and improvements in management encourage upgrading. Special economic zones can be a shortcut on the GVC development path when they successfully address specific market and policy failures.

What needs to be done to reap the benefits of global value chains (GVCs)? And what is the role of government policy in facilitating GVC participation and upgrading? Drawing on evidence from chapter 2 on the determinants of GVCs, as well as from cases from around the world, this chapter considers policies to enter and enhance participation in GVCs. It begins by highlighting four areas of policy that would support GVC participation.

First, because factor endowments matter, countries should exploit their comparative advantage by eliminating barriers to investment and ensuring that labor is competitively priced, by avoiding overvalued exchange rates and restrictive regulations.

Lead firms in GVCs are often multinational corporations (MNCs), and so policies aimed at attracting foreign direct investment (FDI) are especially important for GVC participation. As a starting point, countries should facilitate the establishment and operation of businesses (the agenda is outlined in the World Bank's *Doing Business* reports). An investment policy should facilitate GVC-oriented FDI and support investors throughout the investment life cycle. Relying on well-planned investment promotion strategies, countries such as Costa Rica, Malaysia, and Morocco have successfully attracted transformative GVC investments by large MNCs.

Second, because market size matters, countries need to liberalize trade to expand access to markets and inputs. By liberalizing imports of inputs and eliminating unnecessary nontariff measures (NTMs), a country can expand its sources of supply, as well as the possible roles it can play in the value chain. For example, the large unilateral tariff cuts by Peru in the first decade of the 2000s are associated with lower import costs, faster productivity growth, and expansion and diversification of GVC exports.[1] Liberalization in destination markets can expand market access. For example, preferential trade agreements (PTAs) have acted as a catalyst for GVC entry for a wide range of countries, including Bangladesh, the Dominican Republic, Honduras, Lesotho, Madagascar, and Mauritius.

Goods and services are increasingly linked, and so liberalizing the trade in services is an important part of any strategy for promoting GVCs. Policies should therefore seek to improve the environment for e-commerce, liberalize telecommunications services, and promote free movement of data, as well as support access to other important service inputs such as transport, finance, accounting, and other business support services.

Third, because geography matters, countries can overcome remoteness by improving their connectivity and lowering trade costs. Some countries are disadvantaged naturally by being landlocked or in remote locations. Others are disadvantaged by policy restrictions on transport services and by bureaucratic actions such as slow, costly, unpredictable border procedures. GVCs rely on the fast and predictable movement of goods. For many goods traded among GVCs, a day's delay is equal to imposing a tariff in excess of 1 percent. Improving customs and border procedures, promoting competition in transport services, improving port structure and governance, opening the domestic market to global providers of third-party logistics and express delivery services, and improving information and communication technology (ICT) connectivity—all are strategies that can reduce trade costs related to time and uncertainty.

Fourth, because institutional quality matters, countries need to strengthen enforcement of contracts, protection of property rights, and regulatory standards. GVCs thrive on the flexible formation of networks of firms. Contract enforcement ensures that legal arrangements within a network are stable and predictable. Protecting intellectual property rights creates an environment for more innovative and complex value chains, and it can be supported through deep PTAs. Governments can also facilitate participation in GVCs by strengthening their national certification and testing capacity to ensure compliance with international standards, public and private. Pakistan's ability to overcome an export ban on fish and expand horticultural exports attests to the value of building a strong national standards regime.

But being in a value chain today does not guarantee that a country will capture significant benefits from participation and that those benefits will grow. Many of the traditional approaches to industrial policy, including tax incentives, subsidies, and local content policies, are more likely to distort than help in today's GVC context, as Brazil's poor experience of promoting localization in the automotive sector illustrates. However, a range of proactive policies can enhance GVC participation.

Countries can promote linkages between domestic small and medium enterprises (SMEs) and GVC lead firms by coordinating local suppliers, providing access to information about supply opportunities, and supporting training and capacity building of SMEs. There are many examples of successful supplier linkage programs such as those in Chile and Guinea in mining, Kenya and Mozambique in agriculture, and the Czech Republic in the electronics and automotive sectors. Governments can also help domestic suppliers gain access to finance and technology to support raising productivity and meeting global standards.

Countries can strengthen sector-specific human capital through targeted workforce development strategies, involving close coordination between the public and private sectors. The Penang Skills Development Centre in Malaysia, an industry-led training center, has played an important role in supporting Malaysia's upgrading in the electronics and engineering GVCs. Countries can also support firms in their efforts to upgrade management capabilities and strengthen the capacity for innovation. Turkey's upgrading into the branded segment of the apparel GVC was supported by both government and private sector initiatives, including workforce training, consulting and design services, and incentives for investment in research and development (R&D) and technology.

Governments can also strengthen national innovation systems to support upgrading in GVCs. Germany's dense networks of public-private collaboration involving foreign and local industry, academia, and government research institutions is one example of an effective model.

This chapter also considers whether and how special economic zones (SEZs) may be used as a shortcut on the GVC development path, recognizing that delivering on the policies just outlined is a medium-term agenda. SEZs can be successful when they address specific market failures. Getting conditions right, even in a restricted geographical area, requires careful planning and implementation to ensure that the needed resources—such as labor, land, water, electricity, and telecommunications—are readily available, that there are no unnecessary regulatory barriers, and that connectivity is seamless. The relatively few successful zone programs in places such as China, Panama, and the United Arab Emirates, and emerging in Ethiopia, offer important lessons for how best to take advantage of the instrument to establish an environment for different types of GVC participation.

Facilitating participation

Take advantage of factor endowments and eliminate restrictions in factor markets

As described in chapter 2, factor endowments matter for a country's entry and positioning in GVCs, and that is not surprising. Investment in most commodity GVCs (as well as the travel and tourism services GVCs) depends on access to *natural resources* such as land,

specific climatic conditions, and mineral resources. A move to basic manufacturing GVCs often relies on access to *low-cost labor*, while moving into more advanced and innovative activities requires higher levels of *human capital*. And entry in almost all GVCs requires access to capital—especially *foreign direct investment* in most developing countries. But just having favorable endowments is no guarantee of success. National policies fundamentally shape the price of factor endowments and how well they are able to contribute to GVC participation.

Natural resources

Despite having favorable conditions for agricultural production, many countries have a regulatory and institutional environment that undermines investment prospects in the sector. Surveys of agribusiness investors[2] have identified land acquisition as a special concern. Lack of proper land registries and weak legal systems in many countries make it impossible to enforce land titles. The situation is aggravated in regions such as Sub-Saharan Africa, where countries may have parallel (and often conflicting) customary and statutory land tenure systems. In postconflict environments, forced displacement, land occupations, and loss of official title deeds may make it impossible to secure tenure. For example, in Liberia, despite the government granting large concessions to international investors in rubber and palm oil, competing land claims and community conflicts have resulted in investors managing to plant only on a small portion of the land concession, and the surrounding smallholders have been unable to secure finance to plant without land titles. The ensuing lack of production scale has also made it uneconomic for the lead firms to invest in processing facilities.

Governments should have a clear legal framework for land policy, along with a legal and administrative apparatus that can enforce land rights, while recognizing various acceptable forms of tenure. Such objectives can be supported by adopting a proactive process of engagement, beyond simply consultation, with communities likely to be affected by large investments in agriculture. For example, in Ghana the government has published guidelines on community engagement practices to help facilitate large-scale commercial agriculture investments.

For countries with large mineral endowments, the main issues revolve around the terms of concession agreements. Most notably, such terms relate to royalty and tax payments, but they also may include local content requirements, such as requiring investors to hire a certain share of local staff, to purchase from local companies, or to carry out value-added processing in the country. Mining investments typically require large amounts of capital up front, with returns over the long term. Thus investors face many uncertainties, including production costs and future trends in commodity prices. Governments can reduce uncertainty by having legal frameworks such as mining codes or mining laws that clearly establish the terms under which mining concessions will operate. Botswana, Chile, and Namibia have high-quality policy environments,[3] whereas Zimbabwe, which nationalized and partly nationalized various mining sectors over the past decade and most recently threatened an export ban on platinum, is rated as having one of the least favorable policy environments for mining investment.

Human capital

The empirical findings on the importance of low-cost labor for GVC entry in basic manufacturing is supported by the evidence of foreign investment in GVC-intensive sectors such as apparel. The shift of manufacturing to China and Vietnam, and now (as wages rise in these countries) to Bangladesh, Cambodia, and Ethiopia, reflects the importance of low-cost labor in this sector. At times, investors exploit large labor cost wedges in local environments—for example, when South Africa's apparel production moved just over the border to Lesotho[4] and when apparel factory clusters emerged on the Dominican Republic's border with Haiti.

But many countries with low levels of per capita income and large pools of moderately skilled, under-employed labor find themselves priced out of the market for GVC investments in basic manufacturing activities because of uncompetitive labor costs. For example, a recent study using World Bank survey data on 5,500 companies in 29 countries found that for any given level of GDP, labor is substantially costlier for manufacturing firms located in Sub-Saharan Africa.[5] As shown in figure 7.1, the average labor costs in Bangladesh are in line with the average GDP per capita, whereas in comparator countries in Africa they are often almost twice that average. Only Ethiopia has wage levels on a par with those in Bangladesh.

Addressing rigid labor regulatory policies, while ensuring protection of workers and appropriately sharing the gains from GVC trade (see chapter 8), is one step governments can take toward more competitively priced labor. But regulation is just one contributor to labor price gaps. Overvalued exchange rates are a significant threat to competitively priced labor.

Figure 7.1 Manufacturing labor costs are out of line with national income levels in Sub-Saharan Africa but not in Bangladesh

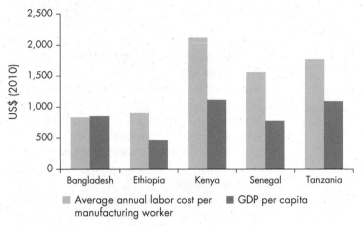

Source: WDR 2020 team, using data from Gelb et al. (2017).

They raise the prices of domestic resources relative to imports, thereby deterring international investments in labor-intensive activities and making domestic investors more likely to import capital equipment to substitute for high-priced domestic labor. Historically, countries with competitive or undervalued exchange rates have undergone greater structural change[6]—the experiences of China and the Republic of Korea stand out here. Because overvalued exchange rates are common in countries that heavily rely on natural resources, they pose a threat when these countries transition into basic manufacturing value chains. For example, an overvalued exchange rate was a major factor in the failure of Trinidad and Tobago to develop its manufacturing sector.[7] Beyond the exchange rate, workers in many countries have high reservation wages because of the high cost of living in urban and peri-urban areas. For example, in urban areas of Sub-Saharan Africa workers often face high costs for food and housing, along with high transport costs, which can consume up to 50 percent of wages.

Therefore, getting the price of labor right requires policies that go well beyond the realm of labor and policies to support urbanization and public services. Governments also have to address other fundamental investment climate constraints, such as poor infrastructure, as well as skill mismatches, which compound labor price gaps by suppressing productivity growth.

As countries look to upgrade in GVCs, policy priorities shift to the quality rather than the quantity of human capital. Higher value-added positions in GVCs require both high-level technical skills and adaptability because changing technologies rapidly reshape the kinds of skills needed. Research in Costa Rica and the Dominican Republic has found that large differences in the investments of each country in human capital is one of the primary explanations for the different development trajectories of the two countries over recent decades. Costa Rica's success in diversifying away from apparel to high-technology exports was supported by public social spending that averaged close to 20 percent of GDP in the 1980s and 1990s. By contrast, in the Dominican Republic, which struggled to move away from low value-added apparel exports, public social spending during this time averaged just 5 percent of GDP, the lowest in all of the countries in Latin America.[8]

Foreign capital

In developing countries, foreign capital is especially important for GVC integration.[9] Foreign investors bring with them the technology, managerial expertise, and established market relationships needed for GVC integration. Thus policies and strategies to attract and retain FDI are important for countries seeking to participate in GVCs.

Attracting and retaining FDI in a GVC context requires a well-formulated investment policy. Certainly, the core elements of investment policy—what sectors are open to foreign investment, what assets may be foreign-owned, what rules exist for capital flows and repatriation of profits, what form the taxation regime takes, and what fiscal and nonfiscal incentives (such as work permits) are available—are central to FDI decision making. But in the GVC world, where investments are fundamentally linked to import–export relationships, trade policy is equally important. Similarly, because of the service intensity of GVCs, domestic regulatory policy, including the role of state-owned enterprises (SOEs) and competition in infrastructural and business services, plays a big part in defining the attractiveness of a location for GVC-linked investments. Facilitating FDI for GVCs requires, then, effective coordination of investment, trade, and domestic regulatory policies.

Political stability, investor protection, and a business-friendly regulatory environment are especially important in attracting FDI. However, FDI is not homogenous. Investors with different motives consider different factors in their decision to invest. For example, MNCs that primarily seek access to natural resources—such as in extractive industries—care about access to land and resources, whereas market-seeking FDI tends to give priority to the size and purchasing power of the domestic market. Efficiency-seeking FDI, which characterizes most noncommodity GVC investments, focuses on factors that affect production and trade costs (box 7.1).

Box 7.1 Determinants of efficiency-seeking investment

For multinational corporations (MNCs), what are the most important determinants of efficiency-seeking foreign direct investment (FDI)? Compared with investors with other motivations, efficiency-seeking firms, which connect countries directly to GVCs, find the following factors more important (figure B7.1.1):[a]

- *Characteristics of host countries.* Most are important, especially low-cost labor and inputs, which 66 percent of firms involved in efficiency-seeking investment find important or critically important, compared with only 39 percent of investors with other motivations.
- *Investment policy factors.* These factors include investment protection guarantees, owning all equity, hiring expatriate staff, importing production inputs, ease of obtaining approvals, bilateral investment treaties, and preferential trade agreements (PTAs). PTAs were found to be important or critically important by 65 percent of firms involved in efficiency-seeking investment, compared with only 45 percent of investors with other motivations.

- *Incentives.* Sixty-three percent of efficiency-seeking investors rate incentives as important or critically important, in contrast with 43 percent of investors with other motivations. These firms rated eight different incentive instruments more highly than other investors, with an average difference of about 13 percentage points.
- *Capacity and skills of local suppliers.* This factor was rated important or critically important by 77 percent of MNCs engaged in efficiency-seeking FDI, compared with 70 percent of investors with other motivations. To promote linkages, 55 percent of MNCs involved in efficiency-seeking FDI have internal "talent scouts" to find local suppliers, compared with only 45 percent of investors involved in other types of FDI.
- *Investment promotion agencies (IPAs).* Fifty-two percent of efficiency-seeking investors identify IPA services as important or critically important, compared with 37 percent of investors involved in other types of FDI.

(Box continues next page)

Figure B7.1.1 MNCs involved in efficiency-seeking FDI are more selective

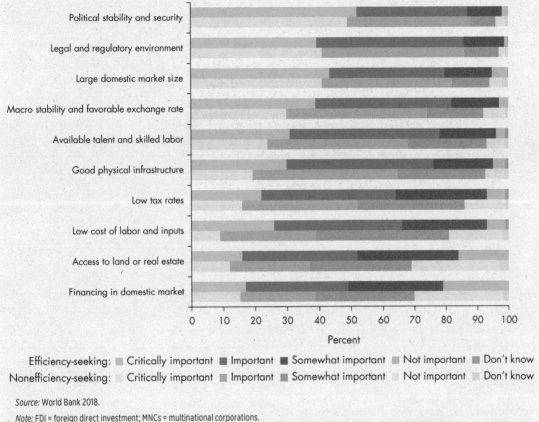

Efficiency-seeking: ■ Critically important ■ Important ■ Somewhat important ■ Not important ■ Don't know
Nonefficiency-seeking: ■ Critically important ■ Important ■ Somewhat important ■ Not important ■ Don't know

Source: World Bank 2018.

Note: FDI = foreign direct investment; MNCs = multinational corporations.

a. This overview of locational determinants of FDI is based on findings from the World Bank's 2017 Global Investment Competitiveness survey on investor perceptions and preferences (World Bank 2018).

Beyond policy, strategies and tactics—and their implementation—matter for attracting and retaining GVC investors. Proactive efforts to attract and facilitate foreign investment, through the use of investment promotion agencies (IPAs), can help overcome problems of information asymmetry and coordination failures that may restrict FDI.[10] IPAs typically carry out image-building campaigns, undertake investment generation through targeted efforts to identify and attract specific investors, help investors to establish their businesses, and lobby government for investor-friendly policies. Research has shown that IPAs can contribute to larger FDI flows[11] (figure 7.2) and can be highly cost-effective, with one study finding that every $1 spent on investment promotion yields $189

in FDI inflows, for a cost of just $78 to create one job in the promoted sectors.[12] IPAs can also improve the quality of investments and contribute to economic transformation by exploiting comparative advantage. For example, Costa Rica, Malaysia, and Morocco successfully attracted transformative, efficiency-seeking investments by large MNCs using well-targeted investment promotion strategies that built off core policies of macroeconomic stability and skills development. These economies saw a boost in revealed comparative advantage and better integration into GVCs.[13]

Liberalize trade to expand markets

Market size matters because larger markets enable firms to benefit from returns to scale in terms of both

Figure 7.2 Better-quality investment promotion agencies attract more FDI inflows

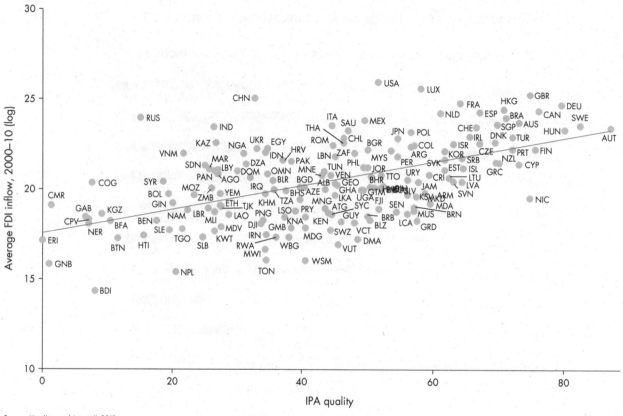

Source: Harding and Javorcik 2012.

Note: The IPI quality rating is based on the World Bank's Global Investment Promotion Benchmarking (GIPB) series. The figure shows the average results of GIPB scores from the 2006, 2009, and 2012 GIPB series. FDI = foreign direct investment; IPA = investment promotion agency. For country abbreviations, see International Organization for Standardization (ISO), https://www.iso.org/obp/ui/#search.

production efficiencies and an ability to make the most of knowledge and technologies. But as chapter 1 describes, domestic market size is less relevant in a GVC world because scale economies can be reaped through deeper specialization and global market integration. This offers a critical shortcut for small developing countries. Taking advantage of this opportunity requires liberalized trade policies that support integration. Indeed, as chapter 2 notes, countries with low tariffs and greater market access are more likely to participate in GVCs.

Tariffs

Worldwide, most-favored-nation (MFN) tariffs fell by about a third between 2001 and 2013.[14] Of this liberalization, more than half was the result of countries cutting tariffs on their own initiative. This reduction included unilateral cuts of between 10 and 20 percent in ad valorem tariffs by India, Morocco, Nigeria, Peru, and Tunisia, and between 5 and 10 percent by Bangladesh, Kenya, and Mexico. Although there

is still scope for an international effort to lower tariffs—bilaterally, regionally, or in a multilateral round (chapter 8)—the scope for countries to engage in unilateral liberalization remains substantial.

Tariff schedules that place higher duties on processed goods than on unprocessed goods—a feature known as tariff escalation—have particularly negative effects on developing countries in GVCs. Escalation acts as a barrier preventing developing countries from upgrading to higher value-added segments of the value chain, potentially locking them into lower-value, limited-processing activities. Trade agreements have significantly reduced the extent of tariff escalation in high-income countries, but the process needs to go further, especially for agricultural products.

High tariffs and tariff escalation can undermine the development of regional value chains. For example, in southern Africa, despite the customs union of Botswana, Eswatini, Lesotho, Namibia, and South Africa, as well as the expressed strategic interests in developing regional agriculture value chains, protection of domestic agricultural interests has resulted in multiple trade restrictions, including seasonal import bans and quotas, as well as duties of up to 40 percent on grain, feed, dairy, and poultry products.

Moreover, in many parts of the world tariffs and other forms of trade protectionism have seen a resurgence over the last two years, fueled in part by tensions between the United States and China. In the age of GVCs, where hyperspecialization and distribution of tasks across borders ensure that trade costs are incurred multiple times, this new wave of protectionism is likely to have significant negative implications. They will arise not only directly from higher trade costs but also from the costs of trade policy uncertainty, which can make firms reluctant to invest in supply chains and thus result in long-lasting disruptions in global investment and production.

Finally, as discussed in detail in box 2.5 in chapter 2, governments can exploit the opportunities created by PTAs, particularly when they offer duty-free market access, to catalyze GVC entry. This was apparent during the period of the Multifibre Arrangement (MFA) quota system, when footloose GVC investors sought opportunities to exploit unused quotas. For example, Korean investors kickstarted the apparel GVC in Bangladesh and Honduras; Taiwanese investors initiated the sector in Lesotho and Swaziland

(now Eswatini); and Mauritian investors established some of the first apparel manufacturing facilities in Madagascar. Preferential arrangements such as the African Growth and Opportunity Act (AGOA) and the Everything but Arms (EBA) initiative of the European Union, along with regional trade agreements such as the Caribbean Basin Initiative (later the Dominican Republic–Central America Free Trade Agreement, DR–CAFTA) played a similar role. Recent fragmentation in the global trading system may in fact create opportunities for countries to exploit PTAs as a channel for GVC entry.

Nontariff measures

The use of NTMs is increasingly widespread. The share of tariff lines covered by NTMs averages about 40 percent for the least developed and developing countries and more than 60 percent for developed countries. The trade covered by such measures is even higher (figure 7.3, panel a). Moreover, multiple NTMs are often applied to the same product category (figure 7.3, panel b).

Although it may appear that countries are simply substituting tariff protection for NTM protection, this is not necessarily the case. NTMs such as quantitative restrictions and nonautomatic licensing have effects similar to those of tariffs, and they serve primarily to

Figure 7.3 Nontariff measure use increases by development status

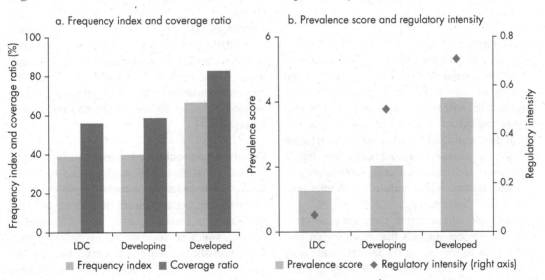

Source: UNCTAD and World Bank 2018.

Note: Panel a: The frequency index captures a country's share of traded product lines subject to at least one nontariff measure (NTM). The coverage ratio captures a country's share of trade subject to NTMs. Unlike the frequency index, it is weighted by import values instead of traded product lines. Panel b: The prevalence score indicates a country's average number of distinct NTMs applied on regulated products. In doing so, it measures the diversity of NTM types applied and provides some indication of the intensity of regulation. The regulatory intensity adjusts the prevalence score for differences in regulatory intensity and trade importance across products. In doing so, it adjusts for the fact that some products are more traded and regulated than others such as medicines. Computed as an average for a country, the regulatory intensity is normalized by the average number of measures for each product around the world and then weighted by its importance in world trade. LDC = least developed country.

restrict trade—indeed, such NTMs can inhibit GVC formation. But a large share of modern NTMs are regulatory in nature. Technical barriers to trade (TBTs) and sanitary and phytosanitary (SPS) measures are at least ostensibly designed to protect human, animal, and plant life; health; and the environment. Moreover, their application is regulated by World Trade Organization (WTO) agreements. Higher-income countries, which tend to have lower tariffs, are more likely to make extensive use of TBTs and SPS measures.

However, regulatory measures, even when they have legitimate goals, can pose challenges for low- and middle-income countries as their producers strive to meet more stringent standards, which may be costly. For exporters, failure to meet standards—such as those for quality and traceability in agriculture—can lock firms out of markets. For importers, inappropriate standards may exclude firms from some valuable opportunities for GVC participation. For example, importers in many South Asian countries find it difficult to import synthetic yarn and fabrics, which inhibits their apparel producers from serving the market for higher value-added segments such as athletic wear.

On the other hand, the emergence of well-defined product standards can help firms in developing countries overcome technical, informational, and reputational barriers to market access and so play an important role in facilitating GVC participation and upgrading (this issue is discussed in more detail later in this chapter).

Trade in services

For many developing countries, the best opportunities for GVC integration will not come through natural resources or manufacturing, but instead through integration in services GVCs, notably through sectors such as tourism and business process outsourcing. And as discussed in chapter 1, even manufacturing and natural resources–focused GVCs are highly service-intensive. Thus eliminating impediments to trade and investment in services is a high priority to promote GVC participation.

The limited information on trade and investment policy for services suggests that much higher barriers remain to liberalizing the services trade than the goods trade. The World Bank's Services Trade Restrictions Database reveals that, although public monopolies are now rare and few service markets are completely closed, numerous restrictions remain on entry, ownership, and operations.[15] Even where there is little explicit discrimination against foreign providers, market access is often unpredictable because the allocation of new licenses remains opaque and highly discretionary in many countries.

Across regions, some of the fastest-growing countries in Asia and the oil-rich Gulf states have highly restrictive policies in services, while some of the poorest countries are remarkably open, as measured by the World Bank's Services Trade Restrictiveness Index, which takes values from 0 for completely open regimes to 100 for completely closed (map 7.1). Across sectors, professional and transport services are among the most protected in both industrial and developing countries, whereas retail, telecommunications, and even finance tend to be more open.

National decisions to open markets to certain types of services trade are critical for GVCs. Among those types are third-party logistics providers and express delivery services. In addition, much of the innovation in value chains takes place at the downstream end, through retailers. It may be easier for large retailers to take advantage of new supply chain technologies to enhance GVC productivity than for the more traditional small retailers to do so, and even easier for e-commerce firms.[16] Thus policies that restrict the entry of large retailers (either domestic or foreign) can have a negative impact on efforts to exploit the full efficiencies of GVCs. To the extent that advanced supply chain technologies complement e-commerce, interventions to improve the enabling environment for e-commerce and policies to enable the free movement of data are likely to complement the development of GVCs. Liberalizing telecommunications services, including access to the Internet, is essential to facilitating the flow of information between buyers and sellers needed to promote GVCs (box 7.2). In addition, countries can remove impediments to importing services.[17] Initiatives such as liberalization of professional licensing are possible subjects for regional cooperation.

Enhance connectivity to lower trade costs

Beyond tariffs, the cost of moving goods remains a substantial impediment to trade. Supply chains go where the logistics are smooth. To compete in GVCs, firms need to respond quickly to any changes in demand, which is costly when intermediate inputs face border delays that necessitate maintaining inventories. Supply chain efficiency has therefore emerged as an important determinant of trade performance. Improving supply chain–related trade costs associated with border administration and transport and communications infrastructure halfway to global best practice would, it is estimated, produce global GDP gains up to six times larger than the elimination of all

Map 7.1 Services trade remains restricted in many countries

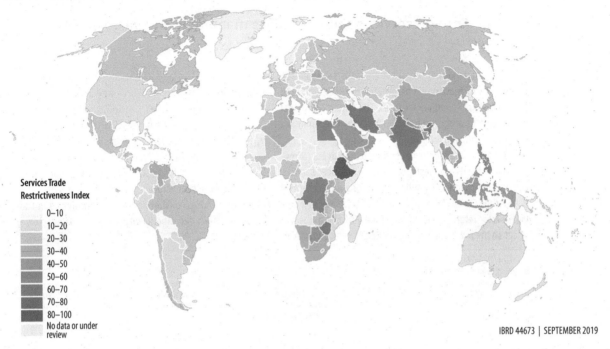

Services Trade Restrictiveness Index

- 0–10
- 10–20
- 20–30
- 30–40
- 40–50
- 50–60
- 60–70
- 70–80
- 80–100
- No data or under review

IBRD 44673 | SEPTEMBER 2019

Source: Borchert, Gootiiz, and Mattoo 2014.

Note: The World Bank's Services Trade Restrictions Database covers 103 countries (79 developing) and financial, basic telecommunications, transport, distribution, and selected professional services. Data were collected between 2008 and 2010. The Services Trade Restrictiveness Index (STRI) takes on values from 0 to 100, where 0 indicates a country is completely open to trade without restrictions, and 100 indicates a country is completely closed to trade.

Box 7.2 Foreign services firms in India's manufacturing value chains

India offers a powerful example of how foreign services firms help support greater participation in manufacturing value chains. Conventional explanations of the modest resurgence of Indian manufacturing since the early 1990s have focused on policy reforms in manufacturing industries. However, a central factor lies outside manufacturing in the services sector. Reforms in the 1990s visibly transformed services sectors, with greater openness and improved regulation leading to dramatic growth in domestic and foreign investment. Indian manufacturing firms were no longer at the mercy of inefficient public monopolies; they could now source services from a wide range of domestic and foreign providers operating in an increasingly competitive environment. As a result, they had access to better, newer, more reliable, and more diverse business services. These improvements enhanced firms' abilities to invest in new business opportunities and better production technology, to exploit economies of scale by concentrating production

in fewer locations, to efficiently manage inventories, and to coordinate decisions with suppliers and customers.

To analyze the link between service reforms and manufacturing productivity in India, Arnold et al. (2016) collected detailed information on the pace of reform across Indian services sectors, focusing on entry and operational restrictions. To make this information amenable to econometric analysis, the investigators aggregated it into time-varying reform indexes. They then related the total factor productivity (TFP) of about 4,000 manufacturing firms to the state of liberalization in the services sectors, taking into account other aspects of openness such as tariffs on output and intermediate inputs, as well as foreign direct investment (FDI) in the final and intermediate goods sectors.

The results suggested that pro-competitive reforms in banking, transport, insurance, and telecommunications boosted the productivity of both foreign and locally owned manufacturing firms. A one standard deviation increase in

(Box continues next page)

Box 7.2 Foreign services firms in India's manufacturing value chains *(continued)*

the aggregated index of services liberalization resulted in a productivity increase of 11.7 percent for domestic firms and 13.2 percent for foreign enterprises. The largest additional effect was for transport reforms, followed by telecommunications and banking reforms.

Several other studies have confirmed that access to low-cost, high-quality (domestic or foreign) producer services can promote productivity and economic growth.[a] Firm-level data for the Czech Republic for 1998–2003 reveal that services sector reforms leading to greater FDI had a positive effect on the productivity of domestic firms in downstream

manufacturing.[b] Similarly, another study demonstrates that substantial FDI inflows in producer services sectors in Chile had a positive effect on the TFP of Chilean manufacturing firms.[c] The same study suggests that foreign investment in services fosters innovation in manufacturing and offers opportunities for laggard firms to catch up with industry leaders.[d] These benefits arise not just from foreign investment but also from cross-border trade in services. For example, services offshoring by high-income countries tends to raise the productivity of their manufacturing sectors.[e]

a. Hoekman and Mattoo (2008).
b. Arnold, Javorcik, and Mattoo (2011).
c. Fernandes and Paunov (2012).
d. Similar results have been found for Sub-Saharan Africa (Arnold, Mattoo, and Narciso 2008) and Indonesia (Duggan, Rahardja, and Varela 2015).
e. Amiti and Wei (2009a). Although offshoring of services has both positive and negative effects on domestic employment, Amiti and Wei (2009b) show that, at least for the United States, it tends on average to enhance domestic employment.

tariffs.[18] One aspect of these costs is trade facilitation and logistics. Delays due to shipping and border procedures have a negative effect on trade comparable to that of tariffs. A day's delay reduces trade by more than 1 percent in Africa,[19] and a day's reduction in inland transit times can boost exports by as much as 7 percent.[20]

Figure 7.4 shows the estimated tariff equivalent of a day's delay in shipping for a wide variety of product categories. The time costs in trade are significant for products with complex value chains such as motor vehicles; perishable products such as fruits and vegetables; and textiles and apparel, both of which involve complex GVCs and changes in fashion that reduce their shelf life. By contrast, traders are willing to wait longer for goods such as live animals, leather goods, and wood and forestry products.

GVCs are impeded not only by the slow movement of goods but also by their unpredictable movement, which disrupts the ability of a value chain to perform its steps in the appropriate sequence. In Sub-Saharan Africa, the slowness and unpredictability of land transport impeded the formation of GVCs in almost all countries until very recently.[21]

Many poor, remote, landlocked countries are underserved by international shipping and air cargo services. In part, this is a vicious circle—because of weak economic activity few shippers schedule service to such countries, which increases trade costs. However,

countries can take measures unilaterally to promote increased connectivity and cost-effectiveness:

• *Rebalance and repurpose trade infrastructure.* For many developing countries, particularly in Sub-Saharan Africa, Central Asia, and parts of Latin America, trade infrastructure has been established primarily around extractive sectors. Such infrastructure, built around bulk and direct connections between often rural areas (such as mining locations) and ports, may not be supportive of the environment needed for value chain–oriented sectors, which may require denser, multimodal infrastructure. A study of port costs in South Africa found that, although export charges for mining commodities were well below the global average in 2014, charges for containerized exports were almost twice the global average.[22]

• *Improve port infrastructure and governance.*[23] There are vast differences between the world's most and least efficient ports in terms of the time it takes to unload ships, cargo dwell time (the time it takes for a container to be available for pickup after being unloaded from a ship), and the adequacy of warehouses and port customs procedures. Technological solutions do exist, such as use of electronics at customs or improvement in gantry cranes, but the reforms needed may be obstructed because some stakeholders benefit from delays.

Figure 7.4 Shipping delays matter more for products with complex value chains

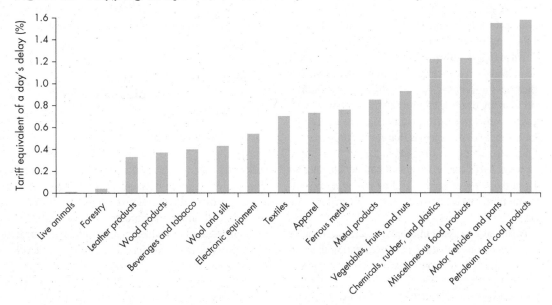

Source: WDR 2020 team, using data from Minor (2013), based on USAID (2007).

Note: The tariff equivalent on the y-axis is measured as the percentage of an ad valorem tariff economically equivalent to a day's delay in shipping. For example, a day's delay in moving chemicals, rubber, and plastics is equivalent in economic terms to imposing a 1.2 percent tariff on imports of the same goods.

- *Improve connectivity of landlocked countries and of remote regions within countries.* Although landlocked and remote regions tend to be poorer (20 of 54 low-income countries were landlocked in 2011, compared with 3 of 35 high-income countries), human action adds to naturally high trade costs. For example, road transport cartels emerge in environments where roads are of low quality.[24] Cooperation between landlocked and transit countries may reduce costs, as well as cooperation between remote neighboring countries in the recognition of transit rights for trucking, harmonization of rules on transport (such as axle weight loads and insurance), and treatment of goods in transit. "Hard" multimodal infrastructure (rail, road, air, and pipeline) should complement "soft" initiatives such as pursuing better border procedures through trade facilitation.

Indeed, unilateral regulatory reforms to improve trade facilitation could have a significant impact on GVC competitiveness. Such reforms include modernization of customs systems and reforms and harmonization of customs rules and procedures such as implementing effective risk management systems, replacing paper-based documentation with electronic-based documentation, and improving transparency through trade information portals and single windows.[25] A concerted effort to implement the provisions of the WTO's Trade Facilitation Agreement could go a long way in this area. In Albania, a risk management reform that sharply reduced the number of physical inspections of shipments shortened clearance times, reduced uncertainty of clearance, and expanded imports (figure 7.5).[26]

GVC integration can also be supported by liberalization of trade and transport services, including opening domestic markets to global providers of

Figure 7.5 Customs reform can reduce delay and expand imports: Evidence from Albania

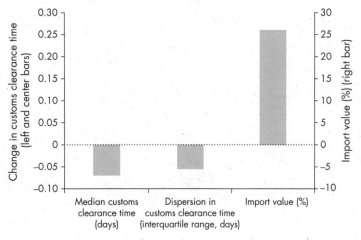

Source: Fernandes, Hillberry, and Mendoza-Alcántara 2019.

Note: It is assumed that the probability that a shipment is inspected falls from 50 percent or more to under 50 percent.

third-party logistics and express delivery services. Advances in logistics include not only those related to companies (some of which are engaging directly in shipping and road and air transport), but also those related to freight forwarders, customs brokers, loaders and unloaders, "pick and pack" warehouses, and many other types of services. At the high end, the coordination of many of these services by a third-party logistics company can be critical in the design of a local or global supply chain (such as that for the organization of disc drive manufacturing in Thailand).[27] The supply of such services can be expanded both by liberalizing FDI in the relevant sectors and by removing impediments to doing business domestically in the same sectors.

Finally, as discussed in chapter 6, ICT is critical as a facilitator of information and coordination in value chains, especially for countries that are peripherally located. The Philippines is an example of a peripheral country that has utilized ICT to participate in relatively high-value segments of services GVCs. However, many developing countries have an insufficient ICT infrastructure and its pricing is uncompetitive. Moreover, the ICT capabilities of many smaller companies are limited. Governments can support efforts to improve ICT capabilities by investing in infrastructure (including "last mile" broadband), promoting competition in ICT markets, and ensuring that ICT

skills development is pervasive and deep, including through technical and vocational education systems and through support of firms seeking to invest in ICT systems/applications and training.

Strengthen institutions for contracts, intellectual property protection, and standards

Contract enforcement

Coordination of a GVC involves managing large networks of firms, which must share dispersed knowledge and often commit assets to relationships with specific partners. It is therefore essential that the partners in a GVC enter and enforce complex contracts. In an environment in which contract enforcement is relatively weak, the formation and ongoing conduct of GVCs are inhibited.

Litigation between pairs of U.S. firms reveals that contract enforcement issues are most prevalent in relationships between firms and their suppliers of professional services, including insurance, business services, and financial services (figure 7.6). This finding implies that the supply of such services may be lower where the legal institutions to enforce contracts are weak. Since such institutions are generally weaker in lower-income countries, this accounts in part for the scarcity of business services in those countries (figure 7.7).[28]

Figure 7.6 Contract enforcement intensity is higher in services sectors: Evidence from the United States

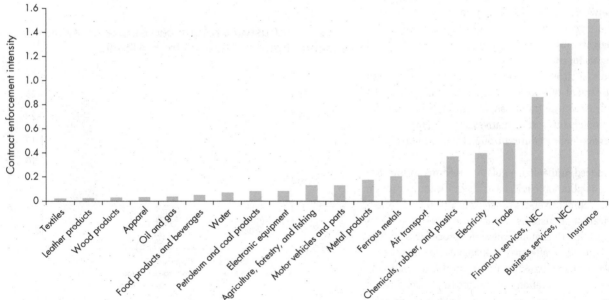

Source: WDR 2020 team, using data from Boehm (2018).

Note: See Boehm (2018) for method of calculating contract enforcement intensity. NEC = not elsewhere classified.

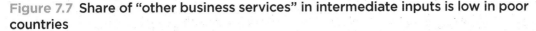

Figure 7.7 Share of "other business services" in intermediate inputs is low in poor countries

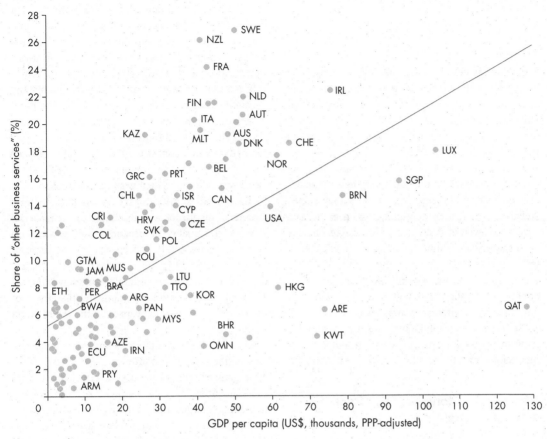

Source: WDR 2020 team, based on Boehm (2018).

Note: PPP = purchasing power parity. For country abbreviations, see International Organization for Standardization (ISO), https://www.iso.org/obp/ui/#search.

A survey of GVC sectors across 14 countries in Sub-Saharan Africa found that just 43 percent of lead firms outsourced critical business and technical services, with the majority choosing to bring the required expertise in-house.[29] Results from the survey suggest that this choice is driven in part by lack of access to a sufficient breadth of quality suppliers (reflecting barriers to trade and investment in services, among other things). Weak legal and regulatory enforcement mechanisms also contribute significantly to the underdevelopment of local markets for services.

Intellectual property rights protection

Complex and innovative GVCs can be influenced by a country's contract enforcement in the realm of intellectual property (IP). The very nature of outsourcing involves the application of know-how (such as design, engineering, production, and business processes) and may include formal licensing or some other form of technology transfer. Outsourcing is based on

contracting relationships with independent suppliers, raising the risk of replication of designs, technologies, and processes. How different national systems deal with contractual frictions and incomplete contracts is therefore important in driving firm choices of location and sourcing, as well as firm boundaries (what they outsource) in GVCs.[30] According to the evidence, countries with stronger IP protections tend to attract more FDI and receive more technology flows through licensing and royalties.[31] Weak intellectual property rights (IPR) protection and weak contract enforcement more broadly not only limit access to GVCs, but also are a significant barrier to countries seeking to secure higher value-added activities in GVCs.

Rules on protection of IPRs have become a common feature of PTAs over the last two decades either through specific provisions in trade agreements or as part of a bilateral investment treaty. However, the specificity and strength of IPR provisions vary across agreements, with PTAs led by high-income countries (especially the United States and the European Union) most commonly paying significant attention to IPRs. By contrast, many other PTAs lack adequate provisions for IPR protection.[32]

Standards

Standards for health, safety, the environment, labor, and quality are imposed by governments primarily to protect consumers, workers, and the environment. But in a GVC world, lead firms are increasingly applying standards across global supply chains. Driven by national regulatory pressures, but even more by consumer and social demands, private standards are growing in importance. On the one hand, these standards establish barriers to entry into global supply chains, and more so for firms in developing countries that may have lower levels of skills, knowledge, and technology. On the other hand, through standards, knowledge and technology from FDI can be transferred in a codified way to firms and workers in developing countries, offering them a shortcut to GVC entry, even where the broader policy environment may be weak.

Recent research highlights how, by overcoming problems of asymmetric information and negative reputational effects, the adoption of global standards supports entry and upgrading in GVCs by firms in developing countries.[33] The research points out that although traditional factor endowment and demand-based explanations imply low-quality production from developing countries, in fact quality varies markedly across sectors within countries.[34] Certification of standards offers a way to overcome information asymmetries and signal the quality and capability of suppliers down the value chain. Without compliance, firms have limited opportunities to enter such GVCs. In the absence of a credible authority to enforce warranty contract and certification, repeated interactions—such as through long-term contracts in GVCs—can alleviate a quality signaling problem.[35]

Case studies and impact evaluations indicate that small institutional or technological changes can improve the quality of products dramatically in a very short time, and the effects can be long-lasting.[36] For example, in only three years the quality of Malian cotton doubled because of implementation of a credible quality certification program, and the effects of the system remained 10 years after the intervention (figure 7.8).[37]

Because adoption of private standards takes advantage of the relational nature of GVCs (that is, they are organized and governed by lead firms), they are especially attractive as a channel for GVC entry and upgrading. But governments can play a critical facilitating role through support for standards institutions. They can adopt flexible regulatory regimes based on principles of equivalence, which would help ensure compatibility between national and global standards. Governments can also promote the adoption of standards through both regulatory enforcement and advocating the adoption of voluntary standards. Most important, governments can build the capacity for domestic inspection, testing, and certification and open the domestic market to international agencies. Effective and efficient quality infrastructure, appropriately recognized internationally, is a precondition for delivering such demonstrable compliance. For example, Pakistan's development of a robust national quality standards regime helped to lift the European Union's ban on the country's fish exports and facilitated rapid growth in mango and mandarin exports by ensuring full traceability in the supply chain.

Many countries reform their national infrastructure institutions in line with their trade, competitiveness, and regional integration frameworks. Efficient and effective standards institutions and mutual recognition by trading partners are essential enablers of trade facilitation. Some countries find it more feasible to share quality infrastructure services

Figure 7.8 Certification had long-lasting effects on quality in Mali's cotton sector

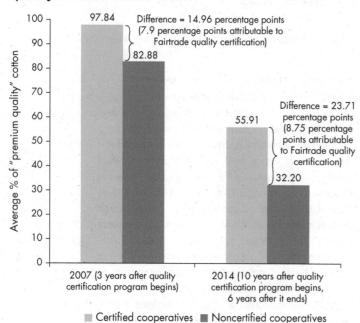

Certified cooperatives   Noncertified cooperatives

Sources: Auriol, Balineau, and Bonneton, forthcoming; Balineau 2013.

Note: The intervention was implementation of a Fairtrade quality certification in 2004. The figure shows the percentage of "premium quality" cotton from cooperatives that participated in the certification program versus those that did not—three years after implementation (2007) and 10 years after implementation (2014).

within a regional construct. For example, a laboratory for mass and volume in Trinidad and Tobago serves as a reference laboratory for 12 standards bodies in the Caribbean region.

Policies to enhance benefits

As governments seek to facilitate entry into GVCs and upgrade to higher technology and value-added activities within GVCs, most will seek to go beyond "getting the basics right" and undertake proactive policies, including industrial policy. Some of the most successful efforts to leverage manufacturing exports for development, including those by China, Korea, and, more recently, Vietnam, have been closely associated with the adoption of government-led industrial policies. On the other hand, outside of these East Asian experiences, industrial policy has been implemented extensively with limited success. Although many of the traditional approaches to industrial policy are likely to be ineffective in today's GVC context, that is not to say that government can do nothing. In fact, a range of proactive policies show significant promise for supporting enhanced GVC participation, including: (1) promoting linkages between domestic suppliers—typically SMEs—and GVC lead firms; (2) building sector-specific skills and management capabilities; and (3) strengthening national and regional innovation systems.

Minimize the use of "traditional" distortionary instruments

Standard industrial policy approaches of the past relied on tax incentives, subsidies, and other protectionist measures designed to build domestic supply chains in targeted sectors. Such instruments may have a role to play if they help overcome a market failure (such as information asymmetries), address a coordination failure (such as requirements for complementary investments in supply chains), or help capture an externality (such as technology spillovers). Indeed, countries such as Indonesia, South Africa, and Vietnam have commonly used such subsidies to attract FDI. Too often, however, these instruments have proven ineffective or have created efficiency-sapping distortions by contributing to rent seeking and misallocation of capital. They are also increasingly problematic in a GVC environment, where full supply chain development is not necessary and trade integration is paramount.

These traditional approaches have a number of other drawbacks as well. First, in the GVC context, which often finds national governments having weaker bargaining power than that of the global lead firms, there is a significant risk that subsidies will amount largely to a transfer of rents to private investors at the expense of social returns. Second, subsidies may distort market outcomes (even when they seek to address a market failure). And, third, subsidies often create a political economy problem: once in place they are difficult to remove because the beneficiaries lobby to maintain them.

Subsidy-like support for GVC firms, whether foreign investors or network lead firms, is also likely to have a "beggar thy neighbor" aspect and create trade tensions. If all countries offered subsidies, the result would be global welfare losses and a race to the bottom.[38] In fact, in recent years more than half the potentially distortionary trade policy instruments employed worldwide have involved subsidies, export-related measures (including subsidies), trade-related investment measures, or FDI measures (figure 7.9). Under WTO rules, countries that find themselves importing cheap subsidized goods are allowed to impose countervailing duties; they may also impose antidumping measures that target specific firms or sectors. Thus any gains in exports that stem from subsidies (which for the most part are prohibited by the WTO) may be reversed by action by the other country. By the end of 2018, 218 instances of countervailing duties had been notified to the WTO and were currently in force.

Figure 7.9 Subsidies account for more than half of distortionary trade policy instruments worldwide

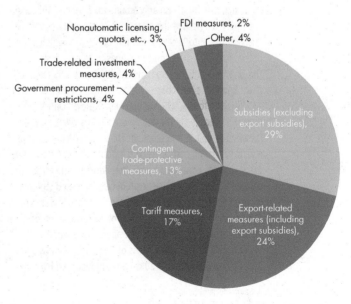

Nonautomatic licensing, quotas, etc., 3%

FDI measures, 2%

Other, 4%

Trade-related investment measures, 4%

Government procurement restrictions, 4%

Subsidies (excluding export subsidies), 29%

Contingent trade-protective measures, 13%

Tariff measures, 17%

Export-related measures (including export subsidies), 24%

Source: WDR 2020 team using data from Global Trade Alert (https://www.globaltradealert.org/).

Note: Data are from November 2018. FDI = foreign direct investment.

Of these, 162 were applied either to metals and metal products or to chemicals, rubber, and plastics and products thereof, suggesting that trade in those sectors is particularly distorted by subsidies. In addition, charges of export subsidies can entangle countries in WTO disputes about both the subsidies and the countervailing duties in response.

Local content policies have been similarly problematic. For example, in an effort to develop backward linkages many countries employ local content requirements either as conditions for foreign investments or as requirements that foreign investors must meet to access public procurement (box 7.3). In the absence of quality local suppliers, however, such requirements can backfire, restricting investment.

Similarly, in many natural resource sectors policy makers may focus on developing forward linkages—and raising domestic value added—by requiring local

---

Box 7.3 Local content requirements are a mismatch in the global auto industry

The global auto industry is characterized by extended value chains, with parts and components produced on a large scale and exported worldwide to maximize efficiency. Both Brazil and South Africa have invested heavily in and significantly protected development of their domestic automotive sectors over the past two decades. And yet, despite the huge costs, the countries are struggling to maintain competitiveness, and the long-term sustainability of the sectors remains in question.

Brazil
Notwithstanding already high levels of protection (roughly 60 percent local content requirement), automotive imports in Brazil rose in the late 2000s, prompting the domestic industry to lobby the government for further protection. The Inovar-Auto policy (2011–17) imposed additional local content requirements, this time including incentives for R&D spending, structured primarily around tax benefits. Although the policy diminished the effects of Brazil's 2014 economic crisis on the auto sector, it did not boost productivity, nor did it improve export competitiveness.[a] Indeed, a study of the 12 largest automakers between 2007 and 2015 revealed that average production per automaker declined from 233,186 units to 195,747 units per year. Scale efficiency likely worsened because of the overinvestment that was incentivized by the policy, and employment levels did not change. Meanwhile, rising costs, declining productivity, and declining profit margins continued across the industry. And although competition among domestic producers increased (the policy attracted new market entrants and increased investments from existing producers), prices went up because domestic automakers were protected from import competition.

Inovar-Auto is in the process of being replaced by Rota 2030, a new policy for the automotive industry, which came into effect in 2019. Rota 2030 seeks to simplify complex local content rules and increase R&D spending requirements in part through additional government grants. Energy efficiency targets, vehicle identification, structural performance, and incentives for electric cars are also included. Like Inovar-Auto, however, the policy continues to focus on the domestic market over exports, and importers will be excluded from the program, suggesting that it may not be enough to bring Brazil's auto industry into modern value chains, which thrive on global content.

South Africa
The mixed performance of South Africa's extensive incentives and policy interventions in the automotive sector demonstrates how difficult it is to use industrial policies in an environment in which the comparative advantage is uncertain. The automotive sector has benefitted from state support since its inception, starting with the Motor Industry Development Programme (MIDP) from 1995 to 2012, which was replaced by the Automotive Production and Development Programme from 2013. The program started with extensive protection from import competition and local content requirements under the MIDP, shifting more recently to some liberalization and investor subsidies. Several major automakers operate in South Africa, and they have created some 150,000 jobs in the industry, but it has never managed to thrive on its own. Although the auto sector has become more competitive over time, it has not performed nearly as well as those in Mexico and Thailand, which benefit from better connectivity with both the Asian production hub and global consumer demand. South African producers export largely to receive duty drawbacks on imports, while linkages to local suppliers remain limited.[b]

a. Sturgeon, Chagas, and Barnes (2017).
b. Black, Barnes, and Monaco (2018).

processing or by taxing exports of unprocessed or semiprocessed commodities. Such strategies have the potential to overcome coordination failures and unlock profitable, value-adding investments, but they are highly context-dependent and are determined by a combination of market power and the basic economics of production and transport. For example, Botswana's dominant position as a source of high-quality diamonds enabled the government to negotiate a relocation of De Beers's sorting, aggregation, and sales operations from London to Gaborone, which has contributed to substantially strengthening Botswana's value-added position in the diamond value chain. Elsewhere, export taxes have helped tip the balance to expand domestic processing of agricultural products such as cashews in India and Vietnam. On the other hand, the literature is filled with examples of poorly designed export bans or taxes that have contributed to collapsing prices for farmers or production (such as cashews in Mozambique and maize in Malawi and Tanzania) or otherwise created serious distortions across the value chain (for example, Argentina's 2006 beef export ban).

Promote domestic supply chain linkages and FDI spillovers

Establishing linkages between lead firms and domestic SME suppliers is the starting point for leveraging spillovers and upgrading in GVCs. The extent of supply linkages varies dramatically across countries and GVC sectors (figure 7.10). Although some of the variation is structural in nature, there is scope for significant densification of GVCs in many developing countries. Support for building these domestic supply linkages would be an important proactive government policy that would help reap the benefits of GVCs.

Realizing the potential of GVCs for productivity gains through spillovers of knowledge and technology is by no means guaranteed. Indeed, the barriers to spillovers may be even higher than they are in non-GVC environments. GVCs, with their global governance of supply chains and often footloose investing, create an environment in which foreign investors may have little incentive to invest in research and labor market integration in host countries and in which technologies and processes for production may be significantly disconnected from local realities. The implication is that the process of upgrading within GVCs may be curtailed, risking the sustainability of investment in the first place because the attractiveness of a location remains reliant on access to inputs (labor or natural resources) whose price cannot remain

Figure 7.10 The share of locally supplied inputs in GVCs varies by sector and country

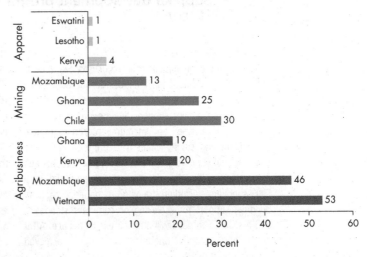

Source: Farole and Winkler (2014), based on 400 surveys of lead firms and suppliers conducted between March 2012 and October 2012.

suppressed indefinitely. This scenario is apparent in many countries that have participated in apparel GVCs. For example, although Lesotho and Swaziland (now Eswatini) experienced the rapid transformation of their economies when they attracted foreign investment in apparel GVCs, after more than 20 years that sector remains almost wholly disengaged from the domestic economy and no upgrading of the sector has taken place. As a result, uncertainties over trade preferences and wage pressures constantly threaten the viability of investments.

Governments can play a role in providing the information needed to bring local SMEs together with FDI through supplier linkage programs (box 7.4). Where the local supplier base is fragmented and characterized by very small, often informal, enterprises, coordination of suppliers through cooperative structures or associations can be important for helping producers achieve greater scale, allowing for investments in common goods, and pooling knowledge and expertise. It can also enable suppliers to engage more effectively with lead firms.

Governments can help deepen domestic supply chain relationships through broad reforms of their country's investment climate. This is particularly critical for domestic investors, who may not be in a position to benefit from targeted investment incentives or SEZ programs that are available to large foreign investors. Moreover, and at minimum, governments must be sure to avoid displaying a bias against domestic investors. For example, many SEZs, either by rule or de facto, exclude domestic investors, especially

Box 7.4 Supplier development programs help deliver inclusive, sustainable GVCs

Guinea Linkages Program[a]

As part of the development of a major iron ore mine in Guinea, the International Finance Corporation (IFC), together with lead investors Rio Tinto and Guinea Alumina, initiated a pilot supplier linkage programmed at integrating local small and medium enterprises (SMEs) into the mining supply chain. The program combined informational support of mining procurement teams and comprehensive supply-side support for potential local SME suppliers, including training, managerial capacity building, support for achieving procurement standards, and assistance in gaining better access to finance. After just a couple years of operation, the program achieved significant results:

- More than 100 local SMEs upgraded their capacity through the program.
- Over $9.1 million in new contracts were signed between local businesses and international mining companies.
- Over 700 new jobs were created in local businesses as a part of the mining sector's supply chain.

Chile's World-Class Supplier Development Program[b]

Chile's World-Class Supplier Development Program was launched in 2008 by BHP Billiton, and it has since expanded to include other mining companies such as Codelco. The program is coordinated by Fundación Chile, a nonprofit corporation that is seeking to support technology transfer and innovation and increase the competitiveness of Chilean firms across the economy. The project's goal is to create 250 world-class suppliers in Chile by 2020. The model encourages mining companies to identify areas in which innovative solutions could contribute to operational efficiency across their operations and identify local suppliers who have the capacity to work on the problem. The selection procedure is rigorous—only 16 percent of identified projects at Codelco reached the implementation stage. Selection criteria include economic benefits, replicability, urgency of the problem, technological risk, and impact on health, safety, and the environment. Through 2014, more than 70 projects were implemented, and a number of suppliers have expanded exports as a result.

Malaysia's Industrial Linkages Program[c]

Established in 1996, Malaysia's Industrial Linkages Program (ILP) is a cluster-based program centered on fiscal incentives for both multinational corporations (MNCs) and SMEs. It includes components of business matching, support for skills development, access to industrial sites, and financing for SMEs. SMEs become eligible to participate in the program if they meet certain criteria. Most important, they must supply at least one MNC and manufacture a product on the "List of Promoted Activities and Products." Once accepted, they receive fiscal benefits, allowing them a tax exemption of 100 percent of statutory income and an investment tax allowance of 60 percent on qualifying capital expenditures incurred within five years. They are also offered "matching services" from SME Corporation Malaysia (the country's SME agency), which facilitates relationships with the MNCs to support upgrading. In its first decade of operation, more than 900 SMEs were registered with ILP, of which 128 were linked to MNCs.

Czech Pilot Supplier Development Program[d]

Through CzechInvest, the Czech investment promotion agency, the Czech government implemented a pilot National Supplier Development Program from 2000 to 2002 in the electronics and automotive sectors. The motivation for the program was to raise local content in these sectors to widen foreign direct investment benefits to the local economy and strengthen these sectors.[e] The program, which was demand-driven, sought to improve the competitiveness of Czech SMEs, thereby enabling them to enter GVCs by becoming suppliers to MNCs. A dozen MNCs were involved in the project, and 45 SMEs received targeted training based on needs uncovered during business reviews. An evaluation revealed that within 18 months of completion of the program, one-third of participants had gained new business, which they attributed to the program, benefiting from contracts worth $46 million for the period 2000–2003. The share of components sourced from Czech companies by the MNCs participating in the program correspondingly increased, from a rate of 0–5 percent at the start to 2.5–30 percent by 2004. Driven by supply-side improvements in export performance, the Czech Republic experienced significant gains in global market shares and continual improvement in product quality.

a. World Bank (2015).
b. Farole and Winkler (2014).
c. Malaysia Ministry of International Trade and Industry (2019).
d. Malinska and Martin (2000–2002).
e. The country had been one of the most successful at attracting FDI since the fall of communism in the 1990s, but relatively few of the investments were felt by the local economy.

local SMEs, by imposing minimum size requirements, mandating establishment of a new business entity, and placing restrictions on mixing domestic and export businesses, among other things. Moreover, physical (customs gates) and financial controls, along with financial incentives (for example, firms inside SEZs can import inputs duty-free but must pay the value added tax or deal with complex drawback arrangements when buying from a local supplier) may prove to be barriers for local SMEs taking advantage of GVC opportunities. By contrast, in Bangladesh the government intervened directly to address two specific investment climate constraints faced by local manufacturers in the apparel GVC by introducing a bonded warehouse scheme that enabled duty-free imports for export production and a "back-to-back" letter of credit that would allow manufacturers to obtain credit for input purchases secured by export orders.

Governments also play a central role in building a local absorptive capacity. Research shows that direct technical assistance from lead firms—either through formal linkage programs or as part of the normal firm-client relationship—is one of the biggest sources of spillovers to local suppliers.[39] However, strengthening the absorptive capacity of local firms and workers also depends on government policies to support, among other things, access to finance and technology, as well as skills development.

For local SMEs to absorb spillovers from GVC participation, ongoing investments are required in technology, process improvements, and training. In fact, lack of financing is one of the main obstacles to GVC participation among suppliers in developing economies (figure 7.11). Policies that facilitate access to credit via financial sector reforms, the provision of information, as well as incentives such as matching grants and loan guarantees can play an important role. Beyond pure financing, incentives can be made available to support technology transfer and licensing, a major source of spillovers for local suppliers in GVCs.

New financial technologies are helping GVC suppliers improve their access to supply chain financing, effectively leveraging the higher credit rating of their global buyers to access financing on better terms. Tools such as electronic invoices and e-receivables speed and improve communication among customs brokers, freight forwarders, transportation carriers, government agencies, and banks. For example, seven global banks recently announced formation of the Trade Information Network to digitize trade finance. Other examples of financial technology (fintech) innovations include the use of "smart" factory technology, which collects frequent data on production and assembly lines and can be used for credit scoring, and Bluetooth scales, which are used in agribusiness chains to accurately weigh farmers' harvests and provide real-time

Figure 7.11 Lack of financing impedes low-income country suppliers the most from entering or moving up in GVCs

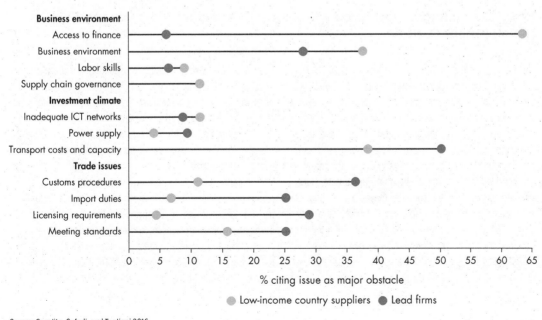

% citing issue as major obstacle

● Low-income country suppliers   ● Lead firms

Source: Cusolito, Safadi, and Taglioni 2016.

Note: ICT = information and communication technology.

lines of credit at the point of sale. In addition, new models reward firms that have better sustainability ratings with cheaper financing to support the significant costs imposed on SMEs to meet international standards. For example, Puma, BNP Paribas, and the fintech firm GT Nexus offer better receivable financing (discount) terms to suppliers who score high on Puma's sustainability index. Levi's has a comparable arrangement with its suppliers through the Global Trade Supplier Finance program of the International Finance Corporation (IFC). Investors are also designing "green" bonds that pool smaller loans for GVC suppliers to invest in environmentally friendly technology.

Invest in sector-specific skills, management, and innovation capabilities

Developing sector-specific skills

Although human capital development is a long-term process going back to foundational education and early childhood development, much can be done to build industry-specific skills. In many developing countries, there are large gaps between the outputs of traditional education and skills development institutions and the needs of employers.[40] Targeted workforce development strategies can bridge these gaps, ideally linking lead firms and local institutions, including universities and vocational and technical centers. The German model, which includes a dual education system and coordination through works councils, is being adapted to other countries. Other examples, such as the Penang Skills Development Centre in Malaysia (box 7.5), illustrate how governments, in coordination with the private sector, can build strongly territorialized capabilities through an industry or cluster-led skills development initiative.

Turkey is an example of a country that has managed to successfully move up the value chain in the apparel GVC. Its firms are assuming design roles and even building global brands. This achievement has been supported by both the private and public sectors and their active workforce development efforts. For example, the Istanbul Textile and Apparel Exporter Associations (ITKIB) partnered with the private sector and government agencies to promote vocational training in fashion design. The Istanbul Fashion Academy is a partnership of the European Union and ITKIB. The Small and Medium Industry Development Organization (KOSGEB), a quasi-governmental organization, has also been involved in workforce development; it provides marketing support, training, and consulting services. The movement into own branding has also been supported by government incentives, including reimbursement of up to 60 percent of the cost of personnel expenses for a maximum of three years (including training and recruiting highly qualified personnel), machinery, equipment and software, consultancy, and R&D-related materials.

Box 7.5 Building a workforce with industry-specific skills: Penang Skills Development Centre

The Penang Skills Development Centre (PSDC), the first industry-led training center established in Malaysia, was conceived in 1989 in response to an urgent sense that if Penang was going to continue to attract foreign direct investment (FDI), its human capital would have to be trained to keep pace with changes in technology. Although the state and federal governments launched the initiative and provided the land and some financial support, Malaysian and foreign private companies played the leading role in establishing the center. Not only did these companies furnish the initial trainers and equipment, but they also designed the training programs to meet their needs.

PSDC has more than 200 members and operates as a nonprofit society. Its mission is to pool resources among the free industrial zones and industrial estates in Penang to provide up-to-date training and educational programs in support of operational requirements and to stay abreast of technology. The center operates on a full-cost basis—companies (FDI and local) pay to send employees for training. To ensure that the training meets the needs of industry, the programs are continually upgraded and adapted to evolving skill needs.

The center has trained more than 200,000 workers by means of more than 10,000 courses, pioneered local industry development initiatives, provided input and helped formulate national policies for human capital development, and contributed directly to the Malaysian workforce transformation initiatives. Meanwhile, the PSDC model has been adopted throughout the country—skills development centers operate in almost all states in Malaysia.

Source: Adapted from Farole (2011).

Governments can also facilitate access to skilled labor by ensuring open labor markets and helping match investors' needs with the available local skills. In many developing counties, lack of skills in technical and managerial positions is a binding constraint to upgrading in value chains. Pervasive skills gaps often result in a large wage premium for these positions, as well as in professions such as accounting and engineering. Nevertheless, explicit policies to promote "localization" of skilled jobs often result in investors facing high barriers to obtaining work permits to bring in skilled workers. By contrast, some countries actively help GVC investors identify skilled labor. For example, the Chengdu Hi-tech Industrial Development Zone gives priority to talent recruitment, assisting companies in the zone with their recruitment efforts both within China and abroad.

Developing management and firm capabilities

Although most skills development policies target workers, an equally important constituency typically undersupported is firms and their managers. According to a growing body of research, firms differ greatly in management capabilities and practices, especially in developing countries, where productivity and profitability vary significantly.[41] Governments can support firm upgrading and boost firm productivity by correcting market failures, including encouraging firms to improve their managerial practices and build relationships with buyers.

Recent studies point to several market failures that result in firms underinvesting in management. Information asymmetries are manifested in managers who "don't know what they don't know," and therefore they systematically misdiagnose the quality of the organization and management of their company.[42] These asymmetries are further compounded by uncertainties about the returns on investments in improving management and organization, as well as lack of information on the quality of providers of management consulting services.[43] When firms do invest in improving management, they not only experience much higher profits, productivity, and job growth,[44] but also improve product quality and increase the likelihood of exporting.[45] In Mexico, firms in the top decile of the managerial practices index are more than seven times more likely to participate in GVCs than firms in the bottom decile (figure 7.12). This and other evidence from developed and developing countries indicate that financial incentives or direct support to firms to facilitate improvements in management is not only a cost-effective way to

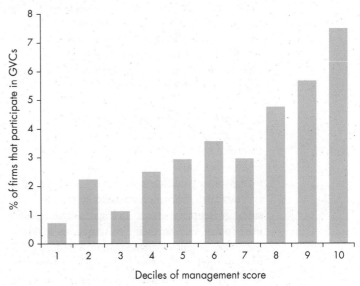

Figure 7.12 Managerial know-how is associated with greater GVC participation in Mexico

Source: WDR 2020 team, using data from ENAPROCE 2015. See appendix A for a description of the databases used in this Report.

boost productivity, but also a useful tool to support GVC integration.

Another type of market failure takes the form of uncertainty and limited information about demand. Firms are then unwilling to invest in searching for potential buyers when competitors may also benefit from their investments. This failure especially affects young firms, which are often more productive than incumbents but less likely to survive adverse shocks because of underdeveloped relationships with buyers.[46] In this context, helping firms discover markets and building relationships with clients can improve product quality and raise overall productivity. For example, in a randomized controlled trial in which Egyptian carpet producers were given access to demand from high-income foreign markets (such as the United States and the European Union), the treated firms experienced a 16–26 percent increase in profits, driven by higher quality and learning-by-doing as their product quality improved over time.[47]

The ability of firms to effectively match the needs of foreign buyers—a core requirement of participating in GVCs—requires a combination of good management and actively accumulating demand. Successful programs to support supplier development, such as those in Chile and the Czech Republic, typically combine interventions that address both supply-side and demand-side market failures. In Chile, the Chilean Innovation Agency (CORFO) set up a large matching grant program in which lead firms would apply for support for their SME suppliers and CORFO would cofinance a six-month consulting diagnostic and up to three years of diagnostic implementation. An evaluation of the impact of the program revealed significant increases in supplier survival, sales, employment, and salaries, as well as positive effects on the sales and exporting likelihood of the lead firms two years after joining the program.[48]

Strengthening innovation systems

The capacity of national and regional innovation systems also needs to expand.[49] The range of technical, engineering, and managerial skills to sustain complex manufacturing, much less innovation-intensive GVCs, is substantial. Although innovation systems—universities, government, firms, and specialized research institutions—vary in their configurations and role, the desired outputs of an innovation system's capabilities are similar. Whatever forms such systems take, knowledge must flow among firms, government, and universities. Agglomerations of innovation—such as Silicon Valley in California, Cambridge (U.K.), Bangalore, London, Berlin, and Dublin—are a feature of this stage. Governments can even establish innovation parks to induce agglomerations of innovators.

The German innovation system primarily focuses on developing complex innovations along known technology trajectories. The existing knowledge in auto manufacturing, mechanical and electrical engineering, and chemicals is mature enough that incremental improvements tend to have clear market applications. In turn, the development of both services and advanced manufacturing is a central determinant of the long-run rate of economic growth.[50]

The development of a rich national innovation system involves a great deal of networking and a wide variety of institutions—in effect, value chains of knowledge. In Germany, knowledge-intensive service sectors include both traditional professional services such as marketing and advertising and technology-based services such as software and computer systems design and R&D. A wide array of institutions mediate the relationship among private sector R&D, the university system, and the government, fulfilling the functions of coordination and cooperation. These institutions vary both in their focus on nonappropriable basic research versus marketable applied research and in their mix of private and public funding. The Max Planck Institutes, "'Blue List" institutes, national research centers, and subnationally focused "Länder" institutes are largely publicly funded institutions that focus on basic research. Universities receive a mix of public and private funding. The Fraunhofer Society is responsible for applied contract-based research that bridges basic research and industrial demand. Emerging new forms of cooperation within the innovation system, mainly privately funded, involve the creation of institutions to bridge the existing centers of knowledge and skills. Of these, new forms of collaboration between universities and industry have proliferated.

Consider special economic zones as a possible shortcut to GVC participation

Delivering on the policy priorities outlined in this chapter is no easy task, least of all for developing countries, which almost by definition face significant weaknesses across many of these policy areas. What then can these countries and the firms operating in them do to improve their chances for GVC participation in the short term, while taking the steps needed to improve the policy environment over the medium term? This section discusses the possibility of using SEZs as a means of shortcutting GVC participation.

SEZs are demarcated geographical areas within a country's national boundaries where the rules of business are generally more liberal than those that prevail in the national territory. Specifically, most economic zones create a "special" regime (box 7.6) that usually confers four main advantages to investors relative to what they could normally receive in the domestic environment:

- *Infrastructure* (including serviced land, factory shells, and utilities) that is easier to access and more reliable than is normally available domestically
- A *customs regime* that includes efficient customs administration and (usually) access to imported inputs free of tariffs and duties
- A *regulatory and administrative regime* that includes streamlined procedures for company setup, licensing, and operations
- A *fiscal regime* that includes reduction or elimination of corporate taxes, the value added tax, and other taxes; labor contributions; and sometimes training or other subsidies.[51]

SEZs are designed to facilitate trade and attract FDI, but governments may also seek to take advantage of other potential benefits of SEZs. Examples are capturing agglomeration economies,[52] which happens through exploiting backward and forward linkages;[53] labor pooling, which facilitates matching between firms and workers;[54] and technology spillovers.[55] In some countries, SEZs have been used to pilot experimental policy reforms. In China, for example,

Box 7.6 Clarifying the terminology: SEZs versus industrial parks

The term *special economic zone (SEZ)* may be used to refer to any one of the similar spatial industrial instruments known as free zones, free economic zones, export processing zones, industrial zones, economic and technology development zones, high-tech zones, science and innovation parks, free ports, and enterprise zones.[a] Even though the terms *SEZ* and *industrial park* are often used interchangeably, there are important policy and operational differences between the two.

Industrial parks are property developments that are zoned for industry or manufacturing activity. A government or a private property developer may prepare services sites or even build infrastructure, but industrial parks are not necessarily governed by any special fiscal, customs, or regulatory regime. Thus industrial parks are not necessarily SEZs.

An SEZ may take the form of an industrial park, or an industrial park may be located in it. However, what makes an SEZ "special" is that it operates within a special regulatory regime, typically covering customs (such as duty-free imports and exports), fiscal issues (such as taxation), and potentially a broad range of special regulatory regimes (such as on company registration and labor). SEZs may be geared to manufacturing, but often they accommodate mixed-use development, including services, and also may include commercial and residential activities.

These differences matter because they have important implications when choosing between an SEZ and an industrial park. When governments are dealing with land constraints, when they need to concentrate infrastructure investment, or when they are primarily seeking to promote agglomeration but do not need to create a policy and regulatory environment that differs from the existing domestic environment, an industrial park is likely to be sufficient. It is only when a special regulatory regime is needed and there are good reasons why this cannot be done nationally that an SEZ is the appropriate instrument.

a. Zeng (2015).

---

financial, legal, labor, and even pricing reforms were introduced first within its SEZs before being extended to the rest of the economy.

Whatever the objective, one the main attractions of SEZs as an instrument has always been the idea that they can act as a shortcut to infrastructure investments or policy reforms that would take many years to deliver, if at all, across a country. Instead of building infrastructure or enacting a policy everywhere, which could be financially, technically, and politically infeasible, a country could concentrate its efforts on one or two specific locations where the environment could be designed specifically to meet the needs of GVC investors or where difficult policy reforms could be contained.

SEZs: A mixed record

In some countries, the SEZ model has delivered spectacularly, playing a catalytic role in growth and structural transformation. Examples include China and Korea, which used SEZs as a platform to support the development of export-oriented manufacturing. In Latin America, the Dominican Republic, El Salvador, and Honduras, among other countries, have used free zones to take advantage of preferential access to U.S. markets and have generated large-scale manufacturing sectors in economies previously reliant on agricultural commodities. In the Middle East and North Africa, SEZs have played an important role in catalyzing export-oriented diversification in countries such as the Arab Republic of Egypt, Morocco, and the United Arab Emirates. And in Sub-Saharan Africa, SEZs in Mauritius have been a central policy tool supporting a highly successful process of economic diversification and industrialization.

And yet despite these success stories, SEZs have a mixed record (box 7.7). In some countries, the zones have failed to attract investors, leaving "white elephants" that inflicted both fiscal and political damage. In other countries, SEZs have been exploited by investors to take advantage of tax breaks without delivering substantial employment or export earnings. And in many countries, traditional export processing zone programs have been successful in attracting investment and creating employment in the short term but have failed to sustain competitiveness in the face of rising wages or eroding trade preferences.[56]

Overall, any kind of empirical assessment of SEZs (beyond individual zones and country programs) and their determinants has proven difficult. Even the most serious studies have tended to be plagued by small sample sizes and difficulty in obtaining comparable

Box 7.7 Comparing SEZ experiences: China, India, and Sub-Saharan Africa

China

China's special economic zones (SEZs) have been a well-documented global success story. They account for about 22 percent of its GDP, 46 percent of foreign direct investment (FDI), and 60 percent of exports, generating more than 30 million jobs,[a] or about 60 percent of global employment in SEZs.[b] An analysis of panel data for 270 cities at the prefecture level over 23 years shows that opening a major zone in a city led to an increase in GDP of 12 percent on average in the postreform years, with the effect depending on the type of zone. The long-term (cumulative) effect of an SEZ could be a roughly 20 percent increase in GDP.[c] Another analysis of 321 prefecture-level cities between 1978 and 2008 finds that on average an SEZ program increases per capita FDI by 21.7 percent and the growth rate of FDI by 6.9 percentage points.[d] Moreover, the average wage of workers in municipalities with an SEZ increased by 8 percent more than that of the control group, against a 5 percent rise in the cost of living.[e]

The performance of Chinese zones has not, however, been uniformly outstanding. As zones have proliferated, especially at the provincial level, their marginal impact has diminished.[f] In addition, many zones have suffered from environmental degradation, as well as from challenges in social services delivery, including inadequate health, education, and transport services. They have also lacked cultural and recreational activities for workers. In the 2000s, China responded by shutting down a large number of poorly planned industrial zones, improving the coordination between zones and urban and regional planning, and seeking to increase the role of market forces.

India[g]

Over time in India, policy decisions have contributed to erosion of the "specialness" of SEZs. For example, the overall incentive and support package available to firms in the domestic tariff area (DTA) is often more beneficial and easier to use than the zone-specific incentives. In addition, firms in the DTA can access the domestic market. With the proliferation of new free trade agreements with Japan, the Republic of Korea, and member countries of the Association of Southeast Asian Nations (ASEAN), exporters in the DTA can import with reduced or no duties from these countries instead of importing tariffed goods from zones. By contrast, India's SEZ policy framework restricts market access to the DTA, thereby constraining value chain development.

Suppliers and ancillary units co-locating within the SEZ to supply anchor investors are unable to claim income tax exemptions. Such tensions, a direct result of competing policy objectives, have limited the development of linkages between zones and the DTA, further eroding the "special" environment of zones in India.

The Indian experience suggests that zone performance depends on operational factors working in tandem rather than a single dominant factor. Zone performance, often measured by export growth, ability to attract investors, and other indicators, is a complex function of internal and external factors. In India, almost all zones with higher exports are in states with a supportive regulatory environment, are close to seaports, and have access to skilled labor through proximity to urban centers. Several were set up by the central government under the previous export promotion regime, giving investors a sense of confidence. New zones set up as public-private partnerships offer superior infrastructure and quick approvals, attracting more investors. But some zones could not sustain operations because of inexperienced private developers and underinvestment in infrastructure improvements, despite having state support.

Sub-Saharan Africa

Several Sub-Saharan countries launched zone programs as far back as the early 1970s, but most came into being in the 1990s or 2000s. Modern SEZs did not appear until after 2006. The early SEZ record in Africa is less than spectacular. Except for Mauritius and some modest achievements in Kenya, Lesotho, and Madagascar, most Sub-Saharan SEZ programs have not had a transformative impact. A 2011 analysis comparing African SEZs with those in other parts of the world developed several stylized facts:

- The takeoff of export growth in African SEZs was less significant than that outside of Africa.
- SEZs accounted for a smaller share of industrial employment (except in Lesotho) and much smaller absolute levels of industrial employment than that enjoyed outside of Africa.
- Although structural transformation of exports, as measured by diversification into manufacturing, took place fairly rapidly in SEZ-intensive countries outside Africa, it has been more limited in Africa.
- African SEZs have provided weaker enabling conditions than those in the rest of the world.[h]

(Box continues next page)

Despite relatively weak performance to date, SEZ programs remain highly popular across the continent, and policy makers seem determined to learn from the lessons of the past, both within Africa and globally. As a result, some countries, such as Ghana, Kenya, South Africa, and Tanzania, have revisited and reformed their SEZ programs in recent years. Other recently developed zones, such as Gabon's Nkok SEZ, a public-private partnership involving Olam International, the Africa Finance Corporation, and the Republic of Gabon, are showing significant promise. And early evidence from the rapidly developing SEZ program in Ethiopia, including at Bole Lemi, Eastern, and especially Hawassa, suggests that Ethiopia may have the conditions and approach to make SEZs a successful instrument of GVC integration.

a. Zeng (2010).
b. Farole (2011, 43).
c. Alder, Shao, and Zilibotti (2013).
d. Wang (2013).
e. Zeng (2015).
f. Wang (2013).
g. This section relies on Saurav (n.d.).
h. Farole (2011).

measures of SEZ performance. More recent work examines 346 zones in 22 countries across the developing world and Korea using night lights data from satellite observations as a novel way of measuring zone activity.[57] One critical finding of the study, which reinforces conclusions from previous work,[58] is that SEZs find it difficult to significantly outperform the underlying economy. Few of the zones included in the study experienced growth much higher than the national average, and many grew at a rate lower than the national average. SEZs tend to perform better in national economies that are open, growing, and competitive than in those that are not.

Lessons for successful implementation of SEZs

SEZs are not easy to get right. And even successful SEZs usually take a decade or more to start showing results. Policy makers should approach SEZs with a clear objective, a long-term commitment, and a strong technical team. Among the many lessons that they should take to heart in planning SEZs are concentrating on only the best location; understanding the market and leveraging comparative advantage; and, most important, ensuring that zones are "special."

A consistent finding from empirical research is that location choice is critical to success. International experience supports that finding, with SEZs flourishing in core areas and around gateway infrastructure (seaports, airports). Cities offer features that tend to be essential to the success of large-scale, labor-intensive SEZs, including access to deep and specialized labor pools, specialized suppliers and business services, social infrastructure, and connectivity to national and global markets. Yet governments continue to try (and fail) to use zones as regional development tools. The majority of countries with zones decide to locate at least one in a "lagging" or remote region, and few have done enough to address the infrastructure connectivity, labor skills, and supply access that these regions tend to lack. Not surprisingly, foreign investors typically shun these locations in favor of more central ones—a preference that has been on display in Bangladesh, Indonesia, Thailand, and Turkey, among other countries.[59]

Although SEZs are often implemented specifically to catalyze the development of new sectors, a location's comparative advantage remains essential. An extensive market assessment will reveal what factors drive investment decision making, and a realistic assessment of the location will reveal what it has to offer. Gaps between comparative advantage and SEZ targeting may explain why countries that have specialized in natural resources but do not have competitively priced labor and efficient infrastructure (such as Ghana, Kuwait, Nigeria, and to some degree Indonesia and Peru) have struggled to develop manufacturing-oriented zones. Mauritius is a good example of a country that has leveraged the zone instrument over several phases to exploit evolving sources of comparative advantage. The export processing zone model, so successful in transforming Mauritius from its reliance on sugar and vanilla plantations to becoming a major apparel exporter, eventually became obsolete. However, as its source of comparative advantage moved away from low wages, the government returned to the zone instrument to promote emerging industries such as ICT and financial services.[60]

With a clear understanding of investors' needs, countries can design and deliver zones that fully overcome the existing constraints to investment. If investors need reliable electricity, the SEZs should guarantee no downtime. If they need smooth customs clearance as a priority, SEZs should ensure that customs authorities resolve all possible reasons for delays. Too often SEZs are not, in fact, special. For example, a survey of global SEZ investors found that infrastructure (especially electricity quality) was among their top considerations in choosing an investment location, and that customs and trade issues were also a high priority. However, that survey also found that although successful global SEZs in the survey virtually eliminated downtime from electrical power outages, issues with electricity remained fairly frequent in the African SEZs, even though there were some improvements compared with the situation in the rest of the country. As for customs clearance, the times at seaports were actually worse in the SEZ than outside the SEZ in half of the African countries surveyed.

Finally, it is important to recognize that SEZs cannot overcome all the constraints that may restrict access to GVCs. Once outside the gates of an SEZ, problems of poor infrastructure, predatory institutions, and lack of safety and security may become binding. Such problems can affect SEZ inputs and outputs traveling between the zone and the port. They can also affect the managers and workers who must go in and out of the zone on a daily basis. More broadly, macro factors, such as a volatile exchange rate, may present problems that are difficult to shield from SEZ investors.

Policies for upgrading

This chapter has highlighted a broad range of policies that can help countries to accelerate GVC participation, to deepen the levels of participation, and to capture more of the gains from GVCs. But some policies are more salient than others, depending on the stage of GVC participation. Figure 7.13 is a summary of the policies that countries should consider as they plan their transition to the next stage of GVC participation.

Transitioning from commodities specialization to limited manufacturing GVCs

To move into downstream manufacturing from a commodities base, a country would likely have to acquire new technological and managerial capabilities.

Attracting FDI would be the quickest way to amass such capabilities. A country would, then, have to address its business climate constraints and establish simple procedures for registering foreign investors. Foreign investors will also want to be assured of basic political stability and rule of law, but deep institutional reforms may not be critical at this stage. Competitive labor costs are important at this point, but less so for GVCs that involve processing of natural resources (such as agriprocessing) and more so for those that mainly make use of imported inputs (such as apparel and electronics).

Because imported inputs play a large role in basic manufacturing GVCs, countries should give priority to measures that would support trade, including those that would improve physical connectivity, in particular through critical trade-related physical infrastructure such as ports and first-generation trade facilitation reforms. Tariff reforms—at least for selected goods—may ensure access to competitively priced inputs or involve the use of a mechanism such as bonded warehouses, duty drawbacks, or SEZs. Finally, countries should seek to secure market access through PTAs.

Transitioning to advanced manufacturing and services

Transitioning to advanced manufacturing and services GVCs presents a much bigger challenge than that to basic manufacturing. Examples of such sectors are motor vehicles, medical devices, aerospace, and precision instruments. Countries that have recently succeeded in one or more of these sectors, though not necessarily on the aggregate, include Costa Rica (box 7.8), Poland, Turkey, and Vietnam. Moving into these activities requires a step change in the policy environment.

Although labor costs still matter for some parts of the value chain—for example, in the final assembly of electronics and in some auto components such as ignition wiring sets—advanced manufacturing GVCs typically require a more highly educated workforce. The range of technical, engineering, and managerial skills needed to sustain complex manufacturing is substantial. Improvements are needed in national education and employability policies and programs, but because many of these skills may be firm-specific, a policy environment that is open to bringing in foreign skilled labor and that incentivizes foreign investors to invest in training and transfer tacit knowledge is needed as well. Policies that prescribe the use of domestic partners or force technology transfers can be inhibiting. Finally, because domestic supply capabilities will be increasingly important for advanced manufacturing

Figure 7.13 Different policy priorities underpin the transitions between types of GVC participation

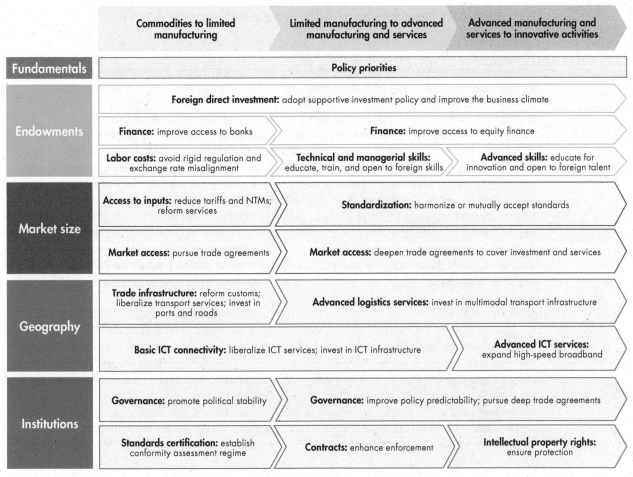

	Commodities to limited manufacturing	Limited manufacturing to advanced manufacturing and services	Advanced manufacturing and services to innovative activities
Fundamentals	Policy priorities		
Endowments	**Foreign direct investment:** adopt supportive investment policy and improve the business climate		
	Finance: improve access to banks	**Finance:** improve access to equity finance	
	Labor costs: avoid rigid regulation and exchange rate misalignment	**Technical and managerial skills:** educate, train, and open to foreign skills	**Advanced skills:** educate for innovation and open to foreign talent
Market size	**Access to inputs:** reduce tariffs and NTMs; reform services	**Standardization:** harmonize or mutually accept standards	
	Market access: pursue trade agreements	**Market access:** deepen trade agreements to cover investment and services	
Geography	**Trade infrastructure:** reform customs; liberalize transport services; invest in ports and roads	**Advanced logistics services:** invest in multimodal transport infrastructure	
	Basic ICT connectivity: liberalize ICT services; invest in ICT infrastructure		**Advanced ICT services:** expand high-speed broadband
Institutions	**Governance:** promote political stability	**Governance:** improve policy predictability; pursue deep trade agreements	
	Standards certification: establish conformity assessment regime	**Contracts:** enhance enforcement	**Intellectual property rights:** ensure protection

Source: WDR 2020 team.

Note: ICT = information and communication technology; NTMs = nontariff measures.

and services GVCs, policies that promote linkages, build managerial capabilities, and facilitate upgrading of domestic SMEs come into play as countries look toward making this transition.

The demand for lower trade costs is even greater for complex manufactures than for simpler ones. Lower tariffs are important, including zero-tariff treatment of regional partners through trade agreements (see chapter 9). Trusted trader programs, which expedite customs procedures for shipments of established value chain firms, are also useful at this stage. But access to low-cost inputs must go beyond a limited range of goods inputs. Countries at this stage must liberalize access to competitive services inputs, including through trade and investment reforms. They must ensure that the domestic regulatory environment does not restrict competition by either limiting access by foreign services providers or protecting

state-owned or other domestic firms. One particular area in which services inputs matter is transport and logistics. At this stage of GVC development, trade facilitation becomes more complex and critical, requiring the development of a competitive logistics services sector. Linked to this is the need for high-quality, competitively priced ICT infrastructure and services to help coordinate increasingly complex activities and value chains.

At the institutional level, the shift to advanced manufacturing GVCs demands that greater attention be paid to contract enforcement and protection of intellectual property. The capacity of national innovation systems also must expand. Although universities, government, firms, and specialized research institutions play various roles in national innovation systems, the desired outputs of an innovation system's capabilities are similar.

Box 7.8 Costa Rica moves into the medical devices GVC

As part of a concerted strategy to upgrade beyond basic light manufacturing exports (notably apparel), Costa Rica sought integration into higher value-added GVCs. The country has been highly successful, achieving a 10-fold increase in foreign direct investment (FDI) and GVC participation in less than 30 years. Costa Rica's shift to higher value-added GVCs has included semiconductors (the country famously attracted large-scale investment from Intel), global shared services, and medical devices, a value chain in which Costa Rica has been particularly successful in upgrading its position over the last two decades (figure B7.8.1). Its success can be attributed to effective public policy on issues such as workforce development, technology acquisition, and regulatory alignment, supported by high-quality trade and investment institutions.[a]

Workforce development

The number of workers required to produce medical devices to standard specifications is unusually high compared with that in other manufacturing sectors because of the fatal consequences of human error and the potential for liability suits. Although Costa Rica is not the lowest-cost source of labor, the training of its workforce more than offsets this factor. Direct labor for medical devices tends to be drawn from technical high school graduates, whereas the university system provides specialized workers such as material handlers, engineers, and microbiologists.

Technology and management practices

The technology required to produce medical devices is proprietary. Similarly, the management practices required to secure regulatory approval for such devices in foreign markets are mostly found in firms with prior experience. Because foreign firms bring with them "follow-on" suppliers in the medical devices GVC (who are also foreign investors), this GVC activity has grown rapidly in Costa Rica. Linkages to Costa Rican domestic firms have been concentrated in areas such as packaging but are gradually deepening to include manufacture of parts and components.

Regulatory alignment

The regulatory systems of the European Union, Japan, and the United States categorize medical devices according to the risk facing the consumer: more stringent regulations apply to higher-risk devices. Items such as elastic bandages, blood pressure cuffs, and X-ray film may be regulated lightly as Class I, whereas more stringent Class III regulations are applied to devices implanted in the human body such as pacemakers, artificial heart valves, and silicone breast

Figure B7.8.1 Costa Rica's medical device exports have increased in volume and sophistication since 2000

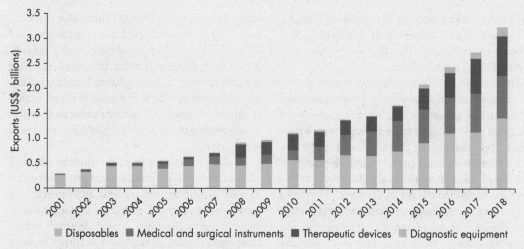

Source: WDR 2020 team, based on data from Bamber and Gereffi (2013).

(Box continues next page)

implants. An increasing number of Class III products are being fabricated in Costa Rica, reflecting the growing confidence in the capabilities of producers to follow strict regulatory protocols. Regulatory cooperation across borders is also important. The Latin American headquarters of the U.S. Food and Drug Administration opened in San José in 2011 to enable access to regulatory information and to work with local regulatory authorities, industries, and academics.

Trade and investment institutions

Costa Rica has a unique nongovernmental organization, CINDE, that is devoted to promoting economic growth through FDI. CINDE provides a forum in which firms can share information and address challenges in coordinating with other government and nongovernment actors. Among

the government actors are PROCOMER, the export promotion organization, and COMEX, the Ministry of Foreign Trade, responsible for trade policy and trade negotiations and for fulfilling an investment promotion role. CINDE has enjoyed a high level of government support and strong partnerships since the late 1990s when it landed Intel, Abbott Laboratories (now Hospira), P&G, and other anchor investors in the country's most dynamic sectors. It has continually sharpened its focus, from an all-purpose development agency when it was founded in the mid-1980s to a full-blown investment promotion agency attracting and expanding FDI projects by the turn of the century. CINDE has also improved its service offering beyond attracting investors; it now accompanies strategic investors through their investment cycle.

a. Bamber and Gereffi (2013).

Transitioning to innovative activities

As countries move toward high-income status, innovation becomes the main determinant of GVC participation. Such status is normally delivered either entirely through services or in GVCs that are highly services-intensive. Because of the growing intertwining of services and manufacturing, the development of services in GVCs is not entirely autonomous.[61] Nevertheless, high-income countries have been able to establish leading positions in services value chains ranging from research and consulting to motion pictures to software design. Some middle-income countries have established positions in services value chains as well—Nollywood in Nigeria, call centers in the Philippines, and software, call centers, and Bollywood in India.

Overall, the policy priorities needed to support innovation and advanced services GVCs are similar to those needed for advanced manufacturing, although some policies are of even greater importance such as those for technical and managerial skills and for access to advanced services. To maintain international collaboration in services, national markets must be open to foreign participation—not only for cross-border supply and commercial presences but also for the temporary movement of national persons. Workers holding higher education degrees are needed to produce innovative services. A business environment

that supports start-ups and SMEs is also essential—many service firms are small start-ups that are "born global."[62]

Innovation and advanced services GVCs also require a high-quality institutional environment that includes intellectual property rights protection and strong contract enforcement capabilities. They require, as well, policies that support a high-quality and flexible innovation ecosystem, including advanced ICT infrastructure and services; strong academic, private sector, and government partnerships; and a supportive R&D policy that incentivizes collaborative research and development.

Notes

1. Pierola, Fernandes, and Farole (2018).
2. UNCTAD and World Bank (2018).
3. Stedman and Green (2018).
4. Morris and Staritz (2017).
5. Gelb et al. (2017).
6. Rodrik (2008).
7. Conrad and Jagessar (2018).
8. Sánchez-Ancochea (2006).
9. This section relies on material from Echandi (2019).
10. World Bank (2020).
11. Charlton and Davis (2007); Morisset and Andrews-Johnson (2004); Wells and Wint (2000).
12. Harding and Javorcik (2011).
13. Freund and Moran (2017).

14. Bureau, Guimbard, and Jean (2016).
15. See appendix A for a description of the databases used in this Report.
16. Ferrantino and Koten (2019).
17. Huria et al. (2019).
18. WEF (2013).
19. Djankov, Freund, and Pham (2010).
20. Freund and Rocha (2011).
21. Christ and Ferrantino (2011).
22. Pieterse et al. (2016).
23. Londoño-Kent and Kent (2003); Raballand et al. (2012). Some issues with transport may require regional or multilateral coordination, such as anticompetitive conduct in shipping and air markets (Clark, Dollar, and Micco 2004; Fink, Mattoo, and Neagu 2002) and low connectivity in remoter developing countries (Arvis and Shepherd 2011).
24. Arvis et al. (2011).
25. World Bank (2012).
26. Fernandes, Hillberry, and Mendoza-Alcántara (2019).
27. Hiratsuka (2006).
28. Boehm (2018).
29. Farole (2016).
30. Antràs and Yeaple (2013).
31. Smith (2001).
32. Fink (2011).
33. Auriol, Balineau, and Bonneton (forthcoming).
34. Henn et al. (2017).
35. Auriol, Balineau, and Bonneton (forthcoming).
36. Balineau (2013); Bold et al. (2017).
37. Auriol, Balineau, and Bonneton (forthcoming).
38. See the discussion in chapter 3 on the consequences of tax competition and the discussion in chapter 9 on tax cooperation.
39. Farole and Winkler (2014).
40. Fernández-Stark, Bamber, and Gereffi (2012).
41. See for example, Bloom and Van Reenen (2006, 2010); Bloom et al. (2019).
42. Bloom et al. (2013, 2019).
43. Cirera and Maloney (2017).
44. Bloom et al. (2013); Bloom, Dressel, and Yam (2018); Bruhn, Karlan, and Schoar (2018).
45. Bloom et al. (2018).
46. Foster, Haltiwanger, and Syverson (2016).
47. Atkin, Khandelwal, and Osman (2017).
48. Arráiz, Henríquez, and Stucchi (2011).
49. Fagerberg and Srholec (2008).
50. Koschatzky and Stahlecker (2010).
51. FIAS (2008).
52. UNIDO (2009).
53. Ottaviano and Puga (1998).
54. Combes and Duranton (2006).
55. Rodríguez-Pose and Crescenzi (2008).
56. Farole (2011).
57. Frick, Rodríguez-Pose, and Wong (2019).
58. See Farole (2011).
59. See Farole, Norman, and Kilroy (2014); Rothenberg et al. (2017).
60. Farole (2011).
61. Kommerskollegium (2012).
62. Knight and Cavusgil (2004).

References

Alder, Simon Francis, Lisheng Shao, and Fabrizio Zilibotti. 2013. "Economic Reforms and Industrial Policy in a Panel of Chinese Cities." CEPR Discussion Paper DP9748, Center for Economic Policy Research, London.

Amiti, Mary, and Shang-Jin Wei. 2009a. "Service Offshoring and Productivity: Evidence from the U.S." World Economy 32 (2): 203–20.

———. 2009b. "Does Service Offshoring Lead to Job Losses? Evidence from the United States." In International Trade in Services and Intangibles in the Era of Globalization, edited by Marshall Reinsdorf and Matthew J. Slaughter, 227–43. National Bureau of Economic Research Studies in Income and Wealth Series 69. Chicago: University of Chicago Press.

Antràs, Pol, and Stephen Ross Yeaple. 2013. ""Multinational Firms and the Structure of International Trade." NBER Working Paper 18775 (February), National Bureau of Economic Research, Cambridge, MA.

Arnold, Jens Matthias, Beata Smarzynska Javorcik, Molly Lipscomb, and Aaditya Mattoo. 2016. "Services Reform and Manufacturing Performance: Evidence from India." Economic Journal 126 (590): 1–39.

Arnold, Jens Matthias, Beata Smarzynska Javorcik, and Aaditya Mattoo. 2011. "Does Services Liberalization Benefit Manufacturing Firms? Evidence from the Czech Republic." Journal of International Economics 85 (1): 136–46.

Arnold, Jens Matthias, Aaditya Mattoo, and Gaia Narciso. 2008. "Services Inputs and Firm Productivity in Sub-Saharan Africa: Evidence from Firm-Level Data." Journal of African Economies 17 (4): 578–99.

Arráiz, Irani, Francisca Henríquez, and Rodolfo Stucchi. 2011. "Impact of the Chilean Supplier Development Program on the Performance of SMEs and Their Large Firm Customers." OVE Working Paper OVE/WP–04/11 (May), Office of Evaluation and Oversight, Inter-American Development Bank, Washington, DC.

Arvis, Jean-François, Robin Carruthers, Graham Smith, and Christopher Willoughby. 2011. Connecting Landlocked Developing Countries to Markets: Trade Corridors in the 21st Century. Directions in Development: Trade Series. Washington, DC: World Bank.

Arvis, Jean-François, and Ben Shepherd. 2011. "The Air Connectivity Index: Measuring Integration in the Global Air Transport Network." Policy Research Working Paper 5722, World Bank, Washington, DC.

Atkin, David, Amit Kumar Khandelwal, and Adam Osman. 2017. "Exporting and Firm Performance: Evidence from a Randomized Experiment." Quarterly Journal of Economics 132 (2): 551–615.

Auriol, Emmanuelle, Gaëlle Balineau, and Nicolas Bonneton. Forthcoming. "The Economics of Quality in Developing Countries."

Balineau, Gaëlle. 2013. "Disentangling the Effects of Fair Trade on the Quality of Malian Cotton." World Development 44 (April): 241–55.

Bamber, Penny, and Gary Gereffi. 2013. "Costa Rica in the Medical Devices Global Value Chain: Opportunities for Upgrading." Research Report (August 20), Global Value Chains Center, Duke University, Durham, NC.

Black, Anthony, Justin Barnes, and Lorenza Monaco. 2018. "Structural Transformation in the Auto Sector: Industrial Policy, State-Business Bargaining, and Supply Chain Development." Draft Project Report (March 15), Industrial Development Think Tank, Center for Competition, Regulation, and Economic Development, and SARChI Chair in Industrial Development, University of Johannesburg, Johannesburg, South Africa.

Bloom, Nicholas, Erik Brynjolfsson, Lucia Foster, Ron Jarmin, Megha Patnaik, Itay Saporta-Eksten, and John Van Reenen. 2019. "What Drives Differences in Management Practices?" *American Economic Review* 109 (5): 1648–83.

Bloom, Nicholas, Leonie Dressel, and Emilie Yam. 2018. "Management Delivers: Why Firms Should Invest in Better Business Practices." IGC Growth Brief 14 (March), International Growth Center, London.

Bloom, Nicholas, Benn Eifert, Aprajit Mahajan, David McKenzie, and John Roberts. 2013. "Does Management Matter? Evidence from India." *Quarterly Journal of Economics* 128 (1): 1–51.

Bloom, Nicholas, Kalina Manova, John Van Reenen, Stephen Teng Sun, and Zhihong Yu. 2018. "Managing Trade: Evidence from China and the U.S." NBER Working Paper 24718 (June), National Bureau of Economic Research, Cambridge, MA.

Bloom, Nicholas, and John Van Reenen. 2006. "Measuring and Explaining Management Practices across Firms and Countries." NBER Working Paper 12216 (May), National Bureau of Economic Research, Cambridge, MA.

———. 2010. "Why Do Management Practices Differ across Firms and Countries?" *Journal of Economic Perspectives* 24 (1): 203–24.

Boehm, Johannes. 2018. "The Impact of Contract Enforcement Costs on Value Chains and Aggregate Productivity." Sciences Po Economics Discussion Paper 2018–12, Department of Economics, Sciences Po, Paris.

Bold, Tessa, Kayuki C. Kaizzi, Jakob Svensson, and David Yanagizawa-Drott. 2017. "Lemon Technologies and Adoption: Measurement, Theory, and Evidence from Agricultural Markets in Uganda." *Quarterly Journal of Economics* 132 (3): 1055–1100.

Borchert, Ingo, Batshur Gootiiz, and Aaditya Mattoo. 2014. "Policy Barriers to International Trade in Services: Evidence from a New Database." *World Bank Economic Review* 28 (1): 162–88.

Bruhn, Miriam, Dean Karlan, and Antoinette Schoar. 2018. "The Impact of Consulting Services on Small and Medium Enterprises: Evidence from a Randomized Trial in Mexico." *Journal of Political Economy* 126 (2): 635–87.

Bureau, Jean-Christophe, Houssein Guimbard, and Sébastien Jean. 2016. "Competing Liberalizations: Tariffs and Trade in the 21st Century." CEPII Working Paper 2016–12 (May), Centre d'Etudes Prospectives et d'Informations Internationales, Paris.

Charlton, Andrew, and Nicholas Davis. 2007. "Does Investment Promotion Work?" *B. E. Journal of Economic Analysis and Policy* 7 (1): 1–21.

Christ, Nannette, and Michael Joseph Ferrantino. 2011. "Land Transport for Export: The Effects of Cost, Time, and Uncertainty in Sub-Saharan Africa." *World Development* 39 (10): 1749–59.

Cirera, Xavier, and William F. Maloney. 2017. *The Innovation Paradox: Developing-Country Capabilities and the Unrealized Promise of Technological Catch-Up*. Washington, DC: World Bank.

Clark, Ximena, David Dollar, and Alejandro Micco. 2004. "Port Efficiency, Maritime Transport Costs, and Bilateral Trade." *Journal of Development Economics* 75 (2): 417–50.

Combes, Pierre-Philippe, and Gilles Duranton. 2006. "Labour Pooling, Labour Poaching, and Spatial Clustering." *Regional Science and Urban Economics* 36 (1): 1–28.

Conrad, Daren, and Jaymieon Jagessar. 2018. "Real Exchange Rate Misalignment and Economic Growth: The Case of Trinidad and Tobago." *Economies* 6 (52): 1–23.

Cusolito, Ana Paula, Raed Safadi, and Daria Taglioni. 2016. *Inclusive Global Value Chains: Policy Options for Small and Medium Enterprises and Low-Income Countries*. Directions in Development: Trade Series. Washington, DC: World Bank and Organisation for Economic Co-operation and Development.

Djankov, Simeon, Caroline L. Freund, and Cong S. Pham. 2010. "Trading on Time." *Review of Economics and Statistics* 92 (1): 166–73.

Duggan, Victor, Sjamsu Rahardja, and Gonzalo J. Varela. 2015. "Revealing the Impact of Relaxing Service Sector FDI Restrictions on Productivity in Indonesian Manufacturing." Policy Note 5, World Bank, Jakarta, Indonesia.

Echandi, Roberto. 2019. "Connecting the Dots between International Trade and Investment Regulation, Investment Climate Reform and Development." Revised working paper, World Bank, Washington, DC.

Fagerberg, Jan, and Martin Srholec. 2008. "National Innovation Systems, Capabilities, and Economic Development." *Research Policy* 37 (9): 1417–35.

Farole, Thomas. 2011. *Special Economic Zones in Africa: Comparing Performance and Learning from Global Experience*. Directions in Development: Trade Series. Washington, DC: World Bank.

———. 2016. "Factory Southern Africa? SACU in Global Value Chains." World Bank, Washington, DC.

Farole, Thomas, Martin Norman, and Austin Kilroy. 2014. "Special Economic Zones (SEZs) and Cities: Opportunities for Mutual Benefit in South Africa." Reimbursable Advisory Services, World Bank, Washington, DC.

Farole, Thomas, and Deborah Elisabeth Winkler, eds. 2014. *Making Foreign Direct Investment Work for Sub-Saharan Africa: Local Spillovers and Competitiveness in Global Value Chains*. Directions in Development: Trade Series. Washington, DC: World Bank.

Fernandes, Ana Margarida, Russell Henry Hillberry, and Alejandra Mendoza-Alcántara. 2019. "Trade Effects of Customs Reform: Evidence from Albania." Paper presented at Department of Economics Spring Seminar, University of Nebraska, Lincoln, January 18.

Fernandes, Ana Margarida, and Caroline Paunov. 2012. "Foreign Direct Investment in Services and Manufacturing Productivity: Evidence for Chile." *Journal of Development Economics* 97 (2): 305–21.

Fernández-Stark, Karina, Penny Bamber, and Gary Gereffi. 2012. "Upgrading in Global Value Chains: Addressing the Skills Challenge in Developing Countries." Research Report (September 26), Global Value Chains Center, Duke University, Durham, NC.

Ferrantino, Michael Joseph, and Emine Elcin Koten. 2019. "Understanding Supply Chain 4.0 and Its Potential Impact on Global Value Chains." In *Global Value Chain Development Report 2019: Technological Innovation, Supply Chain Trade, and Workers in a Globalized World*, 103–19. Geneva: World Trade Organization.

FIAS (Facility for Investment Climate Advisory Services). 2008. "Special Economic Zones: Performance, Lessons Learned, and Implications for Zone Development." Report 45869 (April), World Bank, Washington, DC.

Fink, Carsten. 2011. "Intellectual Property Rights." In *Preferential Trade Agreement Policies for Development: A Handbook*, edited by Jean-Pierre Chauffour and Jean-Christophe Maur, 387–405. Washington, DC: World Bank.

Fink, Carsten, Aaditya Mattoo, and Ileana Cristina Neagu. 2002. "Trade in International Maritime Services: How Much Does Policy Matter?" *World Bank Economic Review* 16 (1): 81–108.

Foster, Lucia, John Haltiwanger, and Chad Syverson. 2016. "The Slow Growth of New Plants: Learning about Demand?" *Economica* 83 (329): 91–129.

Freund, Caroline L., and Theodore H. Moran. 2017. "Multinational Investors as Export Superstars: How Emerging-Market Governments Can Reshape Comparative Advantage." PIIE Working Paper 17–1 (January), Peterson Institute for International Economics, Washington, DC.

Freund, Caroline L., and Nadia Rocha. 2011. "What Constrains Africa's Exports?" *World Bank Economic Review* 25 (3): 361–86.

Frick, Susanne A., Andrés Rodríguez-Pose, and Michael D. Wong. 2019. "Toward Economically Dynamic Special Economic Zones in Emerging Countries." *Economic Geography* 95 (1): 30–64.

Gelb, Alan, Christian J. Meyer, Vijaya Ramachandran, and Divyanshi Wadhwa. 2017. "Can Africa Be a Manufacturing Destination? Labor Costs in Comparative Perspective." CGD Working Paper 466 (October), Center for Global Development, Washington, DC.

Harding, Torfinn, and Beata Smarzynska Javorcik. 2011. "Roll Out the Red Carpet and They Will Come: Investment Promotion and FDI Inflows." *Economic Journal* 121 (557): 1445–76.

———. 2012. "Investment Promotion and FDI Inflows: Quality Matters." Department of Economics Discussion Paper 612 (June), University of Oxford, Oxford, U.K.

Henn, Christian, Chris Papageorgiou, Jose Manuel Romero, and Nikola Spatafora. 2017. "Export Quality in Advanced and Developing Economies: Evidence from a New Data Set." Policy Research Working Paper 8196, World Bank, Washington, DC.

Hiratsuka, Daisuke. 2006. "Vertical Intra-Regional Production Networks in East Asia: A Case Study of the Hard Disc Drive Industry." In *East Asia's De Facto Economic Integration*, edited by Daisuke Hiratsuka, 181–99. Institute of Developing Economies–Japan External Trade Organization Series. London: Palgrave Macmillan.

Hoekman, Bernard, and Aaditya Mattoo. 2008. "Services Trade and Growth." Policy Research Working Paper 4461, World Bank, Washington, DC.

Huria, Sughanda, Ruchita Manghnani, Sebastian Saez, and Eric van der Marel. 2019. "Servicification of Indian Manufacturing." World Bank, Washington, DC.

Knight, Gary A., and S. Tamar Cavusgil. 2004. "Innovation, Organizational Capabilities, and the Born-Global Firm." *Journal of International and Business Studies* 35 (2): 124–41.

Kommerskollegium (National Board of Trade). 2012. "Everybody Is in Services: The Impact of Servicification in Manufacturing on Trade and Trade Policy." Kommerskollegium, Stockholm.

Koschatzky, Knut, and Thomas Stahlecker. 2010. "The Emergence of New Modes of R&D Services in Germany." *Services Industry Journal* 30 (5): 685–700.

Londoño-Kent, María del Pilar, and Paul E. Kent. 2003. "A Tale of Two Ports: The Cost of Inefficiency." Research Report (December), World Bank, Washington, DC.

Malaysia Ministry of International Trade and Industry. 2019. "SME Development," accessed at miti.gov.my/index.php /pages/view/1801 October 3, 2019.

Malinska, Jana, and Stephen Martin. 2000–2002. "Czech Supplier Development Programme in Electronics and Automotive. http://www3.weforum.org/docs/Manufacturing _Our_Future_2016/Case_Study_13.pdf.

Minor, Peter J. 2013. "Time as a Barrier to Trade: A GTAP Database of Ad Valorem Trade Time Costs." ImpactEcon, Boulder, CO.

Morisset, Jacques, and Kelly Andrews-Johnson. 2004. "The Effectiveness of Promotion Agencies at Attracting Foreign Direct Investment." FIAS Occasional Paper 16, Facility for Investment Climate Advisory Services, World Bank, Washington, DC.

Morris, Mike, and Cornelia Staritz. 2017. "Industrial Upgrading and Development in Lesotho's Apparel Industry: Global Value Chains, Foreign Direct Investment, and Market Diversification." Oxford Development Studies 45 (3): 303–20.

Ottaviano, Gianmarco, and Diego Puga. 1998. "Agglomeration in the Global Economy: A Survey of the 'New Economic Geography.'" *World Economy* 21 (6): 707–31.

Pierola, Martha Denisse, Ana Margarida Fernandes, and Thomas Farole. 2018. "The Role of Imports for Exporter Performance in Peru." *World Economy* 41 (2): 550–72.

Pieterse, Duncan, Thomas Farole, Martin Odendaal, and Andre Steenkamp. 2016. "Supporting Export Competitiveness through Port and Rail Network Reforms: A Case Study of South Africa." Policy Research Working Paper 7532, World Bank, Washington, DC.

Raballand, Gaël, Salim Refas, Monica Beuran, and Gözde Isik. 2012. *Why Does Cargo Spend Weeks in Sub-Saharan African Ports? Lessons from Six Countries.* Directions in Development: Trade Series. Washington, DC: World Bank.

Rodríguez-Pose, Andrés, and Riccardo Crescenzi. 2008. "Research and Development, Spillovers, Innovation Systems, and the Genesis of Regional Growth in Europe." *Regional Studies* 42 (1): 51–67.

Rodrik, Dani. 2008. "The Real Exchange Rate and Economic Growth." *Brookings Papers on Economic Activity* 39 (2): 365–439.

Rothenberg, Alexander D., Samuel Bazzi, Shanthi Nataraj, and Amalavoyal V. Chari. 2017. *When Regional Policies Fail: An Evaluation of Indonesia's Integrated Economic Development Zones.* Santa Monica, CA: RAND Corporation. https://www.rand.org/pubs/working_papers/WR1183.html.

Sánchez-Ancochea, Diego. 2006. "Development Trajectories and New Comparative Advantages: Costa Rica and the Dominican Republic under Globalization." *World Development* 34 (6): 996–1015.

Saurav, Abhishek. No date. "Performance of Special Economic Zones in India: Experience and Lessons." Background note prepared for this Report.

Smith, Pamela J. 2001. "How Do Foreign Patent Rights Affect U.S. Exports, Affiliate Sales, and Licenses?" *Journal of International Economics* 55 (2): 411–39.

Stedman, Ashley, and Kenneth P. Green. 2018. "Fraser Institute Annual Survey of Mining Companies, 2018." Fraser Institute, Vancouver, Canada.

Sturgeon, Timothy J., Leonardo Lima Chagas, and Justin Barnes. 2017. *Inovar Auto: Evaluating Brazil's Automotive Industrial Policy to Meet the Challenges of Global Value Chains.* Washington, DC: World Bank.

UNCTAD (United Nations Conference on Trade and Development) and World Bank. 2018. "The Unseen Impact of Non-tariff Measures: Insights from a New Database." Report UNCTAD DC:/DITC/TAB/2018/2, UNCTAD, Geneva.

UNIDO (United Nations Industrial Development Organization). 2009. *Industrial Development Report 2009; Breaking In and Moving Up: New Industrial Challenges for the Bottom Billion and the Middle-Income Countries.* Vienna: UNIDO.

USAID (U.S. Agency for International Development). 2007. "Calculating Tariff Equivalents for Time in Trade." USAID, Washington, DC.

Wang, Jin. 2013. "The Economic Impact of Special Economic Zones: Evidence from Chinese Municipalities." *Journal of Development Economics* 101 (March): 133–47.

WEF (World Economic Forum). 2013. *Enabling Trade: Valuing Growth Opportunities.* Geneva: WEF.

Wells, Louis T., Jr., and Alvin G. Wint. 2000. "Marketing a Country: Promotion as a Tool for Attracting Foreign Investment." FIAS Occasional Paper 13 (March). Facility for Investment Climate Advisory Services, World Bank, Washington, DC.

World Bank. 2012. "Developing a Trade Information Portal." Report 83273 (July), World Bank, Washington, DC.

———. 2015. "A Practical Guide to Increasing Mining Local Procurement in West Africa." Report AUS6324 (February), World Bank, Washington, DC.

———. 2018. *Global Investment Competitiveness Report 2017/2018: Foreign Investor Perspectives and Policy Implications.* Washington, DC: World Bank.

———. 2020. *Foreign Direct Investment as a Key Driver for Global Value Chains.* Washington, DC: World Bank.

Zeng, Douglas Zhihua. 2010. *Building Engines for Growth and Competitiveness in China: Experience with Special Economic Zones and Industrial Clusters.* Directions in Development: Countries and Regions. Washington, DC: World Bank.

———. 2015. "Global Experiences with Special Economic Zones: Focus on China and Africa." Policy Research Working Paper 7240, Washington, DC, World Bank.

8

Policies for inclusion and sustainability

Key findings

- **Developing countries would benefit from policies that spread the jobs and earnings gains from global value chain (GVC) participation across society.** Access to child care and training programs support jobs for women and youth, respectively. Smallholders need assistance, such as extension services and access to finance, to integrate into agricultural value chains. GVC lead firms, labor, and governments can work together to protect workers' safety and rights.

- **Industrial countries would benefit from adjustment policies for workers displaced by technology, trade, and the expansion of GVCs.** Placement services, training, and mobility support can help workers transition to more productive jobs.

- **Policy can mitigate negative environmental consequences and promote the adoption of environmentally friendly technologies.** Pricing the environmental costs of production and distribution appropriately will encourage conservation and cleaner technologies. In addition, regulation is needed for specific pollutants and industries.

- **These national measures can be complemented by global cooperation on the environment and working conditions.** Standardized international data will help expose poor production practices and induce firms to improve.

The policies and institutions that maximize the aggregate gains from participation in global value chains (GVCs) will not necessarily ensure that these gains are shared—across locations, across skill levels, and across different groups in society such as women and youth (chapter 3). They may even exacerbate the negative environmental consequences of GVCs (chapter 5). In this context, ensuring the inclusiveness and sustainability of the GVC model calls for considering policies in three areas that support broader gains among workers and mitigate their negative social and environmental consequences.

First, developing countries would benefit from policies that spread the jobs and earnings gains from GVC participation across society, thereby helping to lift the bottom 40 percent. For countries participating in agriculture value chains, policies that support the integration of smallholders are particularly important. As countries move into basic manufacturing, lower-skilled poor workers will benefit most from policies that support comparative advantage and incentivize investment in labor-intensive activities.

Policies should also support the inclusion of women and youth in GVCs, including by providing access to child care and training programs and by addressing legal and social barriers to employment and earnings. For example, in Côte d'Ivoire a project to develop the cashew value chain—supported by investments in feeder roads, reform of agricultural extension services, and improved access to finance—is expected to raise earnings for 225,000 smallholder farmers and create at least 12,000 processing jobs, with half going to women.

Significant shortfalls in worker safety standards are still common in the supply chains of many global brands, particularly among their second- and third-tier suppliers, as incidents such as the 2013 Rana Plaza garment factory disaster in Bangladesh attest. Although most global brands have developed social and environmental compliance standards for their global supply chains, broader initiatives bringing lead firms together with suppliers, trade unions, and civil society are becoming more common. For example, the International Labour Organization-International Finance Corporation (ILO-IFC) Better Work program, which covers nearly 2.5 million workers in 1,700 GVC-linked garment factories in eight countries, has demonstrated that improved compliance with labor standards can lead to higher productivity and profits. Meanwhile, governments are moving toward "binding due diligence," whereby lead firms are legally responsible for compliance across their entire supply

chains. Yet a role remains for national governments to safeguard the protection of workers in GVCs through, for example, collective bargaining, freedom of association, and social dialogue.

Second, in advanced countries the welfare of workers left behind in communities where factories have closed is the primary threat to the sustainability of trade and GVCs. In response, labor adjustment policies can be used to ensure that workers have the skills to move to new industries and places. By contrast, using trade restrictions or rigid labor policies to protect existing jobs is unsustainable and will slow economic transformation and long-run income growth. Place-based interventions should take into account local endowments and favor targeted initiatives to address coordination failures over broad-based investment subsidies.

Third, policies can mitigate negative environmental consequences and promote the adoption of environmentally friendly technologies. An important first step is to set a price on environmental degradation. Prices of goods should reflect both their economic and socioenvironmental costs, and trade should be carried out based on comparative advantage that accounts for these costs. In addition to pricing, there is also a role for regulation, especially for specific pollutants and industries.

These national measures can be complemented by global cooperation to deal directly with the environment, as well as to ensure that trade agreements are consistent with environmental goals. International treaties such as the 2015 Paris Agreement on climate change include requirements on environmental protection for signatories at all income levels. Recent major trade agreements, such as the Comprehensive and Progressive Agreement for Trans-Pacific Partnership (CPTPP) and the new European Union (EU) free trade agreements, include environmental provisions.

Finally, standardized international data on the environmental consequences of firms in GVCs can expose poor production practices and incentivize firms to improve.

Sharing the gains

Exploit comparative advantage to ensure jobs-rich investment in GVCs

Jobs are the most direct and important channel through which GVCs contribute to poverty reduction and shared prosperity. Chapter 3 describes the strong links between GVCs and job creation at both the national and the firm level. Importantly, it shows that job growth in GVCs is associated with both greater use of imported inputs and greater use of technology. Thus, although the higher imported inputs and capital intensity of GVC production may mean less labor is needed per unit of output, the output boost induced by GVC participation means more jobs are created overall. Chapter 3 also points out that GVCs are, on the whole, inclusive; they are both pro-poor and a significant source of jobs for women. These positive outcomes can be facilitated by supportive domestic policies.

Create jobs in sectors that absorb poor and low-skilled workers

For many developing countries, particularly those selling only commodities, ensuring GVCs benefit the poorest will come primarily through integrating smallholders into agriculture value chains and home-based workers into manufacturing and services GVCs. Integration of smallholders is particularly important for Africa, where 55 percent of jobs and more than 70 percent of the earnings of the poor are reliant on the agriculture sector.[1]

As discussed in chapter 2, foreign direct invest-ment (FDI) may play a critical role in supporting the development of agriculture value chains. Lead firms help solve many of the challenges of raising small-holder productivity by providing access to inputs, technical support, finance, and markets. The integra-tion of smallholders with offtakers or directly with processors supports greater value addition at the farmgate through a range of services such as tech-nology transfer, quality or certification premiums, and continual access to the market. For example, the rapid development of floriculture value chains across East Africa, which opened up many jobs and earnings opportunities for smallholder farmers and women in packing and distribution, was made possible through subcontracting models organized by lead firms.

Smallholder integration in GVCs is, however, not a panacea. A case study in Côte d'Ivoire and Ghana on participation in the pineapple and cocoa value chains found that, although participation leads to better growing processes, larger yields, and higher incomes for successful commercial farmers, it is also associated with an increase in casual labor hiring, as well as dis-placement of farmers from land because of their weak bargaining positions and scant knowledge of their rights to land ownership.[2] Moreover, the near-collapse of Ghana's export pineapple sector in the mid-2000s was due in part to smallholders' lack of organization, which contributed to overproduction and inflexibility in response to changing market demand.

Therefore, governments have an important role to play both in facilitating lead firm investment and in supporting smallholder integration in agricultural GVCs. Policies for the former include many of those discussed in chapter 7—notably, trade and investment policy and infrastructure. Policies for the latter include the provision of agricultural extension services, access to risk management instruments such as insurance, and assistance with convening and coordinating smallholders to exploit scale through cooperatives and other producer organizations.

Finally, as countries seek to move downstream from natural resources and integrate into manu-facturing and services value chains, the objective of delivering jobs for the current stock of poor workers calls for policies that reinforce comparative advantage.[3] This means, for example, a relatively small, agriculturally rich country would focus on agriprocessing, or a large, low-skilled labor surplus country would implement policies conducive to attracting light manufacturing GVCs. For example, Côte d'Ivoire and Rwanda adopted strategies to expand agriculture value added and increase pro-cessing to raise returns to smallholder coffee farm-ers (box 8.1). Ethiopia, by leveraging FDI in industrial parks, developed labor-intensive light manufactur-ing to absorb labor transitioning away from agricul-ture. And Morocco upgraded to high-value manufac-turing to create jobs for an underemployed skilled population. These strategies offer a contrast with strategies that attempt to promote the development of high-technology, innovation-driven value chain nodes—strategies that in the same countries, even if successful, would unlikely have significant impacts on lower-skilled workers and could contribute to wage polarization.

At the heart of policies that reinforce compara-tive advantage are those that minimize distortions of market prices—of land, labor, and capital—so that factors flow smoothly to the sectors and places where comparative advantage can be best exploited. These include economywide policies to support land mar-ket reforms, competition, open labor markets, and access to finance, along with investments in critical infrastructure.

In low-income, labor surplus countries with large pools of unskilled labor transitioning from the agri-culture sector, externalities arising from the diver-gence between the market price and the opportunity cost of labor may call for additional targeted incen-tives for the private sector to invest in labor-intensive activities.[4]

Box 8.1 Taking advantage of comparative advantage: Agribusiness GVCs deliver more and better jobs in Côte d'Ivoire and Rwanda

Côte d'Ivoire's cashew value chain

Cashews are Côte d'Ivoire's third-ranking export after cacao and refined petroleum products, and they are an important source of cash for smallholders and processors in the poorer north of the country. Although Côte d'Ivoire produces 23 percent of the world's cashew supply, fewer than 7 percent of raw cashew nuts are processed domestically. Low yields and low quality are a result of poorly maintained plantations, lack of quality stock and inputs, weak extension services, losses in postharvest handling and storage, and lack of finance for improvements. With coordinated support from the World Bank and the International Finance Corporation, and working closely with the private sector, a comprehensive program to upgrade the cashew sector and increase domestic value addition was put in place. In 2017 the program established four cashew "platforms" and eight satellite hubs that provide training, access to inputs, and market information, along with processing demonstration units. The program was supported with access to new sources of finance for smallholders, notably through the introduction of a warehouse receipts system that enables processors to use unprocessed nuts as collateral for working capital loans. About 225,000 cashew farmers are expected to benefit from the upgrading and improved value chain integration.

Source: World Bank (2018).

Rwanda's coffee value chain

In the late 1990s, as Rwanda looked to rebuild its economy and create jobs and earnings opportunities after a civil war, it faced structural challenges to developing internationally competitive tradables. For one thing, it is small and land-locked and in a poor and fragile neighborhood. The coffee sector was historically the country's main export crop and a major source of earnings for up to half a million rural Rwandans. But at the end of the 1990s, fallout from the civil war helped put the sector on the verge of collapse because of the low quantity and quality of its product. To address this challenge, the country put in place a strategy, completed in 2002, to raise production and move to a higher value-added position in the coffee GVC. Working closely with the private sector and nongovernmental organizations, the government introduced a two-pronged approach: (1) upgrade technology and increase production and (2) boost skills and improve quality.

These interventions proved to be a critical turning point for the sector and spurred upgrading along the coffee value chain. The upgrading was manifested in more skilled farming techniques, better use of technologies, and higher productivity. During the first five years of implementing the National Coffee Strategy, private investment in coffee washing stations grew by an average of 120 percent a year in locations with the highest cherry availability (the fruit that contains the coffee bean), water supplies, and road linkages. The total number of coffee washing stations rose from just two in the entire country in 1998 to 299 as of early 2015. Meanwhile, the higher-quality coffee began to merit higher prices, with Rwandan coffee now fetching a premium in international markets. According to the U.S. Agency for International Development (USAID), as a result of the reforms in the coffee GVC, approximately 50,000 rural households have seen their incomes from coffee production more than double, and some 2,000 jobs have been created in coffee washing stations.

Source: Adapted from Karuretwa (2016).

Create jobs for women and youth

The propensity of GVCs to employ women and youth is partly related to the sectors and activities that lend themselves to outsourcing and global relocation, which in turn are associated with some of the negative consequences of GVCs, especially those around low wages and poor working conditions. Nevertheless, the potential of GVCs to employ large numbers of young female workers means they may play a major role in supporting many countries' efforts to increase female labor force participation and reduce youth NEETs (not in employment, education, or training). In Bangladesh, more than 3 million women, mainly young rural–urban migrants, gained employment in the garment sector as it integrated into GVCs in the early 2000s, contributing to an almost 10 percentage point rise in the rate of female labor force participation in just a decade.

Education and skills development policy is the starting point for helping youth to take advantage of the opportunities for employment in GVCs. The *World Development Report 2019: The Changing Nature of*

Work highlighted the rapidly changing demand for skills, along with the growing importance of advanced cognitive skills, sociobehavioral skills, and, most important, adaptability to changing circumstances and to "unlearn and relearn quickly."[5] Research shows increasingly large payoffs from such adaptability—for example, in Armenia and Georgia the ability to solve problems and learn new skills yields a wage premium of nearly 20 percent.[6]

GVCs are at the forefront of these changing demands for skills, but in many if not most countries there remains a large gap between the needs of employers and the approaches of education and skills development institutions. Countries need to work toward a system that emphasizes the employability of youth and facilitates the transition from study to work. Promising policy directions include adoption of dual education systems that provide flexibility for combining general and vocational education, development of vocational training curricula with private sector participation to ensure relevance to employer needs, and expanded use of innovative apprentice models that give youth an opportunity to learn from working. Public-private models are often used to develop pathways to GVC-specific employment. For example, in Kenya the national coffee board and industry bodies have teamed up with Kimathi University of Technology to develop a coffee diploma program that combines classroom training on technology and quality management with an industry placement of three to six months.

Governments can help facilitate women's access to jobs in GVCs by enacting policies that support women's participation in the economy. Such policies could establish the legal and regulatory environment for access to quality child care, facilitate access to safe transport, as well as ensure that women are protected from unfair treatment. For example, recent research by the World Bank's Women, Business, and the Law project shows that in the Middle East and North Africa region women have on average less than half the legal rights of men in measured areas. Box 8.2 highlights two contrasting approaches to integration of female workers in GVC factories—one that brought women workers to the factories and another that brought factories to women workers.

Private enterprises have a role to play through training and development programs and ensuring fair promotion practices. In Bangladesh, for example, an initiative in partnership with the ILO-IFC Better Work program developed, implemented, and evaluated an innovative training program for women operatives in 28 apparel factories. Of the 144 women who attended the training program, 92 were offered a promotion and higher salary within weeks of completing the program. The evaluation also found that average efficiency increased by 5 percent, and absenteeism fell in line where trained female supervisors worked.

Balance adequate wages with sustaining competitiveness

The inclusivity and social sustainability of GVCs depend not only on the scale and distribution of jobs in GVCs, but also on the quality of those jobs. Here the concept of job quality incorporates both wages (or earnings more broadly) and working conditions, including working hours, benefits, the health and safety environment, treatment of workers, and the degree to which workers have voice and agency to help shape employers' decisions on issues that affect workers. This concept is in line with Sustainable Development Goal 8 of United Nations Agenda 2030, which highlights the importance of ensuring improvements in working conditions—combining aspects such as productive employment, social protection, social dialogue, and rights at work—together with economic growth. The issue of job quality is particularly relevant to labor-intensive GVCs, where outsourcing to developing country locations is fundamentally motivated by the desire to access low-cost labor.[7]

Because many of the most prominent GVCs involve outsourcing of low-skill, labor-intensive activities, the very low nominal wages in some countries often grab the world's attention. For example, recent news articles have noted that t-shirts are being produced for charities or high-profile brands in factories paying less than 50 cents an hour. Certainly, to readers in high-income countries where even the lowest-skilled factory jobs pay 20–30 times that level, this is a shockingly low wage. However, this does not necessarily mean that low wages are a problem in GVCs. As discussed in chapter 3, firms operating in GVCs tend to pay higher wages than firms operating in direct trade only.[8] What matters more is whether the wages on offer are in line with productivity and whether they offer a reasonable "living wage" for workers.

GVCs can be problematic if they contribute to the emergence of "low wage traps"—that is, where wage suppression is used to maintain international competitiveness. Although low wage traps are not inherent to GVCs, the globalized and footloose nature of GVC production in some sectors may make them more likely, particularly where lead firms in GVCs use international production cost comparisons to maintain

Box 8.2 A tale of two economic zones: Initiatives to promote women's employment in garment GVCs in Bangladesh and Jordan

Bangladesh

In Bangladesh, women's integration into the workforce of garment factories in export processing zones (EPZs)—mostly in Dhaka and Chittagong—was almost immediate. Because the EPZs were located in Bangladesh's largest cities, urban women faced somewhat lower transport and social barriers to working in GVC factories. The challenge in Bangladesh was how to make these same opportunities available to rural women for whom these constraints were binding. An innovative pilot project, the Northern Areas Reduction of Poverty Initiative, supported by the World Bank in cooperation with the Bangladesh Export Processing Zones Authority, brought women from the poorest regions of northern Bangladesh into Dhaka for training and employment in the EPZ-based garment factories. The program gave women and the local community the information and awareness they needed to overcome social stigmas. Women also received transport, living stipends, and comprehensive technical and life skills training, followed by employment. The results of the pilot were positive: more than 6,000 women (two-thirds of those who completed training) took up employment in the garment factories at earnings above the industry average. And positive spillovers from the pilot are evident. Many of the constraints of information and social norms have been overcome,

opening up new opportunities for other women in these northern villages.[a]

Jordan

Jordan's qualified industrial zones (QIZs), established in the late 1990s, were expected to not only generate exports by integrating Jordan into the garment GVC, but also create large-scale employment for women in a country in which the female labor force participation is among the lowest in the world. The QIZs were able to attract investment and create jobs, but manufacturers faced large barriers in integrating local women into the factories in the QIZs because of lack of transport and perceptions of the safety and social acceptability of working in these factories. As a result, virtually all the jobs created for women in the initial stages of the QIZs were taken up by migrant workers, mostly from South and Southeast Asia. In response, the government created satellite production units in rural areas around the villages in which women resided, supported by substantial financial incentives for manufacturers to hire through these satellite units. The initiative, which was launched in 2010, has shown positive results, even if on a small scale: as of August 2017, approximately 3,300 jobs had been created in 12 satellite factories, with a 90 percent female workforce.[b]

a. World Bank (2017).
b. Davis (2017).

---

pricing pressure on suppliers in developing countries. Moreover, because GVCs can emerge as enclaves or dominant sectors in developing country economies, there is a risk that employers take advantage of monopsony and political power in labor bargaining. For example, in Bangladesh garment factory owners have managed, despite repeated large-scale protests, to avoid any real term increase in garment factory wages. Depressed wages can be particularly problematic for low-income workers in developing countries where GVC integration is associated with rapid urbanization and where housing and transport costs are rising far more quickly than overall inflation rates.

In this context, policies should protect workers' earnings while maintaining competitiveness to attract GVC investment. Collective bargaining can be an effective mechanism for negotiating the appropriate wage

levels. Minimum wages also play an important role. Virtually all countries have some minimum wage for regular workers, although it varies dramatically (even considering differences in purchasing power) from just $2 a month in Burundi and Uganda to more than $2,900 a month in Norway.[9] Minimum wages should be set at a level that, at the very least, protects workers from poverty and vulnerability,[10] while also keeping an eye on firm competitiveness. Perhaps most important, they should be raised at regular intervals and through a systematic and transparent process,[11] which includes tripartite social dialogue. Minimum wage indexation should be linked to both productivity growth and the cost of living, avoiding excessively sharp increases during significant economic downturns. Meanwhile, the impact of minimum wage on workers is unequal and depends on compliance and enforcement, as well as the degree of segmentation between formal and informal workers. Thus a minimum wage should be seen as just one mechanism for supporting inclusivity in GVCs.

In some countries, distortions in the domestic market may drive a significant wedge between a living wage for workers and the wage at which firms can remain competitive in international markets. Government policy can help bridge this gap—over the medium term by addressing the market failure and over the short term by undertaking interventions that change relative prices. In South Africa, the government introduced a wage subsidy for youth workers and later extended it to all workers based in special economic zones (SEZs). Governments may also seek to raise net returns to workers by, for example, lowering the cost of transport to access jobs through transport subsidies or investments in public transport services or by lowering the costs of housing through social housing schemes or unlocking the constraints to private housing construction. Such instruments are often incorporated directly into SEZs, with SEZ-based employers routinely providing transport for workers and in some cases providing housing in on-site dormitories.

As countries shift from commodity and basic manufacturing GVCs to advanced manufacturing and innovation-based GVCs, wages are less fundamental to competitiveness. However, in many developing countries the problem is lack of a sufficient base of skilled workers (particularly technical workers), which in turn creates large wage premiums that not only contribute to polarization but also undermine competitiveness. Because skilled workers in these GVCs typically complement unskilled workers, the lack of skilled workers also has a negative impact on inclusion. Aside from the obvious role of education and skills-development policy, countries should be open to the immigration of skilled workers as a strategy for both competitiveness and inclusion.

Protecting the well-being of workers is about more than wages

But workers care about more than just wages. Evidence from Vietnam shows that workers' reported well-being is affected also by incentive structures, benefits packages, training, absence of sexual harassment, strikes, and health and safety. Beyond wages, occupational health and safety affect well-being at four times the rate of any other measure of working conditions, such as number of hours worked.[12] Yet working conditions are commonly found to fall short of international standards in GVC supplier countries,

ranging from violations of core labor standards such as child labor, forced labor, lack of freedom of association, and exploitative and abusive practices to unsafe working conditions, low wages, excessive working hours, and precarious contracts. Although serious breaches of standards are becoming less common in the direct supplier networks of multinationals, they remain a problem and are rife in second- and third-tier suppliers. Widely publicized examples, such as the Rana Plaza disaster in Bangladesh in 2013, in which more than 1,100 garment workers lost their lives, and the Baldia textile factory fire, which killed close to 300 workers in Pakistan in 2012, are well known. However, below the radar millions of workers in globally linked industries work daily in vulnerable situations. Although poor working conditions in Dickensian factories tend to garner the most attention, similar problems exist in global commodity chains such as agriculture[13] and even in high-technology value chains, as confirmed by recent news reports documenting the casualization, discrimination, harassment, and retaliation encountered in some of the world's largest technology multinationals.

Many of the specific features of poor working conditions (particularly around workplace safety) are less a feature of GVCs themselves than of the labor markets in countries to which GVC activities are outsourced. In fact, like wages, working conditions in GVC-linked enterprises tend to be better on average than in those enterprises in the same country operating outside of GVCs. And yet aside from the fact that the GVC model enables global enterprises (and consumers) to profit from offshoring to avoid the costs of protecting workers, GVCs may also exacerbate the problems of poor working conditions by creating incentives for GVC-linked suppliers in developing countries to similarly seek to cut these costs. For example, an underlying factor in Bangladesh's Rana Plaza disaster was the common practice of first-tier suppliers subcontracting work to smaller, often informal, producers to reduce costs and avoid scrutiny from lead firms.

Even where developing countries have robust national policy regimes in place to support international labor standards, those regimes are ultimately only as good as their enforcement capacity. It is here that many developing countries come undone. Lack of technical capacity and financial resources, corruption, and distorted incentives are all powerful forces that undermine both national and private standards designed to promote quality jobs in GVCs. As countries engage more deeply in GVCs, investing in upgrading the capacity and governance of their labor regulatory regimes will be increasingly critical to both protect workers and maintain the "national brand" for supply chain compliance.

In response to concerns about working conditions in GVC supply chains, over the last decade or more most global brands have developed social and environmental compliance standards for supply chains. Such initiatives, which increasingly involve global framework agreements between trade unions and multinational enterprises, have succeeded in improving working conditions, particularly those related to occupational health and safety and other measurable standards. In recent years, the limitations of unilateral brand initiatives have been addressed somewhat by multistakeholder initiatives that bring together lead firms and suppliers, trade unions, civil society, and, in some cases, national governments. One example is the ILO-IFC Better Work program noted earlier and described in box 8.3.[14]

Despite the success of private and public-private initiatives, they are limited in scope and coverage. At the very least, national governments must play a supportive role in facilitating compliance through

Box 8.3 Transparency promotes compliance with labor standards and improves working conditions

According to global evidence from the International Labour Organization-International Finance Corporation (ILO-IFC) Better Work program, garment factories in GVCs are more productive and more profitable when they comply with labor standards[a]—especially those aimed at ensuring freedom of association and collective bargaining,[b] improving workers' sense of physical security and assurance of wage payments, and eliminating sexual harassment[c] and verbal abuse.[d]

Greater transparency on working conditions in GVCs plays a role in promoting compliance with labor standards. In Vietnam, for example, the noncompliance rates of firms in the apparel sector declined with each additional year of program participation (figure B8.3.1, panel a), and the introduction of a policy to publicly disclose the firms that fail to meet key labor standards has also improved firm compliance (figure B8.3.1, panel b).[e]

Figure B8.3.1 Working conditions improved in apparel sector firms participating in the ILO-IFC Better Work Vietnam program

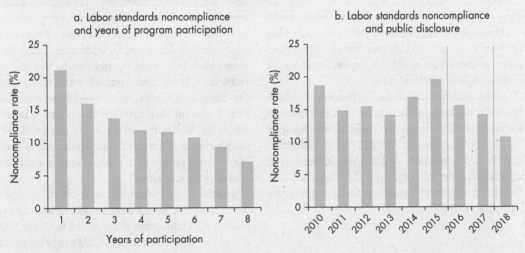

Source: Hollweg (2019).

Note: Panel a plots the average noncompliance rate of firms for each year of program participation in Better Work Vietnam (2010–18). Panel b plots the average noncompliance rate of firms over time since Better Work Vietnam was launched in 2010. The policy of public disclosure of firms that failed to meet key labor standards was announced in 2015 and implemented in 2017. IFC = International Finance Corporation; ILO = International Labour Organization.

a. ILO and IFC (2016).
b. Brown et al. (2015).
c. Brown and Lin (2014).
d. Rourke (2014).
e. Hollweg (2019).

regulatory enforcement, even if their capacity is often weak. In addition, they can, in partnership with the private sector, support their GVC-linked enterprises, and especially small and medium enterprises (SMEs), in meeting the international standards on wages and working conditions.[15] A starting point is for countries to adopt international labor standards—notably ILO's core conventions.[16] By doing so, countries send an important signal to GVC investors that they will not engage in a race to the bottom on wages and working conditions. To make the standards effective, however, countries need to strengthen the monitoring and enforcement capacity of labor inspection regimes and build robust labor market institutions, including support for collective bargaining, freedom of association, and social dialogue.

In addition, a shortcoming of most of the initiatives targeting working conditions in GVC supply chains is that they are nonbinding on the lead firm and tend to rely on a "name and shame" approach. Increasingly, however, governments in countries where lead firms are based are responding to demands from civil society to introduce "binding due diligence"—that is, lead firms are legally responsible for standards across their supply chains (including subcontractors), particularly around issues of labor and human rights, but potentially also with respect to the environment, industrial relations, consumer protection, and corporate governance. Most notably, in 2017 France enacted the Duty of Vigilance Law, which requires large French companies to publish and implement a vigilance plan in order to identify and prevent human rights risks linked to their activities. Other European countries are considering similar measures.

Some international trade agreements include specific provisions on labor rights.[17] For example, following its participation in the U.S.–Cambodia Bilateral Textile Trade Agreement (USCBTTA), Cambodia ratified the ILO conventions on forced labor, freedom of association, collective bargaining, discrimination, and child labor, with positive spillovers for labor conditions in apparel factories.[18]

Managing adjustment

As highlighted in chapter 3 and recent research,[19] because GVC trade tends to strongly reinforce comparative advantage, lower-skilled workers in high-income countries, and the places in which they are concentrated, typically lose out as countries upgrade in GVCs. In this context, there is a role for policy to manage the adjustment process for workers who may be displaced during the transitions across GVC development stages, as well as the places where those workers are concentrated.

"Flexicurity" approaches can help manage adjustment while maintaining competitiveness

Labor market policies can provide a cushion when workers lose jobs and offer assistance in finding new employment. Income protection policies, such as unemployment and disability insurance, along with other forms of social protection, aim to mitigate the income losses of workers without taking steps to return them to work. And active labor market policies (ALMPs), including employment services (such as counseling, job search assistance, and intermediation), training, wage subsidies, and entrepreneurship programs are designed to match displaced workers with income-earning opportunities.[20]

Because GVC employers need to compete in absolute terms in global markets, restrictive labor market policies can be a barrier to investment. To balance inclusion and competitiveness, countries may combine greater labor market flexibility (that is, limiting labor regulations that significantly restrict employers, while maintaining adequate protection of workers) with highly supportive social protection and complementary social insurance.

This approach, proposed in *World Development Report 2019*,[21] calls for a stronger and expanded socially supported minimum level of income, complemented by mandated social insurance and more flexibility in labor markets. For example, Denmark's "flexicurity" model gives businesses the freedom to hire and fire workers with relatively limited restrictions, while providing a generous, broad-based unemployment benefit system that cushions the negative income effects on displaced workers. A key feature of Denmark's system is the significant investment in active labor market programs to enhance employability and connect workers to jobs.

Despite having relatively low levels of unemployment, Denmark invests more heavily in labor market policies than other countries (figure 8.1). A large share of this spending is devoted to ALMPs to help workers in sectors or regions undergoing adjustments. By contrast, in the United States minimal, broad-based protection is the norm, and ALMPs are deployed narrowly for specific "trade adjustment assistance."

Designing and delivering labor market programs remain a challenge, particularly in low- and middle-income countries. In these countries, lower formal education in the workforce limits the benefits of vocational training, higher labor market informality limits

Figure 8.1 Denmark invests more than other OECD countries to support workers

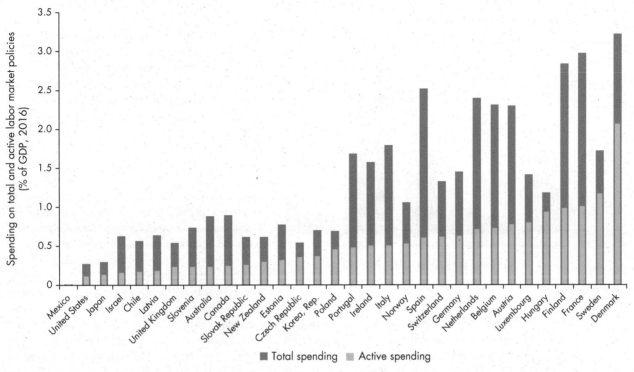

Source: Adapted from Bown and Freund 2019.

Note: Data for France, Italy, and Spain are for 2015, and data for the United Kingdom are for 2011.

the reach of adjustment beyond the formal economy, and a weak institutional capacity limits the ability to ascertain eligibility and control fraud. Because such programs are expensive, they are also difficult to implement in countries facing significant fiscal constraints. However, evidence suggests that they pay off to both protect workers and maintain political support for open trade. Denmark, for example, has not experienced the kind of backlash against trade experienced by many industrial countries.

Support for people in left-behind places can target services, skills training, and mobility

The challenge of labor adjustment is fundamentally linked to the spatial distribution of economic activity in GVCs both across and *within* countries. These spatial patterns of development are relevant at the initial stages of GVC integration and throughout the stages of upgrading. As countries integrate globally, GVC investment tends to concentrate in the places within countries that are well connected to regional and global markets (figure 8.2). This concentration may aggravate existing disparities by reinforcing the competitiveness of leading regions, especially where large

infrastructure gaps and regulatory barriers prevent the integration of domestic markets.[22]

As a result, the dislocations that come with GVC adjustments do not happen just to people; they also happen to places. Examples are easy to find. Detroit and other Rust Belt cities in the United States have seen automotive and other machinery and equipment manufacturing offshored to lower-cost locations like Mexico. Similarly, industrial production has shifted out of places like northeastern France and Germany's Ruhr Valley and toward locations in central and eastern Europe. In many developing countries, both former industrial hubs and agricultural hinterlands may no longer be able to rely on captive domestic markets—examples are Bulawayo in Zimbabwe and East London in South Africa. The effects can be long-lasting. Research in Brazil has found that regions affected by trade liberalization faced sharply lower formal sector employment and earnings even after 20 years.[23] Wherever places are facing adjustment, there has emerged a strong political imperative for targeted, place-based policies designed to create new sources of demand to absorb displaced workers in the short term and to shift the local economy onto a more sustainable path for the future.

Figure 8.2 Industrial development was uneven across regions of Mexico during the period of strong international market integration

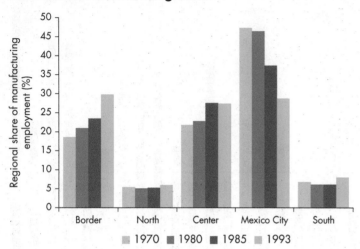

Source: Hanson 1998.

Policies addressing these increasing regional inequalities must target the people in them, a principle that is set out clearly in *World Development Report 2009: Reshaping Economic Geography*.[24] Policy measures might include launching retraining programs and removing barriers to labor mobility, including lack of access to information on job opportunities and subsidies for relocation. China's relaxation of strict controls on internal mobility and the integration of Germany after 1989 are natural experiments that prove the positive effects of promoting labor mobility, not just on the individuals who migrate, but also on the places both receiving *and* sending migrants.

Spatially targeted interventions work best when designed with a clear understanding of the structural conditions of the region. Regions that are peripheral and sparse in population may well have niche opportunities that can be exploited, but interventions should give priority to raising welfare, strengthening human capital, and promoting mobility. By contrast, regions that have sufficient density and relatively good market access are candidates for place-based interventions that aim to overcome coordination failures blocking investment and preventing the formation of productive agglomerations.

The traditional subsidies used to attract (usually foreign) investors to regions lagging or suffering from trade adjustment have largely been ineffective, for several reasons. For one thing, the level of subsidy required to overcome constraints such as poor infrastructure, distance to markets, and lack of agglomeration is usually infeasibly large. For another, there

is a major risk that, with fiscal incentives, regions within the same country will engage in territorial competition and a race to the bottom. The fiscal wars fought by Brazilian states competing for global automotive investment in the 1990s are instructive. Investment subsidies amounted to massive transfers to private—mainly foreign—investors at a huge fiscal cost but with a limited impact on job creation, no guarantees of sustainability through development of local supply chains, and the potential of undermining the competitiveness of the overall sector.[25] Moreover, governments face risks in offering large incentives to attract investment in footloose activities such as garment manufacturing, which may relocate quickly in response to political factors, global market conditions, or the removal of subsidies such as recently for Foxconn and Amazon in the United States.

Recent proposals have called for shifting from targeting investment broadly to deploying a geographically targeted wage subsidy or a hiring tax credit that directly targets job creation in regions that are affected by trade adjustment or are otherwise lagging.[26] Such approaches may indeed be effective for supporting increased investment and targeted employment, as discussed previously in this Report. However, because they do nothing to change the structure of the local economy, they are likely to be effective only in the short run in the absence of complementary interventions.

Environmental sustainability

Chapter 5 highlights how GVCs can have significant negative environmental impacts. These impacts include both the aggregate global effects of GVC-oriented production and distribution systems and the place-specific effects of the concentration of GVC activities in a country or region. And yet, as outlined in chapter 5, GVCs also offer opportunities to support environmentally sustainable production models, especially if countries adopt appropriate policies. Building environmental sustainability directly into both the production and governance models guiding GVCs will be increasingly critical to their ongoing viability. That effort will require a combination of appropriate pricing, regulations, and cooperative arrangements.

Both pricing environmental degradation and mandating sustainable production, in particular for local pollutants, are needed to counter the negative impacts on the environment of the scale and composition effects discussed in chapter 5. Effective policy support in the form of carbon taxes or tradable emissions permits, regulations such as low-carbon fuel standards, and restrictions on the use of fossil fuels are needed.

For example, the International Maritime Organization (IMO) has committed to an energy transition in shipping to zero-emissions fuels.[27] The combination of taxes on shipping fuels and regulations could support fully exploiting the existing energy efficiency potential and developing alternative fuels and other innovative solutions. The challenge, however, is that ships are highly mobile: they travel mostly in international waters and can easily be registered anywhere. Thus regional or—ideally—global cooperative solutions are preferable.

Pricing environmental degradation

Pigouvian taxes equivalent to the environmental harm inflicted by an activity (for example, a tax on carbon) would reduce the use of energy and lead to more innovation in energy-efficient products. Not pricing the environmental costs implies a subsidy for fuels. Using the difference between existing and efficient (inclusive of environmental costs) prices, the International Monetary Fund (IMF) estimates that the unpriced externality caused by fossil fuels is more than 10 times the direct financial subsidy.[28]

What can countries do? Many still have energy subsidies in place that lead to excess pollution. The subsidies are often regressive because the poor tend to have smaller houses and fewer appliances and thus use less energy. Removing explicit fuel subsidies shifts business incentives away from energy-intensive production toward labor. Shifting from a system that is subsidizing carbon emissions or is neutral to taxing those emissions is optimal.

To minimize distortions of trade, the most efficient implementation of a carbon price would be through an international agreement on a "carbon price floor."[29] Universal adoption may, however, suffer from free-rider problems for public goods. Some observers have suggested that incentives to join the agreement could be strengthened if participating countries agree to grant preferential access to each other's markets.[30]

Countries can also act unilaterally. To maintain competitiveness, they can tax the consumption of pollution-intensive goods rather than their production (box 8.4). Different forms of consumption-based carbon pricing are available, but a simple design consistent with trade law is to tax carbon in much the same way that countries use corrective taxes for tobacco or alcohol—they apply a consumption-based excise tax. In many countries, both imported and domestically produced alcohol are taxed alike when they are consumed within the country, but alcohol headed for export is exempt from the tax. This way, corrective taxes can be applied unilaterally without harming external competitiveness and in compliance with trade law.[31]

The same policy design could be used for taxing the environmental costs of traded commodities. For example, a country could tax carbon-intensive aluminum by setting an excise tax according to the social cost of the emissions typically released per ton of the metal. The tax would be levied at the same rate for all aluminum used in the country, but not for exports. The efficiency of the tax scheme could be further improved by granting output-based tax rebates to domestic and overseas firms that adopt low-emissions production techniques.

Despite the clear efficiency of a carbon tax, its feasibility from a political perspective is far from guaranteed. Unlike regulations, which hide the additional costs to consumers, carbon taxes are very visible. In late 2018, when France announced an increase in fuel taxes in part to help the country transition to renewable energies, it stoked a reaction from the *gilets jaunes* (or yellow vests) movement (according to French law, all vehicles must carry yellow vests in case of emergency). Large, at times violent, protests broke out across the country, led by commuters—many from rural areas—and those in the transport industry. Protestors argued that the rise in fuel taxes imposed a disproportionate burden on the poorest in society, particularly those living in nonurban areas who were already suffering from stagnating incomes and poor public transport services. Meanwhile, large multinationals—deemed to bear greater responsibility for rising emissions worldwide—could find ways to minimize their tax burden and still reap large profits. Ultimately, the government was forced to withdraw the proposed tax increase.

Mandating more sustainable production

Countries can also use regulatory (command-and-control) policy to deal with externalities from traded commodities, especially to maintain clean water, prevent overfishing and overfarming, curb emissions and specific pollutants, and reduce the production of disposable, single-use goods. For example, agricultural runoff contaminated with high levels of pesticide and fertilizer residue, as well as organic matter and sediment, is the primary source of water pollution in many countries, particularly high-income and middle-income ones. A 2018 report by the Food and Agriculture Organization (FAO) on the topic identifies the regulatory measures needed to reduce agriculture-related water pollution, such as water quality standards and pollution discharge permits.[32] China, the world's largest pork producer, adopted new laws in 2015 to manage runoff from pig farms and to

Box 8.4 Cost-effectiveness and equitability of environmental regulation

The year 2020 marks the 100th anniversary of British economist Arthur Pigou's description of environmental pollution as "externalities" and his suggestion that they be addressed with taxes.[a] Pollution taxes are more cost-effective than other types of environmental regulations—that is, such taxes reduce pollution the most per dollar of cost or, equivalently, taxes cost the least per ton of pollution reduced. They are also more robust to tax evasion than direct taxes and are a fiscally efficient means of domestic resource mobilization because their coverage extends to the informal sector.

Despite that cost-effectiveness and despite the advocacy of such taxes by economists, policy makers worldwide have largely chosen other types of regulations over pollution taxes. Many claim that the burden of paying pollution taxes would be unfair, or regressive, falling disproportionately on poor households and poor countries. But the evidence that pollution taxes harm poor people is not straightforward. Richer people are indirectly responsible for more pollution because they spend more money and consume more goods whose production generates pollution. Thus if one follows Pigou's 100-year-old advice and taxes pollution, rich households would pay more than poor households in absolute terms. But that spending on polluting goods may constitute a larger share of poor households' incomes. In relative terms, then, those tax payments could fall disproportionally on the poor. Which effect prevails varies across economies. In lower-income countries, these taxes tend to be regressive, with overall positive effects on equity.[b] Furthermore, a proportion of the environmental tax burden may fall onto capital factor incomes. Since capital is highly unequally distributed, studies considering these General Equilibrium effects find a progressive impact.[c]

That general argument—that pollution taxes are worse for poor households—fails to consider the case in their favor for two further reasons. First, it ignores what happens to the tax revenues. If revenues are distributed to rich households or used to fund programs that mostly benefit rich households, they would, of course, be regressive. But if the revenues are paid to or fund programs for poor households, that can offset the higher tax burden on poorer people. If the revenues are divided evenly, there would be a net benefit to poorer households. Poor consumers would pay more in taxes as a share of their income, but would receive an even larger share of the dividends.

A second shortfall of the regressivity argument is that policies enacted in lieu of pollution taxes can be worse for poor households, no matter what is done with the revenue. Consider energy efficiency mandates—the type of technical rules that require appliances, buildings, and vehicles to use less energy in their operation. For vehicles, these take the form of fuel economy standards that amount to a tax on gas guzzlers and a subsidy for efficient cars. Whereas a gas tax targets fuel directly, a fuel economy standard effectively taxes vehicles based on their fuel-consuming attributes.

If U.S. households were taxed based on the vehicles they own in a way designed to mimic a fuel economy standard and raise the same revenue as a $0.29 a gallon gas tax, poor households would pay an extra $92 a year and rich households an extra $260. Even if all the revenue were refunded evenly, or if the tax subsidy combinations were designed to be revenue neutral, poor households' net tax rebates would be lower with the fuel economy standard than the gas tax. Fuel economy standards are therefore both less cost-effective and less progressive than Pigou's 100-year-old, mostly disregarded suggestion.

Source: WDR 2020 team, based on Levinson (2019).

Note: Data are from the 2009 National Household Travel Survey, conducted by the U.S. Federal Highway Administration (https://nhts.ornl.gov/). Data include all 101,000 households surveyed, including those without vehicles.

a. Pigou (1920).
b. Dorband et al. (2019).
c. Beck et al. (2015); Dissou and Siddiqui (2014); Metcalf and Hassett (2012); Rausch, Metcalf, and Reilly (2011).

institute more efficient, sustainable farming methods. In fisheries, quota systems are used to prevent overfishing, although there is concern that quotas, which are based on commercial considerations, may be too high to prevent the depletion of certain fish stocks. The European Union has committed to basing all fishing quotas on scientific advice (the "maximum sustainable yield") by 2020.[33]

How to reduce and eliminate the consumption of disposable goods such as single-use plastics is a growing concern. The European Union announced in March 2019 that single-use plastics will be banned as of 2021 and has implemented a target to recycle 90 percent of plastic beverage bottles by 2029. Canada announced a similar measure in May 2019, banning single-use plastic items such as bags, straws, cutlery, and stirring sticks as of 2021. Many more countries have long imposed bans on single-use plastic bags, including Bangladesh (2002), Kenya (2017), and Rwanda (2008). In Kenya, the acts of manufacturing and importing plastic bags incur penalties ranging between $19,000 and $38,000 and jail terms of up to four years. Although some large firms have announced the elimination of certain single-use plastics in their supply chain, government measures are needed to achieve broad-based change across society.

Developing countries sometimes worry that environmental policies would be to their economic disadvantage. However, the economic literature over the last 30 years on "double dividends" and the "economic co-benefits of environmental policies" finds that internalizing external costs through fiscal policy raises economic development more often than it deflects it.[34] It is precisely in those economic circumstances characteristic of developing countries—informality,[35] difficulty in raising domestic tax revenue,[36] a highly distorted preexisting tax system,[37] and high air pollution levels,[38] among others—that the probability of a double dividend is higher.

Other policies can be used to further stimulate sustainable production and consumption. For example, a number of governments are exploring feebates, which combine a surcharge for energy-inefficient production with rebates for energy-efficient production.[39] Policy makers also need to take into account behavioral biases to changing habits. People may stick to old habits for lack of sufficient incentives to switch to more sustainable production or consumption. They may also not be aware of better alternatives. In this latter case, labels and certification schemes for sustainability standards can help. Standards, and in particular private standards, play an increasingly important role in GVCs.

A private sector solution to externalities from traded products is sustainability certification. Such certificates were first issued in the timber market, specifically as a solution for trade, and now they are spreading to other commodities. Sustainability certificates can greatly improve the sustainability of trade, but they also have their limits. Governments are increasingly recognizing the importance of working with large international corporations and other private sector actors to help them establish and phase in higher standards in their production networks. In some cases, governments and stock exchanges are making mandatory sustainability reporting by large multinationals and their suppliers.[40]

Using trade policy and agreements?

In most countries, import tariffs and nontariff barriers are substantially lower on dirty industries than on clean industries, measured as carbon dioxide (CO_2) emissions per dollar of output.[41] These dirtier industries, such as fuel, tend to be located upstream in the value chain and face lower tariffs (as discussed in terms of tariff escalation in chapter 7). The greater environmental protection of downstream industries is explained by the fact that downstream industries lobby for relatively low tariffs on their inputs and relatively high tariffs on competing goods. If countries applied similar trade policies to clean and dirty goods, global CO_2 emissions may decline substantially without a fall in global real income.[42]

In addition to greater market access, countries upstream in the chain may be reluctant to raise environmental standards because of fear of losing investors. This reluctance leads to a "regulatory chill" in which regulatory progress stalls across policy areas that affect foreign investors. The extent of a regulatory chill is a function not of whether firms will actually relocate, but of whether governments believe their threats to do so.[43] Evidence from the economic literature (and the World Bank's operational experience) indicates that governments tend to believe these threats, even when they are not credible.[44] International investment agreements, especially those with investor-state dispute settlement (ISDS) provisions, seem to be particularly vulnerable to regulatory chill.[45] A solution is not to forgo ISDS provisions, which can help compensate for weak institutions, but to exclude environmental and health provisions.

Both international climate agreements and trade and investment agreements can be used to help address the risk of regulatory chill and to implement environmental regulations. International treaties such as the Paris Agreement include ambitious commitments for environmental protection and emissions reduction. Recent trade agreements have taken into account the need for environmental policy. Countries that do not adhere to environmental commitments risk losing the preferential market access in the agreements. Deep trade agreements also increasingly include environmental provisions. For example, the Comprehensive and Progressive Agreement for Trans-Pacific Partnership (CPTPP) has an environmental chapter that promotes sustainable fisheries (see chapter 9). And new agreements include trade-exposed industries in environmental policies without the need for exemptions for competitiveness problems and without violations of trade law.[46]

Encouraging green goods and environmentally friendly production?

Production subsidies are typically considered distortionary because they encourage production above the efficient level. They are especially worrisome in industries such as agriculture and mining, where overuse is particularly harmful to the environment. However, if the good or production process has a positive externality, the standard argument changes.

In particular, there is a possible argument for subsidizing green goods, especially in industries where costs fall with higher production. The electric vehicle sector, for example, was fostered by government interventions tailored to stimulate supply and demand in both China and the United States. Indeed, such subsidies hastened the economic viability of the sector. Similarly, deployment incentives have been important for solar photovoltaic firms in China, Europe, and Latin America, especially for new projects. But such incentives must be weighed carefully because they can distort trade and become fiscally burdensome to governments.

Trade agreements on environmental goods can also promote their use, effectively lowering their cost relative to other goods. In the summer of 2014, a group of nearly 50 members of the World Trade Organization launched negotiations to reduce tariffs on green goods. Relatively few developing countries signed on because their tariffs tend to be relatively higher on

the targeted goods and the agreement would have required more liberalization from them. In addition, the large countries could not agree on the final list of products. The agreement therefore remains stalled. And yet the goals of the agreement remain desirable: increase trade, reduce the price of environmental goods, and reduce CO_2 emissions. If the agreement one day becomes a multilateral one, the magnitude of the identified impacts would increase substantially.[47]

Chapter 7 discusses the role that SEZs and industrial parks could play in stimulating GVC production. For their part, governments could induce GVC firms to opt for industrial parks that encourage the use of environmentally friendly production techniques. Worldwide, more than 300 industrial parks now consider themselves to be eco-industrial parks (EIPs)—a number that is expected to rise. In many countries, governments have become more conscious of green approaches to manufacturing, and lead firms, concerned about their reputation, are eager to improve the sustainability of production (box 8.5).

Finally, better metrics are needed for monitoring environmental practices to understand problem firms, industries, and regions and encourage upgrading. Transparent, consistent, and standardized

Box 8.5 Green industrial parks support sustainable production and attract better investors

In 2018, 40 countries, including Argentina, Bangladesh, China, Colombia, the Arab Republic of Egypt, India, Indonesia, the Republic of Korea, Lebanon, Mauritania, Morocco, Thailand, Turkey, and Vietnam, were home to more than 300 eco-industrial parks (EIPs) and special economic zones (SEZs).[a] (Figure B8.5.1 shows the worldwide growth in the number of EIPs from 1985 to 2015.) Because in many countries a high share of export-oriented industrial production is located in industrial parks located in SEZs, a correspondingly high share of industrial emissions originates from them—not only air and water pollution but also greenhouse gases. For three reasons, then, SEZs and industrial parks are relevant to pollution control and GVCs.[b]

First, GVCs are now in a position to create strong incentives for more sustainable production in SEZs. A major issue for many developing countries is attracting foreign investment, diversifying export baskets, and creating better jobs. But in many old-style SEZs, the environmental standards

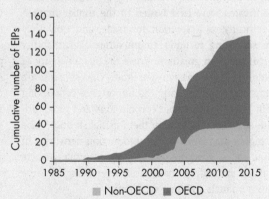

Figure B8.5.1 The number of eco-industrial parks grew rapidly from 1985 to 2015

Source: Kechichian and Jeong 2016.

Note: EIPs = eco-industrial parks; OECD = Organisation for Economic Co-operation and Development.

(Box continues next page)

Box 8.5 Green industrial parks support sustainable production and attract better investors *(continued)*

were low, with an industrialization model based on the attractiveness of low production costs and taxes. Under emerging laws on sustainability reporting, companies with headquarters in many industrialized countries are liable for risks along their value chains. To reduce those risks and ensure the traceability and quality of final products, companies are now seeking more transparency along value chains.

Second, as in other policy areas, SEZs offer an avenue for policy experimentation in making industrial parks sustainable. New environmental policies and disciplines can be implemented in a more manageable environment, such as promoting recycling, provisioning renewable energy and other green infrastructure, constructing environmentally friendly buildings, and reusing and commercializing waste products. Because waste reuse and energy cogeneration can be designed to link firms within the same SEZ, some of these policies can take advantage of the ecosystem aspects of SEZs (industrial symbiosis).

In a bid to address the negative environmental impacts of the concentration of industrial production, the World Bank, in partnership with the United Nations Industrial Development Organization (UNIDO) and Deutsche Gesellschaft für Internationale Zusammenarbeit (GIZ),

developed in 2017 an international framework to guide policy makers in establishing environmentally sustainable EIPs. Meanwhile, EIPs are becoming increasingly important for overcoming sustainability challenges within the scope of the United Nations' Sustainable Development Goals. Countries such as Denmark, France, Japan, and Korea, among many others, have leveraged EIPs to promote more inclusive and sustainable action to improve industrial competitiveness in line with climate change goals.[c]

Third, from the perspective of an industrial park operator or developer, offering environmentally sustainable facilities is an opportunity to attract higher-quality and higher-paying tenants, which GVC firms tend to be. With thousands of industrial parks globally, operators are seeking a more sustainable and competitive operating environment in order to differentiate themselves from the more basic industrial parks. For example, Hawassa industrial park in Ethiopia adopted zero-liquid discharge technologies for wastewater treatment to attract high-end apparel manufacturers. Vietnam recently issued guidelines for improved environmental performance in its industrial parks. These approaches improve socioenvironmental performance without the need for more regulations.

a. Kechichian and Jeong (2016); UNIDO, World Bank, and GIZ (2017).
b. Special economic zones are spaces in a country intended to attract industrial production by offering companies locating there special concessions on taxes, tariffs, and regulations. Chapter 7 describes SEZs in more detail.
c. UNIDO, World Bank, and GIZ (2017).

information on how firms produce is not available. Multiple sets of sustainability standards exist, from public to private and from mandatory to voluntary, but they are not standardized, and ratings of the same firms often differ widely across them. An international agency tasked with these ratings could shed light on firms' activities and offer incentives for changes in behavior.

Notes

1. Beegle, Coudouel, and Monsalve (2018).
2. Elbehri and Benali (2013).
3. Lin (2012).
4. Robalino and Walker (2017).
5. World Bank (2019b, 72).
6. World Bank (2019b).
7. ILO and IFC (2016).
8. McMillan and Verduzco-Gallo (2011); Shingal (2015).

9. World Bank's Doing Business database (2018). See appendix A for a description of the databases used in this Report.
10. Increasingly, many jurisdictions are including calculations of a living wage in efforts to establish the level of a minimum wage.
11. Kuddo, Robalino, and Weber (2015).
12. Domat et al. (2013).
13. Barrientos et al. (2016).
14. Hollweg (2019).
15. ILO (2016, 2017).
16. Covering freedom of association, right to collective bargaining, elimination of forced and compulsory labor, abolition of child labor, and elimination of discrimination with respect to employment and occupation.
17. Evans (2019).
18. Wetterberg (2011).
19. Farole, Hollweg, and Winkler (2018).
20. Bown and Freund (2019).
21. World Bank (2019b).

22. Farole (2013).
23. Dix-Carneiro and Kovak (2017).
24. World Bank (2009).
25. Rodriguez-Pose and Arbix (2001).
26. Austin, Glaeser, and Summers (2018); Hendrickson, Muro, and Galston (2018).
27. IMO (2018a, 2018b).
28. The estimates are based on a price gap analysis that takes as the reference price a calculation of externalities based on detailed country data. This calculation controls for the true comparative advantages for hosting polluting industries, such as having a low population density or (more controversially) a low value of statistical life. For estimates, see Coady et al. (2017, 2019), and for the method for calculating them, see Parry et al. (2014).
29. Cramton et al. (2017); Farid et al. (2016); Weitzman (2017).
30. Gollier and Tirole (2015); Nordhaus (2015).
31. Trachtman (2017).
32. Mateo-Sagasta, Zadeh, and Turral (2018).
33. "Managing Fisheries," Common Fisheries Policy, Directorate-General for Maritime Affairs and Fisheries, European Commission, Brussels, https://ec.europa.eu/fisheries/cfp/fishing_rules_en.
34. Pigato (2019).
35. Bento, Jacobsen, and Liu (2018).
36. Liu (2013).
37. Parry and Bento (2000).
38. Parry, Veung, and Heine (2015).
39. Fay et al. (2015).
40. See World Business Council for Sustainable Reporting "Reporting Exchange" for a database on mandatory regulation in sustainability reporting. https://www.reportingexchange.com/ and https://www.cdsb.net/sites/default/filescdsb_report_1_esg.pdf.
41. Shapiro (2019).
42. Shapiro (2019).
43. Neumayer (2001).
44. Zarsky (2006).
45. Examples include countries allowing mining in forest protection areas (Brown 2013; Gross 2003) and repealing science-based environmental regulations on oil mining because of threats of investor-state disputes (Tienhaara 2011).
46. Böhringer, Rosendahl, and Storrøsten (2017); Trachtman (2017).
47. European Commission (2016).

References

Austin, Benjamin, Edward L. Glaeser, and Lawrence H. Summers. 2018. "Saving the Heartland: Place-Based Policies in 21st Century America." BPEA Conference Draft (March 8–9), Brookings Papers on Economic Activity, Brookings Institution, Washington, DC.

Barrientos, Stephanie Ware, Peter Knorringa, Barbara Evers, Margareet Visser, and Maggie Opondo. 2016. "Shifting Regional Dynamics of Global Value Chains: Implications for Economic and Social Upgrading in African Horticulture." Environment and Planning A: Economy and Space 48 (7): 1266–83.

Beck, Marisa, Nicholas Rivers, Randall Wigle, and Hidemichi Yonezawa. 2015. "Carbon Tax and Revenue Recycling: Impacts on Households in British Columbia." Resource and Energy Economics 41: 40–69.

Beegle, Kathleen, Aline Coudouel, and Emma Monsalve, eds. 2018. Realizing the Full Potential of Social Safety Nets in Africa. Africa Development Forum Series. Washington, DC: Agence Française de Développement and World Bank.

Bento, Antonio M., Mark R. Jacobsen, and Antung A. Liu. 2018. "Environmental Policy in the Presence of an Informal Sector." Journal of Environmental Economics and Management 90 (July): 61–77.

Böhringer, Christoph, Knut Einar Rosendahl, and Halvor Briseid Storrøsten. 2017. "Robust Policies to Mitigate Carbon Leakage." Journal of Public Economics 149 (May): 35–46

Bown, Chad P., and Caroline L. Freund. 2019. "Active Labor Market Policies: Lessons from Other Countries for the United States." PIIE Working Paper 19-2 (January), Peterson Institute for International Economics, Washington, DC.

Brown, Drusilla, Rajeev Dehejia, Raymond Robertson, George Domat, and Selven Veeraragoo. 2015. "Are Sweatshops Profit-Maximizing? Answer: No; Evidence from Better Work Vietnam." Better Work Discussion Paper 17 (March), International Labour Office, Geneva. https://users.nber.org/~rdehejia/papers/DP%2017%20web.pdf.

Brown, Drusilla, and Xirong Lin. 2014. "Sexual Harassment in the Workplace: How Does It Affect Firm Performance and Profits?" Better Work Discussion Paper 16 (November), International Labour Office, Geneva. https://betterwork.org/blog/portfolio/sexual-harassement-in-the-workplace-how-does-it-affect-firm-performance-and-profits/.

Brown, Julia G. 2013. "International Investment Agreements: Regulatory Chill in the Face of Litigious Heat?" Western Journal of Legal Studies 3 (1): 47–74.

Coady, David P., Ian W. H. Parry, Nghia-Piotr Trong Le, and Baoping Shang. 2019. "Global Fossil Fuel Subsidies Remain Large: An Update Based on Country-Level Estimates." IMF Working Paper WP/19/89 (May 2), International Monetary Fund, Washington, DC.

Coady, David P., Ian W. H. Parry, Louis Sears, and Baoping Shang. 2017. "How Large Are Global Fossil Fuel Subsidies?" World Development 91 (March): 11–27.

Cramton, Peter, David J. C. MacKay, Axel Ockenfels, and Steve Stoft, eds. 2017. Global Carbon Pricing: The Path to Climate Cooperation. Cambridge, MA: MIT Press.

Davis, Michelle. 2017. "Satellite Factories Create More Jobs for Women in Rural Jordan." Jobs and Development (blog), December 7. https://blogs.worldbank.org/jobs/satellite-factories-create-more-jobs-women-rural-jordan.

Dissou, Yazid, and Muhammad Shahid Siddiqui. 2014. "Can Carbon Taxes Be Progressive?" Energy Economics 42: 88–100.

Dix-Carneiro, Rafael, and Brian K. Kovak. 2017. "Trade Liberalization and Regional Dynamics." American Economic Review 107 (10): 2908–46.

Domat, George, Paris Adler, Rajeev Dehejia, Drusilla Brown, and Raymond Robertson. 2013. "Do Factory Managers

Know What Workers Want? Manager-Worker Information Asymmetries and Pareto Optimal Working Conditions." Better Work Discussion Paper 10 (June), International Labour Office, Geneva. https://betterwork .org/global/wp-content/uploads/DP-10-web.pdf.

Dorband, Ira Irina, Michael Jakob, Matthias Kalkuhl, and Jan Christoph Steckel. 2019. "Poverty and Distributional Effects of Carbon Pricing in Low- and Middle-Income Countries: A Global Comparative Analysis." *World Development* 115: 246–57.

Elbehri, Aziz, and Marwan Benali. 2013. "A Historical Comparative Analysis of Commodity Development Models in West Africa and Implications for Staple Food Value Chains." In *Rebuilding West Africa's Food Potential: Policies and Market Incentives for Smallholder-Inclusive Food Value Chains*, edited by Aziz Elbehri, 43–81. Rome: Food and Agriculture Organization of the United Nations.

European Commission. 2016. *Trade Sustainability Impact Assessment on the Environmental Goods Agreement*. Final Report. Brussels: Directorate-General for Trade, European Commission.

Evans, Alice. 2019. "Incentivising Pro-Labour Reforms." CID Faculty Working Paper 349 (March), Center for International Development, Harvard University, Cambridge, MA.

Farid, Mai, Michael Keen, Michael G. Papaioannou, Ian W. H. Parry, Catherine A. Pattillo, and Anna Ter-Martirosyan. 2016. "After Paris: Fiscal, Macroeconomic, and Financial Implications of Global Climate Change." IMF Staff Discussion Note 16/01 (January), International Monetary Fund, Washington, DC.

Farole, Thomas, ed. 2013. *The Internal Geography of Trade: Lagging Regions and Global Markets*. Directions in Development: Trade Series. Washington, DC: World Bank.

Farole, Thomas, Claire H. Hollweg, and Deborah Elisabeth Winkler. 2018. "Trade in Global Value Chains: An Assessment of Labor Market Implications." Jobs Working Paper 18 (July 16), World Bank, Washington, DC.

Fay, Marianne, Stephane Hallegatte, Adrien Vogt-Schilb, Julie Rozenberg, Ulf Narloch, and Tom Kerr. 2015. *Decarbonizing Development: Three Steps to a Zero-Carbon Future.* Climate Change and Development. Washington, DC: World Bank.

Gollier, Christian, and Jean Tirole. 2015. "Negotiating Effective Institutions against Climate Change." *Economics of Energy and Environmental Policy* 4 (2): 5–27.

Gross, Stuart G. 2003. "Inordinate Chill: BITS, Non-NAFTA MITS, and Host-State Regulatory Freedom; An Indonesian Case Study." *Michigan Journal of International Law* 24 (3): 893–960.

Hanson, Gordon H. 1998. "North American Economic Integration and Industry Location." *Oxford Review of Economic Policy* 14 (2): 30–44.

Hendrickson, Clara, Mark Muro, and William A. Galston. 2018. "Countering the Geography of Discontent: Strategies for Left-Behind Places." Brookings Institution, Washington, DC.

Hollweg, Claire H. 2019. "Firm Compliance and Public Disclosure in Vietnam." Policy Research Working Paper 9026, World Bank, Washington, DC.

ILO (International Labour Organization). 2016. *Assessment of Labour Provisions in Trade and Investment Arrangements.* Studies on Growth with Equity Series. Geneva: International Labour Office. https://www.ilo.org/wcmsp5 /groups/public/---dgreports/---inst/documents/publi cation/wcms_498944.pdf.

———. 2017. *Handbook on Assessment of Labour Provisions in Trade and Investment Arrangements*. Growth with Equity Series. Geneva: International Labour Office. https:// www.ilo.org/global/publications/books/WCMS_564702 /lang—en/index.htm.

ILO (International Labour Organization) and IFC (International Finance Corporation). 2016. "Progress and Potential: How Better Work Is Improving Garment Workers' Lives and Boosting Factory Competitiveness." International Labour Office, Geneva. https://betterwork .org/dev/wp-content/uploads/2016/09/BW-Progress-and -Potential_Web-final.pdf.

IMO (International Maritime Organization). 2018a. "Marine Litter." In Focus, IMO, London. http://www.imo.org/en /MediaCentre/HotTopics/marinelitter/Pages/default.aspx.

———. 2018b. "UN Body Adopts Climate Change Strategy for Shipping." Press Briefing 06, April 13, IMO, London. http:// www.imo.org/en/MediaCentre/PressBriefings/Pages /06GHGinitialstrategy.aspx.

Karuretwa, Kaliza. 2016. "Case 14: Rwanda Coffee Sector." Case Studies on the Future of Manufacturing, World Economic Forum Global Agenda Council on the Future of Manufacturing, World Economic Forum, Geneva.

Kechichian, Etienne, and Mi Hoon Jeong. 2016. "Mainstreaming Eco-Industrial Parks." World Bank, Washington, DC.

Kuddo, Arvo, David Alejandro Robalino, and Michael Weber. 2015. "Balancing Regulations to Promote Jobs: From Employment Contracts to Unemployment Benefits." World Bank, Washington, DC.

Levinson, Arik. 2019. "Energy Efficiency Standards Are More Regressive than Energy Taxes: Theory and Evidence." *Journal of the Association of Environmental and Resource Economists* 6 (1): 7–36.

Lin, Justin Yifu. 2012. *The Quest for Prosperity: How Developing Economies Can Take Off.* Princeton, NJ: Princeton University Press.

Liu, Antung Anthony. 2013. "Tax Evasion and Optimal Environmental Taxes." *Journal of Environmental Economics and Management* 66 (3): 656–70.

Mateo-Sagasta, Javier, Sara Marjani Zadeh, and Hugh Turral. 2018. *More People, More Food, Worse Water? A Global Review of Water Pollution from Agriculture.* Colombo, Sri Lanka: International Water Management Institute; Rome: Food and Agriculture Organization of the United Nations. http:// www.fao.org/3/ca0146en/CA0146EN.pdf.

McMillan, Margaret S., and Íñigo Verduzco-Gallo. 2011. "New Evidence on Trade and Employment: An Overview." In *Trade and Employment: From Myths to Facts*, edited by Marion Jansen, Ralf Peters, and José Manuel Salazar-Xirinachs, 23–60. Geneva: International Labour Office.

Metcalf, Gilbert, and Kevin Hassett. 2012. "Distributional Impacts in a Comprehensive Climate Policy Package." In *The Design and Implementation of U.S. Climate Policy,* edited by Don Fullerton and Catherine Wolfram. Chicago: University of Chicago Press.

Neumayer, Eric. 2001. "Do Countries Fail to Raise Environmental Standards? An Evaluation of Policy Options Addressing 'Regulatory Chill.'" *International Journal of Sustainable Development* 4 (3): 231–44.

Nordhaus, William. 2015. "Climate Clubs: Overcoming Free-Riding in International Climate Policy." *American Economic Review* 105 (4): 1339–70.

Parry, Ian W. H., and Antonio M. Bento. 2000. "Tax Deductions, Environmental Policy, and the 'Double Dividend' Hypothesis." *Journal of Environmental Economics and Management* 39 (1): 67–96.

Parry, Ian W. H., Dirk Heine, Eliza Lis, and Shanjun Li. 2014. *Getting Energy Prices Right: From Principle to Practice*. Washington, DC: International Monetary Fund.

Parry, Ian W. H., Chandara Veung, and Dirk Heine. 2015. "How Much Carbon Pricing Is in Countries' Own Interests? The Critical Role of Co-benefits." *Climate Change Economics* 6 (4): 1–26.

Pigato, Miria A., ed. 2019. *Fiscal Policies for Development and Climate Action*. International Development in Focus Series. Washington, DC: World Bank.

Pigou, Arthur Cecil. 1920. *The Economics of Welfare*. London: Macmillan.

Rausch, Sebastian, Gilbert Metcalf, and John Reilly. 2011. "Distributional Impacts of Carbon Pricing: A General Equilibrium Approach with Micro-Data for Households." *Energy Economics* 33 (S1): S20–S33.

Robalino, David Alejandro, and David Ian Walker. 2017. "Guidance Note: Economic Analysis of Jobs Investment Projects." Jobs Working Paper 7 (August), World Bank, Washington, DC.

Rodríguez-Pose, Andrés, and Glauco Arbix. 2001. "Strategies of Waste: Bidding Wars in the Brazilian Automobile Sector." *International Journal of Urban and Regional Research* 25 (1): 134–54.

Rourke, Emily L. 2014. "Is There a Business Case against Verbal Abuse? Incentive Structure, Verbal Abuse, Productivity, and Profits in Garment Factories." Better Work Discussion Paper 15 (September), International Labour Office, Geneva. https://betterwork.org/global/wp-content/uploads/2014/09/DP-15-web.pdf.

Shapiro, Joseph S. 2019. "The Environmental Bias of Trade Policy." Paper presented at the Association of Environmental and Resource Economists' Summer Conference, Lake Tahoe, NV, May 30–31.

Shingal, Anirudh. 2015. "Labour Market Effects of Integration into GVCs: Review of Literature." R4D Working Paper 2015/10, Swiss Programme for Research on Global Issues for Development, Swiss National Science Foundation, Bern, Switzerland.

Tienhaara, Kyla. 2011. "Regulatory Chill and the Threat of Arbitration: A View from Political Science." In *Evolution in Investment Treaty Law and Arbitration*, edited by Chester Brown and Kate Miles, 606–28. Cambridge, U.K.: Cambridge University Press.

Trachtman, Joel P. 2017. "WTO Law Constraints on Border Tax Adjustment and Tax Credit Mechanisms to Reduce the Competitive Effects of Carbon Taxes." *National Tax Journal* 70 (2): 469–94.

UNIDO (United Nations Industrial Development Organization), World Bank, and GIZ (Deutsche Gesellschaft für Internationale Zusammenarbeit). 2017. "An International Framework for Eco-Industrial Parks." December, World Bank, Washington, DC.

Weitzman, Martin L. 2017. "How a Minimum Carbon-Price Commitment Might Help to Internalize the Global Warming Externality." In *Global Carbon Pricing: The Path to Climate Collaboration*, edited by Peter Cramton, David J. C. MacKay, Axel Ockenfels, and Steven Stoft, 125–48. Cambridge, MA: MIT Press.

Wetterberg, Ana. 2011. "Public-Private Partnership in Labor Standards Governance: Better Factories Cambodia." *Public Administration and Development* 31 (1): 64–73.

World Bank. 2009. *World Development Report 2009: Reshaping Economic Geography*. Washington, DC: World Bank.

———. 2017. "In Bangladesh, Empowering and Employing Women in the Garments Sector." World Bank, Washington, DC. https://www.worldbank.org/en/news/feature/2017/02/07/in-bangladesh-empowering-and-employing-women-in-the-garments-sector.

———. 2018. "Maximizing Finance for Development: Côte d'Ivoire, Improving Opportunities through Cashew Value Chains." MFD Brief 06/2018 (June), World Bank, Washington, DC.

———. 2019a. *Women, Business, and the Law 2019: A Decade of Reform*. Washington, DC: World Bank.

———. 2019b. *World Development Report 2019: The Changing Nature of Work*. Washington, DC: World Bank.

Zarsky, Lyuba. 2006. "From Regulatory Chill to Deepfreeze?" *International Environmental Agreements: Politics, Law and Economics* 6 (4): 395–99.

PART V

How can international cooperation help?

Cooperation on trade

Key findings

- **Developing countries have benefited from the rules-based trade system,** with its guarantees against trade discrimination, incentives to reform, assured market access, and dispute settlement.

- **The international trade system is especially valuable in a global value chain (GVC) world.** Policy action or inaction in one country can affect producers and consumers in other countries.

- **Increasing pressure on the global trading system, manifested in protectionism and policy uncertainty, puts these benefits at risk.** These pressures arise, first, from the growing symmetry in the economic size of countries and the persistent asymmetry in their levels of protection; second, from the failure to use domestic policies to address labor market dislocation and growing inequality in some advanced countries.

- **To sustain beneficial trade openness,** countries need to deepen traditional trade cooperation to address remaining barriers to trade in goods and services, as well as other measures that distort trade, such as subsidies and the activities of state-owned enterprises.

- **Meaningful outcomes may be possible** if the major developing country traders engage as equal partners and even leaders instead of seeking special and differential treatment; if the large advanced countries continue to place their faith in rules-based negotiations instead of resorting to unilateral protection; and if countries together define a negotiating agenda that reflects both development and business priorities.

Developing countries have benefited enormously from the rules-based multilateral trade system. In fact, it is hard to imagine any current global value chain (GVC) operating outside of the membership of the World Trade Organization (WTO). The trade system has provided countries with incentives to reform, market access around the globe, and recourse in case of disputes, even against the trade heavyweights. Estimates suggest that acceding to the WTO boosts a developing country's growth rate by 2 percent a year for five years after joining, if the country made reforms upon accession.[1] The tariffs they face fall significantly. For example, 90 percent of U.S. tariff lines applied to WTO members are below 10 percent, whereas for nonmembers 50 percent of products are subject to tariffs of more than 30 percent. Developing countries also have had success in WTO dispute settlement, even against the WTO's largest members. For example, Indonesia recently won a case against the European Union (EU) about antidumping measures for biodiesel products.

Supporting the rules-based trade system is therefore important for development, but a series of events have weakened it. The failure of the WTO's Doha Round, which began in 2001, was the first strike, and recent disputes among members have further damaged the system. Regional initiatives such as the European Union and the North American Free Trade Agreement (NAFTA) have also been hurt by disagreements among member countries. In view of this trade climate, this chapter and the next argue that (1) the multilateral trade system matters profoundly in a GVC world; (2) the system is under stress because of tensions between the existing rules and the forces of economic convergence; and (3) revival of the system will depend on deepening trade cooperation and extending cooperation to new areas.

The multilateral trade system is especially important for GVCs because the costs of protection are magnified when goods and services cross borders multiple times. Similarly, the gains from a coordinated reduction of barriers to trade are even larger for GVCs than for conventional trade. Trade and investment policies must be known and predictable to encourage firms to invest in long-term international relationships. To address this need, international trade agreements include rules to enhance the transparency of national policies and help reduce policy uncertainty through legally binding commitments. Trade agreements and WTO commitments can also help to discipline the protectionist impact of differences in regulatory regimes.

But rapidly growing trade, especially with low-income countries, has put pressure on both existing and new industries in advanced countries. Although the rapid trade growth of the 1990s and early 2000s supported overall income growth, it also created winners and losers. Those forces were magnified with the expansion of GVCs because of the hyperspecialization that GVCs produced. Some manufacturing communities in advanced countries experienced large job losses as imports took market shares from domestic firms. And as developing country production grew rapidly, exporters from advanced countries—the traditional supporters of open trade policies—also experienced more intense competition at home and in other markets. Because some of the new developing country markets were still relatively protected and their exporters were supported by the state, trust in the trade system to ensure equal treatment eroded.

In addition to the challenges presented by the growing competition, the new global economy produced other significant risks that led to disenchantment (discussed in more detail in chapter 10). A greater share of the burden for resource mobilization shifted to workers as capital became much harder to tax in a GVC world. Because firms operate around the world and a high share of value added has become virtual, they can easily shift profits to low-tax jurisdictions. The new global economy also sparked concerns about market failure in international markets where regulation remains mostly national. Concerns ranged from abuse of privacy in data-based services to anticompetitive practices in platform-based services. Some developing countries also became disenchanted with the international trade system, especially in light of the failed Doha Development Agenda because the areas that matter the most to them, such as agriculture and apparel, have failed to be liberalized.

The path forward will require more cooperation between the new players in global trade, the large developing countries, and the incumbents, the large advanced countries. The large developing countries were mostly inactive during earlier episodes of reciprocal liberalization, but they have now grown to a size where their exports and their markets matter. Traditional trade negotiations may deliver more meaningful outcomes if the major developing country traders engage as equal partners, and even leaders, instead of seeking special and differential treatment (box 9.1); if the large industrial countries continue to place their faith in rules-based negotiations instead of resorting to unilateral protection; and if all countries together define a negotiating agenda that reflects both development and business priorities.

To sustain trade openness, the first priority is to deepen traditional trade cooperation to address the

Box 9.1 Special and differential treatment for developing countries

An important feature of the World Trade Organization (WTO) is the approach it takes to the disparities in the economic size and capacity of its members. This approach is encapsulated in the principle of special and differential treatment (SDT) for developing countries—a feature of the trade system almost since its origins. SDT arose because the export earnings of developing countries were insufficient for development needs and unpredictable because of the fluctuations in commodity prices. The solution was to give developing countries more flexibility in tariff setting and more access to markets in developed countries.

SDT also served a purpose for developed countries; it made negotiations easier because those countries could exchange market access among a small group without having to reach consensus with the full membership of the predecessor of the WTO, the General Agreement on Tariffs and Trade (GATT). At a time when developing countries accounted for less than a third of global exports, this approach made sense to developed countries. However, times have changed, and with developing countries accounting for nearly 45 percent of global exports, it is no longer palatable to developed nations.

A peculiar feature of SDT is that countries can declare themselves developing countries on a particular issue to avoid full commitments. For example, Japan and the Republic of Korea used SDT to postpone commitments to changing from a quota system to a tariff system on rice in the Uruguay Round. The WTO does not define what constitutes a developing country, leaving it to members to self-determine their status. Outside of the group of 47 (UN-defined) least developed countries (LDCs)—the only distinct group of developing countries formally identified in the WTO—there are no criteria that allow differentiation between developing countries. WTO members have not been able to agree on criteria to differentiate between countries and determine when graduation should occur.

Notwithstanding the rhetoric by opponents and proponents of SDT, building blocks for a more differentiated approach toward addressing economic development disparities have gradually emerged. In practice, differentiation has been negotiated on an issue-specific basis. An important example is the classification of developing countries based on per capita GDP and export competitiveness in the WTO's Agreement on Subsidies and Countervailing Measures. Other examples include the flexible approach taken in the WTO's Trade Facilitation Agreement (TFA) to scheduling commitments by developing countries and the ability of developing countries to link implementation of specific TFA provisions to technical assistance. The TFA embodies a new approach toward SDT that is not centered on exemptions for developing countries. Instead, it lets countries decide on the sequencing of implementation, depending on which elements of the agreement are priorities from a national perspective and commitments by high-income countries to assist those countries that request it to implement specific provisions.

Studies reveal that traditional SDT has not served developing countries well.[a] Their trade interests, such as agriculture and apparel, have been liberalized slowly or not at all. It has also lessened the ability of the trade system to act as an external force for domestic reform. As a result, tariffs in developing countries are on average bound at the WTO at 30 percentage points above actual levels. Meanwhile, tariff liberalization among developing countries has been largely unilateral; it has not occurred from external negotiations. Studies also find that developing countries have had limited gains from trade preferences, another dimension of SDT, because of their unilateral and uncertain nature and associated conditions, such as restrictive rules of origin.

a. See, for example, Ornelas (2016).

remaining barriers to trade in goods and services, as well as other measures that distort trade. Alongside such an effort, cooperation should be widened beyond trade policy to include taxes, regulation, and infrastructure, as discussed in more detail in chapter 10.

The case for cooperation

GVCs span boundaries, and policy action or inaction in one country can affect producers and consumers in other countries. International cooperation can help address the policy spillovers and achieve better development outcomes in several ways.

First, because the costs of protection are magnified when goods and services cross borders multiple times, the gains from a coordinated reduction of barriers to trade are even larger for GVCs than for standard trade. Because foreign investment and GVCs are inextricably linked, creating an open and secure climate for investment is vital for GVC participation, especially by capital-scarce countries. International cooperation has so far delivered greater openness in goods and services, but significant barriers remain.

Second, access to information about trade and investment policies and their predictability is important for firms, especially when investing in international relationships. To address this need, international trade agreements include rules to enhance the transparency of national policies and to help reduce policy uncertainty through legally binding commitments. But the failure of countries to honor WTO requirements that they provide regular notifications of subsidies and other measures that affect trade has led to policy opaqueness and has caused trade tensions. Similarly, large wedges between legal bindings and applied policies in both goods and services have perpetuated policy uncertainty (box 9.2).

Box 9.2 A story of the demise of most-favored-nation status foretold?

This is not the first time the world economy has confronted a situation in which the most powerful country moves away from a policy of nondiscriminatory openness. A surprising aspect of British trade policy in the 19th century was its nonexclusivity. With a share of world exports of more than 20 percent, Britain sought and obtained not preferred access to resources and markets but a commitment to nondiscriminatory trade (figure B9.2.1). Combined with its unilateral adoption of a free trade policy applied on a most-favored-nation (MFN) or nondiscriminatory basis, this approach defined the "free trade imperialism" that prevailed during Pax Britannica, beginning in the early 19th century and peaking in the mid-19th century. This stance was largely maintained until the early 20th century. That commitment first faltered when the United States and Germany threatened British dominance toward the end of the 19th century, causing its share of world trade to dip below 15 percent, and collapsed around the time of the Great Depression when Britain's share fell below 10 percent, leading to a policy of imperial preferences as well as increased protection.

Figure B9.2.1 shows that the events during Pax Britannica bear an uncanny resemblance to the U.S. role as a pillar of the multilateral trading system during Pax Americana in the 20th century. The U.S. share of world trade had reached 20 percent before World War II. In 1947 the United States

Figure B9.2.1 Shifts in trade shares and changes in policy stances of the United Kingdom and the United States since 1800

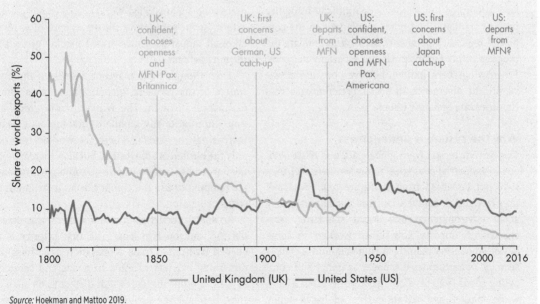

Source: Hoekman and Mattoo 2019.

Note: MFN = most-favored-nation.

(Box continues next page)

Box 9.2 A story of the demise of most-favored-nation status foretold?
(continued)

was, unquestioned, the dominant power in the world economy and played a central role in the creation of the General Agreement on Tariffs and Trade (GATT). It accommodated the formation of the European Economic Community (EEC) without departing from its MFN policy itself, and when it began to feel the discriminatory effects of European integration, it pushed for reductions in MFN tariffs through multilateral GATT negotiations (in the Kennedy and Tokyo Rounds) rather than through unilateral action. The U.S. commitment first wavered at the end of the 1970s when Japan emerged as a major trader and the U.S. share of world trade fell below 15 percent. But the United States relaxed when Japan did not threaten to cause a further decline in share and because the Uruguay Round negotiations led to

the successful expansion of policy coverage of the trade system to areas in which the United States had a comparative advantage—services and innovation.

As the U.S. share of global exports declined, the United States retreated from nondiscrimination. Unexpectedly rapid growth by China and other emerging economies in the late 1990s and the 2000s drove the U.S. share of global exports below 10 percent, which seems to be a critical threshold inducing the incumbent power to depart from an MFN policy. The result was first an attempt to negotiate modern-day "imperial preferences" under the Comprehensive and Progressive Agreement for Trans-Pacific Partnership (CPTPP) beginning in 2008, before the recent recourse to discriminatory tariffs and bilateralism.

Third, many of the policies affecting GVCs are regulatory, including technical regulations, sanitary and phytosanitary measures, and a range of regulations for services. Trade agreements and WTO commitments have made some progress in disciplining the protectionist impacts of these measures, but they tend to view the measures primarily through a producer-centric market-access lens. Accordingly, countries have attempted to harmonize or mutually recognize product standards and other regulations in the context of regional agreements, seeking to emulate the progress in the European Union, especially in goods. Progress has been limited, however, because of the significant divergence in social preferences across countries on regulatory issues.

Why the system is under stress

The current retreat from globalization is most obvious in industrial countries: many workers feel they have not benefited from it (figure 9.1); firms feel they face unfair competition; and consumers worry about environmental and social standards associated with imports. Low-skilled workers in some advanced-country manufacturing communities have seen job opportunities disappear as imports of competing goods from developing countries grow. Meanwhile, market- and private enterprise–based policy regimes tend to be not well suited to softening the pain associated with adjustment. Sharp adjustments in trade patterns have also threatened the existing

international order, potentially exacerbating tensions between countries (box 9.2).

A consequence is growing political sensitivity to the plight of industrial workers in advanced countries, whose incomes have stagnated during periods of rapid globalization. There is evidence that trade contributed to job loss in some countries, but technological change reduced the number of jobs in manufacturing for unskilled workers to a much greater extent. At the same time, the emergence of winner-takes-all industries concentrated income growth in the top 1 percent.

Even though trade may not have been the only source of the problem, globalization makes remedial action difficult. The winners from globalization—internationally mobile capital and skills—are increasingly hard to tax. Therefore, workers bear not only the burden of adjustment, but also, increasingly, the burden of taxation (figure 9.2). And governments are tempted to use trade policy as an instrument of social protection.

To sustain beneficial trade openness, it is essential to "walk on two legs." The first priority is to deepen traditional trade cooperation to address the remaining barriers to trade in goods and services, as well as other measures that distort trade such as subsidies and the activities of state-owned enterprises (SOEs). In parallel, cooperation should be widened beyond trade policy to include taxes, regulation, and infrastructure (the subject of the next chapter).

Figure 9.1 Attitudes toward trade differ in the sluggish North and the dynamic South

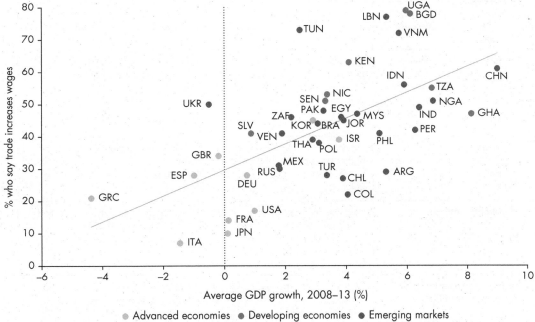

Sources: WDR 2020 team, based on Pew Research Center, Spring 2014 Global Attitudes Survey, Q28 (https://www.pewresearch.org/global/2014/06/05/spring-2014-survey-data/); GDP annual growth: International Monetary Fund's World Economic Outlook database, April 2014. See appendix A for a description of the databases used in this Report.

Note: For country abbreviations, see International Organization for Standardization (ISO), https://www.iso.org/obp/ui/#search.

Table 9.1 lists the policy areas in which national incentives can produce an outcome that is bad for all or most countries and a cooperative solution that is better for all.

Deepening trade cooperation

Because the costs of protection are magnified when goods and services cross borders multiple times, the gains from coordinated reduction of barriers to trade are even larger from GVCs than from standard trade. And because foreign investment and GVCs are linked, creating an open and secure climate for investment is vital for GVC participation, especially for capital-scarce countries. International cooperation has so far delivered greater openness, if unevenly:

- For goods, multilateral and preferential initiatives have worked in tandem to reduce the tariffs on goods and to greatly enhance market access for the poorest countries. But problems remain from a GVC perspective: high tariffs in many of the poorest developing countries hurt GVC participation by increasing the transaction costs of acquiring inputs even when they are notionally tariff-exempt. Tariff escalation in

Figure 9.2 Corporate tax rates and personal income tax rates for the top 1 percent have fallen, but the rate for the median worker increased in 65 economies between 1980 and 2007

Source: Egger, Nigai, and Strecker 2019.

Table 9.1 Policy rationale, externalities, and cooperative solutions

Policy area	National motive	International externality	Cooperative solution
Tariffs and other restrictions on trade and investment	Improve terms of trade; protect special interests; gain revenue	Negative impact on trading partners and possible prisoner's dilemma	Mutually agreed reduction in protection plus legal binding to reduce policy uncertainty
Subsidies	Support infant, senescent, or strategic industries or stages of production; address market failures (e.g., positive environmental externalities)	Negative impact on trading partners' industries but positive impact on foreign consumers—at least in the short run	Disciplines on use of specific types of subsidies and other forms of assistance such as tax incentives
Regulatory requirements	Protect consumers, the environment, and intellectual property rights	Industries in trading partners face higher costs for compliance, but benefit from enhanced supply of public goods	Regulatory cooperation in the form of harmonization, mutual recognition, or exporter regulatory commitments
Corporate taxes, investment incentives, FDI policies	Attract investment	Negative impacts on other investment locations and tax jurisdictions, potential tax competition, and a race to the bottom	Tax cooperation (e.g., the existing BEPS initiative at the OECD); destination-based taxes
Competition law, public ownership and control	Promote contestable markets; provide public goods	Abuse of market power; foreclosure of ability of firms to compete on a level playing field	Cooperation and common disciplines to control firm behavior
Investment in trade-facilitating infrastructure	Reduce trade costs	Positive externality for trading partners; potential coordination failure and underinvestment	Investment coordination to exploit synergies across countries and forms of infrastructure

Source: WDR 2020 team.

Note: BEPS = base erosion and profit shifting; FDI = foreign direct investment; OECD = Organisation for Economic Co-operation and Development.

important destination markets inhibits processing activities in agroindustry and other labor-intensive areas such as apparel and leather goods. And restrictive rules of origin curtail sourcing options.

- For services, international negotiations have not delivered much liberalization beyond that undertaken unilaterally. Important GVC-relevant services, such as air and maritime transport, for which liberalization needs to be coordinated, have typically been excluded from negotiations.
- For investment in goods, there are no multilateral rules, and the relevant policies are covered by a patchwork of preferential trade agreements (PTAs) and bilateral investment treaties (BITs).
- As for subsidies, trade rules have sought to allow space for legitimate use while preventing protectionist abuse, but recent frictions suggest that they have not succeeded.

Two policy areas in which international cooperation can help developing countries engage in GVCs are in reducing tariffs and restrictions in services both at home and abroad.

Tariffs and tariff preferences

A new International Trade Centre (ITC)–World Bank Database on Deep Integration Agreements reveals that unilateral, multilateral, and preferential liberalization has reduced trade-weighted average tariff rates to less than 5 percent for most industrial countries.[2] Preferential liberalization has reduced the applied tariffs confronting many countries to a fraction of the most-favored-nation (MFN) rate. Although preferential liberalization has targeted highly protected sectors, pockets of protection remain for agricultural products, textiles, and footwear—areas of export interest for developing countries (figure 9.3).

There is greater room for further liberalization in lower-income countries. Low-income and lower-middle-income countries still have average trade-weighted preferential tariff levels of over 5 percent (figure 9.4 , panel a). When preferential tariffs are split by level of development of the importing and exporting countries, trade-weighted preferential tariffs imposed by countries in the South on other countries (in both the South and North) are more than double those imposed by the North (figure 9.4, panel b).

Figure 9.3 Tariffs have been liberalized across sectors, but pockets of protection remain

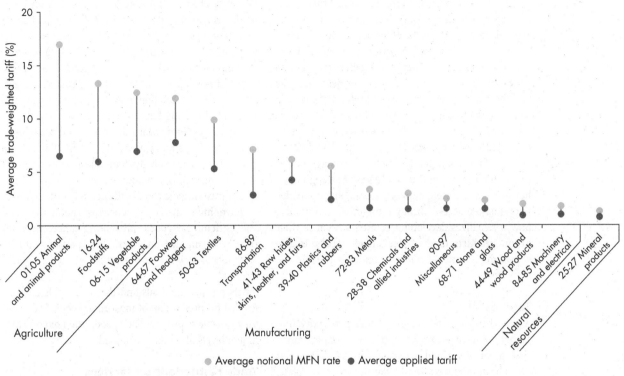

● Average notional MFN rate   ● Average applied tariff

Source: Espitia et al. 2018.

Note: MFN = most-favored-nation. The numbers on the x-axis are Harmonized System two-digit industrial codes.

Figure 9.4 There is room for further liberalization

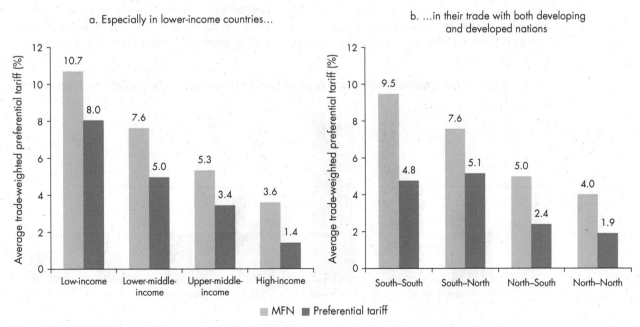

a. Especially in lower-income countries…

b. …in their trade with both developing and developed nations

■ MFN   ■ Preferential tariff

Source: Espitia et al. 2018.

Note: MFN = most-favored-nation.

North–South tariffs are on average higher than North–North tariffs because many of the goods developing countries export, such as agriculture and apparel, face tariff peaks. However, within product categories, low income countries do receive higher preference margins, averaging 3 percentage points above other countries.[3] Some countries, such as Lesotho and Afghanistan, receive preference margins as much as 10 percentage points. In contrast, several countries outside the global trade system, such as Cuba and the Democratic People's Republic of Korea, face tariffs on their goods about 5 percentage points higher than other countries. The variation highlights how the trade system supports developing countries with market access through preferences, but also how it penalizes developing countries because their export products tend to face higher tariffs. It also shows the additional hurdles countries outside the trade system face.

Tariff escalation

A goal of many developing countries is to move into higher value-added production. For example, coffee bean producers would like to sell roasted coffee, and cocoa bean producers would like to export chocolate. One difficulty, though, is that tariffs on processed goods tend to be higher than tariffs on raw materials or semiprocessed goods in many of the largest markets. This *tariff escalation* is designed to protect the high value-added industries, while allowing producers access to imported inputs. Tariff escalation implies especially high rates of effective protection on final goods because not only are these goods protected against competing imported goods, but they also are relatively cheap to produce because tariffs on intermediates are below the average tariffs on other goods.[4]

All countries and groups have some degree of tariff escalation. It is particularly pernicious in middle-income countries, where processed goods face average tariffs of over 10 percent (figure 9.5). From a GVC perspective, tariff escalation tends to push countries into backward participation.

Examining industrial and agricultural goods separately reveals distinct patterns (figure 9.6). High tariffs on raw materials in low-income countries can prevent them from joining the later stages of supply chains. By contrast, middle- and high-income countries tend to have high tariffs on processed nonagricultural and agricultural goods, preventing other countries from accessing their markets. These patterns hit low-income countries twice. First, they suffer a self-inflicted wound from the relatively high domestic tariffs on raw materials and the semifinished goods needed for production of most final goods. Second, if they are able to produce final goods, their exports face higher levels of protection abroad.

Trade restrictions on services

As for services, trade agreements have not done much to deliver liberalization. The General Agreement on Trade in Services (GATS) emerged from the Uruguay Round as a framework for negotiating liberalization, but there was limited liberalization of access to markets. In telecommunications services, however, the GATS did have a mutually reinforcing relationship with a broader liberalization trend. For example,

Figure 9.5 Most countries impose higher tariffs on semifinished and finished goods

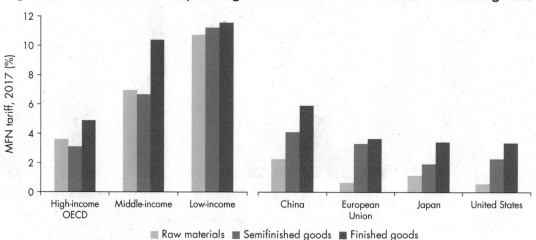

Source: WDR 2020 team, based on World Bank's WITS database.

Note: MFN = most-favored-nation; OECD = Organisation for Economic Co-operation and Development.

Figure 9.6 Low-income countries are penalized by tariff escalation both at home and in their destination markets

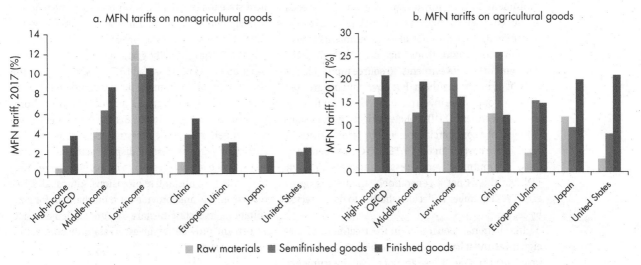

a. MFN tariffs on nonagricultural goods

b. MFN tariffs on agricultural goods

■ Raw materials ■ Semifinished goods ■ Finished goods

Source: WDR 2020 team, based on World Bank's WITS database.

Note: MFN = most-favored-nation; OECD = Organisation for Economic Co-operation and Development.

several countries that were not ready to open markets immediately nevertheless chose to commit themselves legally to opening up at specific points in the future—an exercise that lent credibility to reform programs. Unfortunately, the Doha negotiations in services fell victim to the broader negotiating inertia, and the initial offers did not promise any meaningful liberalization.

Typically excluded from services agreements are air and maritime transport services—two services vital for connectivity and participation in GVCs. In international transport, it takes two to liberalize. Zambia cannot unilaterally introduce greater competition on the Lusaka–London or Lusaka–Johannesburg air routes. Both the United Kingdom and South Africa also need to agree to allow entry by third-country airlines on each route. Both industrial and developing countries use restrictive bilateral air service agreements to fragment the international market into a series of route-specific duopolies. The WTO would have been a natural platform to negotiate liberalization, but powerful members have ensured that air traffic rights are excluded from its scope.

Trade-related regulatory costs

An important area of traditional trade cooperation relevant to GVC participation is the concerted action to reduce the trade costs associated with trade-related regulation. Examples are customs clearance procedures; enforcement of product health, safety, and environmental standards; control of

counterfeit imports; and rules to establish the origin of products needed in applying trade preference programs and PTAs. Both WTO and PTA disciplines ensure that traders know what the rules are and that enforcement procedures are predictable. Governments are increasingly cooperating to facilitate trade by agreeing on good practices to reduce trade costs without undermining regulatory goals such as product safety and tax collection.

Complying with standards is critical to participating in GVCs. Two WTO agreements—one on sanitary and phytosanitary measures and one on technical barriers to trade—encourage the adoption of international standards where they exist and require that national product standards have a scientific basis, do not restrict trade unnecessarily, and are applied on a nondiscriminatory basis.

International standards are being developed not by the WTO but by specialist organizations. For example, international standards for phytosanitary measures, which are particularly significant for agriculture GVCs, are developed and adopted by contracting parties to the International Plant Protection Convention. These standards provide countries with harmonized guidance on the implementation of regulations in the trade of plants, plant products, and conveyances that may carry pests and diseases of plants.

Gaps in rules

The gaps in multilateral rules are in at least two important GVC-relevant areas: investment and subsidies.

Investment

The WTO has uneven rules for policies affecting investment. Policies for foreign investment in goods are not covered. The existing national treatment rule[5] on the goods trade does not allow governments to give incentives or require firms, including those benefiting from foreign investments, to source inputs locally instead of importing them. But governments are free to restrict or provide investment incentives for foreign direct investment (FDI). Policies affecting the establishment of a commercial presence by foreign firms in services are covered in the GATS. WTO members may make commitments on access to markets through FDI, but this is not a general obligation—it is up to each WTO member to decide whether to do so, sector by sector.

International cooperation in the treatment of foreign investment has mainly taken the form of bilateral investment treaties. These are not always instruments of liberalization in terms of market access; instead, they provide foreign investors with protection against governments taking action against them once they have entered the country. The main goals are to ensure that foreign investors are treated the same as domestic investors and to put in place international arbitration mechanisms to determine the appropriate compensation for a foreign investor if the host government takes actions to expropriate the investment. The arbitration dimension of BITs has been contested in recent years, resulting in revisions of the regime by some jurisdictions.

Increasingly, PTAs are providing for both investment liberalization and investment protection.[6] Liberalization may include access during the preestablishment or entry phase of investment, including national treatment, which requires the host state to remove all discriminatory market access barriers and allow foreign investors to invest on the same terms as domestic investors. Investor protections in PTAs generally grant national treatment to other members of PTAs and MFN treatment once the investment has been made (in the postestablishment phase) and cover direct and indirect forms of expropriation (figure 9.7). Finally, dispute settlement plays a prominent role in the investment chapters of PTAs, particularly investor–state dispute settlement provisions, which allow investors to bring disputes relating to the treaty's substantive provisions. Almost all PTAs that cover this area provide for a mechanism for consultations and state-to-state dispute settlement, and 77 percent provide for investor–state dispute settlement provisions.

Subsidies

Subsidies, like taxes, are an important policy tool that governments can use to pursue a number of legitimate goals. Often, they are the best way to address market failures that lead to the underprovision of certain goods. They can also be used to promote social objectives such as supporting access to basic services in marginalized areas. But subsidies also can have distortive effects, including on trade. They may undermine the benefits of trade and investment by distorting international prices or limiting market access, such as when they are granted with the condition that local content be used. Such a condition can have negative welfare effects on other trading partners and the global economy. Ensuring that subsidies pursue

Figure 9.7 A majority of PTAs protect investors from discrimination and expropriation

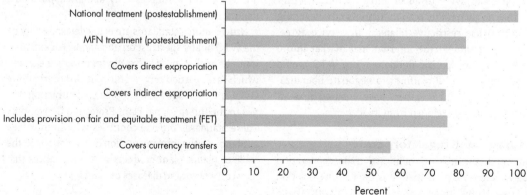

Source: Mattoo, Rocha, and Ruta, forthcoming.

Note: National treatment requires imported products to be treated no less favorably than "like domestic products." MFN = most-favored-nation; PTAs = preferential trade agreements.

desirable goals and are not captured by special groups to further their own interests is a challenge. Trade rules have sought to allow space for legitimate goals while preventing protectionist ones, but it is not clear they have succeeded.

The impact of a subsidy is less clear in a GVC world in terms of the resulting distortion, as well as who benefits from a "subsidy" and who might be hurt.[7] The most obvious feature of a subsidy is that it can be targeted to specific stages of production or types of economic activity—presumably associated with immediate or future spillover benefits—rather than entire industries. That feature may imply that location decisions are more responsive than others to financial incentives. In relational GVCs, subsidies can help overcome a market failure in which investment in specific goods is too low because of incomplete contracts.

The two sides of a subsidy

The first order of business in considering a subsidy is to identify and define its spillovers. Subsidies used by a country to support local firms may have adverse effects on the firms producing similar goods or services. Therefore, the potential for welfare-reducing subsidy competition between jurisdictions is significant. U.S. states "spend" some $80 billion a year on tax incentives and subsidies of investments, reflecting vigorous competition to attract investment.[8] This competition increases state-level welfare by attracting firms, increasing employment, and raising wages, but it generates beggar-thy-neighbor effects. Although large potential gains can accrue at the state level from subsidizing investment, such subsidies distort resource allocation by making inputs too cheap and generating excessive entry. The cost to the United States as a whole is significant—if states were to refrain from subsidy competition, manufacturing real income in the United States would be 3.9 percent higher.[9]

Although investment subsidies may have negative welfare spillovers, they can also achieve outcomes sought by governments, such as generating local employment. A U.K. program that offers investment subsidies to firms in depressed areas on the condition they create or safeguard manufacturing jobs in these areas has positive effects on employment, investment, and net entry. A 10 percent investment subsidy generates about a 7 percent increase in manufacturing employment. The "cost per job" has been estimated at $6,300, suggesting that investment subsidies can be cost-effective.[10]

These examples illustrate the trade-offs associated with subsidies and raise several questions from a trading system perspective. How large are any spillovers? What types of subsidies generate the greatest adverse effects for other countries and for the trade system? Are subsidies achieving government objectives, or are they likely to be captured by special interests? All these questions require better information and further analysis.

As discussed in chapter 8, about half of all trade-related policy measures imposed by governments since 2009 take the form of subsidies or some type of support for exports. These subsidies are only partially covered by WTO disciplines.

WTO subsidy rules

WTO subsidy rules have significant gaps—they do not cover investment incentives or support received by services activities, and only partially do they discipline the behavior of SOEs. Most PTAs do little more than the WTO on subsidies, but the European Union is a major exception. For SOEs, however, several recent deep PTAs, such as the Comprehensive and Progressive Agreement for Trans-Pacific Partnership (CPTPP) and the United States–Mexico–Canada Agreement (USMCA), do go beyond the WTO.

Much of the focus of WTO members has been on agricultural subsidies, but their views have changed in recent years. Many high-income countries have long supported their agriculture sectors through a variety of policy instruments, including border barriers and production subsidies. The WTO Agreement on Agriculture negotiated during the Uruguay Round significantly reduced the ability of members to use agricultural subsidies and encouraged governments to decouple support from production. In 2015 WTO members agreed to ban agricultural export subsidies. Although other agricultural support continues to be trade-distorting, it is much less so than in the 1980s and 1990s because of the shift to decoupling support from production and linking it to achievement of equity, environmental, and sustainability goals as opposed to increasing output. Since the early 2000s, the Organisation for Economic Co-operation and Development (OECD) has seen a remarkable reduction in production support (figure 9.8), but there has been an increase in support in large emerging economies such as China. These trends illustrate the value and feasibility of cooperation to reduce the negative spillovers created by subsidies. But further cooperation is needed to address the increase in farm support not decoupled from production in countries such as China and the United States.[11]

Nondistorting forms of support are positively associated with agri-food GVC participation and the generation of domestic value added.[12] Conversely,

Figure 9.8 Agricultural producer support converged across some high-income and lower-income countries from 2000 to 2017

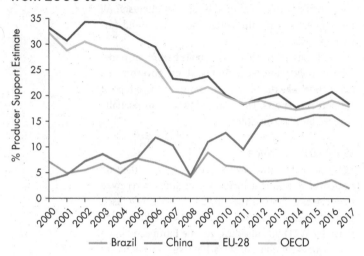

Source: WDR 2020 team, using data from the Organisation for Economic Co-operation and Development's (OECD's) Producer and Consumer Support Estimates database.

Note: EU-28 refers to the 28 member countries of the European Union.

subsidies linked to output and market price support measures lower the benefits of GVC participation. Distortionary payments increase forward GVC participation in OECD member countries but decrease the domestic returns to participation in agri-food GVCs because the subsidy acts as a tax on other contributing sectors. Cooperation to limit subsidies and distortions in agri-food sectors may thus enhance the domestic value added captured through participation in GVCs.[13]

A separate WTO Agreement on Subsidies and Countervailing Measures (ASCM) pertaining to subsidies on nonagricultural goods seeks to limit their use while granting flexibility to developing countries. The ASCM has a twofold objective: (1) to prevent the use of subsidies to circumvent market access (tariff) concessions and (2) to regulate countervailing duties (CVDs) used to offset the harmful effects on domestic producers of the foreign subsidization of goods.[14] Export subsidies are prohibited. All other subsidies can be used, but they could lead to the imposition of CVDs in destination markets.[15] *De minimis* provisions allow developing countries to use subsidies subject to certain thresholds.[16] However, the WTO rules are not concerned with why a government has implemented a subsidy, such as whether it can be justified by a market failure.[17]

WTO disciplines on SOEs are limited, with only a provision for state trading enterprises to require firms granted exclusive or special privileges in trading to abide by the nondiscrimination rules. The growth of

the Chinese economy has resulted in a substantial increase in the relative weight of SOEs in the global economy. In 2006, 4 percent of the world's top 1,000 firms were Chinese, and by 2014, 14 percent were Chinese, of which 70 percent were state-owned.[18] SOEs are also active in other emerging and developed countries, often in cross-border mergers and acquisitions, engaging in outward FDI. Concerns are frequently expressed about the potential of SOEs to distort competition, reflecting views that SOEs are effectively subsidized through soft loans, guarantees, and direct subsidies, among other things. They also may benefit from indirect subsidies for factor inputs such as energy and land, as well from protection from foreign competition (reflected, for example, in FDI restrictions, joint venture requirements, and preferential access to public procurement).[19] Many SOEs operate in GVC-intensive sectors, both upstream in energy and downstream in transport.

Disciplines on SOEs are included in recent PTAs such as the CPTPP and USMCA, and the relevant provisions are enforceable through dispute settlement procedures. These disciplines require SOEs to make purchases and sales on the basis of commercial considerations, and specify that subsidies granted to SOEs, both direct fiscal transfers and indirect subsidies, are actionable and that signatories may not discriminate in favor of SOEs (that is, they must apply the national treatment principle). The agreements also include provisions requiring signatories to list their SOEs and publish data on measures used to assist them. As just noted, incentives to attract investment are not covered by WTO rules.

Current WTO rules on countervailing action are directed at the domestic industry: if a sufficiently large share of the industry agrees it is being injured by a foreign subsidy, action can be initiated. In a GVC setting, the high import content of total value added embodied in a final good means subsidies will benefit foreign interests as well as local ones. The current concept of injury may need to be reconsidered. Because any GVC spans firms in different countries, it may be more appropriate to focus on the effects of subsidies on GVCs as a whole.

Strengthening subsidy rules
Concerns and conflicts about the effects of subsidies and the potential competition-distorting role of SOEs in the international economy call for revisiting the WTO rules. Such efforts can take different forms, ranging from "soft law"—agreement on guidelines—to enforceable treaty commitments. In 2018 the European Union, Japan, and the United States launched a

trilateral process to identify ways to strengthen disciplines on subsidies, suggesting expansion of the list of prohibited subsidies in the WTO to include SOEs, open-ended financial guarantees, subsidies to insolvent or failing companies with no credible restructuring plan, and preferential pricing for inputs. A necessary condition for meaningful outcomes is that developing countries, especially the larger emerging economies, participate in such deliberations.

Transparency, transparency, transparency

A first step—and a core part of any revision of subsidy rules—is transparency. Cooperation to ensure transparency and allow assessments of the effects of subsidies can benefit both the subsidizing country and the trade system. The WTO requires members to regularly notify subsidy programs, but often compliance is neither timely nor comprehensive. In part this may reflect capacity constraints; in part it may reflect a decision to not notify subsidies.

New rules could build on the EU experience. EU member states must comply with transparency obligations for state aid allocations of more than €500,000, including the name of the beneficiary and the amount of aid granted. These data are accompanied by evaluation of selected large state aid schemes to assess their impact and guide possible improvements in the design of programs as well as the subsidy rules. Lessons learned from the processes used by EU member states and the European Commission to report data on subsidies could inform changes by the WTO.

Transparency could be bolstered through a collective effort to compile information on subsidies (going beyond reliance on notifications by countries) and to launch a process of dialogue and deliberation in the WTO to define a negotiating agenda. This effort may be more effective if undertaken plurilaterally, centered on the major trading powers, but any initiative in this area should be open to all countries and be informed by economic analysis of the (spillover) effects of different types of subsidies. An important challenge in defining possible rules and related cooperation is to agree on what in principle constitutes desirable (globally welfare-enhancing) policies and what types of subsidies are more likely to generate undesirable spillover effects, based on empirical analysis and evidence. In the WTO working group on investment set up after the WTO's Singapore ministerial meeting in 1996, it became clear early on that many governments were not willing to discuss and consider disciplines to address the spillover effects of investment incentives and subsidies, removing much of the potential rationale for a multilateral agreement.

Substantive disciplines

A precondition for considering how and where to revisit WTO rules is agreement on what types of support are a problem and where there should be a presumption that a measure is not trade-distorting or not large enough to matter. It is desirable to move toward an approach that devotes more attention to the aims and effects of subsidies and prioritizes rule making for subsidies that are more likely to have adverse spillovers on low-income countries, while enabling the use of subsidy instruments to address market failures.

There may also be lessons from the European Union because it is the only international integration effort that ensures a level playing field for firms in the integrated market. Subsidies are covered by EU competition policy disciplines, and four criteria determine whether state aid is illegal: (1) state resources (a subsidy or tax expenditure) lead to (2) a selective advantage for a firm or activity that (3) distorts competition and (4) affects trade between member states. This also applies to undertakings to which member states have granted special or exclusive rights (such as to SOEs). Subsidies falling under a General Block Exemption Regulation are deemed to raise few or no concerns about distorting competition in the EU market. These include regional aid (including for ports and airports); aid for small and medium enterprises (SMEs); and aid for research and development and innovation, broadband infrastructures, energy and the environment, employment and training, natural disasters, sports, and culture.

In 2017 EU member states spent €116.2 billion, or 0.76 percent of the European Union's GDP, on state aid. More than 90 percent of total state aid was allocated to horizontal objectives of common interest, such as environmental protection; regional development; and research, development, and innovation. Agreeing to a set of subsidies deemed not to cause spillover concerns along the lines of the European Union could help differentiate between subsidies that are not considered to have harmful trade spillover effects and those that may have such consequences and should be actionable.

The elements of progress are already embodied in WTO agreements, including the green box approach used in the Agreement on Agriculture, which exempts subsidies that cause minimal distortion to trade and includes social and environmental programs. The agreement also gives developing countries additional flexibility in providing domestic support. The green box approach was also incorporated on a provisional basis in the WTO agreement on subsidies and countervailing measures that expired in 1999. Revisiting it is one possible factor in balancing stronger disciplines on subsidies with recognition that many types of subsidies fulfill an important function in addressing market failures. Moreover, the various de minimis provisions included in these WTO agreements for developing countries are a way of recognizing that the spillover effects created by subsidies used by low-income countries are likely to be small from a systemic perspective.

All this suggests that any new subsidy rules should consider, in a way that current WTO rules do not, the motivation for a policy that may give rise to negative spillovers. Such rules should cover all subsidy-like policies to encompass services and investment incentives, as well as the agricultural domestic support policies that have long been an interest of the WTO membership—and that matter most for many developing countries.

Deep integration agreements and GVCs

Trade cooperation can be characterized as either "shallow" or "deep."[20] Shallow cooperation is limited to commitments to enhance the transparency and visibility of extant trade policies and reduce or eliminate trade barriers such as tariffs and quotas. It gives countries discretion in setting nontariff measures that could affect trade. Its basic requirement is "national treatment," which requires imported products to be treated no less favorably than "like domestic products."

Deep agreements go beyond national treatment by including commitments on the substance of nontariff measures. Examples include agreements to protect certain types of intellectual property, to adopt common approaches to regulating the services sectors, or to implement a competition law that embodies criteria that mirror those of trading partners. A feature of deep trade agreements is that many provisions are enforceable: they specify precise legally binding obligations, and trading partners can raise objections and take action if a signatory does not live up to its commitments.[21]

In some situations, cooperation may not require binding disciplines. If the problem is a coordination failure, all that may be required is information and agreement to apply a given norm at the national level. An example is an agreement on technical standards to allow equipment, vessels, or network infrastructure to connect. In many circumstances, soft law cooperation will center on international monitoring and mechanisms that elicit dialogue and analysis to allow learning and identification of good practices. This is an important role of institutions

such as OECD and the Asia-Pacific Economic Cooperation forum.

Deep integration agreements can fill some of the gaps in the WTO on investment-related policies, SOEs, and services. They do so, however, on a preferential basis: the benefits of market access are limited to partners. They may also offer a way of bundling disciplines on a range of GVC-relevant issues. Evidence suggests that these bundles affect the joint evolution of GVCs and FDI.

Deep trade agreements boost GVC participation

There is a strong correlation between GVC-related trade and the depth of PTAs (figure 9.9). Adding a provision to a PTA boosts the domestic value added of intermediate goods and services exports (forward GVC linkages) by 0.48 percent, while an additional provision in a PTA increases the foreign value added of intermediate goods and services exports (backward GVC linkages) by 0.38 percent.[22] Although deep PTAs boost trade between their members,[23] this effect is stronger for GVC trade, which is consistent with the view that policy spillovers are more relevant to GVCs than to standard trade. Indeed, deep trade agreements improve forward linkages, especially for more complex GVCs, which export intermediates across borders two or more times.[24] Conversely, the unraveling of deep trade agreements can have an adverse effect on GVCs (box 9.3).

Figure 9.9 Deep trade agreements are associated with GVC integration

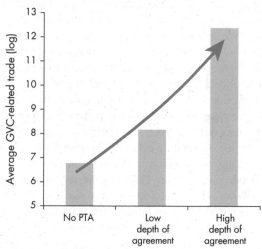

Source: Laget et al. 2018.

Note: The estimator is the Poisson Pseudo Maximum Likelihood (PPML). GVC-related trade is defined as trade in parts and components. PTA = preferential trade agreement.

Box 9.3 The impact of Brexit on GVC trade

How will Brexit affect trade between the United Kingdom and the European Union (EU)? One difficulty in addressing this question lies in the lack of systematic information on the content of trade agreements, which makes it difficult to assess precisely the impact that a set of common rules has on trade flows.[a] A recent study uses the information available on the content of trade agreements to assess the impact of Brexit on goods, services, and value-added trade.[b] Specifically, it augments a standard gravity model of trade to quantify the effect that the "depth" of the EU agreements has on U.K. trade and then use the estimates from this analysis to evaluate the future of U.K.–EU trade relations under different post-Brexit scenarios. In a first step, the study examines the extent to which EU membership contributed to boosting U.K. trade, notably GVC trade.[c] It finds that EU membership increased goods, services, and value-added trade for member countries and that this impact has been even stronger for the United Kingdom (figure B9.3.1). Following its membership in the European Union, the United Kingdom's services trade more than doubled; its intermediates value added in gross exports (forward linkages) increased by 31 percent; and the foreign value added in U.K. exports (backward linkages) increased by 37 percent.

In a second step, the study examines the impact that Brexit can have on U.K.–EU trade relations going forward. Three distinct scenarios are considered, varying by the decreasing depth of the post-Brexit agreement between the United Kingdom and the rest of the European Union. The first scenario is a "soft" Brexit, assuming that the post-Brexit arrangement between the United Kingdom and the European Union will be as deep as the agreement the European Union has with Norway. In the second scenario, the United Kingdom and the European Union will sign an agreement as deep as the average agreement the European Union currently has with third countries. The third "hard" scenario has no agreement.

Under all scenarios, bilateral U.K.–EU trade declines, and the drop is sharper the lower the depth of the post-Brexit arrangement relative to the depth of the EU agreement. In terms of value-added trade, the decline ranges from 6 percent for the "softer" scenario to 28 percent for the "harder" Brexit scenario. The largest declines are for U.K. services trade.

Figure B9.3.1 Trade impacts of membership in the European Union on the United Kingdom and other EU members

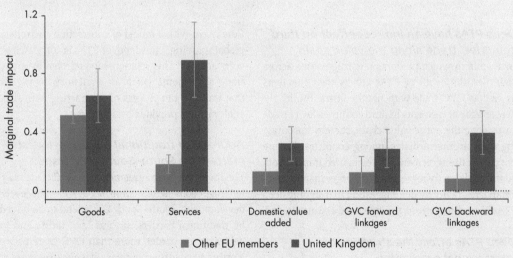

Source: Mulabdic, Osnago, and Ruta 2017.

Note: The figure reports the coefficients and confidence intervals of an augmented gravity equation, capturing the marginal impact on trade of a deep trade agreement and its statistical significance. In each category, the blue bar represents the coefficient for all countries in the sample, except the United Kingdom (for which the red bar is the coefficient). For example, a coefficient of 0.5 for goods trade indicates that country-pairs that signed the deepest trade agreement increased their total bilateral trade in goods by 69 percent (exp 0.5–1.0). The United Kingdom was not affected more than the average in terms of goods trade. The estimator is the Poisson Pseudo Maximum Likelihood (PPML). All specifications include bilateral fixed effects and country-time fixed effects. Ninety percent confidence intervals are constructed using robust standard errors, clustered by country-pair.

(Box continues next page)

Box 9.3 The impact of Brexit on GVC trade *(continued)*

Table B9.3.1 Changes in the United Kingdom's bilateral trade with the European Union under three Brexit scenarios

Percent

Type of trade	"Norway" (or "soft") scenario	"Average PTA" scenario	"No agreement" (or "hard") scenario
Goods	–12	–38	–50
Services	–16	–48	–62
Domestic value added	–6	–20	–28
GVC forward linkages	–5	–18	–26
GVC backward linkages	–7	–25	–34

Source: Mulabdic, Osnago, and Ruta 2017.

Note: The depth of the post-Brexit arrangement falls from a score of 44 to 36 (the number of legally enforceable policy areas covered by the agreement) in the "Norway" scenario, to 14 in the "average PTA" scenario, and to 0 in the "no agreement" scenario. PTA = preferential trade agreement.

Table B9.3.1 summarizes results of the study. These predictions are average effects because it takes time for trade flows to respond to changes in trade costs, and so the impact in the short run is expected to be smaller than in the longer term. Moreover, they are made under the assumption that entry and exit from an agreement are symmetric processes because the predictions are based on the impact that EU membership had on U.K.–EU trade. Because firms have already paid sunk costs to enter the market, the trade effect of a breakup can be less than what a gravity model predicts.

a. A way around this problem is to make assumptions about how different scenarios will lower trade costs (Dhingra et al. 2016) or to identify trade agreements that have diverse content (Baier et al. 2008).
b. Mulabdic, Osnago, and Ruta (2017).
c. The analysis uses data from the World Bank's WIOD database on goods, services, and value-added trade and World Bank data on the content of deep agreements (Hofmann, Osnago, and Ruta 2019) to estimate a gravity equation augmented with a measure of depth for the period 1995–2011. The effect of common trade rules on U.K. imports and exports of goods, services, and value added is quantified by interacting the depth of trade agreements with dummies identifying the United Kingdom.

Deep PTAs have an indirect effect on third countries' trade along the value chain

In a world in which production is fragmented across countries, the depth of PTAs affects their members as well as GVC trade with nonmembers. Intuitively, deeper trade agreements in third countries lower trade costs along the entire value chain, thereby encouraging trade in intermediates among countries that are not part of the agreement. The estimated impact from augmented gravity regressions are larger than those of a standard gravity model, suggesting that signing deep PTAs has indirect effects through third-country trade.[25]

Deep PTAs affect the structure of international production

Deep trade agreements also affect FDI and, more generally, the way in which goods are traded internationally (within firms or at arm's length). The underlying idea is that deep PTAs affect firms' make-or-buy decisions—that is, whether producers outsource to trading partners' suppliers or vertically integrate production processes with affiliates in foreign economies.

Consistent with a model of contractual frictions and global sourcing,[26] the depth of PTAs is correlated with vertical FDI.[27] This relationship is driven by areas in trade agreements (such as regulatory cooperation) that improve the process of contracting with suppliers for inputs provided by suppliers.

Addressing traditional trade barriers still matters for South–South GVC trade

The impact of deep agreements on GVC trade may be heterogeneous across countries at different levels of development. South–South GVCs tend to be impeded by traditional barriers, such as high tariffs and long delays at the border, more than GVC trade between North and South economies. Evidence suggests that PTAs boost South–South GVC integration by going further in policy areas under the current WTO mandate (such as tariffs, customs, and services), whereas North–South GVCs are primarily affected by commitments in areas such as investment, competition, and intellectual property rights protection not covered by the WTO.[28]

Table 9.2 Existing trade agreements in Africa are relatively shallow

Policy area	African Continental Free Trade Area (AfCFTA)[a]	Common Market for Eastern and Southern Africa (COMESA)	East African Community (EAC)	Economic Community of West African States (ECOWAS)	Southern African Customs Union (SACU)	Southern African Development Community (SADC)	West African Economic and Monetary Union (WAEMU)
Tariffs on manufacturing goods	✔	✔	✔	✔	✔	✔	✔
Tariffs on agricultural goods	✔	✔	✔	✔	✔	✔	✔
Export taxes	✔	✔	✔			✔	✔
Customs	✔	✔	✔	✔	✔	✔	
Competition policy	✔	✔	✔				✔
State aid	?	✔	✔				
Antidumping	✔	✔	✔	✔		✔	
Countervailing measures	✔		✔			✔	
Agreement on Trade-Related Aspects of Intellectual Property Rights (TRIPS)	✔					✔	
State trading enterprise (STE)	✔						
Technical barrier to trade (TBT)	✔		✔		✔	✔	
General Agreement on Trade in Services (GATS)	✔			✔		✔	
Sanitary and phytosanitary (SPS)	✔	✔	✔			✔	
Movement of capital	✔	✔	✔	✔			✔
Public procurement	?						
Intellectual property rights (IPRs)	✔						
Investment	✔	✔					
Environmental laws	?						
Labor market regulation	?						
Agreement on Trade-Related Investment Measures (TRIMs)	?						

Source: WDR 2020 team, based on Hofmann, Osnago, and Ruta 2019.

a. The depth of AfCFTA is based on the text of the Agreement Establishing the African Continental Free Trade Area ("Kigali Draft Text," March 2018). Several AfCFTA details are still being negotiated. It is unknown if any commitments will be included in the areas of state aid, public procurement, environment, labor market regulation, and TRIMs.

These findings provide useful guidance for South–South integration initiatives, such as the African Continental Free Trade Area (AfCFTA). It is far more ambitious than the existing PTAs in Africa (table 9.2). Because bilateral trade protection among African countries affects backward and forward participation in agriculture and food GVCs,[29] the immediate challenge for AfCFTA negotiations for GVC integration is to address the distortions created by traditional barriers to trade within Africa (box 9.4).

Box 9.4 How the African Continental Free Trade Area (AfCFTA) can support integration into GVCs

AfCFTA will likely boost trade and deepen regional integration in Africa, with positive effects on growth and poverty reduction. The agreement, now ratified by 27 countries, has become legally binding and entered into force in May 2019. The first phase of negotiations will consider trade in goods and services, as well as procedures for dispute settlement. This phase will include negotiations on rules of origin, which are likely to have an important role in enabling the development of regional value chains. The second phase will cover the rules defining investment, competition, and intellectual property rights.

There is widespread optimism throughout the continent that increased trade integration will strengthen the emerging regional value chains and enable firms throughout Africa to participate in GVCs. Creating an integrated and much larger market can attract market-seeking foreign direct investment, especially if some of the deeper integration ambitions are also realized. Similarly, a well-staffed AfCFTA secretariat with clear monitoring and enforcement capacities can help ensure that commitments are fully implemented, leading to greater policy predictability. Some institutions such as the African Export-Import Bank are seeking to develop facilities to help governments address adjustment costs. However, it is unclear whether such efforts will be sufficient. As for most free trade agreements (FTAs), governments will have to look for ways to support those workers who may lose from the adjustment-related aspects of greater trade openness.

There is, however, reason for caution at this stage. Despite a long history of hope for greater integration in Africa, the efforts to date have fallen short. Here, the development of integrated trade and production networks in Asia provides some lessons. Implementing trade facilitation commitments and improving border management can reduce trade costs within Africa and also reduce distances to global hubs. The impact of AfCFTA depends, then, on much more than tariff reduction; some of the largest gains would come from effectively tackling nontariff barriers

(NTBs) to trade in goods and services and implementing trade facilitation measures. World Bank staff estimates indicate that reduction of tariffs alone is expected to increase the welfare of AfCFTA members by 0.2 percent. Reducing NTBs in goods and services by half would increase welfare gains by 1.6 percent. Full implementation of the World Trade Organization's Trade Facilitation Agreement (TFA) would bring the overall welfare gains to 5 percent by 2035 (compared with the baseline). However, the aggregate results mask heterogeneity of impacts across countries. Even though AfCFTA is expected to benefit all members, welfare gains by 2035 will range from 0.4 percent to 19 percent (figure B9.4.1). Thus the impact of the agreement will depend on its depth and the extent to which it covers NTBs and services, especially in backbone sectors such as transport and logistics, and on the respective export basket and economic structure of each country.

AfCFTA will also provide an opportunity to build on efforts by the many regional economic communities to develop integrated regional value chains (RVCs) to support growth and industrial development. In the recent past, these efforts have suffered from the fragmented and piecemeal engagement of the private sector and the capacity, political economy, and coordination challenges that lead to the "implementation gap" in regional commitments.[a] Ongoing initiatives by regional communities, national governments, and donors are seeking to identify and address policy and regulatory constraints to cross-border trade, such as in the soya RVC in southern Africa, the dairy RVC in East Africa, and the leather RVC in the Common Market for Eastern and Southern Africa (COMESA) region. The benefit of structuring interventions and support around individual RVCs is that it allows participants to focus on required policy reforms and needed investments to address market failures and to create mutually beneficial outcomes. This in turn can create demonstration effects and reduce cross-cutting barriers across sectors that can be scaled up across RVCs spanning subgroups of countries.

(Box continues next page)

Figure B9.4.1 AfCFTA members benefit from reductions in tariffs, nontariff measures, and implementation of the World Trade Organization's Trade Facilitation Agreement

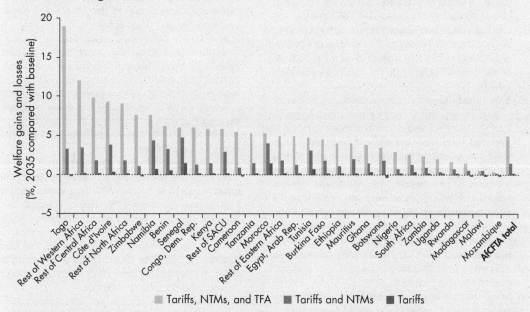

Legend: ■ Tariffs, NTMs, and TFA   ■ Tariffs and NTMs   ■ Tariffs

Source: Maliszewska, Osorio-Rodarte, and van der Mensbrugge, forthcoming.

Note: The figure shows the percentage change in welfare in 2035 compared with the baseline. Tariffs refers to full elimination of tariffs in trade within the African Continental Free Trade Area (AfCFTA); NTMs refers to halving the nontariff measures (NTMs) in goods and services; and TFA refers to full implementation of the World Trade Organization's Trade Facilitation Agreement. *Rest of Central Africa* includes Angola, Central African Republic, Chad, Republic of Congo, Equatorial Guinea, Gabon, and São Tomé and Príncipe; *rest of Eastern Africa* includes Burundi, Comoros, Djibouti, Eritrea, Mayotte, Seychelles, Somalia, South Sudan, and Sudan; *rest of North Africa* includes Algeria, Libya, and Western Sahara; *rest of SACU (South African Customs Union)* includes Eswatini and Lesotho; *rest of Western Africa* includes Cabo Verde, The Gambia, Guinea-Bissau, Liberia, Mali, Mauritania, Niger, Saint Helena, and Sierra Leone.

a. Vanheukelom and Bertelsmann-Scott (2016); World Bank (2017, 2019).

Notes

1. Tang and Wei (2009).
2. The website for this database is still under construction.
3. Competition adjusted preference margins are calculated as the difference between the weighted average tariff rate applied to the rest of the world and that applied to the beneficiary country, holding weights constant based on preference-granting country imports.
4. Corden (1971).
5. National treatment is specified by the WTO (in Article III of the General Agreement on Tariffs and Trade), as well as in most preferential trade agreements. It requires imported products to be treated no less favorably than "like domestic products."
6. Crawford and Kotschwar (2018).
7. Hoekman (2016).

8. Ossa (2015).
9. Ossa (2015).
10. Criscuolo et al. (2012).
11. OECD (2018).
12. Greenville, Kawasaki, and Beaujeu (2017).
13. Greenville, Kawasaki, and Beaujeu (2017).
14. Adverse effects include injury to a domestic industry, nullification or impairment of tariff concessions, or serious prejudice to the country's interests. Serious prejudice arises if subsidies are used to cover the operating losses of a firm or industry or if debt relief is granted for government-held liabilities. Serious prejudice may arise if the subsidy reduces exports of other WTO members, results in significant price undercutting, or increases the world market share of the subsidizing country in a

primary product. WTO disciplines focus on the amount of assistance given and not on the extent to which a subsidy harms trading partners. Subsidies below 5 percent ad valorem are not actionable. See Hoekman and Kostecki (2009).

15. In response to subsidies, other countries can impose CVDs on subsidized imports that injure a domestic industry (with duties up to the amount of the subsidy paid) or request a government to withdraw a prohibited subsidy or withdraw or modify an actionable subsidy. In case of noncompliance, the injured WTO member can take countermeasures against the subsidizing state up to the amount of the subsidy paid (in the case of a prohibited subsidy) or up to the amount of the injury suffered by the domestic industry (in the case of an actionable subsidy).

16. If the subsidy is less than 2 percent of the per unit value of products exported, developing countries are exempt from CVDs (for less developed countries the threshold is 3 percent). De minimis also applies if the import market share of a developing country is below 4 percent, and the aggregate share of all developing countries is below 9 percent of total imports. The ASCM also exempts nations with per capita incomes below $1,000 from the WTO prohibition on the use of export subsidies and precludes CVDs on associated exports if global market shares are less than 3.5 percent for a product. De minimis provisions are also included in the WTO Agreement on Agriculture, permitting support up to 10 percent of output in developing countries.

17. In the Uruguay Round, a third category, nonactionable subsidies, was included in the ASCM spanning environmental, R&D, and regional subsidies. This provision was time-bound and lapsed at the end of 1999 because a consensus could not be reached to extend it.

18. Freund and Sidhu (2017).

19. See, for example, USTR (2018) for arguments to this effect. Empirical evidence suggests that SOEs are less profitable and less productive than private firms in their respective sectors. See European Commission (2016) for the European Union; Harrison et al. (2019) for China; and Kowalski et al. (2013) and OECD (2016) for a broad sample of countries.

20. Lawrence, Bressand, and Ito (1996).

21. Ederington and Ruta (2016).

22. Laget et al. (2018). For other research on the relationship between deep PTAs and GVCs see Dhingra, Freeman, and Mavroeidi (2018); Johnson and Noguera (2017); Orefice and Rocha (2014).

23. Mattoo, Mulabdic, and Ruta (2017).

24. Laget et al. (2018).

25. Laget et al. (2018) build on the approach by Noguera (2012) to investigate this mechanism through a gravity model augmented to account for third-country effects.

26. Antràs and Helpman (2008).

27. Osnago, Rocha, and Ruta (2017, 2019).

28. Laget et al. (2018).

29. Balié et al. (2017).

References

Antràs, Pol, and Elhanan Helpman. 2008. "Contractual Frictions and Global Sourcing." In *The Organization of Firms in a Global Economy*, edited by Elhanan Helpman, Dalia Marin, and Thierry Verdier, 9–54. Cambridge, MA: Harvard University Press.

Baier, Scott L., Jeffrey H. Bergstrand, Peter Egger, and Patrick A. McLaughlin. 2008. "Do Economic Integration Agreements Actually Work? Issues in Understanding the Causes and Consequences of the Growth of Regionalism." *World Economy* 31 (4): 461–97.

Balié, Jean, Davide Del Prete, Emiliano Magrini, Pierluigi Montalbano, and Silvia Nenci. 2017. "Agriculture and Food Global Value Chains in Sub-Saharan Africa: Does Bilateral Trade Policy Impact on Backward and Forward Participation?" DISSE Working Paper 4/17, Dipartimento di scienze sociali ed economiche, University of Rome–Sapienza, Rome.

Corden, W. M. 1971. *The Theory of Protection*. Oxford, U.K.: Oxford University Press.

Crawford, Jo-Ann, and Barbara Kotschwar. 2018. "Investment Provisions in Preferential Trade Agreements: Evolution and Current Trends." WTO Staff Working Paper ERSD-2018–14 (December), Economic Research and Statistics Division, World Trade Organization (WTO), Geneva.

Criscuolo, Chiara, Ralf Martin, Henry Overman, and John Van Reenen. 2012. "The Causal Effects of an Industrial Policy." NBER Working Paper 17842, National Bureau of Economic Research, Cambridge, MA.

Dhingra, Swati, Rebecca Ann Freeman, and Eleonora Mavroeidi. 2018. "Beyond Tariff Reductions: What Extra Boost from Trade Agreement Provisions?" CEPR Discussion Paper 12795 (March), Centre for Economic Policy Research, London.

Dhingra, Swati, Gianmarco Ottaviano, Thomas Sampson, and John Van Reenen. 2016. "The Consequences of Brexit for UK Trade and Living Standards." CEP Brexit Analysis 2, Centre for Economic Performance, London School of Economics, London.

Ederington, Josh, and Michele Ruta. 2016. "Non-Tariff Measures and the World Trading System." Policy Research Working Paper 7661, World Bank, Washington, DC.

Egger, Peter H., Sergey Nigai, and Nora Margot Strecker. 2019. "The Taxing Deed of Globalization." *American Economic Review* 109 (2): 353–90.

Espitia, Alvaro, Aaditya Mattoo, Mondher Mimouni, Xavier Pichot, and Nadia Rocha. 2018. "How Preferential Is Preferential Trade?" Policy Research Working Paper 8446, World Bank, Washington, DC.

European Commission. 2016. "State-Owned Enterprises in the EU: Lessons Learnt and Ways Forward in a Post-Crisis Context." European Economy Institutional Paper 31 (July), European Union, Luxembourg.

Freund, Caroline L., and Dario Sidhu. 2017. "Global Competition and the Rise of China." PIIE Working Paper 17–3 (February), Peterson Institute for International Economics, Washington, DC.

Greenville, Jared, Kentaro Kawasaki, and Raphaël Beaujeu. 2017. "How Policies Shape Global Food and Agriculture Value Chains." OECD Food, Agriculture, and Fisheries Paper 100, Organisation for Economic Co-operation and Development, Paris.

Harrison, Ann E., Marshall Meyer, Peichun Wang, Linda Zhao, and Minyuan Zhao. 2019. "Can a Tiger Change Its Stripes? Reform of Chinese State-Owned Enterprises in the Penumbra of the State." NBER Working Paper 25475 (January), National Bureau of Economic Research, Cambridge, MA.

Hoekman, Bernard M. 2016. "Subsidies, Spillovers, and WTO Rules in a Value-Chain World." *Global Policy* 7 (3): 351–59.

Hoekman, Bernard M., and Michel M. Kostecki. 2009. *The Political Economy of the World Trading System: The WTO and Beyond*, 3rd ed. Oxford, U.K.: Oxford University Press.

Hoekman, Bernard M., and Aaditya Mattoo. 2019. "Altered States: Rethinking International Trade Cooperation." Unpublished working paper, World Bank, Washington, DC.

Hofmann, Claudia, Alberto Osnago, and Michele Ruta. 2019. "The Content of Preferential Trade Agreements." *World Trade Review* 18 (3): 365–98.

Johnson, Robert Christopher, and Guillermo Noguera. 2017. "A Portrait of Trade in Value-Added over Four Decades." *Review of Economics and Statistics* 99 (5): 896–911.

Kowalski, Przemyslaw, Max Büge, Monika Sztajerowska, and Matias Egeland. 2013. "State-Owned Enterprises: Trade Effects and Policy Implications." OECD Trade Policy Paper 147, Organisation for Economic Co-operation and Development, Paris.

Laget, Edith, Alberto Osnago, Nadia Rocha, and Michele Ruta. 2018. "Deep Trade Agreements and Global Value Chains." Policy Research Working Paper 8491, World Bank, Washington, DC.

Lawrence, Robert Z., Albert Bressand, and Takatoshi Ito. 1996. *A Vision for the World Economy: Openness, Diversity, and Cohesion*. Integrating National Economies Series. Washington, DC: Brookings Institution Press.

Maliszewska, Maryla, Israel Osorio-Rodarte, and Dominique van der Mensbrugge. Forthcoming. "Making the Most of the Africa Continental Free Trade Area: Assessment of the Impacts on Trade, Growth and Poverty Reduction." World Bank, Washington, DC.

Mattoo, Aaditya, Alen Mulabdic, and Michele Ruta. 2017. "Trade Creation and Trade Diversion in Deep Agreements." Policy Research Working Paper 8206, World Bank, Washington, DC.

Mattoo, Aaditya, Nadia Rocha, and Michele Ruta. Forthcoming. *Handbook of Deep Integration Agreements*. Washington, DC: World Bank.

Mulabdic, Alen, Alberto Osnago, and Michele Ruta. 2017. "Trading Off a 'Soft' and 'Hard' Brexit." *VOX CEPR Policy Portal*, January 23, Centre for Economic Policy Research, London. https://voxeu.org/article/trading-soft-and-hard-brexit.

Noguera, Guillermo. 2012. "Trade Costs and Gravity for Gross and Value Added Trade." Unpublished job market paper, Columbia University, New York.

OECD (Organisation for Economic Co-operation and Development). 2016. *State-Owned Enterprises as Global Competitors: A Challenge or an Opportunity?* Paris: OECD.

———. 2018. *Agricultural Policy Monitoring and Evaluation 2018*. Paris: OECD.

Orefice, Gianluca, and Nadia Rocha. 2014. "Deep Integration and Production Networks: An Empirical Analysis." *World Economy* 37 (1): 106–36.

Ornelas, Emanuel. 2016. "Special and Differential Treatment for Developing Countries." In *Handbook of Commercial Policy*, vol. 1A, edited by Kyle Bagwell and Robert W. Staiger, 369–432. *Handbooks in Economics*. Amsterdam: Elsevier.

Osnago, Alberto, Nadia Rocha, and Michele Ruta. 2017. "Do Deep Trade Agreements Boost Vertical FDI?" *World Bank Economic Review* 30 (1): 119–25.

———. 2019. "Deep Trade Agreements and Vertical FDI: The Devil Is in the Details." *Canadian Journal of Economics* 52 (November).

Ossa, Ralph. 2015. "A Quantitative Analysis of Subsidy Competition in the U.S." NBER Working Paper No. 20975, National Bureau of Economic Research, Cambridge, MA.

Tang, Man-Keung, and Shang-Jin Wei. 2009. "The Value of Making Commitments Externally: Evidence from WTO Accessions." *Journal of International Economics* 78 (2): 216–29.

USTR (U.S. Office of the Trade Representative). 2018. *Findings of the Investigation into China's Acts, Policies, and Practices Related to Technology Transfer, Intellectual Property, and Innovation under Section 301 of the Trade Act of 1974*. Washington, DC: USTR.

Vanheukelom, Jan, and Talitha Bertelsmann-Scott. 2016. "The Political Economy of Regional Integration in Africa: The Southern African Development Community (SADC)." European Centre for Development Policy Management, Maastricht, the Netherlands.

World Bank. 2017. "Supporting Africa's Transformation: Regional Integration and Cooperation Assistance Strategy for the Period FY18–FY23." Report 121912-AFR (December 15), World Bank, Washington, DC.

———. 2019. *Africa's Pulse: Analysis of Issues Shaping Africa's Economic Future*. Vol. 19. Washington, DC: World Bank.

Cooperation beyond trade

Key findings

- **Sustaining openness to trade and global value chains (GVCs)** requires cooperation beyond trade policy on taxes, regulation, competition policy, and infrastructure.

- **GVCs exacerbate the problems of tax avoidance and tax competition between potential host countries.** International cooperation is necessary to enable countries to raise tax revenues and to ensure that conditions of competition are not distorted. Ultimately, a joint approach to greater use of destination-based corporate taxation could eliminate the incentive to shift profits and compete over taxes. Meanwhile, other measures against tax base erosion and income shifting could enhance domestic resource mobilization.

- **Domestic regulation is insufficient to address international market failures, such as privacy concerns related to cross-border data transfers.** Cooperation by data-destination countries to protect foreign consumer data could reassure data-source countries that their commitments to openness will not put their citizens' data at risk.

- **Anticompetitive behavior by GVC firms can affect the distribution of gains from GVC participation.** Enhanced international cooperation around competition law enforcement would enable countries to overcome jurisdictional and capacity constraints to combat anticompetitive practices.

- **Coordination between countries on investment in transport and communication infrastructure can improve international connectivity.** Gains are larger when governments collaborate to expedite trade simultaneously.

To sustain trade openness, it is essential to "walk on two legs." The previous chapter looked at the first leg—deepening traditional liberalization and removing distortions. This chapter looks at the second leg—widening cooperation beyond trade policy to include taxes, regulation, competition policy, and infrastructure. Enhanced cooperation among countries on *taxes* is needed to reduce both the incentives for governments to engage in inefficient tax competition and the opportunities for firms to shift profits to low-tax jurisdictions. Such steps will help governments mobilize the resources necessary to pay for labor adjustment programs and build the infrastructure needed for economic growth. Cooperation among countries on *regulation* and *competition policy* can reassure consumers that greater openness need not imply vulnerability to fraud or anticompetitive practices. Finally, cooperation and assistance on *infrastructure* can help poorer countries remedy the energy and connectivity gaps that have limited their participation in trade and global value chains (GVCs).

Tax competition and profit shifting may be affecting both the ability of countries to join GVCs and their benefits. Multinationals encourage competition between potential hosts, which results in countries using fiscal incentives to win them. GVCs have thus made it hard for countries to tax profits, especially those of firms reliant on patents for their profits, which can easily be shifted to low-tax jurisdictions. As a result, a greater share of the burden for resource mobilization has fallen on workers. International cooperation may be needed to enable states to raise tax revenues in a GVC world and to ensure that conditions of competition are not distorted. The Organisation for Economic Co-operation and Development (OECD) has already taken steps to address tax base erosion and profit shifting (BEPS) by multinationals, including changes in the transfer pricing of intermediate inputs, especially for intangibles such as services and intellectual property. These problems, as well as tax competition, may ultimately best be addressed by a destination-based corporate tax, similar to a value added tax (VAT), in all countries, which would eliminate the incentive to shift profits and compete for taxes. The consequences of such a tax for revenue in small developing countries would, however, have to be considered. A destination-based tax may not be immediately feasible, but transitional arrangements could begin to alleviate the resource mobilization problem.

The new economy has also raised concerns about market failure in international markets where regulation is still mostly at the national level, ranging from abuse of privacy in data-based services to anticompetitive practices in platform-based services. International market failures could be addressed cooperatively in several areas that matter for GVCs. For example, for cross-border, data-based services, addressing market failures efficiently is not possible without the cooperation of the regulator in the data-destination country. Governments may fear opening markets if the gains from liberalization are likely to be eroded by anticompetitive practices in both goods and services—practices for which there is growing evidence. Cooperative solutions that support innovation and efficiency while protecting consumers will be needed to maintain an open trade system in these goods and services. But developing countries must not be left out of such cooperation; multilateral trade rules require that they be given an opportunity to join any such agreements.

Finally, more cooperation is needed on infrastructure gaps. Coordination failures in infrastructural investment affect GVC investment, expansion, and upgrading. Multinational agreements can help address this problem. Consider the Trade Facilitation Agreement (TFA) of the World Trade Organization (WTO), which encourages countries to coordinate improvements in trade facilitation. Each country does not fully internalize the benefits to foreign traders of reductions in domestic trade costs, and gains are larger when governments on both sides of the border invest in expediting trade simultaneously. The WTO agreement addresses this coordination problem and provides low-income countries with financial assistance for the necessary investments. A similar approach could exploit synergies in other infrastructure investments in transport, energy, and communications.

Taxes

Although GVCs are not the cause of the tax competition between governments or the tax avoidance by firms, they do magnify the challenges facing the international tax system (see chapter 3). Firms are more sensitive to tax differences when factors of production are mobile and production processes are fragmented across countries. Cross-border trade between corporate affiliates creates opportunities for tax avoidance because multinational enterprises can reduce their tax burden by manipulating transfer prices and other artificial mechanisms. Profit shifting has become easier for firms and harder for governments to identify as the importance of intangible assets and the digital delivery of services has grown.

A global consensus is emerging around the need to reform international corporate taxation. As long as the current system relies on the physical location where value is created (and booked) for tax purposes, it is open to abuse and compromises the revenue collection efforts of governments.[1] As elaborated in chapter 3, an estimated 30 percent of global cross-border corporate investment stocks are routed through offshore hubs, and the associated tax losses for developing countries amount to about $100 billion.[2] Overall, non-OECD countries lose out on approximately 1.3 percent of GDP as a result of profit shifting.[3]

International efforts are already well under way to address tax avoidance by large multinational firms. New measures are contained in the OECD/G20 Inclusive Framework on BEPS, including updated guidance on transfer pricing.[4] Transparency in international tax matters is being enhanced by an OECD initiative that supports the exchange of data between tax administrations.[5] And overall coordination between governments in implementing the BEPS measures is supported through the Multilateral Convention to Implement Tax Treaty Related Measures to Prevent BEPS, which enables quick updates to international tax treaties between signatory governments.[6]

Although countries have made significant progress within the BEPS framework in reducing opportunities for corporate profit shifting and base erosion, implementation of the relevant measures by developing countries is still lagging.[7] Guidance on when and how to apply transfer pricing methods leaves firms and tax administrations with significant discretion.[8] The complexity of many BEPS rules and lack of data, particularly on segments of GVCs located in other jurisdictions, pose further obstacles. As a result, developing countries find it difficult to implement key parts of the BEPS package.

More important, however, the current BEPS package fails to address inefficient tax competition. The revenue losses from tax competition are estimated to outweigh those of tax avoidance.[9] Indeed, reducing the opportunities for tax avoidance by firms increases the incentives for tax competition between governments.[10] For example, analysis suggests that the 2017 U.S. federal corporate income tax reform, which combined a cut in the headline rate with tighter rules to prevent profit shifting, provoked other countries to reduce their headline rates by about four points to compete.[11] Meanwhile, regional coordination could be helpful for aligning policy makers' incentives on taxes, but in practice such efforts fall short in eliminating undesirable forms of tax competition.[12] For example,

the West African Economic and Monetary Union (WAEMU) has instituted legal arrangements for tax coordination that are among the most advanced in the world, but because of gaps in implementation they are ineffective in many areas.[13]

Tax competition is a legitimate fiscal policy tool that countries can use in aligning their tax systems with development priorities to, for example, attract foreign direct investment (FDI) that supports high-quality and sustainable jobs, as well as technology transfers that spur productivity spillovers. Yet often tax competition results in inefficient outcomes with costs exceeding benefits.[14] This situation leads to negotiated tax breaks to attract foreign investment that benefit favored businesses and economic sectors, while undermining competition and producing little in terms of jobs added or productivity enhanced.

Finally, the BEPS package does not extend taxing rights over corporate income to countries where a firm has no presence but makes sales (market countries). Traditionally, the income of affiliates of a multinational corporation (MNC) is taxed in the country where production takes place, with the "residence" country in which the MNC's headquarters is physically located taxing the residual profits. Safeguards (antiabuse measures) are in place in many jurisdictions to prevent profit shifting between them purely for lowering an MNC's aggregate tax bill. However, the digitalization of the economy has spurred many market countries to contest this distribution of taxing rights. The Internet makes it possible for companies to generate vast profits in countries in which they have no physical presence and are not liable for corporate income taxes. Profit may be generated out of intangible assets that are difficult to tax, such as customer data. In the absence of a coordinated solution at the global level, countries are threatening to impose income taxes on companies that generate income from economic activities in their country even if they do not have a physical presence in that country (so-called destination-based income taxes).[15]

Against this backdrop, the OECD/G20 Inclusive Framework is negotiating larger reforms of the international corporate tax architecture.[16] To further advance the agenda, other proposals and analyses have been developed by the International Monetary Fund (IMF),[17] the World Bank,[18] and academia.[19] The various reform options come with different costs and benefits for developing countries from both an administrative and a revenue generation perspective.[20]

Two of the OECD/G20 Inclusive Framework reform proposals embody stronger antiabuse rules within the current international tax framework: the *income inclusion rule* and the *base-eroding payment rule,* together known as the global antibase erosion (GLoBE) proposal. The income inclusion rule allows countries in which MNCs are headquartered (the residence country) to tax income held by MNC subsidiaries in low-tax jurisdictions abroad. This rule does not directly benefit developing countries, which typically are not residence countries for major MNCs. However, it does offer those countries an indirect benefit by reducing the incentive for tax competition between countries. The base-eroding payment rule would not allow MNCs to take deductions for payments to related parties abroad if those payments are suspected of being motivated by tax avoidance and are not subject to a minimum effective tax rate in the foreign country. Although such a rule is relatively straightforward to enforce by means of MNC self-assessment and disclosure obligations, it is difficult to identify base eroding payments if they go first through intermediate countries that meet the minimum effective rate. Where successful, however, the rule can directly help developing countries to raise revenue.[21]

A third option, the *diverted profits rule,* would provide developing countries with a more direct benefit and could be adopted as part of any reform package that includes antiabuse measures. This option is not currently under consideration by the OECD/G20 Inclusive Framework. A diverted profits rule would reallocate profits posted in (very) low-tax jurisdictions over and above that allocable to any productive activities in those entities. These residual profits would then be allocated more fairly across jurisdictions in which MNCs operate based on a formula using a set of factors that indicate profit generation such as assets, labor, and sales. A main advantage of this rule is that it would allocate low-taxed profits to all countries in the same GVC instead of to the parent entity. A main obstacle will be reaching agreement between countries on a formula for distributing low-taxed profits.[22]

Two proposals considered by the OECD/G20 Inclusive Framework—*user value* and *marketing intangibles*—grant greater taxing rights to the destination countries in which goods and services are consumed. These proposals would allocate to source countries only a portion of residual profits, with the allocation formula based on the value of the market. Destination countries would then have the right to tax businesses that interact with their economies—either through the location of users or through links to certain marketing intangibles such as market research or brands/trademarks—even if those businesses have no physical presence there. Again, however, the benefits reaped by developing countries depend on the specific design. For example, by focusing on where consumption takes place, these two proposals may disadvantage countries with production- or resource-based economies. These options are also highly complex, creating implementation challenges for low-capacity tax administrations.[23]

The reform options currently under consideration by the OECD/G20 Inclusive Framework would go a long way toward correcting the distortions present in the current system. However, alternatives, such as a destination-based cash flow tax (DBCFT), could eliminate tax competition and avoidance more completely.[24] With a DBCFT, taxes are collected in the destination country, thereby extending the OECD/G20 Inclusive Framework proposals that focus on the reallocation of residual profits. This tax would eliminate the incentive for firms to shift profits between affiliates and for governments to lower tax rates to compete for investment. Moreover, unlike the OECD/G20 Inclusive Framework's GLoBE proposal, governments would not need to agree on a minimum tax rate.

The DBCFT would replace the existing corporate income tax with a new tax on the receipts of corporations less their expenditures, similar to a VAT. It would tax all cash inflows (from sales of products, services, and real assets, borrowing, and the receipt of interest, but excluding injections of equity) with a deduction for all cash outflows (purchase of materials, products, labor, and other services, real assets, lending, repayment of borrowing, and interest payments, but excluding equity repurchases and dividends).[25] However, to eliminate the incentive for tax competition it would include a "border adjustment": receipts from exports would not be included, but imports consumed locally would be taxed at the domestic rate. Like the VAT, it is a domestic tax based on the location of sales to consumers (the "destination" of the product) rather than on the location of profits, production, or corporate residence.[26] As such, the DBCFT removes incentives for tax competition and tax avoidance by MNCs.[27] But by exempting the labor element of value added from taxation, it provides an incentive for job creation.

Based on the prevailing tax rates, global adoption of a DBCFT system could have significant redistributive effects on revenues across countries.[28] Countries with trade deficits, limited revenues from natural resources, and low per capita income would be more likely to benefit under such a tax, at least initially.[29]

Importantly, countries that lose from a switch to a destination-based system can raise tax rates to compensate because pressures from profit shifting and tax competition are removed.[30]

Skepticism about the feasibility of a destination-based system is valid. MNCs that currently engage in aggressive tax planning would lose and are likely to resist such a system, as occurred recently in the United States.[31] Unilateral adoption would in the immediate term increase the prices of imported items and lower export prices, which should result in an exchange rate adjustment that would fully offset such price effects. But the need for such a large and immediate appreciation presents an important risk of major economic distortions. Border adjustment for direct taxes may also raise questions about WTO consistency, compared with that for indirect taxes such as the VAT where it is explicitly allowed. However, because the DBCFT is economically equivalent to a VAT plus a wage subsidy, both of which are WTO-compatible, technical adjustments in the form of the tax may be made to achieve compliance.[32] Furthermore, a globally coordinated switch to a DBCFT may be more generally acceptable. Another concern is that administering and enforcing such a tax could be complex, but perhaps not much more so than current rules or those experienced under a VAT.[33]

Notwithstanding the OECD/G20 Inclusive Framework's ongoing negotiations, governments in developing countries can take immediate steps to address issues related to profit shifting and tax competition, primarily by adopting stronger antiabuse rules—mechanical, simple, and transparent. Countries can greatly benefit from the application of mechanical rules for transfer pricing in some GVCs where application of the arm's-length principle is straightforward.[34] Countries also need to revise their tax treaty networks to renegotiate or cancel cost-ineffective tax treaties.[35] Depending on how the ongoing efforts unfold to reach a consensus on rule design by 2020, developing countries should also consider adopting the antiabuse GLoBE proposals, supplemented with a diverted profit rule.

Observers are optimistic that the final solution proposed by the OECD/G20 Inclusive Framework will move toward granting greater taxing rights to jurisdictions where users and markets are located and incorporating stronger antiabuse rules. Such proposals are a step in the right direction—but only when low-capacity countries can implement them easily and allocation rules do not compromise the taxing ability of producer and resource countries.

Regulation

In the conventional producer-centric view, regulatory cooperation is a complement to liberalization. In the alternative consumer-centric view, regulatory cooperation is a precondition for liberalization. Both are important in facilitating the operation of GVCs.[36]

Producer-centric cooperation to address regulatory heterogeneity

Regulatory heterogeneity can impede the compatibility of parts that is vital for GVCs. It arises when requirements differ across countries because of differences either in institutions (leading typically to "horizontal" differentiation, such as in electrical plugs and legal services) or in social preferences (leading to "vertical" differentiation, such as in the stringency of food, paint, or financial regulations). The traditional case for regulatory cooperation arises from the fact that regulatory heterogeneity segments international markets in a way that prevents the exploitation of economies of scale in production. For example, because each East African country has its own regulatory requirements for service professionals, compliance costs cannot be spread out over the provision of professional services in other East African countries but must be incurred separately in each market. According to one estimate, the European Union (EU) stock of FDI could increase by 20–35 percent if regulatory heterogeneity were reduced in response to a common services regulation directive.[37]

Such regulatory heterogeneity cannot be addressed by imposing traditional trade disciplines because the problem is not due to protectionist or explicit anticompetitive intent. But there is an economic cost of such heterogeneity because each country is independently choosing its regulations without considering their negative impacts on foreign producers and thus on competition. There are, then, potential gains from international cooperation in which each country forgoes the benefits of maintaining different nationally optimal regulations for the benefits of integrating markets through some form of regulatory convergence.

In some cases, regulatory cooperation could be far-reaching and lead to harmonization or mutual recognition, which would eliminate the costs of regulatory heterogeneity for firms and liberate them from the uncertainty of discretionary licensing.[38] In other cases, regulatory cooperation could be valuable even if it only involves greater mutual understanding of how regulatory discretion in each jurisdiction will be exercised because that, too, would lend predictability to commitments.

Consumer-centric regulatory cooperation to address international externalities

The alternative case for regulatory cooperation arises because regulators in the jurisdiction of the exporter do not consider the consequences of market failure for consumers in the jurisdiction of the importer. For example, weak data protection in a country that exports data processing services can compromise the privacy of citizens of other countries. An increase in the concentration and anticompetitive practices of producers in one market can lead to exploitation of downstream consumers in another market. And poor regulation of medicines, hospitals, and universities in one country can hurt the health and human capital of foreign citizens who receive or visit for treatment or education.

Conventional trade negotiations and rulemaking are primarily concerned with reciprocal liberalization of import policy (figure 10.1). Accordingly, rules and commitments focus on tying the hands of importers: tariffs are bound; quotas are prohibited or restrained; discrimination against imports and trading partners is prohibited or restrained; and further disciplines may be imposed on importing country product standards—such as the requirement that rules be "necessary" to achieving a legitimate objective. For the most part, trade rules do not concern themselves with exporter disciplines or commitments. The rare examples for goods include prohibitions or restraints on export subsidies, quotas, and agricultural assistance.

This asymmetric structure of trade rules in which rules and commitments are directed entirely toward importing countries and none (or very few) toward exporting countries is not conducive to consumer-centric regulatory cooperation. The result is importing countries' unwillingness to give up protection or regulatory discretion, or both. The solution may be mutually binding commitments by exporting and importing countries.[39] The exporting countries would make regulatory commitments to looking after the interests of consumers in importing countries, and in return the importing countries would make commitments to allowing access to their markets (represented by the diagonal arrow in figure 10.1).

Data flows

The ability to move data freely across borders underpins a growing range of economic activity and

Figure 10.1 Regulatory commitments by exporters can be exchanged for import liberalization commitments

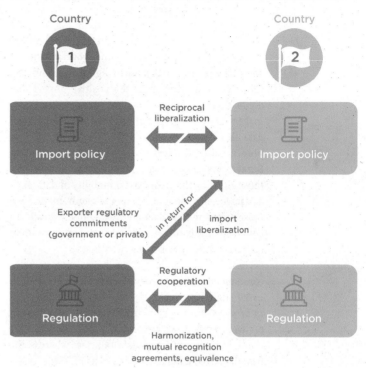

Source: WDR 2020 team.

international trade. The McKinsey Global Institute has estimated that cross-border data flows were 45 times larger in 2015 than in 2014, and about 12 percent of the international trade in goods was through global e-commerce platforms such as Alibaba and Amazon.[40] The U.S. International Trade Commission estimates that in 2014 global digital trade, including data processing and other data-based services, led to a more than 3.4 percent increase in U.S. GDP by increasing productivity and lowering the costs of trade.[41] Recent empirical research finds that restrictions on data flows have significant negative consequences on the productivity of local companies using digital technologies and, in particular, on trade in services. These estimates underscore the importance of cross-border data flows for diffusing knowledge and technology and for enabling the fragmentation of production of goods and services across countries.

But international data flows also raise concerns. The provision online of search, communication, health, education, retail, and financial services relies on, or could lead to, the collection of personal data. Because of the global nature of the Internet, such data can be quickly and easily transferred to third parties in other jurisdictions. This transfer can undermine domestic privacy goals when the personal data of citizens flow to jurisdictions that do not offer comparable levels of privacy protection, prompting domestic regulators to limit the free flow of data across borders.

These concerns are prompting governments to apply new regulatory policies to digital trade and data flows, severely dampening the positive impact that digital trade has on the economy.[42] Meanwhile, policy makers are paying special attention to cross-border data flows, and so restrictions on data flows have been trending upward in recent years (figure 10.2). Burdensome data policies can be split into two types: those affecting the cross-border mobility of data, such as data localization or local storage requirements, and those affecting how data are treated domestically. In both cases, the pattern emerging from a wide swath of countries is rising policy restrictiveness.

Restrictions on data flows have large negative consequences on the productivity of local companies using digital technologies and especially on trade in services. Studies show that countries would gain on average about 4.5 percent in productivity if they removed their restrictive data policies, whereas the benefits of reducing data restrictions on trade in services would on average be about 5 percent.[43]

Figure 10.2 Countries' restrictions on data flows increased from 2006 to 2016

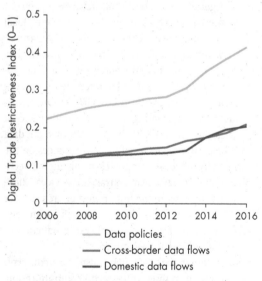

Data policies

Cross-border data flows

Domestic data flows

Source: Ferracane, Lee-Makiyama, and van der Marel 2018.

Note: This figure is based on the ECIPE Digital Trade Restrictiveness Index (DTRI), which ranges from 0 (completely open) to 1 (virtually restricted), with higher levels indicating increasing data restrictiveness. The index covers 64 countries representing more than 95 percent of the value-added content of gross exports.

In May 2018, the European Union implemented the world's most comprehensive data protection regime, the General Data Protection Regulation (GDPR), which replaced its 1995 Data Protection Directive. Under the GDPR, personal data are allowed out of the European Union only under strict conditions. One option is for the non-EU country to adopt a privacy regime whose level of protection is "essentially equivalent" to that guaranteed within the European Union.[44] In other options, firms can accept Binding Corporate Rules (BCRs) or use Standard Contractual Clauses (SCCs), which are mechanisms to authorize companywide or transaction-specific data transfers, respectively.

These new regulations are likely to especially affect services GVCs that depend on data flows. Such data flows drive the most dynamic exports of developing countries—digitally delivered data processing and data-related business services. These services, ranging from financial accounting and tax returns to health transcriptions and diagnostics, contributed to the more than $50 billion in developing country exports to the European Union in 2015—one-fifth of them from Africa.

Here, developing countries face a dilemma: either they must adopt EU-like national privacy regulations or their firms must incur the firm-specific costs of using BCRs or the transaction-specific costs of using SCCs. The GDPR offers a balance between privacy and the economic and trade opportunities from data flows that may not be optimal for developing countries.[45] A GDPR-based national privacy law would impose the same high standard on all firms, even when they sell at home, leading to higher economywide costs of doing business. The adoption of tough standards is likely to reduce the scope to use personal data to improve access to domestic services, such as by opening new credit bureaus, and to reduce the competitiveness of digital exports in third markets such as the United States that do not require GDPR-like privacy standards. Overall, then, BCRs and SCCs have proved costly and time-consuming. A survey in India of the impact of the earlier, less-stringent EU Data Protection Directive revealed that the process to ensure that firms complied took over six months, and 90 percent of the respondents used transaction-specific contracts that involved on average a complex process lasting more than three months.[46] As many as two-thirds of the surveyed services exporters claimed a significant loss of business opportunities because of the requirements.

Because privacy regulations affect the international data transfers on which the digital trade depends, developing countries could in principle challenge at the WTO the consistency of the GDPR with EU trade commitments. But WTO litigation is unlikely to address the underlying challenge raised by the GDPR: how to preserve digital trade opportunities while maintaining nationally desired privacy standards. Even so, WTO litigation could induce the European Union to be more flexible in its application of the GDPR and offer other countries opportunities to negotiate arrangements like the one with the United States.

The EU–U.S. Privacy Shield offers a way of resolving the conflict between regulatory heterogeneity and international data flows (a subject discussed in more detail shortly). Whereas traditional trade agreements are geared toward an exchange of market access commitments, the Privacy Shield is an innovative bargain: the destination country for the data promises to protect the privacy of foreign citizens consistent with their own national standards. In return, the source country commits to not restricting the flow of data. The rules on digital trade in the Comprehensive and Progressive Agreement for Trans-Pacific Partnership (CPTPP) reflect a similar bargain in a multicountry context.[47] In conjunction with progress toward developing common privacy standards in OECD countries and the Asia–Pacific Economic Cooperation (APEC) forum, such cross-border commitments can help create a framework for global privacy protection that also supports digital trade.

The approaches described here, however, risk excluding some developing countries that may not be able to make credible regulatory commitments in the near term, leading to a pattern of trade based on existing mutual trust rather than comparative advantage. Fortunately, the existing multilateral rules, notably provisions on mutual recognition agreements in the WTO's General Agreement on Trade in Services (GATS), can help protect the interests of excluded countries. Some developing countries are participating in the CPTPP, in which the provisions on data flows are matched by provisions on protecting privacy and preventing fraud. Developing countries also should take advantage of the U.S. Clarifying Lawful Overseas Use of Data (CLOUD) Act, which has created the basis for new agreements to supplement older and slower mutual legal assistance treaties.

Table 10.1 is an overview of the different approaches to cross-border data flows of some of the major privacy arrangements in place. Each privacy mechanism relies on some convergence toward common privacy principles (whether in the European Union or among a set of countries).

In 2016 the United States and the European Union concluded the Privacy Shield—an arrangement that the EU Commission has deemed "adequate" under the EU Data Protection Directive—thereby enabling the transfer of personal information from the European Union to U.S. participating businesses.[48] Under the Privacy Shield, U.S. companies self-certify individually or through an industry body to the U.S. Department of Commerce that they will protect personal data consistent with the Privacy Shield, which largely reflects the main elements of the EU Data Protection Directive.[49] U.S. businesses are required to publish their privacy policies, and the Privacy Shield gives the U.S. Federal Trade Commission jurisdiction over such businesses if they breach their own policies. In addition, the United States provides various means of redress for people whose personal data has been compromised, including a direct complaint to the business or a complaint to the U.S. Department of Commerce.

Such an agreement with the European Union gives participating U.S. firms two big advantages over the existing options. First, unlike in the case of BCRs and SCCs, the firms are not required to establish a costly presence in the European Union because domestic regulators assess conformity with EU standards at home. Second, unlike in the case of a national adequacy determination by the European Union, firms are not obliged to adopt more stringent and costlier standards for data involving transactions at home or with countries less demanding than the European Union.

The CPTPP provision on data flows requires that "each Party shall allow the cross-border transfer of information by electronic means, including personal information, when this activity is for the conduct of the business of a covered person." It also prohibits data localization, stating that "no Party shall require a covered person to use or locate computing facilities in that Party's territory as a condition for conducting business in that territory." At the same time, the CPTPP breaks new ground by obligating data-destination countries to prevent fraud and deception and protect personal information. In particular, "each Party shall adopt or maintain a legal framework that provides for the protection of the personal information of the users of electronic commerce." Moreover, "each Party shall endeavor to adopt non-discriminatory practices in protecting users of electronic commerce from personal information protection violations occurring within its jurisdiction."

Such reciprocal obligations on data source and destination countries are a perfect example of the type of

Table 10.1 Regulation of international transfers of personal information, by privacy regime

Regime attribute	EU Data Protection Directive and EU GDPR	EU–U.S. Privacy Shield	CPTPP and USMCA	APEC CBPR	OECD privacy principles
Privacy principles	Determined by EU	Determined by EU, but recognizes that U.S. promise of privacy protection for EU citizens is equivalent to that of EU	Determined by each party, taking into account "principles and guidelines of relevant international bodies"	Common APEC privacy principles based on OECD privacy floor, which domestic privacy regimes can go beyond	Common OECD privacy principles
Scope	Applies to all firms collecting data on EU citizens no matter where the firms are located	Applies to U.S. firms participating in the Privacy Shield and collecting data on EU citizens	Requires each party to "endeavor to adopt non-discriminatory practices in protecting users of electronic commerce from personal information protection violations occurring within its jurisdiction"	Applies to APEC CBPR–compliant[a] organizations collecting personal information from APEC economies	Applies to data controllers—entities that decide about the content and use of personal data, without regard for location of data
Enforcement	In case of a national adequacy finding, the data destination country enforces In case of BCRs and SCCs, the data source EU country enforces against local entity	United States (data-destination country) enforces—that is, EU recognizes U.S. enforcement procedures	Unspecified—depends on national privacy law	Data source country enforces through APEC Accountability Agent[b] and Privacy Enforcement Authority (PEA),[c] with cross-border enforcement cooperation facilitated by APEC Cross-Border Privacy Rules[d]	Data source country enforces against data controller

Source: Mattoo and Meltzer 2018.

Note: APEC = Asia–Pacific Economic Cooperation; BCRs = Binding Corporate Rules; CBPR = Cross-Border Privacy Rules; CPTPP = Comprehensive and Progressive Agreement for Trans-Pacific Partnership; EU = European Union; GDPR = General Data Protection Regulation; OECD = Organisation for Economic Co-operation and Development; SCCs = Standard Contractual Clauses; USMCA = United States–Mexico–Canada Agreement.

a. An entity is CBPR-compliant when its self-assessment of compliance with its own data privacy policies compared with those of the APEC Privacy Framework has been reviewed by an APEC-recognized Accountability Agent.
b. An APEC Accountability Agent has met the APEC recognition criteria to the satisfaction of the APEC economies.
c. A Privacy Enforcement Authority is any public body responsible for enforcing privacy law that can conduct investigations or pursue enforcement proceedings.
d. Endorsed by APEC ministers in 2009, a Cross-border Privacy Enforcement Arrangement (CPEA) is a voluntary framework that aims to facilitate cooperation among PEAs in enforcing the CBPR, such as parallel or joint investigations or enforcement actions. Information sharing and cooperation are also encouraged with privacy enforcement authorities outside of APEC.

regulatory cooperation needed to reassure data-source countries that their commitments to openness will not place their consumers at the mercy of indifferent foreign regulators.

Countries can be expected to self-select into these arrangements, as members of APEC, OECD, the European Union, and the United States are already doing, and gradually widen and deepen them. The African Union's Convention on Cyber Security and Personal Data Protection, adopted in 2014, has been ratified into domestic law by five members to date and signed by nine others.[50] In the transitional phase, multilateral rules can fulfil two important roles. GATS Article III on transparency and Article VII on recognition agreements can help ensure that the emerging arrangements between sets of countries are fully transparent. More important, GATS Article VII can help ensure that any such arrangements do not discriminate against, and are open to participation by, third countries.

Competition policy

Anticompetitive practices in international markets can affect the distribution of gains from participating in GVCs. Because GVCs span many markets, action against anticompetitive practices must take into account the behavior that reduces the availability or raises the prices of the end product (to the detriment

Figure 10.3 Cartel episodes and significant overcharges have been observed across all regions

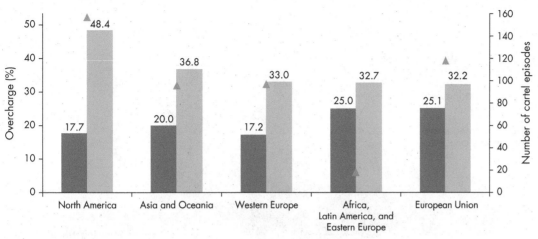

Sources: World Bank and OECD (2017), with elaboration on data (485 decisions) from Connor (2014).

of buyers) as well as of intermediates (to the detriment of rivals). An examination of 1,530 cartel cases involving overcharges across countries reveals that the mean average overcharge is at least 49 percent, and 80 percent where cartels are strongest.[51] The largest overcharges have been observed in North America (figure 10.3). The price-raising effect of such behavior may foreclose the ability of producers to participate in a value chain or limit their profits and thus their opportunities for expansion.[52]

The effects of these practices can fall outside the jurisdiction of national competition authorities where the firms are based. And the firms can be outside the jurisdictions of the authorities where the effects are felt. Overall, then, one set of authorities is not mandated to address the effects, and the other set—even if it could in principle enforce the law under the effects doctrine[53]—is, in practice, not able to do so without collaboration among jurisdictions. Meaningful international cooperation on the enforcement of competition policy would reassure countries facing jurisdictional constraints or limited enforcement capacity that the gains from GVC participation will not be appropriated by firms behaving anticompetitively.[54]

The negative spillovers of anticompetitive practices

Anticompetitive behavior by companies at one stage of production, whether abuse of a dominant position or restrictive business practices, can reduce the

benefits accruing to participants at another stage of production. The cross-border nature of GVCs means that restrictive practices often also have a cross-border dimension. For example, in 2009 the South African Competition Commission detected a cartel among four large cement producers involving market allocation and price-fixing in South African provinces as well as in Botswana and Namibia. Since the cartel was broken up, prices and margins for downstream firms in the region have declined by 7.5–9.7 percent.[55] In 2015 Colombia's Superintendence of Industry and Commerce fined 12 sugar mills, 14 individuals, two companies, and three business associations a total of $91 million for agreeing to prevent sugar imports from Bolivia, Costa Rica, El Salvador, and Guatemala and for allocating clients.[56] Food processing associations in Colombia had reported sugar overcharges of 45 percent[57] affecting food value chains and confectionary exports that account for 13 percent of overall food exports.[58]

In 2016 the European Commission prosecuted a cartel case against major European truck producers that had colluded on pricing and the timing to introduce new emissions technologies—and had agreed to pass on the cost of such systems to buyers of trucks.[59] Intermediate input suppliers may also collude to raise prices for parts needed by lead firms. Automotive parts makers in Europe were first investigated in 2010–12, and eventually more than a dozen specific cartels for a range of car parts were identified by the authorities. The European Union alone imposed more than

Figure 10.4 The European Commission has imposed large fines on car parts cartels since 2013

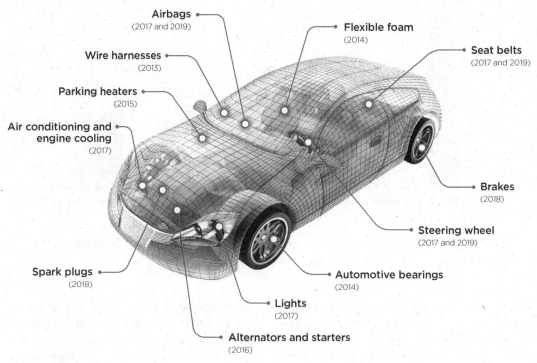

Airbags
(2017 and 2019)

Flexible foam
(2014)

Wire harnesses
(2013)

Seat belts
(2017 and 2019)

Parking heaters
(2015)

Air conditioning and
engine cooling
(2017)

Brakes
(2018)

Steering wheel
(2017 and 2019)

Spark plugs
(2018)

Automotive bearings
(2014)

Lights
(2017)

Alternators and starters
(2016)

Source: European Commission 2019.

€2 billion in fines in 15 separate rulings pertaining to various car parts producers (figure 10.4).

Anticompetitive practices have also been identified in services sectors central to global production networks, such as finance and transport, as well as in new digital services in search, advertising, communication, and distribution. For example, fines of $1 billion or more were levied by the United Kingdom's Financial Conduct Authority, the United States' Commodity Futures Trading Commission, and Swiss regulators on the world's biggest banks—Barclays, JPMorgan Chase, Royal Bank of Scotland, Citigroup, and Creditbank—for manipulating foreign exchange markets. The rigging apparently took place through information sharing and coordinated trading.

Various cartels involving as many as 16 freight forwarders have been discovered in key destination markets for GVCs. Between 2002 and 2007, freight forwarding companies were investigated in the United States for price-fixing, with 16 companies pleading guilty by 2011. The total fines levied by the U.S. Department of Justice amounted to $100 million.[60] In 2009 Japan issued a cease and desist order to 12 of the same freight forwarding companies for similar conduct during the same period, with a joint fine of ¥9 billion,[61]

and in 2012 the European Union uncovered four cartels in the international air freight forwarding market (between six and nine of the same companies were in each cartel).[62] The companies were charged with coordinating conduct such as currency adjustment and peak season surcharges.

Anticompetitive behavior is also commonly found among services related to port transport, such as handling and towage services. In 2019 the Guyana Competition and Consumer Affairs Commission (CCAC) fined five terminal operators almost $4 million each for colluding to fix prices for the haulage of containers—an arrangement facilitated by the national shipping association.[63] And in 2017 the German and Dutch competition agencies collaborated in investigating a cartel in harbor and towage services dating back to 2000/2001. Four companies were fined a total of €13 million for allocating orders between them in accordance with turnover targets.[64]

In 2010 the European Commission fined 11 air cargo carriers nearly €1 billion for operating a worldwide cartel that affected cargo services within the European Economic Area (EEA).[65] The carriers coordinated their action on surcharges for fuel and security without discounts over a six-year period. The European

Commission's fines on the air cargo carriers were reduced by 50 percent in relation to sales between the EEA and third countries to take into account the fact that the harm of the cartel fell outside of the EEA's jurisdiction. International maritime transport has also regularly been a target of enforcement: in 2018 the European Union levied $458 million in fines on four maritime car carriers for customer allocation and price-fixing for deep-sea transport of vehicles.[66]

Digital companies are also attracting attention from national competition authorities. Large multi-sided markets created through the inherent network effects of individual platforms are vulnerable to monopolistic behavior, and platform firms can exploit user data to stifle competition. In early 2019, the United States launched a Technology Task Force to monitor competition in U.S. technology markets, particularly those in which platforms compete.[67] Australia, the European Union, Germany, and the United Kingdom have also initiated multistakeholder inquiries into competition in digital markets. Meanwhile, competition authorities continue to police specific instances of anticompetitive behavior. For example, the European Commission is pursuing a review of smartphone chargers that could have implications for Apple because the iPhone's charger departs from the micro-USB connectors used by the rest of the industry through voluntary agreement.[68] Abuse of dominance was a recurring theme in three EU investigations into Google between 2017 and 2019, resulting in fines totaling $9.3 billion (EU regulations permit fines of up to 10 percent of a company's annual global turnover). Brazil (2013), the Russian Federation (2015), and India (2018), among other countries, have also launched investigations into Google for abuse of dominance in web search advertising and bundling of search results as the default on Android mobile devices.

The ability of platform companies to use data collected through their platforms to stifle competition is also a concern. Brazil's 2013 investigation of Google also examined whether the company was scraping (extracting) relevant competitive content (such as product reviews) held by rival search websites in order to strengthen Google's own search services. In 2018 the European Union opened a preliminary investigation into how Amazon uses data on third-party vendors operating on its platform because of concerns that the data allow Amazon to identify product trends early and promote its own brands.[69]

Mergers and acquisitions create similar concerns about their effects on market competition. In the United States, Amazon's acquisition of the supermarket chain Whole Foods in 2017 raised concerns about the use of consumer data.[70] In 2019 Mexico's Federal Economic Competition Commission (COFECE) blocked a merger between Walmart and Cornershop, a Mexican platform that delivers groceries from online retailers such as Costco, Chedraui, and Walmart.[71] According to COFECE's decision, the merger could unduly displace competitors in the provision of logistical services, and the market power of the merged economic entity could inhibit the development of new platforms.

It is not known how much cartels affect GVCs and cost consumers in developing countries, but the spillover effects of foreign cartels clearly can be significant.

The empowered: Not very concerned

In 2018 over 130 jurisdictions had a competition law in place, up from fewer than 50 in the early 1990s.[72] The growth in the number of competition agencies has been associated with an increase in the number of cartels prosecuted each year. Between 1989 and 2016, 953 cartel investigations led to fines totaling $112 billion. While large, the number is much less than total overcharges to buyers, which are estimated to exceed $1 trillion.[73]

A central feature of competition law, however, is that it is directed at the effects of anticompetitive practices on *national* consumers and markets. Addressing the effects of behavior by national firms on a foreign market is not part of the mandate of national competition agencies. For example, Section 3 of South Africa's Competition Act states that it "applies to all economic activity, within, or having an effect within, the Republic." It does allow foreign agencies to investigate anticompetitive behavior that has an impact both on South Africa and the region and share information, but only if the companies concerned agree to this. For the most part, however, countries must rely on self-defense to combat anticompetitive behavior with effects on their markets, whether it involves locally established firms or companies headquartered in foreign countries or MNCs.

The concerned: Not fully empowered

Competition laws generally permit action against anticompetitive practices that have effects on the domestic market, but developing countries may not have adequate capacity or jurisdiction to act. The effectiveness of this "effects doctrine" depends on the capacity of authorities to identify, investigate, and if necessary fine foreign firms for anticompetitive behavior. Small or low-income countries may not be able to do so. Competition law enforcement capacities vary widely across developing countries. Whereas in Latin America, agencies in Brazil, Chile, Colombia, Mexico, and Peru apply sophisticated investigative tools to detect several major cartel agreements each year, many of their regional peers have fined only a few firms for such conduct in over a decade. Cartel enforcement in Africa and Asia is quite limited with very few exceptions. In 2017–18, only the Arab Republic of Egypt and South Africa imposed significant cartel fines on the African continent.[74] In one case, foreign exchange firms without a local presence were excluded from prosecution in South African courts for colluding on fixing exchange rates.[75] Similarly, differences in capacity to act imply that many developing countries are less able than more advanced countries to defend the interests of their consumers from anticompetitive behavior.

Few, if any, complementary investigations have been pursued of South African firms that have engaged in anticompetitive behavior in other countries in southern Africa, nor have any claims been made for damages, even though in many of these cases the firms operate in neighboring countries.[76] Zambia is a notable exception. Its competition authority has jurisdiction over Zambian markets and can investigate and sanction foreign companies that have Zambian operations. In 2013 it prosecuted a fertilizer cartel that was uncovered in South Africa and fined the participants $20 million.[77] For companies domiciled in foreign countries, it collaborates with other national and regional authorities, such as the Common Market for Eastern and Southern Africa (COMESA) Competition Commission, to sanction those companies in the event their anticompetitive practices have an effect on the Zambian market.

The limited scope of existing multilateral and plurilateral cooperation

In 2003 efforts to launch negotiations on a multilateral agreement on competition policy in the WTO failed to attain the needed consensus. The WTO services agreement does contain a provision on anticompetitive practices (GATS Article IX), but it provides only for an exchange of information and consultation. Since then, the International Competition Network, in conjunction with deliberations in OECD and the United Nations Conference on Trade and Development (UNCTAD), has established a basis for international cooperation between agencies. This effort has been complemented with bilateral agreements between agencies to cooperate in different areas. Moreover, preferential trade agreements (PTAs) are increasingly including chapters on competition policy. In free trade agreements, these generally establish a basic framework of principles such as transparency, due process, assistance (for example, exchange of nonconfidential information), and nondiscrimination. Moreover, technical competition commitments are directed at antitrust enforcement and merger control, even though in some PTAs they are not binding and cannot be challenged through the dispute settlement provisions of PTAs. Competition commitments in PTAs have helped to promote regional market integration. In common markets, regional secretariats may investigate cases. An example is the COMESA Competition Commission, which has the mandate to investigate cases that affect two or more COMESA members, and it has vetted merger cases. But besides antitrust, PTAs have included a number of sector-specific commitments to eliminate domestic rules that facilitate anticompetitive practices. These provisions typically target domestic rules that reinforce dominance or discrimination in favor of domestic firms, such as in the case of agribusiness and investment chapters.[78]

Cooperation can increase the effectiveness of enforcement through sharing information and enhancing the joint capacity to investigate and act. The car parts cartel cases described earlier involved cooperation by 13 jurisdictions, including Brazil, Canada, China, the European Union, India, Japan, the Republic of Korea, South Africa, and the United States, with some 70 companies investigated for price-fixing and bid rigging for more than 100 products.[79] The same is true of large or complex merger cases. The acquisition of Lafarge (France) by Holcim (Swiss), two large cement and concrete producers with global operations, involved seven competition agencies in countries outside the European Economic Area: Brazil, Canada, India, Mauritius, the Philippines, South Africa, and the United States.[80] However, Holcim-Lafarge operates in some 80 countries, and most did not investigate the merger or require remedies even though many may be negatively affected.[81]

International agreements on cross-border regulatory cooperation

Despite the efforts to cooperate in investigations of anticompetitive practices, what has not changed is the explicit nationalist focus of competition laws. Competition law enforcement is premised on self-help. There are no examples of international cooperation among countries to enforce competition rules to protect the interests of foreign consumers, although foreign consumers may be incidental beneficiaries of case-specific collaboration between agencies in two affected jurisdictions.

One corrective step would be to provide foreign jurisdictions with information on the foreign effects of anticompetitive practices under investigation when such effects are identified. Agreeing to explicitly assess such effects could also be an element of a plurilateral agreement to assist developing countries in addressing restrictive business practices that harm their consumers or firms. In one further step, countries would end existing exemptions for export cartels from the scope of their national competition laws.[82] For example, the United States and the European Union, which are home to many services multinationals, could begin by ending exemptions from the scope of their competition law collusive practices whose effects are felt outside their jurisdiction. This could be pursued through a plurilateral agreement—in the WTO, OECD, or UNCTAD—among the largest jurisdictions. In a more ambitious step, countries could change national legislation to require nationals not to harm foreigners abroad by conduct that is illegal at home.[83] Such a change could be accompanied by recognition of the right of foreign consumers to challenge anticompetitive practices by services firms in the national courts of countries whose citizens own or control these firms.

Such a deal could be part of a broader trade agreement obliging importing countries to liberalize and exporting countries to regulate. For example, Zambia could assert that opening its market to South African firms would be conditional on a commitment by South African authorities to investigate anticompetitive behavior in Zambia by firms based in South Africa, or to assist the local authorities in doing so. In principle, it would be in South Africa's interest to provide such reassurance.

Regional cooperation between developing countries

In parallel, deepening regional cooperation enforcement of competition policy offers a mechanism for many developing countries to protect their consumers and firms from foreign anticompetitive behavior. An option is to form a regional competition agency to which national competition agencies could pass jurisdiction in specific circumstances, just as EU member states pass jurisdiction to the European Commission when circumstances warrant. For example, in a cost-saving move Dominica, Grenada, St. Kitts and Nevis, St. Lucia, and St. Vincent and the Grenadines established in May 2000, with World Bank support,

the Eastern Caribbean Telecommunications Authority (ECTEL), the world's first regional telecommunications authority. Although the member countries retained their sovereign power over licensing and regulation, ECTEL provides technical expertise, advice, and support for national regulations. Apart from the economies of scale in establishing a common regulator, there are at least three other advantages of such an arrangement. It promotes the development of harmonized and transparent regulation in the region, allows for greater independence (and thus credibility) in regulatory advice, and enhances bargaining power in negotiations with incumbents and potential entrants. In fact, there is evidence that the creation of ECTEL, along with other reforms, prompted a decline in the price of a daytime call to the United States of between 24 and 42 percent in these countries.

However, creating a supranational competition law regime should be a mechanism for strengthening competition rather than weakening national competition law regimes. The competition legal regime of the West African Economic and Monetary Union (WAEMU) prohibits parallel national competition rules. Thus Côte d'Ivoire and Senegal, among others, are barred from implementing their national competition laws. Meanwhile, WAEMU itself has limited resources to implement competition law enforcement, which is therefore mostly ineffective in the entire region.[84]

Infrastructure

The failure of countries to coordinate the provision of infrastructure impedes GVC investment, expansion, and upgrading. Each country does not fully internalize the benefits to foreign traders of reductions in domestic trade costs, and so gains are larger when governments on both sides of the border invest in expediting trade simultaneously. The WTO Trade Facilitation Agreement addresses the coordination problem and provides low-income countries with financial assistance for the necessary investments.

Coordinated efforts to develop infrastructure can enhance international connectivity (box 10.1). For any country, building a railway or a road has some value, but it also has value to the countries around it because improvements in one part of the transport network reduce shipping times for all countries in the network. If each country alone decided how to invest in infrastructure, spillovers to other countries would not be taken into account. This is even truer for transport infrastructure that crosses one or more borders.

Box 10.1 International cooperation on transport infrastructure

Of the many examples of international cooperation on transport infrastructure, the two most well known are the European Union's Trans-European Transport Network (TEN-T) and China's Belt and Road Initiative (BRI). TEN-T is an effort to develop a Europe-wide network of roads, railway lines, inland waterways, maritime shipping routes, ports, airports, and railroad terminals. The TEN-T will require building new physical infrastructure; adopting innovative digital technologies, alternative fuels, and universal standards; and modernizing and upgrading the existing infrastructure and platforms. Although the scope of the BRI is still taking shape, it is structured around two main components, underpinned by significant infrastructure investments: the Silk Road Economic Belt (the "Belt") and the New Maritime Silk Road (the "Road"). The overland Belt will link China to Central and South Asia and onward to Europe, and the maritime Road will link China to Southeast Asia, the Gulf countries, East Africa and North Africa, and on to Europe.

Transport infrastructure that improves international connectivity can have a significant impact on international trade and GVC integration. Time delays are a barrier to international trade. This is even truer for goods and services produced in GVCs because their production relies on the timely delivery of time-sensitive inputs.[a] The importance of time as a trade barrier is well established in the literature.[b] By one estimate for a sample of 126 countries, a one-day delay in shipping time reduces trade by at least 1 percent.[c] The World Trade Organization (WTO) finds that delays and border costs can be equivalent to a 134 percent ad valorem tariff on a product in high-income countries and a 219 percent tariff equivalent in developing countries.[d]

An analysis of the impacts of transport projects linked to the Belt and Road Initiative reveals the relevance of international cooperation in infrastructure for GVCs (figure B10.1.1). For economies along the Belt and the Road, as well as for non–Belt and Road countries, the effects of infrastructure investment on GDP are larger when the model accounts for cross-border input–output linkages. When a sector experiences a decrease in the price of its imported inputs as shipping times and trade costs fall, it passes on the associated reduction in production costs to downstream industries, propagating the benefits across the world. These input–output linkages lead to a potentially complex reallocation of comparative advantage, production, and trade, thereby increasing welfare.

International cooperation on infrastructure also comes with its challenges. Large cross-border infrastructure

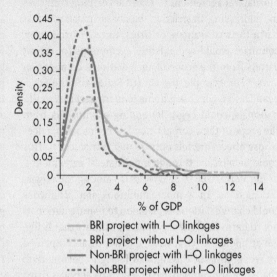

Figure B10.1.1 Impact of China's Belt and Road Initiative transport projects with and without input–output linkages

- BRI project with I–O linkages
- BRI project without I–O linkages
- Non-BRI project with I–O linkages
- Non-BRI project without I–O linkages

Source: de Soyres, Mulabdic, and Ruta 2019.

Note: In this figure, de Soyres, Mulabdic, and Ruta (2019) build on Caliendo and Parro (2015)—a Ricardian model with sectoral linkages, trade in intermediate goods, and sectoral heterogeneity—to allow for changes in trade costs stemming from improvements in transportation infrastructure connecting multiple countries—improvements financed through domestic taxation. The model highlights the impact on trade and GDP of infrastructure investments linked to the Belt and Road Initiative (BRI) through cross-border input–output linkages.

projects have major impacts on public finances and generally have asymmetric effects on the trade and GDP of individual countries. Countries that build and pay for large sections of a project may not gain the most from it. Indeed, analysis suggests that the BRI transport project increases overall welfare for the economies along the Belt and Road by up to 2.8 percent, but three countries (Azerbaijan, Mongolia, and Tajikistan) will experience welfare losses because the infrastructure costs will outweigh gains through trade.[e] This raises the difficult question of equitable financing of common infrastructure projects. Furthermore, the welfare effects of BRI transport projects would increase by a factor of four if participating countries would reduce by half the delays at borders and tariffs, which highlights the importance of complementary policy reforms. Put differently, lack of such reforms severely limits the gains from international cooperation on infrastructure.

a. Baniya, Rocha, and Ruta (2019).
b. Djankov, Freund, and Pham (2010); Hummels and Schaur (2012, 2013).
c. Djankov, Freund, and Pham (2010).
d. Baniya, Rocha, and Ruta (2019).
e. de Soyres, Mulabdic, and Ruta (2019).

For any country, the timing of investments by neighboring countries in their infrastructure is relevant because the value of one's investment depends on the investment decisions of others. The ultimate impact of a country's investments also depends on the policy choices of other countries, such as the standards they use when building infrastructure or the procedures that countries use to clear goods at the border.

But common transport infrastructure also creates challenges. One is that it has significant implications for public finances and may have asymmetric effects on the trade and GDP of individual countries. This asymmetry raises the possibility that the countries that build—and bear the cost of—large sections of the project may not be the ones that will gain the most from it.[85] Another challenge is the need to ensure mutual compatibility in standards. An example of how slight differences in infrastructure standards can disrupt trade is the rail gauge—that is, the distance between the two rails that form a railway track. Trains cannot easily cross borders if the rail gauge standards differ across countries. Russia used broad-gauge track (1,520 millimeters, or roughly 5 feet) in the 19th century to protect it from the entry of trains from the west, which ran on standard-gauge track (1,435 millimeters). For Russia, the 85-millimeter (or 3-inch) difference served a strategic military purpose because troops and material could not easily enter the country by rail. But in more tranquil times, the same 85 millimeters have become a high trade barrier, preventing goods from seamlessly crossing borders. Broad-gauge tracks are still used in successor states of the Soviet Union such as the Kyrgyz Republic, Tajikistan, and Uzbekistan, exacerbating the transport challenges that these countries face because they are landlocked. In part because of the extensive delays when changing cargo at borders, only about 5 percent of the goods transported between Asia and Europe move by rail.

Synergies can arise across different types of infrastructure. For example, it is much cheaper to bundle the laying of fiber-optic cable with the building of electric or gas lines, roads, or railways than to create communications, transport, and energy connectivity separately. Such bundling has the further advantage of not prejudging the future importance of different types of international flows. It also does not presume the evolution of comparative advantage in any specific direction: a country is equipped to export goods by road or rail and digital services by cable.

Seamless travel across borders requires cooperation not just on physical infrastructure, but also on soft infrastructure. When people cross borders, there are two sets of checks: one for exit and one for entry. The same is true for goods, but the delays tend to be even longer than those for people because of complex regulations and taxes that differ across products and countries. However, there is little a government can do to ensure short customs transit times for its firms' exports when they reach their destination.

Cooperation on policy and trade facilitation can together go a long way toward eliminating delays at borders. For example, for many years Guatemala and Honduras required identical paperwork and duplicate processes on both sides of the border, but the red tape was still expensive and time-consuming for businesses. Some truck drivers even brought hammocks to the border so they could wait out the lengthy process in comfort. When both countries moved from a free trade area to a customs union, eliminating the need for complex rules of origin, transit times fell from 10 hours to just 15 minutes and trade increased by 7 percent.[86] Now paperwork is handled by a single online instrument. At the border, a digital reader device instantly scans a Quick Response (QR) code and quickly certifies—online—whether an importer has already paid the VAT on the goods in the destination country.[87] Another example is East Africa, where a combination of procedural simplification, introduction of one-stop border posts, harmonization of vehicle standards, and enforcement of dwell time limits helped to reduce the time to cross at the Malaba border post from two days to six hours for loaded trucks.[88]

Trade facilitation has become an increasingly common feature of trade agreements. It encourages coordination and cooperation among customs authorities, expanding the benefits from improvements on both sides of the border. For example, the Comprehensive and Progressive Agreement for Trans-Pacific Partnership commits members to adopting predictable and transparent procedures and the advance electronic submission of import requirements. A problem, however, is that the reform requires a capacity, both technical and monetary, that many developing countries lack.

The WTO Trade Facilitation Agreement ratified in 2017 allows developing countries to reform at their own pace and with assistance provided by advanced countries. It serves as an example for other areas in which cooperation and capacity are constraints on trade. As of August 2019, more than 63 percent of WTO members implemented the TFA, including 100 percent of developed members, 62.5 percent of developing members, and 26.8 percent of least developed countries.

Notes

1. This section is on direct taxation. GVCs also pose challenges for indirect taxes such as the VAT, although these are more tractable (see Clavey et al. 2019).
2. UNCTAD (2015).
3. Crivelli, de Mooij, and Keen (2016).
4. The Inclusive Framework on BEPS, adopted by over 130 countries, was launched in 2013. For more information, see "International Collaboration to End Tax Avoidance," Organisation for Economic Co-operation and Development, Paris, http://www.oecd.org/tax/beps/.
5. See "Global Forum on Transparency and Exchange of Information for Tax Purposes," Organisation for Economic Co-operation and Development, Paris, https://www.oecd.org/tax/transparency/.
6. See "Multilateral Convention to Implement Tax Treaty Related Measures to Prevent BEPS," Organisation for Economic Co-operation and Development, Paris, https://www.oecd.org/tax/treaties/multilateral -convention-to-implement-tax-treaty-related-measures -to-prevent-beps.htm.
7. Beer and Loeprick (2015) suggest that the most relevant indicator of transfer pricing rules adoption are effective documentation requirements. From 1994 to 2014, the number of countries with "effective" transfer pricing documentation rules increased from four to more than 80 (Cooper et al. 2016). Although that is a substantial increase, it did not result in comprehensive coverage of countries. Similarly, as of 2012 only 34 developing countries had formal transfer pricing rules (de Mooij and Liu 2018).
8. The split profit method is particularly useful in the GVC context where comparable market-based pricing is not available for benchmarking transfer pricing. It is recognized as one of the methods for transfer pricing in the BEPS package, but the OECD guidance did not stipulate how and when practitioners should perform a "value chain analysis" to determine whether the profit split method is the most appropriate method to price a related party transaction. Also, during consultations, transfer pricing experts disagreed over what constitutes a value chain analysis, and ultimately the 2018 guidance did not cover the topic.
9. OECD (2015).
10. IMF (2019).
11. Beer, Klemm, and Matheson (2018).
12. Quak (2018).
13. See Mansour and Rota-Graziosi (2013).
14. See PCT (2015).
15. In July 2019, France introduced a digital services tax (DST) of 3 percent on revenue from digital services earned in France by large companies (some 30 mostly U.S.-based multinational companies). The European Union has considered but not agreed on a DST. The United Kingdom is planning to introduce a 2 percent DST in April 2020, and other European countries such as Austria, the Czech Republic, Italy, Poland, and Spain are signaling that they may introduce such a tax.
16. OECD (2019).
17. IMF (2019).
18. Pemberton and Loeprick (2019).
19. Auerbach et al. (2017).
20. Clavey et al. (2019).
21. For comparison, the U.S. Congress's Joint Committee on Taxation estimated the revenue impact of the Base Erosion and Anti-abuse Tax (BEAT) at $149.6 billion over 2018–27. See U.S. Congress, Joint Committee on Taxation (2017).
22. Pemberton and Loeprick (2019).
23. A third OECD/G20 Inclusive Framework proposal, *significant economic presence*, targets highly digitalized businesses and taxes revenues of such firms even if they lack a physical presence. The allocation of profits would be by formula.
24. Auerbach et al. (2017).
25. Auerbach et al. (2017).
26. Auerbach (2017b).
27. IMF (2019).
28. Hebous, Klemm, and Stausholm (2019).
29. Hebous, Klemm, and Stausholm (2019).
30. Auerbach (2017a).
31. This includes highly leveraged firms because debt-financed investments would no longer be subsidized. See Avi-Yonah and Clausing (2019).
32. Grinberg (2017); Schön (2016).
33. Auerbach and Holtz-Eakin (2016); Auerbach et al. (2017).
34. PCT (2017).
35. Beer and Loeprick (2018).
36. Although the focus here is on mandatory regulation, similar factors arise in the context of private standard setting by lead firms in GVCs (including large retailers), or collaborative efforts by firms and nongovernmental organizations to set standards for products or production processes used by firms that participate in the supply chain, such as the Global Food Safety Initiative (GFSI) and GLOBALG.A.P.
37. de Bruijn, Kox, and Lejour (2008).
38. Trachtman (2014).
39. Mattoo (2018).
40. MGI (2016).
41. USITC (2014).
42. Ferracane, Kren, and van der Marel (2018); Ferracane, Lee-Makiyama, and van der Marel (2018).
43. Ferracane, Kren, and van der Marel (2018); Ferracane, Lee-Makiyama, and van der Marel (2018).
44. Schrems v. Data Prot. Comm'r, I.E.H.C. 310 (2014) at para. 73.
45. Members of the Fortune 500 would need to spend on average $16 million each to avoid falling foul of the European Union's GDPR, according to estimates reported in the *Financial Times* (Khan 2017). Each company is expected to hire on average five dedicated privacy employees (such as data protection officers) and another five employees to deal partially with the new rules. Financial services and technology companies face the biggest compliance costs.
46. NASSCOM-DSCI (2013).
47. The recent United States–Mexico–Canada Agreement (USMCA) follows the example of the CPTPP.
48. European Commission (2017).

49. U.S. Department of Commerce (2016).
50. "List of Countries Which Have Signed, Ratified/Acceded to the African Union Convention on Cyber Security and Personal Data Protection," https://au.int/sites /default/files/treaties/29560-sl-AFRICAN%20UNION%20 CONVENTION%20ON%20CYBER%20SECURITY%20 AND%20PERSONAL%20DATA%20PROTECTION.pdf.
51. Connor (2014).
52. Issues that may be of concern to firms participating in GVCs or to end consumers—such as the governance of GVCs and the allocation of total profits associated with the operation of a GVC along the value chain as a whole— are not matters that can be typically addressed through competition law.
53. Most modern competition law regimes follow the effects test. Under that test, a state has jurisdiction over anticompetitive conduct when that conduct has produced significant and foreseeable effects in the relevant jurisdiction, regardless of whether the acts subject to a complaint took place within the territory of that state. This test allows the reach of the domestic jurisdiction's competition laws to extend outside the state's borders. However, it also excludes jurisdiction over conduct in foreign countries that does not have significant and foreseeable domestic effects, and thus limits the likelihood for clashes in competition law enforcement between different jurisdictions. Jurisdictions such as Canada, France, Japan, and the United Kingdom have adopted an effects-based approach to jurisdiction (Zanettin 2002).
54. Francois and Wooton (2001).
55. Govinda, Khumalo, and Mkhwanazi (2014).
56. OECD (2016).
57. *El Espectador* (2015).
58. "Colombia," Observatory of Economic Complexity, Macro Connections Group, MIT Media Lab, Massachusetts Institute of Technology, Cambridge, MA, https://atlas .media.mit.edu/en/profile/country/col/#Exports.
59. The companies involved were Daimler, DAF, Iveco, MAN, Scania, and Volvo/Renault. See "Antitrust/Cartel Cases: 39824 Trucks," European Commission, http:// ec.europa.eu/competition/elojade/isef/case_details.cfm? proc_code=1_39824.
60. https://www.carteldigest.com/cartel-detail-page.cfm? itemID=44.
61. Japan Fair Trade Commission (2009).
62. European Commission (2012).
63. Guyana Competition and Consumer Affairs Commission (2019).
64. Germany Bundeskartellamt (2017); Netherlands Authority for Consumers and Markets (2017).
65. European Commission (2010).
66. Simpson Thacher (2019).
67. FTC (2019).
68. In 2009, 10 leading mobile phone manufacturers signed a memorandum of understanding (MoU) committing them to using micro-USB connectors for chargers. As an exception, manufacturers could continue to use their own connector if they offered an adapter, which allowed Apple to continue using its own connector. The MoU expired in 2012. See "One Mobile Phone Charger for All Campaign," European Commission, http://ec.europa.eu /growth/sectors/electrical-engineering/red-directive /common-charger_en.
69. Chee (2018).
70. Petro (2017).
71. Solomon (2019).
72. Anderson, Müller, and Sen (2018).
73. Connor (2016).
74. Morgan Lewis (2019).
75. South Africa Competition Tribunal (2019).
76. Roberts, Vilakazi, and Simbanegavi (2017).
77. *Daily Nation* (2013).
78. Licetti, Miralles, and Teh (2019).
79. See Connor (2012) and Linklaters (2018).
80. The merged entity was required to divest some operations in many of the countries concerned—see Holcim and Lafarge (2015). A noteworthy feature of this case was the recognition of the value chain nature of activities. The U.S. Federal Trade Commission and the Canadian Competition Bureau cooperated in order to ensure remedies would not disrupt cross-border supply chains. Thus Holcim was required to divest all its operations in Canada but also to sell several U.S. plants deemed to be critical to the Canadian operation as part of an integrated package to a single buyer. See Competition Bureau (2015).
81. Fox (2015).
82. Behavior that has an effect only on foreign markets cannot be addressed by national competition agencies.
83. Fox (2015); Hoekman and Sabel (2019).
84. Senegal faces an additional contradiction as the Economic Community of West African States (ECOWAS) does foresee the application of national competition law for conduct that does not affect trade among its member states.
85. de Soyres, Mulabdic, and Ruta (2019).
86. Gain and Alfaro de Morán (2019).
87. Gain and Alfaro de Morán (2019).
88. Kunaka, Raballand, and Fitzmaurice (2019).

References

Anderson, Robert D., Anna Caroline Müller, and Nivedita Sen. 2018. "Competition Policy in WTO Accessions: Filling in the Blanks in the International Trading System." In *Trade Multilateralism in the Twenty-First Century: Building the Upper Floors of the Trading System through WTO Accessions*, edited by Alexei Kireyev and Chiedu Osakwe, 299–319. Cambridge, U.K.: Cambridge University Press.

Auerbach, Alan Jeffrey. 2017a. "Demystifying the Destination-Based Cash Flow Tax." NBER Working Paper 23881 (September), National Bureau of Economic Research, Cambridge, MA.

———. 2017b. "Understanding the Destination-Based Approach to Business Taxation." *VOX CEPR Policy Portal*, October 26, Centre for Economic Policy Research, London. https://voxeu.org/article/understanding-destination -based-approach-business-taxation.

Auerbach, Alan Jeffrey, Michael P. Devereux, Michael Keen, and John Vella. 2017. "Destination-Based Cash Flow

Taxation." Working Paper WP 17/01, Centre for Business Taxation, Oxford University, Oxford, U.K.

Auerbach, Alan Jeffrey, and Douglas Holtz-Eakin. 2016. "The Role of Border Adjustments in International Taxation." *Research*, November 30, American Action Forum, Washington, DC. http://www.americanactionforum.org /research/14344/.

Avi-Yonah, Reuven S., and Kimberly Clausing. 2019. "Problems with Destination-Based Corporate Taxes and the Ryan Blueprint." *Columbia Journal of Tax Law* 8 (2): 229–56.

Baniya, Suprabha, Nadia Rocha, and Michele Ruta. 2019. "Trade Effects of the New Silk Road: A Gravity Analysis." Policy Research Working Paper 8694, World Bank, Washington, DC.

Beer, Sebastian, Alexander Klemm, and Thornton Matheson. 2018. "Tax Spillovers from U.S. Corporate Income Tax Reform." IMF Working Paper WP/18/166 (July), International Monetary Fund, Washington, DC.

Beer, Sebastian, and Jan Loeprick. 2015. "Taxing Income in the Oil and Gas Sector: Challenges of International and Domestic Profit Shifting." WU International Taxation Research Paper 2015–18, Vienna University of Economics and Business, Vienna.

———. 2018. "The Cost and Benefits of Tax Treaties with Investment Hubs: Findings from Sub-Saharan Africa." Policy Research Working Paper 8623, World Bank, Washington, DC.

Caliendo, Lorenzo, and Fernando Parro. 2015. "Estimates of the Trade and Welfare Effects of NAFTA." *Review of Economic Studies* 82 (1): 1–44.

Chee, Foo Yun. 2018. "Amazon's Use of Merchant Data under EU Microscope." *Reuters*, September 19. https:// www.reuters.com/article/us-eu-amazon-com-antitrust /amazons-use-of-merchant-data-under-eu-microscope-id USKCN1LZ1UV.

Clavey, Colin, Jonathan Leigh Pemberton, Jan Loeprick, and Marijn Verhoeven. 2019. "International Tax Reform, Digitization, and Developing Economies." Unpublished working paper, World Bank, Washington, DC.

Competition Bureau. 2015. "Holcim/Lafarge Merger: Competition Bureau Accepts the Sale of All of Holcim's Operations in Canada." News release, May 4, Competition Bureau, Government of Canada, Ottawa. http://www .competitionbureau.gc.ca/eic/site/cb-bc.nsf/eng/03919 .html.

Connor, John M. 2012. "Multiple Prosecutions Point to Huge Damages from Auto-Parts Cartels." AAI Working Paper 12-06 (December 11), American Antitrust Institute, Washington, DC.

———. 2014. "Cartel Overcharges." In *The Law and Economics of Class Actions*, edited by James Langenfeld, 249–387. Vol. 26 of *Research in Law and Economics*. Bingley, U.K.: Emerald Publishing.

———. 2016. "The Private International Cartels (PIC) Data Set: Guide and Summary Statistics, 1990–July 2016." Revised 2d ed. (August 9), SSRN eLibrary. http://dx.doi .org/10.2139/ssrn.2821254.

Cooper, Joel, Randall Fox, Jan Loeprick, and Komal Mohindra. 2016. *Transfer Pricing and Developing Economies: A Handbook for Policy Makers and Practitioners*. Directions in Development: Public Sector Governance Series. Washington, DC: World Bank.

Crivelli, Ernesto, Ruud Aloysius de Mooij, and Michael Keen. 2016. "Base Erosion, Profit Shifting, and Developing Countries." *FinanzArchiv: Public Finance Analysis* 72 (3): 268–301.

Daily Nation. 2013. "Omnia, Nyiombo Face Prosecution." June 6. https://www.zambiadailynation.com/2013/06/06 /omnia-nyiombo-face-prosecution/.

de Bruijn, Roland, Henk Kox, and Arjan Lejour. 2008. "Economic Benefits of an Integrated European Market for Services." *Journal of Policy Modeling* 30 (2): 301–19.

de Mooij, Ruud Aloysius, and Li Liu. 2018. "At a Cost: The Real Effects of Transfer Pricing Regulations." IMF Working Paper WP/18/69 (March 23), International Monetary Fund, Washington, DC.

de Soyres, François, Alen Mulabdic, and Michele Ruta. 2019. "Common Transport Infrastructure: A Quantitative Model and Estimates from the Belt and Road Initiative." Policy Research Working Paper 8801, World Bank, Washington, DC.

Djankov, Simeon, Caroline L. Freund, and Cong S. Pham. 2010. "Trading on Time." *Review of Economics and Statistics* 92 (1): 166–73.

El Espectador. 2015. "Supuesto cartel del azúcar se remontaría a 1998." June 2. https://www.elespectador.com /noticias/economia/cartel-del-azucar-se-remontaria-1998 -articulo-564010.

European Commission. 2010. "Antitrust: Commission Fines 11 Air Cargo Carriers €799 Million in Price Fixing Cartel." Press release, November 9. https://europa.eu/rapid /press-release_IP-10-1487_en.htm.

———. 2012. "Antitrust: Commission Imposes €169 Million Fine on Freight Forwarders for Operating Four Price Fixing Cartels." Press release, March 28. https://europa.eu /rapid/press-release_IP-12-314_en.htm.

———. 2017. "First Annual Review of the EU–U.S. Privacy Shield." Fact Sheet (October 18), European Commission, Brussels.

———. 2019. "Antitrust: Commission Fines Car Safety Equipment Suppliers €368 Million in Cartel Settlement." Press release (March 5), European Commission, Brussels. http:// europa.eu/rapid/press-release_IP-19-1512_en.htm.

Ferracane, Martina Francesca, Janez Kren, and Erik van der Marel. 2018. "Do Data Policy Restrictions Impact the Productivity Performance of Firms and Industries?" ECIPE Digital Trade Estimates Working Paper 1, European Center for International Political Economy, Brussels.

Ferracane, Martina Francesca, Hosuk Lee-Makiyama, and Erik van der Marel. 2018. "Digital Trade Restrictiveness Index." European Centre for International Political Economy, Brussels.

Fox, Eleanor M. 2015. "Antitrust without Borders: From Roots to Codes to Networks." E15 Initiative Think Piece (September), International Centre for Trade and Sustainable Development and World Economic Forum, Geneva.

Francois, Joseph Francis, and Ian Wooton. 2001. "Market Structure, Trade Liberalization, and the GATS." CEPR Discussion Paper 2669 (January), Centre for Economic Policy Research, London.

FTC (U.S. Federal Trade Commission). 2019. "FTC's Bureau of Competition Launches Task Force to Monitor Technology Markets." Press release, February 26, Washington, DC. https://www.ftc.gov/news-events/press-releases/2019/02/ftcs-bureau-competition-launches-task-force-monitor-technology.

Gain, Bill, and Mayra Alfaro de Morán. 2019. "Leave Your Hammocks at Home: How a Customs Union between Guatemala and Honduras Cut Trade Times from 10 Hours to 15 Minutes." *Trade Post* (blog), January 30, World Bank, Washington, DC. https://blogs.worldbank.org/trade/leave-your-hammocks-home-how-customs-union-between-guatemala-and-honduras-cut-trade-times-10-hours.

Germany Bundeskartellamt. 2017. "Bundeskartellamt Imposes Fines on Harbour Towage Service Providers." Press release, December 18. https://www.bundeskartellamt.de/SharedDocs/Meldung/EN/Pressemitteilungen/2017/18_12_2017_Hafenschlepper.html.

Govinda, Hariprasad, Junior Khumalo, and Siphamandla Mkhwanazi. 2014. "On Measuring the Economic Impact: Savings to the Consumer Post Cement Cartel Bust." Paper presented at Competition Commission and Tribunal's Eighth Annual Conference on Competition Law, Economics, and Policy, Johannesburg, September 4–5.

Grinberg, Itai. 2017. "A Destination-Based Cash Flow Tax Can Be Structured to Comply with World Trade Organization Rules." *National Tax Journal* 70 (4): 803–18.

Guyana Competition and Consumer Affairs Commission. 2019. "CCAC Rules against Shipping Body in Price-Fixing Complaint." Press release, April 12. https://ccac.gov.gy/ccac-rules-against-shipping-body-in-price-fixing-complaint/.

Hebous, Shafik, Alexander D. Klemm, and Saila Stausholm. 2019. "Revenue Implications of Destination-Based Cash-Flow Taxation." IMF Working Paper WP/19/7 (January 15), International Monetary Fund, Washington, DC.

Hoekman, Bernard M., and Charles Sabel. 2019. "Open Plurilateral Agreements, International Regulatory Cooperation, and the WTO." EUI Working Paper RSCAS 2019/10, Robert Schuman Centre for Advanced Studies, European University Institute, San Domenico di Fiesole, Italy.

Holcim and Lafarge. 2015. "Holcim and Lafarge Obtain Merger Clearances in the United States and Canada Paving the Way to Closing Their Merger." News release, May 4, Lafarge, Paris; Holcim, Zurich. https://www.lafargeholcim.com/sites/lafargeholcim.com/files/atoms/files/05042015-press_finance-lafargeholcim_usa_canada_clearance_merger-uk.pdf.

Hummels, David L., and Georg Schaur. 2012. "Time as a Trade Barrier." NBER Working Paper 17758 (January), National Bureau of Economic Research, Cambridge, MA.

———. 2013. "Time as a Trade Barrier." *American Economic Review* 103 (7): 2935–59.

IMF (International Monetary Fund). 2019. "Corporate Taxation in the Global Economy." Policy Paper 19/007 (March 10), IMF, Washington, DC. https://www.imf.org/en/Publications/Policy-Papers/Issues/2019/03/08/Corporate-Taxation-in-the-Global-Economy-46650.

Japan Fair Trade Commission. 2009. "Cease and Desist Order and Surcharge Payment Order against Air Freight Forwarders." Press release, March 18. https://www.jftc.go.jp/en/pressreleases/yearly-2009/mar/individual-000056.html.

Khan, Mehreen. 2017. "Companies Face High Cost to Meet New EU Data Protection Rules." *Financial Times*, November 19. https://www.ft.com/content/0d47ffe4-ccb6-11e7-b781-794ce08b24dc.

Kunaka, C. G. Raballand, and M. Fitzmaurice. 2019. "How Trucking Services Have Improved and May Contribute to Economic Development." In *Industries without Smokestacks: Industrialization in Africa Reconsidered*, edited by Richard S. Newfarmer, John Page, and Finn Tarp. New York: Oxford University Press. http://fdslive.oup.com/www.oup.com/academic/pdf/openaccess/9780198821885.pdf.

Licetti, M., G. Miralles, and R. Teh. 2019. "Competition-Related Provision in Preferential Trade Agreements." In *Handbook of Deep Integration Agreements*, chap. 8. Washington, DC: World Bank.

Linklaters. 2018. "Pressure Points: Global Cartel Enforcement in 2018." *Insights* (April), Linklaters, London. https://www.linklaters.com/en-us/insights/publications/2018/april/global-cartel-enforcement-in-2018.

Mansour, Mario, and Grégoire Rota-Graziosi. 2013. "Tax Coordination, Tax Competition, and Revenue Mobilization in the West African Economic and Monetary Union." IMF Working Paper WP/13/163 (July), International Monetary Fund, Washington, DC.

Mattoo, Aaditya. 2018. "Services Globalization in an Age of Insecurity: Rethinking Trade Cooperation." Policy Research Working Paper 8579, World Bank, Washington, DC.

Mattoo, Aaditya, and Joshua P. Meltzer. 2018. "International Data Flows and Privacy: The Conflict and Its Resolution." *Journal of International Economic Law* 21 (4): 769–89.

MGI (McKinsey Global Institute). 2016. *Digital Globalization: The New Era of Global Flows*. New York: McKinsey.

Morgan Lewis. 2019. "Global Cartel Enforcement Report, Year-End 2018." Morgan, Lewis, and Bockius, Washington, DC.

NASSCOM-DSCI (National Association of Software and Services Companies–Data Security Council of India). 2013. "NASSCOM Update on EU Data Protection Regime." NASSCOM, New Delhi.

Netherlands Authority for Consumers and Markets. 2017. "Collaboration between Bundeskartellamt and ACM Leads to Settlements in Towage Sector." News, December 18. https://www.acm.nl/en/publications/collaboration-between-bundeskartellamt-and-acm-leads-settlements-towage-sector.

OECD (Organisation for Economic Co-operation and Development). 2015. *Measuring and Monitoring BEPS, Action 11: 2015 Final Report*. Paris: OECD. http://www.oecd.org/ctp/measuring-and-monitoring-beps-action-11-2015-final-report-9789264241343-en.htm.

———. 2016. "Annual Report on Competition Policy Developments in Colombia, 2015." Report DAF/COMP/AR(2016)11 (June 13), Competition Committee, Directorate for Financial and Enterprise Affairs, OECD, Paris.

———. 2019. "Programme of Work to Develop a Consensus Solution to the Tax Challenges Arising from the Digitalisation of the Economy: Inclusive Framework on BEPS."

May 31, OECD/G20 Base Erosion and Profit Shifting Project, OECD, Paris.

PCT (Platform for Collaboration on Tax). 2015. "Options for Low-Income Countries' Effective and Efficient Use of Tax Incentives for Investment: A Report to the G-20 Development Working Group by the IMF, OECD, UN, and World Bank." October 15, International Monetary Fund; Center for Tax Policy and Administration, Organisation for Economic Co-operation and Development; United Nations; and World Bank, Washington, DC.

———. 2017. "Update on Activities of the Platform for Collaboration on Tax." June 27, International Monetary Fund; Center for Tax Policy and Administration, Organisation for Economic Co-operation and Development; United Nations; and World Bank, Washington, DC.

Pemberton, Jonathan Leigh, and Jan Loeprick. 2019. "Low Tax Jurisdictions and Preferential Regimes: Policy Gaps in Developing Economies." Policy Research Working Paper 8778, World Bank, Washington, DC.

Petro, Greg. 2017. "Amazon's Acquisition of Whole Foods Is about Two Things: Data and Product." *Forbes*, August 2. https://www.forbes.com/sites/gregpetro/2017/08/02/amazons-acquisition-of-whole-foods-is-about-two-things-data-and-product/#12062f86a808.

Quak, Evert-jan. 2018. "Tax Coordination and Tax Harmonisation within the Regional Economic Communities in Africa." K4D Helpdesk Report (May 4), Institute of Development Studies, Brighton, U.K.

Roberts, Simon, Thando Selaelo Vilakazi, and Witness Simbanegavi. 2017. "Competition, Regional Integration, and Inclusive Growth in Africa: A Research Agenda." In *Competition Law and Economic Regulation in Southern Africa: Addressing Market Power in Southern Africa*, edited by Jonathan Klaaren, Simon Roberts, and Imraan Valodia, 263–87. Johannesburg: WITS University Press.

Schön, Wolfgang. 2016. "Destination-Based Income Taxation and WTO Law: A Note." In *Practical Problems in European and International Tax Law: Essays in Honour of Manfred Mössner*, edited by Heike Jochum, Peter Essers, Michael Lang, Norbert Winkeljohann, and Bertil Wiman, 429–51. Amsterdam: International Bureau of Fiscal Documentation.

Simpson Thacher. 2019. "2018 Global Cartel Enforcement Report." January, Simpson Thacher, New York. https://www.stblaw.com/docs/default-source/Publications/globalcartelenforcementreport_january2019.pdf.

Solomon, Daina Beth. 2019. "Exclusive: Mexico Blamed Walmart's Size, Access to Rivals' Data in Blocking App Deal." Reuters, June 14. https://www.reuters.com/article/us-walmart-mexico-exclusive/exclusive-mexico-blamed-walmarts-size-access-to-rivals-data-in-blocking-app-deal-idUSKCN1TF2IF.

South Africa Competition Tribunal. 2019. "Order and Reasons: Banks/FOREX Pre-Trial Matter." June 12. https://www.comptrib.co.za/info-library/case-press-releases/order-and-reasons-banks-forex-pre-trial-matter.

Trachtman, Joel P. 2014. "Mutual Recognition of Services Regulation at the WTO." In *WTO Domestic Regulation and Services Trade: Putting Principles into Practice*, edited by Aik Hoe Lim and Bart De Meester, 110–26. New York: Cambridge University Press.

UNCTAD (United Nations Conference on Trade and Development). 2015. *World Investment Report 2015: Reforming International Investment Governance*. Geneva: UNCTAD.

U.S. Congress, Joint Committee on Taxation. 2017. "Estimated Budget Effects of the Conference Agreement for H.R. 1, the 'Tax Cuts and Jobs Act': Fiscal Years 2018–2027." Document JCX-67-17 (December 18), Washington, DC. https://www.jct.gov/publications.html?func=startdown&id=5053.

U.S. Department of Commerce. 2016. "Privacy Shield Framework." Notice, *Federal Register* 81 (148), August 2, International Trade Administration, U.S. Department of Commerce, Washington, DC.

USITC (United States International Trade Commission). 2014. *Digital Trade in the U.S. and Global Economies, Part 2*. Publication 4485, Investigation 332–540 (August). Washington, DC: USITC.

World Bank and OECD (Organisation for Economic Co-operation and Development). 2017. *A Step Ahead: Competition Policy for Shared Prosperity and Inclusive Growth*. Washington, DC: World Bank.

Zanettin, Bruno. 2002. *Cooperation between Antitrust Agencies at the International Level*. Oxford, U.K.: Hart Publishing.

Appendix A
Databases used in this Report

Country-specific and firm-level databases are used in some chapters.

China Customs Statistics
China Customs Statistics cover the merchandise passing through its customs, including goods from abroad entering customs warehouses, bonded areas, or special economic zones and goods leaving these areas for shipment abroad; goods for inward or outward processing or assembling and subsequent reexportation or reimportation; goods on lease for one year or more; goods imported or exported by foreign-invested enterprises; and international aid or donations. Since 2014, duty-free goods have been included in China Customs Statistics. Since 2016, the countertrade of border residents has been included as "other" in Customs Statistics.
http://english.customs.gov.cn/Statistics/Statistics?ColumnId=7

Deep Trade Agreements
This World Bank database on the content of preferential trade agreements (PTAs) covers 189 countries and maps 52 provisions in 279 PTAs notified to the World Trade Organization and signed between 1958 and 2015. It also includes information on the legal enforceability of each provision.
https://datacatalog.worldbank.org/dataset/content-deep-trade-agreements

Developing Countries' Trade and Market Access in the European Union and the United States
Compiled by the World Bank, this database builds on existing national data sources for imports and tariffs covering the period 1997–2017: Eurostat's COMEXT and the European Commission's TARIC data sources for the European Union and the U.S. Census and U.S. International Trade Commission (USITC) data sources for the United States.
https://datacatalog.worldbank.org/dataset/developing-countries%E2%80%99-trade-and-market-access-european
-union-and-united-states-introducing

Doing Business
The World Bank's Doing Business database provides objective measures of business regulations and their enforcement across 190 economies covering the period 2004–18. Economies are ranked on their ease of doing business from 1 to 190.
https://datacatalog.worldbank.org/dataset/doing-business

Economic Census (Mexico)
The Economic Census includes all establishments producing goods, sellers of goods, and service providers to generate Mexico's economic indicators at a high level of geographic, sectoral, and thematic detail. The Economic Census is conducted every five years by Mexico's National Institute of Statistics and Geography (INEGI). Data are for 1993–2013. The data are proprietary, and access requires permission from the issuing agency.
https://en.www.inegi.org.mx/programas/ce/2014

ENAPROCE (Mexico)

The National Survey on Productivity and Competitiveness of Micro, Small and Medium Enterprises (ENAPROCE) 2015 is conducted by Mexico's National Institute of Statistics and Geography (INEGI). The data are proprietary, and access requires permission from the issuing agency.

https://www.inegi.org.mx/programas/enaproce/2015/

Enterprise Surveys (Vietnam)

Since 2001, Vietnam's General Statistics Office (GSO) has conducted an annual census of enterprises operating in Vietnam. It covers all enterprises with more than 10 workers, and firms with fewer than 10 workers are surveyed. The data are proprietary, and access requires permission from the issuing agency.

https://www.gso.gov.vn/Default_en.aspx?tabid=491

Enterprise Surveys (World Bank)

The World Bank's Enterprise Surveys offer an expansive array of economic data on 140,000 firms in 141 countries covering the period 2002–18.

https://www.enterprisesurveys.org/

Eora

The Eora global supply chain database consists of a multiregion input–output (MRIO) table model that provides high-resolution input–output tables with matching environmental and social satellite accounts for 190 countries for the period 1990–2015. Eora26 is a complete global MRIO table, plus environmental satellite accounts, in a harmonized 26-sector classification. Eora is free for academic use at degree-granting academic institutions. All other users must license the data.

https://worldmrio.com/

EU-KLEMS

This database, a project of the European Union (EU), measures economic growth, productivity, employment creation, capital formation, and technological change at the industry level for all EU member states covering the period 1995–2015.

http://www.euklems.net

Exiobase

Exiobase is a global detailed multiregional environmental extended supply-use table (MR-SUT) and input–output table (MR-IOT) covering 44 countries and five rest-of-world regions over the period 1995–2011 (version 3). The data are proprietary, and access requires a license from the issuing agency.

https://www.exiobase.eu/

Exporter Dynamics Database

This World Bank database includes indicators on exporter dynamics and concentration for 70 countries based on exporter-level customs data, most commonly covering the period 2005–12 and in some cases up to 2014.

https://www.worldbank.org/en/research/brief/exporter-dynamics-database

Global Trade Alert

Global Trade Alert provides information on more than 10,000 state interventions since November 2008 that are likely to affect foreign commerce. It includes those affecting trade in goods and services, foreign investment, and labor force migration.

https://www.globaltradealert.org

GSMA Intelligence

GSMA publishes mobile operator data, analysis, and forecasts covering the performance of all 1,400-plus operators and 1,200-plus mobile virtual network operators across 4,400 networks, 65 groups, and 237 countries and territories worldwide. Full unrestricted access to all data sets, tools, and research is available by subscription.

https://www.gsmaintelligence.com

International Federation of Robotics

The International Federation of Robotics provides worldwide market data on robotics surveys, studies, and statistics. Robotics data are based on annual surveys of robot suppliers and currently cover 75 countries (about 90 percent of the industrial robots market). The data are available for purchase.
https://ifr.org/

IPUMS USA

IPUMS USA collects, preserves, and harmonizes U.S. Census microdata and provides access to this data with enhanced documentation. Data include decennial censuses from 1790 to 2010 and American Community Surveys since 2000.
https://usa.ipums.org/usa/

Large and Medium Manufacturing Industry Survey (Ethiopia)

This census of large and medium manufacturing industries is conducted by the Ethiopian Central Statistical Agency and includes establishments with at least 10 employees. It covers the period 1996–2017. The data are proprietary, and access requires permission from the issuing agency.
http://www.csa.gov.et/survey-report/category/17-large-and-medium-manufacturing-industry-survey

Penn World Table

The Penn World Table (PWT) contains information on the relative levels of income, output, input, and productivity worldwide. To date, 10 releases are available, differing in their country and period coverage. The most recent, the PWT 9.1 version, covers 182 countries over the period 1950–2017.
https://www.rug.nl/ggdc/productivity/pwt/

Pew Research Center

The Pew Research Center is a nonpartisan fact tank that informs the public about the issues, attitudes, and trends shaping the world. It conducts public opinion polling, demographic research, media content analysis, and other empirical social science research. The center does not take policy positions. It is a subsidiary of the Pew Charitable Trusts.
https://www.pewresearch.org/

Producer and Consumer Support Estimates

Agricultural policies address a wide range of issues, including providing sufficient food at reasonable prices for consumers, ensuring food safety, and improving environmental quality. The Organisation for Economic Co-operation and Development (OECD) has developed agricultural support indicators that, despite this diversity, express policy measures with numbers in a comparable way across OECD and other countries covering the period 1986–2017.
https://www.oecd.org/countries/ukraine/producerandconsumersupportestimatesdatabase.htm

Regional Trade Agreements

The Regional Trade Agreements (RTAs) database was launched in 2009 as part of the Transparency Mechanism for RTAs of the World Trade Organization (WTO). It was developed and is maintained by the RTA Section of the WTO Trade Policies Review Division. The database is a repository of the legal texts and annexes of all RTAs notified to the WTO, preferential tariff and trade data provided by RTA parties, and other related documents. It currently covers 219 countries/territories over the period 1948–2019.
https://rtais.wto.org/UI/PublicMaintainRTAHome.aspx

Services Trade Restrictions Database

This World Bank database provides comparable information on services trade policy measures for 103 countries, five sectors (telecommunications, finance, transportation, retail, and professional services), and key modes of delivery (modes 1, 3, and 4). The data are based on surveys that were mostly conducted in 2008.
https://datacatalog.worldbank.org/dataset/services-trade-restrictions-database

TiVA

The Trade in Value Added (TiVA) database, compiled by the Organisation for Economic Co-operation and Development (OECD), considers the value added by each country in the production of goods and services that are consumed worldwide. The latest (2018) release covers 64 economies over the period 2005–15 for 36 industries at the International Standard Industrial Classification Revision 4 (ISIC Rev. 4) level.

https://www.oecd.org/sti/ind/measuring-trade-in-value-added.htm

UN Comtrade

UN Comtrade is a repository of official international trade statistics and relevant analytical tables. All data are available through the API portal.

https://comtrade.un.org

UN Trade Statistics

This United Nations database covers international merchandise trade statistics, trade in services, and tourism statistics.

https://unstats.un.org/unsd/tradekb/default.aspx/

UNCTAD-WB Nontariff Barriers

This joint United Nations Conference on Trade and Development–World Bank database includes ad valorem equivalents (AVEs) of nontariff measures (NTMs), defined as the uniform tariffs that have the same trade impacts on the import of a product because of the presence of the NTMs. AVEs are available for 40 importing countries, as well as for the European Union and 200 exporting countries at the cross-sectional level. The AVE estimation is based on data in the World Bank's World Integrated Trade Solution and World Development Indicators databases.

https://datacatalog.worldbank.org/dataset/ad-valorem-equivalent-non-tariff-measures

U.S. Census

The mission of the U.S. Census Bureau is to serve as the United States' leading provider of quality data about its people and economy.

http://census.gov

WDI

World Development Indicators (WDI) is the primary World Bank collection of development indicators, compiled from officially recognized international sources. It presents the most current and most accurate global development data available and includes national, regional, and global estimates for 216 economies over the period 1960–2018.

https://datacatalog.worldbank.org/dataset/world-development-indicators

WIOD

In the 2013 World Input–Output Database (WIOD), the World Input–Output Tables and underlying data cover 40 countries and a model for the rest of the world for the period 1995–2011. Data for 35 sectors are classified according to the International Standard Industrial Classification Revision 3 (ISIC Rev. 3). The tables adhere to the 1993 version of the System of National Accounts. In the 2016 WIOD database, the World Input–Output Tables and underlying data cover 43 countries and a model for the rest of the world for the period 2000–2014. Data for 56 sectors are classified according to the International Standard Industrial Classification Revision 4 (ISIC Rev. 4). The tables adhere to the 2008 version of the System of National Accounts. This is a collaborative project led by researchers at the University of Groningen.

http://www.wiod.org/home

WITS

The World Bank's World Integrated Trade Solution (WITS) database provides access to international merchandise trade, tariff, and nontariff measure data.

https://wits.worldbank.org/about_wits.html

Women, Business, and the Law
Women, Business, and the Law is a World Bank Group project collecting unique data on the laws and regulations that restrict women's economic opportunities. The data offer objective and measurable benchmarks for global progress toward gender equality and cover 187 economies over the period 2009–18.
https://datacatalog.worldbank.org/dataset/women-business-and-law

World Bank Group–LinkedIn Digital Data for Development, Jobs, Skills, and Migration
These data sets cover four categories of metrics: (1) industry employment shifts, (2) talent migration, (3) industry skills needs, and (4) skill penetration. LinkedIn and the World Bank Group plan to refresh the data annually at a minimum. The data sets cover 140 economies and the period 2015–18.
https://datacatalog.worldbank.org/dataset/world-bank-group-linkedin-dashboard-dataset

World Economic Outlook
The World Economic Outlook (WEO) database of the International Monetary Fund (IMF) contains selected macroeconomic data series from the statistical appendix of the *World Economic Outlook* report, which presents the IMF staff's analysis and projections of economic developments at the global level, in major country groups, and in many individual countries. The WEO is released in April and September/October each year, is available for the period 1980 to the present for 194 economies, and also includes forecasts.
https://www.imf.org/external/pubs/ft/weo/2019/01/weodata/index.aspx

World Telecommunication/ICT Indicators
Sponsored by the International Telecommunication Union (ITU), the United Nations specialized agency for information and communication technologies (ICTs), the World Telecommunication/ICT Indicators database contains time series data for the years 1960, 1965, 1970, and annually from 1975 to 2018 for more than 200 economies and 180 telecommunication/ICT statistics.
https://www.itu.int/en/ITU-D/Pages/About.aspx

Worldscope
Worldscope, under the auspices of the University of British Columbia, offers fundamental data on the world's leading public and private companies, including annual and interim/quarterly data, detailed historical financial statement content, per share data, calculated ratios, and pricing and textual information. It covers over 80,000 companies across more than 120 countries and the period 1980 to the present. The data are proprietary, and access requires permission from the issuing agency.
http://resources.library.ubc.ca/page.php?id=2165

WTO I-TIP
The World Trade Organization's Integrated Trade Intelligence Portal (I-TIP) provides a single entry point for information compiled by the WTO on over 25,000 trade policy measures. I-TIP Goods provides comprehensive information on nontariff measures applied by WTO members to the merchandise trade. I-TIP Services, a joint initiative of the WTO and the World Bank, is a set of linked databases that provide information on members' commitments under the WTO's General Agreement on Trade in Services (GATS), services commitments in regional trade agreements, applied measures in services, and services statistics.
https://www.wto.org/english/res_e/statis_e/itip_e.htm

Appendix B
Glossary

advanced manufacturing and services GVC. A country is part of an advanced manufacturing and services global value chain if it exports a high share of manufacturing and business services and has high backward GVC integration (see box 1.3).

agribusiness or agrifood. The business of agricultural production and food processing.

backward GVC participation. Importing inputs to produce goods or services that are exported.

commodities GVCs. A country is part of a commodities global value chain if it predominantly exports commodities produced by agriculture and mining and has a small share of manufacturing exports and limited backward GVC integration (see box 1.3).

co-movement. The common movement of two or more entities.

deep integration agreement. Trade agreement that not only contains rules on tariffs and nontariff trade restrictions, but also regulates the business environment in other ways. Issues of deep integration include competition policy, investor rights, product standards, public procurement, and intellectual property rights.

exchange rate elasticity of exports. The percentage increase in exports associated with a 1 percent change in the exchange rate. It is a measure of the responsiveness of exports to changes in currency value.

forward GVC participation. Exporting domestically produced inputs to partners for the production of goods or services that they export.

global production network. An organizational arrangement comprising interconnected actors coordinated by a global lead firm and producing goods or services across different countries and regions.

global value chain (GVC). The series of stages required to produce a good or service that is sold to consumers, with each stage adding value and with at least two stages conducted in different countries.

GVC activities (or stages). The activities required to produce a good or service in the context of a global value chain. Spread across several locations, these activities span the conception of the good or service to its end use and include research, design, production, marketing, and distribution.

GVC intensification. An increase in the participation of a country, sector, or firm in a global value chain.

GVC participation (or integration). The engagement of a country, sector, or firm in at least one stage of a global value chain. Overall participation may take the form of two broad types: backward or forward participation.

innovative activities GVC. A country is part of an innovative activities global value chain if it has high backward GVC integration, spends a large share of its GDP on research and development, and receives a large share of GDP from intellectual property (see box 1.3).

lead firm. A firm that is the hierarchically dominant actor within a global value chain.

limited manufacturing GVC. A country is part of a limited manufacturing global value chain if it exports a limited set of manufacturing products, often alongside commodities exports, and has medium backward GVC integration (see box 1.3).

production fragmentation. The distribution of the production process across different countries and regions.

relational GVC. A global value chain in which actors are engaged in long-term firm-to-firm relationships rather than anonymous spot market transactions.

sticky or rigid GVC relationship. A business relationship within a global value chain that is not easily changed. For example, it can correspond to a trade flow involving a supplier trading a product that is precisely customized for the buyer and for which the buyer cannot easily find another supplier.

trade diversion. The process of diverting trade from a more efficient exporter to a less efficient one by means of a free trade agreement or a customs union. For example, when two countries sign a trade agreement, they could reduce their imports from the rest of the world and source their imports from each other. To the extent that this strategy of import reallocation has been triggered by the trade agreement, it can be considered a trade diversion.